Symmetry in the
Mathematical Inequalities

Symmetry in the Mathematical Inequalities

Editors

Nicusor Minculete
Shigeru Furuichi

MDPI • Basel • Beijing • Wuhan • Barcelona • Belgrade • Manchester • Tokyo • Cluj • Tianjin

Editors
Nicusor Minculete
Transilvania University
of Brasov
Romania

Shigeru Furuichi
Nihon University
Japan

Editorial Office
MDPI
St. Alban-Anlage 66
4052 Basel, Switzerland

This is a reprint of articles from the Special Issue published online in the open access journal *Symmetry* (ISSN 2073-8994) (available at: https://www.mdpi.com/journal/symmetry/special_issues/symmetry_mathematical_inequalities).

For citation purposes, cite each article independently as indicated on the article page online and as indicated below:

LastName, A.A.; LastName, B.B.; LastName, C.C. Article Title. *Journal Name* **Year**, *Volume Number*, Page Range.

ISBN 978-3-0365-4005-4 (Hbk)
ISBN 978-3-0365-4006-1 (PDF)

© 2022 by the authors. Articles in this book are Open Access and distributed under the Creative Commons Attribution (CC BY) license, which allows users to download, copy and build upon published articles, as long as the author and publisher are properly credited, which ensures maximum dissemination and a wider impact of our publications.

The book as a whole is distributed by MDPI under the terms and conditions of the Creative Commons license CC BY-NC-ND.

Contents

About the Editors ix

Preface to "Symmetry in the Mathematical Inequalities" xi

Nicușor Minculete
Special Issue Editorial "Symmetry in the Mathematical Inequalities"
Reprinted from: *Symmetry* **2022**, *14*, 774, doi:10.3390/sym14040774 1

Soubhagya Kumar Sahoo, Muhammad Tariq, Hijaz Ahmad, Jamshed Nasir, Hassen Aydi and Aiman Mukheimer
New Ostrowski-Type Fractional Integral Inequalities via Generalized Exponential-Type Convex Functions and Applications
Reprinted from: *Symmetry* **2021**, *13*, 1429, doi:10.3390/sym13081429 7

Xianyong Huang, Shanhe Wu and Bicheng Yang
A More Accurate Half-Discrete Hilbert-Type Inequality Involving One upper Limit Function and One Partial Sum
Reprinted from: *Symmetry* **2021**, *13*, 1548, doi:10.3390/sym13081548 25

Thanin Sitthiwirattham, Ghulam Murtaza, Muhammad Aamir Ali, Sotiris K. Ntouyas, Muhammad Adee and Jarunee Soontharanon
On Some New TrapezoidalType Inequalities for Twice (p, q) Differentiable Convex Functions in Post-Quantum Calculus
Reprinted from: *Symmetry* **2021**, *13*, 1605, doi:10.3390/sym13091605 37

Thanin Sitthiwirattham, Hüseyin Budak, Hasan Kara, Muhammad Aamir Ali and Jiraporn Reunsumrit
On Some New Fractional Ostrowski- and Trapezoid-Type Inequalities forFunctions of Bounded Variations with Two Variables
Reprinted from: *Symmetry* **2021**, *13*, 1724, doi:10.3390/sym13091724 49

Ifra Bashir Sial, Muhammad Aamir Ali, Ghulam Murtaza, Sotiris K. Ntouyas, Jarunee Soontharanon and Thanin Sitthiwirattham
On Some New Inequalities of Hermite–Hadamard Midpoint and Trapezoid Type for Preinvex Functions in (p, q)-Calculus
Reprinted from: *Symmetry* **2021**, *13*, 1864, doi:10.3390/sym13101864 71

Yuanfei Li and Zeng Peng
Continuous Dependence on the Heat Source of 2D Large-Scale Primitive Equations in Oceanic Dynamics
Reprinted from: *Symmetry* **2021**, *13*, 1961, doi:10.3390/sym13101961 89

Slavko Simić and Bandar Bin-Mohsin
Global Bounds for the Generalized Jensen Functional with Applications
Reprinted from: *Symmetry* **2021**, *13*, 2105, doi:10.3390/sym13112105 105

Muhammad Aamir Ali, Hasan Kara, Jessada Tariboon, Suphawat Asawasamrit, Hüseyin Budak and Fatih Hezenci
Some New Simpson's-Formula-Type Inequalities for Twice-Differentiable Convex Functions via Generalized Fractional Operators
Reprinted from: *Symmetry* **2021**, *13*, 2249, doi:10.3390/sym13122249 115

Shiguang Luo, Jincheng Shi and Baiping Ouyang
Phragmén-Lindelöf Alternative Results for a Class of Thermoelastic Plate
Reprinted from: *Symmetry* 2021, 13, 2256, doi:10.3390/sym13122256 . . . . **129**

Tao Zhang, Alatancang Chen, Huannan Shi, B. Saheya and Boyan Xi
Schur-Convexity for Elementary Symmetric Composite Functions and Their Inverse Problems and Applications
Reprinted from: *Symmetry* 2021, 13, 2351, doi:10.3390/sym13122351 . . . . **151**

Shigeru Furuichi and Nicuşor Minculete
Bounds for the Differences between Arithmetic and Geometric Means and Their Applications to Inequalities
Reprinted from: *Symmetry* 2021, 13, 2398, doi:10.3390/sym13122398 . . . . **165**

Miguel J. Vivas-Cortez, Muhammad Aamir Ali, Shahid Qaisar, Ifra Bashir Sial, Sinchai Jansem and Abdul Mateen
On Some New Simpson's Formula Type Inequalities for Convex Functions in Post-Quantum Calculus
Reprinted from: *Symmetry* 2021, 13, 2419, doi:10.3390/sym13122419 . . . . **185**

Xuejiao Chen, Yuanfei Li and Dandan Li
Spatial Decay Bounds for the Brinkman Fluid Equations in Double-Diffusive Convection
Reprinted from: *Symmetry* 2022, 14, 98, doi:10.3390/sym14010098 . . . . **203**

Jiraporn Reunsumrit, Miguel J. Vivas-Cortez, Muhammad Aamir Ali and Thanin Sitthiwirattham
On Generalization of Different Integral Inequalities for Harmonically Convex Functions
Reprinted from: *Symmetry* 2022, 14, 302, doi:10.3390/sym14020302 . . . . **225**

Artion Kashuri, Ravi P. Agarwal, Pshtiwan Othman Mohammed, Kamsing Nonlaopon, Khadijah M. Abualnaja and Yasser S. Hamed
New Generalized Class of Convex Functions and Some Related Integral Inequalities
Reprinted from: *Symmetry* 2022, 14, 722, doi:10.3390/sym14040722 . . . . **239**

About the Editors

Nicusor Minculete (Ph.D.) has been an associate professor at the Department of Mathematics and Computer Science of Transylvania, University of Brașov, Romania, since 2013. His research interests include number theory, Euclidean geometry, inequality, operators, and entropy. He is the author of more than 30 articles, most of which are published in international ISI journals.

Shigeru Furuichi (Ph.D.) received his B.S. degree from Department of Mathematics, Tokyo University of Science, and M.S. and Ph.D. from Department of information Science, Tokyo University of Science, Japan. He was an Assistant Professor and Lecturer from 1997 to 2007 in the Department of Electronics and Computer Science, Tokyo University of Science, Yamaguchi, Japan. He was an Associate Professor from 2008 to 2012 and has been Professor since 2013 in the Department of Information Science, College of Humanities and Sciences, Nihon University. His research interests include inequality, matrices/operators, and entropy. He is the author of more than 150 articles, most of which are published in international ISI journals.

Preface to "Symmetry in the Mathematical Inequalities"

This Special Issue brings together original research papers, in all areas of mathematics, that are concerned with inequalities or the role of inequalities. The research results presented in this Special Issue are related to improvements in classical inequalities, highlighting their applications and promoting an exchange of ideas between mathematicians from many parts of the world dedicated to the theory of inequalities.

This volume will be of interest to mathematicians specializing in inequality theory and beyond. Many of the studies presented here can be very useful in demonstrating new results.

It is our great pleasure to publish this book. All contents were peer-reviewed by multiple referees and published as papers in our Special Issue in the journal Symmetry. These studies give new and interesting results in mathematical inequalities enabling readers to obtain the latest developments in the fields of mathematical inequalities.

Finally, we would like to thank all the authors who have published their valuable work in this Special Issue. We would also like to thank the editors of the journal Symmetry for their help in making this volume, especially Mrs. Teresa Yu.

Nicusor Minculete and Shigeru Furuichi
Editors

Editorial

Special Issue Editorial "Symmetry in the Mathematical Inequalities"

Nicuşor Minculete

Faculty of Mathematics and Computer Science, Transilvania University of Braşov, Iuliu Maniu Street 50, 500091 Braşov, Romania; minculete.nicusor@unitbv.ro

Introduction

The theory of inequalities represents a long-standing topic in many mathematical areas and remains an attractive research domain with many applications. Inequalities Theory represents an old topic of many mathematical areas which still remains an attractive research domain with many applications. The study of convex functions occupied and still occupies a central role in Inequalities Theory because the convex functions develop a series of inequalities.

The research results presented here are concerned with the improvement in classical inequalities resulting from convex functions and highlighting their applications.

Related to probability theory, a convex function applied to the expected value of a random variable is always less than or equal to the expected value of the convex function of the random variable. This result, known as *Jensen's inequality*, underlies many important inequalities.

Another important result related to convex function is the *Hermite–Hadamard inequality*, due to Hermite and Hadamard, which asserts that for every continuous convex function $f : [a,b] \to \mathbb{R}$ the following inequalities hold:

$$f\left(\frac{a+b}{2}\right) \leq \frac{1}{b-a}\int_a^b f(t)dt \leq \frac{f(a)+f(b)}{2}.$$

Related to the Hermite–Hadamard inequality, many mathematicians have worked with great interest to generalise, refine, and extend it for different classes of functions such as quasi-convex functions, log-convex, *r*-convex functions, etc., and apply it for special means (logarithmic mean, Stolarsky mean, etc.).

Ujević in [1] obtained sharp inequalities for Simpson and Ostrowski types. Liu et al., in [2], used the MT-convexity-class-derived Ostrowski fractional inequalities. Kaijser et al., in [3], established Hardy-type inequalities via convexity. Rashid et al., in [4], using generalized *k*-fractional integrals, found Grüss inequalities.

There are many types of inequalities for functionals and inequalities for invertible positive operators. Among these, we found the Jensen functional under superquadraticity conditions and the Jensen functional related to a strongly convex function. Some applications of these functionals are related characterizations of generalized entropies. Generalized entropies have been studied by many researchers. Rényi and Tsallis entropies are well known as one-parameter generalizations of Shannon's entropy, being intensively studied not only in the field of classical statistical physics but also in the field of quantum physics.

Due to the nature of convexity theory, there exists a strong relationship between convexity and symmetry. When working on either of the concepts, it can be applied to the other one as well. Integral inequalities concerned with convexity have a lot of applications in various fields of mathematics in which symmetry has a great part to play.

Recently, fractional calculus has been the center of attraction for researchers in mathematical sciences because of its basic definitions, properties, and applications in tackling real-life problems.

Quantum information theory, an interdisciplinary field that includes computer science, information theory, philosophy, cryptography, and symmetry, has various applications for quantum calculus. The inequalities have a strong association with convex and symmetric convex functions. From the past to the present, various works have been dedicated to Simpson's inequality for differentiable convex functions. Simpson-type inequalities for twice-differentiable functions have been the subject of some research.

This Special Issue brings together original research papers in all areas of mathematics that are concerned with inequalities or their role. The research results presented in this Special Issue are related to the improvement of classical inequalities and highlight their applications, promoting an exchange of ideas between mathematicians from many parts of the world dedicated to the theory of inequalities.

For example, the study of convex functions has occupied a central role in the theory of inequalities because such functions develop a series of inequalities. There is a strong correlation between the concepts of convexity and symmetry. In number theory, a number of inequalities characterize arithmetic functions. Other important types of inequalities are those related to invertible positive operators that have applications in operator equations, network theory, and quantum information theory (inequalities for generalized entropies).

The following manuscripts were selected for publication. The articles were prepared by scientists working in leading universities and research centers in Albania, China, Ecuador, Greece, India, Iraq, Italy, Japan, Pakistan, Romania, Serbia, Saudi Arabia, South Africa, Taiwan, Thailand, Tunisia, Turkey, and the USA.

S. K. Sahoo et al., in the paper "New Ostrowski-Type Fractional Integral Inequalities via Generalized Exponential-Type Convex Functions and Applications" [5], presented some fractional integral inequalities of the Ostrowski type for a new class of convex mapping. Specifically, n-polynomials that are exponentially s-convex via a fractional operator are established. Additionally, they showed a new Hermite–Hadamard fractional integral inequality. Some special cases of the results are discussed as well. Finally, in applications, some new limits for special means of positive real numbers and midpoint formulae are given. These new outcomes yield a few generalizations of the earlier outcomes already published in the literature.

X. Huang et al., in the paper "A More Accurate Half-Discrete Hilbert-Type Inequality Involving One upper Limit Function and One Partial Sum" [6], constructed proper weight coefficients by virtue of the symmetry principle and used them to establish a more accurate half-discrete, Hilbert-type inequality involving one upper limit function and one partial sum. The authors proved the new inequality with the help of the Euler–Maclaurin summation formula and Abel's partial summation formula. Finally, it is illustrated how the obtained results can generate some new half-discrete Hilbert-type inequalities.

T. Sitthiwirattham et al., in the paper "On Some New Trapezoidal Type Inequalities for Twice (p,q) Differentiable Convex Functions in Post-Quantum Calculus" [7], studied a (p,q)-integral identity involving the second (p,q)-derivative and then used this result to prove some new trapezoidal-type inequalities for twice (p,q)-differentiable convex functions. It is also shown that the newly established results are the refinements of some existing results in the field of integral inequalities.

T. Sitthiwirattham et al., in the paper "On Some New Fractional Ostrowski- and Trapezoid-Type Inequalities for Functions of Bounded Variations with Two Variables" [8], proved three identities for functions of bounded variations. Then, by using these equalities, several trapezoid- and Ostrowski-type inequalities were obtained via generalized fractional integrals for the functions of bounded variations with two variables. Moreover, presented some results were presented for Riemann–Liouville fractional integrals by the special choice of the main results. Finally, the connections between their results and those in earlier works were investigated.

I. B. Sial et al., in the paper "On Some New Inequalities of Hermite–Hadamard Midpoint and Trapezoid Type for Preinvex Functions in p,q-Calculus" [9], established some new Hermite–Hadamard-type inequalities for preinvex functions and left–right estimates of newly established inequalities for (p,q)-differentiable pre-invex functions in the context of (p,q)-calculus. The authors also show that the results established in this paper are generalizations of comparable results in the literature of integral inequalities. Analytic inequalities of this nature and especially the techniques involved have applications in various areas in which symmetry plays a prominent role.

Y. Li and P. Zeng, in the paper "Continuous Dependence on the Heat Source of 2D Large-Scale Primitive Equations in Oceanic Dynamics" [10], studied the initial boundary value problem for the two-dimensional primitive equations of large-scale oceanic dynamics. These models are often used to predict the weather and climate change. Using the differential inequality technique, rigorous a priori bounds of the solutions and the continuous dependence on the heat source are established. The application of symmetry in mathematical inequalities are shown in practice.

S. Simić and B. Bin-Mohsin, in the paper "Global Bounds for the Generalized Jensen Functional with Applications" [11], found sharp global bounds for the generalized Jensen functional $J_n(g, h; p, x)$. In particular, exact bounds are determined for the generalized power mean in terms from the class of the Stolarsky means. As a consequence, they obtained the best possible global converses of quotients and differences of the generalized arithmetic, geometric, and harmonic means.

M. A. Ali et al., in the paper "Some New Simpson's–Formula–Type Inequalities for Twice-Differentiable Convex Functions via Generalized Fractional Operators" [12], established a new generalized fractional integral identity involving twice-differentiable functions. The authors used this result to prove some new Simpson's-formula-type inequalities for twice-differentiable convex functions. Furthermore, a few special cases of newly established inequalities were examined, and several new and old Simpson's-formula-type inequalities were obtained. These types of analytic inequalities, as well as the methodologies for solving them, have applications in a wide range of fields where symmetry is crucial.

S. Luo et al., in the paper "Phragmén-Lindelöf Alternative Results for a Class of Thermoelastic Plate" [13], studied the spatial properties of solutions for a class of thermoelastic plates with biharmonic operators. The energy method was used. A differential inequality in which the energy expression was controlled by a second-order differential inequality was deduced. The Phragmén–Lindelöf alternative results of the solutions were obtained by solving the inequality. These results show that the Saint-Venant principle is also valid for the hyperbolic–hyperbolic coupling equations. Their results can been seen as a version of symmetry in inequality for studying the Phragmén–Lindelöf alternative results.

T. Zhang et al., in the paper "Schur-Convexity for Elementary Symmetric Composite Functions and Their Inverse Problems and Applications" [14], investigated the Schur-convexity, Schur-geometric convexity, and Schur-harmonic convexity for the elementary symmetric composite function and its dual form. The inverse problems are also considered. New inequalities on special means are established by using the theory of majorization.

S. Furuichi and N. Minculete, in the paper "Bounds for the Differences between Arithmetic and Geometric Means and Their Applications to Inequalities" [15], provide some bounds for the differences between the weighted arithmetic and geometric means, using known inequalities. It improved the results given by Furuichi–Ghaemi–Gharakhanlu and Sababheh–Choi. The authors also found some bounds on entropies, applying the results in a different approach. Finally, explored certain convex or concave functions are explored, which are symmetric functions on the axis $t = 1/2$.

M. J. Vivas-Cortez et al., in the paper "On Some New Simpson's Formula Type Inequalities for Convex Functions in Post–Quantum Calculus" [16], proved a new (p,q)-integral identity involving a (p,q)-derivative and (p,q)-integral. The newly established identity is then used to show some new Simpson's formula type inequalities for (p,q)-differentiable convex functions. Finally, the newly discovered results are shown to be refinements of comparable results in the literature. Analytic inequalities of this type, as well as the techniques used to solve them, have applications in a variety of fields where symmetry is important.

X. Chen et al., in the paper "Spatial Decay Bounds for the Brinkman Fluid Equations in Double-Diffusive Convection" [17], studied the Brinkman equations pipe flow, which includes the salinity and the temperature. Assuming that the fluid satisfies nonlinear boundary conditions at the finite end of the cylinder, using the symmetry of differential inequalities and the energy analysis methods, the exponential decay estimates for homogeneous Brinkman equations are established.

J. Reunsumrit et al., in the paper "On Generalization of Different Integral Inequalities for Harmonically Convex Functions" [18], proved a parameterized integral identity involving differentiable functions. Then, for differentiable harmonically convex functions, they use this result to establish some new inequalities of a midpoint type, trapezoidal type, and Simpson type. Analytic inequalities of this type, as well as the approaches for solving them, have applications in a variety of domains where symmetry is important. Finally, several particular cases of recently discovered results are discussed, as well as applications to the special means of real numbers.

A. Kashuri et al., in the paper "New Generalized Class of Convex Functions and Some Related Integral Inequalities" [19], studied the new generic class of functions called the (n, m)-generalized convex and studied its basic algebraic properties. The Hermite–Hadamard inequality for the (n, m)-generalized convex function, for the products of two functions and of this type, were proven. Moreover, this class of functions was applied to several known identities; midpoint-type inequalities of Ostrowski and Simpson were derived. Our results are extensions of many previous contributions related to integral inequalities via different convexities.

This volume will be of interest to mathematicians specializing in inequalities theory and beyond. Many of the results presented here can be very useful in demonstrating new results.

Funding: The research was funded by the Transilvania University of Braşov. There is no third-party funding received in relation to this article.

Institutional Review Board Statement: Not applicable.

Informed Consent Statement: Not applicable.

Data Availability Statement: Not applicable.

Conflicts of Interest: The author declares no conflict of interest.

References

1. Ujević, N. Sharp inequalities of Simpson type and Ostrowski type. *Comput. Math. Appl.* **2004**, *48*, 145–151. [CrossRef]
2. Liu, W.; Wen, W.; Park, J. Ostrowski type fractional integral inequalities for MT-convex functions. *Math. Notes* **2015**, *16*, 249–256. [CrossRef]
3. Kaijser, S.; Nikolova, L.; Persson, L.E.; Wedestig, A. Hardy type inequalities via convexity. *Math. Inequal. Appl.* **2005**, *8*, 403–417. [CrossRef]
4. Rashid, S.; Jarad, F.; Noor, M.A.; Noor, K.I.; Baleanu, D.; Liu, J.B. On Grüss inequalities within generalized k–fractional integrals. *Adv. Differ. Equ.* **2020**, *2020*, 203. [CrossRef]
5. Sahoo, S.K.; Tariq, M.; Ahmad, H.; Nasir, J.; Aydi, H.; Mukheimer, A. New Ostrowski–Type Fractional Integral Inequalities via Generalized Exponential–Type Convex Functions and Applications. *Symmetry* **2021**, *13*, 1429. [CrossRef]
6. Huang, X.; Wu, S.; Yang, B. A More Accurate Half–Discrete Hilbert–Type Inequality Involving One upper Limit Function and One Partial Sum. *Symmetry* **2021**, *13*, 1548. [CrossRef]
7. Sitthiwirattham, T.; Murtaza, G.; Ali, M.A.; Ntouyas, S.K.; Adeel, M.; Soontharanon, J. On Some New Trapezoidal Type Inequalities for Twice (p,q) Differentiable Convex Functions in Post–Quantum Calculus. *Symmetry* **2021**, *13*, 1605. [CrossRef]
8. Sitthiwirattham, T.; Budak, H.; Kara, H.; Ali, M.A.; Reunsumrit, J. On Some New Fractional Ostrowski– and Trapezoid–Type Inequalities for Functions of Bounded Variations with Two Variables. *Symmetry* **2021**, *13*, 1724. [CrossRef]
9. Sial, I.B.; Ali, M.A.; Murtaza, G.; Ntouyas, S.K.; Soontharanon, J.; Sitthiwirattham, T. On Some New Inequalities of Hermite–Hadamard Midpoint and Trapezoid Type for Preinvex Functions in p,q–Calculus. *Symmetry* **2021**, *13*, 1864. [CrossRef]
10. Li, Y.; Zeng, P. Continuous Dependence on the Heat Source of 2D Large–Scale Primitive Equations in Oceanic Dynamics. *Symmetry* **2021**, *13*, 1961. [CrossRef]
11. Simić, S.; Bin-Mohsin, B. Global Bounds for the Generalized Jensen Functional with Applications. *Symmetry* **2021**, *13*, 2105. [CrossRef]

12. Ali, M.A.; Kara, H.; Tariboon, J.; Asawasamrit, S.; Budak, H.; Hezenci, F. Some New Simpson's–Formula–Type Inequalities for Twice–Differentiable Convex Functions via Generalized Fractional Operators. *Symmetry* **2021**, *13*, 2249. [CrossRef]
13. Luo, S.; Shi, J.; Ouyang, B. Phragmén-Lindelöf Alternative Results for a Class of Thermoelastic Plate. *Symmetry* **2021**, *13*, 2256. [CrossRef]
14. Zhang, T.; Chen, A.; Shi, H.; Saheya, B.; Xi, B. Schur–Convexity for Elementary Symmetric Composite Functions and Their Inverse Problems and Applications. *Symmetry* **2021**, *13*, 2351. [CrossRef]
15. Furuichi, S.; Minculete, N. Bounds for the Differences between Arithmetic and Geometric Means and Their Applications to Inequalities. *Symmetry* **2021**, *13*, 2398. [CrossRef]
16. Vivas-Cortez, M.J.; Ali, M.A.; Qaisar, S.; Sial, I.B.; Jansem, S.; Mateen, A. On Some New Simpson's Formula Type Inequalities for Convex Functions in Post–Quantum Calculus. *Symmetry* **2021**, *13*, 2419. [CrossRef]
17. Chen, X.; Li, Y.; Li, D. Spatial Decay Bounds for the Brinkman Fluid Equations in Double–Diffusive Convection. *Symmetry* **2022**, *14*, 98. [CrossRef]
18. Reunsumrit, J.; Vivas-Cortez, M.J.; Ali, M.A.; Sitthiwirattham, T. On Generalization of Different Integral Inequalities for Harmonically Convex Functions. *Symmetry* **2022**, *14*, 302. [CrossRef]
19. Kashuri, A.; Agarwal, R.P.; Mohammed, P.O.; Nonlaopon, K.; Abualnaja, K.M.; Hamed, Y.S. New Generalized Class of Convex Functions and Some Related Integral Inequalities. *Symmetry* **2022**, *14*, 722. [CrossRef]

Article

New Ostrowski-Type Fractional Integral Inequalities via Generalized Exponential-Type Convex Functions and Applications

Soubhagya Kumar Sahoo [1], Muhammad Tariq [2], Hijaz Ahmad [3], Jamshed Nasir [4], Hassen Aydi [5,6,7,*] and Aiman Mukheimer [8]

[1] Department of Mathematics, Institute of Technical Education and Research, Siksha O Anusandhan University, Bhubaneswar 751030, India; soubhagyakumarsahoo@soa.ac.in
[2] Department of Basic Sciences and Related Studies, Mehran University of Engineering and Technology, Jamshoro 76062, Pakistan; captaintariq2187@gmail.com
[3] Section of Mathematics, International Telematic University Uninettuno, Corso Vittorio Emanuele II 39, 00186 Roma, Italy; hijaz555@gmail.com
[4] Department of Mathematics & Statistics, Virtual University of Pakistan, Lahore Campus 54000, Pakistan; jnasir143@gmail.com
[5] Institut Supérieur d'Informatique et des Techniques de Communication, Université de Sousse, Hammam Sousse 4000, Tunisia
[6] Department of Mathematics and Applied Mathematics, Sefako Makgatho Health Sciences University, Ga-Rankuwa P.O. Box 60, South Africa
[7] China Medical University Hospital, China Medical University, Taichung 40402, Taiwan
[8] Department of Mathematics and General Sciences, Prince Sultan University, P. O. Box 66833, Riyadh 11586, Saudi Arabia; mukheimer@psu.edu.sa
* Correspondence: hassen.aydi@isima.rnu.tn

Abstract: Recently, fractional calculus has been the center of attraction for researchers in mathematical sciences because of its basic definitions, properties and applications in tackling real-life problems. The main purpose of this article is to present some fractional integral inequalities of Ostrowski type for a new class of convex mapping. Specifically, n–polynomial exponentially s–convex via fractional operator are established. Additionally, we present a new Hermite–Hadamard fractional integral inequality. Some special cases of the results are discussed as well. Due to the nature of convexity theory, there exists a strong relationship between convexity and symmetry. When working on either of the concepts, it can be applied to the other one as well. Integral inequalities concerned with convexity have a lot of applications in various fields of mathematics in which symmetry has a great part to play. Finally, in applications, some new limits for special means of positive real numbers and midpoint formula are given. These new outcomes yield a few generalizations of the earlier outcomes already published in the literature.

Keywords: Ostrowski inequality; Hölder's inequality; power mean integral inequality; n-polynomial exponentially s-convex function

1. Introduction

The theory of inequalities along with convexity property plays an essential part in present-day mathematical investigation. Numerical analysis relies on numerous mathematical inequalities such as the Simpson inequality, Hermite–Hadamard inequality, Bullen-type inequality, Ostrowski inequality, etc. Recently, a broad exploration has been completed on acquiring different variants of traditional inequalities using different methodologies. An exceptionally intriguing methodology is to obtain a fractional version of the inequalities. Inequalities associated with various forms of fractional operator such as Riemann–Liouville fractional operator, Conformable, Katugampola fractional operator, Tempered fractional operator, Generalized proportional fractional, Weighted fractional operator, Caputo fractional operator, etc. assume a critical part in the foundation of the unique solution for fractional differential equations. For some recent articles on fractional inequalities, see References [1–8].

The concept of convexity plays a strong role in the field of mathematical inequalities and mathematical analysis due to the beautiful nature of its classical definition and its algebraic properties. Recently, many authors have explored the close relationship and interrelated work on convexity and symmetry. They have also explained that due to the strong relationship between them, while working on any one of the concepts it can be applied to the other one as well. Convexity theory has gained a lot of attention in recent years and many generalizations and refinements of convexity analysis for inequalities have been found (see, for example [9–15]).

Fractional operator examines the integrals and derivatives of any order $\alpha > 0$ be it real or complex valued. It was introduced by Leibniz and Marquis de l'Hospital in 1695 by talking about the differentiation of functions. In any case, it encountered a fast development throughout the limited time.

In the theory of integral inequalities, Sarikaya et al. [6] introduced the application of fractional integral operator by establishing the fractional analogues of classical Hermite–Hadamard's inequality using convexity. In [16], Dragomir for the first time established fractional versions of Ostrowski-type inequalities.

In 1938, Ostrowski introduced the following useful and interesting integral inequality, (see [17], page: 468).

Let $\varphi : J \subseteq \mathbb{R} \to \mathbb{R}$ be a differentiable mapping on J^o, the interior of the interval J, such that $\varphi \in \mathcal{L}[\eta_1, \eta_2]$, where $\eta_1, \eta_2 \in J$ with $\eta_2 > \eta_1$. If $|\varphi'(z)| \leq K$, for all $z \in [\eta_1, \eta_2]$, then the following inequality holds:

$$\left| \varphi(z) - \frac{1}{\eta_2 - \eta_1} \int_{\eta_1}^{\eta_2} \varphi(\chi) d\chi \right| \leq K(\eta_2 - \eta_1) \left[\frac{1}{4} + \frac{\left(z - \frac{\eta_1 + \eta_2}{2}\right)^2}{(\eta_2 - \eta_1)^2} \right] \qquad (1)$$

holds, where K is the Lipschitz constant which is equal to $\sup \left\{ \left| \frac{\varphi(\chi) - \varphi(\phi)}{\chi - \phi} \right| ; \chi \neq \phi \right\}$. The above result (1) is famously known as the Ostrowski inequality. For recent results and related generalizations, variants and extensions about the Ostrowski inequality (see [18–23]). This inequality gives us an upper bound for the approximation of the integral average $\frac{1}{\eta_2 - \eta_1} \int_{\eta_1}^{\eta_2} \varphi(\chi) d\chi$ by the value of $\varphi(u)$ at the point $\chi \in [\eta_1, \eta_2]$.

The Ostrowski inequality has a great number of applications in different fields of mathematical analysis such as numerical analysis and especially in the theory of approximations. This type of analytic inequality and especially the techniques used in this article have applications in various fields in which symmetry plays a significant role.

In the wake of contemplating writing about convexity theory, propelled and motivated by the continuous generalizations and exploration in this interesting field, we discovered that there exists an exceptional class of convexity known as exponential convexity and recently a great number of researchers are working on this concept for its enhancement. Antczak [24] and Dragomir [25] presented the class of exponential-type convexity. Consequently, Awan [26] contemplated and examined another class of exponential convex function. Very recently, Mahir Kadakal and İşcan [27] presented another meaning of exponential-type convexity. Studying the above-mentioned papers, we have introduced a new definition in this aspect which is called n–polynomial exponential s–convex function. Applying this new definition, we have presented our main results as refinements of the Ostrowski inequality. This is the novelty of our proposed work.

The objective of this paper is to obtain some new novel refinements of Ostrowski's inequality basically using n–polynomial exponential s–convex function for fractional calculus. We initially attain a new fractional version of the Hermite–Hadamard inequality using a new class of convexity, namely n–polynomial exponential s–convex function. We additionally investigate some important special cases that can be concluded from the presented results of the article. In Sections 6 and 7, we present a few applications of the presented results. We trust that the thoughts and strategies introduced in this paper will rouse intrigued researchers for further research.

Recently, it has been seen that many scientists are interested in big data analysis, deep learning and information theory using the concept of exponentially convex functions. Hence, we believe that the concept of n–polynomial exponentially convex function using fractional operator can attract the interest of such scientists for further development in the field of deep learning, data analysis and information theory.

Motivated by the advancement of the theory of fractional calculus, ongoing research and literature about integral inequality and convexity, the present paper is structured in the following way: First, in Section 2, we will give some necessary known definitions and literature. Second, in Section 3, we will explore the concept of n–polynomial exponentially s–convex function. In addition, algebraic properties and examples for the newly introduced definition are elaborated. In Section 4, we attain a new fractional version of the Hermite—Hadamard-type inequality. Furthermore, in Section 5, we investigate some novel refinements of the Ostrowski-type inequality and some special cases via the Riemann–Liouville fractional integral operator. Finally, in the next Section, we present some applications to special means and midpoint formula.

2. Preliminaries

In this Section, we recall some known concepts.

Definition 1 ([28]). *Let $\varphi : I \subseteq \mathbb{R} \to \mathbb{R}$ be a real-valued function. A function φ is said to be convex, if*

$$\varphi(\chi\eta_1 + (1-\chi)\eta_2) \leq \chi\varphi(\eta_1) + (1-\chi)\varphi(\eta_2), \tag{2}$$

holds for all $\eta_1, \eta_2 \in I$ and $\chi \in [0,1]$.

The Hermite–Hadamard inequality states that if a mapping $\varphi : J \subset \mathbb{R} \to \mathbb{R}$ is convex on J for $\eta_1, \eta_2 \in J$ and $\eta_2 > \eta_1$, then

$$\varphi\left(\frac{\eta_1 + \eta_2}{2}\right) \leq \frac{1}{\eta_2 - \eta_1} \int_{\eta_1}^{\eta_2} \varphi(\chi)d\chi \leq \frac{\varphi(\eta_1) + \varphi(\eta_2)}{2}. \tag{3}$$

Interested readers can refer to [8,29].

Definition 2 ([30]). *A function $\varphi : [0, +\infty) \to \mathbb{R}$ is said to be s–convex in the second sense for a real number $s \in (0,1]$ or φ belongs to the class of K_s^2, if*

$$\varphi(\chi\eta_1 + (1-\chi)\eta_2) \leq \chi^s \varphi(\eta_1) + (1-\chi)^s \varphi(\eta_2) \tag{4}$$

holds for all $\eta_1, \eta_2 \in [0, +\infty)$ and $\chi \in [0,1]$.

Breckner in his article [31] introduced s–convex functions. Hudzik presented several properties and connections with s–convexity in the first sense in [32]. Usually, when we put $s = 1$ for s–convexity, it reduces to usual convexity. In [29], Dragomir et al. proved a generalized Hadamard's inequality, which holds for s–convex functions in the second sense.

Recently, many researchers have investigated the importance and development of the theory of exponentially convex functions. The fruitful importance of exponential-type convexity is that it can be used to manipulate for statistical learning, image processing, stochastic optimization and sequential prediction. In 2020, Kadakal and İşcan investigated a new class of exponential convexity, which is stated as follows:

Definition 3 ([27]). A nonnegative real-valued function $\varphi : J \subset \mathbb{R} \to \mathbb{R}$ is known to be an exponential convex function if the following inequality holds:

$$\varphi(\chi\eta_1 + (1-\chi)\eta_2) \leq (e^\chi - 1)\varphi(\eta_1) + \left(e^{(1-\chi)} - 1\right)\varphi(\eta_2). \quad (5)$$

Definition 4 ([33]). A nonnegative real-valued function $\psi : I \to \mathbb{R}$ is called n–polynomial convex, if

$$\psi(\chi\eta_1 + (1-\chi)\eta_2) \leq \frac{1}{n}\sum_{i=1}^{n}[1-(1-\chi)^i]\psi(\eta_1) + \frac{1}{n}\sum_{i=1}^{n}[1-\chi^i]\psi(\eta_2), \quad (6)$$

holds for every $\eta_1, \eta_2 \in I$, $\chi \in [0,1]$, $s \in [0,1]$ and $n \in \mathbb{N}$.

Definition 5 (see, for details, [6]). Let $\varphi \in \mathcal{L}[\eta_1, \eta_2]$. Then the fractional integrals $J^\alpha_{\eta_1^+}$ and $J^\alpha_{\eta_2^-}$ of order $\alpha > 0$ are defined by

$$J^\alpha_{\eta_1^+}\varphi(x) := \frac{1}{\Gamma(\alpha)}\int_{\eta_1}^{x}(x-z)^{\alpha-1}\varphi(z)dz \quad (0 \leq \eta_1 < x < \eta_2)$$

and

$$J^\alpha_{\eta_2^-}\varphi(x) := \frac{1}{\Gamma(\alpha)}\int_{x}^{\eta_2}(z-x)^{\alpha-1}\varphi(z)dz \quad (0 \leq \eta_1 < x < \eta_2),$$

respectively.

3. Generalized Exponentially s–Convex Function

Definition 6. Let $n \in \mathbb{N}$ and $s \in (0,1]$. Then the nonnegative real-valued function $\varphi : J \subset \mathbb{R} \to \mathbb{R}$ is known to be an n–polynomial exponentially s–convex function if the inequality holds:

$$\varphi(\chi\eta_1 + (1-\chi)\eta_2) \leq \frac{1}{n}\sum_{i=1}^{n}(e^{s\chi} - 1)^i\varphi(\eta_1) + \frac{1}{n}\sum_{i=1}^{n}\left(e^{s(1-\chi)} - 1\right)^i\varphi(\eta_2). \quad (7)$$

We represent the class of all n–polynomial exponentially type convex functions on the interval J as $POLEXPC(J)$ for each $\eta_1, \eta_2 \in J$ and $\chi \in [0,1]$.

Remark 1. In Definition 6, if $n = s = 1$, then the 1-polynomial exponentially s- convex function reduces to the classical exponential-type convexity given by İşcan in [27].

Remark 2. The range of the exponentially s–convex functions for some fixed $s \in [\ln 2.4, 1]$ is $[0, +\infty)$.

Lemma 1. For all $\chi \in [0,1]$ and for some fixed $s \in [\ln 2.4, 1]$ the following inequalities $\frac{1}{n}\sum_{i=1}^{n}(e^{s\chi}-1)^i \geq \chi^s$ and $\frac{1}{n}\sum_{i=1}^{n}(e^{s(1-\chi)}-1)^i \geq (1-\chi)^s$ hold.

Proof. Now, we will prove the first inequality i.e., $\frac{1}{n}\sum_{i=1}^{n}(e^{s\chi}-1)^i \geq \chi^s$ for all $\chi \in [0,1]$ and $s \in [\ln 2.4, 1]$ and $n \in \mathbb{N}$.

The following inequality is well-known as Bernoulli inequality in mathematical analysis

$$(-1+e^{s\chi})^i \geq 1 + ie^{s\chi}$$
$$\implies -1 + (-1+e^{s\chi})^i \geq ie^{s\chi}$$
$$\implies \frac{-1+(-1+e^{s\chi})^i}{ie^{s\chi}} \leq 1$$

Thus, we have
$$\frac{1}{n}\sum_{i=1}^{n}(e^{s\chi}-1)^{i-1} = \frac{1-(-1+e^{s\chi})^n}{ne^{s\chi}} \leq 1$$

$$n(e^{s\chi}-1)\left[-1+\frac{1}{n}\sum_{i=1}^{n}(e^{s\chi}-1)^{i-1}\right] = -n(e^{s\chi}-1) + \frac{1}{n}\sum_{i=1}^{n}(e^{s\chi}-1)^i \leq 0$$

Hence,
$$\chi^s \leq \frac{1}{n}\sum_{i=1}^{n}(e^{s\chi}-1)^i$$

Consequently, similar computation proves
$$(1-\chi)^s \leq \frac{1}{n}\sum_{i=1}^{n}(e^{s(1-\chi)}-1)^i.$$

□

Proposition 1. *Every nonnegative s–convex function is an n–polynomial exponentially s–convex function for $s \in [\ln 2.4, 1]$.*

Proof. Applying Lemma 1 and $s \in [\ln 2.4, 1]$, we have
$$\varphi(\chi\eta_1 + (1-\chi)\eta_2) \leq \chi^s \varphi(\eta_1) + (1-\chi)^s \varphi(\eta_2)$$
$$\leq \frac{1}{n}\sum_{i=1}^{n}(e^{s\chi}-1)^i \varphi(\eta_1) + \frac{1}{n}\sum_{i=1}^{n}\left(e^{(1-\chi)s}-1\right)^i \varphi(\eta_2).$$

□

Remark 3. *If in the above proposition $s = 1$, then every nonnegative convex function is an n–polynomial exponentially s–convex function for $s \in [\ln 2.4, 1]$.*

Now, we will make some examples in the support of the newly introduced function.

Example 1. *Since, $\varphi(x) = e^x$ is a nonnegative convex function for all $x > 0$. Using Remark 3, it is also an n–polynomial exponentially s–convex function for $s \in [\ln 2.4, 1]$.*

Example 2. *Since, $\varphi(x) = c$ is a nonnegative convex function on R for any $c \geq 0$, using Remark 3, it is also an n–polynomial exponentially s–convex function for $s \in [\ln 2.4, 1]$.*

Example 3. *Since $\varphi(x) = \frac{1}{x}$ for all $x > 0$, is a nonnegative convex function, using Remark 3, it is also an n–polynomial exponentially s–convex function for $s \in [\ln 2.4, 1]$.*

Example 4. *Since $\varphi(x) = \frac{q}{m+q}x^{\frac{m}{q}+1}$ for $m > 1$ and $q \geq 1$, is a nonnegative convex function. Using Proposition 3, it is also an n–polynomial exponentially s–convex function for $s \in [\ln 2.4, 1]$.*

Example 5. *Dragomir [29] clearly investigated and proved that the function $\varphi(x) = x^{ls}$, $x > 0$ is an s–convex function, for the above-mentioned conditions $s \in (0,1)$ and $1 \leq l \leq \frac{1}{s}$. In addition, using Proposition 1, it is also an n–polynomial exponentially s–convex function for $s \in [\ln 2.4, 1]$.*

Remark 4. *If we assign $n = 2$ in Definition 7, we obtain the following definition for 2-polynomial exponentially s-convex function.*

$$\varphi(\chi\eta_1 + (1-\chi)\eta_2) \leq \left(\frac{e^{2s\chi} - e^{s\chi}}{2}\right)\varphi(\eta_1) + \left(\frac{e^{2s(1-\chi)} - e^{s(1-\chi)}}{2}\right)\varphi(\eta_2). \quad (8)$$

4. Hermite–Hadamard Type Inequality via Fractional Operator

In this Section, we present one Hermite—Hadamard-type inequality for the n–polynomial exponentially s–convex function.

Theorem 1. *Let $\varphi : \mathbb{A} = [\eta_1, \eta_2] \to \mathbb{R}$ be a positive function with $0 \leq \eta_1 \leq \eta_2$ and φ be an integrable function on the closed interval sets η_1 and η_2. If φ is an n–polynomial exponentially s–convex function, then the following inequality for fractional integral with $\alpha > 0$ and $s \in [\ln 2.4, 1]$ holds:*

$$\frac{1}{\frac{1}{n}\sum_{i=1}^{n}\left(e^{\frac{s}{2}} - 1\right)^i} \leq \frac{\Gamma(\alpha+1)}{(\eta_2 - \eta_1)^\alpha}\left[J_{\eta_1^+}^\alpha \varphi(\eta_2) + J_{\eta_2^-}^\alpha \varphi(\eta_1)\right] \quad (9)$$

$$\leq \alpha[\varphi(\eta_1) + \varphi(\eta_2)]\int_0^1 \chi^{\alpha-1}\left\{\frac{1}{n}\sum_{i=1}^{n}(e^{s\chi} - 1)^i + \frac{1}{n}\sum_{i=1}^{n}\left(e^{s(1-\chi)} - 1\right)^i\right\}d\chi.$$

Proof. Let $z_1, z_2 \in \mathbb{A}$. Then, using the definition of n–polynomial exponentially s–convex function φ on $\mathbb{A}$, we have

$$\varphi\left(\frac{z_1 + z_2}{2}\right) \leq \frac{1}{n}\sum_{i=1}^{n}\left(e^{\frac{s}{2}} - 1\right)^i [\varphi(z_1) + \varphi(z_2)] \quad (10)$$

Suppose $z_1 = \chi\eta_2 + (1-\chi)\eta_1$ and $z_2 = \chi\eta_1 + (1-\chi)\eta_2$.

Then (10) leads to

$$\varphi\left(\frac{\eta_1 + \eta_2}{2}\right) \leq \frac{1}{n}\sum_{i=1}^{n}\left(e^{\frac{s}{2}} - 1\right)^i [\varphi(\chi\eta_2 + (1-\chi)\eta_1) + \varphi(\chi\eta_1 + (1-\chi)\eta_2)]. \quad (11)$$

Now, multiplying both sides of (11) by $\chi^{\alpha-1}$ and then, integrating the resultant inequality with respect to χ over [0,1] and, we obtain

$$\frac{1}{\alpha}\varphi\left(\frac{\eta_1 + \eta_2}{2}\right) \leq \frac{1}{n}\sum_{i=1}^{n}\left(e^{\frac{s}{2}} - 1\right)^i\left[\int_0^1 \chi^{\alpha-1}\varphi(\chi\eta_2 + (1-\chi)\eta_1)d\chi + \int_0^1 \chi^{\alpha-1}\varphi(\chi\eta_1 + (1-\chi)\eta_2)d\chi\right]$$

Hence, we obtain

$$\frac{1}{\frac{1}{n}\sum_{i=1}^{n}\left(e^{\frac{s}{2}} - 1\right)^i}\varphi\left(\frac{\eta_1 + \eta_2}{2}\right) \leq \frac{\Gamma(\alpha+1)}{(\eta_2 - \eta_1)^\alpha}\left[J_{\eta_1^+}^\alpha \varphi(\eta_2) + J_{\eta_2^-}^\alpha \varphi(\eta_1)\right].$$

The proof of the first part of the inequality (9) is complete.

Next, we prove the second part of the inequality (9) using the fact that φ is an exponentially s–convex function, we obtain

$$\varphi(\chi\eta_2 + (1-\chi)\eta_1) \leq \frac{1}{n}\sum_{i=1}^{n}(e^{s\chi} - 1)^i \varphi(\eta_2) + \frac{1}{n}\sum_{i=1}^{n}\left(e^{s(1-\chi)} - 1\right)^i \varphi(\eta_1) \quad (12)$$

and

$$\varphi(\chi\eta_1 + (1-\chi)\eta_2) \leq \frac{1}{n}\sum_{i=1}^{n}(e^{s\chi} - 1)^i \varphi(\eta_1) + \frac{1}{n}\sum_{i=1}^{n}\left(e^{s(1-\chi)} - 1\right)^i \varphi(\eta_2). \quad (13)$$

Upon adding the above inequalities, we obtain

$$\varphi(\chi\eta_2 + (1-\chi)\eta_1) + \varphi(\chi\eta_1 + (1-\chi)\eta_2) \tag{14}$$
$$\leq [\varphi(\eta_1) + \varphi(\eta_2)]\left\{\frac{1}{n}\sum_{i=1}^{n}(e^{s\chi}-1)^i + \frac{1}{n}\sum_{i=1}^{n}\left(e^{s(1-\chi)}-1\right)^i\right\}.$$

Now, multiplying both sides of (14) by $\chi^{\alpha-1}$, integrating the resultant inequality with respect to χ over [0,1] and then using the change of variable technique, we obtain

$$\frac{\Gamma(\alpha)}{(\eta_2-\eta_1)^\alpha}\left[J^\alpha_{\eta_1^+}\varphi(\eta_2) + J^\alpha_{\eta_2^-}\varphi(\eta_1)\right]$$
$$\leq [\varphi(\eta_1) + \varphi(\eta_2)]\int_0^1 \chi^{\alpha-1}\left\{\frac{1}{n}\sum_{i=1}^{n}(e^{s\chi}-1)^i + \frac{1}{n}\sum_{i=1}^{n}\left(e^{s(1-\chi)}-1\right)^i\right\}d\chi,$$

Consequently,

$$\frac{\Gamma(\alpha+1)}{(\eta_2-\eta_1)^\alpha}\left[J^\alpha_{\eta_1^+}\varphi(\eta_2) + J^\alpha_{\eta_2^-}\varphi(\eta_1)\right]$$
$$\leq \alpha[\varphi(\eta_1) + \varphi(\eta_2)]\int_0^1 \chi^{\alpha-1}\left\{\frac{1}{n}\sum_{i=1}^{n}(e^{s\chi}-1)^i + \frac{1}{n}\sum_{i=1}^{n}\left(e^{s(1-\chi)}-1\right)^i\right\}d\chi.$$

This completes rest of the proof. □

Remark 5. *Exclusively, in Theorem 1, If we assign $\alpha = 1$, then we attain*

$$\frac{1}{2\frac{1}{n}\sum_{i=1}^{n}\left(e^{\frac{s}{2}}-1\right)^i}\varphi\left(\frac{\eta_1+\eta_2}{2}\right) \leq \frac{1}{\eta_2-\eta_1}\int_{\eta_1}^{\eta_2}\varphi(\chi)\,d\chi \tag{15}$$
$$\leq \frac{1}{n}\sum_{i=1}^{n}\left(\frac{e^s-s-1}{s}\right)^i\left[\varphi(\eta_1) + \varphi(\eta_2)\right].$$

Remark 6. *Exclusively, in Theorem 1, If we assign $n = s = \alpha = 1$, then it reduces to [Theorem 3.1, [27]].*

In the next section, we establish new Ostrowski-type inequalities for n–polynomial exponentially s–convexity via Riemann–Liouville fractional integral. A useful and interesting feature of our results is that they provide new estimates on these type of inequalities for fractional integrals.

5. Ostrowski-Type Inequalities for n–Polynomial Exponentially s–Convexity via Fractional Integral

To prove our results, we need the following identity (see [34,35]).

Lemma 2. *Suppose a mapping $\varphi : J \subseteq R \to R$ is differentiable on J°, where $\eta_1, \eta_2 \in J$ with $\eta_1 < \eta_2$. If $\varphi' \in \mathcal{L}[\eta_1, \eta_2]$, for all $z \in [\eta_1, \eta_2]$ and $\alpha > 0$, then the following equality holds:*

$$\left(\frac{(z-\eta_1)^\alpha + (\eta_2-z)^\alpha}{\eta_2-\eta_1}\right)\varphi(z) - \frac{\Gamma(\alpha+1)}{\eta_2-\eta_1}\{J^\alpha_{z^-}\varphi(\eta_1) + J^\alpha_{z^+}\varphi(\eta_2)\}$$
$$= \frac{(z-\eta_1)^{\alpha+1}}{\eta_2-\eta_1}\int_0^1 \chi^\alpha \varphi'(\chi z + (1-\chi)\eta_1)\,d\chi - \frac{(\eta_2-z)^{\alpha+1}}{\eta_2-\eta_1}\int_0^1 \chi^\alpha \varphi'(\chi z + (1-\chi)\eta_2)\,d\chi, \tag{16}$$

where Γ is the Euler gamma function.

Theorem 2. *Suppose a mapping $\varphi : J \subseteq R \to R$ is differentiable on J°, where $\eta_1, \eta_2 \in J$ with $\eta_1 < \eta_2$. If $|\varphi'|$ is n-polynomial exponentially s−convex on $[\eta_1, \eta_2]$ for some $s \in (0,1]$, $\varphi' \in \mathcal{L}[\eta_1, \eta_2]$ and $|\varphi'(z)| \leq K$, for all $z \in [\eta_1, \eta_2]$, $\alpha > 0$, then the following inequality holds:*

$$\left| \left(\frac{(z-\eta_1)^\alpha + (\eta_2-z)^\alpha}{\eta_2 - \eta_1} \right) \varphi(z) - \frac{\Gamma(\alpha+1)}{\eta_2 - \eta_1} \{ J_{z^-}^\alpha \varphi(\eta_1) + J_{z^+}^\alpha \varphi(\eta_2) \} \right|$$

$$\leq \frac{K}{n(\eta_2 - \eta_1)}$$

$$\times \Bigg[(z-\eta_1)^{\alpha+1} \bigg\{ \sum_{i=1}^n \left(\frac{\gamma(\alpha+1,-s) - \Gamma(\alpha+1)}{(-s)^\alpha s} - \frac{1}{\alpha+1} \right)^i$$

$$- \sum_{i=1}^n \left(\frac{(\gamma(\alpha+1,s) - \Gamma(\alpha+1))e^s}{s^{\alpha+1}} + \frac{1}{\alpha+1} \right)^i \bigg\}$$

$$+ (\eta_2-z)^{\alpha+1} \bigg\{ \sum_{i=1}^n \left(\frac{\gamma(\alpha+1,-s) - \Gamma(\alpha+1)}{(-s)^\alpha s} - \frac{1}{\alpha+1} \right)^i$$

$$- \sum_{i=1}^n \left(\frac{(\gamma(\alpha+1,s) - \Gamma(\alpha+1))e^s}{s^{\alpha+1}} + \frac{1}{\alpha+1} \right)^i \bigg\} \Bigg]. \quad (17)$$

Proof. From Lemma 2, n-polynomial exponentially s−convexity of $|\varphi'|$ and $|\varphi'(z)| \leq K$, we have

$$\left| \left(\frac{(z-\eta_1)^\alpha + (\eta_2-z)^\alpha}{\eta_2 - \eta_1} \right) \varphi(z) - \frac{\Gamma(\alpha+1)}{\eta_2 - \eta_1} \{ J_{z^-}^\alpha \varphi(\eta_1) + J_{z^+}^\alpha \varphi(\eta_2) \} \right|$$

$$\leq \frac{(z-\eta_1)^{\alpha+1}}{\eta_2 - \eta_1} \int_0^1 \chi^\alpha |\varphi'(\chi z + (1-\chi)\eta_1)| d\chi + \frac{(\eta_2 - z)^{\alpha+1}}{\eta_2 - \eta_1} \int_0^1 \chi^\alpha |\varphi'(\chi z + (1-\chi)\eta_2)| d\chi.$$

$$\leq \frac{(z-\eta_1)^{\alpha+1}}{\eta_2 - \eta_1} \int_0^1 \chi^\alpha \bigg\{ \frac{1}{n} \sum_{i=1}^n (e^{s\chi} - 1)^i |\varphi'(z)| + \frac{1}{n} \sum_{i=1}^n \left(e^{s(1-\chi)} - 1 \right)^i |\varphi'(\eta_1)| \bigg\} d\chi$$

$$+ \frac{(\eta_2 - z)^{\alpha+1}}{\eta_2 - \eta_1} \int_0^1 \chi^\alpha \bigg\{ \frac{1}{n} \sum_{i=1}^n (e^{s\chi} - 1)^i |\varphi'(z)| + \frac{1}{n} \sum_{i=1}^n \left(e^{s(1-\chi)} - 1 \right)^i |\varphi'(\eta_1)| \bigg\} d\chi$$

$$\leq \frac{(z-\eta_1)^{\alpha+1}}{\eta_2 - \eta_1} \bigg\{ |\varphi'(z)| \int_0^1 \chi^\alpha \frac{1}{n} \sum_{i=1}^n (e^{s\chi} - 1)^i d\chi + |\varphi'(\eta_1)| \int_0^1 \chi^\alpha \frac{1}{n} \sum_{i=1}^n \left(e^{s(1-\chi)} - 1 \right)^i d\chi \bigg\}$$

$$+ \frac{(\eta_2 - z)^{\alpha+1}}{\eta_2 - \eta_1} \bigg\{ |\varphi'(z)| \int_0^1 \chi^\alpha \frac{1}{n} \sum_{i=1}^n (e^{s\chi} - 1)^i d\chi + |\varphi'(\eta_2)| \int_0^1 \chi^\alpha \frac{1}{n} \sum_{i=1}^n \left(e^{s(1-\chi)} - 1 \right)^i d\chi \bigg\}$$

$$\leq \frac{K}{n(\eta_2 - \eta_1)}$$

$$\times (z-\eta_1)^{\alpha+1} \bigg\{ \sum_{i=1}^n \left(\frac{\gamma(\alpha+1,-s) - \Gamma(\alpha+1)}{(-s)^\alpha s} - \frac{1}{\alpha+1} \right)^i$$

$$- \sum_{i=1}^n \left(\frac{(\gamma(\alpha+1,s) - \Gamma(\alpha+1))e^s}{s^{\alpha+1}} + \frac{1}{\alpha+1} \right)^i \bigg\}$$

$$+ \frac{K}{n(\eta_2 - \eta_1)}$$

$$\times (\eta_2-z)^{\alpha+1} \bigg\{ \sum_{i=1}^n \left(\frac{\gamma(\alpha+1,-s) - \Gamma(\alpha+1)}{(-s)^\alpha s} - \frac{1}{\alpha+1} \right)^i$$

$$- \sum_{i=1}^n \left(\frac{(\gamma(\alpha+1,s) - \Gamma(\alpha+1))e^s}{s^{\alpha+1}} + \frac{1}{\alpha+1} \right)^i \bigg\}.$$

After further simplifications, proof of Theorem 17 will be completed. □

Corollary 1. *If we assign* $n = 1$ *in Theorem 2, then*

$$\left|\left(\frac{(z-\eta_1)^\alpha + (\eta_2-z)^\alpha}{\eta_2-\eta_1}\right)\varphi(z) - \frac{\Gamma(\alpha+1)}{\eta_2-\eta_1}\{J^\alpha_{z^-}\varphi(\eta_1) + J^\alpha_{z^+}\varphi(\eta_2)\}\right|$$

$$\leq \frac{K}{(\eta_2-\eta_1)}$$

$$\times \left[(z-\eta_1)^{\alpha+1}\left\{\left(\frac{\gamma(\alpha+1,-s)-\Gamma(\alpha+1)}{(-s)^\alpha s}-\frac{1}{\alpha+1}\right)\right.\right.$$

$$\left.-\left(\frac{(\gamma(\alpha+1,s)-\Gamma(\alpha+1))e^s}{s^{\alpha+1}}+\frac{1}{\alpha+1}\right)\right\}$$

$$+ (\eta_2-z)^{\alpha+1}\left\{\left(\frac{\gamma(\alpha+1,-s)-\Gamma(\alpha+1)}{(-s)^\alpha s}-\frac{1}{\alpha+1}\right)\right.$$

$$\left.\left.-\left(\frac{(\gamma(\alpha+1,s)-\Gamma(\alpha+1))e^s}{s^{\alpha+1}}+\frac{1}{\alpha+1}\right)\right\}\right].$$

Corollary 2. *If we assign* $s = 1$ *in Theorem 2, then*

$$\left|\left(\frac{(z-\eta_1)^\alpha + (\eta_2-z)^\alpha}{\eta_2-\eta_1}\right)\varphi(z) - \frac{\Gamma(\alpha+1)}{\eta_2-\eta_1}\{J^\alpha_{z^-}\varphi(\eta_1) + J^\alpha_{z^+}\varphi(\eta_2)\}\right|$$

$$\leq \frac{K}{n(\eta_2-\eta_1)}$$

$$\times \left[(z-\eta_1)^{\alpha+1}\left\{\sum_{i=1}^n \left(\frac{\gamma(\alpha+1,-1)-\Gamma(\alpha+1)}{(-1)^\alpha}-\frac{1}{\alpha+1}\right)^i\right.\right.$$

$$\left.-\sum_{i=1}^n \left((\gamma(\alpha+1,1)-\Gamma(\alpha+1))e+\frac{1}{\alpha+1}\right)^i\right\}$$

$$+ (\eta_2-z)^{\alpha+1}\left\{\sum_{i=1}^n \left(\frac{\gamma(\alpha+1,-1)-\Gamma(\alpha+1)}{(-1)^\alpha}-\frac{1}{\alpha+1}\right)^i\right.$$

$$\left.\left.-\sum_{i=1}^n \left((\gamma(\alpha+1,1)-\Gamma(\alpha+1))e+\frac{1}{\alpha+1}\right)^i\right\}\right].$$

Corollary 3. *If we assign* $\alpha = 1$ *in Theorem 2, then*

$$\left|\varphi(z) - \frac{1}{\eta_2-\eta_1}\int_{\eta_1}^{\eta_2}\varphi(\chi)d\chi\right|$$

$$\leq \frac{K}{(\eta_2-\eta_1)n}\left[(z-\eta_1)^2\left\{\sum_{i=1}^n\left(\frac{2+2(s-1)e^s-s^2}{2s^2}\right)^i + \sum_{i=1}^n\left(\frac{2e^s-s^2-2s-2}{2s^2}\right)^i\right\}\right.$$

$$\left.+ (\eta_2-z)^2\left\{\sum_{i=1}^n\left(\frac{2+2(s-1)e^s-s^2}{2s^2}\right)^i + \sum_{i=1}^n\left(\frac{2e^s-s^2-2s-2}{2s^2}\right)^i\right\}\right].$$

Corollary 4. *If we assign* $\alpha = 1$ *and* $z = \eta_1$ *in Theorem 2, then*

$$\left|\varphi(\eta_1) - \frac{1}{\eta_2-\eta_1}\int_{\eta_1}^{\eta_2}\varphi(\chi)d\chi\right|$$

$$\leq \frac{K}{(\eta_2-\eta_1)n}\left[(\eta_2-\eta_1)^2\left\{\sum_{i=1}^n\left(\frac{2+2(s-1)e^s-s^2}{2s^2}\right)^i + \sum_{i=1}^n\left(\frac{2e^s-s^2-2s-2}{2s^2}\right)^i\right\}\right].$$

Corollary 5. *If we assign $\alpha = 1$ and $z = \eta_2$ in Theorem 2, then*

$$\left| \varphi(\eta_2) - \frac{1}{\eta_2 - \eta_1} \int_{\eta_1}^{\eta_2} \varphi(\chi) d\chi \right|$$

$$\leq \frac{K}{(\eta_2 - \eta_1)n} \left[(\eta_2 - \eta_1)^2 \left\{ \sum_{i=1}^{n} \left(\frac{2 + 2(s-1)e^s - s^2}{2s^2} \right)^i + \sum_{i=1}^{n} \left(\frac{2e^s - s^2 - 2s - 2}{2s^2} \right)^i \right\} \right].$$

Theorem 3. *Suppose a mapping $\varphi : J \subseteq R \to R$ is differentiable on J°, where $\eta_1, \eta_2 \in J$ with $\eta_1 < \eta_2$. If $|\varphi'|^q$ is n–polynomial exponentially s–convex on $[\eta_1, \eta_2]$ for some $s \in (0, 1]$, $q > 1$, $q^{-1} = 1 - p^{-1}$, $\varphi' \in \mathcal{L}[\eta_1, \eta_2]$ and $|\varphi'(z)| \leq K$, for all $z \in [\eta_1, \eta_2]$, with $\alpha > 0$, then the following inequality holds:*

$$\left| \left(\frac{(z - \eta_1)^\alpha + (\eta_2 - z)^\alpha}{\eta_2 - \eta_1} \right) \varphi(z) - \frac{\Gamma(\alpha + 1)}{\eta_2 - \eta_1} \{ J_{z^-}^\alpha \varphi(\eta_1) + J_{z^+}^\alpha \varphi(\eta_2) \} \right|$$

$$\leq \frac{2^{\frac{1}{q}} K}{\sqrt[q]{n}(\eta_2 - \eta_1)} \left(\frac{1}{\alpha p + 1} \right)^{\frac{1}{p}}$$

$$\times \left[(z - \eta_1)^{\alpha+1} \left\{ \sum_{i=1}^{n} \left(\frac{e^s - s - 1}{s} \right)^i \right\}^{\frac{1}{q}} + (\eta_2 - z)^{\alpha+1} \left\{ \sum_{i=1}^{n} \left(\frac{e^s - s - 1}{s} \right)^i \right\}^{\frac{1}{q}} \right]. \quad (18)$$

Proof. Applying Lemma 2 and the well-known Hölder's inequality, we have

$$\left| \left(\frac{(z - \eta_1)^\alpha + (\eta_2 - z)^\alpha}{\eta_2 - \eta_1} \right) \varphi(z) - \frac{\Gamma(\alpha + 1)}{\eta_2 - \eta_1} \{ J_{z^-}^\alpha \varphi(\eta_1) + J_{z^+}^\alpha \varphi(\eta_2) \} \right|$$

$$\leq \frac{(z - \eta_1)^{\alpha+1}}{\eta_2 - \eta_1} \int_0^1 \chi^\alpha |\varphi'(\chi z + (1 - \chi)\eta_1)| \, d\chi + \frac{(\eta_2 - z)^{\alpha+1}}{\eta_2 - \eta_1} \int_0^1 \chi^\alpha |\varphi'(\chi z + (1 - \chi)\eta_2)| \, d\chi$$

$$\leq \frac{(z - \eta_1)^{\alpha+1}}{\eta_2 - \eta_1} \left(\int_0^1 \chi^{\alpha p} d\chi \right)^{\frac{1}{p}} \left(\int_0^1 |\varphi'(\chi z + (1 - \chi)\eta_1)|^q d\chi \right)^{\frac{1}{q}}$$

$$+ \frac{(\eta_2 - z)^{\alpha+1}}{\eta_2 - \eta_1} \left(\int_0^1 \chi^{\alpha p} d\chi \right)^{\frac{1}{p}} \left(\int_0^1 |\varphi'(\chi z + (1 - \chi)\eta_2)|^q d\chi \right)^{\frac{1}{q}}. \quad (19)$$

Since $|\varphi'|^q$ is n–polynomial exponentially s–convex and $|\varphi'(z)| \leq K$, we obtain

$$\int_0^1 |\varphi'(\chi z + (1 - \chi)\eta_1)|^q d\chi = \int_0^1 \left\{ \frac{1}{n} \sum_{i=1}^{n} (e^{s\chi} - 1)^i |\varphi'(z)|^q + \frac{1}{n} \sum_{i=1}^{n} \left(e^{s(1-\chi)} - 1 \right)^i |\varphi'(\eta_1)|^q \right\} d\chi$$

$$\leq K^q \frac{1}{n} \sum_{i=1}^{n} \left(\frac{e^s - s - 1}{s} \right)^i + K^q \frac{1}{n} \sum_{i=1}^{n} \left(\frac{e^s - s - 1}{s} \right)^i$$

$$\leq 2K^q \frac{1}{n} \sum_{i=1}^{n} \left(\frac{e^s - s - 1}{s} \right)^i \quad (20)$$

and

$$\int_0^1 |\varphi'(\chi z + (1 - \chi)\eta_2)|^q d\chi = \int_0^1 \left\{ \frac{1}{n} \sum_{i=1}^{n} (e^{s\chi} - 1)^i |\varphi'(z)|^q + \frac{1}{n} \sum_{i=1}^{n} \left(e^{s(1-\chi)} - 1 \right)^i |\varphi'(\eta_2)|^q \right\} d\chi$$

$$\leq K^q \frac{1}{n} \sum_{i=1}^{n} \left(\frac{e^s - s - 1}{s} \right)^i + K^q \frac{1}{n} \sum_{i=1}^{n} \left(\frac{e^s - s - 1}{s} \right)^i$$

$$\leq 2K^q \frac{1}{n} \sum_{i=1}^{n} \left(\frac{e^s - s - 1}{s} \right)^i. \quad (21)$$

By connecting (20) and (21) with (19), we have the desired inequality (18). □

Corollary 6. *If we assign $n = 1$ in Theorem 3, then*

$$\left|\left(\frac{(z-\eta_1)^\alpha + (\eta_2-z)^\alpha}{\eta_2-\eta_1}\right)\varphi(z) - \frac{\Gamma(\alpha+1)}{\eta_2-\eta_1}\{J_{z^-}^\alpha \varphi(\eta_1) + J_{z^+}^\alpha \varphi(\eta_2)\}\right|$$

$$\leq \frac{2^{\frac{1}{q}}K}{(\eta_2-\eta_1)}\left(\frac{1}{\alpha p + 1}\right)^{\frac{1}{p}}$$

$$\times \left[(z-\eta_1)^{\alpha+1}\left(\frac{e^s - s - 1}{s}\right)^{\frac{1}{q}} + (\eta_2-z)^{\alpha+1}\left(\frac{e^s - s - 1}{s}\right)^{\frac{1}{q}}\right].$$

Corollary 7. *If we assign $s = 1$, in Theorem 3, then*

$$\left|\left(\frac{(z-\eta_1)^\alpha + (\eta_2-z)^\alpha}{\eta_2-\eta_1}\right)\varphi(z) - \frac{\Gamma(\alpha+1)}{\eta_2-\eta_1}\{J_{z^-}^\alpha \varphi(\eta_1) + J_{z^+}^\alpha \varphi(\eta_2)\}\right|$$

$$\leq \frac{2^{\frac{1}{q}}K}{\sqrt[q]{n}(\eta_2-\eta_1)}\left(\frac{1}{\alpha p + 1}\right)^{\frac{1}{p}}\left[(z-\eta_1)^{\alpha+1}\left\{\sum_{i=1}^{n}(e-2)^i\right\}^{\frac{1}{q}} + (\eta_2-z)^{\alpha+1}\left\{\sum_{i=1}^{n}(e-2)^i\right\}^{\frac{1}{q}}\right].$$

Corollary 8. *If we assign $\alpha = 1$, in Theorem 3, then*

$$\left|\varphi(z) - \frac{1}{\eta_2-\eta_1}\int_{\eta_1}^{\eta_2}\varphi(\chi)d\chi\right|$$

$$\leq \frac{2^{\frac{1}{q}}K}{(\eta_2-\eta_1)\sqrt[q]{n}}\left(\frac{1}{p+1}\right)^{\frac{1}{p}}\left[(z-\eta_1)^2\left\{\sum_{i=1}^{n}\left(\frac{e^s-s-1}{s}\right)^i\right\}^{\frac{1}{q}} + (\eta_2-z)^2\left\{\sum_{i=1}^{n}\left(\frac{e^s-s-1}{s}\right)^i\right\}^{\frac{1}{q}}\right]. \quad (22)$$

Corollary 9. *If we assign $\alpha = 1$ and $z = \eta_1$ in Theorem 3, then*

$$\left|\varphi(\eta_1) - \frac{1}{\eta_2-\eta_1}\int_{\eta_1}^{\eta_2}\varphi(\chi)d\chi\right|$$

$$\leq \frac{2^{\frac{1}{q}}K}{(\eta_2-\eta_1)\sqrt[q]{n}}\left(\frac{1}{p+1}\right)^{\frac{1}{p}}\left[(\eta_2-\eta_1)^2\left\{\sum_{i=1}^{n}\left(\frac{e^s-s-1}{s}\right)^i\right\}^{\frac{1}{q}}\right]. \quad (23)$$

Corollary 10. *If we assign $\alpha = 1$ and $z = \eta_2$ in Theorem 3, then*

$$\left|\varphi(\eta_2) - \frac{1}{\eta_2-\eta_1}\int_{\eta_1}^{\eta_2}\varphi(\chi)d\chi\right|$$

$$\leq \frac{2^{\frac{1}{q}}K}{(\eta_2-\eta_1)\sqrt[q]{n}}\left(\frac{1}{p+1}\right)^{\frac{1}{p}}\left[(\eta_2-\eta_1)^2\left\{\sum_{i=1}^{n}\left(\frac{e^s-s-1}{s}\right)^i\right\}^{\frac{1}{q}}\right]. \quad (24)$$

Theorem 4. *Suppose a mapping $\varphi : J \subseteq R \to R$ is differentiable on J^o, where $\eta_1, \eta_2 \in J$ with $\eta_1 < \eta_2$. Let $q \geq 1$ and $q^{-1} = 1 - p^{-1}$. If $|\varphi'|^q$ is n–polynomial exponentially s–convex on*

$[\eta_1, \eta_2]$ for some $s \in (0,1]$, $\varphi' \in \mathcal{L}[\eta_1, \eta_2]$ and $|\varphi'(z)| \leq K$, for all $z \in [\eta_1, \eta_2]$, with $\alpha > 0$, then the following inequality holds:

$$\left| \left(\frac{(z-\eta_1)^\alpha + (\eta_2-z)^\alpha}{\eta_2 - \eta_1} \right) \varphi(z) - \frac{\Gamma(\alpha+1)}{\eta_2 - \eta_1} \{ J_{z^-}^\alpha \varphi(\eta_1) + J_{z^+}^\alpha \varphi(\eta_2) \} \right|$$

$$\leq \frac{K}{\sqrt[q]{n}(\eta_2 - \eta_1)} \left(\frac{1}{\alpha+1} \right)^{1-\frac{1}{q}}$$

$$\times \left[(z-\eta_1)^{\alpha+1} \left\{ \sum_{i=1}^{n} \left(\frac{\gamma(\alpha+1,-s) - \Gamma(\alpha+1)}{(-s)^\alpha s} - \frac{1}{\alpha+1} \right)^i \right. \right.$$

$$\left. - \sum_{i=1}^{n} \left((\gamma(\alpha+1,s) - \Gamma(\alpha+1))s^{-\alpha-1}e^s - \frac{1}{\alpha+1} \right)^i \right\}^{\frac{1}{q}}$$

$$+ (\eta_2 - z)^{\alpha+1} \left\{ \sum_{i=1}^{n} \left(\frac{\gamma(\alpha+1,-s) - \Gamma(\alpha+1)}{(-s)^\alpha s} - \frac{1}{\alpha+1} \right)^i \right.$$

$$\left. \left. - \sum_{i=1}^{n} \left((\gamma(\alpha+1,s) - \Gamma(\alpha+1))s^{-\alpha-1}e^s - \frac{1}{\alpha+1} \right)^i \right\}^{\frac{1}{q}} \right]. \quad (25)$$

Proof. Using Lemma 2 and power mean inequality, we have

$$\left| \left(\frac{(z-\eta_1)^\alpha + (\eta_2-z)^\alpha}{\eta_2 - \eta_1} \right) \varphi(z) - \frac{\Gamma(\alpha+1)}{\eta_2 - \eta_1} \{ J_{z^-}^\alpha \varphi(\eta_1) + J_{z^+}^\alpha \varphi(\eta_2) \} \right|$$

$$\leq \frac{(z-\eta_1)^{\alpha+1}}{\eta_2 - \eta_1} \int_0^1 \chi^\alpha |\varphi'(\chi z + (1-\chi)\eta_1)| \, d\chi + \frac{(\eta_2-z)^{\alpha+1}}{\eta_2 - \eta_1} \int_0^1 \chi^\alpha |\varphi'(\chi z + (1-\chi)\eta_2)| \, d\chi$$

$$\leq \frac{(z-\eta_1)^{\alpha+1}}{\eta_2 - \eta_1} \left(\int_0^1 \chi^\alpha d\chi \right)^{1-\frac{1}{q}} \left(\int_0^1 \chi^\alpha |\varphi'(\chi z + (1-\chi)\eta_1)|^q d\chi \right)^{\frac{1}{q}}$$

$$+ \frac{(\eta_2-z)^{\alpha+1}}{\eta_2 - \eta_1} \left(\int_0^1 \chi^\alpha d\chi \right)^{1-\frac{1}{q}} \left(\int_0^1 \chi^\alpha |\varphi'(\chi z + (1-\chi)\eta_2)|^q d\chi \right)^{\frac{1}{q}} \quad (26)$$

Since, $|\varphi'|^q$ is n-polynomial exponentially s-convexity and $|\varphi'(z)| \leq K$, we obtain

$$\int_0^1 \chi^\alpha |\varphi'(\chi z + (1-\chi)\eta_1)|^q \, d\chi$$

$$= \int_0^1 \chi^\alpha \left\{ \frac{1}{n} \sum_{i=1}^n (e^{s\chi} - 1)^i |\varphi'(z)|^q + \frac{1}{n} \sum_{i=1}^n \left(e^{s(1-\chi)} - 1 \right)^i |\varphi'(\eta_1)|^q \right\} d\chi$$

$$\leq \frac{K^q}{n} \left\{ \sum_{i=1}^n \left(\frac{\gamma(\alpha+1,-s) - \Gamma(\alpha+1)}{(-s)^\alpha s} - \frac{1}{\alpha+1} \right)^i \right.$$

$$\left. - \sum_{i=1}^n \left((\gamma(\alpha+1,s) - \Gamma(\alpha+1))s^{-\alpha-1}e^s - \frac{1}{\alpha+1} \right)^i \right\} \quad (27)$$

Consequently, similar computation gives

$$\int_0^1 \chi^\alpha |\varphi'(\chi z + (1-\chi)\eta_2)|^q \, d\chi$$

$$= \int_0^1 \chi^\alpha \left\{ \frac{1}{n} \sum_{i=1}^n (e^{s\chi} - 1)^i |\varphi'(z)|^q + \frac{1}{n} \sum_{i=1}^n \left(e^{s(1-\chi)} - 1 \right)^i |\varphi'(\eta_2)|^q \right\} d\chi$$

$$\leq \frac{K^q}{n} \left\{ \sum_{i=1}^n \left(\frac{\gamma(\alpha+1,-s) - \Gamma(\alpha+1)}{(-s)^\alpha s} - \frac{1}{\alpha+1} \right)^i \right.$$

$$\left. - \sum_{i=1}^n \left((\gamma(\alpha+1,s) - \Gamma(\alpha+1))s^{-\alpha-1}e^s - \frac{1}{\alpha+1} \right)^i \right\}. \quad (28)$$

By connecting (27) and (28) with (26), we obtain the desired result (25). □

Corollary 11. *If we assign $n = 1$ in Theorem 4, then*

$$\left| \left(\frac{(z-\eta_1)^\alpha + (\eta_2-z)^\alpha}{\eta_2-\eta_1} \right) \varphi(z) - \frac{\Gamma(\alpha+1)}{\eta_2-\eta_1} \{J^\alpha_{z-}\varphi(\eta_1) + J^\alpha_{z+}\varphi(\eta_2)\} \right|$$

$$\leq \frac{K}{(\eta_2-\eta_1)} \left(\frac{1}{\alpha+1} \right)^{1-\frac{1}{q}}$$

$$\times \left[(z-\eta_1)^{\alpha+1} \left\{ \frac{\gamma(\alpha+1,-s) - \Gamma(\alpha+1)}{(-s)^\alpha s} - (\gamma(\alpha+1,s) - \Gamma(\alpha+1))s^{-\alpha-1}e^s - \frac{2}{\alpha+1} \right\}^{\frac{1}{q}} \right.$$

$$+ (\eta_2-z)^{\alpha+1} \left\{ \frac{\gamma(\alpha+1,-s) - \Gamma(\alpha+1)}{(-s)^\alpha s} - (\gamma(\alpha+1,s) - \Gamma(\alpha+1))s^{-\alpha-1}e^s - \frac{2}{\alpha+1} \right\}^{\frac{1}{q}} \right].$$

Corollary 12. *If we assign $s = 1$, in Theorem 4, then*

$$\left| \left(\frac{(z-\eta_1)^\alpha + (\eta_2-z)^\alpha}{\eta_2-\eta_1} \right) \varphi(z) - \frac{\Gamma(\alpha+1)}{\eta_2-\eta_1} \{J^\alpha_{z-}\varphi(\eta_1) + J^\alpha_{z+}\varphi(\eta_2)\} \right|$$

$$\leq \frac{K}{\sqrt[q]{n}(\eta_2-\eta_1)} \left(\frac{1}{\alpha+1} \right)^{1-\frac{1}{q}}$$

$$\times \left[(z-\eta_1)^{\alpha+1} \left\{ \sum_{i=1}^{n} \left(\frac{\gamma(\alpha+1,-1) - \Gamma(\alpha+1)}{(-1)^\alpha} - \frac{1}{\alpha+1} \right)^i \right. \right.$$

$$- \sum_{i=1}^{n} \left((\gamma(\alpha+1,1) - \Gamma(\alpha+1))e - \frac{1}{\alpha+1} \right)^i \right\}^{\frac{1}{q}}$$

$$+ (\eta_2-z)^{\alpha+1} \left\{ \sum_{i=1}^{n} \left(\frac{\gamma(\alpha+1,-1) - \Gamma(\alpha+1)}{(-1)^\alpha} - \frac{1}{\alpha+1} \right)^i \right.$$

$$\left. \left. - \sum_{i=1}^{n} \left((\gamma(\alpha+1,1) - \Gamma(\alpha+1))e - \frac{1}{\alpha+1} \right)^i \right\}^{\frac{1}{q}} \right].$$

Corollary 13. *If we assign $\alpha = 1$, in Theorem 4, then*

$$\left| \varphi(z) - \frac{1}{\eta_2-\eta_1} \int_{\eta_1}^{\eta_2} \varphi(\chi)d\chi \right|$$

$$\leq \frac{K}{\sqrt[q]{n}(\eta_2-\eta_1)2^{1-\frac{1}{q}}} \left[(z-\eta_1)^2 \left\{ \sum_{i=1}^{n} \left(\frac{2 + (2s-2)e^s - s^2}{2s^2} \right)^i + \sum_{i=1}^{n} \left(\frac{2e^s - s^2 - 2s - 2}{2s^2} \right)^i \right\}^{\frac{1}{q}} \right.$$

$$\left. + (\eta_2-z)^2 \left\{ \sum_{i=1}^{n} \left(\frac{2 + (2s-2)e^s - s^2}{2s^2} \right)^i + \sum_{i=1}^{n} \left(\frac{2e^s - s^2 - 2s - 2}{2s^2} \right)^i \right\}^{\frac{1}{q}} \right].$$

Corollary 14. *If we assign $\alpha = 1$ and $z = \eta_1$ in Theorem 4, then*

$$\left| \varphi(\eta_1) - \frac{1}{\eta_2-\eta_1} \int_{\eta_1}^{\eta_2} \varphi(\chi)d\chi \right|$$

$$\leq \frac{K}{\sqrt[q]{n}(\eta_2-\eta_1)2^{1-\frac{1}{q}}} \left[(\eta_2-\eta_1)^2 \left\{ \sum_{i=1}^{n} \left(\frac{2 + (2s-2)e^s - s^2}{2s^2} \right)^i + \sum_{i=1}^{n} \left(\frac{2e^s - s^2 - 2s - 2}{2s^2} \right)^i \right\}^{\frac{1}{q}} \right].$$

Corollary 15. *If we assign $\alpha = 1$ and $z = \eta_2$ in Theorem 4, then*

$$\left|\varphi(\eta_2) - \frac{1}{\eta_2 - \eta_1}\int_{\eta_1}^{\eta_2}\varphi(x)dx\right|$$
$$\leq \frac{K}{\sqrt[q]{n}(\eta_2-\eta_1)2^{1-\frac{1}{q}}}\left[(\eta_2-\eta_1)^2\left\{\sum_{i=1}^{n}\left(\frac{2+(2s-2)e^s-s^2}{2s^2}\right)^i + \sum_{i=1}^{n}\left(\frac{2e^s - s^2 - 2s - 2}{2s^2}\right)^i\right\}^{\frac{1}{q}}\right].$$

6. Applications

We recall the following special means for different positive real numbers η_1, η_2 and $\eta_1 < \eta_2$ as follows:

1. The arithmetic mean:
$$A(\eta_1, \eta_2) = \frac{\eta_1 + \eta_2}{2}.$$

2. The Harmonic mean:
$$H(\eta_1, \eta_2) = \frac{2\eta_1\eta_2}{\eta_1 + \eta_2}, \quad \eta_1, \eta_2 > 0.$$

3. The logarithmic mean:
$$L = L(\eta_1, \eta_2) = \frac{\eta_2 - \eta_1}{\ln \eta_2 - \ln \eta_1}, \quad \eta_1 \neq \eta_2.$$

4. The generalized logarithmic mean:
$$L_r(\eta_1, \eta_2) = \left[\frac{\eta_2^{r+1} - \eta_1^{r+1}}{(r+1)(\eta_2 - \eta_1)}\right]^{\frac{1}{r}}; \quad r \in \mathbb{R}\setminus\{-1, 0\}.$$

5. The Identric mean:
$$I(\eta_1, \eta_2) = \begin{cases} \eta_1 & \eta_1 = \eta_2 \\ \frac{1}{e}\left(\frac{\eta_2^{\eta_2}}{\eta_1^{\eta_1}}\right)^{\frac{1}{\eta_2-\eta_1}} & \eta_1 \neq \eta_2 \end{cases}.$$

Proposition 2. *Let $0 < \eta_1 < \eta_2$. Then for some fixed $s \in [\ln 2.4, 1)$, we obtain*

$$|\ln I(\eta_1, \eta_2) - \ln A(\eta_1, \eta_2)|$$
$$\leq (\eta_2 - \eta_1)\frac{K}{2n}\left\{\sum_{i=1}^{n}\left(\frac{2 + 2(s-1)e^s - s^2}{2s^2}\right)^i + \sum_{i=1}^{n}\left(\frac{2e^s - s^2 - 2s - 2}{2s^2}\right)^i\right\}.$$

Proof. The assertion follows from Corollary 3 by letting $z = \frac{\eta_1 + \eta_2}{2}$ and $\varphi(z) = -\ln z$. □

Note: Estimation of "K" for the above Proposition 2 is as follows:

$$\varphi(z) = -\ln z \implies |\varphi'(z)| = \frac{1}{z} \leq K = |\varphi'(\eta_1)| = \frac{1}{\eta_1}.$$

Proposition 3. *Let $0 < \eta_1 < \eta_2$ and $q > 1$. Then for some fixed $s \in [\ln 2.4, 1)$, we obtain*

$$\left|H(\eta_1, \eta_2) - L^{-1}(\eta_1, \eta_2)\right| \leq 2^{\frac{1}{q}-1}\frac{K}{\sqrt[q]{n}}(\eta_2 - \eta_1)\left(\frac{1}{p+1}\right)^{\frac{1}{p}}\left\{\sum_{i=1}^{n}\left(\frac{e^s - s - 1}{s}\right)^i\right\}^{\frac{1}{q}}.$$

Proof. The assertion follows from Corollary 8 by letting $z = \frac{\eta_1 + \eta_2}{2}$ and $\varphi(z) = \frac{1}{z}$. □

Note: *Estimation of "K" for the above Proposition 3 is as follows:*

$$\varphi(z) = \frac{1}{z} \implies |\varphi'(z)| = \frac{1}{z^2} \leq K = |\varphi'(\eta_1)| = \frac{1}{\eta_1^2}$$

Proposition 4. *Let $0 < \eta_1 < \eta_2$. Then for some fixed $s \in [\ln 2.4, 1)$, we obtain*

$$\left| A^{ls}(\eta_1, \eta_2) - L^{ls}_{ls}(\eta_1, \eta_2) \right|$$

$$\leq (\eta_2 - \eta_1) \frac{K}{2n} \left\{ \sum_{i=1}^{n} \left(\frac{2 + 2(s-1)e^s - s^2}{2s^2} \right)^i + \sum_{i=1}^{n} \left(\frac{2e^s - s^2 - 2s - 2}{2s^2} \right)^i \right\}.$$

Proof. The assertion follows from Corollary 3 by letting $z = \frac{\eta_1 + \eta_2}{2}$ and $\varphi(z) = z^{ls}$. □

Note: *Estimation of "K" for the above Proposition 4 is as follows:*

$$\varphi(z) = z^{ls} \implies |\varphi'(z)| = ls(z)^{ls-1} \leq K = |\varphi'(\eta_2)| = ls(\eta_2)^{ls-1}$$

Proposition 5. *Let $0 < \eta_1 < \eta_2$. Then for some fixed $s \in [\ln 2.4, 1)$, we obtain*

$$\left| A^{ls}(\eta_1, \eta_2) - L^{ls}_{ls}(\eta_1, \eta_2) \right|$$

$$\leq 2^{\frac{1}{q}-1} \frac{K}{\sqrt[q]{n}} (\eta_2 - \eta_1) \left(\frac{1}{p+1} \right)^{\frac{1}{p}} \left\{ \sum_{i=1}^{n} \left(\frac{e^s - s - 1}{s} \right)^i \right\}^{\frac{1}{q}}.$$

Proof. The assertion follows from Corollary 8 by letting $z = \frac{\eta_1 + \eta_2}{2}$ and $\varphi(z) = z^{ls}$. □

Note: *Similarly, one can estimate the value of "K" as estimated in the above propositions (see Propositions 2–4).*

Proposition 6. *Let $0 < \eta_1 < \eta_2$. Then for some fixed $s \in [\ln 2.4, 1)$, we obtain*

$$|G^s(\alpha, \beta) - L(\alpha^s, \beta^s)|$$

$$\leq (\eta_2 - \eta_1) \frac{K}{2n} \left\{ \sum_{i=1}^{n} \left(\frac{2 + 2(s-1)e^s - s^2}{2s^2} \right)^i + \sum_{i=1}^{n} \left(\frac{2e^s - s^2 - 2s - 2}{2s^2} \right)^i \right\}.$$

Proof. The assertion follows from Corollary 3 by letting $z = \frac{\eta_1 + \eta_2}{2}$, $\varphi(z) = e^{sz}, z > 0$ and $\alpha = e^{\eta_1}, \beta = e^{\eta_2}$. □

Note: *Similarly, one can estimate the value of "K" as estimated in the above propositions (see Propositions 2–4).*

7. Midpoint Formula

Since in [36], suppose d is the division $\eta_1 = x_0 < x_1 < x_2 < ... < x_n = \eta_2$ of the interval $[\eta_1, \eta_2]$ and consider the quadrature formula

$$\int_{\eta_1}^{\eta_2} \varphi(\chi) d\chi = T(\varphi, d) + E(\varphi, d), \tag{29}$$

where $T(\varphi, d) = \sum_{j=1}^{n-1} \varphi\left(\frac{x_j + x_{j+1}}{2}\right) h_j$, is the midpoint version and $E(\varphi, d)$ denotes the approximation error and $h_j = x_{j+1} - x_j$, for $j = 0, 1, 2, ..., n-1$.

Proposition 7. Suppose a mapping $\varphi : I \subset [0, \infty) \to \mathbb{R}$ is differentiable on I° such that $\varphi' \in L[\eta_1, \eta_2]$, where $\eta_1, \eta_2 \in I$ with $\eta_2 > \eta_1$. If $|\varphi'|$ is n–polynomial exponentially s–convex on $[\eta_1, \eta_2]$, then for every division d of $[\eta_1, \eta_2]$, the midpoint error satisfy

$$|E(\varphi, d)| \leq \frac{K}{2n} \sum_{j=0}^{n-1} h_j^2 \left\{ \sum_{i=1}^{n} \left(\frac{2 + 2(s-1)e^s - s^2}{2s^2} \right)^i + \sum_{i=1}^{n} \left(\frac{2e^s - s^2 - 2s - 2}{2s^2} \right)^i \right\}.$$

Proof. Since applying Corollary 3 with n–polynomial exponentially s–convexity and $z = \frac{\eta_1 + \eta_2}{2}$ on the subinterval $[x_j, x_{j+1}]$

$$\left| h_j \varphi \left(\frac{x_j + x_{j+1}}{2} \right) - \int_{x_j}^{x_{j+1}} \varphi(x) dx \right| \leq \frac{h_j^2 K}{2n}$$

$$\times \left\{ \sum_{i=1}^{n} \left(\frac{2 + 2(s-1)e^s - s^2}{2s^2} \right)^i + \sum_{i=1}^{n} \left(\frac{2e^s - s^2 - 2s - 2}{2s^2} \right)^i \right\}.$$

Summing over j from 0 to $n-1$ and taking into account that $|\varphi'|$ is n–polynomial exponentially s–convex, we obtain, by the triangle inequality

$$\left| \int_{\eta_1}^{\eta_2} \varphi(\chi) d\chi - T(\varphi, d) \right|$$

$$\leq \left| \sum_{j=0}^{n-1} \left\{ \int_{x_j}^{x_{j+1}} \varphi(x) dx - \varphi\left(\frac{x_j + x_{j+1}}{2} \right) h_j \right\} \right|$$

$$\leq \sum_{j=0}^{n-1} \left| \left\{ \int_{x_j}^{x_{j+1}} \varphi(x) dx - \varphi\left(\frac{x_j + x_{j+1}}{2} \right) h_j \right\} \right|$$

$$\leq \frac{K}{2n} \sum_{j=0}^{n-1} h_j^2 \times \left\{ \sum_{i=1}^{n} \left(\frac{2 + 2(s-1)e^s - s^2}{2s^2} \right)^i + \sum_{i=1}^{n} \left(\frac{2e^s - s^2 - 2s - 2}{2s^2} \right)^i \right\}.$$

which completes the proof. □

Note: Similarly, one can estimate the value of "K" as estimated in the above propositions (see Propositions 2–4).

Proposition 8. Suppose a mapping $\varphi : I \subset [0, \infty) \to \mathbb{R}$ is differentiable on I° such that $\varphi' \in L[\eta_1, \eta_2]$, where $\eta_1, \eta_2 \in I$ with $\eta_2 > \eta_1, q > 1$, for $s \in [\ln 2.4, 1)$ in (29), for every division d of $[\eta_1, \eta_2]$. If $|\varphi'|^q$ is n–polynomial exponentially s–convex on $[\eta_1, \eta_2]$, then the midpoint error satisfy

$$|E(\varphi, d)| \leq 2^{\frac{1}{q}-1} \frac{K}{\sqrt[q]{n}} \sum_{j=0}^{n-1} h_j^2 \times \left(\frac{1}{p+1} \right)^{\frac{1}{p}} \left\{ \sum_{i=1}^{n} \left(\frac{e^s - s - 1}{s} \right)^i \right\}^{\frac{1}{q}}.$$

Proof. By applying the same technique as in proposition (7) but using the Corollary 8 with $z = \frac{\eta_1 + \eta_2}{2}$. □

Note: Similarly, one can estimate the value of "K" as estimated in the above propositions (see Propositions 2–4).

8. Conclusions

In this article, we have taken into consideration a critical extension of convexity that is referred to as n-polynomial exponentially s-convex functions and acquired a new Hermite–Hadamard-type inequality and some novel refinements of Ostrowski-type inequalities. We also presented some applications of our established results to special means of two positive real numbers and midpoint formula. In the future, new inequalities for other n-polynomial convex functions can be obtained by using the techniques used in this article.

Author Contributions: Conceptualization, S.K.S., M.T., H.A. (Hijaz Ahmad), J.N., H.A. (Hassen Aydi); methodology, S.K.S., M.T., H.A. (Hijaz Ahmad), J.N., H.A. (Hassen Aydi); validation, S.K.S., M.T., H.A. (Hijaz Ahmad), J.N., H.A. (Hassen Aydi), A.M.; investigation, S.K.S., M.T., H.A. (Hijaz Ahmad), J.N., H.A. (Hassen Aydi); writing— original draft preparation, S.K.S., M.T.; writing—review and editing, S.K.S., M.T., H.A. (Hijaz Ahmad), J.N., H.A. (Hassen Aydi), A.M.; supervision, S.K.S., M.T., H.A. (Hassen Aydi). All authors have read and agreed to the final version of the manuscript.

Funding: Research group Nonlinear Analysis Methods in Applied Mathematics (NAMAM) group number RG-DES-2017-01-17, Prince Sultan University.

Institutional Review Board Statement: Not applicable.

Informed Consent Statement: Not applicable.

Data Availability Statement: No data and materials were used to support this study.

Acknowledgments: The last author would like to thank Prince Sultan University for funding this work through research group Nonlinear Analysis Methods in Applied Mathematics (NAMAM) group number RG-DES-2017-01-17.

Conflicts of Interest: The authors declare that they have no competing interests.

References

1. Mohammed, P.O.; Brevik, I. A new version of the Hermite–Hadamard inequality for Riemann–Liouville fractional integrals. *Symmetry* **2020**, *12*, 610. [CrossRef]
2. Mohammed, P.O.; Sarikaya, M.Z.; Baleanu, D. On the generalized Hermite–Hadamard inequalities via the tempered fractional integrals. *Symmetry* **2020**, *12*, 595. [CrossRef]
3. Mohammed, P.O.; Abdeljawad, T. Modification of certain fractional integral inequalities for convex functions. *Adv. Differ. Equ.* **2020**, *2020*, 1–22. [CrossRef]
4. Vivas-Cortez, M.; Kashuri, A.; Hernández, J.E.H. Trapezium–type inequalities for Raina's fractional integrals operator using generalized convex functions. *Symmetry* **2020**, *12*, 1034. [CrossRef]
5. Butt, S.I.; Nadeem, M.; Qaisar, S.; Akdemir, A.O.; Abdeljawad, T. Hermite–Jensen–Mercer type inequalities for conformable integrals and related results. *Adv. Differ. Equ.* **2020**, *1*, 1–24. [CrossRef]
6. Sarikaya, M.Z.; Set, E.; Yaldiz, H.; Başak, N. Hermite–Hadamard inequalities for fractional integrals and related fractional inequalities. *Math. Comput. Model.* **2013**, *57*, 2403–2407. [CrossRef]
7. Mohammed, P.O.; Aydi, H.; Kashuri, A.; Hamed, Y.S.; Abualnaja, K.M. Midpoint inequalities in fractional calculus defined using positive weighted symmetry function kernels. *Symmetry* **2021**, *13*, 550. [CrossRef]
8. Kilbas, A.A.; Srivastava, H.M.; Trujillo, J.J. *Theory and Applications of Fractional Differential Equations*; Elsevier: Amsterdam, The Netherlands, 2006.
9. Xi, B.Y.; Qi, F. Some integral inequalities of Hermite–Hadamard type for convex functions with applications to means. *J. Funct. Spaces Appl.* **2012**, *2012*, 980438. [CrossRef]
10. Özcan, S.; İşcan, İ. Some new Hermite-Hadamard type integral inequalities for the s–convex functions and theirs applications. *J. Inequal. Appl.* **2019**, *201*, 1–14.
11. Mehren, K.; Agarwal, P. New Hermite–Hadamard type integral inequalities for the convex functions and theirs applications. *J. Comp. Appl. Math.* **2019**, *350*, 274–285. [CrossRef]
12. Butt, S.I.; Kashuri, A.; Tariq, M.; Nasir, J.; Aslam, A.; Geo, W. n–polynomial exponential–type p–convex function with some related inequalities and their applications. *Heliyon* **2020**, *6*, e05420. [CrossRef] [PubMed]
13. Zhang, K.S.; Wan, J.P. p–convex functions and their applications. *Pure Appl. Math.* **2017**, *23*, 130–133
14. Butt, S.I.; Tariq, M.; Aslam, A.; Ahmad, H.; Nofel, T.A. Hermite–Hadamard type inequalities via generalized harmonic exponential convexity. *J. Funct. Spaces* **2021**. [CrossRef]
15. Butt, S.I.; Kashuri, A.; Tariq, M.; Nasir, J.; Aslam, A.; Geo, W. Hermite–Hadamard type inequalities via n–polynomial exponential–type convexity and their applications. *Adv. Differ. Equ.* **2020**, *508*, 1–25. [CrossRef]
16. Dragomir, S.S. Ostrowski type inequalities for Riemann–Liouville fractional integrals of absolutely continuous functions in terms of norms. *RGMIA Res. Rep. Collect.* **2017**, *20*, 49.
17. Mitrinovic, D.S.; Pecaric, J.; Fink, A.M. *Inequalities Involving Functions and Their Integrals and Derivatives*; Springer Science and Business Media: Berlin/Heidelberg, Germany, 1991; Volume 53, 603p
18. Alomari, M.; Darus, M. Some Ostrowski type inequalities for quasi-convex functions with applications to special means. *RGMIA Res. Rep. Coll* **2010**, *13696936*, 1–9

19. Cerone, P.; Dragomir, S.S. Ostrowski type inequalities for functions whose derivatives satisfy certain convexity assumptions. *Demonstr. Math.* **2004**, *37*, 299–308. [CrossRef]
20. Alomari, M.; Darus, M.; Dragomir, S.S.; Cerone, P. Ostrowski type inequalities for functions whose derivatives are s–convex in the second sense. *Appl. Math. Lett.* **2010**, *23*, 1071–1076. [CrossRef]
21. Dragomir, S.S. On the Ostrowski's integral inequality for mappings with bounded variation and applications. *Math. Ineq. Appl.* **1998**, *1*, 59–66. [CrossRef]
22. Set, E.; Sarikaya, M.Z.; Özdemir, M.E. Some Ostrowski's Type Inequalities for Functions whose Second Derivatives are s–Convex in the Second Sense and Applications. *arXiv* **2010**, arXiv:1006.2488.
23. Pachpatte, B.G. On an inequality of Ostrowski type in three independent variables. *J. Math. Anal. Appl.* **2000**, *249*, 583–591. [CrossRef]
24. Antczak, T. On (p,r)-invex set and functions. *J. Math. Anal. Appl.* **2001**, *263*, 355–379. [CrossRef]
25. Dragomir, S.S.; Gomm, I. Some Hermite-Hadamard's Inequality functions whose exponentials are convex. *Babes Bolyani Math.* **2005**, *60*, 527–534.
26. Awan, M.U.; Noor, M.A.; Noor, K.I. Hermite-Hadamard type inequalities for exponentially convex function. *Appl. Math. Inf. Sci.* **2018**, *12*, 405–409. [CrossRef]
27. Kadakal, M.; İşcan, İ. Exponential type convexity and some related inequalities. *J. Inequal. Appl.* **2020**, *2020*, 1–9. [CrossRef]
28. Niculescu, C.P.; Persson, L.E. *Convex Functions and Their Applications*; Springer: New York, NY, USA, 2006.
29. Dragomir, S.S.; Fitzpatrik, S. The Hadamard inequality for s–convex functions in the second sense. *Demonstr. Math.* **1999**, *32*, 687–696. [CrossRef]
30. Set, E.; Özdemir, M.E.; Sarikaya, M.Z. New inequalities of Ostrowski's type for s–convex functions in the second sense with applications. *arXiv* **2010**, arXiv:1005.0702.
31. Breckner, W.W. Stetigkeitsaussagen für eine Klasse verallgemeinerter konvexer funktionen in topologischen linearen Raumen. *Pupl. Inst. Math.* **1978**, *23*, 13–20.
32. Hudzik, H.; Maligranda, L. Some remarks on s-convex functions. *Aequ. Math.* **1994**, *48*, 100–111. [CrossRef]
33. Toplu, T.; Kadakal, M.; İşcan, İ. On n-polynomial convexity and some relatd inequalities. *AIMS* **2020**, *5*, 1304–1318. [CrossRef]
34. Noor, M.A.; Noor, K.I.; Awan, M.U. Fractional Ostrowski inequalities for s-Godunova-Levin functions. *Int. J. Anal. Appl.* **2014**, *5*, 167–173.
35. Set, E. New inequalities of Ostrowski type for mappings whose derivatives are s-convex in the second sense via fractional integrals. *Comput. Math. Appl.* **2012**, *63*, 1147–1154. [CrossRef]
36. Kirmaci, U.S.; Özdemir, M.E. On some inequalities for differentiable mappings and applications to special means of real numbers and to midpoint formula. *Appl. Math. Comput.* **2004**, *153*, 361–368. [CrossRef]

Article

A More Accurate Half-Discrete Hilbert-Type Inequality Involving One upper Limit Function and One Partial Sum

Xianyong Huang [1], Shanhe Wu [2,*] and Bicheng Yang [3]

1. Department of Mathematics, Guangdong University of Education, Guangzhou 510303, China; huangxianyong@gdei.edu.cn
2. Department of Mathematics, Longyan University, Longyan 364012, China
3. Institute of Applied Mathematics, Longyan University, Longyan 364012, China; bcyang@gdei.edu.cn
* Correspondence: shanhewu@lyun.edu.cn

Abstract: In this paper, by virtue of the symmetry principle, we construct proper weight coefficients and use them to establish a more accurate half-discrete Hilbert-type inequality involving one upper limit function and one partial sum. Then, we prove the new inequality with the help of the Euler–Maclaurin summation formula and Abel's partial summation formula. Finally, we illustrate how the obtained results can generate some new half-discrete Hilbert-type inequalities.

Keywords: weight coefficient; Euler–Maclaurin summation formula; Abel's partial summation formula; half-discrete Hilbert-type inequality; upper limit function

1. Introduction

The celebrated Hardy–Hilbert's inequality reads as:

$$\sum_{m=1}^{\infty}\sum_{n=1}^{\infty}\frac{a_m b_n}{m+n} < \frac{\pi}{\sin(\pi/p)}\left(\sum_{m=1}^{\infty} a_m^p\right)^{\frac{1}{p}}\left(\sum_{n=1}^{\infty} b_n^q\right)^{\frac{1}{q}}, \tag{1}$$

where $p > 1$, $\frac{1}{p}+\frac{1}{q}=1$, $a_m, b_n \geq 0$, $0 < \sum_{m=1}^{\infty} a_m^p < \infty$ and $0 < \sum_{n=1}^{\infty} b_n^q < \infty$, the constant factor $\frac{\pi}{\sin(\pi/p)}$ is the best possible (see [1], Theorem 315).

A more accurate form of (1) was provided in ([1], Theorem 323), as follows:

$$\sum_{m=1}^{\infty}\sum_{n=1}^{\infty}\frac{a_m b_n}{m+n-1} < \frac{\pi}{\sin(\pi/p)}\left(\sum_{m=1}^{\infty} a_m^p\right)^{\frac{1}{p}}\left(\sum_{n=1}^{\infty} b_n^q\right)^{\frac{1}{q}}. \tag{2}$$

In 2006, by introducing parameters $\lambda_i \in (0,2]\,(i=1,2), \lambda_1 + \lambda_2 = \lambda \in (0,4]$, an extension of (1) was provided by [2] as follows:

$$\sum_{m=1}^{\infty}\sum_{n=1}^{\infty}\frac{a_m b_n}{(m+n)^\lambda} < B(\lambda_1,\lambda_2)\left[\sum_{m=1}^{\infty} m^{p(1-\lambda_1)-1} a_m^p\right]^{\frac{1}{p}}\left[\sum_{n=1}^{\infty} n^{q(1-\lambda_2)-1} b_n^q\right]^{\frac{1}{q}}, \tag{3}$$

where the constant factor $B(\lambda_1, \lambda_2)$ is the best possible, and the beta function is defined as:

$$B(u,v) = \int_0^\infty \frac{t^{u-1}}{(1+t)^{u+v}} dt \quad (u,v > 0).$$

Obviously, when $\lambda = 1, \lambda_1 = \frac{1}{q}, \lambda_2 = \frac{1}{p}$, inequality (2) reduces to (1); when $p = q = 2$, $\lambda_1 = \lambda_2 = \frac{\lambda}{2}$, inequality (2) reduces to the inequality presented by Yang in [3].

Recently, applying inequality (3) and Abel's summation by parts formula, Adiyasuren et al. [4] gave a new inequality with the kernel $\frac{1}{(m+n)^\lambda}$ involving two partial sums. Inequality (1), with its integral analogues, is playing an important role in analysis and its applications (see [5–8]).

In 1934, a half-discrete Hilbert-type inequality was given as follows ([1], Theorem 351): assuming that $K(t)\,(t>0)$ is a decreasing function, $0<\phi(s):=\int_0^\infty K(t)t^{s-1}dt<\infty$, $a_n \geq 0$, such that $0<\sum_{n=1}^\infty a_n^p<\infty$, we have:

$$\int_0^\infty x^{p-2}(\sum_{n=1}^\infty K(nx)a_n)^p dx < \phi^p(\frac{1}{q})\sum_{n=1}^\infty a_n^p. \qquad (4)$$

In 2016, Hong et al. [9] considered some equivalent statements of the extensions of (1) with the best possible constant factor related to several parameters. Some extensions of inequality (4) were given by [10–15]. Recently, Yang et al. [16,17] gave reverse half-discrete Hardy–Hilbert's inequalities and dealt with their equivalent statements of the best possible constant factor related to several parameters.

In this article, following the method of [2,4,9], in the light of the symmetry principle, we construct proper weight coefficients and use them to establish a more accurate half-discrete Hilbert-type inequality involving one upper limit function and one partial sum. Subsequently, we prove this new inequality by means of the Hermite–Hadamard inequality, Euler–Maclaurin summation formula and Abel's partial summation formula. As an extension of the obtained results, the equivalent statements of the best possible constant factor related to several parameters are discussed. It is shown that some new half-discrete Hilbert-type inequalities can be derived from the special cases of our main results.

2. Some Lemmas

In what follows, we suppose that $p>1$, $\frac{1}{p}+\frac{1}{q}=1$, $\eta\in[0,\frac{1}{4}]$, $\lambda\in(0,2]$, $\lambda_1\in(0,\lambda+1)$, $\lambda_2\in(0,\frac{1}{2}]\cap(0,\lambda+1)$, $\hat{\lambda}_1:=\frac{\lambda-\lambda_2}{p}+\frac{\lambda_1}{q}$, $\hat{\lambda}_2:=\frac{\lambda-\lambda_1}{q}+\frac{\lambda_2}{p}$. We also assume that $f(x)(\geq 0)$ is a Lebesgue integrable function in any interval $(0,b]\,(b>0)$, and define the upper limit function $F(x):=\int_0^x f(t)dt\,(x\geq 0)$ with the partial sums as follows:

$$A_n := \sum_{k=1}^n a_k (a_n \geq 0, n \in \mathbb{N} := \{1, 2, \cdots\}),$$

which satisfies $F(x) = o(e^{tx})$, $A_n = o(e^{t(n-\eta)})\,(t>0; x, n \to \infty)$:

$$0 < \int_0^\infty x^{-p\hat{\lambda}_1-1}F^p(x)dx < \infty \text{ and } 0 < \sum_{n=1}^\infty (n-\eta)^{-q\hat{\lambda}_2-1}A_n^q < \infty. \qquad (5)$$

Lemma 1. *(i) Let $(-1)^i\frac{d^i}{dt^i}g(t)>0, t\in[m,\infty)\,(m\in\mathbb{N})$ with $g^{(i)}(\infty)=0\,(i=0,1,2,3)$, and let $P_i(t), B_i\,(i\in\mathbb{N})$ be the Bernoulli functions and the Bernoulli numbers of i-order. Then, we have ([5]):*

$$\int_m^\infty P_{2q-1}(t)g(t)dt = -\varepsilon_q\frac{B_{2q}}{2q}g(m)\,(0<\varepsilon_q<1; q\in\mathbb{N}). \qquad (6)$$

In particular, for $q=1$, in view of $B_2=\frac{1}{6}$, we have:

$$-\frac{1}{12}g(m) < \int_m^\infty P_1(t)g(t)dt < 0; \qquad (7)$$

For $q=2$, in view of $B_4=-\frac{1}{30}$, it follows that:

$$0 < \int_m^\infty P_3(t)g(t)dt < \frac{1}{120}g(m). \qquad (8)$$

(ii) If $h(t)(>0) \in C^3[m,\infty), h^{(i)}(\infty) = 0$ $(i = 0,1,2,3)$, then we have the following Euler–Maclaurin summation formula:

$$\sum_{k=m}^{\infty} h(k) = \int_m^{\infty} h(t)dt + \frac{1}{2}h(m) + \int_m^{\infty} P_1(t)h'(t)dt, \tag{9}$$

where:

$$\int_m^{\infty} P_1(t)h'(t)dt = -\frac{1}{12}h'(m) + \frac{1}{6}\int_m^{\infty} P_3(t)h'''(t)dt. \tag{10}$$

Lemma 2. Let $s \in (0,4], s_2 \in (0, \frac{3}{2}] \cap (0,s), k_s(s_i) := B(s_i, s - s_i)$ $(i = 1,2)$, and let $\omega(s_2, x)$ denote the following weight coefficient:

$$\omega(s_2, x) := x^{s-s_2} \sum_{n=1}^{\infty} \frac{(n-\eta)^{s_2-1}}{(x+n-\eta)^s} \ (x \in \mathbb{R}_+ := (0,\infty)) \tag{11}$$

Then, we have the following inequalities:

$$0 < k_s(s_2)(1 - O(\frac{1}{x^{s_2}})) < \omega(s_2, x) < k_s(s_2), \tag{12}$$

where we indicate $O(\frac{1}{x^{s_2}}) := \frac{1}{k_s(s_2)}\int_0^{\frac{1-\eta}{x}} \frac{u^{s_2-1}}{(1+u)^s}du > 0$.

Proof. For fixed $x \in \mathbb{R}_+$, we define a function $g(x,t)$ by:

$$g(x,t) := \frac{(t-\eta)^{s_2-1}}{(x+t-\eta)^s}(t \in (\eta, \infty)),$$

which implies that $g(x,t) > 0$ $(t \in I_\eta)$ and $g \in C^\infty(I_\eta)$, where $I_\eta := (\eta, \infty)$. In the following, we consider two cases of $s_2 \in (0,1) \cap (0,s)$ and $s_2 \in [1, \frac{3}{2}] \cap (0,s)$ to prove inequalities (12).
(i) For $s_2 \in (0,1) \cap (0,s)$, since:

$$(-1)^i \frac{\partial^i}{\partial t^i} g(x,t) > 0 (t > \eta; i = 0,1,2),$$

by the Hermite–Hadamard inequality, setting $u = \frac{t-\eta}{x}$, we have:

$$\omega(s_2, x) = x^{s-s_2} \sum_{n=1}^{\infty} g(x,n) < x^{s-s_2}\int_{\frac{1}{2}}^{\infty} g(x,t)dt$$

$$= x^{s-s_2}\int_{\frac{1}{2}}^{\infty} \frac{(t-\eta)^{s_2-1}}{(x+t-\eta)^s}dt = \int_{\frac{\frac{1}{2}-\eta}{x}}^{\infty} \frac{u^{s_2-1}}{(1+u)^s}du$$

$$\leq \int_0^{\infty} \frac{u^{s_2-1}}{(1+u)^s}du = B(s_2, s-s_2) = k_s(s_2).$$

On the other hand, in view of the decreasingness property of series, setting $u = \frac{t-\eta}{x}$, we obtain:

$$\omega(s_2, x) = x^{s-s_2}\sum_{n=1}^{\infty} g(x,n) > x^{s-s_2}\int_1^{\infty} g(x,t)dt$$

$$= \int_{\frac{1-\eta}{x}}^{\infty} \frac{u^{s_2-1}}{(1+u)^s}du = B(s_2, s-s_2) - \int_0^{\frac{1-\eta}{x}} \frac{u^{s_2-1}}{(1+u)^s}du$$

$$= k_s(s_2)(1 - O(\frac{1}{x^{s_2}})) > 0,$$

where $O(\frac{1}{x^{s_2}}) = \frac{1}{k_s(s_2)} \int_0^{\frac{1-\eta}{x}} \frac{u^{s_2-1}}{(1+u)^s} du > 0$, which satisfies:

$$0 < \int_0^{\frac{1-\eta}{x}} \frac{u^{s_2-1}}{(1+u)^s} du < \int_0^{\frac{1-\eta}{x}} u^{s_2-1} du = \frac{1}{s_2}\left(\frac{1-\eta}{x}\right)^{s_2} (x \in \mathbb{R}_+).$$

In this case, we obtain (12).

(ii) For $s_2 \in [1, \frac{3}{2}] \cap (0, s)$, by (9), we have:

$$\sum_{n=1}^{\infty} g(x,n) = \int_1^{\infty} g(x,t)dt + \frac{1}{2}g(x,1) + \int_1^{\infty} P_1(t)\frac{\partial}{\partial t}g(x,t)dt$$
$$= \int_{\eta}^{\infty} g(x,t)dt - h(x),$$

where $h(x)$ is defined by:

$$h(x) := \int_{\eta}^{1} g(x,t)dt - \frac{1}{2}g(x,1) - \int_1^{\infty} P_1(t)\frac{\partial}{\partial t}g(x,t)dt.$$

We obtain $-\frac{1}{2}g(x,1) = \frac{-(1-\eta)^{s_2-1}}{2(x+1-\eta)^s}$, and then integrating by parts, it follows that:

$$\int_{\eta}^{1} g(x,t)dt = \int_{\eta}^{1} \frac{(t-\eta)^{s_2-1}}{(x+t-\eta)^s} dt = \frac{1}{s_2}\int_{\eta}^{1} \frac{d(t-\eta)^{s_2}}{(x+t-\eta)^s} = \frac{1}{s_2}\frac{(t-\eta)^{s_2}}{(x+t-\eta)^s}\Big|_{\eta}^{1} + \frac{s}{s_2}\int_{\eta}^{1} \frac{(t-\eta)^{s_2} dt}{(x+t-\eta)^{s+1}}$$

$$= \frac{1}{s_2}\frac{(1-\eta)^{s_2}}{(x+1-\eta)^s} + \frac{s}{s_2(s_2+1)}\int_{\eta}^{1} \frac{1}{(x+1-\eta)^{s+1}} d(t-\eta)^{s_2+1}$$

$$> \frac{1}{s_2}\frac{(1-\eta)^{s_2}}{(x+1-\eta)^s} + \frac{s}{s_2(s_2+1)}\left[\frac{(t-\eta)^{s_2+1}}{(x+t-\eta)^{s+1}}\Big|_{\eta}^{1} + \frac{s(s+1)}{s_2(s_2+1)(x+1-\eta)^{s+2}}\int_{\eta}^{1}(t-\eta)^{s_2+1} dt\right]$$

$$= \frac{1}{s_2}\frac{(1-\eta)^{s_2}}{(x+1-\eta)^s} + \frac{s}{s_2(s_2+1)}\frac{(1-\eta)^{s_2+1}}{(x+1-\eta)^{s+1}} + \frac{s(s+1)(1-\eta)^{s_2+2}}{s_2(s_2+1)(s_2+2)(x+1-\eta)^{s+2}}.$$

We find:

$$-\frac{\partial}{\partial t}g(x,t) = -\frac{(s_2-1)(t-\eta)^{s_2-2}}{(x+t-\eta)^s} + \frac{s(t-\eta)^{s_2-1}}{(x+t-\eta)^{s+1}}$$
$$= \frac{(1-s_2)(t-\eta)^{s_2-2}}{(x+t-\eta)^s} + \frac{s(t-\eta)^{s_2-2}}{(x+t-\eta)^s} - \frac{sx(t-\eta)^{s_2-2}}{(x+t-\eta)^{s+1}}$$
$$= \frac{(s+1-s_2)(t-\eta)^{s_2-2}}{(x+t-\eta)^s} - \frac{sx(t-\eta_2)^{s_2-2}}{(x+t-\eta)^{s+1}},$$

additionally, for $s_2 \in [1, \frac{3}{2}] \cap (0, s)$, it follows that:

$$(-1)^i \frac{\partial^i}{\partial t^i}\left[\frac{(t-\eta)^{s_2-2}}{(x+t-\eta)^s}\right] > 0, (-1)^i \frac{\partial^i}{\partial t^i}\left[\frac{(t-\eta)^{s_2-2}}{(x+t-\eta)^{s+1}}\right] > 0 (t > \eta; i = 0,1,2,3).$$

By (8), (9) and (10), setting $a := 1-\eta(\in [\frac{3}{4}, 1])$, we obtain:

$(s+1-s_2)\int_1^{\infty} P_1(t)\frac{(t-\eta)^{s_2-2}}{(x+t-\eta)^s}dt > -\frac{s+1-s_2}{12(x+1-\eta)^s}a^{s_2-2},$

$-xs\int_1^{\infty} P_1(t)\frac{(t-\eta)^{s_2-2}}{(x+t-\eta)^{s+1}}dt > \frac{xs}{12(x+1-\eta)^{s+1}}a^{s_2-2} - \frac{xs}{720}\left[\frac{(t-\eta)^{s_2-2}}{(x+t-\eta)^{s+1}}\right]''_{t=1}$

$> \frac{(x+1-\eta)s-as}{12(x+1-\eta)^{s+1}}a^{s_2-2} - \frac{(x+1-\eta)s}{720}\left[\frac{(s+1)(s+2)a^{s_2-2}}{(x+1-\eta)^{s+3}} + \frac{2(s+1)(2-s_2)a^{s_2-3}}{(x+1-\eta)^{s+2}} + \frac{(2-s_2)(3-s_2)a^{s_2-4}}{(x+1-\eta)^{s+1}}\right].$

$= \frac{sa^{s_2-2}}{12(x+1-\eta)^s} - \frac{sa^{s_2-1}}{12(x+1-\eta)^{s+1}} - \frac{s}{720}\left[\frac{(s+1)(s+2)a^{s_2-2}}{(x+1-\eta)^{s+2}} + \frac{2(s+1)(2-s_2)a^{s_2-3}}{(x+1-\eta)^{s+1}} + \frac{(2-s_2)(3-s_2)a^{s_2-4}}{(x+1-\eta)^s}\right],$

and then we have:
$$h(x) > \frac{a^{s_2-4}}{(x+1-\eta)^s}h_1 + \frac{sa^{s_2-3}}{(x+1-\eta)^{s+1}}h_2 + \frac{s(s+1)a^{s_2-2}}{(x+1-\eta)^{s+2}}h_3,$$

where h_i ($i=1,2,3$) are indicated as:
$$h_1 := \frac{a^4}{s_2} - \frac{a^3}{2} - \frac{(1-s_2)a^2}{12} - \frac{s(2-s_2)(3-s_2)}{720},$$
$$h_2 := \frac{a^4}{s_2(s_2+1)} - \frac{a^2}{12} - \frac{(s+1)(2-s_2)}{360},$$
$$h_3 := \frac{a^4}{s_2(s_2+1)(s_2+2)} - \frac{s+2}{720}.$$

For $s \in (0,4], s_2 \in [1, \frac{3}{2}] \cap (0,s), a \in [\frac{3}{4}, 1]$, we find:
$$h_1 > \frac{a^2}{12s_2}[s_2^2 - (6a+1)s_2 + 12a^2] - \frac{1}{90}.$$

In view of:
$$\frac{d}{da}[s_2^2 - (6a+1)s_2 + 12a^2] = 6(4a - s_2) \geq 6(4 \cdot \frac{3}{4} - \frac{3}{2}) > 0, \text{ and}$$

$$\frac{d}{ds_2}[s_2^2 - (6a+1)s_2 + 12a^2] = 2s_2 - (6a+1)$$
$$\leq 2 \cdot \frac{3}{2} - (6 \cdot \frac{3}{4} + 1) = 3 - \frac{11}{2} < 0,$$

we obtain:
$$h_1 \geq \frac{(3/4)^2}{12(3/2)}[(\frac{3}{2})^2 - (6 \cdot \frac{3}{4} + 1)\frac{3}{2} + 12(\frac{3}{4})^2] - \frac{1}{90}$$

$$h_2 > a^2(\frac{4a^2}{15} - \frac{1}{12}) - \frac{1}{72} \geq (\frac{3}{4})^2[\frac{4}{15}(\frac{3}{4})^2 - \frac{1}{12}] - \frac{1}{72} = \frac{3}{80} - \frac{1}{72} > 0,$$

$$h_3 \geq \frac{8a^4}{105} - \frac{6}{720} \geq \frac{8}{105}(\frac{3}{4})^4 - \frac{1}{120} = \frac{27}{1120} - \frac{1}{120} > 0,$$

and then we obtain $h(x) > 0$.

On the other hand, similar to the above, we have:
$$\sum_{n=1}^{\infty} g(x,n) = \int_1^\infty g(x,t)dt + \frac{1}{2}g(x,1) + \int_1^\infty P_1(t)\frac{\partial}{\partial t}g(x,t)dt$$
$$= \int_1^\infty g(x,t)dt + H(x),$$

where $H(x)$ is indicated as:
$$H(x) := \frac{1}{2}g(x,1) + \int_1^\infty P_1(t)\frac{\partial}{\partial t}g(x,t)dt.$$

Thus, we obtain that $\frac{1}{2}g(x,1) = \frac{a^{s_2-1}}{2(x+1-\eta)^s}$ and:
$$\frac{\partial}{\partial t}g(x,t) = -\frac{(s+1-s_2)(t-\eta)^{s_2-2}}{(x+t-\eta)^s} + \frac{sx(t-\eta)^{s_2-2}}{(x+t-\eta)^{s+1}}.$$

For $s_2 \in (0, \frac{3}{2}] \cap (0,s), 0 < s \leq 4$, by (7), we obtain:
$$-(s+1-s_2)\int_1^\infty P_1(t)\frac{(t-\eta)^{s_2-2}}{(x+t-\eta)^s}dt > 0,$$

$$xs\int_1^\infty P_1(t)\frac{(t-\eta)^{s_2-2}}{(x+t-\eta)^{s+1}}dt > \frac{-xs}{12(x+1-\eta)^{s+1}}a^{s_2-2} = \frac{-(x+1-\eta)s+as}{12(x+1-\eta)^{s+1}}a^{s_2-2}$$

$$= \frac{-s}{12(x+1-\eta)^s}a^{s_2-2} + \frac{s}{12(x+1-\eta)^{s+1}}a^{s_2-1} > \frac{-s}{12(x+1-\eta)^s}a^{s_2-2}.$$

Hence, we have:

$$H(x) > \frac{a^{s_2-1}}{2(x+1-\eta)^s} - \frac{sa^{s_2-2}}{12(x+1-\eta)^s} = (\tfrac{a}{2} - \tfrac{s}{12})\frac{a^{s_2-2}}{(x+1-\eta)^s}$$

$$\geq (\tfrac{1}{2}\cdot\tfrac{3}{4} - \tfrac{4}{12})\frac{a^{s_2-2}}{(x+1-\eta)^s} = (\tfrac{3}{8} - \tfrac{1}{3})\frac{a^{s_2-2}}{(x+1-\eta)^s} > 0.$$

Therefore, we obtain:

$$\int_1^\infty g(x,t)dt < \sum_{n=1}^\infty g(x,n) < \int_\eta^\infty g(x,t)dt \, (x > 0)$$

In view of the results obtained in the case (i), we obtain (12). This completes the proof of lemma 2. □

Lemma 3. *Let $s \in (0,4], s_1 \in (0,s), s_2 \in (0,\tfrac{3}{2}] \cap (0,s)$. Then, we have the following more accurate half-discrete Hardy–Hilbert inequality:*

$$I = \int_0^\infty \sum_{n=1}^\infty \frac{a_n f(x)}{(x+n-\eta)^s}dx \leq (k_s(s_2))^{\frac{1}{p}}(k_s(s_1))^{\frac{1}{q}}$$

$$\times \left\{\int_0^\infty x^{p[1-(\frac{s-s_2}{p}+\frac{s_1}{q})]-1}f^p(x)dx\right\}^{\frac{1}{p}}\left\{\sum_{n=1}^\infty (n-\eta)^{q[1-(\frac{s-s_1}{q}+\frac{s_2}{p})]-1}a_n^q\right\}^{\frac{1}{q}}. \quad (13)$$

Proof. For $s_1 \in (0,s)$, setting $u = \frac{x}{n-\eta}$, we have the following expression of the weight coefficient:

$$w(s_1,n) := (n-\eta)^{s-s_1}\int_0^\infty \frac{x^{s_1-1}}{(x+n-\eta)^s}dx = \int_0^\infty \frac{u^{s_1-1}}{(u+1)^s}du = k_s(s_1) \, (n \in \mathbb{N}). \quad (14)$$

By using Hölder's inequality [18], we obtain:

$$I = \int_0^\infty \sum_{n=1}^\infty \frac{1}{(x+n-\eta)^s}\left[\frac{x^{(1-s)1/q}}{(n-\eta)^{(1-s_2)/p}}f(x)\right]\left[\frac{(n-\eta)^{(1-s_2)/p}}{x^{(1-s)1/q}}a_n\right]dx$$

$$\leq [\int_0^\infty \sum_{n=1}^\infty \frac{1}{(x+n-\eta)^s}\frac{x^{(1-s_1)(p-1)}}{(n-\eta)^{1-s_2}}f^p(x)dx]^{\frac{1}{p}}$$

$$\times [\sum_{n=1}^\infty \int_0^\infty \frac{1}{(x+n-\eta)^s}\frac{(n-\eta)^{(1-s_2)(q-1)}}{x^{1-s_1}}dx a_n^q]^{\frac{1}{q}}$$

$$= \left\{\int_0^\infty \omega(s_2,x)x^{p[1-(\frac{s-s_2}{p}+\frac{s_1}{q})]-1}f^p(x)dx\right\}^{\frac{1}{p}}$$

$$\times \left\{\sum_{n=1}^\infty w(s,1n)(n-\eta)^{q[1-(\frac{s-s_1}{q}+\frac{s_2}{p})]-1}a_n^q\right\}^{\frac{1}{q}}.$$

Then, by (12) and (14), we derive inequality (13). The Lemma 3 is proved. □

Remark 1. *In (13), for $s = \lambda + 2 \in (2,4], \lambda \in (0,2], s_1 = \lambda_1 + 1 \in (1,s), \lambda_1 \in (0,\lambda+1)$,*

$$s_2 = \lambda_2 + 1 \in (1,\tfrac{3}{2}], \lambda_2 \in (0,\tfrac{1}{2}] \cap (0,\lambda+1)$$

30

Replacing $f(x)$ (resp. a_n) by $F(x)$ (resp. A_n), in view of Lemma 3 and (5), we have:

$$\int_0^\infty \sum_{n=1}^\infty \frac{A_n}{(x+n-\eta)^{\lambda+2}} F(x)dx < (k_{\lambda+2}(\lambda_2+1))^{\frac{1}{p}} (k_{\lambda+2}(\lambda_1+1))^{\frac{1}{q}}$$

$$\times \left[\int_0^\infty x^{-p\hat{\lambda}_1-1} F^p(x) dx\right]^{\frac{1}{p}} \left[\sum_{n=1}^\infty (n-\eta)^{-q\hat{\lambda}_2-1} A_n^q\right]^{\frac{1}{q}}. \quad (15)$$

Lemma 4. *For $t > 0$, we have:*

$$\int_0^\infty e^{-tx} f(x) dx = t \int_0^\infty e^{-tx} F(x) dx, \quad (16)$$

$$\sum_{n=1}^\infty e^{-t(n-\eta)} a_n \leq t \sum_{n=1}^\infty e^{-t(n-\eta)} A_n. \quad (17)$$

Proof. Integration by parts, in view of $F(0) = 0$, $F(x) = o(e^{tx})$ $(t > 0; x \to \infty)$, it follows that:

$$\int_0^\infty \sum_{n=1}^\infty \frac{A_n}{(x+n-\eta)^{\lambda+2}} F(x)dx < (k_{\lambda+2}(\lambda_2+1))^{\frac{1}{p}} (k_{\lambda+2}(\lambda_1+1))^{\frac{1}{q}}$$

$$= \lim_{x\to\infty} e^{-tx} F(x) + t\int_0^\infty e^{-tx} F(x)dx = t\int_0^\infty e^{-tx} F(x)dx,$$

and then (16) follows.

In view of $A_n e^{-t(n-\eta)} = o(1) (n \to \infty)$, by Abel's summation by parts formula, we obtain:

$$\sum_{n=1}^\infty e^{-t(n-\eta)} a_n = \lim_{n\to\infty} A_n e^{-t(n-\eta)} + \sum_{n=1}^\infty A_n [e^{-t(n-\eta)} - e^{-t(n-\eta+1)}]$$

$$= \sum_{n=1}^\infty A_n [e^{-t(n-\eta)} - e^{-t(n-\eta+1)}] = (1-e^{-t}) \sum_{n=1}^\infty e^{-t(n-\eta)} A_n.$$

Since $1 - e^{-t} < t (t > 0)$, we have (17). The Lemma 4 is proved. □

3. Main Results

Theorem 1. *Let $p > 1$, $\frac{1}{p} + \frac{1}{q} = 1$, $\eta \in [0, \frac{1}{4}]$, $\lambda \in (0,2]$, $\lambda_1 \in (0, \lambda+1)$, $\lambda_2 \in (0, \frac{1}{2}] \cap (0, \lambda+1)$, $\hat{\lambda}_1 := \frac{\lambda-\lambda_2}{p} + \frac{\lambda_1}{q}$, $\hat{\lambda}_2 := \frac{\lambda-\lambda_1}{q} + \frac{\lambda_2}{p}$. Then, we have the following half-discrete Hilbert-type inequality:*

$$I := \int_0^\infty \sum_{n=1}^\infty \frac{a_n}{(x+n-\eta)^\lambda} f(x) dx < \frac{\Gamma(\lambda+2)}{\Gamma(\lambda)} (k_{\lambda+2}(\lambda_2+1))^{\frac{1}{p}} (k_{\lambda+2}(\lambda_1+1))^{\frac{1}{q}}$$

$$\times \left[\int_0^\infty x^{-p\hat{\lambda}_1-1} F^p(x) dx\right]^{\frac{1}{p}} \left[\sum_{n=1}^\infty (n-\eta)^{-q\hat{\lambda}_2-1} A_n^q\right]^{\frac{1}{q}}. \quad (18)$$

In particular, for $\lambda_1 + \lambda_2 = \lambda (\in (0,2]) (\lambda_1 \in (0,\lambda), \lambda_2 \in (0, \frac{1}{2}] \cap (0,\lambda))$, we have:

$$\int_0^\infty \sum_{n=1}^\infty \frac{a_n}{(x+n-\eta)^\lambda} f(x) dx < \lambda_1 \lambda_2 B(\lambda_1, \lambda_2)$$

$$\times \left[\int_0^\infty x^{-p\lambda_1-1} F^p(x) dx\right]^{\frac{1}{p}} \left[\sum_{n=1}^\infty (n-\eta)^{-q\lambda_2-1} A_n^q\right]^{\frac{1}{q}}. \quad (19)$$

Proof. Since for $\lambda > 0$, we have:
$$\frac{1}{(x+n-\eta)^\lambda} = \frac{1}{\Gamma(\lambda)} \int_0^\infty t^{\lambda-1} e^{-(x+n-\eta)t} dt,$$

it follows that:
$$I = \frac{1}{\Gamma(\lambda)} \int_0^\infty \sum_{n=1}^\infty a_n f(x) \int_0^\infty t^{\lambda-1} e^{-(x+n-\eta)t} dt dx$$
$$= \frac{1}{\Gamma(\lambda)} \int_0^\infty t^{\lambda-1} \int_0^\infty e^{-xt} f(x) dx \sum_{n=1}^\infty e^{-(n-\eta)t} a_n dt$$
$$\leq \frac{1}{\Gamma(\lambda)} \int_0^\infty t^{\lambda+1} \int_0^\infty e^{-xt} F(x) dx \sum_{n=1}^\infty e^{-(n-\eta)t} A_n dt$$
$$= \frac{1}{\Gamma(\lambda)} \int_0^\infty \sum_{n=1}^\infty A_n F(x) \int_0^\infty t^{(\lambda+2)-1} e^{-(x+n-\eta)t} dt dx$$
$$= \frac{\Gamma(\lambda+2)}{\Gamma(\lambda)} \int_0^\infty \sum_{n=1}^\infty \frac{A_n}{(x+n-\eta)^{\lambda+2}} F(x) dx$$

By applying (15), we obtain (18).
In particular, for $\lambda_1 + \lambda_2 = \lambda (\in (0,2]) (\lambda_1 \in (0,\lambda), \lambda_2 \in (0,\frac{1}{2}] \cap (0,\lambda))$, one has:

$$k_{\lambda+2}(\lambda_2+1) = k_{\lambda+2}(\lambda_1+1) = B(\lambda_1+1, \lambda_2+1)$$
$$= \frac{\Gamma(\lambda_1+1)\Gamma(\lambda_2+1)}{\Gamma(\lambda+2)} = \frac{\lambda_1 \lambda_2 \Gamma(\lambda_1)\Gamma(\lambda_2)}{\Gamma(\lambda+2)} = \frac{\Gamma(\lambda)}{\Gamma(\lambda+2)} \lambda_1 \lambda_2 B(\lambda_1, \lambda_2).$$

Hence, it follows from (18) that:
$$\int_0^\infty \sum_{n=1}^\infty \frac{a_n}{(x+n-\eta)^\lambda} f(x) dx < \lambda_1 \lambda_2 B(\lambda_1, \lambda_2)$$
$$\times [\int_0^\infty x^{-p\lambda_1-1} F^p(x) dx]^{\frac{1}{p}} [\sum_{n=1}^\infty (n-\eta)^{-q\lambda_2-1} A_n^q]^{\frac{1}{q}}, \qquad (20)$$

which is the desired inequality (19). □

Remark 3. *Putting $\eta = 0$ in (20), we have:*
$$\int_0^\infty \sum_{n=1}^\infty \frac{a_n}{(x+n)^\lambda} f(x) dx < \lambda_1 \lambda_2 B(\lambda_1, \lambda_2)$$
$$\times [\int_0^\infty x^{-p\lambda_1-1} F^p(x) dx]^{\frac{1}{p}} [\sum_{n=1}^\infty n^{-q\lambda_2-1} A_n^q]^{\frac{1}{q}}. \qquad (21)$$

Namely, (18) given by Theorem 1 is a more accurate extension of (21) above. It should be noted that here the statement of "more accurate inequality" borrows from the statement mentioned at the beginning of the paper on the comparison between inequalities (1) and (2) described in the previous literature.

Theorem 2. *If $\lambda - \lambda_1 \leq \frac{1}{2}$, then the following statements (i), (ii) and (iii), associated with Theorem 1, are equivalent:*

(i) $(k_{\lambda+2}(\lambda_2+1))^{\frac{1}{p}} (k_{\lambda+2}(\lambda_1+1))^{\frac{1}{q}} \leq k_{\lambda+2}(\frac{\lambda-\lambda_2}{p} + \frac{\lambda_1}{q} + 1);$
(ii) $\lambda_1 + \lambda_2 = \lambda(\in (0,2]), where \lambda_1 \in (0,\lambda), \lambda_2 \in (0,\frac{1}{2}] \cap (0,\lambda);$
(iii) *The constant factor:*

$$\frac{\Gamma(\lambda+2)}{\Gamma(\lambda)} (k_{\lambda+2}(\lambda_2+1))^{\frac{1}{p}} (k_{\lambda+2}(\lambda_1+1))^{\frac{1}{q}}$$

in (19) is the best possible.

Proof. "(i)⇒(ii)". By using Hölder inequality with weight, we obtain:

$$k_{\lambda+2}(\tfrac{\lambda-\lambda_2}{p}+\tfrac{\lambda_1}{q}+1)$$
$$=\int_0^\infty \frac{1}{(1+u)^{\lambda+2}}u^{\frac{\lambda-\lambda_2}{p}+\frac{\lambda_1}{q}}du = \int_0^\infty \frac{1}{(1+u)^{\lambda+2}}(u^{\frac{\lambda-\lambda_2}{p}})(u^{\frac{\lambda_1}{q}})du$$
$$\leq [\int_0^\infty \frac{1}{(1+u)^{\lambda+2}}u^{\lambda-\lambda_2}du]^{\frac{1}{p}}[\int_0^\infty \frac{1}{(1+u)^{\lambda+2}}u^{\lambda_1}du]^{\frac{1}{q}}$$
$$= [\int_0^\infty \frac{1}{(1+v)^{\lambda+2}}v^{(\lambda_2+1)-1}dv]^{\frac{1}{p}}[\int_0^\infty \frac{1}{(1+u)^{\lambda+2}}u^{(\lambda_1+1)-1}du]^{\frac{1}{q}}$$
$$= (k_{\lambda+2}(\lambda_2+1))^{\frac{1}{p}}(k_{\lambda+2}(\lambda_1+1))^{\frac{1}{q}}. \tag{22}$$

In view of inequality (i), we conclude that (22) keeps the form of equality.

We observe that (22) keeps the form of equality if and only if there exist constants A and B, such that they are not both zero and $Au^{\lambda-\lambda_2}=Bu^{\lambda_1}$ a.e. in $\mathbb{R}_+$ (see [18]). Assuming that $A \neq 0$, we have $u^{\lambda-\lambda_2-\lambda_1}=\frac{B}{A}$ a.e. in $\mathbb{R}_+$, and then $\lambda-\lambda_2-\lambda_1=0$, namely, $\lambda_1+\lambda_2=\lambda(\in(0,2])$, where, $\lambda_1 \in (0,\lambda), \lambda_2 \in (0,\tfrac{1}{2}]\cap(0,\lambda)$.

"(ii)⇒(iii)". For $\lambda_1+\lambda_2=\lambda(\in(0,2])$, $\lambda_1 \in (0,\lambda), \lambda_2 \in (0,\tfrac{1}{2}]\cap(0,\lambda)$, (19) reduces to (20). For any $0<\varepsilon<\min\{p\lambda_1,q\lambda_2\}$, we set:

$$\tilde{f}(x) := \begin{cases} 0, 0<x<1, \\ x^{\lambda_1-\frac{\varepsilon}{p}-1}, x \geq 1 \end{cases}, \tilde{a}_n := n^{\lambda_2-\frac{\varepsilon}{q}-1}(n \in \mathbb{N})$$

Then, it follows that:

$$\tilde{F}(x) := \int_0^x \tilde{f}(t)dt \leq \begin{cases} 0, 0<x<1, \\ \frac{1}{\lambda_1-\frac{\varepsilon}{p}}x^{\lambda_1-\frac{\varepsilon}{p}}, x \geq 1 \end{cases},$$

$$\tilde{A}_n := \sum_{k=1}^n \tilde{a}_k = \sum_{k=1}^n k^{\lambda_2-\frac{\varepsilon}{q}-1} < \int_0^n t^{\lambda_2-\frac{\varepsilon}{q}-1}dt = \frac{1}{\lambda_2-\frac{\varepsilon}{q}}n^{\lambda_2-\frac{\varepsilon}{q}}(n \in \mathbb{N}).$$

If there exists a positive constant $M \leq \lambda_1\lambda_2 B(\lambda_1,\lambda_2)$ such that (20) is valid when replacing $\lambda_1\lambda_2 B(\lambda_1,\lambda_2)$ by M, then, in particular for $\eta=0$, by substitution of $f(x)=\tilde{f}(x), a_n=\tilde{a}_n$, $F(x)=\tilde{F}(x)$ and $A_n=\tilde{A}_n$ in (21), we have:

$$\tilde{I} := \int_0^\infty \sum_{n=1}^\infty \frac{\tilde{a}_n \tilde{f}(x)}{(x+n)^\lambda}dx < M(\int_0^\infty x^{-p\lambda_1-1}\tilde{F}^p(x)dx)^{\frac{1}{p}}(\sum_{n=1}^\infty n^{-q\lambda_2-1}\tilde{A}_n^q)^{\frac{1}{q}}. \tag{23}$$

In the following, we show that $\lambda_1\lambda_2 B(\lambda_1,\lambda_2) \leq M$, and then $M = \lambda_1\lambda_2 B(\lambda_1,\lambda_2)$ is the best possible constant factor in (20).

By (23) and the decreasingness property of series, we obtain:

$$\tilde{I} < M\frac{1}{\lambda_1-\frac{\varepsilon}{p}}(\int_1^\infty x^{-p\lambda_1-1}x^{p\lambda_1-\varepsilon}dx)^{\frac{1}{p}}\frac{1}{\lambda_2-\frac{\varepsilon}{q}}(\sum_{n=1}^\infty n^{-q\lambda_2-1}n^{q\lambda_2-\varepsilon})^{\frac{1}{q}}$$

$$= M(\tfrac{1}{\lambda_1-\frac{\varepsilon}{p}})(\tfrac{1}{\lambda_2-\frac{\varepsilon}{q}})(\int_1^\infty x^{-\varepsilon-1}dx)^{\frac{1}{p}}(1+\sum_{n=2}^\infty n^{-\varepsilon-1})^{\frac{1}{q}}$$

$$< M(\tfrac{1}{\lambda_1-\frac{\varepsilon}{p}})(\tfrac{1}{\lambda_2-\frac{\varepsilon}{q}})(\int_1^\infty x^{-\varepsilon-1}dx)^{\frac{1}{p}}(1+\int_1^\infty y^{-\varepsilon-1}dy)^{\frac{1}{q}}$$

$$= \frac{M}{\varepsilon}(\tfrac{1}{\lambda_1-\frac{\varepsilon}{p}})(\tfrac{1}{\lambda_2-\frac{\varepsilon}{q}})(\varepsilon+1)^{\frac{1}{q}}.$$

By (11) (for $\eta = 0$), setting $\tilde{\lambda}_2 = \lambda_2 - \frac{\varepsilon}{q} \in (0, \frac{1}{2}) \cap (0, \lambda) (0 < \tilde{\lambda}_1 = \lambda_1 + \frac{\varepsilon}{q} < \lambda)$, we obtain:

$$\tilde{I} = \int_1^\infty [x^{(\lambda_1+\frac{\varepsilon}{q})} \sum_{n=1}^\infty \frac{1}{(x+n)^\lambda} n^{(\lambda_2-\frac{\varepsilon}{q})-1}]x^{-\varepsilon-1}dx$$
$$= \int_1^\infty \omega(\tilde{\lambda}_2, x)x^{-\varepsilon-1}dx > B(\tilde{\lambda}_1, \tilde{\lambda}_2) \int_1^\infty [1 - O(\frac{1}{x^{\tilde{\lambda}_2}})]x^{-\varepsilon-1}dx$$
$$= B(\tilde{\lambda}_1, \tilde{\lambda}_2)[\int_1^\infty x^{-\varepsilon-1}dx - \int_1^\infty O(\frac{1}{x^{\lambda_2+\frac{\varepsilon}{p}+1}})dx]$$
$$= \frac{1}{\varepsilon}B(\lambda_1 + \frac{\varepsilon}{q}, \lambda_2 - \frac{\varepsilon}{q})(1 - \varepsilon O(1)).$$

Then, in virtue of the above results, we have:

$$B(\lambda_1 + \frac{\varepsilon}{q}, \lambda_2 - \frac{\varepsilon}{q})(1 - \varepsilon O(1)) < \varepsilon \tilde{I} < M(\frac{1}{\lambda_1 - \frac{\varepsilon}{p}})(\frac{1}{\lambda_2 - \frac{\varepsilon}{q}})(\varepsilon + 1)^{\frac{1}{q}}.$$

Putting $\varepsilon \to 0^+$, in view of the continuity of the beta function, we obtain $\lambda_1 \lambda_2 B(\lambda_1, \lambda_2) \leq M$. Hence, $M = \lambda_1 \lambda_2 B(\lambda_1, \lambda_2)$ is the best possible constant factor in (20).

"(iii)⇒(i)". Since $\lambda - \lambda_1 \leq \frac{1}{2}$, for $\hat{\lambda}_1 = \frac{\lambda-\lambda_2}{p} + \frac{\lambda_1}{q}, \hat{\lambda}_2 = \frac{\lambda-\lambda_1}{q} + \frac{\lambda_2}{p}$, we find:

$$\hat{\lambda}_1 + \hat{\lambda}_2 = \frac{\lambda - \lambda_2}{p} + \frac{\lambda_1}{q} + \frac{\lambda - \lambda_1}{q} + \frac{\lambda_2}{p} = \lambda, 0 < \hat{\lambda}_1, \hat{\lambda}_2 < \frac{\lambda}{p} + \frac{\lambda}{q} = \lambda,$$

$\hat{\lambda}_2 \leq \frac{1/2}{p} + \frac{1/2}{q} = \frac{1}{2}$, and $\hat{\lambda}_1 \hat{\lambda}_2 B(\hat{\lambda}_1, \hat{\lambda}_2) \in \mathbf{R}_+$.

If the constant factor $\frac{\Gamma(\lambda+2)}{\Gamma(\lambda)}(k_{\lambda+2}(\lambda_2 + 1))^{\frac{1}{p}}(k_{\lambda+2}(\lambda_1 + 1))^{\frac{1}{q}}$ in (19) is the best possible, then by (21) (for $\lambda_i = \hat{\lambda}_i (i = 1, 2)$), we have:

$$\frac{\Gamma(\lambda + 2)}{\Gamma(\lambda)}(k_{\lambda+2}(\lambda_2 + 1))^{\frac{1}{p}}(k_{\lambda+2}(\lambda_1 + 1))^{\frac{1}{q}}$$

$$\leq \hat{\lambda}_1 \hat{\lambda}_2 B(\hat{\lambda}_1, \hat{\lambda}_2) = \frac{\Gamma(\lambda+2)}{\Gamma(\lambda)} k_{\lambda+2}(\hat{\lambda}_1 + 1)$$
$$= \frac{\Gamma(\lambda+2)}{\Gamma(\lambda)} k_{\lambda+2}(\frac{\lambda-\lambda_2}{p} + \frac{\lambda_1}{q} + 1)(\in \mathbf{R}_+),$$

namely, statement (i) is valid.

Hence, the statements (i), (ii) and (iii) are equivalent. This completes the proof of Theorem 2. □

Remark 4. Putting $\eta = \frac{1}{4}$ in (20), we acquire:

$$\int_0^\infty \sum_{n=1}^\infty \frac{a_n}{(x+n-\frac{1}{4})^\lambda} f(x)dx < \lambda_1 \lambda_2 B(\lambda_1, \lambda_2)$$

$$\times [\int_0^\infty x^{-p\lambda_1-1} F^p(x)dx]^{\frac{1}{p}} [\sum_{n=1}^\infty (n-\frac{1}{4})^{-q\lambda_2-1} A_n^q]^{\frac{1}{q}} \quad (24)$$

In particular, for $\lambda = 1, \lambda_1 = \lambda_2 = \frac{1}{2}$, we have the following Hilbert-type inequality with the best possible constant factor $\frac{\pi}{4}$

$$\int_0^\infty \sum_{n=1}^\infty \frac{a_n}{x+n-\frac{1}{4}} f(x)dx < \frac{\pi}{4} [\int_0^\infty x^{-\frac{p}{2}-1} F^p(x)dx]^{\frac{1}{p}} [\sum_{n=1}^\infty (n-\frac{1}{4})^{-\frac{q}{2}-1} A_n^q]^{\frac{1}{q}}. \quad (25)$$

4. Conclusions

In this paper, based on the weight coefficients and the idea of introducing parameters, by applying Hermite–Hadamard inequality, the Euler–Maclaurin summation formula and Abel's summation by parts formula, a more accurate half-discrete Hilbert-type inequality involving one upper limit function as well as one partial sum is given in Theorem 1. The equivalent statements of the best possible constant factor related to several parameters are considered in Theorem 2. As applications of the main results, some new inequalities are proposed in Remarks 3 and 4. Our results would provide a significant supplement to the study of half-discrete Hilbert-type inequality.

Author Contributions: B.Y. carried out the mathematical studies, participated in the sequence alignment and drafted the manuscript. S.W. and X.H. participated in the design of the study and performed the numerical analysis. All authors contributed equally to the preparation of this paper. All authors have read and agreed to the published version of the manuscript.

Funding: This work is supported by the National Natural Science Foundation (No. 61772140, No.12071491), the Characteristic Innovation Project of Guangdong Provincial Colleges and Universities (No.2020KTSCX088), the Construction Project of Teaching Quality and Teaching Reform in Guangdong Undergraduate Colleges and Universities in 2018 (Speciality of Financial Mathematics), and the Natural Science Foundation of Fujian Province of China (No. 2020J01365).

Institutional Review Board Statement: Not applicable.

Informed Consent Statement: Not applicable.

Data Availability Statement: The data used to support the findings of this study are included within the article.

Conflicts of Interest: The authors declare that they have no competing interest.

References

1. Hardy, G.H.; Littlewood, J.E.; Polya, G. *Inequalities*; Cambridge University Press: Cambridge, UK, 1934.
2. Krnić, M.; Pečarić, J. Extension of Hilbert's inequality. *J. Math. Anal. Appl.* **2006**, *324*, 150–160. [CrossRef]
3. Yang, B. On a generalization of Hilbert's double series theorem. *Math. Inequalities Appl.* **2002**, *18*, 197–204. [CrossRef]
4. Adiyasuren, V.; Batbold, T.; Azar, L.E. A new discrete Hilbert-type inequality involving partial sums. *J. Inequalities Appl.* **2019**, *2019*, 127. [CrossRef]
5. Yang, B.C. *The Norm of Operator and Hilbert-Type Inequalities*; Science Press: Beijing, China, 2009.
6. Krnić, M.; Pečarić, J. General Hilbert's and Hardy's inequalities. *Math. Inequal. Appl.* **2005**, *8*, 29–51. [CrossRef]
7. Perić, I.; Vuković, P. Multiple Hilbert's type inequalities with a homogeneous kernel. *Banach J. Math. Anal.* **2011**, *5*, 33–43. [CrossRef]
8. Adiyasuren, V.; Batbold, T.; Krnić, M. Hilbert-type inequalities involving differential operators, the best constants, and applications. *Math. Inequalities Appl.* **2015**, 111–124. [CrossRef]
9. Hong, Y.; Wen, Y.M. A necessary and sufficient condition of that Hilbert type series inequality with homogeneous kernel has the best constant factor. *Ann. Math.* **2016**, *37*, 329–336.
10. Rassias, M.T.; Yang, B. On half-discrete Hilbert's inequality. *Appl. Math. Comput.* **2013**, *220*, 75–93. [CrossRef]
11. Yang, B.C.; Krnić, M. A half-discrete Hilbert-type inequality with a general homogeneous kernel of degree 0. *J. Math. Inequal.* **2012**, *6*, 401–417.
12. Rassias, M.T.; Yang, B. A multidimensional half-discrete Hilbert-type inequality and the Riemann zeta function. *Appl. Math. Comput.* **2013**, *225*, 263–277. [CrossRef]
13. Rassias, M.T.; Yang, B. On a multidimensional half-discrete Hilbert-type inequality related to the hyperbolic cotangent function. *Appl. Math. Comput.* **2014**, *242*, 800–813. [CrossRef]
14. Yang, B.C.; Debnath, L. *Half-Discrete Hilbert-Type Inequalities*; World Scientific Publishing: Singapore, 2014.
15. Huang, Z.; Yang, B. Equivalent property of a half-discrete Hilbert's inequality with parameters. *J. Inequalities Appl.* **2018**, *2018*. [CrossRef] [PubMed]
16. Yang, B.; Wu, S.; Wang, A. On a Reverse Half-Discrete Hardy-Hilbert's Inequality with Parameters. *Mathematics* **2019**, *7*, 1054. [CrossRef]
17. Wang, A.-Z.; Yang, B.-C.; Chen, Q. Equivalent properties of a reverse half-discrete Hilbert's inequality. *J. Inequalities Appl.* **2019**, *2019*. [CrossRef]
18. Kuang, J.C. *Applied Inequalities*; Shangdong Science and Technology Press: Jinan, China, 2004.

Article

On Some New Trapezoidal Type Inequalities for Twice (p, q) Differentiable Convex Functions in Post-Quantum Calculus

Thanin Sitthiwirattham [1,*,†], Ghulam Murtaza [2,*,†], Muhammad Aamir Ali [3,*,†], Sotiris K. Ntouyas [4,5,†], Muhammad Adeel [2,†] and Jarunee Soontharanon [6,†]

[1] Mathematics Department, Faculty of Science and Technology, Suan Dusit University, Bangkok 10300, Thailand
[2] Department of Mathematics, University of Management and Technology, Lahore 54700, Pakistan; F2019349078@umt.edu.pk
[3] Jiangsu Key Laboratory for NSLSCS, School of Mathematical Sciences, Nanjing Normal University, Nanjing 210023, China
[4] Department of Mathematics, University of Ioannina, 45110 Ioannina, Greece; sntouyas@uoi.gr
[5] Nonlinear Analysis and Applied Mathematics (NAAM)—Research Group, Department of Mathematics, Faculty of Science, King Abdulaziz University, Jeddah 21589, Saudi Arabia
[6] Department of Mathematics, Faculty of Applied Science, King Mongkut's University of Technology North Bangkok, Bangkok 10800, Thailand; jarunee.s@sci.kmutnb.ac.th
* Correspondence: thanin_sit@dusit.ac.th (T.S.); ghulammurtaza@umt.edu.pk (G.M.); mahr.muhammad.aamir@gmail.com (M.A.A.)
† These authors contributed equally to this work.

Abstract: Quantum information theory, an interdisciplinary field that includes computer science, information theory, philosophy, cryptography, and symmetry, has various applications for quantum calculus. Inequalities has a strong association with convex and symmetric convex functions. In this study, first we establish a (p,q)-integral identity involving the second (p,q)-derivative and then we used this result to prove some new trapezoidal type inequalities for twice (p,q)-differentiable convex functions. It is also shown that the newly established results are the refinements of some existing results in the field of integral inequalities. Analytic inequalities of this nature and especially the techniques involved have applications in various areas in which symmetry plays a prominent role.

Keywords: Hermite–Hadamard inequality; (p,q)-calculus; convex functions

1. Introduction

In convex functions theory, Hermite–Hadamard (HH) inequality is very important, and was discovered by C. Hermite and J. Hadamard independently (see, also [1,2], p. 137).

$$\Pi\left(\frac{\pi_1 + \pi_2}{2}\right) \leq \frac{1}{\pi_2 - \pi_1} \int_{\pi_1}^{\pi_2} \Pi(\varkappa) d\varkappa \leq \frac{\Pi(\pi_1) + \Pi(\pi_2)}{2} \tag{1}$$

where Π is a convex function. In the case of concave mappings, the above inequality satisfies in reverse order.

On the other hand, several works in the field of q-analysis, beginning with Euler, have been implemented in order to master the mathematics that underpins quantum computing. The term q-calculus creates a link between mathematics and physics. It's used in combinatorics, number theory, basic hypergeometric functions, orthogonal polynomials, and other fields, as well as relativity theory, mechanics, and quantum theory [3,4]. In quantum information theory, it has many applications [5–7] and it not only has a link with the estimations calculus, but also to affine algebraic geometry including the famous Jacobian Conjecture [8,9]. Euler used the q-parameter in Newton's work on infinite series, which is why he is thought to be inventor of this important branch of mathematics.

The concept of q-calculus that is known to be calculus without limits was given by Jackson [10,11] for the first time in a proper way. The notions about the q-fractional integral and q-Riemann–Liouville fractional integral was given by Al-Salam [12] in 1996. Since the research increased gradually in this field, therefore Tariboon and Ntouyas [13] gave the idea about the $_{\pi_1}D_q$-difference operator and $_{q\pi_1}$-integral. The notions about the $^{\pi_2}D_q$-difference operator and q^{π_2}-integral were given by Bermudo et al. [14] very recently in 2020. Sadjang [15] generalized the concept of q-calculus by introducing the concepts of (p,q)-calculus. Soontharanon et al. [16] introduced the concepts of fractional (p,q)-calculus later on. The (p,q)-variant of $_{\pi_1}D_q$-difference operator and $_{q\pi_1}$-integral was introduced by Tunç and Göv [17]. Recently, in 2021, Chu et al. introduced the notions of $^{\pi_2}D_{p,q}$ derivative and $(p,q)^{\pi_2}$-integral in [18].

Many integral inequalities for many sorts of functions have indeed been investigated employing quantum as well as post-quantum integrals. For example, the HH inequalities and their right–left estimates for convex and coordinated convex functions via $_{\pi_1}D_q, ^{\pi_2}D_q$-derivatives and $_{q\pi_1}, q^{\pi_2}$-integrals were given by different authors in [19–27]. Noor et al. [28] used the pre-invexity to prove HH inequalities in the setup of q-calculus. Some parameterized q-integral inequalities for generalized quasi-convex functions established by Nwaeze et al. [29]. Khan et al. used the notions of Green functions to establish some new inequalities of HH type in [30]. Budak et al. [31], Ali et al. [32,33] and Vivas-Cortez et al. [34] proved some new boundaries for Simpson's and Newton's type inequalities for convex and coordinated convex functions in the setting of q-calculus. One can consult [35–37] for q-Ostrowski's inequalities for convex and coordinated convex functions. In [38], the authors generalized the results of [21] and proved HH type inequalities and their left estimates using $_{\pi_1}D_{p,q}$-difference operator and $(p,q)_{\pi_1}$-integral. Recently, in [39], the authors established the right estimates of HH type inequalities proved by Kunt et al. [38]. For (p,q)-Ostrowski type inequalities, one can consult [18]. The results proved in [14] were generalized in [40].

Inspired by the ongoing studies, we establish some new post-quantum trapezoidal type inequalities for (p,q)-differentiable convex functions through the (p,q)-integral. Furthermore, we prove that the newly established inequalities are the extensions of some already given inequalities.

The organization of this paper is as follows: In Section 2, a short explanation of the concepts of q-calculus and some associated works in this direction are given. In Section 3,, we review the notions of (p,q)-derivatives and integrals. In Section 4, the trapezoidal type inequalities for twice (p,q)-differentiable functions via (p,q)-integrals are presented. The relationship between the results provided here and comparable outcomes in the literature are also taken into account. Section 5 provides some findings as well as other study directions.

2. Quantum Derivatives and Integrals

In this portion, we recall a few known definitions and related inequalities in q-calculus. Set the following notation ([4]):

$$[n]_q = \frac{1-q^n}{1-q} = 1+q+q^2+...+q^{n-1}, \quad q \in (0,1).$$

The q-Jackson integral of a mapping Π from 0 to π_2 is given by Jackson [11], which is defined as:

$$\int_0^{\pi_2} \Pi(\varkappa) \, d_q\varkappa = (1-q)\pi_2 \sum_{n=0}^{\infty} q^n \Pi(\pi_2 q^n), \text{ where } 0 < q < 1 \qquad (2)$$

provided that the sum converges absolutely. Moreover, over the interval $[\pi_1, \pi_2]$, he gave the following integral of a mapping Π:

$$\int_{\pi_1}^{\pi_2} \Pi(\varkappa) \, d_q\varkappa = \int_0^{\pi_2} \Pi(\varkappa) \, d_q\varkappa - \int_0^{\pi_1} \Pi(\varkappa) \, d_q\varkappa.$$

Definition 1 ([13]). *The q_{π_1}-derivative of mapping $\Pi : [\pi_1, \pi_2] \to \mathbb{R}$ is defined as:*

$$_{\pi_1}D_q\Pi(\varkappa) = \frac{\Pi(\varkappa) - \Pi(q\varkappa + (1-q)\pi_1)}{(1-q)(\varkappa - \pi_1)}, \; \varkappa \neq \pi_1. \tag{3}$$

For $\varkappa = \pi_1$, we state $_{\pi_1}D_q\Pi(\pi_1) = \lim_{\varkappa \to \pi_1} {}_{\pi_1}D_q\Pi(\varkappa)$ if it exists and it is finite.

Definition 2 ([14]). *The q^{π_2}-derivative of mapping $\Pi : [\pi_1, \pi_2] \to \mathbb{R}$ is given as:*

$$^{\pi_2}D_q\Pi(\varkappa) = \frac{\Pi(q\varkappa + (1-q)\pi_2) - \Pi(\varkappa)}{(1-q)(\pi_2 - \varkappa)}, \; \varkappa \neq \pi_2. \tag{4}$$

For $\varkappa = \pi_2$, we state $^{\pi_2}D_q\Pi(\pi_2) = \lim_{\varkappa \to \pi_2} {}^{\pi_2}D_q\Pi(\varkappa)$ if it exists and it is finite.

Definition 3 ([13]). *The q_{π_1}-definite integral of mapping $\Pi : [\pi_1, \pi_2] \to \mathbb{R}$ on $[\pi_1, \pi_2]$ is defined as:*

$$\int_{\pi_1}^{\varkappa} \Pi(\tau) \, _{\pi_1}d_q\tau = (1-q)(\varkappa - \pi_1) \sum_{n=0}^{\infty} q^n \Pi(q^n\varkappa + (1-q^n)\pi_1), \; \varkappa \in [\pi_1, \pi_2]. \tag{5}$$

On the other side, the following concept of q-definite integral is stated by Bermudo et al. [14]:

Definition 4 ([14]). *The q^{π_2}-definite integral of mapping $\Pi : [\pi_1, \pi_2] \to \mathbb{R}$ on $[\pi_1, \pi_2]$ is given as:*

$$\int_{\varkappa}^{\pi_2} \Pi(\tau) \, ^{\pi_2}d_q\tau = (1-q)(\pi_2 - \varkappa) \sum_{n=0}^{\infty} q^n \Pi(q^n\varkappa + (1-q^n)\pi_2), \; \varkappa \in [\pi_1, \pi_2]. \tag{6}$$

Remark 1. *If Π is a symmetric function, that is $\Pi(t) = f(\pi_1 + \pi_2 - t)$, then we have the following relation*

$$\int_{\pi_1}^{\pi_2} \Pi(t) \, _{\pi_1}d_qt = \int_{\pi_1}^{\pi_2} \Pi(t) \, ^{\pi_2}d_qt.$$

3. Post-Quantum Derivatives and Integrals

In this section, we review some fundamental notions and notations of (p,q)-calculus. The $[n]_{p,q}$ is said to be (p,q)-integers and expressed as:

$$[n]_{p,q} = \frac{p^n - q^n}{p - q}$$

with $0 < q < p \leq 1$. The $[n]_{p,q}!$ and $\begin{bmatrix} n \\ k \end{bmatrix}!$ are called (p,q)-factorial and (p,q)-binomial, respectively, and expressed as:

$$[n]_{p,q}! = \prod_{k=1}^{n} [k]_{p,q}, \; n \geq 1, \; [0]_{p,q}! = 1,$$

$$\begin{bmatrix} n \\ k \end{bmatrix}! = \frac{[n]_{p,q}!}{[n-k]_{p,q}![k]_{p,q}!}.$$

Definition 5 ([15]). *The (p,q)-derivative of mapping $\Pi : [\pi_1, \pi_2] \to \mathbb{R}$ is given as:*

$$D_{p,q}\Pi(\varkappa) = \frac{\Pi(p\varkappa) - \Pi(q\varkappa)}{(p-q)\varkappa}, \quad \varkappa \neq 0 \tag{7}$$

with $0 < q < p \leq 1$.

Definition 6 ([17]). *The $(p,q)_{\pi_1}$-derivative of mapping $\Pi : [\pi_1, \pi_2] \to \mathbb{R}$ is given as:*

$$_{\pi_1}D_{p,q}\Pi(\varkappa) = \frac{\Pi(p\varkappa + (1-p)\pi_1) - \Pi(q\varkappa + (1-q)\pi_1)}{(p-q)(\varkappa - \pi_1)}, \quad \varkappa \neq \pi_1 \tag{8}$$

with $0 < q < p \leq 1$.

For $\varkappa = \pi_1$, we state $_{\pi_1}D_{p,q}\Pi(\pi_1) = \lim_{\varkappa \to \pi_1} {_{\pi_1}}D_{p,q}\Pi(\varkappa)$ if it exists and it is finite.

Definition 7 ([18]). *The $(p,q)^{\pi_2}$-derivative of mapping $\Pi : [\pi_1, \pi_2] \to \mathbb{R}$ is given as:*

$$^{\pi_2}D_{p,q}\Pi(\varkappa) = \frac{\Pi(q\varkappa + (1-q)\pi_2) - \Pi(p\varkappa + (1-p)\pi_2)}{(p-q)(\pi_2 - \varkappa)}, \quad \varkappa \neq \pi_2. \tag{9}$$

For $\varkappa = \pi_2$, we state $^{\pi_2}D_{p,q}\Pi(\pi_2) = \lim_{\varkappa \to \pi_2} {^{\pi_2}}D_{p,q}\Pi(\varkappa)$ if it exists and it is finite.

Remark 2. *It is clear that if we use $p = 1$ in (8) and (9), then the equalities (8) and (9) reduce to (3) and (4), respectively.*

Definition 8 ([17]). *The definite $(p,q)_{\pi_1}$-integral of mapping $\Pi : [\pi_1, \pi_2] \to \mathbb{R}$ on $[\pi_1, \pi_2]$ is stated as:*

$$\int_{\pi_1}^{\varkappa} \Pi(\tau) \, _{\pi_1}d_{p,q}\tau = (p-q)(\varkappa - \pi_1) \sum_{n=0}^{\infty} \frac{q^n}{p^{n+1}} \Pi\left(\frac{q^n}{p^{n+1}}\varkappa + \left(1 - \frac{q^n}{p^{n+1}}\right)\pi_1\right) \tag{10}$$

with $0 < q < p \leq 1$.

Definition 9 ([18]). *The definite $(p,q)^{\pi_2}$-integral of mapping $\Pi : [\pi_1, \pi_2] \to \mathbb{R}$ on $[\pi_1, \pi_2]$ is stated as:*

$$\int_{\varkappa}^{\pi_2} \Pi(\tau) \, ^{\pi_2}d_{p,q}\tau = (p-q)(\pi_2 - \varkappa) \sum_{n=0}^{\infty} \frac{q^n}{p^{n+1}} \Pi\left(\frac{q^n}{p^{n+1}}\varkappa + \left(1 - \frac{q^n}{p^{n+1}}\right)\pi_2\right) \tag{11}$$

with $0 < q < p \leq 1$.

Remark 3. *It is evident that if we pick $p = 1$ in (10) and (11), then the equalities (10) and (11) change into (5) and (6), respectively.*

Remark 4. *If we take $\pi_1 = 0$ and $\varkappa = \pi_2 = 1$ in (10), then we have*

$$\int_0^1 \Pi(\tau) \, _0d_{p,q}\tau = (p-q) \sum_{n=0}^{\infty} \frac{q^n}{p^{n+1}} \Pi\left(\frac{q^n}{p^{n+1}}\right).$$

Similarly, by taking $\varkappa = \pi_1 = 0$ and $\pi_2 = 1$ in (11), then we obtain that

$$\int_0^1 \Pi(\tau) \, ^1d_{p,q}\tau = (p-q) \sum_{n=0}^{\infty} \frac{q^n}{p^{n+1}} \Pi\left(1 - \frac{q^n}{p^{n+1}}\right).$$

In [38], Kunt et al. proved the following HH type inequalities for convex functions via $(p,q)_{\pi_1}$-integral:

Theorem 1. *For a convex mapping $\Pi : [\pi_1, \pi_2] \to \mathbb{R}$, which is differentiable on $[\pi_1, \pi_2]$, the following inequalities hold for $(p,q)_{\pi_1}$-integral:*

$$\Pi\left(\frac{q\pi_1 + p\pi_2}{[2]_{p,q}}\right) \leq \frac{1}{p(\pi_2 - \pi_1)} \int_{\pi_1}^{p\pi_2+(1-p)\pi_1} \Pi(\varkappa) \,_{\pi_1}d_{p,q}\varkappa \leq \frac{q\Pi(\pi_1) + p\Pi(\pi_2)}{[2]_{p,q}} \qquad (12)$$

where $0 < q < p \leq 1$.

Lemma 1 ([40]). *We have the following equalities:*

$$\int_{\pi_1}^{\pi_2} (\pi_2 - \varkappa)^\alpha \,_{\pi_2}d_{p,q}\varkappa = \frac{(\pi_2 - \pi_1)^{\alpha+1}}{[\alpha + 1]_{p,q}}$$

$$\int_{\pi_1}^{\pi_2} (\varkappa - \pi_1)^\alpha \,_{\pi_1}d_{p,q}\varkappa = \frac{(\pi_2 - \pi_1)^{\alpha+1}}{[\alpha + 1]_{p,q}}$$

where $\alpha \in \mathbb{R} - \{-1\}$.

Remark 5. *If Π is a symmetric function, that is $\Pi(t) = f(\pi_1 + \pi_2 - t)$, then we have following relation*

$$\int_{\pi_1}^{p\pi_2+(1-p)\pi_1} \Pi(t) \,_{\pi_1}d_{p,q}t = \int_{p\pi_1+(1-p)\pi_2}^{\pi_2} \Pi(t) \,^{\pi_2}d_q t.$$

4. Post-Quantum Trapezoidal Type Inequalities

In this section, we prove some new trapezoidal type inequalities for twice (p,q)-differentiable convex functions using the (p,q)-integrals.

Lemma 2. *Consider a mapping $\Pi : I = [\pi_1, \pi_2] \to \mathbb{R}$, which is twice (p,q)-differentiable and $^{\pi_2}D^2_{p,q}\Pi$ is continuous and integrable on I. Then, the following equality holds:*

$$\frac{p\Pi(p\pi_1 + (1-p)\pi_2) + q\Pi(\pi_2)}{[2]_{p,q}} - \frac{1}{\pi_2 - \pi_1} \int_{p^2\pi_1+(1-p^2)\pi_2}^{\pi_2} \Pi(\varkappa) \,^{\pi_2}d_{p,q}\varkappa$$

$$= \frac{q^2(\pi_2 - \pi_1)^2}{[2]_{p,q}} \int_0^1 p\tau(1 - q\tau) \,^{\pi_2}D^2_{p,q}\Pi(\tau\pi_1 + (1-\tau)\pi_2) d_{p,q}\tau, \qquad (13)$$

where $0 < q < p \leq 1$.

Proof. Consider

$$^{\pi_2}D^2_{p,q}\Pi(\tau\pi_1 + (1-\tau)\pi_2)$$

$$= {}^{\pi_2}D_{p,q}\left[\frac{\Pi(q\tau\pi_1 + (1-q\tau)\pi_2) - \Pi(p\tau\pi_1 + (1-p\tau)\pi_2)}{(p-q)(\pi_2 - \pi_1)\tau}\right]$$

$$= \frac{p\Pi(q^2\tau\pi_1 + (1-q^2\tau)\pi_2) - [2]_{p,q}\Pi(pq\tau + (1-pq\tau)\pi_2) + q\Pi(p^2\tau\pi_1 + (1-p^2\tau)\pi_2)}{pq(p-q)^2(\pi_2 - \pi_1)^2\tau^2}.$$

Now, from Definition 9, we have

$$\int_0^1 p\tau(1-q\tau)\,{}^{\pi_2}D^2_{p,q}\Pi(\tau\pi_1+(1-\tau)\pi_2)\,d_{p,q}\tau$$

$$= \int_0^1 p\tau(1-q\tau)\left[\frac{\begin{array}{c}p\Pi(q^2\tau\pi_1+(1-q^2\tau)\pi_2)-(p+q)\Pi(pq\tau\\+(1-pq\tau)\pi_2)+q\Pi(p^2\tau\pi_1+(1-p^2\tau)\pi_2)\end{array}}{pq(p-q)^2(\pi_2-\pi_1)^2\tau^2}\right]d_{p,q}\tau$$

$$= \frac{1}{q(p-q)^2(\pi_2-\pi_1)^2}$$

$$\times\left[\begin{array}{c}\int_0^1 \frac{p\Pi(q^2\tau\pi_1+(1-q^2\tau)\pi_2)-(p+q)\Pi(pq\tau\pi_1+(1-pq\tau)\pi_2)+q\Pi(p^2\tau\pi_1+(1-p^2\tau)\pi_2)}{\tau}d_{p,q}\tau\\ -pq\int_0^1\Pi(q^2\tau\pi_1+(1-q^2\tau)\pi_2)d_{p,q}\tau+q[2]_{p,q}\int_0^1\Pi(pq\tau\pi_1+(1-pq\tau)\pi_2)d_{p,q}\tau\\ -q^2\int_0^1\Pi(p^2\tau\pi_1+(1-p^2\tau)\pi_2)d_{p,q}\tau\end{array}\right]$$

$$= \frac{1}{q(p-q)^2(\pi_2-\pi_1)^2}\left[\begin{array}{c}p(p-q)\sum_{n=0}^{\infty}\Pi\left(\frac{q^{n+2}}{p^{n+1}}\pi_1+(1-\frac{q^{n+2}}{p^{n+1}})\pi_2\right)\\ -(p^2-q^2)\sum_{n=0}^{\infty}\Pi\left(\frac{q^{n+1}}{p^n}\pi_1+(1-\frac{q^{n+1}}{p^n})\pi_2\right)\\ +q(p-q)\sum_{n=0}^{\infty}\Pi\left(\frac{q^n}{p^{n-1}}\pi_1+(1-\frac{q^n}{p^{n-1}})\pi_2\right)\\ -pq(p-q)\sum_{n=0}^{\infty}\frac{q^n}{p^{n+1}}\Pi\left(\frac{q^{n+2}}{p^{n+1}}\pi_1+(1-\frac{q^{n+2}}{p^{n+1}})\pi_2\right)\\ +q(p^2-q^2)\sum_{n=0}^{\infty}\frac{q^n}{p^{n+1}}\Pi\left(\frac{q^{n+1}}{p^n}\pi_1+(1-\frac{q^{n+1}}{p^n})\pi_2\right)\\ -q^2(p-q)\sum_{n=0}^{\infty}\frac{q^n}{p^{n+1}}\Pi\left(\frac{q^n}{p^{n+1}}\pi_1+(1-\frac{q^n}{p^{n+1}})\pi_2\right)\end{array}\right]$$

$$= \frac{1}{q(p-q)^2(\pi_2-\pi_1)^2}\left[\begin{array}{c}p(p-q)(\Pi(\pi_2)-\Pi(q\pi_1+(1-q)\pi_2))\\ +q(p-q)(\Pi(p\pi_1+(1-p)\pi_2)-\Pi(\pi_2))\\ -\frac{p^3}{q(\pi_2-\pi_1)}\int_{p^2\pi_1+(1-p^2)\pi_2}^{\pi_2}\Pi(\varkappa)\,{}^{\pi_2}d_{p,q}\varkappa+\frac{p^2}{q}(p-q)\Pi(p\pi_1+(1-p)\pi_2)\\ +p(p-q)\Pi(q\pi_1+(1-q)\pi_2)-\frac{q^2}{\pi_2-\pi_1}\int_{p^2\pi_1+(1-p^2)\pi_2}^{\pi_2}\Pi(\varkappa)\,{}^{\pi_2}d_{p,q}\varkappa\\ +\frac{p[2]_{p,q}}{\pi_2-\pi_1}\int_{p^2\pi_1+(1-p^2)\pi_2}^{\pi_2}\Pi(\varkappa)\,{}^{\pi_2}d_{p,q}\varkappa-(p^2-q^2)\Pi(p\pi_1+(1-p)\pi_2)\end{array}\right]$$

$$= \frac{1}{q(\pi_2-\pi_1)^2}\Pi(\pi_2)+\frac{p}{q^2(\pi_2-\pi_1)^2}\Pi(p\pi_1+(1-p)\pi_2)-\frac{[2]_{p,q}}{q^2(\pi_2-\pi_1)^3}\int_{p^2\pi_1+(1-p^2)\pi_2}^{\pi_2}\Pi(\varkappa)\,{}^{\pi_2}d_{p,q}\varkappa. \quad (14)$$

Now, we have the identity (13) by multiplying both sides of (14) by $\frac{q^2(\pi_2-\pi_1)^2}{[2]_{p,q}}$, and the proof is complete. □

Remark 6. *In Lemma 2, If we set $p=1$, then we have*

$$\frac{\Pi(\pi_1)+q\Pi(\pi_2)}{[2]_q}-\frac{1}{\pi_2-\pi_1}\int_{\pi_1}^{\pi_2}\Pi(\varkappa)\,{}^{\pi_2}d_q\varkappa = \frac{q^2(\pi_2-\pi_1)^2}{[2]_q}\int_0^1 \tau(1-q\tau)\,{}^{\pi_2}D_q^2\Pi(\tau\pi_1+(1-\tau)\pi_2)\,d_q\tau.$$

This is established by Ali et al. in [19].

Remark 7. *In Lemma 2, If we set $p = 1$ and later take the limit as $q \to 1^-$, then we have*

$$\frac{\Pi(\pi_1) + \Pi(\pi_2)}{2} - \frac{1}{\pi_2 - \pi_1} \int_{\pi_1}^{\pi_2} \Pi(\varkappa) d\varkappa = \frac{(\pi_2 - \pi_1)^2}{2} \int_0^1 \tau(1-\tau) \Pi''(\tau\pi_1 + (1-\tau)\pi_2) d\tau.$$

This is established by Alomari et al. in [41].

Theorem 2. *Consider the assumptions in Lemma 2 are valid. If $|^{\pi_2} D_{p,q}^2 \Pi|$ is convex on I, then the following inequality holds:*

$$\left| \frac{p\Pi(p\pi_1 + (1-p)\pi_2) + q\Pi(\pi_2)}{[2]_{p,q}} - \frac{1}{\pi_2 - \pi_1} \int_{p^2\pi_1+(1-p^2)\pi_2}^{\pi_2} \Pi(\varkappa)\, ^{\pi_2} d_{p,q}\varkappa \right|$$

$$\leq \frac{p^3 q^2 (\pi_2 - \pi_1)^2}{[2]_{p,q}[3]_{p,q}[4]_{p,q}} \left[p \left| ^{\pi_2} D_{p,q}^2 \Pi(\pi_1) \right| + (p^2 - p + q^2) \left| ^{\pi_2} D_{p,q}^2 \Pi(\pi_2) \right| \right],$$

where $0 < q < p \leq 1$.

Proof. Taking modulus of (13) and applying the convexity of $\left| ^{\pi_2} D_{p,q}^2 \Pi \right|$, we obtain

$$\left| \frac{p\Pi(p\pi_1 + (1-p)\pi_2) + q\Pi(\pi_2)}{[2]_{p,q}} - \frac{1}{\pi_2 - \pi_1} \int_{p^2\pi_1+(1-p^2)\pi_2}^{\pi_2} \Pi(\varkappa)\, ^{\pi_2} d_{p,q}\varkappa \right|$$

$$\leq \frac{pq^2(\pi_2 - \pi_1)^2}{[2]_{p,q}} \int_0^1 \tau(1-q\tau) \left| ^{\pi_2} D_{p,q}^2 \Pi(\tau\pi_1 + (1-\tau)\pi_2) \right| d_{p,q}\tau$$

$$\leq \frac{pq^2(\pi_2 - \pi_1)^2}{[2]_{p,q}} \int_0^1 \tau(1-q\tau) \left[\tau \left| ^{\pi_2} D_{p,q}^2 \Pi(\pi_1) \right| + (1-\tau) \left| ^{\pi_2} D_{p,q}^2 \Pi(\pi_2) \right| \right] d_{p,q}\tau$$

$$\leq \frac{pq^2(\pi_2 - \pi_1)^2}{[2]_{p,q}} \left[\left| ^{\pi_2} D_{p,q}^2 \Pi(\pi_1) \right| \int_0^1 \tau^2 (1-q\tau) d_{p,q}\tau + \left| ^{\pi_2} D_{p,q}^2 \Pi(\pi_2) \right| \int_0^1 \tau(1-q\tau)(1-\tau) d_{p,q}\tau \right]$$

$$= \frac{pq^2(\pi_2 - \pi_1)^2}{[2]_{p,q}[3]_{p,q}[4]_{p,q}} \left[p^3 \left| ^{\pi_2} D_{p,q}^2 \Pi(\pi_1) \right| + p^2(p^2 - p + q^2) \left| ^{\pi_2} D_{p,q}^2 \Pi(\pi_2) \right| \right]$$

and the proof is completed. □

Remark 8. *In Theorem 2, if we set $p = 1$, then we obtain [19], Theorem 4.*

Remark 9. *In Theorem 2, If we set $p = 1$ and later take the limit as $q \to 1^-$, then we obtain [42], Proposition 2.*

Theorem 3. *Consider the assumptions in Lemma 2 as valid. If $|^{\pi_2} D_{p,q}^2 \Pi|^r, r \geq 1$, is convex on I, then the following inequality holds:*

$$\left| \frac{p\Pi(p\pi_1 + (1-p)\pi_2) + q\Pi(\pi_2)}{[2]_{p,q}} - \frac{1}{\pi_2 - \pi_1} \int_{p^2\pi_1+(1-p^2)\pi_2}^{\pi_2} \Pi(\varkappa)\, ^{\pi_2} d_{p,q}\varkappa \right|$$

$$\leq \frac{p^3 q^2 (\pi_2 - \pi_1)^2}{[2]_{p,q}^{2-\frac{1}{r}}[3]_{p,q}[4]_{p,q}^{\frac{1}{r}}} \left[p \left| ^{\pi_2} D_{p,q}^2 \Pi(\pi_1) \right|^r + (p^2 - p + q^2) \left| ^{\pi_2} D_{p,q}^2 \Pi(\pi_2) \right|^r \right]^{\frac{1}{r}},$$

where $0 < q < p \leq 1$.

Proof. Taking modulus of (13) and applying the power mean inequality, we have

$$\left| \frac{p\Pi(p\pi_1 + (1-p)\pi_2) + q\Pi(\pi_2)}{[2]_{p,q}} - \frac{1}{\pi_2 - \pi_1} \int_{p^2\pi_1 + (1-p^2)\pi_2}^{\pi_2} \Pi(\varkappa)\,{}^{\pi_2}d_{p,q}\varkappa \right|$$

$$\leq \frac{pq^2(\pi_2 - \pi_1)^2}{[2]_{p,q}} \int_0^1 \tau^2(1 - q\tau)\left|{}^{\pi_2}D_{p,q}^2\Pi(\tau\pi_1 + (1-\tau)\pi_2)\right| d_{p,q}\tau$$

$$\leq \frac{pq^2(\pi_2 - \pi_1)^2}{[2]_{p,q}} \left[\int_0^1 \tau(1-q\tau)d_{p,q}\tau \right]^{1-\frac{1}{r}} \left[\int_0^1 \tau(1-q\tau)\left|{}^{\pi_2}D_{p,q}^2\Pi(\tau\pi_1 + (1-\tau)\pi_2)\right|^r d_{p,q}\tau \right]^{\frac{1}{r}}.$$

Now, using the convexity of $\left|{}^{\pi_2}D_{p,q}^2\Pi\right|^r$, we have

$$\left| \frac{p\Pi(p\pi_1 + (1-p)\pi_2) + q\Pi(\pi_2)}{[2]_{p,q}} - \frac{1}{\pi_2 - \pi_1} \int_{p^2\pi_1 + (1-p^2)\pi_2}^{\pi_2} \Pi(\varkappa)\,{}^{\pi_2}d_{p,q}\varkappa \right|$$

$$\leq \frac{pq^2(\pi_2 - \pi_1)^2}{[2]_{p,q}} \left[\int_0^1 \tau(1-q\tau)d_{p,q}\tau \right]^{1-\frac{1}{r}}$$

$$\times \left[\left|{}^{\pi_2}D_{p,q}^2\Pi(\pi_1)\right|^r \int_0^1 \tau^2(1-q\tau)d_{p,q}\tau + \left|{}^{\pi_2}D_{p,q}^2\Pi(\pi_1)\right|^r \int_0^1 \tau(1-q\tau)(1-\tau)\,d_{p,q}\tau \right]^{\frac{1}{r}}$$

$$\leq \frac{pq^2(\pi_2 - \pi_1)^2}{[2]_{p,q}} \left[\frac{p^2}{[2]_{p,q}[3]_{p,q}} \right]^{1-\frac{1}{r}}$$

$$\times \left[\frac{p^3}{[3]_{p,q}[4]_{p,q}} \left|{}^{\pi_2}D_{p,q}^2\Pi(\pi_1)\right|^r + \frac{p^2(p^2 - p + q^2)}{[3]_{p,q}[4]_{p,q}} \left|{}^{\pi_2}D_{p,q}^2\Pi(\pi_2)\right|^r \right]^{\frac{1}{r}}$$

$$= \frac{p^3 q^2(\pi_2 - \pi_1)^2}{[2]_{p,q}^{2-\frac{1}{r}}[3]_{p,q}[4]_{p,q}^{\frac{1}{r}}} \left[p\left|{}^{\pi_2}D_{p,q}^2\Pi(\pi_1)\right|^r + (p^2 - p + q^2)\left|{}^{\pi_2}D_{p,q}^2\Pi(\pi_2)\right|^r \right]^{\frac{1}{r}}$$

which completes the proof. □

Remark 10. *In Theorem 3, if we set $p = 1$, then we obtain [19], Theorem 5.*

Remark 11. *In Theorem 3, if we set $p = 1$ and later take the limit as $q \to 1^-$, then we have*

$$\left| \frac{\Pi(\pi_1) + \Pi(\pi_2)}{2} - \frac{1}{\pi_2 - \pi_1} \int_{\pi_1}^{\pi_2} \Pi(\varkappa)d\varkappa \right| \leq \frac{2^{-\frac{1}{r}}(\pi_2 - \pi_1)^2}{12} \left[|\Pi''(\pi_1)|^r + |\Pi''(\pi_2)|^r \right]^{\frac{1}{r}}.$$

Theorem 4. *Consider the assumptions in Lemma 2 are valid. If $|{}^{\pi_2}D_{p,q}^2\Pi|^r$ is convex on I for some $r > 1$, then we have the following inequality:*

$$\left| \frac{p\Pi(p\pi_1 + (1-p)\pi_2) + q\Pi(\pi_2)}{[2]_{p,q}} - \frac{1}{\pi_2 - \pi_1} \int_{p^2\pi_1 + (1-p^2)\pi_2}^{\pi_2} \Pi(\varkappa)\,{}^{\pi_2}d_{p,q}\varkappa \right|$$

$$\leq \frac{pq^2(\pi_2-\pi_1)^2}{[2]_{p,q}} z^{\frac{1}{s}} \left[\frac{\left|{}^{\pi_2}D_{p,q}^2\Pi(\pi_1)\right|^r + ([2]_{p,q}-1)\left|{}^{\pi_2}D_{p,q}^2\Pi(\pi_2)\right|^r}{[2]_{p,q}} \right]^{\frac{1}{r}},$$

where $z = (p-q) \sum_{n=0}^{\infty} (\frac{q^n}{p^{n+1}})^{s+1} (1 - (\frac{q}{p})^{n+1})^s$, $0 < q < p \leq 1$ and $s = r/(r-1)$.

Proof. Taking the modulus of (13) and applying the Hölder's inequality, we have

$$\left| \frac{p\Pi(p\pi_1 + (1-p)\pi_2) + q\Pi(\pi_2)}{[2]_{p,q}} - \frac{1}{\pi_2-\pi_1} \int_{p^2\pi_1+(1-p^2)\pi_2}^{\pi_2} \Pi(\varkappa) \,{}^{\pi_2}d_{p,q}\varkappa \right|$$

$$\leq \frac{pq^2(\pi_2-\pi_1)^2}{[2]_{p,q}} \left[\int_0^1 (\tau(1-q\tau))^s d_{p,q}\tau \right]^{\frac{1}{s}} \left[\int_0^1 \left|{}^{\pi_2}D_{p,q}^2\Pi(\tau\pi_1 + (1-\tau)\pi_2)\right|^r d_{p,q}\tau \right]^{\frac{1}{r}}.$$

Now, using the convexity of $|{}^{\pi_2}D_{p,q}^2\Pi|^r$, we have

$$\left| \frac{p\Pi(p\pi_1 + (1-p)\pi_2) + q\Pi(\pi_2)}{[2]_{p,q}} - \frac{1}{\pi_2-\pi_1} \int_{p^2\pi_1+(1-p^2)\pi_2}^{\pi_2} \Pi(\varkappa) \,{}^{\pi_2}d_{p,q}\varkappa \right|$$

$$\leq \frac{pq^2(\pi_2-\pi_1)^2}{[2]_{p,q}} \left[\int_0^1 (\tau(1-q\tau))^s d_{p,q}\tau \right]^{\frac{1}{s}}$$

$$\times \left[\left|{}^{\pi_2}D_{p,q}^2\Pi(\pi_1)\right|^r \int_0^1 \tau\, d_{p,q}\tau + \left|{}^{\pi_2}D_{p,q}^2\Pi(\pi_2)\right|^r \int_0^1 (1-\tau)\, d_{p,q}\tau \right]^{\frac{1}{r}}$$

$$= \frac{pq^2(\pi_2-\pi_1)^2}{[2]_{p,q}} z^{\frac{1}{s}} \left[\frac{\left|{}^{\pi_2}D_{p,q}^2\Pi(\pi_1)\right|^r + ([2]_{p,q}-1)\left|{}^{\pi_2}D_{p,q}^2\Pi(\pi_2)\right|^r}{[2]_{p,q}} \right]^{\frac{1}{r}},$$

where

$$z = \int_0^1 (\tau(1-q\tau))^s d_{p,q}\tau = (p-q) \sum_{n=0}^{\infty} (\frac{q^n}{p^{n+1}})^{s+1} \left[1 - (\frac{q}{p})^{n+1} \right]^s.$$

Hence, the proof is completed. □

Remark 12. *In Theorem 4, if we set $p = 1$, then we obtain [19], Theorem 6.*

Remark 13. *In Theorem 4, if we set $p = 1$ and later take the limit as $q \to 1^-$, then we have*

$$\left| \frac{\Pi(\pi_1) + \Pi(\pi_2)}{2} - \frac{1}{\pi_2-\pi_1} \int_{\pi_1}^{\pi_2} \Pi(\varkappa)d\varkappa \right|$$

$$\leq \frac{(\pi_2-\pi_1)^2}{2} (\mathcal{B}(s+1,s+1))^{1/s} \left[\frac{|\Pi''(\pi_1)|^r + |\Pi''(\pi_2)|^r}{2} \right]^{\frac{1}{r}},$$

where $\mathcal{B}(s+1,s+1) = z = \int_0^1 (\tau(1-\tau))^s d\tau$ is the famous Euler's beta function.

Theorem 5. *With the assumptions of Theorem 4, we have the following inequality*

$$\left| \frac{p\Pi(p\pi_1 + (1-p)\pi_2) + q\Pi(\pi_2)}{[2]_{p,q}} - \frac{1}{\pi_2 - \pi_1} \int_{p^2\pi_1 + (1-p^2)\pi_2}^{\pi_2} \Pi(\varkappa)\ ^{\pi_2}d_{p,q}\varkappa \right|$$

$$\leq \frac{pq^2(\pi_2 - \pi_1)^2}{[2]_{p,q}} \left(\frac{1}{[s+1]_{p,q}}\right)^{\frac{1}{s}} \left[z_1 \left|^{\pi_2}D_{p,q}^2\Pi(\pi_1)\right|^r + z_2 \left|^{\pi_2}D_{p,q}^2\Pi(\pi_2)\right|^r\right]^{\frac{1}{r}},$$

where $z_1 = (p-q) \sum_{n=0}^{\infty} \frac{q^{2n}}{p^{2n+2}} \left(1 - \frac{q^{n+1}}{p^{n+1}}\right)^r$ *and* $z_2 = (p-q) \sum_{n=0}^{\infty} \frac{q^n}{p^{n+1}} \left(1 - \frac{q^n}{p^{n+1}}\right) \left(1 - \frac{q^{n+1}}{p^{n+1}}\right)^r$.

Proof. Taking modulus of (13) and applying the Hölder's inequality, we have

$$\left| \frac{p\Pi(p\pi_1 + (1-p)\pi_2) + q\Pi(\pi_2)}{[2]_{p,q}} - \frac{1}{\pi_2 - \pi_1} \int_{p^2\pi_1 + (1-p^2)\pi_2}^{\pi_2} \Pi(\varkappa)\ ^{\pi_2}d_{p,q}\varkappa \right|$$

$$\leq \frac{pq^2(\pi_2 - \pi_1)^2}{[2]_{p,q}} \left[\int_0^1 \tau^s d_{p,q}\tau\right]^{\frac{1}{s}} \left[\int_0^1 (1-q\tau)^r \left|^{\pi_2}D_{p,q}^2\Pi(\tau\pi_1 + (1-\tau)\pi_2)\right|^r d_{p,q}\tau\right]^{\frac{1}{r}}.$$

Now, using the convexity of $|^{\pi_2}D_{p,q}^2\Pi|^r$, we have

$$\left| \frac{p\Pi(p\pi_1 + (1-p)\pi_2) + q\Pi(\pi_2)}{[2]_{p,q}} - \frac{1}{\pi_2 - \pi_1} \int_{p^2\pi_1 + (1-p^2)\pi_2}^{\pi_2} \Pi(\varkappa)\ ^{\pi_2}d_{p,q}\varkappa \right|$$

$$\leq \frac{pq^2(\pi_2 - \pi_1)^2}{[2]_{p,q}} \left(\frac{1}{[s+1]_{p,q}}\right)^{\frac{1}{s}}$$

$$\times \left[\left|^{\pi_2}D_{p,q}^2\Pi(\pi_1)\right|^r \int_0^1 \tau(1-q\tau)^r\,d_{p,q}\tau + \left|^{\pi_2}D_{p,q}^2\Pi(\pi_2)\right|^r \int_0^1 (1-\tau)(1-q\tau)^r\,d_{p,q}\tau\right]^{\frac{1}{r}}$$

$$= \frac{pq^2(\pi_2 - \pi_1)^2}{[2]_{p,q}} \left(\frac{1}{[s+1]_{p,q}}\right)^{\frac{1}{s}} \left[z_1\left|^{\pi_2}D_{p,q}^2\Pi(\pi_1)\right|^r + z_2\left|^{\pi_2}D_{p,q}^2\Pi(\pi_2)\right|^r\right]^{\frac{1}{r}},$$

where

$$z_1 = (p-q) \sum_{n=0}^{\infty} \left(\frac{q^n}{p^{n+1}}\right)^2 \left(1 - \frac{q^{n+1}}{p^{n+1}}\right)^r$$

and

$$z_2 = (p-q) \sum_{n=0}^{\infty} \frac{q^n}{p^{n+1}} \left(1 - \frac{q^n}{p^{n+1}}\right) \left(1 - (\frac{q}{p})^{n+1}\right)^r.$$

Hence, the proof is completed. □

Remark 14. *In Theorem 5, if we set $p = 1$, then we obtain [19], Theorem 7.*

Remark 15. *In Theorem 5, if we put $p = 1$ and later take the limit as $q \to 1^-$, then we have*

$$\left|\frac{\Pi(\pi_1) + \Pi(\pi_2)}{2} - \frac{1}{\pi_2 - \pi_1} \int_{\pi_1}^{\pi_2} \Pi(\varkappa) d\varkappa\right|$$

$$\leq \frac{(\pi_2 - \pi_1)^2}{2} \left(\frac{1}{s+1}\right)^{\frac{1}{s}} \left(\frac{1}{(r+1)(r+2)}\right)^{\frac{1}{r}} \left[(r+2)|\Pi''(\pi_1)|^r + |\Pi''(\pi_2)|^r\right]^{\frac{1}{r}}.$$

5. Conclusions

In this work, we established some new trapezoidal type (p,q)-integral inequalities for twice (p,q)-differentiable convex functions. We deduce that the findings proved in this work are naturally universal and contribute into the theory of inequalities, as well as applications for determining the uniqueness of solutions in quantum boundary value problems, quantum mechanics, and special relativity theory. The findings of this study can be applied to quantum information theory and symmetry. Results for the case of symmetric functions can be obtained by applying the concepts in Remarks 1 and 5, which will be studied in future work. As a future direction, one can find similar inequalities for coordinated convex functions.

Author Contributions: Conceptualization, T.S., S.K.N. and M.A.A.; methodology, T.S., S.K.N. and M.A.A.; formal analysis, T.S., S.K.N., M.A.A., G.M., M.A. and J.S.; funding acquisition, T.S. and J.S. All authors have read and agreed to the published version of the manuscript.

Funding: This research was funded by King Mongkut's University of Technology North Bangkok. Contract no. KMUTNB-63-KNOW-21.

Institutional Review Board Statement: Not applicable.

Informed Consent Statement: Not applicable.

Conflicts of Interest: The authors declare no conflict of interest.

References

1. Dragomir, S.S.; Pearce, C.E.M. *Selected Topics on Hermite-Hadamard Inequalities and Applications*, RGMIA Monographs, Victoria University: Melbourne, Australia, 2000.
2. Pećarixcx, J.E.; Proschan, F.; Tong, Y.L. *Convex Functions, Partial Orderings and Statistical Applications*; Academic Press: Boston, MA, USA, 1992.
3. Ernst, T. *A Comprehensive Treatment of q-Calculus*; Springer: Basel, Switzerland, 2012.
4. Kac, V.; Cheung, P. *Quantum Calculus*; Springer: Berlin/Heidelberg, Germany, 2001.
5. Benatti, F.; Fannes, M.; Floreanini, R.; Petritis, D. *Quantum Information, Computation and Cryptography: An Introductory Survey of Theory, Technology and Experiments*; Springer: Berlin/Heidelberg, Germany, 2010.
6. Bokulich, A.; Jaeger, G. *Philosophy of Quantum Information Theory and Entanglement*, Cambridge University Press: Cambridge, UK, 2010.
7. Szczęśniak, D.; Kais, S. Gap states and valley-spin filtering in transition metal dichalcogenide monolayers. *Phys. Rev. B* **2020**, *101*, 115423. [CrossRef]
8. Belov, A.; Bokut, L.; Rowen, L.; Yu, J.T. The Jacobian Conjecture, Together with Specht and Burnside-Type Problems. In *Automorphisms in Birational and Affine Geometry*; Springer Proceedings in Mathematics and Statistics, 79; Springer: Berlin/Heidelberg, Germany, 2014; pp. 249–285.
9. Ya, A.; Kanel-Belov; Kontsevich, M.L. The Jacobian conjecture is stably equivalent to the Dixmier conjecture. *Mosc. Math. J.* **2007**, *7*, 209–218.
10. Ernst, T. *The History of Q-Calculus and New Method*; Department of Mathematics, Uppsala University: Uppsala, Sweden, 2000.
11. Jackson, F.H. On a q-definite integrals. *Q. J. Pure Appl. Math.* **1910**, *41*, 193–203.
12. Al-Salam, W. Some Fractional q-Integrals and q-Derivatives. *Proc. Edinb. Math. Soc.* **1966**, *15*, 135–140. [CrossRef]
13. Tariboon, J.; Ntouyas, S.K. Quantum calculus on finite intervals and applications to impulsive difference equations. *Adv. Differ. Equ.* **2013**, *2013*, 282. [CrossRef]
14. Bermudo, S.; Kórus, P.; Valdés, J.N. On q-Hermite-Hadamard inequalities for general convex functions. *Acta Math. Hung.* **2020**, *162*, 364–374. [CrossRef]
15. Sadjang, P.N. On the fundamental theorem of (p,q)-calculus and some (p,q)-Taylor formulas. *Results Math.* **2018**, *73*, 1–21.
16. Soontharanon, J.; Sitthiwirattham, T. On Fractional (p,q)-Calculus. *Adv. Differ. Equ.* **2020**, *2020*, 35. [CrossRef]
17. Tunç, M.; Göv, E. Some integral inequalities via (p,q)-calculus on finite intervals. *RGMIA Res. Rep. Coll.* **2016**, *19*, 95.
18. Chu, Y.M.; Awan, M.U.; Talib, S.; Noor, M.A.; Noor, K.I. New post quantum analogues of Ostrowski-type inequalities using new definitions of left-right (p,q)-derivatives and definite integrals. *Adv. Differ. Equ.* **2020**, *2020*, 634. [CrossRef]
19. Ali, M.A.; Budak, H.; Abbas, M.; Chu, Y.-M. Quantum Hermite—Hadamard-type inequalities for functions with convex absolute values of second q^b-derivatives. *Adv. Differ. Equ.* **2021**, *2021*, 7. [CrossRef]
20. Ali, M.A.; Alp, N.; Budak, H.; Chu, Y.-M.; Zhang, Z. On some new quantum midpoint type inequalities for twice quantum differentiable convex functions. *Open Math.* **2021**, *19*, 427–439. [CrossRef]
21. Alp, N.; Sarikaya, M.Z.; Kunt, M.; İşcan, İ. q-Hermite Hadamard inequalities and quantum estimates for midpoint type inequalities via convex and quasi-convex functions. *J. King Saud Univ.-Sci.* **2018**, *30*, 193–203. [CrossRef]

22. Alp, N.; Sarikaya, M.Z. Hermite Hadamard's type inequalities for co-ordinated convex functions on quantum integral. *Appl. Math. E-Notes* **2020**, *20*, 341–356.
23. Budak, H. Some trapezoid and midpoint type inequalities for newly defined quantum integrals. *Proyecciones* **2021**, *40*, 199–215. [CrossRef]
24. Budak, H.; Ali, M.A.; Tarhanaci, M. Some new quantum Hermite-Hadamard-like inequalities for coordinated convex functions. *J. Optim. Theory Appl.* **2020**, *186*, 899–910. [CrossRef]
25. Liu, W.; Hefeng, Z. Some quantum estimates of Hermite-Hadamard inequalities for convex functions. *J. Appl. Anal. Comput.* **2016**, *7*, 501–522.
26. Noor, M.A.; Noor, K.I.; Awan, M.U. Some quantum estimates for Hermite-Hadamard inequalities. *Appl. Math. Comput.* **2015**, *251*, 675–679. [CrossRef]
27. Seksan, J.; Tariboon, J.; Ntouyas, D.K.; Nonlaopon, K. On q-Hermite-Hadamard inequalities for differentiable convex functions. *Mathematics* **2019**, *7*, 632.
28. Noor, M.A.; Noor, K.I.; Awan, M.U. Some quantum integral inequalities via preinvex functions. *Appl. Math. Comput.* **2015**, *269*, 242–251. [CrossRef]
29. Nwaeze, E.R.; Tameru, A.M. New parameterized quantum integral inequalities via η-quasiconvexity. *Adv. Differ. Equ.* **2019**, *2019*, 425. [CrossRef]
30. Khan, M.A.; Noor, M.; Nwaeze, E.R.; Chu, Y.-M. Quantum Hermite–Hadamard inequality by means of a Green function. *Adv. Differ. Equ.* **2020**, *2020*, 99. [CrossRef]
31. Budak, H.; Erden, S.; Ali, M.A. Simpson and Newton type inequalities for convex functions via newly defined quantum integrals. *Math. Meth. Appl. Sci.* **2020**, *44*, 378–390. [CrossRef]
32. Ali, M.A.; Budak, H.; Zhang, Z.; Yildrim, H. Some new Simpson's type inequalities for co-ordinated convex functions in quantum calculus. *Math. Meth. Appl. Sci.* **2021**, *44*, 4515–4540. [CrossRef]
33. Ali, M.A.; Abbas, M.; Budak, H.; Agarwal, P.; Murtaza, G.; Chu, Y.-M. New quantum boundaries for quantum Simpson's and quantum Newton's type inequalities for preinvex functions. *Adv. Differ. Equ.* **2021**, *2021*, 64. [CrossRef]
34. Vivas-Cortez, M.; Ali, M.A.; Kashuri, A.; Sial, I.B.; Zhang, Z. Some New Newton's Type Integral Inequalities for Co-Ordinated Convex Functions in Quantum Calculus. *Symmetry* **2020**, *12*, 1476. [CrossRef]
35. Ali, M.A.; Chu, Y.-M.; Budak, H.; Akkurt, A.; Yildrim, H. Quantum variant of Montgomery identity and Ostrowski-type inequalities for the mappings of two variables. *Adv. Differ. Equ.* **2021**, *2021*, 25. [CrossRef]
36. Ali, M.A.; Budak, H.; Akkurt, A.; Chu, Y.-M. Quantum Ostrowski type inequalities for twice quantum differentiable functions in quantum calculus. *Open Math.* **2021**, *19*, 427–439. [CrossRef]
37. Budak, H.; Ali, M.A.; Alp, N.; Chu, Y.-M. Quantum Ostrowski type integral inequalities. *J. Math. Inequal.* **2021**, in press.
38. Kunt, M.; İşcan, İ.; Alp, N.; Sarikaya, M.Z. (p,q)-Hermite-Hadamard inequalities and (p,q)-estimates for midpoint inequalities via convex quasi-convex functions. *Rev. R. Acad. Cienc. Exactas Fis. Nat. Ser. A Mat.* **2018**, *112*, 969–992. [CrossRef]
39. Latif, M.A.; Kunt, M.; Dragomir, S.S.; İşcan, İ. Post-quantum trapezoid type inequalities. *AIMS Math.* **2020**, *5*, 4011–4026. [CrossRef]
40. Vivas-Cortez, M.; Ali, M.A.; Budak, H.; Kalsoom, H.; Agarwal, P. Some New Hermite—Hadamard and Related Inequalities for Convex Functions via (p,q)-Integral. *Entropy* **2021**, *23*, 828. [CrossRef] [PubMed]
41. Alomari, M.; Darus, M.; Dragomir, S.S. New inequalities of Hermite-Hadamard type for functions whose second derivatives absolute values are quasi-convex. *RGMIA Res. Rep. Coll.* **2009**, *12*. [CrossRef]
42. Sarikaya, M.Z.; Aktan, N. On the generalization of some integral inequalities and their applications. *Math. Comput. Model.* **2011**, *54*, 2175–2182. [CrossRef]

Article

On Some New Fractional Ostrowski- and Trapezoid-Type Inequalities for Functions of Bounded Variations with Two Variables

Thanin Sitthiwirattham [1,*], Hüseyin Budak [2], Hasan Kara [2], Muhammad Aamir Ali [3,*] and Jiraporn Reunsumrit [4]

[1] Mathematics Department, Faculty of Science and Technology, Suan Dusit University, Bangkok 10300, Thailand
[2] Department of Mathematics, Faculty of Science and Arts, Düzce University, 81620 Düzce, Turkey; hsyn.budak@gmail.com or huseyinbudak@duzce.edu.tr (H.B.); hasan64kara@gmail.com or hasan96929@ogr.duzce.edu.tr (H.K.)
[3] Jiangsu Key Laboratory for NSLSCS, School of Mathematical Sciences, Nanjing Normal University, Nanjing 210023, China
[4] Department of Mathematics, Faculty of Applied Science, King Mongkut's University of Technology North Bangkok, Bangkok 10800, Thailand; jiraporn.r@sci.kmutnb.ac.th
* Correspondence: thanin_sit@dusit.ac.th (T.S.); mahr.muhammad.aamir@gmail.com (M.A.A.)

Abstract: In this paper, we first prove three identities for functions of bounded variations. Then, by using these equalities, we obtain several trapezoid- and Ostrowski-type inequalities via generalized fractional integrals for functions of bounded variations with two variables. Moreover, we present some results for Riemann–Liouville fractional integrals by special choice of the main results. Finally, we investigate the connections between our results and those in earlier works. Analytic inequalities of this nature and especially the techniques involved have applications in various areas in which symmetry plays a prominent role.

Keywords: trapezoid-type inequality; fractional integrals; functions of bounded variations

1. Introduction

One of the most important inequalities for bounded functions is the Ostrowski inequality which gives an estimate for the deviation of the values of a smooth function from its mean value. The Ostrowski inequality is stated as follows: if $F : [\kappa_1, \kappa_2] \to \mathbb{R}$ is a differentiable function with a bounded derivative, then the following integral inequality

$$\left| F(\varkappa) - \frac{1}{\kappa_2 - \kappa_1} \int_{\kappa_1}^{\kappa_2} F(\tau) \, d\tau \right| \leq \left[\frac{1}{4} + \frac{(\varkappa - \frac{\kappa_1 + \kappa_2}{2})^2}{(\kappa_2 - \kappa_1)^2} \right] (\kappa_2 - \kappa_1) \|F'\|_\infty \qquad (1)$$

is valid for every $\varkappa \in [\kappa_1, \kappa_2]$, which was proved by Ostrowski in 1938 [1]. Here, the constant $1/4$ is the best possible.

In the recent years, many versions of Ostrowski-type inequalities have been proved for some kinds of function classes, such as convex functions, bounded functions, functions of bounded variation, and so on. For example, Alomari et al. established some Ostrowski-type inequalities for s-convex functions in [2]. Moreover, some papers were devoted to study on Ostrowski-type inequalities for other kinds of convexities [3–6]. On the other hand, Set first proved the fractional version of Ostrowski inequality for s-convex functions via Riemann–Liouville fractional integrals [7]. Furthermore, many studies were focused on the proof of Ostrowski-type inequalities for certain fractional integral operators, such as k-Riemann–Liouville fractional integrals [8], local fractional integrals [9], Raina fractional integrals [10], etc. (see [11–23]). Moreover, by utilizing co-ordinated convex mapping, several Ostrowski inequalities were presented for the Riemann integral and Riemann–Liouville fractional integrals in [24,25], respectively.

On the other hand, Dragomir extended the Ostrowski inequality for functions of bounded variation [26]. Dragomir also proved trapezoid type inequalities and midpoint type inequalities for the functions of bounded variation in [27,28], respectively. In [29], the author presented several Simpson's type inequalities for the mappings of bounded variations. In the literature, many studies were devoted to new versions of Ostrowski-type inequalities for functions of bounded variation. For some of them, please refer to [30–42]. In [43], some important inequalities for the functions of two variables with bounded variation were given and applications in the cubature formula was provided. However, there were some minor errors in the main results of the paper [43] since the Lemma 1 in the published version of [43] is inexact. Moricz has already provided the correct version of the lemma in [44]. In [43], Budak and Sarikaya presented the corrections of these results by using the lemma proved by Moricz. For other papers on inequalities for functions of two variables with bounded variation, see [45–47].

This paper aims to establish some trapezoid and Ostrowski-type inequalities for functions of bounded variations with two variables via generalized fractional integrals. The general structure of the paper consists of six sections including an introduction. The remaining part of the paper proceeds as follows: In Section 2, we first present definitions of the functions of bounded variations and total variations. We also give the definitions of generalized fractional integrals and relations between generalized fractional integrals and other type fractional integrals. In Section 3, we prove three identities for functions of bounded variations with two variables by using the Riemann–Stieltjes integral. Trapezoid- and Ostrowski-type inequalities for functions of bounded variations with two variables are established in Sections 4 and 5, respectively. At the end of the paper, some conclusions and further directions of research are discussed in Section 6.

2. Preliminaries

In this section, we first present the definition of the functions of bounded variation (single and two variables). Then, we summarize the generalized fractional integrals and give the relations between generalized fractional integrals and the other types of fractional integrals.

2.1. Functions of Bounded Variation with One Variable

Definition 1 ([48]). *For any partition $P : \kappa_1 = \varkappa_0 < \varkappa_1 < ... < \varkappa_n = \kappa_2$ of $[\kappa_1, \kappa_2]$ and $\Delta F(\varkappa_i) = F(\varkappa_{i+1}) - F(\varkappa_i)$. If the sum*

$$\sum_{i=1}^{m} |\Delta F(\varkappa_i)|$$

is bounded for all partitions, then the mapping $F(\varkappa)$ is called of bounded variation. We assume that F has a bounded variation on $[\kappa_1, \kappa_2]$, and $\Sigma(P)$ denotes the sum $\sum_{i=1}^{n} |\Delta F(\varkappa_i)|$ corresponding to the partition P of $[\kappa_1, \kappa_2]$. The number

$$\bigvee_{\kappa_1}^{\kappa_2}(F) := \sup\{\Sigma(P) : P \in P([\kappa_1, \kappa_2])\}$$

is called the total variation of F on $[\kappa_1, \kappa_2]$. Here, the family of partitions of $[\kappa_1, \kappa_2]$ is denoted by $P([\kappa_1, \kappa_2])$.

In [26], for the functions of bounded variation, Dragomir proved the following Ostrowski inequality.

Theorem 1. *For the mapping of bounded variation* $F : [\kappa_1, \kappa_2] \to \mathbb{R}$ *on* $[\kappa_1, \kappa_2]$. *The inequality*

$$\left| \frac{1}{\kappa_2 - \kappa_1} \int_{\kappa_1}^{\kappa_2} F(\tau) d\tau - F(\varkappa) \right| \leq \left[\frac{1}{2} + \left| \frac{\varkappa - \frac{\kappa_1 + \kappa_2}{2}}{\kappa_2 - \kappa_1} \right| \right] \bigvee_{\kappa_1}^{\kappa_2} (F) \qquad (2)$$

holds for all $\varkappa \in [\kappa_1, \kappa_2]$. *The constant* $\frac{1}{2}$ *is the best possible.*

2.2. Functions of Bounded Variation with Two Variables

Definition 2. *For any set of points* $(\varkappa_i, \gamma_i)$ $(i = 0, 1, 2, ..., m)$ *satisfying the conditions*

$$\kappa_1 = \varkappa_0 < \varkappa_1 < ... < \varkappa_m = \kappa_2;$$
$$\kappa_3 = \gamma_0 < \gamma_1 < ... < \gamma_m = \kappa_4,$$

if the sum

$$\sum_{i=1}^{m} |\Delta F(\varkappa_i, \gamma_i)|$$

is bounded for all such sets of points, then the mapping $F(\varkappa, \gamma)$ *is called a bounded variation (see [49,50]).*

As a result, the definition of total variation of a function of two variables can be described as follows:

Let F be of bounded variation on $Q = [\kappa_1, \kappa_2] \times [\kappa_3, \kappa_4]$ and $\Sigma(P)$ denotes the sum $\sum_{i=1}^{n} \sum_{j=1}^{m} |\Delta_{11} F(\varkappa_i, \gamma_j)|$ corresponding to the partition P of Q. The number

$$\bigvee_Q (F) := \bigvee_{\kappa_3}^{\kappa_4} \bigvee_{\kappa_1}^{\kappa_2} (F) := \sup\{\Sigma(P) : P \in P(Q)\}$$

is called the total variation of F on Q. Here, the family of partitions of Q is denoted by $P(Q)$.

Lemma 1 ([44]). *If* $F(\tau, \xi)$ *continuous on the* $Q = [\kappa_1, \kappa_2] \times [\kappa_3, \kappa_4]$ *and* $\alpha(\tau, \xi)$ *is of bounded variation, then* $\alpha(\tau, \xi)$ *is integrable with respect to* $F(\tau, \xi)$ *on* Q *in the Riemann–Stieltjes integrable sense and*

$$\int_{\kappa_1}^{\kappa_2} \int_{\kappa_3}^{\kappa_4} F(\tau, \xi) d_\tau d_\xi \alpha(\tau, \xi) \qquad (3)$$

$$= \int_{\kappa_1}^{\kappa_2} \int_{\kappa_3}^{\kappa_4} \alpha(\tau, \xi) d_\tau d_\xi F(\tau, \xi) - \int_{\kappa_1}^{\kappa_2} \alpha(\tau, \kappa_4) d_\tau F(\tau, \kappa_4) + \int_{\kappa_1}^{\kappa_2} \alpha(\tau, \kappa_3) d_\tau F(\tau, \kappa_3)$$

$$- \int_{\kappa_3}^{\kappa_4} \alpha(\kappa_2, \xi) d_\xi F(\kappa_2, \xi) + \int_{\kappa_3}^{\kappa_4} \alpha(\kappa_1, \xi) d_\xi F(\kappa_1, \xi)$$

$$+ F(\kappa_2, \kappa_4) \alpha(\kappa_2, \kappa_4) - F(\kappa_2, \kappa_3) \alpha(\kappa_2, \kappa_3)$$
$$- F(\kappa_1, \kappa_4) \alpha(\kappa_1, \kappa_4) + F(\kappa_1, \kappa_3) \alpha(\kappa_1, \kappa_3).$$

Lemma 2 ([43]). *Assume that* ρ *is integrable with respect to* α *on* Q *and* α *is of bounded variation on* Q, *then*

$$\left| \int_{\kappa_3}^{\kappa_4} \int_{\kappa_1}^{\kappa_2} \rho(\varkappa, \gamma) d_\varkappa d_\gamma \alpha(\varkappa, \gamma) \right| \leq \sup_{(\varkappa, \gamma) \in Q} |\rho(\varkappa, \gamma)| \bigvee_Q (\alpha). \qquad (4)$$

2.3. Generalized Fractional Integrals

In this section, we summarize some fractional integrals which will be used in our main results.

Definition 3 ([51]). *Let $F \in L_1[\kappa_1, \kappa_2]$. The Riemann–Liouville fractional integrals $\mathsf{J}^\alpha_{\kappa_1+}F$ and $\mathsf{J}^\alpha_{\kappa_2-}F$ of order $\alpha > 0$ with $\kappa_1 \geq 0$ are defined by*

$$\mathsf{J}^\alpha_{\kappa_1+}F(\varkappa) = \frac{1}{\Gamma(\alpha)} \int_{\kappa_1}^{\varkappa} (\varkappa - \tau)^{\alpha-1} F(\tau) d\tau, \quad \varkappa > \kappa_1$$

and

$$\mathsf{J}^\alpha_{\kappa_2+}F(\varkappa) = \frac{1}{\Gamma(\alpha)} \int_{\varkappa}^{\kappa_2} (\tau - \varkappa)^{\alpha-1} F(\tau) d\tau, \quad \varkappa < \kappa_2,$$

respectively. Here, $\Gamma(\alpha)$ is the Gamma function and $\mathsf{J}^0_{\kappa_1+}F(\varkappa) = \mathsf{J}^0_{\kappa_2-}F(\varkappa) = F(\varkappa)$.

Definition 4 ([52]). *Let $\rho : [\kappa_1, \kappa_2] \to \mathbb{R}$ be a positive increasing function on (κ_1, κ_2), having a continuous derivative $\rho'(\varkappa)$ on (κ_1, κ_2). The left-sides $(\mathcal{J}^\alpha_{\kappa_1+;\rho}F(\varkappa))$ and right-sides $(\mathcal{J}^\alpha_{\kappa_2-;\rho}F(\varkappa))$ fractional integral of F with respect to the function ρ on $[\kappa_1, \kappa_2]$ of order $\alpha > 0$ are defined by*

$$\mathcal{J}^\alpha_{\kappa_1+;\rho}F(\varkappa) = \frac{1}{\Gamma(\alpha)} \int_{\kappa_1}^{\varkappa} \frac{\rho'(\tau) F(\tau)}{[\rho(\varkappa) - \rho(\tau)]^{1-\alpha}} d\tau, \quad \varkappa > \kappa_1$$

and

$$\mathcal{J}^\alpha_{\kappa_2-;\rho}F(\varkappa) = \frac{1}{\Gamma(\alpha)} \int_{\varkappa}^{\kappa_2} \frac{\rho'(\tau) F(\tau)}{[\rho(\tau) - \rho(\varkappa)]^{1-\alpha}} d\tau, \quad \varkappa < \kappa_2,$$

respectively.

Riemann–Liouville fractional integrals of a function with two variables can be given as follows:

Definition 5. *Let $F \in L_1(\Delta = [\kappa_1, \kappa_2] \times [\kappa_3, \kappa_4])$. The Riemann–Liouville fractional integrals $\mathsf{J}^{\alpha,\beta}_{\kappa_1+,\kappa_3+}F, \mathsf{J}^{\alpha,\beta}_{\kappa_1+,\kappa_4-}F, \mathsf{J}^{\alpha,\beta}_{\kappa_2-,\kappa_3+}F$ and $\mathsf{J}^{\alpha,\beta}_{\kappa_2-,\kappa_4-}F$ of order $\alpha, \beta > 0$ with $\kappa_1, \kappa_3 \geq 0$ are defined by*

$$\mathsf{J}^{\alpha,\beta}_{\kappa_1+,\kappa_3+}F(\varkappa, \gamma) = \frac{1}{\Gamma(\alpha)\Gamma(\beta)} \int_{\kappa_1}^{\varkappa} \int_{\kappa_3}^{\gamma} (\varkappa - \tau)^{\alpha-1} (\gamma - \xi)^{\beta-1} F(\tau, \xi) d\xi d\tau, \quad \varkappa > \kappa_1, \gamma > \kappa_3,$$

$$\mathsf{J}^{\alpha,\beta}_{\kappa_1+,\kappa_4-}F(\varkappa, \gamma) = \frac{1}{\Gamma(\alpha)\Gamma(\beta)} \int_{\kappa_1}^{\varkappa} \int_{\gamma}^{\kappa_4} (\varkappa - \tau)^{\alpha-1} (\xi - \gamma)^{\beta-1} F(\tau, \xi) d\xi d\tau, \quad \varkappa > \kappa_1, \gamma < \kappa_4,$$

$$\mathsf{J}^{\alpha,\beta}_{\kappa_2-,\kappa_3+}F(\varkappa, \gamma) = \frac{1}{\Gamma(\alpha)\Gamma(\beta)} \int_{\varkappa}^{\kappa_2} \int_{\kappa_3}^{\gamma} (\tau - \varkappa)^{\alpha-1} (\gamma - \xi)^{\beta-1} F(\tau, \xi) d\xi d\tau, \quad \varkappa < \kappa_2, \gamma > \kappa_3$$

and

$$\mathsf{J}^{\alpha,\beta}_{\kappa_2-,\kappa_4-}F(\varkappa, \gamma) = \frac{1}{\Gamma(\alpha)\Gamma(\beta)} \int_{\varkappa}^{\kappa_2} \int_{\gamma}^{\kappa_4} (\tau - \varkappa)^{\alpha-1} (\xi - \gamma)^{\beta-1} F(\tau, \xi) d\xi d\tau, \quad \varkappa < \kappa_2, \gamma < \kappa_4,$$

Definition 6 ([53]). *Let $\rho : [\kappa_1, \kappa_2] \to \mathbb{R}$ be a positive increasing function on (κ_1, κ_2), having a continuous derivative $\rho'(\varkappa)$ on (κ_1, κ_2) and let $\omega : [\kappa_3, \kappa_4] \to \mathbb{R}$ be a positive increasing function* on $(\kappa_3, \kappa_4]$, having a continuous derivative $\omega'(\gamma)$ on (κ_3, κ_4). If $F \in L_1(\Delta)$, then for $\alpha, \beta > 0$, the generalized fractional integral operators for functions of two variables are defined by

$$\mathcal{J}^{\alpha,\beta}_{\kappa_1+,\kappa_3+;\rho,\omega}F(\varkappa,\gamma) = \frac{1}{\Gamma(\alpha)\Gamma(\beta)} \int_{\kappa_1}^{\varkappa}\int_{\kappa_3}^{\gamma} \frac{\rho'(\tau)}{[\rho(\varkappa)-\rho(\tau)]^{1-\alpha}} \frac{\omega'(\xi)}{[\omega(\gamma)-\omega(\xi)]^{1-\beta}} F(\tau,\xi)d\xi d\tau,$$

$\varkappa > \kappa_1, \gamma > \kappa_3,$ (5)

$$\mathcal{J}^{\alpha,\beta}_{\kappa_1+,\kappa_4-;\rho,\omega}F(\varkappa,\gamma) = \frac{1}{\Gamma(\alpha)\Gamma(\beta)} \int_{\kappa_1}^{\varkappa}\int_{\gamma}^{\kappa_4} \frac{\rho'(\tau)}{[\rho(\varkappa)-\rho(\tau)]^{1-\alpha}} \frac{\omega'(\xi)}{[\omega(\xi)-\omega(\gamma)]^{1-\beta}} F(\tau,\xi)d\xi d\tau,$$

$\varkappa > \kappa_1, \gamma < \kappa_4,$ (6)

$$\mathcal{J}^{\alpha,\beta}_{\kappa_2-,\kappa_3+;\rho,\omega}F(\varkappa,\gamma) = \frac{1}{\Gamma(\alpha)\Gamma(\beta)} \int_{\varkappa}^{\kappa_2}\int_{\kappa_3}^{\gamma} \frac{\rho'(\tau)}{[\rho(\tau)-\rho(\varkappa)]^{1-\alpha}} \frac{\omega'(\xi)}{[\omega(\gamma)-\omega(\xi)]^{1-\beta}} F(\tau,\xi)d\xi d\tau,$$

$\varkappa < \kappa_2, \gamma > \kappa_3$ (7)

and

$$\mathcal{J}^{\alpha,\beta}_{\kappa_2-,\kappa_4-;\rho,\omega}F(\varkappa,\gamma) = \frac{1}{\Gamma(\alpha)\Gamma(\beta)} \int_{\varkappa}^{\kappa_2}\int_{\gamma}^{\kappa_4} \frac{\rho'(\tau)}{[\rho(\tau)-\rho(\varkappa)]^{1-\alpha}} \frac{\omega'(\xi)}{[\omega(\xi)-\omega(\gamma)]^{1-\beta}} F(\tau,\xi)d\xi d\tau,$$

$\varkappa < \kappa_2, \gamma < \kappa_4,$ (8)

respectively.

By using Definition 6, well-known fractional integrals can be obtained by some special choices. For example:

1. If we choose $\alpha = \beta = 1$, the operators (5)–(8) reduce to the double Riemann integral;
2. Considering $\rho(\tau) = \tau$ and $\omega(\xi) = \xi$, then the operators (5)–(8) reduce to the Riemann–Liouville fractional integrals $J^{\alpha,\beta}_{\kappa_1+,\kappa_3+}F(\varkappa,\gamma)$, $J^{\alpha,\beta}_{\kappa_1+,\kappa_4-}F(\varkappa,\gamma)$ $J^{\alpha,\beta}_{\kappa_2-,\kappa_3+}F(\varkappa,\gamma)$ and $J^{\alpha,\beta}_{\kappa_2-,\kappa_4-}F(\varkappa,\gamma)$, respectively;
3. For $\rho(\tau) = \ln \tau$ and $\omega(\xi) = \ln \xi$, the operators (5)–(8) reduce to the Hadamard fractional integrals $I^{\alpha,\beta}_{\kappa_1+,\kappa_3+}F(\varkappa,\gamma)$, $I^{\alpha,\beta}_{\kappa_1+,\kappa_4-}F(\varkappa,\gamma)$, $I^{\alpha,\beta}_{\kappa_2-,\kappa_3+}F(\varkappa,\gamma)$ and $I^{\alpha,\beta}_{\kappa_2-,\kappa_4-}F(\varkappa,\gamma)$, respectively.

3. Some Equalities for Functions of Bounded Variations with Two Variables

Firstly, we define the following functions which will be used frequently:

$$M^{\alpha}_{\rho}(\kappa_1,\varkappa) = \frac{[\rho(\varkappa)-\rho(\kappa_1)]^{\alpha}}{\Gamma(\alpha+1)},$$

$$N^{\beta}_{\omega}(\kappa_3,\gamma) = \frac{[\omega(\gamma)-\omega(\kappa_3)]^{\beta}}{\Gamma(\beta+1)},$$

$$M^{\alpha}_{\rho}(\kappa_2,\varkappa) = \frac{[\rho(\kappa_2)-\rho(\varkappa)]^{\alpha}}{\Gamma(\alpha+1)}$$

and

$$N^{\beta}_{\omega}(\kappa_4,\gamma) = \frac{[\omega(\kappa_4)-\omega(\gamma)]^{\beta}}{\Gamma(\beta+1)}$$

$$M^{\alpha}_{\rho}(\kappa_1, \kappa_2; \varkappa) = [\rho(\varkappa) - \rho(\kappa_1)]^{\alpha} + [\rho(\kappa_2) - \rho(\varkappa)]^{\alpha}$$

$$N^{\beta}_{\varpi}(\kappa_3, \kappa_4; \gamma) = [\varpi(\gamma) - \varpi(\kappa_3)]^{\beta} + [\varpi(\kappa_4) - \varpi(\gamma)]^{\beta}$$

for $(\varkappa, \gamma) \in \Delta$. We also denote

$$\begin{aligned}
\mathcal{K}_1 &= M^{\alpha}_{\rho}(\kappa_1, \varkappa) N^{\beta}_{\varpi}(\kappa_3, \gamma) F(\kappa_1, \kappa_3) + M^{\alpha}_{\rho}(\kappa_1, \varkappa) N^{\beta}_{\varpi}(\kappa_4, \gamma) F(\kappa_1, \kappa_4) \\
&\quad + M^{\alpha}_{\rho}(\kappa_2, \varkappa) N^{\beta}_{\varpi}(\kappa_3, \gamma) F(\kappa_2, \kappa_3) + M^{\alpha}_{\rho}(\kappa_2, \varkappa) N^{\beta}_{\varpi}(\kappa_4, \gamma) F(\kappa_2, \kappa_4)
\end{aligned}$$

for $(\varkappa, \gamma) \in \Delta$.

Throughout this paper, we denote the second partial derivative $\frac{\partial^2 F}{\partial \tau \partial \xi}$ by $F_{\tau\xi}$. Moreover, let $\rho : [\kappa_1, \kappa_2] \to \mathbb{R}$ be a positive increasing function on $(\kappa_1, \kappa_2]$, having a continuous derivative $\rho'(\varkappa)$ on (κ_1, κ_2) and let $\varpi : [\kappa_3, \kappa_4] \to \mathbb{R}$ be a positive increasing function on $(\kappa_3, \kappa_4]$, having a continuous derivative $\varpi'(\gamma)$ on (κ_3, κ_4).

Now, we are in position to prove the following identity:

Lemma 3. *If $F : \Delta \to \mathbb{R}$ be a mapping of bounded variation on Δ, then for $\alpha, \beta > 0$, we have the following equality:*

$$\begin{aligned}
&\mathcal{K}_1 - N^{\beta}_{\varpi}(\kappa_3, \gamma) \left[\mathcal{J}^{\alpha}_{\kappa_1+;\rho} F(\varkappa, \kappa_3) + \mathcal{J}^{\alpha}_{\kappa_2-;\rho} F(\varkappa, \kappa_3) \right] \\
&- N^{\beta}_{\varpi}(\kappa_4, \gamma) \left[\mathcal{J}^{\alpha}_{\kappa_1+;\rho} F(\varkappa, \kappa_4) + \mathcal{J}^{\alpha}_{\kappa_2-;\rho} F(\varkappa, \kappa_4) \right] \\
&- M^{\alpha}_{\rho}(\kappa_1, \varkappa) \left[\mathcal{J}^{\beta}_{\kappa_3+;\varpi} F(\kappa_1, \gamma) + \mathcal{J}^{\beta}_{\kappa_4-;\varpi} F(\kappa_1, \gamma) \right] \\
&- M^{\alpha}_{\rho}(\kappa_2, \varkappa) \left[\mathcal{J}^{\beta}_{\kappa_3+;\varpi} F(\kappa_2, \gamma) + \mathcal{J}^{\beta}_{\kappa_4-;\varpi} F(\kappa_2, \gamma) \right] + \mathcal{J}^{\alpha,\beta}_{\kappa_1+,\kappa_3+;\rho,\varpi} F(\varkappa, \gamma) \\
&+ \mathcal{J}^{\alpha,\beta}_{\kappa_1+,\kappa_4-;\rho,\varpi} F(\varkappa, \gamma) + \mathcal{J}^{\alpha,\beta}_{\kappa_2-,\kappa_3+;\rho,\varpi} F(\varkappa, \gamma) + \mathcal{J}^{\alpha,\beta}_{\kappa_2-,\kappa_4-;\rho,\varpi} F(\varkappa, \gamma) \\
&= \frac{1}{\Gamma(\alpha+1)\Gamma(\beta+1)} [I_1 - I_2 - I_3 + I_4],
\end{aligned}$$

where

$$I_1 = \int_{\kappa_1}^{\varkappa} \int_{\kappa_3}^{\gamma} (\rho(\varkappa) - \rho(\tau))^{\alpha} (\varpi(\gamma) - \varpi(\xi))^{\beta} d_{\tau} d_{\xi} F(\tau, \xi),$$

$$I_2 = \int_{\kappa_1}^{\varkappa} \int_{\gamma}^{\kappa_4} (\rho(\varkappa) - \rho(\tau))^{\alpha} (\varpi(\xi) - \varpi(\gamma))^{\beta} d_{\tau} d_{\xi} F(\tau, \xi),$$

$$I_3 = \int_{\varkappa}^{\kappa_2} \int_{\kappa_3}^{\gamma} (\rho(\tau) - \rho(\varkappa))^{\alpha} (\varpi(\gamma) - \varpi(\xi))^{\beta} d_{\tau} d_{\xi} F(\tau, \xi),$$

$$I_4 = \int_{\varkappa}^{\kappa_2} \int_{\gamma}^{\kappa_4} (\rho(\tau) - \rho(\varkappa))^{\alpha} (\varpi(\xi) - \varpi(\gamma))^{\beta} d_{\tau} d_{\xi} F(\tau, \xi).$$

Proof. By using Lemma 1, we have

$$\begin{aligned}
I_1 &= \int_{\kappa_1}^{\varkappa} \int_{\kappa_3}^{\gamma} (\rho(\varkappa) - \rho(\tau))^{\alpha} (\varpi(\gamma) - \varpi(\xi))^{\beta} d_{\tau} d_{\xi} F(\tau, \xi) \qquad (9) \\
&= (\varpi(\gamma) - \varpi(\kappa_3))^{\beta} (\rho(\varkappa) - \rho(\kappa_1))^{\alpha} F(\kappa_1, \kappa_3) - \Gamma(\alpha+1)(\varpi(\gamma)
\end{aligned}$$

$$-\varpi(\kappa_3))^\beta \mathcal{J}^\alpha_{\kappa_1+;\rho} F(\varkappa,\kappa_3) - \Gamma(\beta+1)(\rho(\varkappa) - \rho(\kappa_1))^\alpha \mathcal{J}^\beta_{\kappa_3+;\varpi} F(\kappa_1,\gamma)$$

$$+\Gamma(\alpha+1)\Gamma(\beta+1)\mathcal{J}^{\alpha,\beta}_{\kappa_1+\kappa_3+;\rho,\varpi} F(\varkappa,\gamma).$$

Similarly, we obtain

$$I_2 = -(\rho(\varkappa) - \rho(\kappa_1))^\alpha (\varpi(\kappa_4) - \varpi(\gamma))^\beta F(\kappa_1,\kappa_4) + \Gamma(\alpha+1)(\varpi(\kappa_4) \quad (10)$$

$$-\varpi(\gamma))^\beta \mathcal{J}^\alpha_{\kappa_1+;\rho} F(\varkappa,\kappa_4) + \Gamma(\beta+1)(\rho(\varkappa) - \rho(\kappa_1))^\alpha \mathcal{J}^\beta_{\kappa_4-;\varpi} F(\kappa_1,\gamma)$$

$$-\Gamma(\alpha+1)\Gamma(\beta+1)\mathcal{J}^{\alpha,\beta}_{\kappa_1+\kappa_4-;\rho,\varpi} F(\varkappa,\gamma),$$

$$I_3 = -(\rho(\kappa_2) - \rho(\varkappa))^\alpha (\varpi(\gamma) - \varpi(\kappa_3))^\beta F(\kappa_2,\kappa_3) + \Gamma(\alpha+1)(\varpi(\gamma) \quad (11)$$

$$-\varpi(\kappa_3))^\beta \mathcal{J}^\alpha_{\kappa_2-;\rho} F(\varkappa,\kappa_3) + \Gamma(\beta+1)(\rho(\kappa_2)$$

$$-\rho(\varkappa))^\alpha \mathcal{J}^\beta_{\kappa_3+;\varpi} F(\kappa_2,\gamma) - \Gamma(\alpha+1)\Gamma(\beta+1)\mathcal{J}^{\alpha,\beta}_{\kappa_2-\kappa_3+;\rho,\varpi} F(\varkappa,\gamma)$$

and

$$I_4 = (\rho(\kappa_2) - \rho(\varkappa))^\alpha (\varpi(\kappa_4) - \varpi(\gamma))^\beta F(\kappa_2,\kappa_4) - \Gamma(\alpha+1)(\varpi(\kappa_4) \quad (12)$$

$$-\varpi(\gamma))^\beta \mathcal{J}^\alpha_{\kappa_2-;\rho} F(\varkappa,\kappa_4) - \Gamma(\beta+1)(\rho(\kappa_2)$$

$$-\rho(\varkappa))^\alpha \mathcal{J}^\beta_{\kappa_4-;\varpi} F(\kappa_2,\gamma) + \Gamma(\alpha+1)\Gamma(\beta+1)\mathcal{J}^{\alpha,\beta}_{\kappa_2-\kappa_4-;\rho,\varpi} F(\varkappa,\gamma).$$

By equalities (9)–(12), we establish

$$\kappa_1 - N^\beta_\varpi(\kappa_3,\gamma)\left[\mathcal{J}^\alpha_{\kappa_1+;\rho} F(\varkappa,\kappa_3) + \mathcal{J}^\alpha_{\kappa_2-;\rho} F(\varkappa,\kappa_3)\right] - N^\beta_\varpi(\kappa_4,\gamma)$$

$$\times\left[\mathcal{J}^\alpha_{\kappa_1+;\rho} F(\varkappa,\kappa_4) + \mathcal{J}^\alpha_{\kappa_2-;\rho} F(\varkappa,\kappa_4)\right] - M^\alpha_\rho(\kappa_1,\varkappa)\left[\mathcal{J}^\beta_{\kappa_3+;\varpi} F(\kappa_1,\gamma) + \mathcal{J}^\beta_{\kappa_4-;\varpi} F(\kappa_1,\gamma)\right]$$

$$-M^\alpha_\rho(\kappa_2,\varkappa)\left[\mathcal{J}^\beta_{\kappa_3+;\varpi} F(\kappa_2,\gamma) + \mathcal{J}^\beta_{\kappa_4-;\varpi} F(\kappa_2,\gamma)\right] + \mathcal{J}^{\alpha,\beta}_{\kappa_1+,\kappa_3+;\rho,\varpi} F(\varkappa,\gamma)$$

$$+\mathcal{J}^{\alpha,\beta}_{\kappa_1+,\kappa_4-;\rho,\varpi} F(\varkappa,\gamma) + \mathcal{J}^{\alpha,\beta}_{\kappa_2-,\kappa_3+;\rho,\varpi} F(\varkappa,\gamma) + \mathcal{J}^{\alpha,\beta}_{\kappa_2-,\kappa_4-;\rho,\varpi} F(\varkappa,\gamma)$$

$$= \frac{1}{\Gamma(\alpha+1)\Gamma(\beta+1)}[I_1 - I_2 - I_3 + I_4]$$

which completes the proof. □

Lemma 4. *If* $F : \Delta \to \mathbb{R}$ *be a mapping of bounded variation on* Δ*, then for* $\alpha, \beta > 0$*, we have the following equality*

$$F(\varkappa,\gamma) - \frac{\Gamma(\alpha+1)}{M^\alpha_\rho(\kappa_1,\kappa_2;\varkappa)}\left[\mathcal{J}^\alpha_{\varkappa-;\rho} F(\kappa_1,\gamma) + \mathcal{J}^\alpha_{\varkappa+;\rho} F(\kappa_2,\gamma)\right]$$

$$-\frac{\Gamma(\beta+1)}{N_\varpi^\beta(\kappa_3,\kappa_4;\gamma)}\left[\mathcal{J}_{\gamma-;\varpi}^\beta F(\varkappa,\kappa_3)+\mathcal{J}_{\gamma+;\varpi}^\beta F(\varkappa,\kappa_4)\right]$$

$$+\frac{\Gamma(\alpha+1)\Gamma(\beta+1)}{M_\rho^\alpha(\kappa_1,\kappa_2;\varkappa)N_\varpi^\beta(\kappa_3,\kappa_4;\gamma)}\left[\mathcal{J}_{\varkappa-,\gamma-;\rho,\varpi}^{\alpha,\beta}F(\kappa_1,\kappa_3)+\mathcal{J}_{\varkappa-,\gamma+;\rho,\varpi}^{\alpha,\beta}F(\kappa_1,\kappa_4)\right.$$

$$\left.+\mathcal{J}_{\varkappa+,\gamma-;\rho,\varpi}^{\alpha,\beta}F(\kappa_2,\kappa_3)+\mathcal{J}_{\varkappa+,\gamma+;\rho,\varpi}^{\alpha,\beta}F(\kappa_2,\kappa_4)\right]$$

$$=\frac{1}{M_\rho^\alpha(\kappa_1,\kappa_2;\varkappa)N_\varpi^\beta(\kappa_3,\kappa_4;\gamma)}[I_5-I_6-I_7+I_8]$$

where

$$I_5=\int_{\kappa_1}^{\varkappa}\int_{\kappa_3}^{\gamma}(\rho(\tau)-\rho(\kappa_1))^\alpha(\varpi(\xi)-\varpi(\kappa_3))^\beta d_\tau d_\xi F(\tau,\xi),$$

$$I_6=\int_{\kappa_1}^{\varkappa}\int_{\gamma}^{\kappa_4}(\rho(\tau)-\rho(\kappa_1))^\alpha(\varpi(\kappa_4)-\varpi(\xi))^\beta d_\tau d_\xi F(\tau,\xi),$$

$$I_7=\int_{\varkappa}^{\kappa_2}\int_{\kappa_3}^{\gamma}(\rho(\kappa_2)-\rho(\tau))^\alpha(\varpi(\xi)-\varpi(\kappa_3))^\beta d_\tau d_\xi F(\tau,\xi)$$

and

$$I_8=\int_{\varkappa}^{\kappa_2}\int_{\gamma}^{\kappa_4}(\rho(\kappa_2)-\rho(\tau))^\alpha(\varpi(\kappa_4)-\varpi(\xi))^\beta d_\tau d_\xi F(\tau,\xi).$$

Proof. By using Lemma 1, we have

$$I_5 = \int_{\kappa_1}^{\varkappa}\int_{\kappa_3}^{\gamma}(\rho(\tau)-\rho(\kappa_1))^\alpha(\varpi(\xi)-\varpi(\kappa_3))^\beta d_\tau d_\xi F(\tau,\xi) \tag{13}$$

$$= (\varpi(\gamma)-\varpi(\kappa_3))^\beta(\rho(\varkappa)-\rho(\kappa_1))^\alpha F(\varkappa,\gamma)-\Gamma(\alpha+1)(\varpi(\gamma)-\varpi(\kappa_3))^\beta \mathcal{J}_{\varkappa-;\rho}^\alpha F(\kappa_1,\gamma)$$

$$-\Gamma(\beta+1)(\rho(\varkappa)-\rho(\kappa_1))^\alpha \mathcal{J}_{\gamma-;\varpi}^\beta F(\varkappa,\kappa_3)+\Gamma(\alpha+1)\Gamma(\beta+1)\mathcal{J}_{\varkappa-,\gamma-;\rho,\varpi}^{\alpha,\beta}F(\kappa_1,\kappa_3).$$

Similarly, we obtain

$$I_6 = \int_{\kappa_1}^{\varkappa}\int_{\gamma}^{\kappa_4}(\rho(\tau)-\rho(\kappa_1))^\alpha(\varpi(\kappa_4)-\varpi(\xi))^\beta d_\tau d_\xi F(\tau,\xi) \tag{14}$$

$$= -(\rho(\varkappa)-\rho(\kappa_1))^\alpha(\varpi(\kappa_4)-\varpi(\gamma))^\beta F(\varkappa,\gamma)+\Gamma(\alpha+1)(\varpi(\kappa_4)-\varpi(\gamma))^\beta \mathcal{J}_{\varkappa-;\rho}^\alpha F(\kappa_1,\gamma)$$

$$+\Gamma(\beta+1)(\rho(\varkappa)-\rho(\kappa_1))^\alpha \mathcal{J}_{\gamma+;\varpi}^\beta F(\varkappa,\kappa_4)-\Gamma(\alpha+1)\Gamma(\beta+1)\mathcal{J}_{\varkappa-,\gamma+;\rho,\varpi}^{\alpha,\beta}F(\kappa_1,\kappa_4),$$

$$I_7 = \int_{\varkappa}^{\kappa_2}\int_{\kappa_3}^{\gamma}(\rho(\kappa_2)-\rho(\tau))^\alpha(\varpi(\xi)-\varpi(\kappa_3))^\beta d_\tau d_\xi F(\tau,\xi) \tag{15}$$

$$= -(\rho(\kappa_2)-\rho(\varkappa))^\alpha(\varpi(\gamma)-\varpi(\kappa_3))^\beta F(\varkappa,\gamma)+\Gamma(\alpha+1)(\varpi(\gamma)-\varpi(\kappa_3))^\beta \mathcal{J}_{\varkappa+;\rho}^\alpha F(\kappa_2,\gamma)$$

$$+\Gamma(\beta+1)(\rho(\kappa_2)-\rho(\varkappa))^\alpha \mathcal{J}_{\gamma-;\varpi}^\beta F(\varkappa,\kappa_3)-\Gamma(\alpha+1)\Gamma(\beta+1)\mathcal{J}_{\varkappa+,\gamma-;\rho,\varpi}^{\alpha,\beta}F(\kappa_2,\kappa_3)$$

and

$$I_8 = \int_{\varkappa}^{\kappa_2}\int_{\gamma}^{\kappa_4}(\rho(\kappa_2)-\rho(\tau))^{\alpha}(\omega(\kappa_4)-\omega(\xi))^{\beta}d_{\tau}d_{\xi}F(\tau,\xi) \qquad (16)$$

$$= (\rho(\kappa_2)-\rho(\varkappa))^{\alpha}(\omega(\kappa_4)-\omega(\gamma))^{\beta}F(\varkappa,\gamma) - \Gamma(\alpha+1)(\omega(\kappa_4)-\omega(\gamma))^{\beta}\mathcal{J}_{\varkappa+;\rho}^{\alpha}F(\kappa_2,\gamma)$$

$$-\Gamma(\beta+1)(\rho(\kappa_2)-\rho(\varkappa))^{\alpha}\mathcal{J}_{\gamma+;\omega}^{\beta}F(\varkappa,\kappa_4) + \Gamma(\alpha+1)\Gamma(\beta+1)\mathcal{J}_{\varkappa+,\gamma+;\rho,\omega}^{\alpha,\beta}F(\kappa_2,\kappa_4).$$

Using equalities (13)–(16), we have the desired result. □

Lemma 5. *If $F : \Delta \to \mathbb{R}$ be a mapping of bounded variation on Δ, then for $\alpha, \beta > 0$, we have the following equality*

$$\frac{F(\kappa_2,\kappa_4)+F(\kappa_2,\kappa_3)+F(\kappa_1,\kappa_4)+F(\kappa_1,\kappa_3)}{4} \qquad (17)$$

$$-\frac{1}{4M_{\rho}^{\alpha}(\kappa_1,\kappa_2)}\left[\mathcal{J}_{\kappa_2-;\rho}^{\alpha}F(\kappa_1,\kappa_4)+\mathcal{J}_{\kappa_2-;\rho}^{\alpha}F(\kappa_1,\kappa_3)+\mathcal{J}_{\kappa_1+;\rho}^{\alpha}F(\kappa_2,\kappa_4)+\mathcal{J}_{\kappa_1+;\rho}^{\alpha}F(\kappa_2,\kappa_3)\right]$$

$$-\frac{1}{4N_{\omega}^{\beta}(\kappa_3,\kappa_4)}\left[\mathcal{J}_{\kappa_4-;\omega}^{\beta}F(\kappa_2,\kappa_3)+\mathcal{J}_{\kappa_3+;\omega}^{\beta}F(\kappa_2,\kappa_4)+\mathcal{J}_{\kappa_4-;\omega}^{\beta}F(\kappa_1,\kappa_3)+\mathcal{J}_{\kappa_3+;\omega}^{\beta}F(\kappa_1,\kappa_4)\right]$$

$$+\frac{1}{4M_{\rho}^{\alpha}(\kappa_1,\kappa_2)N_{\omega}^{\beta}(\kappa_3,\kappa_4)}\left[\mathcal{J}_{\kappa_2-,\kappa_4-;\rho,\omega}^{\alpha,\beta}F(\kappa_1,\kappa_3)+\mathcal{J}_{\kappa_2-,\kappa_3+;\rho,\omega}^{\alpha,\beta}F(\kappa_1,\kappa_4)\right.$$

$$\left.+\mathcal{J}_{\kappa_1+,\kappa_4-;\rho,\omega}^{\alpha,\beta}F(\kappa_2,\kappa_3)+\mathcal{J}_{\kappa_1+,\kappa_3+;\rho,\omega}^{\alpha,\beta}F(\kappa_2,\kappa_4)\right]$$

$$= \frac{1}{4\Gamma(\alpha+1)\Gamma(\beta+1)}\frac{1}{M_{\rho}^{\alpha}(\kappa_1,\kappa_2)N_{\omega}^{\beta}(\kappa_3,\kappa_4)}$$

$$\times \int_{\kappa_1}^{\kappa_2}\int_{\kappa_3}^{\kappa_2}[(\rho(\kappa_2)-\rho(\tau))^{\alpha}-\rho(\tau)-\rho(\kappa_1))^{\alpha}]$$

$$\times \left[(\omega(\kappa_4)-\omega(\xi))^{\beta}-(\omega(\xi)-\omega(\kappa_3))^{\beta}\right]d_{\tau}d_{\xi}F(\tau,\xi).$$

Proof. For $\varkappa = \kappa_2$ and $\gamma = \kappa_4$ in Equation (13), we have

$$I_9 = \int_{\kappa_1}^{\kappa_2}\int_{\kappa_3}^{\kappa_4}(\rho(\tau)-\rho(\kappa_1))^{\alpha}(\omega(\xi)-\omega(\kappa_3))^{\beta}d_{\tau}d_{\xi}F(\tau,\xi) \qquad (18)$$

$$= (\omega(\kappa_4)-\omega(\kappa_3))^{\beta}(\rho(\kappa_2)-\rho(\kappa_1))^{\alpha}F(\kappa_2,\kappa_4) - \Gamma(\alpha+1)(\omega(\kappa_4)$$

$$-\omega(\kappa_3))^{\beta}\mathcal{J}_{\kappa_2-;\rho}^{\alpha}F(\kappa_1,\kappa_4) - \Gamma(\beta+1)(\rho(\kappa_2)-\rho(\kappa_1))^{\alpha}\mathcal{J}_{\kappa_4-;\omega}^{\beta}F(\kappa_2,\kappa_3)$$

$$+\Gamma(\alpha+1)\Gamma(\beta+1)\mathcal{J}_{\kappa_2-,\kappa_4-;\rho,\omega}^{\alpha,\beta}F(\kappa_1,\kappa_3).$$

For $\varkappa = \kappa_2$ and $\gamma = \kappa_3$ in Equation (14), we have

$$I_{10} = \int_{\kappa_1}^{\kappa_2}\int_{\kappa_3}^{\kappa_4}(\rho(\tau)-\rho(\kappa_1))^{\alpha}(\omega(\kappa_4)-\omega(\xi))^{\beta}d_{\tau}d_{\xi}F(\tau,\xi) \qquad (19)$$

$$-(\rho(\kappa_2)-\rho(\kappa_1))^{\alpha}(\omega(\kappa_4)-\omega(\kappa_3))^{\beta}F(\kappa_2,\kappa_3)$$

$$+\Gamma(\alpha+1)(\varpi(\kappa_4)-\varpi(\kappa_3))^\beta \mathcal{J}^\alpha_{\kappa_2-;\rho}F(\kappa_1,\kappa_3)$$

$$+\Gamma(\beta+1)(\rho(\kappa_2)-\rho(\kappa_1))^\alpha \mathcal{J}^\beta_{\kappa_3+;\varpi}F(\kappa_2,\kappa_4)$$

$$-\Gamma(\alpha+1)\Gamma(\beta+1)\mathcal{J}^{\alpha,\beta}_{\kappa_2-,\kappa_3+;\rho,\varpi}F(\kappa_1,\kappa_4),$$

for $\varkappa=\kappa_1$ and $\gamma=\kappa_4$ in Equation (15), we have

$$I_{11} = \int_{\kappa_1}^{\kappa_2}\int_{\kappa_3}^{\kappa_4}(\rho(\kappa_2)-\rho(\tau))^\alpha(\varpi(\xi)-\varpi(\kappa_3))^\beta d_\tau d_\xi F(\tau,\xi) \quad (20)$$

$$= -(\rho(\kappa_2)-\rho(\kappa_1))^\alpha(\varpi(\kappa_4)-\varpi(\kappa_3))^\beta F(\kappa_1,\kappa_4)$$

$$+\Gamma(\alpha+1)(\varpi(\kappa_4)-\varpi(\kappa_3))^\beta \mathcal{J}^\alpha_{\kappa_1+;\rho}F(\kappa_2,\kappa_4)$$

$$+\Gamma(\beta+1)(\rho(\kappa_2)-\rho(\kappa_1))^\alpha \mathcal{J}^\beta_{\kappa_4-;\varpi}F(\kappa_1,\kappa_3)$$

$$-\Gamma(\alpha+1)\Gamma(\beta+1)\mathcal{J}^{\alpha,\beta}_{\kappa_1+,\kappa_4-;\rho,\varpi}F(\kappa_2,\kappa_3)$$

and finally, for $\varkappa=\kappa_1$ and $\gamma=\kappa_3$ in Equation (16), we find

$$I_{12} = \int_{\kappa_1}^{\kappa_2}\int_{\kappa_3}^{\kappa_4}(\rho(\kappa_2)-\rho(\tau))^\alpha(\varpi(\kappa_4)-\varpi(\xi))^\beta d_\tau d_\xi F(\tau,\xi) \quad (21)$$

$$= (\rho(\kappa_2)-\rho(\kappa_1))^\alpha(\varpi(\kappa_4)-\varpi(\kappa_3))^\beta F(\kappa_1,\kappa_3)$$

$$-\Gamma(\alpha+1)(\varpi(\kappa_4)-\varpi(\kappa_3))^\beta \mathcal{J}^\alpha_{\kappa_1+;\rho}F(\kappa_2,\kappa_3)$$

$$-\Gamma(\beta+1)(\rho(\kappa_2)-\rho(\kappa_1))^\alpha \mathcal{J}^\beta_{\kappa_3+;\varpi}F(\kappa_1,\kappa_4)$$

$$+\Gamma(\alpha+1)\Gamma(\beta+1)\mathcal{J}^{\alpha,\beta}_{\kappa_1+,\kappa_3+;\rho,\varpi}F(\kappa_2,\kappa_4).$$

Using equalities (18)–(21), we establish

$$\frac{1}{4\Gamma(\alpha+1)\Gamma(\beta+1)}\frac{1}{M^\alpha_\rho(\kappa_1,\kappa_2)N^\beta_\varpi(\kappa_3,\kappa_4)}[I_9-I_{10}-I_{11}+I_{12}]$$

$$= \frac{F(\kappa_2,\kappa_4)+F(\kappa_2,\kappa_3)+F(\kappa_1,\kappa_4)+F(\kappa_1,\kappa_3)}{4}$$

$$-\frac{1}{4M^\alpha_\rho(\kappa_1,\kappa_2)}\left[\mathcal{J}^\alpha_{\kappa_2-;\rho}F(\kappa_1,\kappa_4)+\mathcal{J}^\alpha_{\kappa_2-;\rho}F(\kappa_1,\kappa_3)+\mathcal{J}^\alpha_{\kappa_1+;\rho}F(\kappa_2,\kappa_4)+\mathcal{J}^\alpha_{\kappa_1+;\rho}F(\kappa_2,\kappa_3)\right]$$

$$-\frac{1}{4N^\beta_\varpi(\kappa_3,\kappa_4)}\left[\mathcal{J}^\beta_{\kappa_4-;\varpi}F(\kappa_2,\kappa_3)+\mathcal{J}^\beta_{\kappa_3+;\varpi}F(\kappa_2,\kappa_4)+\mathcal{J}^\beta_{\kappa_4-;\varpi}F(\kappa_1,\kappa_3)+\mathcal{J}^\beta_{\kappa_3+;\varpi}F(\kappa_1,\kappa_4)\right]$$

$$+\frac{1}{4M^\alpha_\rho(\kappa_1,\kappa_2)N^\beta_\varpi(\kappa_3,\kappa_4)}\left[\mathcal{J}^{\alpha,\beta}_{\kappa_2-,\kappa_4-;\rho,\varpi}F(\kappa_1,\kappa_3)+\mathcal{J}^{\alpha,\beta}_{\kappa_2-,\kappa_3+;\rho,\varpi}F(\kappa_1,\kappa_4)\right.$$

$$\left.+\mathcal{J}^{\alpha,\beta}_{\kappa_1+,\kappa_4-;\rho,\varpi}F(\kappa_2,\kappa_3)+\mathcal{J}^{\alpha,\beta}_{\kappa_1+,\kappa_3+;\rho,\varpi}F(\kappa_2,\kappa_4)\right]$$

which completes the proof. □

4. Trapezoid-Type Inequalities for Functions of Bounded Variations with Two Variables

In this section, we present some trapezoid-type inequalities for generalized fractional integrals.

Theorem 2. *If $F : \Delta \to \mathbb{R}$ be a mapping of bounded variation on Δ, then for $\alpha, \beta > 0$, we have the following inequality*

$$\left| \kappa_1 - N_\omega^\beta(\kappa_3, \gamma) \left[\mathcal{J}_{\kappa_1+;\rho}^\alpha F(\varkappa, \kappa_3) + \mathcal{J}_{\kappa_2-;\rho}^\alpha F(\varkappa, \kappa_3) \right] \right. \tag{22}$$

$$- N_\omega^\beta(\kappa_4, \gamma) \left[\mathcal{J}_{\kappa_1+;\rho}^\alpha F(\varkappa, \kappa_4) + \mathcal{J}_{\kappa_2-;\rho}^\alpha F(\varkappa, \kappa_4) \right]$$

$$- M_\rho^\alpha(\kappa_1, \varkappa) \left[\mathcal{J}_{\kappa_3+;\omega}^\beta F(\kappa_1, \gamma) + \mathcal{J}_{\kappa_4-;\omega}^\beta F(\kappa_1, \gamma) \right]$$

$$- M_\rho^\alpha(\kappa_2, \varkappa) \left[\mathcal{J}_{\kappa_3+;\omega}^\beta F(\kappa_2, \gamma) + \mathcal{J}_{\kappa_4-;\omega}^\beta F(\kappa_2, \gamma) \right] + \mathcal{J}_{\kappa_1+,\kappa_3+;\rho,\omega}^{\alpha,\beta} F(\varkappa, \gamma)$$

$$\left. + \mathcal{J}_{\kappa_1+,\kappa_4-;\rho,\omega}^{\alpha,\beta} F(\varkappa, \gamma) + \mathcal{J}_{\kappa_2-,\kappa_3+;\rho,\omega}^{\alpha,\beta} F(\varkappa, \gamma) + \mathcal{J}_{\kappa_2-,\kappa_4-;\rho,\omega}^{\alpha,\beta} F(\varkappa, \gamma) \right|$$

$$\leq \frac{1}{\Gamma(\alpha+1)\Gamma(\beta+1)} \left[(\rho(\varkappa) - \rho(\kappa_1))^\alpha (\omega(\gamma) - \omega(\kappa_3))^\beta \bigvee_{\kappa_1}^{\varkappa} \bigvee_{\kappa_3}^{\gamma}(F) \right.$$

$$+ (\rho(\varkappa) - \rho(\kappa_1))^\alpha (\omega(\kappa_4) - \omega(\gamma))^\beta \bigvee_{\kappa_1}^{\varkappa} \bigvee_{\gamma}^{\kappa_4}(F)$$

$$+ (\rho(\kappa_2) - \rho(\varkappa))^\alpha (\omega(\gamma) - \omega(\kappa_3))^\beta \bigvee_{\varkappa}^{\kappa_2} \bigvee_{\kappa_3}^{\gamma}(F)$$

$$\left. + (\rho(\kappa_2) - \rho(\varkappa))^\alpha (\omega(\kappa_4) - \omega(\gamma))^\beta \bigvee_{\varkappa}^{\kappa_2} \bigvee_{\gamma}^{\kappa_4}(F) \right]$$

$$\leq \frac{1}{\Gamma(\alpha+1)\Gamma(\beta+1)} \left[\frac{1}{2}(\rho(\kappa_2) - \rho(\kappa_1)) + \left| \rho(\varkappa) - \frac{\rho(\kappa_1) + \rho(\kappa_2)}{2} \right| \right]^\alpha$$

$$\times \left[\frac{1}{2}(\omega(\kappa_4) - \omega(\kappa_3)) + \left| \omega(\gamma) - \frac{\omega(\kappa_3) + \omega(\kappa_4)}{2} \right| \right]^\beta \bigvee_{\kappa_1}^{\kappa_2} \bigvee_{\kappa_2}^{\kappa_4}(F).$$

Proof. By taking the modulus in Lemma 3, we obtain

$$\left| \kappa_1 - N_\omega^\beta(\kappa_3, \gamma) \left[\mathcal{J}_{\kappa_1+;\rho}^\alpha F(\varkappa, \kappa_3) + \mathcal{J}_{\kappa_2-;\rho}^\alpha F(\varkappa, \kappa_3) \right] \right. \tag{23}$$

$$- N_\omega^\beta(\kappa_4, \gamma) \left[\mathcal{J}_{\kappa_1+;\rho}^\alpha F(\varkappa, \kappa_4) + \mathcal{J}_{\kappa_2-;\rho}^\alpha F(\varkappa, \kappa_4) \right]$$

$$- M_\rho^\alpha(\kappa_1, \varkappa) \left[\mathcal{J}_{\kappa_3+;\omega}^\beta F(\kappa_1, \gamma) + \mathcal{J}_{\kappa_4-;\omega}^\beta F(\kappa_1, \gamma) \right]$$

$$- M_\rho^\alpha(\kappa_2, \varkappa) \left[\mathcal{J}_{\kappa_3+;\omega}^\beta F(\kappa_2, \gamma) + \mathcal{J}_{\kappa_4-;\omega}^\beta F(\kappa_2, \gamma) \right] + \mathcal{J}_{\kappa_1+,\kappa_3+;\rho,\omega}^{\alpha,\beta} F(\varkappa, \gamma)$$

$$\left. + \mathcal{J}_{\kappa_1+,\kappa_4-;\rho,\omega}^{\alpha,\beta} F(\varkappa, \gamma) + \mathcal{J}_{\kappa_2-,\kappa_3+;\rho,\omega}^{\alpha,\beta} F(\varkappa, \gamma) + \mathcal{J}_{\kappa_2-,\kappa_4-;\rho,\omega}^{\alpha,\beta} F(\varkappa, \gamma) \right|$$

$$\leq \frac{1}{\Gamma(\alpha+1)\Gamma(\beta+1)} \left[\left| \int_{\kappa_1}^{\varkappa} \int_{\kappa_3}^{\gamma} (\rho(\varkappa)-\rho(\tau))^\alpha (\varpi(\gamma)-\varpi(\xi))^\beta d_\tau d_\xi F(\tau,\xi) \right| \right.$$

$$+ \left| \int_{\kappa_1}^{\varkappa} \int_{\gamma}^{\kappa_4} (\rho(\varkappa)-\rho(\tau))^\alpha (\varpi(\xi)-\varpi(\gamma))^\beta d_\tau d_\xi F(\tau,\xi) \right|$$

$$+ \left| \int_{\varkappa}^{\kappa_2} \int_{\kappa_3}^{\gamma} (\rho(\tau)-\rho(\varkappa))^\alpha (\varpi(\gamma)-\varpi(\xi))^\beta d_\tau d_\xi F(\tau,\xi) \right|$$

$$+ \left. \left| \int_{\varkappa}^{\kappa_2} \int_{\gamma}^{\kappa_4} (\rho(\tau)-\rho(\varkappa))^\alpha (\varpi(\xi)-\varpi(\gamma))^\beta d_\tau d_\xi F(\tau,\xi) \right| \right].$$

By Lemma, it follows that

$$\left| \int_{\kappa_1}^{\varkappa} \int_{\kappa_3}^{\gamma} (\rho(\varkappa)-\rho(\tau))^\alpha (\varpi(\gamma)-\varpi(\xi))^\beta d_\tau d_\xi F(\tau,\xi) \right| \tag{24}$$

$$\leq \sup_{(\tau,\xi)\in[\kappa_1,\varkappa]\times[\kappa_3,\gamma]} \left| (\rho(\varkappa)-\rho(\tau))^\alpha (\varpi(\gamma)-\varpi(\xi))^\beta \right| \bigvee_{\kappa_1}^{\varkappa} \bigvee_{\kappa_3}^{\gamma} (F)$$

$$= (\rho(\varkappa)-\rho(\kappa_1))^\alpha (\varpi(\gamma)-\varpi(\kappa_3))^\beta \bigvee_{\kappa_1}^{\varkappa} \bigvee_{\kappa_3}^{\gamma} (F).$$

Similarly, we obtain

$$\left| \int_{\kappa_1}^{\varkappa} \int_{\gamma}^{\kappa_4} (\rho(\varkappa)-\rho(\tau))^\alpha (\varpi(\xi)-\varpi(\gamma))^\beta d_\tau d_\xi F(\tau,\xi) \right|$$

$$\leq (\rho(\varkappa)-\rho(\kappa_1))^\alpha (\varpi(\kappa_4)-\varpi(\gamma))^\beta \bigvee_{\kappa_1}^{\varkappa} \bigvee_{\gamma}^{\kappa_4} (F) \tag{25}$$

$$\left| \int_{\varkappa}^{\kappa_2} \int_{\kappa_3}^{\gamma} (\rho(\tau)-\rho(\varkappa))^\alpha (\varpi(\gamma)-\varpi(\xi))^\beta d_\tau d_\xi F(\tau,\xi) \right|$$

$$\leq (\rho(\kappa_2)-\rho(\varkappa))^\alpha (\varpi(\gamma)-\varpi(\kappa_3))^\beta \bigvee_{\varkappa}^{\kappa_2} \bigvee_{\kappa_3}^{\gamma} (F) \tag{26}$$

and

$$\left| \int_{\varkappa}^{\kappa_2} \int_{\gamma}^{\kappa_4} (\rho(\tau)-\rho(\varkappa))^\alpha (\varpi(\xi)-\varpi(\gamma))^\beta d_\tau d_\xi F(\tau,\xi) \right|$$

$$\leq (\rho(\kappa_2)-\rho(\varkappa))^\alpha (\varpi(\kappa_4)-\varpi(\gamma))^\beta \bigvee_{\varkappa}^{\kappa_2} \bigvee_{\gamma}^{\kappa_4} (F). \tag{27}$$

By substituting the inequalities (24)–(27) in Equation (23), we obtain

$$\left| \kappa_1 - N_\varpi^\beta(\kappa_3,\gamma) \left[\mathcal{J}_{\kappa_1+;\rho}^\alpha F(\varkappa,\kappa_3) + \mathcal{J}_{\kappa_2-;\rho}^\alpha F(\varkappa,\kappa_3) \right] \right.$$

$$\left. - N_\varpi^\beta(\kappa_4,\gamma) \left[\mathcal{J}_{\kappa_1+;\rho}^\alpha F(\varkappa,\kappa_4) + \mathcal{J}_{\kappa_2-;\rho}^\alpha F(\varkappa,\kappa_4) \right] \right.$$

$$-M_\rho^\alpha(\kappa_1,\varkappa)\left[\mathcal{J}_{\kappa_3+;\varpi}^\beta F(\kappa_1,\gamma)+\mathcal{J}_{\kappa_4-;\varpi}^\beta F(\kappa_1,\gamma)\right]$$

$$-M_\rho^\alpha(\kappa_2,\varkappa)\left[\mathcal{J}_{\kappa_3+;\varpi}^\beta F(\kappa_2,\gamma)+\mathcal{J}_{\kappa_4-;\varpi}^\beta F(\kappa_2,\gamma)\right]+\mathcal{J}_{\kappa_1+,\kappa_3+;\rho,\varpi}^{\alpha,\beta}F(\varkappa,\gamma)$$

$$\left.+\mathcal{J}_{\kappa_1+,\kappa_4-;\rho,\varpi}^{\alpha,\beta}F(\varkappa,\gamma)+\mathcal{J}_{\kappa_2-,\kappa_3+;\rho,\varpi}^{\alpha,\beta}F(\varkappa,\gamma)+\mathcal{J}_{\kappa_2-,\kappa_4-;\rho,\varpi}^{\alpha,\beta}F(\varkappa,\gamma)\right|$$

$$\leq \frac{1}{\Gamma(\alpha+1)\Gamma(\beta+1)}\left[(\rho(\varkappa)-\rho(\kappa_1))^\alpha(\varpi(\gamma)-\varpi(\kappa_3))^\beta\bigvee_{\kappa_1}^{\varkappa}\bigvee_{\kappa_3}^{\gamma}(F)\right.$$

$$+(\rho(\varkappa)-\rho(\kappa_1))^\alpha(\varpi(\kappa_4)-\varpi(\gamma))^\beta\bigvee_{\kappa_1}^{\varkappa}\bigvee_{\gamma}^{\kappa_4}(F)$$

$$+(\rho(\kappa_2)-\rho(\varkappa))^\alpha(\varpi(\gamma)-\varpi(\kappa_3))^\beta\bigvee_{\varkappa}^{\kappa_2}\bigvee_{\kappa_3}^{\gamma}(F)$$

$$\left.+(\rho(\kappa_2)-\rho(\varkappa))^\alpha(\varpi(\kappa_4)-\varpi(\gamma))^\beta\bigvee_{\varkappa}^{\kappa_2}\bigvee_{\gamma}^{\kappa_4}(F)\right]$$

$$=:Y(\varkappa,\gamma)$$

which gives the first inequality in Equation (22).

By the properties of maximum, we obtain

$$Y(\varkappa,\gamma)$$

$$\leq \max\left\{(\rho(\varkappa)-\rho(\kappa_1))^\alpha(\varpi(\gamma)-\varpi(\kappa_3))^\beta,(\rho(\varkappa)-\rho(\kappa_1))^\alpha(\varpi(\kappa_4)-\varpi(\gamma))^\beta,\right.$$

$$\left.(\rho(\kappa_2)-\rho(\varkappa))^\alpha(\varpi(\gamma)-\varpi(\kappa_3))^\beta,(\rho(\kappa_2)-\rho(\varkappa))^\alpha(\varpi(\kappa_4)-\varpi(\gamma))^\beta\right\}$$

$$\times\left[\bigvee_{\kappa_1}^{\varkappa}\bigvee_{\kappa_3}^{\gamma}(F)+\bigvee_{\kappa_1}^{\varkappa}\bigvee_{\gamma}^{\kappa_4}(F)+\bigvee_{\varkappa}^{\kappa_2}\bigvee_{\kappa_3}^{\gamma}(F)+\bigvee_{\varkappa}^{\kappa_2}\bigvee_{\gamma}^{\kappa_4}(F)\right]$$

$$=\max\{(\rho(\varkappa)-\rho(\kappa_1))^\alpha,(\rho(\kappa_2)-\rho(\varkappa))^\alpha\}\max\left\{(\varpi(\gamma)-\varpi(\kappa_3))^\beta,(\varpi(\kappa_4)-\varpi(\gamma))^\beta\right\}$$

$$\times\bigvee_{\kappa_1}^{\kappa_2}\bigvee_{\kappa_3}^{\kappa_4}(F)$$

$$=\left[\frac{1}{2}(\rho(\kappa_2)-\rho(\kappa_1))+\left|\rho(\varkappa)-\frac{\rho(\kappa_1)+\rho(\kappa_2)}{2}\right|\right]^\alpha$$

$$\times\left[\frac{1}{2}(\varpi(\kappa_4)-\varpi(\kappa_3))+\left|\varpi(\gamma)-\frac{\varpi(\kappa_3)+\varpi(\kappa_4)}{2}\right|\right]^\beta\bigvee_{\kappa_1}^{\kappa_2}\bigvee_{\kappa_3}^{\kappa_4}(F).$$

This completes the proof. □

Corollary 1. *If we take $\rho(\tau)=\tau$, $\tau\in[\kappa_1,\kappa_2]$ and $\varpi(\xi)=\xi$, $\xi\in[\kappa_3,\kappa_4]$ in Theorem 2, then we have the following trapezoid-type inequalities for Riemann–Liouville fractional integrals*

$$\left|\frac{(\varkappa-\kappa_1)^\alpha(\gamma-\kappa_3)^\beta}{\Gamma(\alpha+1)\Gamma(\beta+1)}F(\kappa_1,\kappa_3)+\frac{(\varkappa-\kappa_1)^\alpha(\kappa_4-\gamma)^\beta}{\Gamma(\alpha+1)\Gamma(\beta+1)}F(\kappa_1,\kappa_4)\right.$$

$$+\frac{(\kappa_2-\varkappa)^\alpha(\gamma-\kappa_3)^\beta}{\Gamma(\alpha+1)\Gamma(\beta+1)}F(\kappa_2,\kappa_3)+\frac{(\kappa_2-\varkappa)^\alpha(\kappa_4-\gamma)^\beta}{\Gamma(\alpha+1)\Gamma(\beta+1)}F(\kappa_2,\kappa_4)$$

$$-\frac{(\gamma-\kappa_3)^\beta}{\Gamma(\beta+1)}\left[\mathbf{J}^\alpha_{\kappa_1+}F(\varkappa,\kappa_3)+\mathbf{J}^\alpha_{\kappa_2-}F(\varkappa,\kappa_3)\right]$$

$$-\frac{(\kappa_4-\gamma)^\beta}{\Gamma(\beta+1)}\left[\mathbf{J}^\alpha_{\kappa_1+}F(\varkappa,\kappa_4)+\mathbf{J}^\alpha_{\kappa_2-}F(\varkappa,\kappa_4)\right]$$

$$-\frac{(\varkappa-\kappa_1)^\alpha}{\Gamma(\alpha+1)}\left[\mathbf{J}^\beta_{\kappa_3+}F(\kappa_1,\gamma)+\mathbf{J}^\beta_{\kappa_4-}F(\kappa_1,\gamma)\right]$$

$$-\frac{(\kappa_2-\varkappa)^\alpha}{\Gamma(\alpha+1)}\left[\mathbf{J}^\beta_{\kappa_3+}F(\kappa_2,\gamma)+\mathbf{J}^\beta_{\kappa_4-}F(\kappa_2,\gamma)\right]$$

$$+\mathbf{J}^{\alpha,\beta}_{\kappa_1+,\kappa_3+}F(\varkappa,\gamma)+\mathbf{J}^{\alpha,\beta}_{\kappa_1+,\kappa_4-}F(\varkappa,\gamma)+\mathbf{J}^{\alpha,\beta}_{\kappa_2-,\kappa_3+}F(\varkappa,\gamma)+\mathbf{J}^{\alpha,\beta}_{\kappa_2-,\kappa_4-}F(\varkappa,\gamma)\Bigg|$$

$$\leq \frac{1}{\Gamma(\alpha+1)\Gamma(\beta+1)}$$

$$\times\left[(\varkappa-\kappa_1)^\alpha(\gamma-\kappa_3)^\beta\bigvee_{\kappa_1}^\varkappa\bigvee_{\kappa_3}^\gamma(F)+(\varkappa-\kappa_1)^\alpha(\kappa_4-\gamma)^\beta\bigvee_{\kappa_1}^\varkappa\bigvee_\gamma^{\kappa_4}(F)\right.$$

$$\left.+(\kappa_2-\varkappa)^\alpha(\gamma-\kappa_3)^\beta\bigvee_\varkappa^{\kappa_2}\bigvee_{\kappa_3}^\gamma(F)+(\kappa_2-\varkappa)^\alpha(\kappa_4-\gamma)^\beta\bigvee_\varkappa^{\kappa_2}\bigvee_\gamma^{\kappa_4}(F)\right]$$

$$\leq \frac{1}{\Gamma(\alpha+1)\Gamma(\beta+1)}\left[\frac{\kappa_2-\kappa_1}{2}+\left|\varkappa-\frac{\kappa_1+\kappa_2}{2}\right|\right]^\alpha$$

$$\times\left[\frac{\kappa_4-\kappa_3}{2}+\left|\gamma-\frac{\kappa_3+\kappa_4}{2}\right|\right]^\beta\bigvee_{\kappa_1}^{\kappa_2}\bigvee_{\kappa_2}^{\kappa_4}(F).$$

Corollary 2. *If we take* $\varkappa=\frac{\kappa_1+\kappa_2}{2}$ *and* $\gamma=\frac{\kappa_3+\kappa_4}{2}$ *in Corollary 1, then we have*

$$\left|\frac{F(\kappa_2,\kappa_4)+F(\kappa_2,\kappa_3)+F(\kappa_1,\kappa_4)+F(\kappa_1,\kappa_3)}{4}\right.$$

$$-\frac{2^{\alpha-1}\Gamma(\alpha+1)}{(\kappa_2-\kappa_1)^\alpha}\left[\mathbf{J}^\alpha_{\kappa_1+}F(\varkappa,\kappa_3)+\mathbf{J}^\alpha_{\kappa_2-}F(\varkappa,\kappa_3)\right]$$

$$-\frac{2^{\alpha-1}\Gamma(\alpha+1)}{(\kappa_2-\kappa_1)^\alpha}\left[\mathbf{J}^\alpha_{\kappa_1+}F(\varkappa,\kappa_4)+\mathbf{J}^\alpha_{\kappa_2-}F(\varkappa,\kappa_4)\right]$$

$$-\frac{2^{\beta-1}\Gamma(\beta+1)}{(\kappa_4-\kappa_3)^\beta}\left[\mathbf{J}^\beta_{\kappa_3+}F(\kappa_1,\gamma)+\mathbf{J}^\beta_{\kappa_4-}F(\kappa_1,\gamma)\right]$$

$$-\frac{2^{\beta-1}\Gamma(\beta+1)}{(\kappa_4-\kappa_3)^\beta}\left[\mathbf{J}^\beta_{\kappa_3+}F(\kappa_2,\gamma)+\mathbf{J}^\beta_{\kappa_4-}F(\kappa_2,\gamma)\right]$$

$$\frac{2^{\alpha+\beta-2}\Gamma(\alpha+1)\Gamma(\beta+1)}{(\kappa_2-\kappa_1)^\alpha(\kappa_4-\kappa_3)^\beta}\left[\mathbf{J}^{\alpha,\beta}_{\kappa_1+,\kappa_3+}F(\varkappa,\gamma)+\mathbf{J}^{\alpha,\beta}_{\kappa_1+,\kappa_4-}F(\varkappa,\gamma)\right.$$

$$\left.\left.+\mathbf{J}^{\alpha,\beta}_{\kappa_2-,\kappa_3+}F(\varkappa,\gamma)+\mathbf{J}^{\alpha,\beta}_{\kappa_2-,\kappa_4-}F(\varkappa,\gamma)\right]\right|$$

$$\leq \frac{1}{4}\bigvee_{\kappa_1}^{\kappa_2}\bigvee_{\kappa_2}^{\kappa_4}(F).$$

Remark 1. If we assign $\alpha = \beta = 1$ in Corollary 2, then we have

$$\left| \frac{F(\kappa_2, \kappa_4) + F(\kappa_2, \kappa_3) + F(\kappa_1, \kappa_4) + F(\kappa_1, \kappa_3)}{4} \right.$$

$$- \frac{1}{2(\kappa_2 - \kappa_1)} \left[\int_{\kappa_1}^{\kappa_2} F(\varkappa, \kappa_4) d\varkappa + \int_{\kappa_1}^{\kappa_2} F(\varkappa, \kappa_3) d\varkappa \right]$$

$$- \frac{1}{2(\kappa_4 - \kappa_3)} \left[\int_{\kappa_3}^{\kappa_4} F(\kappa_2, \gamma) d\gamma + \int_{\kappa_3}^{\kappa_4} F(\kappa_1, \gamma) d\gamma \right]$$

$$\left. + \frac{1}{(\kappa_2 - \kappa_1)(\kappa_4 - \kappa_3)} \int_{\kappa_1}^{\kappa_2} \int_{\kappa_3}^{\kappa_4} F(\varkappa, \gamma) d\gamma d\varkappa \right|$$

$$\leq \frac{1}{4} \bigvee_{\kappa_1}^{\kappa_2} \bigvee_{\kappa_3}^{\kappa_4} (F).$$

which is given by Budak and Sarikaya in [43].

Theorem 3. If $F : \Delta \to \mathbb{R}$ be a mapping of bounded variation on Δ, then for $\alpha, \beta > 0$, we have the following inequality

$$\left| \frac{F(\kappa_2, \kappa_4) + F(\kappa_2, \kappa_3) + F(\kappa_1, \kappa_4) + F(\kappa_1, \kappa_3)}{4} \right.$$

$$- \frac{1}{4M_\rho^\alpha(\kappa_1, \kappa_2)} \left[\mathcal{J}_{\kappa_2-;\rho}^\alpha F(\kappa_1, \kappa_4) + \mathcal{J}_{\kappa_2-;\rho}^\alpha F(\kappa_1, \kappa_3) + \mathcal{J}_{\kappa_1+;\rho}^\alpha F(\kappa_2, \kappa_4) + \mathcal{J}_{\kappa_1+;\rho}^\alpha F(\kappa_2, \kappa_3) \right]$$

$$- \frac{1}{4N_\omega^\beta(\kappa_3, \kappa_4)} \left[\mathcal{J}_{\kappa_4-;\omega}^\beta F(\kappa_2, \kappa_3) + \mathcal{J}_{\kappa_3+;\omega}^\beta F(\kappa_2, \kappa_4) + \mathcal{J}_{\kappa_4-;\omega}^\beta F(\kappa_1, \kappa_3) + \mathcal{J}_{\kappa_3+;\omega}^\beta F(\kappa_1, \kappa_4) \right]$$

$$+ \frac{1}{4M_\rho^\alpha(\kappa_1, \kappa_2) N_\omega^\beta(\kappa_3, \kappa_4)} \left[\mathcal{J}_{\kappa_2-,\kappa_4-;\rho,\omega}^{\alpha,\beta} F(\kappa_1, \kappa_3) + \mathcal{J}_{\kappa_2-,\kappa_3+;\rho,\omega}^{\alpha,\beta} F(\kappa_1, \kappa_4) \right.$$

$$\left. \left. + \mathcal{J}_{\kappa_1+,\kappa_4-;\rho,\omega}^{\alpha,\beta} F(\kappa_2, \kappa_3) + \mathcal{J}_{\kappa_1+,\kappa_3+;\rho,\omega}^{\alpha,\beta} F(\kappa_2, \kappa_4) \right] \right|$$

$$\leq \frac{1}{4} \bigvee_{\kappa_1}^{\kappa_2} \bigvee_{\kappa_3}^{\kappa_4} (F).$$

Proof. By using Lemma 2, we have

$$\left| \frac{F(\kappa_2, \kappa_4) + F(\kappa_2, \kappa_3) + F(\kappa_1, \kappa_4) + F(\kappa_1, \kappa_3)}{4} \right.$$

$$- \frac{1}{4M_\rho^\alpha(\kappa_1, \kappa_2)} \left[\mathcal{J}_{\kappa_2-;\rho}^\alpha F(\kappa_1, \kappa_4) + \mathcal{J}_{\kappa_2-;\rho}^\alpha F(\kappa_1, \kappa_3) \right.$$

$$\left. + \mathcal{J}_{\kappa_1+;\rho}^\alpha F(\kappa_2, \kappa_4) + \mathcal{J}_{\kappa_1+;\rho}^\alpha F(\kappa_2, \kappa_3) \right]$$

$$- \frac{1}{4N_\omega^\beta(\kappa_3, \kappa_4)} \left[\mathcal{J}_{\kappa_4-;\omega}^\beta F(\kappa_2, \kappa_3) + \mathcal{J}_{\kappa_3+;\omega}^\beta F(\kappa_2, \kappa_4) \right.$$

$$\left. + \mathcal{J}_{\kappa_4-;\omega}^\beta F(\kappa_1, \kappa_3) + \mathcal{J}_{\kappa_3+;\omega}^\beta F(\kappa_1, \kappa_4) \right]$$

$$+ \frac{1}{4M_\rho^\alpha(\kappa_1,\kappa_2) N_\omega^\beta(\kappa_3,\kappa_4)} \left[\mathcal{J}_{\kappa_2-,\kappa_4-;\rho,\omega}^{\alpha,\beta} F(\kappa_1,\kappa_3) + \mathcal{J}_{\kappa_2-,\kappa_3+;\rho,\omega}^{\alpha,\beta} F(\kappa_1,\kappa_4) \right.$$

$$\left. + \mathcal{J}_{\kappa_1+,\kappa_4-;\rho,\omega}^{\alpha,\beta} F(\kappa_2,\kappa_3) + \mathcal{J}_{\kappa_1+,\kappa_3+;\rho,\omega}^{\alpha,\beta} F(\kappa_2,\kappa_4) \right] \Bigg|$$

$$= \frac{1}{4\Gamma(\alpha+1)\Gamma(\beta+1)} \frac{1}{M_\rho^\alpha(\kappa_1,\kappa_2) N_\omega^\beta(\kappa_3,\kappa_4)}$$

$$\times \left| \int_{\kappa_1}^{\kappa_2}\int_{\kappa_3}^{\kappa_2} [(\rho(\kappa_2)-\rho(\tau))^\alpha - \rho(\tau)-\rho(\kappa_1))^\alpha] \right.$$

$$\left. \times \left[(\omega(\kappa_4)-\omega(\xi))^\beta - (\omega(\xi)-\omega(\kappa_3))^\beta \right] d\tau d\xi F(\tau,\xi) \right|$$

$$\leq \frac{1}{4\Gamma(\alpha+1)\Gamma(\beta+1)} \frac{1}{M_\rho^\alpha(\kappa_1,\kappa_2) N_\omega^\beta(\kappa_3,\kappa_4)}$$

$$\times \sup_{(\tau,\gamma)\in\Delta} |(\rho(\kappa_2)-\rho(\tau))^\alpha - \rho(\tau)-\rho(\kappa_1))^\alpha|$$

$$\times \left| (\omega(\kappa_4)-\omega(\xi))^\beta - (\omega(\xi)-\omega(\kappa_3))^\beta \right| \bigvee_{\kappa_1}^{\kappa_2}\bigvee_{\kappa_3}^{\kappa_4}(F)$$

$$= \frac{1}{4\Gamma(\alpha+1)\Gamma(\beta+1)} \frac{(\rho(\kappa_2)-\rho(\tau))^\alpha (\omega(\kappa_4)-\omega(\xi))^\beta}{M_\rho^\alpha(\kappa_1,\kappa_2) N_\omega^\beta(\kappa_3,\kappa_4)} \bigvee_{\kappa_1}^{\kappa_2}\bigvee_{\kappa_3}^{\kappa_4}(F)$$

$$= \frac{1}{4} \bigvee_{\kappa_1}^{\kappa_2}\bigvee_{\kappa_3}^{\kappa_4}(F).$$

This completes the proof. □

Corollary 3. *If we take $\rho(\tau) = \tau$, $\tau \in [\kappa_1,\kappa_2]$ and $\omega(\xi) = \xi$, $\xi \in [\kappa_3,\kappa_4]$ in Theorem 3, then we have*

$$\left| \frac{F(\kappa_2,\kappa_4) + F(\kappa_2,\kappa_3) + F(\kappa_1,\kappa_4) + F(\kappa_1,\kappa_3)}{4} \right.$$

$$- \frac{\Gamma(\alpha+1)}{4(\kappa_2-\kappa_1)^\alpha} \left[J_{\kappa_2-}^\alpha F(\kappa_1,\kappa_4) + J_{\kappa_2-}^\alpha F(\kappa_1,\kappa_3) + J_{\kappa_1+}^\alpha F(\kappa_2,\kappa_4) + J_{\kappa_1+}^\alpha F(\kappa_2,\kappa_3) \right]$$

$$- \frac{\Gamma(\beta+1)}{4(\kappa_4-\kappa_3)^\beta} \left[J_{\kappa_4-}^\beta F(\kappa_2,\kappa_3) + J_{\kappa_3+}^\beta F(\kappa_2,\kappa_4) + J_{\kappa_4-}^\beta F(\kappa_1,\kappa_3) + J_{\kappa_3+}^\beta F(\kappa_1,\kappa_4) \right]$$

$$+ \frac{\Gamma(\alpha+1)\Gamma(\beta+1)}{4(\kappa_2-\kappa_1)^\alpha(\kappa_4-\kappa_3)^\beta} \left[J_{\kappa_2-,\kappa_4-}^{\alpha,\beta} F(\kappa_1,\kappa_3) + J_{\kappa_2-,\kappa_3+}^{\alpha,\beta} F(\kappa_1,\kappa_4) \right.$$

$$\left. \left. + J_{\kappa_1+,\kappa_4-}^{\alpha,\beta} F(\kappa_2,\kappa_3) + J_{\kappa_1+,\kappa_3+}^{\alpha,\beta} F(\kappa_2,\kappa_4) \right] \right|$$

$$\leq \frac{1}{4} \bigvee_{\kappa_1}^{\kappa_2}\bigvee_{\kappa_3}^{\kappa_4}(F).$$

Remark 2. *If we assign $\alpha = \beta = 1$ in Corollary 3, then we have*

$$\left| \frac{F(\kappa_2,\kappa_4) + F(\kappa_2,\kappa_3) + F(\kappa_1,\kappa_4) + F(\kappa_1,\kappa_3)}{4} \right.$$

$$\left. - \frac{1}{2(\kappa_2-\kappa_1)} \left[\int_{\kappa_1}^{\kappa_2} F(\varkappa,\kappa_4) d\varkappa + \int_{\kappa_1}^{\kappa_2} F(\varkappa,\kappa_3) d\varkappa \right] \right.$$

$$-\frac{1}{2(\kappa_4-\kappa_3)}\left[\int_{\kappa_3}^{\kappa_4}F(\kappa_2,\gamma)d\gamma+\int_{\kappa_3}^{\kappa_4}F(\kappa_1,\gamma)d\gamma\right]$$

$$+\frac{1}{(\kappa_2-\kappa_1)(\kappa_4-\kappa_3)}\int_{\kappa_1}^{\kappa_2}\int_{\kappa_3}^{\kappa_4}F(\varkappa,\gamma)d\gamma d\varkappa\bigg|$$

$$\leq \frac{1}{4}\bigvee_{\kappa_1}^{\kappa_2}\bigvee_{\kappa_3}^{\kappa_4}(F).$$

which is given by Budak and Sarikaya in [43].

Corollary 4. *If we take $\rho(\tau)=\ln\tau$, $\tau\in[\kappa_1,\kappa_2]$ and $\omega(\xi)=\ln\xi$, $\xi\in[\kappa_3,\kappa_4]$ in Theorem 3, then we have the following trapezoid-type inequality for Hadamard fractional integrals*

$$\left|\frac{F(\kappa_2,\kappa_4)+F(\kappa_2,\kappa_3)+F(\kappa_1,\kappa_4)+F(\kappa_1,\kappa_3)}{4}\right.$$

$$-\frac{1}{4M_{\ln}^{\alpha}(\kappa_1,\kappa_2)}\left[I_{\kappa_2-}^{\alpha}F(\kappa_1,\kappa_4)+I_{\kappa_2-}^{\alpha}F(\kappa_1,\kappa_3)+I_{\kappa_1+}^{\alpha}F(\kappa_2,\kappa_4)+I_{\kappa_1+}^{\alpha}F(\kappa_2,\kappa_3)\right]$$

$$-\frac{1}{4N_{\ln}^{\beta}(\kappa_3,\kappa_4)}\left[I_{\kappa_4-}^{\beta}F(\kappa_2,\kappa_3)+I_{\kappa_3+}^{\beta}F(\kappa_2,\kappa_4)+I_{\kappa_4-}^{\beta}F(\kappa_1,\kappa_3)+I_{\kappa_3+}^{\beta}F(\kappa_1,\kappa_4)\right]$$

$$+\frac{1}{4M_{\ln}^{\alpha}(\kappa_1,\kappa_2)N_{\ln}^{\beta}(\kappa_3,\kappa_4)}\left[I_{\kappa_2-,\kappa_4-}^{\alpha,\beta}F(\kappa_1,\kappa_3)+I_{\kappa_2-,\kappa_3+}^{\alpha,\beta}F(\kappa_1,\kappa_4)\right.$$

$$\left.+I_{\kappa_1+,\kappa_4-}^{\alpha,\beta}F(\kappa_2,\kappa_3)+I_{\kappa_1+,\kappa_3+}^{\alpha,\beta}F(\kappa_2,\kappa_4)\right]\bigg|$$

$$\leq \frac{1}{4}\bigvee_{\kappa_1}^{\kappa_2}\bigvee_{\kappa_3}^{\kappa_4}(F).$$

5. Ostrowski-Type Inequalities for Functions of Bounded Variations with Two Variables

In this section, we prove some Ostrowski-type inequalities for generalized fractional integrals.

Theorem 4. *If $F:\Delta\to\mathbb{R}$ be a mapping of bounded variation on Δ, then for $\alpha,\beta>0$, we have the following inequality*

$$\left|F(\varkappa,\gamma)-\frac{\Gamma(\alpha+1)}{M_\rho^\alpha(\kappa_1,\kappa_2;\varkappa)}\left[\mathcal{J}_{\varkappa-;\rho}^\alpha F(\kappa_1,\gamma)+\mathcal{J}_{\varkappa+;\rho}^\alpha F(\kappa_2,\gamma)\right]\right. \tag{28}$$

$$-\frac{\Gamma(\beta+1)}{N_\omega^\beta(\kappa_3,\kappa_4;\gamma)}\left[\mathcal{J}_{\gamma-;\omega}^\beta F(\varkappa,\kappa_3)+\mathcal{J}_{\gamma+;\omega}^\beta F(\varkappa,\kappa_4)\right]$$

$$+\frac{\Gamma(\alpha+1)\Gamma(\beta+1)}{M_\rho^\alpha(\kappa_1,\kappa_2;\varkappa)N_\omega^\beta(\kappa_3,\kappa_4;\gamma)}\left[\mathcal{J}_{\varkappa-,\gamma-;\rho,\omega}^{\alpha,\beta}F(\kappa_1,\kappa_3)+\mathcal{J}_{\varkappa-,\gamma+;\rho,\omega}^{\alpha,\beta}F(\kappa_1,\kappa_4)\right.$$

$$\left.\left.+\mathcal{J}_{\varkappa+,\gamma-;\rho,\omega}^{\alpha,\beta}F(\kappa_2,\kappa_3)+\mathcal{J}_{\varkappa+,\gamma+;\rho,\omega}^{\alpha,\beta}F(\kappa_2,\kappa_4)\right]\right|$$

$$=\frac{1}{M_\rho^\alpha(\kappa_1,\kappa_2;\varkappa)N_\omega^\beta(\kappa_3,\kappa_4;\gamma)}$$

$$\times \left[(\rho(\varkappa) - \rho(\kappa_1))^\alpha (\varpi(\gamma) - \varpi(\kappa_3))^\beta \bigvee_{\kappa_1}^{\varkappa} \bigvee_{\kappa_3}^{\gamma}(F) \right.$$

$$+ (\rho(\varkappa) - \rho(\kappa_1))^\alpha (\varpi(\kappa_4) - \varpi(\gamma))^\beta \bigvee_{\kappa_1}^{\varkappa} \bigvee_{\gamma}^{\kappa_4}(F)$$

$$+ (\rho(\kappa_2) - \rho(\varkappa))^\alpha (\varpi(\gamma) - \varpi(\kappa_3))^\beta \bigvee_{\varkappa}^{\kappa_2} \bigvee_{\kappa_3}^{\gamma}(F)$$

$$\left. + (\rho(\kappa_2) - \rho(\varkappa))^\alpha (\varpi(\kappa_4) - \varpi(\gamma))^\beta \bigvee_{\varkappa}^{\kappa_2} \bigvee_{\gamma}^{\kappa_4}(F) \right]$$

$$\leq \frac{1}{M_\rho^\alpha(\kappa_1, \kappa_2; \varkappa) N_\varpi^\beta(\kappa_3, \kappa_4; \gamma)}$$

$$\times \left[\frac{1}{2}(\rho(\kappa_2) - \rho(\kappa_1)) + \left| \rho(\varkappa) - \frac{\rho(\kappa_1) + \rho(\kappa_2)}{2} \right| \right]^\alpha$$

$$\times \left[\frac{1}{2}(\varpi(\kappa_4) - \varpi(\kappa_3)) + \left| \varpi(\gamma) - \frac{\varpi(\kappa_3) + \varpi(\kappa_4)}{2} \right| \right]^\beta \bigvee_{\kappa_1}^{\kappa_2} \bigvee_{\kappa_2}^{\kappa_4}(F).$$

Proof. By taking the modulus in Lemma 3, we obtain

$$\left| F(\varkappa, \gamma) - \frac{\Gamma(\alpha+1)}{M_\rho^\alpha(\kappa_1, \kappa_2; \varkappa)} \left[\mathcal{J}_{\varkappa-;\rho}^\alpha F(\kappa_1, \gamma) + \mathcal{J}_{\varkappa+;\rho}^\alpha F(\kappa_2, \gamma) \right] \right.$$

$$- \frac{\Gamma(\beta+1)}{N_\varpi^\beta(\kappa_3, \kappa_4; \gamma)} \left[\mathcal{J}_{\gamma-;\varpi}^\beta F(\varkappa, \kappa_3) + \mathcal{J}_{\gamma+;\varpi}^\beta F(\varkappa, \kappa_4) \right]$$

$$+ \frac{\Gamma(\alpha+1)\Gamma(\beta+1)}{M_\rho^\alpha(\kappa_1, \kappa_2; \varkappa) N_\varpi^\beta(\kappa_3, \kappa_4; \gamma)} \left[\mathcal{J}_{\varkappa-,\gamma-;\rho,\varpi}^{\alpha,\beta} F(\kappa_1, \kappa_3) + \mathcal{J}_{\varkappa-,\gamma+;\rho,\varpi}^{\alpha,\beta} F(\kappa_1, \kappa_4) \right.$$

$$\left. \left. + \mathcal{J}_{\varkappa+,\gamma-;\rho,\varpi}^{\alpha,\beta} F(\kappa_2, \kappa_3) + \mathcal{J}_{\varkappa+,\gamma+;\rho,\varpi}^{\alpha,\beta} F(\kappa_2, \kappa_4) \right] \right|$$

$$= \frac{1}{M_\rho^\alpha(\kappa_1, \kappa_2; \varkappa) N_\varpi^\beta(\kappa_3, \kappa_4; \gamma)}$$

$$\times \left[\left| \int_{\kappa_1}^{\varkappa} \int_{\kappa_3}^{\gamma} (\rho(\tau) - \rho(\kappa_1))^\alpha (\varpi(\xi) - \varpi(\kappa_3))^\beta d_\tau d_\xi F(\tau, \xi) \right| \right.$$

$$+ \left| \int_{\kappa_1}^{\varkappa} \int_{\gamma}^{\kappa_4} (\rho(\tau) - \rho(\kappa_1))^\alpha (\varpi(\kappa_4) - \varpi(\xi))^\beta d_\tau d_\xi F(\tau, \xi) \right|$$

$$+ \left| \int_{\varkappa}^{\kappa_2} \int_{\kappa_3}^{\gamma} (\rho(\kappa_2) - \rho(\tau))^\alpha (\varpi(\xi) - \varpi(\kappa_3))^\beta d_\tau d_\xi F(\tau, \xi) \right|$$

$$\left. + \left| \int_{\varkappa}^{\kappa_2} \int_{\gamma}^{\kappa_4} (\rho(\kappa_2) - \rho(\tau))^\alpha (\varpi(\kappa_4) - \varpi(\xi))^\beta d_\tau d_\xi F(\tau, \xi) \right| \right].$$

By Lemma 2, we obtain

$$\left| \int_{\kappa_1}^{\varkappa} \int_{\kappa_3}^{\gamma} (\rho(\tau) - \rho(\kappa_1))^\alpha (\varpi(\xi) - \varpi(\kappa_3))^\beta d_\tau d_\xi F(\tau, \xi) \right|$$

$$\leq (\rho(\varkappa) - \rho(\kappa_1))^\alpha (\varpi(\gamma) - \varpi(\kappa_3))^\beta \bigvee_{\kappa_1}^{\varkappa} \bigvee_{\kappa_3}^{\gamma}(F),$$

$$\left| \int_{\kappa_1}^{\varkappa} \int_{\gamma}^{\kappa_4} (\rho(\tau) - \rho(\kappa_1))^\alpha (\varpi(\kappa_4) - \varpi(\xi))^\beta d_\tau d_\xi F(\tau, \xi) \right|$$

$$\leq (\rho(\varkappa) - \rho(\kappa_1))^\alpha (\varpi(\kappa_4) - \varpi(\gamma))^\beta \bigvee_{\kappa_1}^{\varkappa} \bigvee_{\gamma}^{\kappa_4}(F),$$

$$\left| \int_{\varkappa}^{\kappa_2} \int_{\kappa_3}^{\gamma} (\rho(\kappa_2) - \rho(\tau))^\alpha (\varpi(\xi) - \varpi(\kappa_3))^\beta d_\tau d_\xi F(\tau, \xi) \right|$$

$$\leq (\rho(\kappa_2) - \rho(\varkappa))^\alpha (\varpi(\gamma) - \varpi(\kappa_3))^\beta \bigvee_{\varkappa}^{\kappa_2} \bigvee_{\kappa_3}^{\gamma}(F)$$

and

$$\left| \int_{\varkappa}^{\kappa_2} \int_{\gamma}^{\kappa_4} (\rho(\kappa_2) - \rho(\tau))^\alpha (\varpi(\kappa_4) - \varpi(\xi))^\beta d_\tau d_\xi F(\tau, \xi) \right|$$

$$\leq (\rho(\kappa_2) - \rho(\varkappa))^\alpha (\varpi(\kappa_4) - \varpi(\gamma))^\beta \bigvee_{\varkappa}^{\kappa_2} \bigvee_{\gamma}^{\kappa_4}(F).$$

It follows that

$$\left| F(\varkappa, \gamma) - \frac{\Gamma(\alpha+1)}{M_\rho^\alpha(\kappa_1, \kappa_2; \varkappa)} \left[\mathcal{J}_{\varkappa-;\rho}^\alpha F(\kappa_1, \gamma) + \mathcal{J}_{\varkappa+;\rho}^\alpha F(\kappa_2, \gamma) \right] \right.$$

$$- \frac{\Gamma(\beta+1)}{N_\varpi^\beta(\kappa_3, \kappa_4; \gamma)} \left[\mathcal{J}_{\gamma-;\varpi}^\beta F(\varkappa, \kappa_3) + \mathcal{J}_{\gamma+;\varpi}^\beta F(\varkappa, \kappa_4) \right]$$

$$+ \frac{\Gamma(\alpha+1)\Gamma(\beta+1)}{M_\rho^\alpha(\kappa_1, \kappa_2; \varkappa) N_\varpi^\beta(\kappa_3, \kappa_4; \gamma)} \left[\mathcal{J}_{\varkappa-,\gamma-;\rho,\varpi}^{\alpha,\beta} F(\kappa_1, \kappa_3) + \mathcal{J}_{\varkappa-,\gamma+;\rho,\varpi}^{\alpha,\beta} F(\kappa_1, \kappa_4) \right.$$

$$\left. \left. + \mathcal{J}_{\varkappa+,\gamma-;\rho,\varpi}^{\alpha,\beta} F(\kappa_2, \kappa_3) + \mathcal{J}_{\varkappa+,\gamma+;\rho,\varpi}^{\alpha,\beta} F(\kappa_2, \kappa_4) \right] \right|$$

$$= \frac{1}{M_\rho^\alpha(\kappa_1, \kappa_2; \varkappa) N_\varpi^\beta(\kappa_3, \kappa_4; \gamma)}$$

$$\times \left[(\rho(\varkappa) - \rho(\kappa_1))^\alpha (\varpi(\gamma) - \varpi(\kappa_3))^\beta \bigvee_{\kappa_1}^{\varkappa} \bigvee_{\kappa_3}^{\gamma}(F) \right.$$

$$+ (\rho(\varkappa) - \rho(\kappa_1))^\alpha (\varpi(\kappa_4) - \varpi(\gamma))^\beta \bigvee_{\kappa_1}^{\varkappa} \bigvee_{\gamma}^{\kappa_4}(F)$$

$$+ (\rho(\kappa_2) - \rho(\varkappa))^\alpha (\varpi(\gamma) - \varpi(\kappa_3))^\beta \bigvee_{\varkappa}^{\kappa_2} \bigvee_{\kappa_3}^{\gamma}(F)$$

$$\left. + (\rho(\kappa_2) - \rho(\varkappa))^\alpha (\varpi(\kappa_4) - \varpi(\gamma))^\beta \bigvee_{\varkappa}^{\kappa_2} \bigvee_{\gamma}^{\kappa_4}(F) \right]$$

which completes the proof of first inequality in Equation (28). The proof of the second inequality is obvious from the proof of Theorem 2. □

Remark 3. If we take $\rho(\tau) = \tau$, $\tau \in [\kappa_1, \kappa_2]$ and $\omega(\xi) = \xi$, $\xi \in [\kappa_3, \kappa_4]$ in Theorem 4, then we have the following Ostrowski-type inequalities for Riemann–Liouville fractional integrals

$$\left| F(\varkappa, \gamma) - \frac{\Gamma(\alpha+1)}{(\varkappa-\kappa_1)^\alpha + (\kappa_2-\varkappa)^\alpha} \left[\mathcal{J}^\alpha_{\varkappa-;\rho} F(\kappa_1, \gamma) + \mathcal{J}^\alpha_{\varkappa+;\rho} F(\kappa_2, \gamma) \right] \right.$$
$$- \frac{\Gamma(\beta+1)}{(\gamma-\kappa_3)^\beta + (\kappa_4-\gamma)^\beta} \left[\mathcal{J}^\beta_{\gamma-;\omega} F(\varkappa, \kappa_3) + \mathcal{J}^\beta_{\gamma+;\omega} F(\varkappa, \kappa_4) \right]$$
$$+ \frac{\Gamma(\alpha+1)\Gamma(\beta+1)}{\left[(\varkappa-\kappa_1)^\alpha + (\kappa_2-\varkappa)^\alpha\right]\left[(\gamma-\kappa_3)^\beta + (\kappa_4-\gamma)^\beta\right]} \left[\mathcal{J}^{\alpha,\beta}_{\varkappa-,\gamma-;\rho,\omega} F(\kappa_1, \kappa_3) \right.$$
$$\left. + \mathcal{J}^{\alpha,\beta}_{\varkappa-,\gamma+;\rho,\omega} F(\kappa_1, \kappa_4) + \mathcal{J}^{\alpha,\beta}_{\varkappa+,\gamma-;\rho,\omega} F(\kappa_2, \kappa_3) + \mathcal{J}^{\alpha,\beta}_{\varkappa+,\gamma+;\rho,\omega} F(\kappa_2, \kappa_4) \right] \bigg|$$

$$= \frac{1}{\left[(\varkappa-\kappa_1)^\alpha + (\kappa_2-\varkappa)^\alpha\right]\left[(\gamma-\kappa_3)^\beta + (\kappa_4-\gamma)^\beta\right]}$$
$$\times \left[(\varkappa-\kappa_1)^\alpha (\gamma-\kappa_3)^\beta \bigvee_{\kappa_1}^{\varkappa} \bigvee_{\kappa_3}^{\gamma}(F) + (\varkappa-\kappa_1)^\alpha (\kappa_4-\gamma)^\beta \bigvee_{\kappa_1}^{\varkappa} \bigvee_{\gamma}^{\kappa_4}(F) \right.$$
$$\left. + (\kappa_2-\varkappa)^\alpha (\gamma-\kappa_3)^\beta \bigvee_{\varkappa}^{\kappa_2} \bigvee_{\kappa_3}^{\gamma}(F) + (\kappa_2-\varkappa)^\alpha (\kappa_4-\gamma)^\beta \bigvee_{\varkappa}^{\kappa_2} \bigvee_{\gamma}^{\kappa_4}(F) \right]$$

$$\leq \frac{1}{\left[(\varkappa-\kappa_1)^\alpha + (\kappa_2-\varkappa)^\alpha\right]\left[(\gamma-\kappa_3)^\beta + (\kappa_4-\gamma)^\beta\right]}$$
$$\times \left[\frac{\kappa_2-\kappa_1}{2} + \left|\varkappa - \frac{\kappa_1+\kappa_2}{2}\right| \right]^\alpha \left[\frac{\kappa_4-\kappa_1}{2} + \left|\gamma - \frac{\kappa_3+\kappa_4}{2}\right| \right]^\beta \bigvee_{\kappa_1}^{\kappa_2} \bigvee_{\kappa_2}^{\kappa_4}(F).$$

6. Conclusions

In this paper, we present several trapezoid and Ostrowski-type inequalities for functions of bounded variation with two variables via generalized fractional integrals. It is also shown that several results are given by special cases of the main results. We deduce that the findings proved in this work are naturally universal, contribute to the theory of inequalities and have applications for determining the uniqueness of solutions in fractional boundary value problems. The findings of this study can be applied to symmetry. The results for the case of symmetric functions can be obtained by applying the concepts of symmetric convex functions, which will be studied in future work. It is an interesting and new problem and forthcoming researchers can use the techniques of this study to derive similar inequalities for different kinds of fractional integrals in their future works.

Author Contributions: T.S., H.B., H.K., M.A.A. and J.R. contributed equally to the writing of this paper. All authors have read and agreed to the published version of the manuscript.

Funding: This research was funded by King Mongkut's University of Technology North Bangkok. Contract no. KMUTNB-62-KNOW-26.

Institutional Review Board Statement: Not applicable.

Informed Consent Statement: Not applicable.

Data Availability Statement: Not applicable.

Acknowledgments: The authors would like to express their sincere thanks to the editor and the anonymous reviewers for their helpful comments and suggestions.

Conflicts of Interest: The authors declare no conflict of interest.

References

1. Ostrowski, A. Über die Absolutabweichung einer differentiierbaren Funktion von ihrem Integralmittelwert. *Comment. Math. Helv.* **1938**, *10*, 226–227. [CrossRef]
2. Alomari, M.; Darus, M.; Dragomir, S.S.; Cerone, P. Ostrowski type inequalities for functions whose derivatives are ξ-convex in the second sense. *Appl. Math. Lett.* **2010**, *23*, 1071–1076. [CrossRef]
3. Kavurmaci, H.; Özdemir, M.E. New Ostrowski type inequalities for *m*-convex functions and applications. *Hacet. J. Math. Stat.* **2011**, *40*, 135–145.
4. Matłoka, M. Ostrowski type inequalities for functions whose derivatives are *h*-convex via fractional integrals. *J. Sci. Res. Rep.* **2014**, 1633–1641. [CrossRef]
5. Özdemir, M.E.; Kavurmaci, H.; Set, E. Ostrowski's type inequalities for (α, *m*)-convex function. *Kyungpook Math. J.* **2010**, *50*, 371–378. [CrossRef]
6. Tunç, M. Ostrowski-type inequalities via *h*-convex functions with applications to special means. *J. Inequal. Appl.* **2013**, *2013*, 326. [CrossRef]
7. Set, E. New inequalities of Ostrowski type for mappings whose derivatives are s-convex in the second sense via fractional integrals. *Comput. Math. Appl.* **2012**, *63*, 1147–1154. [CrossRef]
8. Farid, G.; Rehman, A.; Usman, M. Ostrowski type fractional integral inequalities for s-Godunova–Levin functions via *k*-fractional integrals. *Proyecc. J. Math.* **2017**, *36*, 753–767.
9. Sarikaya, M.Z.; Budak, H. Generalized Ostrowski type inequalities for local fractional integrals. *Proc. Am. Math. Soc.* **2017**, *145*, 1527–1538. [CrossRef]
10. Agarwal, R.P.; Luo, M.-J.; Raina, R.K. On Ostrowski type inequalities. *Fasc. Math.* **2016**, *56*, 5–27. [CrossRef]
11. Basci, Y.; Baleanu, D. Ostrowski type inequalities involving ψ-Hilfer fractional integrals. *Mathematics* **2019**, *7*, 770. [CrossRef]
12. Budak, H.; Özçelik, K. Some generalized fractional trapezoid and Ostrowski type inequalities for functions with bounded partial derivatives. *Math. Methods Appl. Sci.* **2021**, 1–21. [CrossRef]
13. Dragomir, S.S. Ostrowski and trapezoid type inequalities for the generalized *k*-ρ-fractional integrals of functions with bounded variation. *Commun. Adv. Math. Sci.* **2017**, *2*, 309–330. [CrossRef]
14. Dragomir, S.S. Ostrowski and trapezoid type inequalities for Riemann–Liouville fractional integrals of absolutely continuous functions with bounded derivatives. *Fract. Differ. Calc.* **2020**, *10*, 307–320. [CrossRef]
15. Dragomir, S.S. On some trapezoid type inequalities for generalized Riemann-Liouville fractional integrals. *RGMIA Res. Rep. Coll.* **2017**, *20*, 12.
16. Dragomir, S.S. On some Ostrowski type inequalities for generalized Riemann–Liouville fractional integrals. *RGMIA Res. Rep. Coll.* **2017**, *20*, 13.
17. Dragomir, S.S. Ostrowski and trapezoid type inequalities for generalized Riemann–Liouville fractional integrals of absolutely continuous functions with bounded derivatives. *RGMIA Res. Rep. Coll.* **2017**, *20*, 19.
18. Dragomir, S.S. Further Ostrowski and trapezoid type inequalities for the generalized Riemann-Liouville fractional integrals of functions with bounded variation. *RGMIA Res. Rep. Coll.* **2017**, *20*, 20.
19. Farid, G.; Usman, M. Ostrowski type *k*-fractional integral inequalities for *MT*-convex and *h*-convex functions. *Nonlinear Funct. Anal. Appl.* **2017**, *22*, 627–639.
20. Gürbüz, M.; Taşdan, Y.; Set, E. Ostrowski type inequalities via the Katugampola fractional integrals. *AIMS Math.* **2020**, *5*, 42–53. [CrossRef]
21. Sarikaya, M.Z.; Filiz, H. Note on the Ostrowski type inequalities for fractional integrals. *Vietnam J. Math.* **2014**, *42*, 187–190. [CrossRef]
22. Sarikaya, M.Z.; Yildiz, M.K. Generalization and improvement of Ostrowski type inequalities. *AIP Conf. Proc.* **2018**, *1991*, 020031.
23. Sarikaya, M.Z.; Budak, H.; Yaldiz, H. Some new Ostrowski type inequalities for co-ordinated convex functions. *Turkish J. Anal. Number Theory* **2014**, *2*, 176–182. [CrossRef]
24. Latif, M.A.; Hussain, S.; Dragomir, S.S. New Ostrowski type inequalities for co-ordinated convex functions. *TJMM* **2012**, *4*, 125–136.
25. Latif, M.A.; Hussain, S. New Ostrowski type inequalities for co-ordinated convex functions via fractional integrals. *J. Fract. Calc. Appl.* **2012**, *2*, 1–15.
26. Dragomir, S.S. On the Ostrowski's integral inequality for mappings with bounded variation and applications. *Math. Inequal. Appl.* **2001**, *4*, 59–66. [CrossRef]
27. Dragomir, S.S. On trapezoid quadrature formula and applications. *Kragujev. J. Math.* **2001**, *23*, 25–36.
28. Dragomir, S.S. On the midpoint quadrature formula for mappings with bounded variation and applications. *Kragujev. J. Math.* **2000**, *22*, 13–19.
29. Dragomir, S.S. On Simpson's quadrature formula for mappings of bounded variation and applications. *Tamkang J. Math.* **1999**, *30*, 53–58. [CrossRef]
30. Alomari, M.W. A generalization of Dragomir's generalization of Ostrowski integral inequality and applications in numerical integration. *Ukr. Math.* **2012**, *64*, 435–450.
31. Alomari, M.W. A Generalization of weighted companion of Ostrowski integral inequality for mappings of bounded variation. *Int. J. Nonlinear Sci. Numer. Simul.* **2020**, *1*, 667–673. [CrossRef]

32. Barnett, N.S.; Dragomir, S.S.; Gomm, I. A companion for the Ostrowski and the generalized trapezoid inequalities. *Math. Comput. Model.* **2009**, *50*, 179–187. [CrossRef]
33. Budak, H.; Sarikaya, M.Z.; Qayyum, A. Improvement in companion of Ostrowski type inequalities for mappings whose first derivatives are of bounded variation and application. *Filomat* **2017**, *31*, 5305–5314. [CrossRef]
34. Budak, H.; Pehlivan, E. Some inequalities for weighted area balance via functions of bounded variation. *Rocky Mt. J. Math.* **2020**, *50*, 455–466. [CrossRef]
35. Budak, H.; Sarikaya, M.Z. On generalization of Dragomir's inequalities. *Turkish J. Anal. Number Theory* **2017**, *5*, 191–196. [CrossRef]
36. Cerone, P.; Dragomir, S.S.; Pearce, C.E.M. A generalized trapezoid inequality for functions of bounded variation. *Turk. J. Math.* **2000**, *24*, 147–163.
37. Dragomir, S.S. The Ostrowski integral inequality for mappings of bounded variation. *Bull. Aust. Math. Soc.* **1999**, *60*, 495–508. [CrossRef]
38. Dragomir, S.S. A companion of Ostrowski's inequality for functions of bounded variation and applications. *Int. J. Nonlinear Anal. Appl.* **2014**, *5*, 89–97.
39. Tseng, K.-L.; Yang, G.-S.; Dragomir, S.S. Generalizations of weighted trapezoidal inequality for mappings of bounded variation and their applications. *Math. Comput. Model.* **2004**, *40*, 77–84. [CrossRef]
40. Tseng, K.-L.; Hwang, S.-R.; Dragomir, S.S. Generalizations of weighted Ostrowski type inequalities for mappings of bounded variation and applications. *Comput. Math. Appl.* **2008**, *55*, 1785–1793. [CrossRef]
41. Tseng, K.-L.; Hwang, S.-R.; Yang, G.-S.; Chu, Y.-M. Improvements of the Ostrowski integral inequality for mappings of bounded variation I. *Appl. Comput. Math.* **2010**, *217*, 2348–2355. [CrossRef]
42. Tseng, K.-L.; Hwang, S.-R.; Yang, G.-S.; Chu, Y.-M. Weighted Ostrowski integral inequality for mappings of bounded variation. *Taiwan. J. Math.* **2011**, *15*, 573–585. [CrossRef]
43. Jawarneh, Y.; Noorani, M.S.M. Inequalities of Ostrowski and Simpson type for mappings of two variables with bounded variation and applications. *TJMM* **2011**, *3*, 81–94, Erratum in **2018**, *10*, 71–74.
44. Moricz, F. Order of magnitude of double Fourier coefficients of functions of bounded variation. *Analysis* **2002**, *22*, 335–345. [CrossRef]
45. Budak, H.; Sarikaya, M.Z. On weighted generalization of trapezoid inequalities for functions of two variables with bounded variation. *Kragujev. J. Math.* **2019**, *43*, 109–122.
46. Budak, H.; Sarikaya, M.Z. A companion of Ostrowski type inequalities for functions of two variables with bounded variation. *J. Adv. Math. Stud.* **2015**, *8*, 170–184.
47. Budak, H.; Sarikaya, M.Z. A companion of generalization of Ostrowski type inequalities for functions of two variables with bounded variation. *Appl. Comput. Math.* **2016**, *15*, 297–312.
48. Schumacher, C.S. *Closer and Closer: Introducing Real Analysis*, 1st ed.; Jones and Bartlett Publishers Inc.: Boston, MA, USA, 2008.
49. Clarkson, J.A.; Adams, C.R. On definitions of bounded variation for functions of two variables. *Bull. Am. Math. Soc.* **1933**, *35*, 824–854. [CrossRef]
50. Clarkson, J.A. On double Riemann-Stieltjes integrals. *Bull. Am. Math. Soc.* **1933**, *39*, 929–936. [CrossRef]
51. Samko, S.G.; Kilbas, A.A.; Marichev, I.O. *Fractional Integrals and Derivatives: Theory and Applications*; Gordon & Breach: Yverdon, Switzerland, 1993.
52. Kilbas, A.A.; Srivastava, H.M.; Trujillo, J.J. *Theory and Applications of Fractional Differential Equations*; North-Holland Mathematics Studies, 204; Elsevier Science B.V.: Amsterdam, The Netherlands, 2006.
53. Budak, H.; Agarwal, P. *On Hermite-Hadamard Type Inequalities for Co-Ordinated Convex Mappings Utilizing Generalized Fractional Integrals*; Accepted as an Book Chaper, Fractional Differentiation and its Applications; Springer: Berlin/Heidelberg, Germany, 24 November 2019.

Article

On Some New Inequalities of Hermite–Hadamard Midpoint and Trapezoid Type for Preinvex Functions in (p, q)-Calculus

Ifra Bashir Sial [1], Muhammad Aamir Ali [2,*], Ghulam Murtaza [3], Sotiris K. Ntouyas [4,5], Jarunee Soontharanon [6] and Thanin Sitthiwirattham [7,*]

[1] School of Mathematical Sciences, Jiangsu University, Zhenjiang 212013, China; ifrabashir92@gmail.com
[2] Jiangsu Key Laboratory for NSLSCS, School of Mathematical Sciences, Nanjing Normal University, Nanjing 210023, China
[3] Department of Mathematics, University of Management and Technology, Lahore 54700, Pakistan; ghulammurtaza@umt.edu.pk
[4] Department of Mathematics, University of Ioannina, 451 10 Ioannina, Greece; sntouyas@uoi.gr
[5] Nonlinear Analysis and Applied Mathematics (NAAM)-Research Group, Department of Mathematics, Faculty of Science, King Abdulaziz University, Jeddah 21589, Saudi Arabia
[6] Department of Mathematics, Faculty of Applied Science, King Mongkut's University of Technology North Bangkok, Bangkok 10800, Thailand; jarunee.s@sci.kmutnb.ac.th
[7] Mathematics Department, Faculty of Science and Technology, Suan Dusit University, Bangkok 10300, Thailand
* Correspondence: mahr.muhammad.aamir@gmail.com (M.A.A.); thanin_sit@dusit.ac.th (T.S.)

Abstract: In this paper, we establish some new Hermite–Hadamard type inequalities for preinvex functions and left-right estimates of newly established inequalities for (p,q)-differentiable preinvex functions in the context of (p,q)-calculus. We also show that the results established in this paper are generalizations of comparable results in the literature of integral inequalities. Analytic inequalities of this nature and especially the techniques involved have applications in various areas in which symmetry plays a prominent role.

Keywords: Hermite–Hadamard inequality; (p,q)-integral; post quantum calculus; convex function

1. Introduction

The Hermite–Hadamard (H-H) inequality, which was independently found by C. Hermite and J. Hadamard, is particularly important in convex function theory (see, [1–3], and also [4], p. 137).

$$\Pi\left(\frac{\pi_1 + \pi_2}{2}\right) \leq \frac{1}{\pi_2 - \pi_1} \int_{\pi_1}^{\pi_2} \Pi(\varkappa) d\varkappa \leq \frac{\Pi(\pi_1) + \Pi(\pi_2)}{2} \qquad (1)$$

where Π is a convex mapping. The aforementioned inequality is true in reverse order for concave maps. Jensen's inequality for convex functions can easily capture this inequality [5]. Several generalizations and extensions to classical convex functions have been proposed in recent years. In [6], the notions about invex function was given that is a significant generalization of convex functions. Weir and Mond introduced the concept of preinvex functions in [7], and it is used in optimization theory in a variety of ways. Prequasi-invex functions are a generalization of the invex functions introduced by Pini in [8]. Following that, the authors looked at some fundamental properties of generalized preinvex functions in [9]. Noor established H-H integral inequalities for preinvex functions in [10–12]. The authors of [13,14] used the ordinary and fractional integrals to calculate the left and right bounds of the H-H inequalities for preinvex functions. More recent results on the integral inequalities for various types of preinvexities can be found in [15–24].

On the other hand, beginning with Euler, various efforts in the subject of q-analysis have been implemented in order to master the mathematics that underpins quantum computing. The phrase q-calculus binds mathematics and physics together. It is employed in subjects including combinatorics, number theory, basic hypergeometric functions, orthogonal polynomials, and others, as well as relativity theory, mechanics, and quantum theory [25,26]. It has numerous applications in quantum information theory [27,28]. Euler is believed to be the creator of this crucial branch of mathematics since he employed the q-parameter in Newton's work on infinite series. Jackson [29,30] introduced the concept of q-calculus, sometimes known as calculus without limits, for the first time in a proper manner. Al-Salam [31] introduced the concepts of q-fractional integral and q-Riemann–Liouville fractional integral in 1996. Because study in this subject is gradually increasing, Tariboon and Ntouyas [32] proposed the $_{\pi_1}D_q$-difference operator and q_{π_1}-integral. Bermudo et al. [33] published their ideas regarding the $^{\pi_2}D_q$-difference operator and q^{π_2}-integral in 2020. By presenting the principles of (p,q)-calculus, Sadjang [34] broadened the concept of q-calculus. Tunç and Göv [35] introduced the (p,q)-variant of the $_{\pi_1}D_q$-difference operator and q_{π_1}-integral. Chu et al. established the concepts of $^{\pi_2}D_{p,q}$-derivative and $(p,q)^{\pi_2}$-integral in [36], in 2021.

Quantum and post-quantum integrals have been used to study a variety of integral inequalities for a variety of functions. For example, multiple authors in [37–45] gave the H-H inequalities and their right-left estimates for convex and co-ordinated convex functions via $_{\pi_1}D_q$, $^{\pi_2}D_q$-derivatives and q_{π_1}, q^{π_2}-integrals. In the setting of q-calculus, Noor et al. [46] employed preinvexity to verify H-H inequalities. Nwaeze et al. [47] discovered several parameterized q-integral inequalities for generalized quasi-convex functions. In [48], Khan et al. used the concept of Green functions to develop some novel H-H type inequalities. In the context of q-calculus, Budak et al. [49], Ali et al. [50,51], and Vivas-Cortez et al. [52] demonstrated new boundaries for Simpson's and Newton's type inequalities for convex and coordinated convex functions. For q-Ostrowski inequality for convex and co-ordinated convex functions, see [53–55]. The authors used the $_{\pi_1}D_{p,q}$-difference operator and the $(p,q)_{\pi_1}$-integral to generalize the results of [39] and show H-H type inequalities and their left estimates [56]. The authors recently established the right estimates of H-H type inequalities shown by Kunt et al. [56] in [57]. Reference [36] can be used to solve (p,q)-Ostrowski type inequalities. The findings in [58] are a generalization of [33].

Inspired by the ongoing studies, we give the generalizations of the results proved in [33,39,41,59] by proving H-H trapezoid and midpoint type inequalities for preinvex functions using the concepts of (p,q)-difference operators and (p,q)-integral.

This paper is organized in the following way: Section 2 introduces the basics of q-calculus and discusses other related research in the field. (p,q)-derivatives and integrals are discussed in Section 3. In Section 4, we show that in the (p,q)-calculus setting, H-H type inequalities exist for preinvex functions. Sections 5 and 6 prove new midpoint and trapezoid type inequalities for differentiable preinvex functions via (p,q)-calculus. The link between the findings reported here and analogous findings in the literature is also taken into account. Section 7 summarize the findings and suggests research topics for the future.

2. Quantum Derivatives and Integrals

This section discusses the key concepts and findings that will be needed to prove our critical findings in the next sections.

Definition 1 ([7,9]). *A set $\omega \subseteq \mathbb{R}^n$ is known as invex with respect to the given $\eta : \mathbb{R}^n \times \mathbb{R}^n \to \mathbb{R}^n$ if*

$$\varkappa + t\eta(\gamma, \varkappa) \in \omega, \, \forall \, \varkappa, \gamma \in \omega, t \in [0,1].$$

The η-connected set is a more frequent name for the invex set ω.

Definition 2 ([7,9]). *Consider an invex set $\omega \subseteq \mathbb{R}^n$ with respect to $\eta : \mathbb{R}^n \times \mathbb{R}^n \to \mathbb{R}^n$. A mapping $\Pi : \omega \to \mathbb{R}$ is called preinvex, if*

$$\Pi(\varkappa + t\eta(\gamma, \varkappa)) \leq t\Pi(\gamma) + (1-t)\Pi(\varkappa), \ \forall \ \varkappa, \gamma \in \omega, t \in [0,1]. \tag{2}$$

If $-\Pi$ is preinvex, the mapping Π is called preconcave.

Remark 1. *Definition 2 becomes the definition of convex functions if $\eta(\gamma, \varkappa) = \gamma - \varkappa$ is set in Definition 2:*

$$\Pi(\varkappa + t(\gamma - \varkappa)) \leq t\Pi(\gamma) + (1-t)\Pi(\varkappa), \ \forall \ \varkappa, \gamma \in \omega, t \in [0,1].$$

Condition C. [9] The function η satisfies the following condition if

$$\begin{aligned} \eta(\gamma, \gamma + t\eta(\varkappa, \gamma)) &= -t\eta(\varkappa, \gamma), \\ \eta(\varkappa, \gamma + \eta(\varkappa, \gamma)) &= (1-t)\eta(\varkappa, \gamma) \end{aligned} \tag{3}$$

for every $\varkappa, \gamma \in \omega$ and any $t \in [0,1]$. Note that for every $\varkappa, \gamma \in \omega$, $t_1, t_2 \in [0,1]$, and from Condition C, we have the following:

$$\eta(\gamma + t_2\eta(\varkappa, \gamma), \gamma + t_1\eta(\varkappa, \gamma)) = (t_2 - t_1)\eta(\varkappa, \gamma).$$

Theorem 1 ([60] (Jensen's inequality for preinvex functions)). *Let $\Pi : \omega \to \mathbb{R}$ be a preinvex function. Let $\gamma_1, \gamma_2, \ldots, \gamma_n \in [0,1]$ be the coefficients such that $\sum_{i=0}^{n} \gamma_i = 1$, and let $t_1, t_2, \ldots, t_n \in [0,1]$ be the coefficients. Then, the inequality*

$$\Pi\left(\sum_{i=1}^{n} \gamma_i(\varkappa + t_i\eta(\gamma, \varkappa))\right) \leq \sum_{i=1}^{n} \gamma_i \Pi(\varkappa + t_i\eta(\gamma, \varkappa)) \tag{4}$$

holds for all $\varkappa, \gamma \in \omega$.

Set the following notation [26]:

$$[n]_q = \frac{1-q^n}{1-q} = 1 + q + q^2 + \ldots + q^{n-1}, \ q \in (0,1).$$

The q-Jackson integral of a mapping Π from 0 to π_2 is given by Jackson [30] which is defined as:

$$\int_0^{\pi_2} \Pi(\varkappa) \, d_q \varkappa = (1-q)\pi_2 \sum_{n=0}^{\infty} q^n \Pi(\pi_2 q^n), \text{ where } 0 < q < 1 \tag{5}$$

assuming that the sum is absolutely convergent. Moreover, over the interval $[\pi_1, \pi_2]$, he gave the following integral of a mapping Π:

$$\int_{\pi_1}^{\pi_2} \Pi(\varkappa) \, d_q \varkappa = \int_0^{\pi_2} \Pi(\varkappa) \, d_q \varkappa - \int_0^{\pi_1} \Pi(\varkappa) \, d_q \varkappa.$$

Definition 3 ([32]). *The q_{π_1}-derivative of mapping $\Pi : [\pi_1, \pi_2] \to \mathbb{R}$ is defined as:*

$$_{\pi_1}D_q\Pi(\varkappa) = \frac{\Pi(\varkappa) - \Pi(q\varkappa + (1-q)\pi_1)}{(1-q)(\varkappa - \pi_1)}, \ \varkappa \neq \pi_1. \tag{6}$$

For $\varkappa = \pi_1$, we state $_{\pi_1}D_q\Pi(\pi_1) = \lim_{\varkappa \to \pi_1} {}_{\pi_1}D_q\Pi(\varkappa)$ if it exists and it is finite.

Definition 4 ([33]). *The q^{π_2}-derivative of mapping $\Pi : [\pi_1, \pi_2] \to \mathbb{R}$ is given as:*

$$^{\pi_2}D_q\Pi(\varkappa) = \frac{\Pi(q\varkappa + (1-q)\pi_2) - \Pi(\varkappa)}{(1-q)(\pi_2 - \varkappa)}, \quad \varkappa \neq \pi_2. \tag{7}$$

For $\varkappa = \pi_2$, we state $^{\pi_2}D_q\Pi(\pi_2) = \lim_{\varkappa \to \pi_2} {}^{\pi_2}D_q\Pi(\varkappa)$ if it exists and it is finite.

Definition 5 ([32]). *The q_{π_1}-definite integral of mapping $\Pi : [\pi_1, \pi_2] \to \mathbb{R}$ on $[\pi_1, \pi_2]$ is defined as:*

$$\int_{\pi_1}^{\varkappa} \Pi(\tau) \, _{\pi_1}d_q\tau = (1-q)(\varkappa - \pi_1) \sum_{n=0}^{\infty} q^n \Pi(q^n \varkappa + (1-q^n)\pi_1), \quad \varkappa \in [\pi_1, \pi_2]. \tag{8}$$

Bermudo et al. [33], on the other hand, state the following concept of the q-definite integral:

Definition 6 ([33]). *The q^{π_2}-definite integral of mapping $\Pi : [\pi_1, \pi_2] \to \mathbb{R}$ on $[\pi_1, \pi_2]$ is given as:*

$$\int_{\varkappa}^{\pi_2} \Pi(\tau) \, ^{\pi_2}d_q\tau = (1-q)(\pi_2 - \varkappa) \sum_{n=0}^{\infty} q^n \Pi(q^n \varkappa + (1-q^n)\pi_2), \quad \varkappa \in [\pi_1, \pi_2]. \tag{9}$$

3. Post-Quantum Derivatives and Integrals

We will go over some basic (p,q)-calculus concepts and notations in this section. The $[n]_{p,q}$ is said to be (p,q)-integers and expressed as:

$$[n]_{p,q} = \frac{p^n - q^n}{p - q}$$

with $0 < q < p \leq 1$. The $[n]_{p,q}!$ and $\begin{bmatrix} n \\ k \end{bmatrix}!$ are called (p,q)-factorial and (p,q)-binomial, respectively, and expressed as:

$$[n]_{p,q}! = \prod_{k=1}^{n} [k]_{p,q}, \quad n \geq 1, \quad [0]_{p,q}! = 1,$$

$$\begin{bmatrix} n \\ k \end{bmatrix}! = \frac{[n]_{p,q}!}{[n-k]_{p,q}![k]_{p,q}!}.$$

Definition 7 ([34]). *The (p,q)-derivative of mapping $\Pi : [\pi_1, \pi_2] \to \mathbb{R}$ is given as:*

$$D_{p,q}\Pi(\varkappa) = \frac{\Pi(p\varkappa) - \Pi(q\varkappa)}{(p-q)\varkappa}, \quad \varkappa \neq 0 \tag{10}$$

with $0 < q < p \leq 1$.

Definition 8 ([35]). *The $(p,q)_{\pi_1}$-derivative of mapping $\Pi : [\pi_1, \pi_2] \to \mathbb{R}$ is given as:*

$$_{\pi_1}D_{p,q}\Pi(\varkappa) = \frac{\Pi(p\varkappa + (1-p)\pi_1) - \Pi(q\varkappa + (1-q)\pi_1)}{(p-q)(\varkappa - \pi_1)}, \quad \varkappa \neq \pi_1 \tag{11}$$

with $0 < q < p \leq 1$.

For $\varkappa = \pi_1$, we state $_{\pi_1}D_{p,q}\Pi(\pi_1) = \lim_{\varkappa \to \pi_1} {}_{\pi_1}D_{p,q}\Pi(\varkappa)$ if it exists and it is finite.

Definition 9 ([36]). *The* $(p,q)^{\pi_2}$-*derivative of mapping* $\Pi : [\pi_1, \pi_2] \to \mathbb{R}$ *is given as:*

$$^{\pi_2}D_{p,q}\Pi(\varkappa) = \frac{\Pi(q\varkappa + (1-q)\pi_2) - \Pi(p\varkappa + (1-p)\pi_2)}{(p-q)(\pi_2 - \varkappa)}, \quad \varkappa \neq \pi_2. \tag{12}$$

For $\varkappa = \pi_2$, *we state* $^{\pi_2}D_{p,q}\Pi(\pi_2) = \lim_{\varkappa \to \pi_2} {}^{\pi_2}D_{p,q}\Pi(\varkappa)$ *if it exists and it is finite.*

Remark 2. *It is clear that if we use* $p = 1$ *in (11) and (12), then the equalities (11) and (12) reduce to (6) and (7), respectively.*

Definition 10 ([35]). *The definite* $(p,q)_{\pi_1}$-*integral of mapping* $\Pi : [\pi_1, \pi_2] \to \mathbb{R}$ *on* $[\pi_1, \pi_2]$ *is stated as:*

$$\int_{\pi_1}^{\varkappa} \Pi(\tau) \, {}_{\pi_1}d_{p,q}\tau = (p-q)(\varkappa - \pi_1) \sum_{n=0}^{\infty} \frac{q^n}{p^{n+1}} \Pi\left(\frac{q^n}{p^{n+1}}\varkappa + \left(1 - \frac{q^n}{p^{n+1}}\right)\pi_1\right) \tag{13}$$

with $0 < q < p \leq 1$.

Definition 11 ([36]). *The definite* $(p,q)^{\pi_2}$-*integral of mapping* $\Pi : [\pi_1, \pi_2] \to \mathbb{R}$ *on* $[\pi_1, \pi_2]$ *is stated as:*

$$\int_{\varkappa}^{\pi_2} \Pi(\tau) \, {}^{\pi_2}d_{p,q}\tau = (p-q)(\pi_2 - \varkappa) \sum_{n=0}^{\infty} \frac{q^n}{p^{n+1}} \Pi\left(\frac{q^n}{p^{n+1}}\varkappa + \left(1 - \frac{q^n}{p^{n+1}}\right)\pi_2\right) \tag{14}$$

with $0 < q < p \leq 1$.

Remark 3. *It is evident that if we pick* $p = 1$ *in (13) and (14), then the equalities (13) and (14) change into (8) and (9), respectively.*

Remark 4. *If we take* $\pi_1 = 0$ *and* $\varkappa = \pi_2 = 1$ *in (13), then we have*

$$\int_0^1 \Pi(\tau) \, {}_0d_{p,q}\tau = (p-q) \sum_{n=0}^{\infty} \frac{q^n}{p^{n+1}} \Pi\left(\frac{q^n}{p^{n+1}}\right).$$

Similarly, by taking $\varkappa = \pi_1 = 0$ *and* $\pi_2 = 1$ *in (14), then we obtain that*

$$\int_0^1 \Pi(\tau) \, {}^1d_{p,q}\tau = (p-q) \sum_{n=0}^{\infty} \frac{q^n}{p^{n+1}} \Pi\left(1 - \frac{q^n}{p^{n+1}}\right).$$

In [56], Kunt et al. proved the following H-H type inequalities for convex functions via the $(p,q)_{\pi_1}$-integral:

Theorem 2. *For a convex mapping* $\Pi : [\pi_1, \pi_2] \to \mathbb{R}$, *which is differentiable on* $[\pi_1, \pi_2]$, *the following inequalities hold for the* $(p,q)_{\pi_1}$-*integral:*

$$\Pi\left(\frac{q\pi_1 + p\pi_2}{[2]_{p,q}}\right) \leq \frac{1}{p(\pi_2 - \pi_1)} \int_{\pi_1}^{p\pi_2 + (1-p)\pi_1} \Pi(\varkappa) \, {}_{\pi_1}d_{p,q}\varkappa \leq \frac{q\Pi(\pi_1) + p\Pi(\pi_2)}{[2]_{p,q}} \tag{15}$$

where $0 < q < p \leq 1$.

Lemma 1 ([58]). *We have the following equalities:*

$$\int_{\pi_1}^{\pi_2} (\pi_2 - \varkappa)^\alpha \, {}^{\pi_2}d_{p,q}\varkappa = \frac{(\pi_2 - \pi_1)^{\alpha+1}}{[\alpha+1]_{p,q}}$$

$$\int_{\pi_1}^{\pi_2} (\varkappa - \pi_1)^\alpha \ _{\pi_1}d_{p,q}\varkappa = \frac{(\pi_2 - \pi_1)^{\alpha+1}}{[\alpha+1]_{p,q}}$$

where $\alpha \in \mathbb{R} - \{-1\}$.

4. New H-H Type Inequalities for Post-Quantum Integrals

We present a new variant of the (p,q)-H-H inequality for preinvex functions in this section. It is also demonstrated that the results presented here are a generalization of some previously published results. For brevity, we use $I = [\pi_2 + \eta(\pi_1, \pi_2), \pi_2]$ and $J = [\pi_1, \pi_1 + \eta(\pi_2, \pi_1)]$.

Theorem 3. *For a differentiable preinvex mapping $\Pi : I \to \mathbb{R}$, the following inequality holds for the $(p,q)^{\pi_2}$-integral:*

$$\Pi\left(\frac{p\eta(\pi_1, \pi_2) + [2]_{p,q}\pi_2}{[2]_{p,q}}\right) \leq \frac{1}{p\eta(\pi_2, \pi_1)} \int_{\pi_2 + p\eta(\pi_1, \pi_2)}^{\pi_2} \Pi(\varkappa) \ ^{\pi_2}d_{p,q}\varkappa$$
$$\leq \frac{p\Pi(\pi_2 + p\eta(\pi_1, \pi_2)) + q\Pi(\pi_2)}{[2]_{p,q}}, \quad (16)$$

where $0 < q < p \leq 1$.

Proof. For preinvex functions, we can use Jensen's inequality

$$\Pi\left(\frac{1}{p\eta(\pi_2, \pi_1)} \int_{\pi_2 + p\eta(\pi_1, \pi_2)}^{\pi_2} \varkappa \ ^{\pi_2}d_{p,q}\varkappa\right) \leq \frac{1}{p\eta(\pi_2, \pi_1)} \int_{\pi_2 + p\eta(\pi_1, \pi_2)}^{\pi_2} \Pi(\varkappa) \ ^{\pi_2}d_{p,q}\varkappa$$

and from the Definition 11, one can easily observe that

$$\frac{1}{p\eta(\pi_2, \pi_1)} \int_{\pi_2 + p\eta(\pi_1, \pi_2)}^{\pi_2} \varkappa \ ^{\pi_2}d_{p,q}\varkappa = \frac{p\eta(\pi_1, \pi_2) + [2]_{p,q}\pi_2}{[2]_{p,q}}.$$

Thus, the first part of the inequality (16) is proved. To prove the second inequality in (16), first, we note that Π is preinvex function and we have

$$\Pi(\pi_2 + t\eta(\pi_1, \pi_2)) \leq t\Pi(\pi_1) + (1-t)\Pi(\pi_2). \quad (17)$$

Applying the $(p,q)^{\pi_2}$-integral on the both sides of (17), we have

$$\frac{1}{p\eta(\pi_2, \pi_1)} \int_{\pi_2 + p\eta(\pi_1, \pi_2)}^{\pi_2} \Pi(\varkappa) \ ^{\pi_2}d_{p,q}\varkappa \leq \frac{p\Pi(\pi_2 + p\eta(\pi_1, \pi_2)) + q\Pi(\pi_2)}{[2]_{p,q}}.$$

Hence, the proof is completed. □

Remark 5. *We obtain Theorem 5 in [59], by letting $p = 1$ in Theorem 3.*

Remark 6. *If we set $p = 1$ in Theorem 3 and later assume that $\eta(\pi_2, \pi_1) = -\eta(\pi_1, \pi_2) = \pi_2 - \pi_1$, then Theorem 3 becomes Theorem 12 in [33].*

Example 1. *Let $\Pi(\varkappa) = -|\varkappa|$. Then, Π is preinvex function with respect to the following bifunction:*

$$\eta(\varkappa, y) = \begin{cases} \varkappa - y, & \text{if } \varkappa y \geq 0 \\ y - \varkappa, & \text{if } \varkappa y \leq 0. \end{cases}$$

1. Let us consider $\pi_1, \pi_2 > 0$, then $\eta(\pi_1, \pi_2) = \pi_1 - \pi_2$ and

$$\Pi\left(\frac{p\eta(\pi_1, \pi_2) + [2]_{p,q}\pi_2}{[2]_{p,q}}\right) = -\frac{p\pi_1 + q\pi_2}{[2]_{p,q}},$$

$$\frac{1}{p\eta(\pi_2, \pi_1)}\int_{\pi_2+p\eta(\pi_1,\pi_2)}^{\pi_2} \Pi(\varkappa)\,^{\pi_2}d_{p,q}\varkappa = -\frac{p\pi_1 + q\pi_2}{[2]_{p,q}}$$

and

$$\frac{p\Pi(\pi_2 + p\eta(\pi_1, \pi_2)) + q\Pi(\pi_2)}{[2]_{p,q}} = -\frac{p\pi_1 + q\pi_2}{[2]_{p,q}}.$$

2. Let $\pi_1, \pi_2 < 0$. Then, $\eta(\pi_1, \pi_2) = \pi_1 - \pi_2$ and

$$\Pi\left(\frac{p\eta(\pi_1, \pi_2) + [2]_{p,q}\pi_2}{[2]_{p,q}}\right) = \frac{p\pi_1 + q\pi_2}{[2]_{p,q}},$$

$$\frac{1}{p\eta(\pi_2, \pi_1)}\int_{\pi_2+p\eta(\pi_1,\pi_2)}^{\pi_2} \Pi(\varkappa)\,^{\pi_2}d_{p,q}\varkappa = \frac{p\pi_1 + q\pi_2}{[2]_{p,q}}$$

and

$$\frac{p\Pi(\pi_2 + p\eta(\pi_1, \pi_2)) + q\Pi(\pi_2)}{[2]_{p,q}} = -\frac{p\pi_1 + q\pi_2}{[2]_{p,q}}.$$

3. Finally, let $\pi_1 < 0 < \pi_2$. Then, $\eta(\pi_1, \pi_2) = \pi_2 - \pi_1$ and

$$\Pi\left(\frac{p\eta(\pi_1, \pi_2) + [2]_{p,q}\pi_2}{[2]_{p,q}}\right) = -\frac{(2p+q)\pi_2 - p\pi_1}{[2]_{p,q}},$$

$$\frac{1}{p\eta(\pi_2, \pi_1)}\int_{\pi_2+p\eta(\pi_1,\pi_2)}^{\pi_2} \Pi(\varkappa)\,^{\pi_2}d_{p,q}\varkappa = -\frac{(2p+q)\pi_2 - p\pi_1}{[2]_{p,q}}$$

and

$$\frac{p\Pi(\pi_2 + p\eta(\pi_1, \pi_2)) + q\Pi(\pi_2)}{[2]_{p,q}} = -\frac{(2p+q)\pi_2 - p\pi_1}{[2]_{p,q}}.$$

It is clear that the Theorem 3 is valid.

Theorem 4. *For a differentiable preinvex mapping $\Pi : J \to \mathbb{R}$, the following inequality holds for $(p,q)_{\pi_1}$-integral:*

$$\Pi\left(\frac{p\eta(\pi_2, \pi_1) + [2]_{p,q}\pi_1}{[2]_{p,q}}\right) \leq \frac{1}{p\eta(\pi_2, \pi_1)}\int_{\pi_1}^{\pi_1+p\eta(\pi_2,\pi_1)} \Pi(\varkappa)\,_{\pi_1}d_{p,q}\varkappa$$
$$\leq \frac{p\Pi(\pi_1) + q\Pi(\pi_1 + \eta(\pi_2, \pi_1))}{[2]_{p,q}}, \qquad (18)$$

where $0 < q < p \leq 1$.

Proof. One can easily obtain the inequality (18) by following the methodology used in the proof of Theorem 3 and taking into account Definition 10 of the $(p,q)_{\pi_1}$-integral. □

Remark 7. *We obtain Theorem 6 in [59] by letting $p = 1$ in Theorem 4.*

Remark 8. *If we set $p = 1$ in Theorem 4 and later assume that $\eta(\pi_2, \pi_1) = \pi_2 - \pi_1$, then Theorem 4 reduces to Theorem 6 in [39].*

5. Midpoint Type Inequalities through $(p,q)^{\pi_2}$-Integral

We present some new midpoint type inequalities using the (p,q)-derivative and integral in this section.

The following crucial lemma is required to prove the main results of this section.

Lemma 2. *Let* $\Pi : I \to \mathbb{R}$ *be a differentiable function on* I°. *If* $^{\pi_2}D_{p,q}\Pi$ *is continuous and integrable on* I, *then we have the following identity:*

$$\eta(\pi_2,\pi_1)\left[\int_0^{\frac{p}{[2]_{p,q}}} qt\,^{\pi_2}D_{p,q}\Pi(t(\pi_2+\eta(\pi_1,\pi_2))+(1-t)\pi_2)d_{p,q}t\right.$$

$$\left.+\int_{\frac{p}{[2]_{p,q}}}^1 (qt-1)\,^{\pi_2}D_{p,q}\Pi(t(\pi_2+\eta(\pi_1,\pi_2))+(1-t)\pi_2)d_{p,q}t\right]$$

$$=\frac{1}{p\eta(\pi_2,\pi_1)}\int_{\pi_2+p\eta(\pi_1,\pi_2)}^{\pi_2}\Pi(\varkappa)\,^{\pi_2}d_{p,q}\varkappa-\Pi\left(\frac{p\eta(\pi_1,\pi_2)+[2]_{p,q}\pi_2}{[2]_{p,q}}\right), \quad (19)$$

where $0 < q < p \leq 1$.

Proof. From Definition 9, we have

$$^{\pi_2}D_{p,q}\Pi(t(\pi_2+\eta(\pi_1,\pi_2))+(1-t)\pi_2)$$
$$=\frac{\Pi(qt(\pi_2+\eta(\pi_1,\pi_2))+(1-qt)\pi_2)-\Pi(pt(\pi_2+\eta(\pi_1,\pi_2))+(1-pt)\pi_2)}{t\eta(\pi_2,\pi_1)(p-q)}. \quad (20)$$

From the left side of equality (19), we have

$$\eta(\pi_2,\pi_1)\left[\int_0^{\frac{p}{[2]_{p,q}}} qt\,^{\pi_2}D_{p,q}\Pi(t(\pi_2+\eta(\pi_1,\pi_2))+(1-t)\pi_2)d_{p,q}t\right.$$

$$\left.+\int_{\frac{p}{[2]_{p,q}}}^1 (qt-1)\,^{\pi_2}D_{p,q}\Pi(t(\pi_2+\eta(\pi_1,\pi_2))+(1-t)\pi_2)d_{p,q}t\right]$$

$$=\eta(\pi_2,\pi_1)\left[\int_0^{\frac{p}{[2]_{p,q}}}\,^{\pi_2}D_{p,q}\Pi(t(\pi_2+\eta(\pi_1,\pi_2))+(1-t)\pi_2)d_{p,q}t\right.$$

$$+\int_0^1 qt\,^{\pi_2}D_{p,q}\Pi(t(\pi_2+\eta(\pi_1,\pi_2))+(1-t)\pi_2)d_{p,q}t$$

$$\left.-\int_0^1\,^{\pi_2}D_{p,q}\Pi(t(\pi_2+\eta(\pi_1,\pi_2))+(1-t)\pi_2)d_{p,q}t\right]. \quad (21)$$

By the equality (14), we have

$$\int_0^{\frac{p}{[2]_{p,q}}}\,^{\pi_2}D_{p,q}\Pi(t(\pi_2+\eta(\pi_1,\pi_2))+(1-t)\pi_2)d_{p,q}t$$

$$=\frac{1}{\eta(\pi_2,\pi_1)(p-q)}\int_0^{\frac{p}{[2]_{p,q}}}\frac{\Pi(qt(\pi_2+\eta(\pi_1,\pi_2))+(1-qt)\pi_2)}{t}d_{p,q}t$$

$$=\frac{1}{\eta(\pi_2,\pi_1)}\left[\sum_{n=0}^\infty \Pi\left(\frac{p}{[2]_{p,q}}\frac{q^{n+1}}{p^{n+1}}(\pi_2+\eta(\pi_1,\pi_2))+\left(1-\frac{p}{[2]_{p,q}}\frac{q^{n+1}}{p^{n+1}}\right)\pi_2\right)\right.$$

$$\left.-\sum_{n=0}^\infty \Pi\left(\frac{p}{[2]_{p,q}}\frac{q^n}{p^n}(\pi_2+\eta(\pi_1,\pi_2))+\left(1-\frac{p}{[2]_{p,q}}\frac{q^n}{p^n}\right)\pi_2\right)\right]$$

$$= \frac{\Pi(\pi_2)}{\eta(\pi_2,\pi_1)} - \frac{1}{\eta(\pi_2,\pi_1)}\Pi\left(\frac{p\eta(\pi_1,\pi_2)+[2]_{p,q}\pi_2}{[2]_{p,q}}\right), \qquad (22)$$

$$\int_0^1 {}^{\pi_2}D_{p,q}\Pi(t(\pi_2+\eta(\pi_1,\pi_2))+(1-t)\pi_2)d_{p,q}t$$

$$= \frac{1}{\eta(\pi_2,\pi_1)(p-q)}\int_0^1 \frac{\Pi(qt(\pi_2+\eta(\pi_1,\pi_2))+(1-qt)\pi_2)}{t} d_{p,q}t$$

$$= \frac{1}{\eta(\pi_2,\pi_1)}\left[\begin{array}{l}\sum_{n=0}^{\infty}\Pi\left(\frac{q^{n+1}}{p^{n+1}}(\pi_2+\eta(\pi_1,\pi_2))+\left(1-\frac{q^{n+1}}{p^{n+1}}\right)\pi_2\right)\\ -\sum_{n=0}^{\infty}\Pi\left(\frac{q^n}{p^n}(\pi_2+\eta(\pi_1,\pi_2))+\left(1-\frac{q^n}{p^n}\right)\pi_2\right)\end{array}\right]$$

$$= \frac{\Pi(\pi_2)-\Pi(\pi_2+\eta(\pi_1,\pi_2))}{\eta(\pi_2,\pi_1)} \qquad (23)$$

and

$$\int_0^1 t\,{}^{\pi_2}D_{p,q}\Pi(t(\pi_2+\eta(\pi_1,\pi_2))+(1-t)\pi_2)d_{p,q}t$$

$$= \frac{1}{\eta(\pi_2,\pi_1)(p-q)}\int_0^1\left[\begin{array}{l}\Pi(qt(\pi_2+\eta(\pi_1,\pi_2))+(1-qt)\pi_2)\\ -\Pi(pt(\pi_2+\eta(\pi_1,\pi_2))+(1-pt)\pi_2)\end{array}\right]d_{p,q}t$$

$$= \frac{1}{\eta(\pi_2,\pi_1)}\left[\begin{array}{l}\sum_{n=0}^{\infty}\frac{q^n}{p^{n+1}}\Pi\left(\frac{q^{n+1}}{p^{n+1}}(\pi_2+\eta(\pi_1,\pi_2))+\left(1-\frac{q^{n+1}}{p^{n+1}}\right)\pi_2\right)\\ -\sum_{n=0}^{\infty}\frac{q^n}{p^{n+1}}\Pi\left(\frac{q^n}{p^n}(\pi_2+\eta(\pi_1,\pi_2))+\left(1-\frac{q^n}{p^n}\right)\pi_2\right)\end{array}\right]$$

$$= \frac{1}{\eta(\pi_2,\pi_1)}\left[\begin{array}{l}\frac{1}{q}\sum_{n=0}^{\infty}\frac{q^{n+1}}{p^{n+1}}\Pi\left(\frac{q^{n+1}}{p^{n+1}}(\pi_2+\eta(\pi_1,\pi_2))+\left(1-\frac{q^{n+1}}{p^{n+1}}\right)\pi_2\right)\\ -\frac{1}{p}\sum_{n=0}^{\infty}\frac{q^n}{p^n}\Pi\left(\frac{q^n}{p^n}(\pi_2+\eta(\pi_1,\pi_2))+\left(1-\frac{q^n}{p^n}\right)\pi_2\right)\end{array}\right]$$

$$= \frac{1}{\eta(\pi_2,\pi_1)}\left[\begin{array}{l}\left(\frac{1}{q}-\frac{1}{p}\right)\sum_{n=0}^{\infty}\frac{q^n}{p^n}\Pi\left(\frac{q^n}{p^n}(\pi_2+\eta(\pi_1,\pi_2))+\left(1-\frac{q^n}{p^n}\right)\pi_2\right)\\ -\frac{1}{q}\Pi((\pi_2+\eta(\pi_1,\pi_2)))\end{array}\right]$$

$$= \frac{1}{\eta(\pi_2,\pi_1)}\left[\frac{p-q}{pq}\sum_{n=0}^{\infty}\frac{q^n}{p^n}\Pi\left(\frac{q^n}{p^n}(\pi_2+\eta(\pi_1,\pi_2))+\left(1-\frac{q^n}{p^n}\right)\pi_2\right)\right.$$
$$\left.-\frac{1}{q}\Pi(\pi_2+\eta(\pi_1,\pi_2))\right]$$

$$= \frac{1}{\eta(\pi_2,\pi_1)}\left[\frac{1}{pq\eta(\pi_2,\pi_1)}\int_{\pi_2+p\eta(\pi_1,\pi_2)}^{\pi_2}\Pi(\varkappa)\,{}^{\pi_2}d_{p,q}\varkappa-\frac{1}{q}\Pi(\pi_2+\eta(\pi_1,\pi_2))\right]. \qquad (24)$$

By using (22)–(24) in (21), we obtain the desired identity (19). Thus, the proof is completed. □

Remark 9. *We obtain Lemma 3 in [59] by letting $p=1$ in Lemma 2.*

Remark 10. *If we use $p=1$ in Lemma 2 and later consider $\eta(\pi_2,\pi_1)=-\eta(\pi_1,\pi_2)=\pi_2-\pi_1$, then Lemma 2 becomes Lemma 2 in [41].*

Theorem 5. *Suppose that the assumptions of Lemma 2 hold. If $\left|{}^{\pi_2}D_{p,q}\Pi\right|$ is a preinvex function over I, then we have the following new inequality:*

$$\left|\frac{1}{p\eta(\pi_2,\pi_1)}\int_{\pi_2+p\eta(\pi_1,\pi_2)}^{\pi_2}\Pi(\varkappa)\,{}^{\pi_2}d_{p,q}\varkappa - \Pi\left(\frac{p\eta(\pi_1,\pi_2)+[2]_{p,q}\pi_2}{[2]_{p,q}}\right)\right|$$
$$\leq \eta(\pi_2,\pi_1)\left[\left(\left|{}^{\pi_2}D_{p,q}\Pi(\pi_1)\right|A_1(p,q)+\left|{}^{\pi_2}D_{p,q}\Pi(\pi_2)\right|A_2(p,q)\right)\right.$$
$$\left.+\left(\left|{}^{\pi_2}D_{p,q}\Pi(\pi_1)\right|A_3(p,q)+\left|{}^{\pi_2}D_{p,q}\Pi(\pi_2)\right|A_4(p,q)\right)\right], \qquad (25)$$

where

$$A_1(p,q) = \frac{qp^3}{[2]_{p,q}^3[3]_{p,q}},$$

$$A_2(p,q) = \frac{q\left(p^3(p^2+q^2-p)+p^2[3]_{p,q}\right)}{[2]_{p,q}^4[3]_{p,q}},$$

$$A_3(p,q) = \frac{q(q+2p)}{[2]_{p,q}} - \frac{q^2(q^2+3p^2+3pq)}{[2]_{p,q}^3[3]_{p,q}},$$

$$A_4(p,q) = \frac{q}{[2]_{p,q}} - \frac{q^2(q+2p)}{[2]_{p,q}^4} - A_3(p,q).$$

Proof. Taking the modulus in Lemma 2 and using the preinvexity of $\left|{}^{\pi_2}D_{p,q}\Pi\right|$, we obtain that

$$\left|\frac{1}{p\eta(\pi_2,\pi_1)}\int_{\pi_2+p\eta(\pi_1,\pi_2)}^{\pi_2}\Pi(\varkappa)\,{}^{\pi_2}d_{p,q}\varkappa - \Pi\left(\frac{p\eta(\pi_1,\pi_2)+[2]_{p,q}\pi_2}{[2]_{p,q}}\right)\right|$$
$$\leq \eta(\pi_2,\pi_1)\left[\int_0^{\frac{p}{[2]_{p,q}}} qt\left|{}^{\pi_2}D_{p,q}\Pi(t(\pi_2+\eta(\pi_1,\pi_2))+(1-t)\pi_2)\right|d_{p,q}t\right.$$
$$+\int_{\frac{p}{[2]_{p,q}}}^1 (1-qt)\left|{}^{\pi_2}D_{p,q}\Pi(t(\pi_2+\eta(\pi_1,\pi_2))+(1-t)\pi_2)\right|d_{p,q}t\Bigg]$$
$$\leq \eta(\pi_2,\pi_1)\left[q\int_0^{\frac{p}{[2]_{p,q}}} t\left(t\left|{}^{\pi_2}D_{p,q}\Pi(\pi_1)\right|+(1-t)\left|{}^{\pi_2}D_{p,q}\Pi(\pi_2)\right|\right)d_{p,q}t\right.$$
$$+\int_{\frac{p}{[2]_{p,q}}}^1 (1-qt)\left(t\left|{}^{\pi_2}D_{p,q}\Pi(\pi_1)\right|+(1-t)\left|{}^{\pi_2}D_{p,q}\Pi(\pi_2)\right|\right)d_{p,q}t\Bigg]. \qquad (26)$$

One can easily compute the integrals that appeared on the right side of the inequality (26)

$$\int_0^{\frac{p}{[2]_{p,q}}} t^2\,d_{p,q}t = \frac{p^3}{[2]_{p,q}^3[3]_{p,q}}, \qquad (27)$$

$$\int_0^{\frac{p}{[2]_{p,q}}} t(1-t)\,d_{p,q}t = \frac{p^3(p^2+q^2-p)+p^2[3]_{p,q}}{[2]_{p,q}^4[3]_{p,q}}, \qquad (28)$$

$$\int_{\frac{p}{[2]_{p,q}}}^1 t(1-qt)\,d_{p,q}t = \frac{q(q+2p)}{[2]_{p,q}} - \frac{q^2(q^2+3p^2+3pq)}{[2]_{p,q}^3[3]_{p,q}}, \qquad (29)$$

$$\int_{\frac{p}{[2]_{p,q}}}^1 (1-t)(1-qt)\,d_{p,q}t = \frac{q}{[2]_{p,q}} - \frac{q^2(q+2p)}{[2]_{p,q}^3}$$

$$-\left(\frac{q(q+2p)}{[2]_{p,q}} - \frac{q^2(q^2+3p^2+3pq)}{[2]_{p,q}^3[3]_{p,q}}\right). \tag{30}$$

Making use of (27)–(30) in (26), gives us the required inequality (25). Hence, the proof is finished. □

Remark 11. *We obtain Theorem 9 in [59] by letting $p = 1$ in Theorem 5.*

Remark 12. *If we take $p = 1$ in Theorem 5 and later consider $\eta(\pi_2, \pi_1) = -\eta(\pi_1, \pi_2) = \pi_2 - \pi_1$, then Theorem 5 reduces to Theorem 5 in [41].*

Theorem 6. *Suppose that the assumptions of Lemma 2 hold. If $\left|{}^{\pi_2}D_{p,q}\Pi\right|^r, r \geq 1$ is a preinvex function over I, then we have the following new inequality:*

$$\left|\frac{1}{p\eta(\pi_2,\pi_1)}\int_{\pi_2+p\eta(\pi_1,\pi_2)}^{\pi_2}\Pi(\varkappa)\,{}^{\pi_2}d_{p,q}\varkappa - \Pi\left(\frac{p\eta(\pi_1,\pi_2)+[2]_{p,q}\pi_2}{[2]_{p,q}}\right)\right|$$

$$\leq \eta(\pi_2,\pi_1)\left(\frac{p^2}{([2]_{p,q})^3}\right)^{1-\frac{1}{r}}\left[\left\{\left|{}^{\pi_2}D_{p,q}\Pi(\pi_1)\right|^r A_1(p,q) + \left|{}^{\pi_2}D_{p,q}\Pi(\pi_2)\right|^r A_2(p,q)\right\}^{\frac{1}{r}}\right.$$

$$\left.+\left\{\left|{}^{\pi_2}D_{p,q}\Pi(\pi_1)\right|^r A_3(p,q) + \left|{}^{\pi_2}D_{p,q}\Pi(\pi_2)\right|^r A_4(p,q)\right\}^{\frac{1}{r}}\right], \tag{31}$$

where $A_1(p,q) - A_4(p,q)$ are given in Theorem 5.

Proof. Taking the modulus in Lemma 2, applying the well-known power mean inequality for (p,q)-integrals and the preinvexity of $\left|{}^{\pi_2}D_{p,q}\Pi\right|^r, r \geq 1$, we have

$$\left|\frac{1}{p\eta(\pi_2,\pi_1)}\int_{\pi_2+p\eta(\pi_1,\pi_2)}^{\pi_2}\Pi(\varkappa)\,{}^{\pi_2}d_{p,q}\varkappa - \Pi\left(\frac{p\eta(\pi_1,\pi_2)+[2]_{p,q}\pi_2}{[2]_{p,q}}\right)\right|$$

$$\leq \eta(\pi_2,\pi_1)\left[\int_0^{\frac{p}{[2]_{p,q}}} qt\left|{}^{\pi_2}D_{p,q}\Pi(t(\pi_2+\eta(\pi_1,\pi_2))+(1-t)\pi_2)\right|d_{p,q}t\right.$$

$$\left.+\int_{\frac{p}{[2]_{p,q}}}^1 (1-qt)\left|{}^{\pi_2}D_{p,q}\Pi(t(\pi_2+\eta(\pi_1,\pi_2))+(1-t)\pi_2)\right|d_{p,q}t\right]$$

$$\leq \eta(\pi_2,\pi_1)\left[\left(\int_0^{\frac{p}{[2]_{p,q}}} qt\,d_{p,q}t\right)^{1-\frac{1}{r}}\right.$$

$$\times\left\{q\int_0^{\frac{p}{[2]_{p,q}}} t\left(t\left|{}^{\pi_2}D_{p,q}\Pi(\pi_1)\right|^r + (1-t)\left|{}^{\pi_2}D_{p,q}\Pi(\pi_2)\right|^r\right)d_{p,q}t\right\}^{\frac{1}{r}}$$

$$+\left(\int_{\frac{p}{[2]_{p,q}}}^1 (1-qt)d_{p,q}t\right)^{1-\frac{1}{r}}$$

$$\left.\times\left\{q\int_{\frac{p}{[2]_{p,q}}}^1 (1-qt)\left(t\left|{}^{\pi_2}D_{p,q}\Pi(\pi_1)\right|^r + (1-t)\left|{}^{\pi_2}D_{p,q}\Pi(\pi_2)\right|^r\right)d_{p,q}t\right\}^{\frac{1}{r}}\right]$$

$$= \eta(\pi_2,\pi_1)\left(\frac{p^2}{([2]_{p,q})^3}\right)^{1-\frac{1}{r}}\left[\left\{\left|{}^{\pi_2}D_{p,q}\Pi(\pi_1)\right|^r A_1(p,q) + \left|{}^{\pi_2}D_{p,q}\Pi(\pi_2)\right|^r A_2(p,q)\right\}^{\frac{1}{r}}\right.$$

$$+\left\{|^{\pi_2}D_{p,q}\Pi(\pi_1)|^r A_3(p,q)+|^{\pi_2}D_{p,q}\Pi(\pi_2)|^r A_4(p,q)\right\}^{\frac{1}{r}}\right]$$

which completes the proof. □

Remark 13. *We obtain Theorem 10 in [59] by letting $p=1$ in Theorem 6.*

Remark 14. *If we put $p=1$ in Theorem 6 and later assume that $\eta(\pi_2,\pi_1)=-\eta(\pi_1,\pi_2)=\pi_2-\pi_1$, then Theorem 6 reduces to Theorem 6 in [41].*

Theorem 7. *Suppose that the assumptions of Lemma 2 hold. If $|^{\pi_2}D_{p,q}\Pi|^r$, $r > 1$ is a preinvex function over I, then we have the following new inequality:*

$$\left|\frac{1}{p\eta(\pi_2,\pi_1)}\int_{\pi_2+p\eta(\pi_1,\pi_2)}^{\pi_2}\Pi(\varkappa)\,^{\pi_2}d_{p,q}\varkappa-\Pi\left(\frac{p\eta(\pi_1,\pi_2)+[2]_{p,q}\pi_2}{[2]_{p,q}}\right)\right|$$

$$\leq q\eta(\pi_2,\pi_1)\left[\left(\left(\frac{p}{[2]_{p,q}}\right)^{s+1}\left(\frac{p-q}{p^{s+1}-q^{s+1}}\right)\right)^{\frac{1}{s}}\left\{\begin{array}{c}|^{\pi_2}D_{p,q}\Pi(\pi_1)|^r\left(\frac{p^2}{[2]_{p,q}^3}\right)\\+|^{\pi_2}D_{p,q}\Pi(\pi_2)|^r\left(\frac{p^3+pq^2+2p^2q-p^2}{[2]_{p,q}^3}\right)\end{array}\right\}^{\frac{1}{r}}\right.$$

$$+\left(\int_{\frac{p}{[2]_{p,q}}}^{1}\left(\frac{1}{q}-t\right)^s d_{p,q}t\right)^{\frac{1}{s}}\left\{\begin{array}{c}|^{\pi_2}D_{p,q}\Pi(\pi_1)|^r\left(\frac{[2]_{p,q}-p^2}{[2]_{p,q}^3}\right)\\+|^{\pi_2}D_{p,q}\Pi(\pi_2)|^r\left(\frac{q[2]_{p,q}^2+p^2-p-q}{[2]_{p,q}^3}\right)\end{array}\right\}^{\frac{1}{r}}\right], \quad (32)$$

where $s+r=sr$.

Proof. Taking the modulus in Lemma 2, by applying the well-known Hölder inequality for definite (p,q)-integrals and the preinvexity of $|^{\pi_2}D_{p,q}\Pi|^r$, $r > 1$, we obtain that

$$\left|\frac{1}{p\eta(\pi_2,\pi_1)}\int_{\pi_2+p\eta(\pi_1,\pi_2)}^{\pi_2}\Pi(\varkappa)\,^{\pi_2}d_{p,q}\varkappa-\Pi\left(\frac{p\eta(\pi_1,\pi_2)+[2]_{p,q}\pi_2}{[2]_{p,q}}\right)\right|$$

$$\leq q\eta(\pi_2,\pi_1)\left[\int_0^{\frac{p}{[2]_{p,q}}}t\,|^{\pi_2}D_{p,q}\Pi(t(\pi_2+\eta(\pi_1,\pi_2))+(1-t)\pi_2)|d_{p,q}t\right.$$

$$\left.+\int_{\frac{p}{[2]_{p,q}}}^{1}\left(\frac{1}{q}-t\right)|^{\pi_2}D_{p,q}\Pi(t(\pi_2+\eta(\pi_1,\pi_2))+(1-t)\pi_2)|d_{p,q}t\right]$$

$$\leq q\eta(\pi_2,\pi_1)\left[\left(\int_0^{\frac{p}{[2]_{p,q}}}t^s d_{p,q}t\right)^{\frac{1}{s}}\right.$$

$$\left\{\int_0^{\frac{p}{[2]_{p,q}}}\left(t|^{\pi_2}D_{p,q}\Pi(\pi_1)|^r+(1-t)|^{\pi_2}D_{p,q}\Pi(\pi_2)|^r\right)d_{p,q}t\right\}^{\frac{1}{r}}$$

$$+\left(\int_{\frac{p}{[2]_{p,q}}}^{1}\left(\frac{1}{q}-t\right)^s d_{p,q}t\right)^{\frac{1}{s}}$$

$$\left.\times\left\{\int_{\frac{p}{[2]_{p,q}}}^{1}\left(t|^{\pi_2}D_{p,q}\Pi(\pi_1)|^r+(1-t)|^{\pi_2}D_{p,q}\Pi(\pi_2)|^r\right)d_{p,q}t\right\}^{\frac{1}{r}}\right]. \quad (33)$$

One can easily evaluate the integrals that appear on the right side of the inequality (33)

$$\left(\int_0^{\frac{p}{[2]_{p,q}}} t^s \, d_{p,q}t\right)^{\frac{1}{s}} = \left(\left(\frac{p}{[2]_{p,q}}\right)^{s+1}\left(\frac{p-q}{p^{s+1}-q^{s+1}}\right)\right)^{\frac{1}{s}} \tag{34}$$

$$\int_0^{\frac{p}{[2]_{p,q}}} t \, d_{p,q}t = \frac{p^2}{[2]_{p,q}^3}, \tag{35}$$

$$\int_0^{\frac{p}{[2]_{p,q}}} (1-t) \, d_{p,q}t = \frac{p^3 + pq^2 + 2p^2q - p^2}{[2]_{p,q}^3}, \tag{36}$$

$$\int_{\frac{p}{[2]_{p,q}}}^1 t \, d_{p,q}t = \frac{[2]_{p,q} - p^2}{[2]_{p,q}^3}, \tag{37}$$

$$\int_{\frac{p}{[2]_{p,q}}}^1 (1-t) \, d_{p,q}t = \frac{q[2]_{p,q}^2 + p^2 - p - q}{[2]_{p,q}^3}. \tag{38}$$

Making use of (34)–(38), gives us the required inequality (32). Hence, the proof is accomplished. □

6. Trapezoidal Type Inequalities through $(p,q)^{\pi_2}$-Integral

In this section, we give some new trapezoidal inequalities by using the (p,q)-derivative and integral.

To prove the main results of this section, we need the following crucial lemma.

Lemma 3. *Let $\Pi : I \to \mathbb{R}$ be a differentiable function on I°. If $^{\pi_2}D_{p,q}\Pi$ is continuous and integrable on I, then we have the following identity:*

$$\frac{p\Pi(\pi_2 + p\eta(\pi_1, \pi_2)) + q\Pi(\pi_2)}{[2]_{p,q}} - \frac{1}{p\eta(\pi_2, \pi_1)} \int_{\pi_2+p\eta(\pi_1,\pi_2)}^{\pi_2} \Pi(\varkappa) \, ^{\pi_2}d_{p,q}\varkappa$$

$$= \frac{q\eta(\pi_2, \pi_1)}{[2]_{p,q}} \int_0^1 \left(1 - [2]_{p,q}t\right) {}^{\pi_2}D_{p,q}\Pi(t(\pi_2 + \eta(\pi_1, \pi_2)) + (1-t)\pi_2) \, d_{p,q}t, \tag{39}$$

where $0 < q < p \leq 1$.

Proof. From (20) and the right side of (39), we obtain that

$$\frac{q\eta(\pi_2, \pi_1)}{[2]_{p,q}} \int_0^1 \left(1 - [2]_{p,q}t\right) {}^{\pi_2}D_{p,q}\Pi(t(\pi_2 + \eta(\pi_1, \pi_2)) + (1-t)\pi_2) \, d_{p,q}t$$

$$= \frac{q\eta(\pi_2, \pi_1)}{[2]_{p,q}} \left[\frac{1}{\eta(\pi_2, \pi_1)(p-q)} \int_0^1 \frac{\Pi(qt(\pi_2 + \eta(\pi_1, \pi_2)) + (1-qt)\pi_2) - \Pi(pt(\pi_2 + \eta(\pi_1, \pi_2)) + (1-pt)\pi_2)}{t} \, d_{p,q}t \right.$$

$$\left. - \frac{[2]_{p,q}}{\eta(\pi_2, \pi_1)(p-q)} \int_0^1 \left[\Pi(qt(\pi_2 + \eta(\pi_1, \pi_2)) + (1-qt)\pi_2) - \Pi(pt(\pi_2 + \eta(\pi_1, \pi_2)) + (1-pt)\pi_2) \right] d_{p,q}t \right].$$

From (23) and (24), we have

$$\frac{q\eta(\pi_2, \pi_1)}{[2]_{p,q}} \int_0^1 \left(1 - [2]_{p,q}t\right) {}^{\pi_2}D_{p,q}\Pi(t(\pi_2 + \eta(\pi_1, \pi_2)) + (1-t)\pi_2) \, d_{p,q}t$$

$$= \frac{q\eta(\pi_2,\pi_1)}{[2]_{p,q}} \left[\frac{\Pi(\pi_2) - \Pi(\pi_2 + \eta(\pi_1,\pi_2))}{\eta(\pi_2,\pi_1)} - \frac{[2]_{p,q}}{\eta(\pi_2,\pi_1)} \left\{ \frac{1}{pq\eta(\pi_2,\pi_1)} \int_{\pi_2+p\eta(\pi_1,\pi_2)}^{\pi_2} \Pi(\varkappa) \,^{\pi_2}d_{p,q}\varkappa - \frac{1}{q}\Pi(\pi_2 + \eta(\pi_1,\pi_2)) \right\} \right]$$

where the identity (39) is obtained and the proof is accomplished. □

Remark 15. We obtain Lemma 2 in [59] by letting $p = 1$ in Lemma 3.

Remark 16. If we adopt $p = 1$ in Lemma 3 and later we assume that $\eta(\pi_2, \pi_1) = -\eta(\pi_1, \pi_2) = \pi_2 - \pi_1$, then Lemma 3 becomes Lemma 1 in [41].

Theorem 8. Suppose that the assumptions of Lemma 3 hold. If $|\,^{\pi_2}D_{p,q}\Pi|$ is a preinvex function over I, then we have the following new inequality:

$$\left| \frac{p\Pi(\pi_2 + p\eta(\pi_1,\pi_2)) + q\Pi(\pi_2)}{[2]_{p,q}} - \frac{1}{p\eta(\pi_2,\pi_1)} \int_{\pi_2+p\eta(\pi_1,\pi_2)}^{\pi_2} \Pi(\varkappa) \,^{\pi_2}d_{p,q}\varkappa \right|$$
$$\leq \frac{q\eta(\pi_2,\pi_1)}{[2]_{p,q}} [|\,^{\pi_2}D_{p,q}\Pi(\pi_1)| A_5(p,q) + |\,^{\pi_2}D_{p,q}\Pi(\pi_2)| A_6(p,q)], \qquad (40)$$

where

$$A_5(p,q) = \int_0^1 t \left| \left(1 - [2]_{p,q}t\right) \right| d_{p,q}t,$$

$$A_6(p,q) = \int_0^1 (1-t) \left| \left(1 - [2]_{p,q}t\right) \right| d_{p,q}t.$$

Proof. Taking the modulus in Lemma 3 and using the preinvexity of $|\,^{\pi_2}D_{p,q}\Pi|$, we have

$$\left| \frac{p\Pi(\pi_2 + p\eta(\pi_1,\pi_2)) + q\Pi(\pi_2)}{[2]_{p,q}} - \frac{1}{p\eta(\pi_2,\pi_1)} \int_{\pi_2+p\eta(\pi_1,\pi_2)}^{\pi_2} \Pi(\varkappa) \,^{\pi_2}d_{p,q}\varkappa \right|$$
$$\leq \frac{q\eta(\pi_2,\pi_1)}{[2]_{p,q}} \int_0^1 t \left| \left(1 - [2]_{p,q}t\right) \right| |\,^{\pi_2}D_{p,q}\Pi(\pi_1)| \, d_{p,q}t$$
$$+ \int_0^1 (1-t) \left| \left(1 - [2]_{p,q}t\right) \right| |\,^{\pi_2}D_{p,q}\Pi(\pi_2)| \, d_{p,q}t$$
$$= \frac{q\eta(\pi_2,\pi_1)}{[2]_{p,q}} [|\,^{\pi_2}D_{p,q}\Pi(\pi_1)| A_5(p,q) + |\,^{\pi_2}D_{p,q}\Pi(\pi_2)| A_6(p,q)]. \qquad (41)$$

Thus, the proof is completed. □

Remark 17. We obtain Theorem 7 in [59] by letting $p = 1$ in Theorem 8.

Remark 18. If we adopt $p = 1$ in Theorem 8 and later we assume that $\eta(\pi_2, \pi_1) = -\eta(\pi_1, \pi_2) = \pi_2 - \pi_1$, then Theorem 8 becomes Theorem 7 in [41].

Theorem 9. Suppose that the assumptions of Lemma 3 hold. If $|\,^{\pi_2}D_{p,q}\Pi|^r$, $r \geq 1$ is a preinvex function over I, then we have the following new inequality:

$$\left| \frac{p\Pi(\pi_2 + p\eta(\pi_1,\pi_2)) + q\Pi(\pi_2)}{[2]_{p,q}} - \frac{1}{p\eta(\pi_2,\pi_1)} \int_{\pi_2+p\eta(\pi_1,\pi_2)}^{\pi_2} \Pi(\varkappa) \,^{\pi_2}d_{p,q}\varkappa \right|$$
$$\leq \frac{q\eta(\pi_2,\pi_1)}{[2]_{p,q}} \left(\int_0^1 |1 - [2]_{p,q}t| \, d_{p,q}t \right)^{1-\frac{1}{r}}$$
$$\times \left[|\,^{\pi_2}D_{p,q}\Pi(\pi_1)|^r A_5(p,q) + |\,^{\pi_2}D_{p,q}\Pi(\pi_2)|^r A_6(p,q) \right]^{\frac{1}{r}}, \qquad (42)$$

where $A_5(p,q)$ and $A_6(p,q)$ are given in Theorem 8.

Proof. Taking the modulus in Lemma 3 and applying the well-known power mean inequality for (p,q)-integrals and the preinvexity of $|{}^{\pi_2}D_{p,q}\Pi|^r, r \geq 1$, we obtain that

$$\left| \frac{p\Pi(\pi_2 + p\eta(\pi_1, \pi_2)) + q\Pi(\pi_2)}{[2]_{p,q}} - \frac{1}{p\eta(\pi_2, \pi_1)} \int_{\pi_2 + p\eta(\pi_1,\pi_2)}^{\pi_2} \Pi(\varkappa) \,{}^{\pi_2}d_{p,q}\varkappa \right|$$

$$\leq \frac{q\eta(\pi_2, \pi_1)}{[2]_{p,q}} \left(\int_0^1 \left|1 - [2]_{p,q}t\right| d_{p,q}t \right)^{1-\frac{1}{r}}$$

$$\times \left[\int_0^1 \left|1 - [2]_{p,q}t\right| \left|{}^{\pi_2}D_{p,q}\Pi(t(\pi_2 + \eta(\pi_1, \pi_2)) + (1-t)\pi_2)\right|^r d_{p,q}t \right]^{\frac{1}{r}}$$

$$\leq \frac{q\eta(\pi_2, \pi_1)}{[2]_{p,q}} \left(\int_0^1 \left|1 - [2]_{p,q}t\right| d_{p,q}t \right)^{1-\frac{1}{r}} \left[\int_0^1 t \left|\left(1 - [2]_{p,q}t\right)\right| \left|{}^{\pi_2}D_{p,q}\Pi(\pi_1)\right|^r d_{p,q}t \right.$$

$$\left. + \int_0^1 (1-t) \left|\left(1 - [2]_{p,q}t\right)\right| \left|{}^{\pi_2}D_{p,q}\Pi(\pi_2)\right|^r d_{p,q}t \right]^{\frac{1}{r}}$$

$$= \frac{q\eta(\pi_2, \pi_1)}{[2]_{p,q}} \left(\int_0^1 \left|1 - [2]_{p,q}t\right| d_{p,q}t \right)^{1-\frac{1}{r}}$$

$$\times \left[\left|{}^{\pi_2}D_{p,q}\Pi(\pi_1)\right|^r A_5(p,q) + \left|{}^{\pi_2}D_{p,q}\Pi(\pi_2)\right|^r A_6(p,q) \right]^{\frac{1}{r}}. \tag{43}$$

Thus, the proof is finished. □

Remark 19. We obtain Theorem 8 in [59] by letting $p = 1$ in Theorem 9.

Remark 20. If we adopt $p = 1$ in Theorem 9 and later we assume that $\eta(\pi_2, \pi_1) = -\eta(\pi_1, \pi_2) = \pi_2 - \pi_1$, then Theorem 9 becomes Theorem 4 in [41].

Theorem 10. Suppose that the assumptions of Lemma 3 hold. If $|{}^{\pi_2}D_{p,q}\Pi|^r, r > 1$ is a preinvex function over I, then we have the following new inequality:

$$\left| \frac{p\Pi(\pi_2 + p\eta(\pi_1, \pi_2)) + q\Pi(\pi_2)}{[2]_{p,q}} - \frac{1}{p\eta(\pi_2, \pi_1)} \int_{\pi_2 + p\eta(\pi_1,\pi_2)}^{\pi_2} \Pi(\varkappa) \,{}^{\pi_2}d_{p,q}\varkappa \right|$$

$$\leq \frac{q\eta(\pi_2, \pi_1)}{[2]_{p,q}} \left(\int_0^1 \left|1 - [2]_{p,q}t\right|^s d_{p,q}t \right)^{\frac{1}{s}} \left[\frac{\left|{}^{\pi_2}D_{p,q}\Pi(\pi_1)\right|^r + \left([2]_{p,q} - 1\right)\left|{}^{\pi_2}D_{p,q}\Pi(\pi_2)\right|^r}{[2]_{p,q}} \right]^{\frac{1}{r}}, \tag{44}$$

where $s + r = sr$.

Proof. Taking the modulus in Lemma 3 and applying the well-known Hölder inequality for (p,q)-integrals and the preinvexity of $|{}^{\pi_2}D_{p,q}\Pi|^r, r > 1$, we obtain that

$$\left| \frac{p\Pi(\pi_2 + p\eta(\pi_1, \pi_2)) + q\Pi(\pi_2)}{[2]_{p,q}} - \frac{1}{p\eta(\pi_2, \pi_1)} \int_{\pi_2 + p\eta(\pi_1,\pi_2)}^{\pi_2} \Pi(\varkappa) \,{}^{\pi_2}d_{p,q}\varkappa \right|$$

$$\leq \frac{q\eta(\pi_2, \pi_1)}{[2]_{p,q}} \left(\int_0^1 \left|1 - [2]_{p,q}t\right|^s d_{p,q}t \right)^{\frac{1}{s}}$$

$$\times \left[\int_0^1 \left|{}^{\pi_2}D_{p,q}\Pi(t(\pi_2 + \eta(\pi_1, \pi_2)) + (1-t)\pi_2)\right|^r d_{p,q}t \right]^{\frac{1}{r}}$$

$$\leq \frac{q\eta(\pi_2,\pi_1)}{[2]_{p,q}} \left(\int_0^1 \left|1-[2]_{p,q}t\right|^s d_{p,q}t \right)^{\frac{1}{s}}$$
$$\times \left[\int_0^1 t \left|{}^{\pi_2}D_{p,q}\Pi(\pi_1)\right|^r d_{p,q}t + \int_0^1 (1-t) \left|{}^{\pi_2}D_{p,q}\Pi(\pi_2)\right|^r d_{p,q}t \right]^{\frac{1}{r}}. \quad (45)$$

We can calculate the integrals that occur on the right side of (45) as follows:

$$\int_0^1 t\, d_{p,q}t = \frac{1}{[2]_{p,q}}, \quad (46)$$

$$\int_0^1 (1-t)\, d_{p,q}t = \frac{[2]_{p,q}-1}{[2]_{p,q}}. \quad (47)$$

Making use of (46) and (47) in (45), gives the desired result. Hence, the proof is completed. □

Remark 21. *The left-right estimates of inequality (18) given in Theorem 4 that we left for the readers can be obtained by using the notions of $(p,q)_{\pi_1}$-derivative and integral, as well as the techniques used in the previous two sections.*

7. Conclusions

In this paper, we proved H-H type inequalities for preinvex functions using the (p,q)-calculus setup. For (p,q)-differentiable preinvex functions, we also proved some new midpoint-formula-type and trapezoid-formula-type inequalities. Furthermore, we demonstrated that the newly discovered inequalities are generalizations of the inequalities for convex functions in (p,q)-calculus. This study's conclusions can be used in symmetry. The results for symmetric functions can be reached by employing the notions of symmetric convex functions, which will be explored further in future work. It is an intriguing and novel problem, and future researchers will be able to obtain similar inequalities for co-ordinated preinvex functions in their studies.

Author Contributions: Conceptualization, I.B.S., M.A.A., G.M., S.K.N., J.S. and T.S.; methodology, I.B.S., M.A.A., G.M., S.K.N., J.S. and T.S.; formal analysis, I.B.S., M.A.A., G.M., S.K.N., J.S. and T.S. All authors have read and agreed to the published version of the manuscript.

Funding: This research was funded by King Mongkut's University of Technology North Bangkok. Contract no. KMUTNB-63-KNOW-21.

Institutional Review Board Statement: Not applicable.

Informed Consent Statement: Not applicable.

Acknowledgments: We thank the referees for their valuable comments.

Conflicts of Interest: The authors declare no conflict of interest.

References

1. Ali, M.A.; Valdes, J.E.N.; Kashuri, A.; Zhang, Z. Fractional non conformable Hermite-Hadamard inequalities for generalized φ-convex functions. *Fasc. Math.* **2020**, *64*, 5–16.
2. Dragomir, S.S.; Pearce, C.E.M. *Selected Topics on Hermite-Hadamard Inequalities and Applications*; RGMIA Monographs; Victoria University: Melbourne, VIC, Australia, 2000.
3. Vivas-Cortez, M.; Korus, P.; Napoles Valdes, J.E. Some generalized Hermite-Hadamard-Fejer inequality for convex functions. *Adv. Differ. Equ.* **2021**, *2021*, 199. [CrossRef]
4. Pečarić, J.E.; Proschan, F.; Tong, Y.L. *Convex Functions, Partial Orderings and Statistical Applications*; Academic Press: Boston, MA, USA, 1992.
5. Napoles Valdes, J.E.; Rabossi, F.; Samaniego, A.D. Convex functions: Ariadne's thread or Charlotte's spiderweb? *Adv. Math. Model. Appl.* **2020**, *5*, 176–191.
6. Hanson, M.A. On sufficiency of the Kuhn-Tucker conditions. *J. Math. Anal. Appl.* **1981**, *80*, 545–550. [CrossRef]
7. Weir, T.; Mond, B. Preinvex functions in multiple objective optimization. *J. Math. Anal. Appl.* **1998**, *136*, 29–38. [CrossRef]

8. Pini, R. Invexity and generalized convexity. *Optimization* **1991**, *22*, 513–525. [CrossRef]
9. Mohan, S.R.; Neogy, S.K. On invex sets and preinvex functions. *J. Math. Anal. Appl.* **1995**, *189*, 901–908. [CrossRef]
10. Noor, M.A. Some new classes of nonconvex functions. *Nonlinear Funct. Anal. Appl.* **2006**, *11*, 165–171.
11. Noor, M.A. On Hadamard integral inequalities invoving two log-preinvex functions. *J. Inequal. Pure Appl. Math.* **2007**, *8*, 1–6.
12. Noor, M.A. Hadamard integral inequalities for product of two preinvex function. *Nonlinear Anal. Forum* **2009**, *14*, 167–173.
13. Barani, A.; Ghazanfari, A.G.; Dragomir, S.S. Hermite-Hadamard inequality for functions whose derivatives absolute values are preinvex. *RGMIA Res. Rep. Coll.* **2011**, *14*, 64. [CrossRef]
14. İşcan, İ. Hermite-Hadamard's inequalities for preinvex function via fractional integrals and related fractional inequalities. *Am. J. Mat. Anal.* **2013**, *1*, 33–38.
15. Awan, M.U.; Talib, S.; Noor, M.A.; Chu, Y.-M.; Noor, K.I. Some trapezium-like inequalities involving functions having strongly n-polynomial preinvexity property of higher order. *J. Funct. Spaces* **2020**, *2020*, 9154139. [CrossRef]
16. Du, T.S.; Liao, J.G.; Li, Y.J. Properties and integral inequalities of Hadamard-Simpson type for the generalized (s,m)-preinvex functions. *J. Nonlinear Sci. Appl.* **2016**, *9*, 3112–3126. [CrossRef]
17. Latif, M.A.; Shoaib, M. Hermite-Hadamard type integral inequalities for differentiable m-preinvex and (α, m)-preinvex functions. *J. Egypt. Math. Soc.* **2015**, *23*, 236–241. [CrossRef]
18. Matloka, M. Relative h-preinvex functions and integral inequalities. *Georgian Math. J.* **2020**, *27*, 285–295. [CrossRef]
19. Mehmood, S.; Zafar, F.; Yasmeen, N. Hermite-Hadamard-Fejér type inequalities for preinvex functions using fractional integrals. *Mathematics* **2019**, *7*, 467. [CrossRef]
20. Mohammed, P.O. New integral inequalities for preinvex functions via generalized beta function. *J. Interdiscip.* **2019**, *22*, 539–549. [CrossRef]
21. Noor, M.A.; Noor, K.I.; Awan, M.U. On Hermite-Hadamard Inequalities for h-Preinvex Functions. *Filomat* **2014**, *28*, 1463–1474. [CrossRef]
22. Özcan, S. Some integral inequalities of Hermite-Hadamard type for multiplicatively preinvex functions. *AIMS Math.* **2020**, *5*, 1505–1518. [CrossRef]
23. Rashid, S.; Latif, M.A.; Hammouch, Z.; Chu, Y.-M. Fractional integral inequalities for strongly h-preinvex functions for a kth order differentiable functions. *Symmetry* **2019**, *11*, 1448. [CrossRef]
24. Sun, W. Some Hermite–Hadamard type inequalities for generalized h-preinvex function via local fractional integrals and their applications. *Adv. Differ. Equ.* **2020**, *2020*, 426. [CrossRef]
25. Ernst, T. *A Comprehensive Treatment of q-Calculus*; Springer: Basel, Switzerland, 2012.
26. Kac, V.; Cheung, P. *Quantum Calculus*; Springer: New York, NY, USA, 2001.
27. Benatti, F.; Fannes, M.; Floreanini, R.; Petritis, D. *Quantum Information, Computation and Cryptography: An Introductory Survey of Theory, Technology and Experiments*; Springer Science and Business Media: Berlin/Heidelberg, Germany, 2010.
28. Bokulich, A.; Jaeger, G. *Philosophy of Quantum Information Theory and Entaglement*; Cambridge Uniersity Press: Cambridge, UK, 2010.
29. Ernst, T. *The History Of Q-Calculus And New Method*; Department of Mathematics, Uppsala University: Uppsala, Sweden, 2000.
30. Jackson, F.H. On a q-definite integrals. *Q. J. Pure Appl. Math.* **1910**, *41*, 193–203.
31. Al-Salam, W. Some fractional q-integrals and q-derivatives. *Proc. Edinb. Math. Soc.* **1966**, *15*, 135–140. [CrossRef]
32. Tariboon, J.; Ntouyas, S.K. Quantum calculus on finite intervals and applications to impulsive difference equations. *Adv. Differ. Equ.* **2013**, *2013*, 282. [CrossRef]
33. Bermudo, S.; Kórus, P.; Valdés, J.N. On q-Hermite-Hadamard inequalities for general convex functions. *Acta Math. Hung.* **2020**, *162*, 364–374. [CrossRef]
34. Sadjang, P.N. On the fundamental theorem of (p,q)-calculus and some (p,q)-Taylor formulas. *Results Math.* **2018**, *73*, 1–21.
35. Tunç, M.; Göv, E. Some integral inequalities via (p,q)-calculus on finite intervals. *RGMIA Res. Rep. Coll.* **2016**, *19*, 1–12.
36. Chu, Y.-M.; Awan, M.U.; Talib, S.; Noor, M.A.; Noor, K.I. New post quantum analogues of Ostrowski-type inequalities using new definitions of left–right (p,q)-derivatives and definite integrals. *Adv. Differ. Equ.* **2020**, *2020*, 634. [CrossRef]
37. Ali, M.A.; Budak, H.; Abbas, M.; Chu, Y.-M. Quantum Hermite–Hadamard-type inequalities for functions with convex absolute values of second q^{π_2}-derivatives. *Adv. Differ. Equ.* **2021**, *2021*, 7. [CrossRef]
38. Ali, M.A.; Alp, N.; Budak, H.; Chu, Y.-M.; Zhang, Z. On some new quantum midpoint type inequalities for twice quantum differentiable convex functions. *Open Math.* **2021**, *19*, 427–439. [CrossRef]
39. Alp, N.; Sarikaya, M.Z.; Kunt, M.; İşcan, İ. q-Hermite Hadamard inequalities and quantum estimates for midpoint type inequalities via convex and quasi-convex functions. *J. King Saud Univ. Sci.* **2018**, *30*, 193–203. [CrossRef]
40. Alp, N.; Sarikaya, M.Z. Hermite Hadamard's type inequalities for co-ordinated convex functions on quantum integral. *Appl. Math. E-Notes* **2020**, *20*, 341–356.
41. Budak, H. Some trapezoid and midpoint type inequalities for newly defined quantum integrals. *Proyecciones* **2021**, *40*, 199–215. [CrossRef]
42. Budak, H.; Ali, M.A.; Tarhanaci, M. Some new quantum Hermite-Hadamard-like inequalities for coordinated convex functions. *J. Optim. Theory Appl.* **2020**, *186*, 899–910. [CrossRef]
43. Jhanthanam, S.; Tariboon, J.; Ntouyas, S.K.; Nonlaopon, K. On q-Hermite-Hadamard inequalities for differentiable convex functions. *Mathematics* **2019**, *7*, 632. [CrossRef]

44. Liu, W.; Hefeng, Z. Some quantum estimates of Hermite-Hadamard inequalities for convex functions. *J. Appl. Anal. Comput.* **2016**, *7*, 501–522.
45. Noor, M.A.; Noor, K.I.; Awan, M.U. Some quantum estimates for Hermite-Hadamard inequalities. *Appl. Math. Comput.* **2015**, *251*, 675–679. [CrossRef]
46. Noor, M.A.; Noor, K.I.; Awan, M.U. Some quantum integral inequalities via preinvex functions. *Appl. Math. Comput.* **2015**, *269*, 242–251. [CrossRef]
47. Nwaeze, E.R.; Tameru, A.M. New parameterized quantum integral inequalities via η-quasiconvexity. *Adv. Differ. Equ.* **2019**, *2019*, 425. [CrossRef]
48. Khan, M.A.; Noor, M.; Nwaeze, E.R.; Chu, Y.-M. Quantum Hermite–Hadamard inequality by means of a Green function. *Adv. Differ. Equ.* **2020**, *2020*, 99. [CrossRef]
49. Budak, H.; Erden, S.; Ali, M.A. Simpson and Newton type inequalities for convex functions via newly defined quantum integrals. *Math. Meth. Appl. Sci.* **2020**, *44*, 378–390. [CrossRef]
50. Ali, M.A.; Budak, H.; Zhang, Z.; Yildrim, H. Some new Simpson's type inequalities for co-ordinated convex functions in quantum calculus. *Math. Meth. Appl. Sci.* **2021**, *44*, 4515–4540. [CrossRef]
51. Ali, M.A.; Abbas, M.; Budak, H.; Agarwal, P.; Murtaza, G.; Chu, Y.-M. New quantum boundaries for quantum Simpson's and quantum Newton's type inequalities for preinvex functions. *Adv. Differ. Equ.* **2021**, *2021*, 64. [CrossRef]
52. Vivas-Cortez, M.; Ali, M.A.; Kashuri, A.; Sial, I.B.; Zhang, Z. Some New Newton's Type Integral Inequalities for Co-Ordinated Convex Functions in Quantum Calculus. *Symmetry* **2020**, *12*, 1476. [CrossRef]
53. Ali, M.A.; Chu, Y.-M.; Budak, H.; Akkurt, A.; Yildrim, H. Quantum variant of Montgomery identity and Ostrowski-type inequalities for the mappings of two variables. *Adv. Differ. Equ.* **2021**, *2021*, 25. [CrossRef]
54. Ali, M.A.; Budak, H.; Akkurt, A.; Chu, Y.-M. Quantum Ostrowski type inequalities for twice quantum differentiable functions in quantum calculus. *Open Math.* **2021**, *19*, 427–439. [CrossRef]
55. Budak, H.; Ali, M.A.; Alp, N.; Chu, Y.-M. Quantum Ostrowski type integral inequalities. *J. Math. Inequal.* **2021**, in press.
56. Kunt, M.; İşcan, İ.; Alp, N.; Sarikaya, M.Z. (p,q)-Hermite-Hadamard inequalities and (p,q)-estimates for midpoint inequalities via convex quasi-convex functions. *Rev. Real Acad. Cienc. Exactas Físicas Nat. Ser. A. Matemáticas* **2018**, *112*, 969–992. [CrossRef]
57. Latif, M.A.; Kunt, M.; Dragomir, S.S.; İşcan, İ. Post-quantum trapezoid type inequalities. *AIMS Math.* **2020**, *5*, 4011–4026. [CrossRef]
58. Vivas-Cortez, M.; Ali, M.A.; Budak, H.; Kalsoom, H.; Agarwal, P. Some New Hermite–Hadamard and Related Inequalities for Convex Functions via (p,q)-Integral. *Entropy* **2021**, *23*, 828. [CrossRef]
59. Sitho, S.; Ali, M.A.; Budak, H.; Ntouyas, S.K.; Tariboon, J. Trapezoid and Midpoint Type Inequalities for Preinvex Functions via Quantum Calculus. *Mathematics* **2021**, *2021*, 1666. [CrossRef]
60. Pavić, Z.; Wu, S.; Novoselac, V. Important inequalities for preinvex functions. *J. Nonlinear Sci. Appl.* **2016**, *9*, 3570–3579. [CrossRef]

Article

Continuous Dependence on the Heat Source of 2D Large-Scale Primitive Equations in Oceanic Dynamics

Yuanfei Li *,† and Peng Zeng †

School of Data Science, Guangzhou Huashang College, Guangzhou 511300, China; zyx1120@gdhsc.edu.cn
* Correspondence: 201610104816@mail.scut.edu.cn
† These authors contributed equally to this work.

Abstract: In this paper, we consider the initial-boundary value problem for the two-dimensional primitive equations of the large-scale oceanic dynamics. These models are often used to predict weather and climate change. Using the differential inequality technique, rigorous a priori bounds of solutions and the continuous dependence on the heat source are established. We show the application of symmetry in mathematical inequalities in practice.

Keywords: a priori bounds; 2D primitive equations; continuous dependence; heat source

1. Introduction

Primitive equations are very useful models which are often used to study the climate and weather prediction. It was Lions, Teman and Wang (see [1–4]) who first started the mathematical study of the primitive equations of the atmosphere, the ocean and the coupled atmosphere–ocean. Assuming that all unknown functions are independent of the latitude y, Petcu et al. [5] obtained the two-dimensional primitive equations of the ocean from the three-dimensional primitive equations. The existence and uniqueness of strong solutions of the primitive equations were derived. In a following paper, Huang and Guo [6] considered the two-dimensional primitive equations of large-scale oceanic motion. They obtained the the existence and uniqueness of global strong solutions. Huang et al. [7] studied the two-dimensional primitive equations of large-scale ocean in geophysics driven by degenerate noise. They proved the asymptotically strong Feller property of the probability transition semigroups. Due to the importance of primitive equations, there are many papers to study the problems (see, e.g., [8–14]).

Recently, many authors began to study the structural stability of large-scale primitive equations. Li [15] obtained the continuous dependence on the viscosity coefficient of primitive equations of the atmosphere with vapor saturation. By using the energy analysis methods, Li [16] proved that the primitive equations of the coupled atmosphere-ocean depended continuously on the boundary parameters. The inspiration of the study came from the fluid equations. There have been a lot of articles in the literature to study the stability of fluid equations (for interest, see [17–29]).

In this paper, we also assume that all the unknown functions are independent of the latitude y as in [5,6]. We consider the following two-dimensional large-scale primitive equations with heat source:

$$\begin{aligned}
&\frac{\partial u}{\partial t} - \mu_1 \Delta u + u\frac{\partial u}{\partial x} + w\frac{\partial u}{\partial z} - fv + \frac{\partial p}{\partial x} = 0,\\
&\frac{\partial v}{\partial t} - \mu_2 \Delta v + u\frac{\partial v}{\partial x} + w\frac{\partial v}{\partial z} + fu = 0,\\
&\frac{\partial p}{\partial z} + \rho g = 0,\\
&\frac{\partial u}{\partial x} + \frac{\partial w}{\partial z} = 0,\\
&\frac{\partial T}{\partial t} - \mu_3 \Delta T + u\frac{\partial T}{\partial x} + w\frac{\partial T}{\partial z} = Q(x,t),\\
&\rho = \rho_0(1 - \beta_T(T - T_{ref})).
\end{aligned} \qquad (1)$$

The domain is defined as

$$\Omega = (0,1) \times (-h, 0),$$

where h is the depth of the oceanic which is always assumed to be a positive constant in this paper. In (1) the unknown functions (u,v), w, ρ, p, T are the horizontal velocity field, the vertical velocity, the density, the pressure, the temperature, respectively. Q is the heat source function which is given. f is a function of the Earth's rotation which is taken to be constant here, and $\mu_i > 0 (i = 1,2,3)$ are the viscosity coefficients. ρ_0, T_{ref} are the reference values of the density and the temperature. β_T is the expansion coefficient (constants), $\Delta = \partial_x^2 + \partial_z^2$. We observe that, in the case of ocean dynamics, one has to add the diffusion-transport equation of the salinity to the system (1). The salinity equation is not present in (1), but this would raise little additional difficulty to take into account the salinity.

The boundary of Ω is denoted by $\partial \Omega$ which can be partitioned into

$$\begin{aligned}
\Gamma_0 &= \{(x,z) \in \overline{\Omega} : 0 < x < 1, \, z = 0\},\\
\Gamma_{-h} &= \{(x,z) \in \overline{\Omega} : 0 < x < 1, \, z = -h\},\\
\Gamma_s &= \{(x,z) \in \overline{\Omega} : x = 0, \text{ or } x = 1, -h \leq z \leq 0\}.
\end{aligned}$$

The system (1) also has the following boundary conditions:

$$\begin{aligned}
&\frac{\partial u}{\partial z} = 0, \quad \frac{\partial v}{\partial z} = 0, \quad w = 0, \quad \frac{\partial T}{\partial z} = -\beta T, \quad \text{on } \Gamma_0,\\
&u = v = w = 0, \quad \frac{\partial T}{\partial z} = 0, \quad \text{on } \Gamma_{-h},\\
&u = v = w = 0, \quad \frac{\partial T}{\partial z} = 0, \quad \text{on } \Gamma_s,
\end{aligned} \qquad (2)$$

where β is a positive constant. In addition, the initial conditions can be written as

$$u(x,z,0) = u_0(x,z), \quad v(x,z,0) = v_0(x,z), \quad T(x,z,0) = T_0(x,z), \quad \text{in } \Omega. \qquad (3)$$

The aim of this paper is to prove the continuous dependence on the heat source of problem (1)–(3) by using the energy methods. This type of study is devoted to know whether a small change in the equation can cause a large change in the solutions. While we take advantage of the mathematical analysis and the symmetry in mathematical inequalities to study these equations, it is helpful for us to know their applicability in physics. Since there will appear some inevitable errors in reality, the study of continuous dependence or convergence results becomes more and more significant. At present, most articles in the literature mainly focused on the existence and long-time behavior of the solutions of the primitive equations. Obviously, the structural stability of the primitive equations has not been paid enough attentions. The research of this paper will bring reference to the study of structural stability of other types of primitive equations.

The present paper is organized as follows. In next section we give some preliminaries of the problem and some well-known inequalities which will be used in the whole paper. We establish rigorous a priori bounds of the solutions in Section 2. In Section 3 we want to prove that the energy is exponential decay with time. Finally, we show how to derive a continuous dependence on the the heat source of our problem in Section 4.

2. Preliminaries of the Problem

We formulate the Equations (1)–(3). Since $w|_{z=-h} = 0$, we integrate the Equation (1)$_4$ from $-h$ to z to obtain

$$w(x,z,t) = w(x,-h,t) - \int_{-h}^{z} \frac{\partial}{\partial x} u(x,\zeta,t)d\zeta = -\frac{\partial}{\partial x}\int_{-h}^{z} u(x,\zeta,t)d\zeta. \quad (4)$$

In view of $w|_{z=0} = 0$

$$\int_{-h}^{0} \frac{\partial}{\partial x} u(x,\zeta,t)d\zeta = \frac{\partial}{\partial x}\int_{-h}^{0} u(x,\zeta,t)d\zeta = 0. \quad (5)$$

This means that $\int_{-h}^{0} u(x,\zeta,t)d\zeta$ is a constant for arbitrary $0 \leq x \leq 1$. Realizing the boundary conditions (2)$_3$ we deduce that

$$\int_{-h}^{0} u(x,\zeta,t)d\zeta = 0.$$

By integrating (1)$_3$ and using (1)$_6$ we have

$$\frac{\partial}{\partial x}p(x,z,t) = \frac{\partial}{\partial x}p_s - \mu\int_{z}^{0}\frac{\partial}{\partial x}T(x,\zeta,t)d\zeta, \quad (6)$$

where $p_s = p(x,0,t)$ is the pressure on the surface of the ocean which is unknown and a function of the horizontal variable only, and $\mu = \rho_0\beta_T$. Inserting (4)–(6) into (1)–(3), our problem can be rewritten as

$$\frac{\partial u}{\partial t} - \mu_1 \Delta u + u\frac{\partial u}{\partial x} - \left(\int_{-h}^{z}\frac{\partial}{\partial x}u(x,\zeta,t)d\zeta\right)\frac{\partial u}{\partial z} - fv + \frac{\partial p_s}{\partial x} - \mu\left(\int_{z}^{0}\frac{\partial}{\partial x}T(x,\zeta,t)d\zeta\right) = 0,$$

$$\frac{\partial v}{\partial t} - \mu_2 \Delta v + u\frac{\partial v}{\partial x} - \left(\int_{-h}^{z}\frac{\partial}{\partial x}u(x,\zeta,t)d\zeta\right)\frac{\partial v}{\partial z} + fu = 0,$$

$$\frac{\partial T}{\partial t} - \mu_3 \Delta T + u\frac{\partial T}{\partial x} - \left(\int_{-h}^{z}\frac{\partial}{\partial x}u(x,\zeta,t)d\zeta\right)\frac{\partial T}{\partial z} = Q,$$

$$\int_{-h}^{0}\frac{\partial}{\partial x}u(x,\zeta,t)d\zeta = 0,$$

$$(7)$$

with the following boundary conditions

$$\left.\frac{\partial u}{\partial z}\right|_{z=0} = \left.\frac{\partial v}{\partial z}\right|_{z=0} = 0, \ u\Big|_{z=-h} = v\Big|_{z=-h} = 0, \ (u,v)\Big|_{\Gamma_s} = 0,$$

$$\left.\frac{\partial T}{\partial z}\right|_{z=0} = -\beta T, \ \left.\frac{\partial T}{\partial z}\right|_{z=-h} = \left.\frac{\partial T}{\partial z}\right|_{\Gamma_s} = 0,$$

$$(8)$$

and the initial conditions

$$(u,v,T)\Big|_{t=0} = (u_0, v_0, T_0). \quad (9)$$

In this paper, we also use some well-known inequalities. We list them here.

Lemma 1. *If $\omega(x) \in C^1(0, h)$ and $\omega(0) = \omega(h) = 0$, then*

$$\int_0^h \omega^2 dx \leq \frac{h^2}{\pi^2} \int_0^h \left(\frac{\partial \omega}{\partial x}\right)^2 dx. \tag{10}$$

For proof of Lemma 2.1 one can see Refs. [30,31].

Lemma 2. *If $\omega(x, z, t)$ is a sufficiently smooth function in $\Omega = (0, 1) \times (-h, 0)$ and $\omega(0, z, t) = \omega(1, z, t) = 0$, then*

$$\left(\int_\Omega \omega^4 dA\right)^{\frac{1}{2}} \leq C\left[\left(\int_\Omega \omega^2 dA\right)^{\frac{1}{2}} \left(\int_\Omega |\nabla \omega|^2 dA\right)^{\frac{1}{2}} + \left(\int_\Omega \omega^2 dA\right)^{\frac{1}{4}} \left(\int_\Omega |\nabla \omega|^2 dA\right)^{\frac{3}{4}}\right],$$

or

$$\left(\int_\Omega \omega^4 dA\right)^{\frac{1}{2}} \leq C\left[\int_\Omega \omega^2 dA + \delta \int_\Omega |\nabla \omega|^2 dA\right], \tag{11}$$

where $\nabla = (\partial_x, \partial_z)$, C is a positive computable constant and δ is a positive arbitrary constant.

Proof. By the Hölder inequality, we then write

$$\int_\Omega \omega^4 dA \leq \int_{-h}^0 \left(\int_0^1 \omega^6 dx\right)^{\frac{1}{2}} \left(\int_0^1 \omega^2 dx\right)^{\frac{1}{2}} dz. \tag{12}$$

Since $\omega(0, z, t) = \omega(1, z, t) = 0$, we have

$$\omega^3 = 3 \int_0^x \omega^2(\xi, z, t) \frac{\partial \omega(\xi, z, t)}{\partial \xi} d\xi = -3 \int_x^1 \omega^2(\xi, z, t) \frac{\partial \omega(\xi, z, t)}{\partial \xi} d\xi. \tag{13}$$

Therefore

$$|\omega|^3 \leq \frac{3}{2} \int_0^1 \omega^2(x, z, t) \left|\frac{\partial \omega(x, z, t)}{\partial x}\right| dx. \tag{14}$$

Then we have

$$\left(\int_0^1 \omega^6 dx\right)^{\frac{1}{2}} \leq \frac{3}{2} \left(\int_0^1 \omega^2 \left|\frac{\partial \omega}{\partial x}\right| dx\right). \tag{15}$$

Inserting (15) into (12) we get

$$\int_\Omega \omega^4 dA \leq \frac{3}{2} \int_{-h}^0 \left(\int_0^1 \omega^2 \left|\frac{\partial \omega}{\partial x}\right| dx\right) \left(\int_0^1 \omega^2 dx\right)^{\frac{1}{2}} dz$$

$$\leq \frac{3}{2} \max_{-h \leq z \leq 0} \left\{\left(\int_0^1 \omega^2 dx\right)^{\frac{1}{2}}\right\} \int_\Omega \omega^2 \left|\frac{\partial \omega}{\partial x}\right| dA. \tag{16}$$

Obviously, we have

$$\omega^2 = 2 \int_{-h}^z \omega(x, \zeta, t) \frac{\partial \omega(x, \zeta, t)}{\partial \zeta} d\zeta + \omega^2(x, -h, t)$$

$$= -2 \int_z^0 \omega(x, \zeta, t) \frac{\partial \omega(x, \zeta, t)}{\partial \zeta} d\zeta + \omega^2(x, 0, t), \tag{17}$$

so,

$$\omega^2 \leq \int_{-h}^0 |\omega| \left|\frac{\partial \omega}{\partial z}\right| dz + \frac{1}{2}[\omega^2(x, 0, t) + \omega^2(x, -h, t)]. \tag{18}$$

To bound the last term of (18), we define a new known function, $f(z)$, satisfying

$$f(0) > 0, \ f(-h) < 0, \ |f'(z)| \leq m_1, \ |f(z)| \leq m_2, \ \text{for} \ -h \leq z \leq 0, \qquad (19)$$

where m_1, m_2 are positive constants. For example, $f(z) = \frac{m_1}{2}(z + \frac{h}{2})$, $m_1 h < 4m_2$ satisfies all the conditions in (19). Using the above estimates and employing the divergence theorem allow us to write

$$\min\{f(0), -f(-h)\}([\omega^2(x,0,t) + \omega^2(x,-h,t)] \leq f(0)\omega^2(x,0,t) - f(-h)\omega^2(x,-h,t)$$

$$= \int_{-h}^0 \frac{\partial}{\partial z}(f\omega^2)dz = \int_{-h}^0 f'(z)\omega^2 dz + 2\int_{-h}^0 f\omega\frac{\partial \omega}{\partial z}dz \qquad (20)$$

$$\leq m_1 \int_{-h}^0 \omega^2 dz + 2m_2 \int_{-h}^0 |\omega|\left|\frac{\partial \omega}{\partial z}\right|dz.$$

Inserting (20) into (18), we have

$$\omega^2 \leq m_3 \int_{-h}^0 \omega^2 dz + m_4 \int_{-h}^0 |\omega|\left|\frac{\partial \omega}{\partial z}\right|dz, \qquad (21)$$

where

$$m_3 = \frac{m_1}{2\min\{f(0),-f(-h)\}}, \ m_4 = 1 + \frac{m_2}{\min\{f(0),-f(-h)\}}. \qquad (22)$$

Therefore

$$\max_{-h \leq z \leq 0}\left\{\left(\int_0^1 \omega^2 dx\right)^{\frac{1}{2}}\right\} \leq \left(m_3 \int_\Omega \omega^2 dA + m_4 \int_\Omega |\omega|\left|\frac{\partial \omega}{\partial z}\right|dA\right)^{\frac{1}{2}}. \qquad (23)$$

Thus, from (16) and (23), by the Hölder inequality we have

$$\int_\Omega \omega^4 dA \leq \frac{3}{2}\Big[m_3 \int_\Omega \omega^2 dA$$

$$+ m_4 \left(\int_\Omega \omega^2 dA\right)^{\frac{1}{2}}\left(\int_\Omega \left|\frac{\partial \omega}{\partial z}\right|^2 dA\right)^{\frac{1}{2}}\Big]^{\frac{1}{2}}\left(\int_\Omega \omega^4 dA\right)^{\frac{1}{2}}\left(\int_\Omega \left|\frac{\partial \omega}{\partial x}\right|^2 dA\right)^{\frac{1}{2}}. \qquad (24)$$

We have after simplification

$$\left(\int_\Omega \omega^4 dA\right)^{\frac{1}{2}} \leq C\Big[\left(\int_\Omega \omega^2 dA\right)^{\frac{1}{2}}\left(\int_\Omega |\nabla\omega|^2 dA\right)^{\frac{1}{2}}$$

$$+ \left(\int_\Omega \omega^2 dA\right)^{\frac{1}{4}}\left(\int_\Omega |\nabla\omega|^2 dA\right)^{\frac{3}{4}}\Big]. \qquad (25)$$

□

3. A priori Estimates

Now we derive some a priori estimates for the solutions of (7)–(9).

3.1. Estimates for $\|u\|_2^2$, $\|v\|_2^2$ and $\|T\|_2^2$

Multiplying Equation $(7)_3$ with T and integrating over Ω and using $(2.5)_2$ we find

$$\frac{1}{2}\frac{d}{dt}\int_\Omega T^2 dA + \mu_3 \int_\Omega |\nabla T|^2 dA = -\mu_3 \int_0^1 T^2 dx|_{z=0} + \int_\Omega TQ dA$$

$$- \int_\Omega \Big[u\frac{\partial T}{\partial x} - \Big(\int_{-h}^z \frac{\partial}{\partial x}u(x,\zeta,t)d\zeta\Big)\frac{\partial T}{\partial z}\Big]T dA. \qquad (26)$$

Integrating by parts we have

$$-\int_\Omega \left[u\frac{\partial T}{\partial x} - \left(\int_{-h}^z \frac{\partial}{\partial x} u(x,\zeta,t)d\zeta\right)\frac{\partial T}{\partial z}\right]TdA = 0. \qquad (27)$$

By the Cauchy–Schwarz inequality and the Hölder inequality we deduce

$$\int_\Omega TQdA \le \frac{1}{2}\int_\Omega T^2 dA + \frac{1}{2}\int_\Omega Q^2 dA. \qquad (28)$$

By (26)–(28) we have

$$\frac{1}{2}\frac{d}{dt}\int_\Omega T^2 dA + \mu_3 \int_\Omega |\nabla T|^2 dA \le \frac{1}{2}\int_\Omega T^2 dA + \frac{1}{2}\int_\Omega Q^2 dA. \qquad (29)$$

By the Gronwall inequality, we have

$$\int_\Omega T^2 dA + 2\mu_3 \int_0^t \int_\Omega |\nabla T|^2 dA d\eta \le \int_\Omega T_0^2 dA \cdot e^t + \int_0^t \int_\Omega e^{t-\eta} Q^2 dA d\eta \\ \doteq F_1(t). \qquad (30)$$

Taking the inner product of Equation $(7)_1$ with u, in $L^2(\Omega)$, we have

$$\frac{1}{2}\frac{d}{dt}\int_\Omega u^2 dA + \mu_1 \int_\Omega |\nabla u|^2 dA = -f\int_\Omega uv dA \\ -\int_\Omega \left[u\frac{\partial u}{\partial x} - \left(\int_{-h}^z \frac{\partial}{\partial x} u(x,\zeta,t)d\zeta\right)\frac{\partial u}{\partial z}\right]u dA \qquad (31) \\ -\int_\Omega \frac{\partial p_s}{\partial x} u dA + \mu \int_\Omega \left(\int_z^0 \frac{\partial}{\partial x} T(x,\zeta,t)d\zeta\right) u dA.$$

An integration leads to

$$-\int_\Omega \left[u\frac{\partial u}{\partial x} - \left(\int_{-h}^z \frac{\partial}{\partial x} u(x,\zeta,t)d\zeta\right)\frac{\partial u}{\partial z}\right]u dA = 0. \qquad (32)$$

Integrating by parts and using $(7)_4$ we get

$$-\int_\Omega \frac{\partial p_s}{\partial x} u dA = -\int_0^1 \frac{\partial p_s}{\partial x}\left(\int_{-h}^0 u dz\right)dx = \int_0^1 p_s \left(\int_{-h}^0 \frac{\partial u}{\partial x} dz\right)dx = 0. \qquad (33)$$

By the Cauchy–Schwarz inequality we have

$$\mu\int_\Omega \left(\int_z^0 \frac{\partial}{\partial x} T(x,\zeta,t)d\zeta\right)u dA = -\mu \int_\Omega \left(\int_z^0 T(x,\zeta,t)d\zeta\right)\frac{\partial u}{\partial x} dA \\ \le \frac{\mu_1}{2}\int_\Omega \left(\frac{\partial u}{\partial x}\right)^2 dA + \frac{h^2\mu^2}{2\mu_1}\int_\Omega T^2 dA. \qquad (34)$$

By (31)–(34) we get

$$\frac{d}{dt}\int_\Omega u^2 dA + \mu_1 \int_\Omega |\nabla u|^2 dA \le -2f\int_\Omega uv dA + \frac{h^2\mu^2}{2\mu_1}\int_\Omega T^2 dA. \qquad (35)$$

Similarly, we can have from $(7)_2$

$$\frac{d}{dt}\int_\Omega v^2 dA + 2\mu_2 \int_\Omega |\nabla v|^2 dA \le 2f\int_\Omega uv dA. \qquad (36)$$

94

Combining (35) and (36) and using (30) we get

$$\frac{d}{dt}\left(\int_\Omega u^2 dA + \int_\Omega v^2 dA\right) + \mu_1 \int_\Omega |\nabla u|^2 dA + 2\mu_2 \int_\Omega |\nabla v|^2 dA \leq \frac{h^2\mu^2}{2\mu_1}F_1(t). \tag{37}$$

We integrate (37) from 0 to t to find

$$\int_\Omega u^2 dA + \int_\Omega v^2 dA + \mu_1 \int_0^t \int_\Omega |\nabla u|^2 dAd\eta + 2\mu_2 \int_0^t \int_\Omega |\nabla v|^2 dAd\eta$$
$$\leq \int_\Omega u_0^2 dA + \int_\Omega v_0^2 dA + \frac{h^2\mu^2}{2\mu_1}\int_0^t F_1(\eta)d\eta \doteq F_2(t). \tag{38}$$

3.2. Estimate for $|T|$

We multiply $(7)_3$ by T^{p-1}, and integrate by parts to find

$$\frac{1}{p}\frac{d}{dt}\int_\Omega T^p dA + \frac{p-1}{p^2}\mu_3 \int_\Omega |\nabla T^{\frac{p}{2}}|^2 dA = -\mu_3\beta \int_0^1 T^p dx|_{z=0} + \int_\Omega QT^{p-1}dA$$
$$- \int_\Omega \left[u\frac{\partial T}{\partial x} - \left(\int_{-h}^z \frac{\partial}{\partial x}u(x,\zeta,t)d\zeta\right)\frac{\partial T}{\partial z}\right]T^{p-1}dA. \tag{39}$$

After integrating by parts on the third term of (39) and realizing the boundary condition (8) we get

$$-\int_\Omega \left[u\frac{\partial T}{\partial x} - \left(\int_{-h}^z \frac{\partial}{\partial x}u(x,\zeta,t)d\zeta\right)\frac{\partial T}{\partial z}\right]T^{p-1}dA = 0. \tag{40}$$

By the Hölder inequality and the Cauchy–Schwarz inequality we have

$$\int_\Omega QT^{p-1}dA \leq \frac{1}{p}\int_\Omega Q^p dA + \frac{p-1}{p}\int_\Omega T^p dA. \tag{41}$$

Therefore,

$$\frac{d}{dt}\int_\Omega T^p dA \leq \int_\Omega Q^p dA + (p-1)\int_\Omega T^p dA. \tag{42}$$

By the Gronwall inequality we have

$$\int_\Omega T^p dA \leq \int_\Omega T_0^p dA \cdot e^{(p-1)t} + \int_0^t \int_\Omega e^{(p-1)(t-\eta)} Q^p dAd\eta.$$

Therefore

$$\left(\int_\Omega T^p dA\right)^{\frac{1}{p}} \leq \left\{\int_\Omega T_0^p dA \cdot e^{(p-1)t} + \int_0^t \int_\Omega e^{(p-1)(t-\eta)} Q^p dAd\eta\right\}^{\frac{1}{p}}. \tag{43}$$

Letting now $p \to \infty$ in (43) we can obtain

$$\sup_\Omega |T| \leq T_m, \tag{44}$$

where $T_m = \sup_\Omega\{||Q||_\infty, ||T_0||_\infty\}$.

3.3. Estimate for $\|\frac{\partial u}{\partial z}\|_{L^4(\Omega)}$

Using $(7)_1$ we start with

$$\int_0^t \int_\Omega \frac{\partial}{\partial z}\Big\{\frac{\partial u}{\partial t} + u\frac{\partial u}{\partial x} - \Big(\int_{-h}^z \frac{\partial}{\partial x}u(x,\zeta,t)d\zeta\Big)\frac{\partial u}{\partial z} - fv + \frac{\partial p_s}{\partial x} \\ - \mu\Big(\int_z^0 \frac{\partial}{\partial x}T(x,\zeta,t)d\zeta\Big) - \mu_1\Delta u\Big\}\frac{\partial u}{\partial z}dAd\eta = 0. \tag{45}$$

Integrating by parts we have

$$\frac{1}{2}\int_\Omega \Big(\frac{\partial u}{\partial z}\Big)^2 dA + \mu_1 \int_0^t \int_\Omega \Big|\nabla\frac{\partial u}{\partial z}\Big|^2 dAd\eta = \frac{1}{2}\int_\Omega \Big(\frac{\partial u_0}{\partial z}\Big)^2 dA \\ - \int_0^t \int_\Omega \Big[u\frac{\partial^2 u}{\partial x \partial z} - \Big(\int_{-h}^z \frac{\partial}{\partial x}u(x,\zeta,\eta)d\zeta\Big)\frac{\partial^2 u}{\partial z^2}\Big]\frac{\partial u}{\partial z}dAd\eta \tag{46} \\ + f\int_0^t \int_\Omega \frac{\partial v}{\partial z}\frac{\partial u}{\partial z}dAd\eta - \mu \int_0^t \int_\Omega \frac{\partial T}{\partial x}\frac{\partial u}{\partial z}dAd\eta.$$

Upon integrating by parts we get

$$-\int_0^t \int_\Omega \Big[u\frac{\partial^2 u}{\partial x \partial z} - \Big(\int_{-h}^z \frac{\partial}{\partial x}u(x,\zeta,\eta)d\zeta\Big)\frac{\partial^2 u}{\partial z^2}\Big]\frac{\partial u}{\partial z}dAd\eta = 0. \tag{47}$$

By (30), (38) and the Hölder inequality we have

$$-\mu \int_0^t \int_\Omega \frac{\partial T}{\partial x}\frac{\partial u}{\partial z}dAd\eta \le \mu\Big(\int_0^t \int_\Omega \Big(\frac{\partial T}{\partial x}\Big)^2 dAd\eta\Big)^{\frac{1}{2}}\Big(\int_0^t \int_\Omega \Big(\frac{\partial u}{\partial z}\Big)^2 dAd\eta\Big)^{\frac{1}{2}} \\ \le \mu\sqrt{\frac{F_1(t)F_2(t)}{2\mu_1\mu_3}}. \tag{48}$$

Inserting the above bounds into (46) we write

$$\frac{1}{2}\int_\Omega \Big(\frac{\partial u}{\partial z}\Big)^2 dA + \mu_1 \int_0^t \int_\Omega \Big|\nabla\frac{\partial u}{\partial z}\Big|^2 dAd\eta \\ \le \frac{1}{2}\int_\Omega \Big(\frac{\partial u_0}{\partial z}\Big)^2 dA + f\int_0^t \int_\Omega \frac{\partial v}{\partial z}\frac{\partial u}{\partial z}dAd\eta \tag{49} \\ + \mu\sqrt{\frac{F_1(t)F_2(t)}{2\mu_1\mu_3}}.$$

We now carry out a similar procedure starting from $(7)_2$ to obtain

$$\frac{1}{2}\int_\Omega \Big(\frac{\partial v}{\partial z}\Big)^2 dA + \mu_2 \int_0^t \int_\Omega \Big|\nabla\frac{\partial v}{\partial z}\Big|^2 dAd\eta \\ = \frac{1}{2}\int_\Omega \Big(\frac{\partial v_0}{\partial z}\Big)^2 dA - f\int_0^t \int_\Omega \frac{\partial v}{\partial z}\frac{\partial u}{\partial z}dAd\eta \\ - \int_0^t \int_\Omega \Big[u\frac{\partial^2 v}{\partial x \partial z} - \Big(\int_{-h}^z \frac{\partial}{\partial x}u(x,\zeta,t)d\zeta\Big)\frac{\partial^2 v}{\partial z^2}\Big]\frac{\partial v}{\partial z}dAd\eta \tag{50} \\ - \int_0^t \int_\Omega \Big[\frac{\partial u}{\partial z}\frac{\partial v}{\partial x} - \frac{\partial u}{\partial x}\frac{\partial v}{\partial z}\Big]\frac{\partial v}{\partial z}dAd\eta.$$

Upon integrating by parts we get

$$-\int_0^t \int_\Omega \Big[u\frac{\partial^2 v}{\partial x \partial z} - \Big(\int_{-h}^z \frac{\partial}{\partial x}u(x,\zeta,t)d\zeta\Big)\frac{\partial^2 v}{\partial z^2}\Big]\frac{\partial v}{\partial z}dAd\eta = 0. \tag{51}$$

Upon using the Cauchy–Schwarz inequality, (11), (38)

$$-\int_0^t \int_\Omega \left[\frac{\partial u}{\partial z}\frac{\partial v}{\partial x} - \frac{\partial u}{\partial x}\frac{\partial v}{\partial z}\right]\frac{\partial v}{\partial z} dAd\eta$$

$$\leq \left[\int_0^t \int_\Omega \left(\frac{\partial v}{\partial x}\right)^2 dAd\eta\right]^{\frac{1}{2}} \left[\int_0^t \int_\Omega \left(\frac{\partial u}{\partial z}\right)^4 dAd\eta\right]^{\frac{1}{4}} \left[\int_0^t \int_\Omega \left(\frac{\partial v}{\partial z}\right)^4 dAd\eta\right]^{\frac{1}{4}}$$

$$+ \left[\int_0^t \int_\Omega \left(\frac{\partial u}{\partial x}\right)^2 dAd\eta\right]^{\frac{1}{2}} \left[\int_0^t \int_\Omega \left(\frac{\partial v}{\partial z}\right)^4 dAd\eta\right]^{\frac{1}{2}}$$

$$\leq \left[\int_0^t \int_\Omega \left(\frac{\partial v}{\partial x}\right)^2 dAd\eta\right]^{\frac{1}{2}} \left[\int_0^t \int_\Omega \left(\frac{\partial u}{\partial z}\right)^2 dAd\eta + \delta_1 \int_0^t \int_\Omega \left|\nabla\frac{\partial u}{\partial z}\right|^2 dAd\eta\right]^{\frac{1}{2}}$$

$$\cdot \left[\int_0^t \int_\Omega \left(\frac{\partial v}{\partial z}\right)^2 dAd\eta + \delta_2 \int_0^t \int_\Omega \left|\nabla\frac{\partial v}{\partial z}\right|^2 dAd\eta\right]^{\frac{1}{2}}$$

$$+ \left[\int_0^t \int_\Omega \left(\frac{\partial u}{\partial x}\right)^2 dAd\eta\right]^{\frac{1}{2}} \left[\int_0^t \int_\Omega \left(\frac{\partial v}{\partial z}\right)^2 dAd\eta + \delta_3 \int_0^t \int_\Omega \left|\nabla\frac{\partial v}{\partial z}\right|^2 dAd\eta\right]$$

$$\leq \frac{1}{2}\left[\int_0^t \int_\Omega \left(\frac{\partial v}{\partial x}\right)^2 dAd\eta\right]^{\frac{1}{2}} \left[\int_0^t \int_\Omega \left(\frac{\partial u}{\partial z}\right)^2 dAd\eta + \delta_1 \int_0^t \int_\Omega \left|\nabla\frac{\partial u}{\partial z}\right|^2 dAd\eta\right] \quad (52)$$

$$+ \frac{1}{2}\left[\int_0^t \int_\Omega \left(\frac{\partial v}{\partial x}\right)^2 dAd\eta\right]^{\frac{1}{2}} \left[\int_0^t \int_\Omega \left(\frac{\partial v}{\partial z}\right)^2 dAd\eta + \delta_2 \int_0^t \int_\Omega \left|\nabla\frac{\partial v}{\partial z}\right|^2 dAd\eta\right]$$

$$+ \left[\int_0^t \int_\Omega \left(\frac{\partial u}{\partial x}\right)^2 dAd\eta\right]^{\frac{1}{2}} \left[\int_0^t \int_\Omega \left(\frac{\partial v}{\partial z}\right)^2 dAd\eta + \delta_3 \int_0^t \int_\Omega \left|\nabla\frac{\partial v}{\partial z}\right|^2 dAd\eta\right]$$

$$\leq \left[\frac{1}{2}\sqrt{\frac{F_2(t)}{2\mu_2}\frac{F_2(t)}{\mu_1}} + \frac{1}{2}\sqrt{\frac{F_2(t)}{2\mu_2}\frac{F_2(t)}{2\mu_2}} + \sqrt{\frac{F_2(t)}{\mu_1}\frac{F_2(t)}{2\mu_2}}\right]$$

$$+ \frac{1}{2}\sqrt{\frac{F_2(t)}{2\mu_2}}\delta_1 \int_0^t \int_\Omega \left|\nabla\frac{\partial u}{\partial z}\right|^2 dAd\eta$$

$$+ \left[\frac{1}{2}\sqrt{\frac{F_2(t)}{2\mu_2}}\delta_2 + \sqrt{\frac{F_2(t)}{\mu_1}}\delta_3\right] \int_0^t \int_\Omega \left|\nabla\frac{\partial v}{\partial z}\right|^2 dAd\eta,$$

where δ_1, δ_2, δ_3 are positive constants which will be given later.

The idea is to insert (51) and (52) into (50) and then choose $\delta_2 = \frac{1}{2}\sqrt{\frac{2\mu_2}{F_2(t)}}\mu_2$, $\delta_3 = \frac{1}{4}\sqrt{\frac{\mu_1}{F_2(t)}}\mu_2$. We may have

$$\frac{1}{2}\int_\Omega \left(\frac{\partial v}{\partial z}\right)^2 dA + \frac{1}{2}\mu_2 \int_0^t \int_\Omega \left|\nabla\frac{\partial v}{\partial z}\right|^2 dAd\eta$$

$$\leq \frac{1}{2}\int_\Omega \left(\frac{\partial v_0}{\partial z}\right)^2 dA - f\int_0^t \int_\Omega \frac{\partial v}{\partial z}\frac{\partial u}{\partial z} dAd\eta \quad (53)$$

$$+ \left[\frac{1}{2}\sqrt{\frac{F_2(t)}{2\mu_2}\frac{F_2(t)}{\mu_1}} + \frac{1}{2}\sqrt{\frac{F_2(t)}{2\mu_2}\frac{F_2(t)}{2\mu_2}} + \sqrt{\frac{F_2(t)}{\mu_1}\frac{F_2(t)}{2\mu_2}}\right]$$

$$+ \frac{1}{2}\sqrt{\frac{F_2(t)}{2\mu_2}}\delta_1 \int_0^t \int_\Omega \left|\nabla\frac{\partial u}{\partial z}\right|^2 dAd\eta.$$

We add (49) and (53) and choose that $\delta_1 = \sqrt{\frac{2\mu_2}{F_2(t)}}\mu_1$ to find

$$\int_\Omega \left(\frac{\partial u}{\partial z}\right)^2 dA + \int_\Omega \left(\frac{\partial v}{\partial z}\right)^2 dA$$

$$+ \mu_1 \int_0^t \int_\Omega \left|\nabla\frac{\partial u}{\partial z}\right|^2 dAd\eta + \mu_2 \int_0^t \int_\Omega \left|\nabla\frac{\partial v}{\partial z}\right|^2 dAd\eta \quad (54)$$

$$\leq F_3(t),$$

where

$$F_3(t) = \int_\Omega \left(\frac{\partial u_0}{\partial z}\right)^2 dA + \int_\Omega \left(\frac{\partial v_0}{\partial z}\right)^2 dA + 2\mu\sqrt{\frac{F_1(t)F_2(t)}{2\mu_1\mu_3}}$$
$$+ \sqrt{\frac{F_2(t)}{2\mu_2}\frac{F_2(t)}{\mu_1}} + \sqrt{\frac{F_2(t)}{2\mu_2}\frac{F_2(t)}{2\mu_2}} + \sqrt{\frac{F_2(t)}{\mu_1}\frac{F_2(t)}{\mu_2}} \quad (55)$$

Using (11) with $\delta = 1$ then we have

$$\int_0^t \int_\Omega \left(\frac{\partial u}{\partial z}\right)^4 dAd\eta \leq C\left(\int_0^t \int_\Omega \left(\frac{\partial u}{\partial z}\right)^2 dAd\eta + \int_0^t \int_\Omega \left|\nabla\frac{\partial u}{\partial z}\right|^2 dAd\eta\right)^2$$
$$\leq C\left(\int_0^t F_3(\eta)d\eta + \frac{1}{\mu_1}F_3(t)\right)^2 \doteq F_4(t). \quad (56)$$

4. Exponential Decay Estimates with Time When $Q = 0$

In this section we want to prove the following theorem basis on Section 3.

Theorem 1. *If $(u_0, v_0, T_0) \in H(\Omega)$, $Q = 0$, then the global weakly strong solution (u, v, T) for the system (7)–(9) satisfies*

$$||u||^2, ||v||^2, ||T||^2, \int_0^t ||\partial_{x_2}T(\eta)||^2 d\eta, \int_0^t ||\partial_{x_2}u(\eta)||^2 d\eta, \int_0^t ||\partial_{x_2}v(\eta)||^2 d\eta$$

decay exponentially with time.

Proof. Since T, u and v satisfy the conditions of Lemma 2.1, we have

$$\int_\Omega \left|\frac{\partial T}{\partial x}\right|^2 dA \geq \pi^2 \int_\Omega T^2 dA,$$
$$\int_\Omega \left|\frac{\partial u}{\partial x}\right|^2 dA \geq \pi^2 \int_\Omega u^2 dA, \quad (57)$$
$$\int_\Omega \left|\frac{\partial v}{\partial x}\right|^2 dA \geq \pi^2 \int_\Omega v^2 dA.$$

It follows from (29) with $Q = 0$ that

$$\frac{1}{2}\frac{d}{dt}\int_\Omega T^2 dA + \pi^2\mu_3 \int_\Omega T^2 dA + \mu_3 \int_\Omega \left|\frac{\partial T}{\partial z}\right|^2 dA \leq 0. \quad (58)$$

So, by the Gronwall inequality, we get

$$\int_\Omega T^2 dA + \mu_3 \int_0^t \int_\Omega \left|\frac{\partial T}{\partial z}\right|^2 dAd\eta \leq \int_\Omega T_0^2 dA \cdot e^{-\tau_1 t}. \quad (59)$$

where $\tau_1 = \pi^2\mu_3$. In view of (35), (36) and (57), we have

$$\frac{d}{dt}\left(\int_\Omega u^2 dA + \int_\Omega v^2 dA\right) + \pi^2\mu_1 \int_\Omega u^2 dA + 2\pi^2\mu_2 \int_\Omega v^2 dA$$
$$+ \mu_1 \int_\Omega \left|\frac{\partial u}{\partial z}\right|^2 dA + \mu_2 \int_\Omega \left|\frac{\partial v}{\partial z}\right|^2 dA \quad (60)$$
$$\leq \frac{h^2\mu^2}{2\mu_1}\int_\Omega T^2 dA.$$

Letting

$$\tau_2 = \pi^2 \min\{\mu_1, 2\mu_2\},$$

and using (59) we may have from (60)

$$\frac{d}{dt}\left(\int_\Omega u^2 dA + \int_\Omega v^2 dA\right) + \tau_2\left(\int_\Omega u^2 dA + \int_\Omega v^2 dA\right)$$
$$+ \mu_1 \int_\Omega \left|\frac{\partial u}{\partial z}\right|^2 dA + \mu_2 \int_\Omega \left|\frac{\partial v}{\partial z}\right|^2 dA \quad (61)$$
$$\leq \frac{h^2\mu^2}{2\mu_1}\int_\Omega T_0^2 dA \cdot e^{-\tau_1 t}.$$

By the Gronwall inequality again, we get

$$\int_\Omega u^2 dA + \int_\Omega v^2 dA + \mu_1 \int_0^t \int_\Omega \left|\frac{\partial u}{\partial z}\right|^2 dA d\eta + \mu_2 \int_0^t \int_\Omega \left|\frac{\partial v}{\partial z}\right|^2 dA d\eta$$
$$\leq \left(\int_\Omega u_0^2 dA + \int_\Omega v_0^2 dA\right) \cdot e^{-\tau_2 t} + \frac{h^2\mu^2}{2\mu_1(\tau_2 - \tau_1)}\int_\Omega T_0^2 dA \cdot e^{-\tau_1 t}, \text{ if } \tau_2 > \tau_1,$$

$$\int_\Omega u^2 dA + \int_\Omega v^2 dA + \mu_1 \int_0^t \int_\Omega \left|\frac{\partial u}{\partial z}\right|^2 dA d\eta + \mu_2 \int_0^t \int_\Omega \left|\frac{\partial v}{\partial z}\right|^2 dA d\eta$$
$$\leq \left(\int_\Omega u_0^2 dA + \int_\Omega v_0^2 dA\right) \cdot e^{-\tau_2 t} + \frac{h^2\mu^2}{2\mu_1(\tau_2 - \tau_1)}\int_\Omega T_0^2 dA \cdot e^{-\tau_2 t}, \text{ if } \tau_2 < \tau_1,$$

$$\int_\Omega u^2 dA + \int_\Omega v^2 dA + \mu_1 \int_0^t \int_\Omega \left|\frac{\partial u}{\partial z}\right|^2 dA d\eta + \mu_2 \int_0^t \int_\Omega \left|\frac{\partial v}{\partial z}\right|^2 dA d\eta$$
$$\leq \left(\int_\Omega u_0^2 dA + \int_\Omega v_0^2 dA\right) \cdot e^{-\tau_2 t} + \frac{h^2\mu^2 t}{2\mu_1}\int_\Omega T_0^2 dA \cdot e^{-\tau_2 t}, \text{ if } \tau_2 = \tau_1.$$

□

5. Continuous Dependence on the Heat Source

Supposing (u^*, v^*, T^*, p_s^*) also be the solutions of (7)–(9) with the same initial-boundary conditions as (u, v, T, p_s), but with different heat source Q^*. Let

$$\tilde{u} = u - u^*, \quad \tilde{v} = v - v^*, \quad \tilde{T} = T - T^*, \quad \tilde{\pi}_s = p_s - p_s^*, \quad \tilde{Q} = Q - Q^*, \quad (62)$$

then $(\tilde{u}, \tilde{v}, \tilde{\pi}_s)$ satisfies the following initial-boundary problem

$$\frac{\partial \tilde{u}}{\partial t} - \mu_1 \Delta \tilde{u} + \tilde{u}\frac{\partial u}{\partial x} - \left(\int_{-h}^z \frac{\partial}{\partial x}\tilde{u}(x,\zeta,t)d\zeta\right)\frac{\partial u}{\partial z} + u^*\frac{\partial \tilde{u}}{\partial x}$$
$$- \left(\int_{-h}^z \frac{\partial}{\partial x}u^*(x,\zeta,t)d\zeta\right)\frac{\partial \tilde{u}}{\partial z} - f\tilde{v} + \frac{\partial \tilde{\pi}_s}{\partial x} - \left(\int_z^0 \frac{\partial}{\partial x}\tilde{T}(x,\zeta,t)d\zeta\right) = 0,$$

$$\frac{\partial \tilde{v}}{\partial t} - \mu_2 \Delta \tilde{v} + \tilde{u}\frac{\partial v}{\partial x} - \left(\int_{-h}^z \frac{\partial}{\partial x}\tilde{u}(x,\zeta,t)d\zeta\right)\frac{\partial v}{\partial z} + u^*\frac{\partial \tilde{v}}{\partial x}$$
$$- \left(\int_{-h}^z \frac{\partial}{\partial x}u^*(x,\zeta,t)d\zeta\right)\frac{\partial \tilde{v}}{\partial z} - f\tilde{u} = 0, \quad (63)$$

$$\frac{\partial \tilde{T}}{\partial t} - \mu_3 \Delta \tilde{T} + \tilde{u}\frac{\partial T}{\partial x} - \left(\int_{-h}^z \frac{\partial}{\partial x}\tilde{u}(x,\zeta,t)d\zeta\right)\frac{\partial T}{\partial z} + u^*\frac{\partial \tilde{T}}{\partial x}$$
$$- \left(\int_{-h}^z \frac{\partial}{\partial x}u^*(x,\zeta,t)d\zeta\right)\frac{\partial \tilde{T}}{\partial z} = \tilde{Q},$$

$$\int_{-h}^0 \frac{\partial}{\partial x}\tilde{u}(x,\zeta,t)d\zeta = 0,$$

$$\left.\frac{\partial \tilde{u}}{\partial z}\right|_{z=0} = 0, \left.\frac{\partial \tilde{v}}{\partial z}\right|_{z=0} = 0, \left.\tilde{u}\right|_{z=-h} = \left.\tilde{v}\right|_{z=-h} = 0, \left.(\tilde{u},\tilde{v})\right|_{\Gamma_s} = 0,$$
$$\left.\frac{\partial \tilde{T}}{\partial z}\right|_{z=0} = -\beta\tilde{T}, \left.\frac{\partial \tilde{T}}{\partial z}\right|_{z=-h} = 0, \left.\frac{\partial \tilde{T}}{\partial x}\right|_{\Gamma_s} = 0, \quad (64)$$

$$(\tilde{u}, \tilde{v}, \tilde{T})\big|_{t=0} = (0, 0, 0). \tag{65}$$

We have the following theorem:

Theorem 2. *Let $(\tilde{u}, \tilde{v}, \tilde{T})$ be the solutions of (63)–(65) with $Q, T_0 \in L^\infty(\Omega)$ and $T_0, u_0, v_0 \in L^2(\Omega)$. Then $(\tilde{u}, \tilde{v}, \tilde{T})$ satisfy the inequality for $\theta > 0, \gamma_1(t) > 0$*

$$\int_\Omega (\tilde{u}^2 + \tilde{v}^2 + \theta \tilde{T}^2) dA + \int_0^t \int_\Omega \left(\frac{1}{2}\mu_1 |\nabla \tilde{u}|^2 + \mu_2 |\nabla \tilde{v}|^2 + \theta \mu_3 |\nabla \tilde{T}|^2\right) dA d\eta$$
$$\leq \gamma_1(t)\theta \int_0^t \int_0^\tau \int_\Omega e^{\int_\tau^t \gamma_1(s) ds} \tilde{Q}^2 dA d\eta d\tau + \theta \int_0^t \int_\Omega \tilde{Q}^2 dA d\eta, \tag{66}$$

which is the continuous dependence result on the heat source Q.

Proof. Now taking the inner product of the first equation of (63) with $\tilde{u}$, in $L^2(\Omega)$, we have

$$\frac{1}{2}\int_\Omega \tilde{u}^2 dA + \mu_1 \int_0^t \int_\Omega |\nabla \tilde{u}|^2 dA d\eta = f \int_0^t \int_\Omega \tilde{u}\tilde{v} dA d\eta - \int_0^t \int_\Omega \frac{\partial \pi_s}{\partial x} \tilde{u} dA d\eta$$
$$+ \mu \int_0^t \int_\Omega \left(\int_z^0 \frac{\partial}{\partial x} \tilde{T}(x, \zeta, \eta) d\zeta\right) \tilde{u} dA d\eta$$
$$- \int_0^t \int_\Omega \left[\tilde{u}\frac{\partial u}{\partial x} - \left(\int_{-h}^z \frac{\partial}{\partial x} \tilde{u}(x, \zeta, \eta) d\zeta\right) \frac{\partial u}{\partial z}\right] \tilde{u} dA d\eta$$
$$- \int_0^t \int_\Omega \left[u^* \frac{\partial \tilde{u}}{\partial x} - \left(\int_{-h}^z \frac{\partial}{\partial x} u^*(x, \zeta, \eta) d\zeta\right) \frac{\partial \tilde{u}}{\partial z}\right] \tilde{u} dA d\eta. \tag{67}$$

An integration by parts leads to

$$- \int_0^t \int_\Omega \left[u^* \frac{\partial \tilde{u}}{\partial x} - \left(\int_{-h}^z \frac{\partial}{\partial x} u^*(x, \zeta, \eta) d\zeta\right) \frac{\partial \tilde{u}}{\partial z}\right] \tilde{u} dA d\eta = 0, \tag{68}$$

$$- \int_0^t \int_\Omega \frac{\partial \pi_s}{\partial x} \tilde{u} dA d\eta = - \int_0^t \int_0^1 \frac{\partial \pi_s}{\partial x} \left(\int_{-h}^0 \tilde{u}(x, z, \eta) dz\right) dx d\eta = 0. \tag{69}$$

By the Hölder inequality, Lemma 2.2, (38), Lemma 2.1, (56) and the AG mean inequality, we have

$$- \int_0^t \int_\Omega \left[\tilde{u}\frac{\partial u}{\partial x} - \left(\int_{-h}^z \frac{\partial}{\partial x} \tilde{u}(x, \zeta, \eta) d\zeta\right) \frac{\partial u}{\partial z}\right] \tilde{u} dA d\eta$$
$$\leq \left[\int_0^t \int_\Omega \left(\frac{\partial u}{\partial x}\right)^2 dA d\eta\right]^{\frac{1}{2}} \left[\int_0^t \int_\Omega \tilde{u}^4 dA d\eta\right]^{\frac{1}{2}}$$
$$+ \left[\int_0^t \int_\Omega \left(\int_{-h}^z \frac{\partial}{\partial x} \tilde{u}(x, \zeta, \eta) d\zeta\right)^2 dA d\eta\right]^{\frac{1}{2}} \left[\int_0^t \int_\Omega \left(\frac{\partial u}{\partial z}\right)^4 dA d\eta\right]^{\frac{1}{4}}$$
$$\cdot \left[\int_0^t \int_\Omega \tilde{u}^4 dA d\eta\right]^{\frac{1}{4}}$$
$$\leq \sqrt{\frac{F_2(t)}{\mu_1}} C \left[\int_0^t \int_\Omega \tilde{u}^2 dA d\eta + \delta_1 \int_0^t \int_\Omega |\nabla \tilde{u}|^2 dA d\eta\right]$$
$$+ \frac{\sqrt{Ch}}{\pi} \sqrt[4]{F_4(t)} \left[\int_0^t \int_\Omega \left(\frac{\partial \tilde{u}}{\partial x}\right)^2 dA d\eta\right]^{\frac{1}{2}} \left[\int_0^t \int_\Omega \tilde{u}^2 dA d\eta\right]$$
$$+ \delta_1 \int_0^t \int_\Omega |\nabla \tilde{u}|^2 dA d\eta\right]^{\frac{1}{2}}$$
$$\leq b_1(t) \int_0^t \int_\Omega \tilde{u}^2 dA d\eta + b_2(t)\delta_1 \int_0^t \int_\Omega |\nabla \tilde{u}|^2 dA d\eta \tag{70}$$

for computable $b_1(t), b_2(t)$ and positive arbitrary constant δ_1.

Applying the Cauchy–Schwarz inequality again we have

$$\mu \int_0^t \int_\Omega \left(\int_z^0 \frac{\partial}{\partial x} \tilde{T}(x,\zeta,\eta) d\zeta \right) \tilde{u} \, dA \, d\eta$$
$$= -\mu \int_0^t \int_\Omega \left(\int_z^0 \tilde{T}(x,\zeta,\eta) d\zeta \right) \frac{\partial \tilde{u}}{\partial x} dA \, d\eta \tag{71}$$
$$\leq \frac{h^2 \mu^2}{\mu_1} \int_0^t \int_\Omega \tilde{T}^2 dA \, d\eta + \frac{\mu_1}{4} \int_0^t \int_\Omega \left(\frac{\partial \tilde{u}}{\partial x} \right)^2 dA \, d\eta.$$

Inserting (68)—(71) into (67) and choosing $\delta_1 = \frac{\mu_1}{4b_2(t)}$ we have

$$\frac{1}{2} \int_\Omega \tilde{u}^2 dA + \frac{1}{2} \mu_1 \int_0^t \int_\Omega |\nabla \tilde{u}|^2 dA \, d\eta \leq f \int_0^t \int_\Omega \tilde{u} \tilde{v} \, dA \, d\eta$$
$$+ \frac{h^2 \mu^2}{\mu_1} \int_0^t \int_\Omega \tilde{T}^2 dA \, d\eta + b_1(t) \int_0^t \int_\Omega \tilde{u}^2 dA \, d\eta. \tag{72}$$

Now, taking the inner product of Equation (63)$_2$ with $\tilde{v}$, we have

$$\frac{1}{2} \int_\Omega \tilde{v}^2 dA + \mu_2 \int_0^t \int_\Omega |\nabla \tilde{v}|^2 dA \, d\eta = -f \int_0^t \int_\Omega \tilde{u} \tilde{v} \, dA \, d\eta$$
$$- \int_0^t \int_\Omega \left[\tilde{u} \frac{\partial v}{\partial x} - \left(\int_{-h}^z \frac{\partial}{\partial x} \tilde{u}(x,\zeta,\eta) d\zeta \right) \frac{\partial v}{\partial z} \right] \tilde{u} \, dA \, d\eta \tag{73}$$
$$- \int_0^t \int_\Omega \left[u^* \frac{\partial \tilde{v}}{\partial x} - \left(\int_{-h}^z \frac{\partial}{\partial x} u^*(x,\zeta,\eta) d\zeta \right) \frac{\partial \tilde{v}}{\partial z} \right] \tilde{v} \, dA \, d\eta.$$

Computing as previous we arrive at

$$\frac{1}{2} \int_\Omega \tilde{v}^2 dA + \frac{1}{2} \mu_2 \int_0^t \int_\Omega |\nabla \tilde{v}|^2 dA \, d\eta \leq -f \int_0^t \int_\Omega \tilde{u} \tilde{v} \, dA \, d\eta + b_3(t) \int_0^t \int_\Omega \tilde{v}^2 dA \, d\eta \tag{74}$$

for computable positive function $b_3(t)$. A combination of (74) and (78) leads to

$$\int_\Omega \tilde{u}^2 dA + \int_\Omega \tilde{v}^2 dA + \mu_1 \int_0^t \int_\Omega |\nabla \tilde{u}|^2 dA \, d\eta + \mu_2 \int_0^t \int_\Omega |\nabla \tilde{v}|^2 dA \, d\eta$$
$$\leq \frac{2h^2 \mu^2}{\mu_1} \int_0^t \int_\Omega \tilde{T}^2 dA \, d\eta + 2b_1(t) \int_0^t \int_\Omega \tilde{u}^2 dA \, d\eta + 2b_3(t) \int_0^t \int_\Omega \tilde{v}^2 dA \, d\eta. \tag{75}$$

We take the inner product of Equation (63)$_3$ with $\tilde{T}$, we have

$$\frac{1}{2} \int_\Omega \tilde{T}^2 dA + \mu_3 \int_0^t \int_\Omega |\nabla \tilde{T}|^2 dA \, d\eta$$
$$= - \int_0^t \int_\Omega \left[\tilde{u} \frac{\partial T}{\partial x} - \left(\int_{-h}^z \frac{\partial}{\partial x} \tilde{u}(x,\zeta,\eta) d\zeta \right) \frac{\partial T}{\partial z} \right] \tilde{T} \, dA \, d\eta$$
$$- \int_0^t \int_\Omega \left[u^* \frac{\partial \tilde{T}}{\partial x} - \left(\int_{-h}^z \frac{\partial}{\partial x} u^*(x,\zeta,\eta) d\zeta \right) \frac{\partial \tilde{T}}{\partial z} \right] \tilde{T} \, dA \, d\eta \tag{76}$$
$$+ \int_0^t \int_\Omega \tilde{Q} \tilde{T} \, dA \, d\eta.$$

On integrating by parts we have

$$- \int_0^t \int_\Omega \left[u^* \frac{\partial \tilde{T}}{\partial x} - \left(\int_{-h}^z \frac{\partial}{\partial x} u^*(x,\zeta,\eta) d\zeta \right) \frac{\partial \tilde{T}}{\partial z} \right] \tilde{T} \, dA \, d\eta = 0. \tag{77}$$

Integrating by parts and using the Hölder inequality, (44), Lemma 3.2, the AG mean inequality we get

$$
\begin{aligned}
&-\int_0^t \int_\Omega \left[\tilde{u}\frac{\partial T}{\partial x} - \left(\int_{-h}^z \frac{\partial}{\partial x}\tilde{u}(x,\zeta,\eta)d\zeta\right)\frac{\partial T}{\partial z}\right]\tilde{T}dAd\eta \\
&= \int_0^t \int_\Omega \tilde{u}T\frac{\partial \tilde{T}}{\partial x}dAd\eta - \int_0^t \int_\Omega \left(\int_{-h}^z \frac{\partial}{\partial x}\tilde{u}(x,\zeta,\eta)d\zeta\right)T\frac{\partial \tilde{T}}{\partial z}dAd\eta \\
&\leq T_m\left(\int_0^t \int_\Omega \left(\frac{\partial \tilde{T}}{\partial x}\right)^2 dAd\eta\right)^{\frac{1}{2}}\left(\int_0^t \int_\Omega \tilde{u}^2 dAd\eta\right)^{\frac{1}{2}} \\
&\quad + T_m\left(\int_0^t \int_\Omega \left(\int_{-h}^z \frac{\partial}{\partial x}\tilde{u}(x,\zeta,\eta)d\zeta\right)^2 dAd\eta\right)^{\frac{1}{2}}\left(\int_0^t \int_\Omega \left(\frac{\partial \tilde{T}}{\partial z}\right)^2 dAd\eta\right)^{\frac{1}{2}} \\
&\leq \frac{1}{2}T_m\delta_2 \int_0^t \int_\Omega \left(\frac{\partial \tilde{T}}{\partial x}\right)^2 dAd\eta + \frac{1}{2\delta_2}T_m\int_0^t\int_\Omega \tilde{u}^2 dAd\eta \\
&\quad + \frac{h^2}{2\pi^2\delta_2}T_m\int_0^t\int_\Omega \left(\frac{\partial \tilde{u}}{\partial x}\right)^2 dAd\eta + \frac{1}{2}\delta_2 T_m \int_0^t\int_\Omega \left(\frac{\partial \tilde{T}}{\partial z}\right)^2 dAd\eta,
\end{aligned}
\tag{78}
$$

where δ_2 is a positive constant.

By the Hölder inequality and the AG mean inequality it follows that

$$\int_0^t \int_\Omega \tilde{Q}\tilde{T} dAd\eta \leq \frac{1}{2}\int_0^t \int_\Omega \tilde{Q}^2 dAd\eta + \frac{1}{2}\int_0^t \int_\Omega \tilde{T}^2 dAd\eta. \tag{79}$$

Inserting (77)–(79) into (76) and choosing $\delta_2 = \frac{\mu_3}{2T_m}$ we get

$$
\int_\Omega \tilde{T}^2 dA + \mu_3 \int_0^t \int_\Omega |\nabla \tilde{T}|^2 dAd\eta \leq \frac{1}{\delta_2}T_m \int_0^t \int_\Omega \tilde{u}^2 dAd\eta + \frac{h^2}{\pi^2\delta_2}T_m\int_0^t\int_\Omega \left(\frac{\partial \tilde{u}}{\partial x}\right)^2 dAd\eta \\
+ \int_0^t \int_\Omega \tilde{T}^2 dAd\eta + \int_0^t \int_\Omega \tilde{Q}^2 dAd\eta.
\tag{80}
$$

Then, using (75) and (80), we find that for a positive constant $\theta = \frac{\pi^2 \delta_2 \mu_1}{2h^2 T_m}$

$$
\int_\Omega \left(\tilde{u}^2 + \tilde{v}^2 dA + \theta\tilde{T}^2\right)dA + \int_0^t\int_\Omega \left(\frac{1}{2}\mu_1|\nabla\tilde{u}|^2 + \mu_2|\nabla\tilde{v}|^2 + \theta\mu_3|\nabla\tilde{T}|^2\right)dAd\eta \\
\leq \gamma_1(t)\int_0^t\int_\Omega \left(\tilde{u}^2 + \tilde{v}^2 + \theta\tilde{T}^2\right)dAd\eta \\
+ \theta\int_0^t\int_\Omega \tilde{Q}^2 dAd\eta,
\tag{81}
$$

where

$$\gamma_1(t) = \max\{1 + \frac{2h^2}{\mu_1\theta}, 2b_1(t) + \frac{T_m\theta}{\delta_2}, 2b_3(t)\}. \tag{82}$$

Therefore

$$\frac{d}{dt}\left\{\int_0^t\int_\Omega (\tilde{u}^2 + \tilde{v}^2 + \theta\tilde{T}^2)dAd\eta \cdot e^{-\int_0^t \gamma_1(s)ds}\right\} \leq \theta\int_0^t\int_\Omega \tilde{Q}^2 dAd\eta \cdot e^{-\int_0^t \gamma_1(s)ds}. \tag{83}$$

An integration of (83) yields that

$$\int_0^t\int_\Omega (\tilde{u}^2 + \tilde{v}^2 + \theta\tilde{T}^2)dAd\eta \leq \theta\int_0^t\int_0^\tau\int_\Omega e^{\int_\tau^t \gamma_1(s)ds}\tilde{Q}^2 dAd\eta d\tau. \tag{84}$$

Then returning to (81), we obtain

$$\int_\Omega (\tilde{u}^2 + \tilde{v}^2 + \theta \tilde{T}^2) dA + \int_0^t \int_\Omega \left(\frac{1}{2}\mu_1 |\nabla \tilde{u}|^2 + \mu_2 |\nabla \tilde{v}|^2 + \theta \mu_3 |\nabla \tilde{T}|^2\right) dA d\eta \qquad (85)$$
$$\leq \gamma_1(t) \theta \int_0^t \int_0^\tau \int_\Omega e^{\int_\tau^t \gamma_1(s) ds} \tilde{Q}^2 dA d\eta d\tau + \theta \int_0^t \int_\Omega \tilde{Q}^2 dA d\eta.$$

6. Conclusions

In this paper, we obtain the continuous dependence of the two-dimensional large-scale primitive equations in oceanic dynamics, where the depth of the ocean is assumed to be a positive constant. When the depth of the ocean is positive but not always a constant, Huang and Guo [32] have obtained the existence and uniqueness of a global strong solution for the problem. The study of the continuous dependence of the primitive equations in this case may be more interesting.

Author Contributions: Conceptualization, and validation, Y.L.; formal analysis and investigation, P.Z. All authors have read and agreed to the published version of the manuscript.

Funding: This research was funded by Key projects of universities in Guangdong Province (NATURAL SCIENCE) (2019KZDXM042) and the Research team project of Guangzhou Huashang College(2021HSKT01).

Institutional Review Board Statement: Not applicable.

Informed Consent Statement: Not applicable.

Data Availability Statement: Not applicable.

Acknowledgments: The authors would like to deeply thank all the reviewers for their insightful and constructive comments.

Conflicts of Interest: The authors declare no conflict of interest.

Sample Availability: Sharing is not applicable to this article, as no new data were created or analyzed in this study.

References

1. Lions, J.L.; Temam, R.; Wang, S. New formulations of the primitive equations of atmosphere and applications. *Nonlinearity* **1992**, *5*, 237–288. [CrossRef]
2. Lions, J.L.; Temam, R.; Wang, S. On the equations of the large-scale ocean. *Nonlinearity* **1999**, *5*, 1007–1053. [CrossRef]
3. Lions, J.L.; Temam, R.; Wang, S. Models of the coupled atmosphere and ocean(CAO I). *Comput. Mech. Adv.* **1993**, *1*, 5–54.
4. Lions, J.L.; Temam, R.; Wang, S. Mathematical theory for the coupled atmosphere-ocean models (CAOIII). *J. Math. Pures Appl.* **1995**, *74*, 105–163.
5. Petcu, M.; Temam, R.; Wirosoetisno, D. Existence and regularity results for the primitive equations in the two dimensions. *Comm. Pure Appl. Anal.* **2004**, *3*, 115–131. [CrossRef]
6. Huang, D.W.; Guo, B.L. On two-dimensional large-scale primitive equations in oceanic dynamics (I). *Appl. Math. Mech.* **2007**, *28*, 581–592. [CrossRef]
7. Huang, D.W.; Shen, T.L.; Zheng, Y. Ergodicity of two-dimensional primitive equations of large scale-ocean in geophysics driven by degenerate noise. *Appl. Math. Lett.* **2020**, *102*, 106146. [CrossRef]
8. Hieber, M.; Hussein, A.; Kashiwabara, T. Global strong L^p well-posedness of the 3D primitive equations with heat and salinity diffusion. *J. Diff. Equ.* **2016**, *261*, 6950–6981. [CrossRef]
9. You, B.; Li, F. Global attractor of the three-dimensional primitive equations of large-scale ocean and atmosphere dynamics. *Z. Angew. Math. Phys.* **2018**, *69*, 114. [CrossRef]
10. Jiu, Q.; Li, M.J.; Wang, F. Uniqueness of the global weak solutions to 2D compressible primitive equations. *J. Math. Anal. Appl.* **2018**, *461*, 1653–1671. [CrossRef]
11. Chiodaroli, E.; Michálek, M. Existence and non-uniqueness of global Weak solutions to inviscid primitive and Boussinesq equations. *Commun. Math. Phys.* **2017**, *353*, 1201–1216. [CrossRef]
12. Sun, J.Y.; Yang, M. Global well-posedness for the viscous primitive equations of geophysics. *Boundary Value Probl.* **2016**, *2016*, 21. [CrossRef]
13. Sun, J.Y.; Cui, S.B. Sharp well-posedness and ill-posedness of the three-dimensional primitive equations of geophysics in Fourier-Besov spaces. *Nonlinear Anal. Real World Appl.* **2019**, *48*, 445–465. [CrossRef]

14. Fang, D.F.; Han, B. Global well-posedness for the 3D primitive equations in anisotropic framework. *J. Math. Anal. Appl.* **2020**, *484*, 123714. [CrossRef]
15. Li, Y.F.; Xiao, S.Z.; Zeng, P. Continuous dependence of primitive equations of the atmosphere with vapor saturation. *J. East China Normal Univ. (Nat. Sci.)* **2021**, *2021*, 34–46.
16. Li, Y.F. Continuous dependence on boundary parameters for three-dimensional viscous primitive equation of large-scale ocean atmospheric dynamics. *J. Jilin Univ. (Sci. Ed.)* **2019**, *57*, 1053–1059.
17. Liu, Y. Continuous dependence for a thermal convection model with temperature-dependent solubility. *Appl. Math. Comput.* **2017**, *308*, 18–30.
18. Li, Y.F.; Xiao, S.Z.; Chen, X.J. Spatial alternative and stability of type III Thermoelastic equations. *Appl. Math. Mech.* **2021**, *42*, 431–440.
19. Li, Y.F.; Shi, J.C.; Zhu, H.S.; Huang, S.Q. Fast growth or decay estimates of Thermoelastic equations in an external domain. *Acta Math. Sci.* **2021**, *41A*, 1042–1052.
20. Li, Y.F.; Xiao, S.Z.; Zeng, P. The applications of some basic mathematical inequalities on the convergence of the primitive equations of moist atmosphere. *J. Math. Inequalit.* **2021**, *15*, 293–304. [CrossRef]
21. Li, Y.F.; Chen, X.J.; Shi, J.C. Structural stability in resonant penetrative convection in a Brinkman-Forchheimer fluid interfacing with a Darcy fluid. *Appl. Math. Opt.* **2021**, *84*, 979–999. [CrossRef]
22. Chen, W.H. Dissipative structure and diffusion phenomena for doubly dissipative elastic waves in two space dimensions. *J. Math. Anal. Appl.* **2020**, *486*, 123922. [CrossRef]
23. Oveissi, S.; Eftekhari, S.A.; Toghraie, D. Longitudinal vibration and instabilities of carbon nanotubes conveying fluid considering size effects of nanoflow and nanostructure. *Phys. E Low-Dimens. Syst. Nanostruct.* **2016**, *2016*, 164–173. [CrossRef]
24. Faridzadeh, M.R.; Semiromi, D.T.; Niroomand, A. Analysis of laminar mixed convection in an inclined square lid-driven cavity with a nanofluid by using an artificial neural network. *Heat Transf. Res.* **2014**, *45*, 361–390. [CrossRef]
25. Oveissi, S.; Toghraie, D.; Eftekhari, S.A. Longitudinal vibration and stability analysis of carbon nanotubes conveying viscous fluid. *Phys. E Low-Dimens. Syst. Nanostr.* **2016**, *2016*, 275–283. [CrossRef]
26. Liu, Y.; Xiao, S.Z.; Lin, C.H. Continuous dependence for the Brinkman-Forchheimer fluid interfacing with a Darcy fluid in a bounded domain. *Math. Comput. Simul.* **2018**, *150*, 66–88. [CrossRef]
27. Scott, N.L.; Straughan, B. Continuous dependence on the reaction terms in porous convection with surface reactions. *Quart. Appl. Math.* **2013**, *71*, 501–508. [CrossRef]
28. Li, Y.F.; Lin, C.H. Continuous dependence for the nonhomogeneous Brinkman-Forchheimer equations in a semi-infinite pipe. *Appl. Math. Comput.* **2014**, *244*, 201–208. [CrossRef]
29. Hameed, A.A.; Harfash, A.J. Continuous dependence of double diffusive convection in a porous medium with temperature-dependent density. *Basrah J. Sci.* **2019**, *37*, 1–15.
30. Hardy, C.H.; Littlewood, J.E.; Polya, G. *Inequalities*; Cambridge University Press: Cambridge, UK, 1953.
31. Mitronovic, D.S. *Analytical Inequalities*; Springer: Berlin/Heidelberg, Germany, 1970.
32. Huang, D.W.; Guo, B.L. On two-dimensional large-scale primitive equations in oceanic dynamics (II). *Appl. Math. Mech. (Engl. Ed.)* **2007**, *28*, 593–600. [CrossRef]

Article

Global Bounds for the Generalized Jensen Functional with Applications

Slavko Simić [1,*] and Bandar Bin-Mohsin [2]

1. Mathematical Institute SANU, 11000 Belgrade, Serbia
2. Department of Mathematics, College of Science, King Saud University, Riyadh 11451, Saudi Arabia; balmohsen@ksu.edu.sa
* Correspondence: ssimic@turing.mi.sanu.ac.rs

Abstract: In this article we give sharp global bounds for the generalized Jensen functional $J_n(g,h;\mathbf{p},x)$. In particular, exact bounds are determined for the generalized power mean in terms from the class of Stolarsky means. As a consequence, we obtain the best possible global converses of quotients and differences of the generalized arithmetic, geometric and harmonic means.

Keywords: Jensen functional; A-G-H inequalities; global bounds; power means; convex functions

MSC: 26D07(26D15)

1. Introduction

Recall that the Jensen functional $J_n(h;\mathbf{p},x)$ is defined on an interval $I \subseteq \mathbb{R}$ by

$$J_n(h;\mathbf{p},x) := \sum_1^n p_i h(x_i) - h(\sum_1^n p_i x_i),$$

where $h: I \to \mathbb{R}$, $\mathbf{x} = (x_1, x_2, \cdots, x_n) \in I^n$ and $\mathbf{p} = \{p_i\}_1^n$ is a positive weight sequence. If h is a convex function on I then the inequality

$$0 \leq J_n(h;\mathbf{p},x)$$

holds for each $\mathbf{x} \in I^n$ and any positive weight sequence $\mathbf{p}$.

If h is a concave function on I then the above inequality is reversed. Those inequalities play a fundamental role in many parts of mathematical analysis and applications. For example, the well-known $\mathcal{A} - \mathcal{G} - \mathcal{H}$ inequality, Holder's inequality, Ky Fan inequality, etc., are proven by the help of Jensen's inequality (cf. [1–6]).

Our aim in this paper is to find the simplest constant C such that

$$0 \leq J_n(h;\mathbf{p},x) \leq C,$$

for any choice of $\mathbf{p}, x$ and thus make this inequality symmetrical.

This will be done by assuming that $\mathbf{x} \in [a,b]^n \subset I^n$, and we shall find some global bounds for the generalized Jensen functional

$$J_n(g,h;\mathbf{p},x) := g(\sum_1^n p_i h(x_i)) - g(h(\sum_1^n p_i x_i)),$$

that is, the bounds not depending on $\mathbf{p}$ or x but only on a, b and functions g and h.

In this sense, a typical result is given by the part of Theorem 1 (below).

For $\mathbf{x} \in [a,b]^n \subset I^n$, let $h : I \to J$ be convex and $g : J \to \mathbb{R}$ be an increasing function. Then

$$0 \le J_n(g, h; \mathbf{p}, x) \le \max_p [g(ph(a) + (1-p)h(b)) - g(h(pa + (1-p)b))].$$

Our global bounds will be entirely presented in terms of elementary means. Recall that the *mean* is a map $M : \mathbb{R}_+ \times \mathbb{R}_+ \to \mathbb{R}_+$, with a property

$$\min(x, y) \le M(x, y) \le \max(x, y),$$

for each $x, y \in \mathbb{R}_+$.

In the sequel we shall use the class of so-called Stolarsky (or extended) two-parametric mean values, defined for positive values of $x, y, x \ne y$ by the following

$$E_{r,s}(x,y) = \begin{cases} \left(\frac{r(x^s - y^s)}{s(x^r - y^r)}\right)^{1/(s-r)}, & rs(r-s) \ne 0 \\ \exp\left(\frac{-1}{s} + \frac{x^s \log x - y^s \log y}{x^s - y^s}\right), & r = s \ne 0 \\ \left(\frac{x^s - y^s}{s(\log x - \log y)}\right)^{1/s}, & s \ne 0, r = 0 \\ \sqrt{xy}, & r = s = 0, \\ x, & y = x > 0. \end{cases}$$

In this form it was introduced by Keneth Stolarsky in [7].

Most of the classical two variable means are special cases of the class E. For example,

$$A(x, y) = E_{1,2}(x, y) = \frac{x+y}{2}$$

is the arithmetic mean;

$$G(x, y) = E_{0,0}(x, y) = E_{-r,r}(x, y) = \sqrt{xy}$$

is the geometric mean;

$$L(x, y) = E_{0,1}(x, y) = \frac{x-y}{\log x - \log y}$$

is the logarithmic mean;

$$I(x, y) = E_{1,1}(x, y) = (x^x/y^y)^{\frac{1}{x-y}}/e$$

is the identric mean, etc.

More generally, the r-th power mean

$$A_r(x, y) = \left(\frac{x^r + y^r}{2}\right)^{1/r}$$

is equal to $E_{r,2r}(x, y)$.

Using the class of Stolarsky means enables our results to be presented in a condensed and applicable way. For example, we give some results regarding $\mathcal{A} - \mathcal{G} - \mathcal{H}$ inequalities, where

$$\mathcal{A}(\mathbf{p}, x) := \sum_1^n p_i x_i;$$

$$\mathcal{G}(\mathbf{p}, x) := \prod_1^n x_i^{p_i};$$

$$\mathcal{H}(\mathbf{p}, x) := \left(\sum_1^n p_i/x_i\right)^{-1},$$

are the generalized arithmetic, geometric and harmonic means, respectively.
Let $\mathbf{x} \in [a,b]^n, 0 < a < b$. Then

$$0 \leq \mathcal{A}(\mathbf{p},x) - \mathcal{H}(\mathbf{p},x) \leq 2(A(a,b) - G(a,b));$$

$$0 \leq \mathcal{A}(\mathbf{p},x) - \mathcal{G}(\mathbf{p},x) \leq A(a,b) - L(a,b) + L(a,b)\log\frac{L(a,b)}{G(a,b)};$$

$$1 \leq \frac{\mathcal{A}(\mathbf{p},x)}{\mathcal{H}(\mathbf{p},x)} \leq \left(\frac{A(a,b)}{G(a,b)}\right)^2;$$

$$1 \leq \frac{\mathcal{G}(\mathbf{p},x)}{\mathcal{H}(\mathbf{p},x)} \leq \frac{I(a,b)L(a,b)}{G^2(a,b)};$$

$$1 \leq \frac{\mathcal{A}(\mathbf{p},x)}{\mathcal{G}(\mathbf{p},x)} \leq \frac{I(a,b)L(a,b)}{G^2(a,b)},$$

where A, G, H, L, I stands for the arithmetic, geometric, harmonic, logarithmic and identric means of positive numbers a and b, respectively.

All bounds above are the best possible.

2. Results and Proofs

Our results concerning global bounds for the generalized Jensen functional are given in the following two assertions.

Theorem 1. *1. For continuous functions g, h let $h : I \to J$ be convex and $g : J \to \mathbb{R}$ be an increasing function or $h : I \to J$ be concave and $g : J \to \mathbb{R}$ be a decreasing function. Then*

$$0 \leq J_n(g,h;\mathbf{p},x) \leq \max_p[g(ph(a) + (1-p)h(b)) - g(h(pa + (1-p)b))].$$

2. If $h : I \to J$ is convex and $g : J \to \mathbb{R}$ is a decreasing function or $h : I \to J$ is concave and $g : J \to \mathbb{R}$ is an increasing function. Then

$$0 \leq -J_n(g,h;\mathbf{p},x) \leq \max_p[g(h(pa + (1-p)b)) - g(ph(a) + (1-p)h(b))].$$

Proof. We shall prove only the part 1. The proof of part 2 of this theorem is analogous.

Therefore, if h is a convex function on J we have $\sum_1^n p_i h(x_i) \geq h(\sum_1^n p_i x_i)$. Since g is an increasing function, it follows that

$$J_n(g,h;\mathbf{p},x) = g(\sum_1^n p_i h(x_i)) - g(h(\sum_1^n p_i x_i)) \geq 0.$$

Similarly, if h is a concave function on J we have $\sum_1^n p_i h(x_i) \leq h(\sum_1^n p_i x_i)$. Since g is a decreasing function, it follows again that

$$J_n(g,h;\mathbf{p},x) \geq 0.$$

On the other hand, since $a \leq x_i \leq b$, there exist non-negative numbers $\lambda_i, \mu_i; \lambda_i + \mu_i = 1$, such that $x_i = \lambda_i a + \mu_i b$, $i = 1, 2, ..., n$.

Hence,

$$J_n(g,h;\mathbf{p},x) = g(\sum_1^n p_i h(x_i)) - g(h(\sum_1^n p_i x_i)) = g(\sum_1^n p_i h(\lambda_i a + \mu_i b)) - g(h(\sum_1^n p_i(\lambda_i a + \mu_i b)))$$

$$\leq g(\sum_1^n p_i(\lambda_i h(a) + \mu_i h(b))) - g(h(a\sum_1^n p_i \lambda_i + b\sum_1^n p_i \mu_i)))$$

$$= g(ph(a) + (1-p)h(b)) - g(h(pa + (1-p)b)) := F(p;a,b) \leq \max_p F(p;a,b),$$

where we denoted $\sum_1^n p_i \lambda_i := p \in [0,1]$.

The second case with concave h and decreasing g leads to the same result. □

Note that the function $F(p;a,b)$ is continuous in p and non-negative with $F(0;a,b) = F(1;a,b) = 0$. Therefore, $\max_p F(p;a,b)$ exists. Another and sometimes difficult problem is to evaluate its exact value (see Open Problem below).

For this cause, we give an estimation of $J_n(g,h;\mathbf{p},x)$ with a unique maximum, which could be easily calculated. This method can be applied to the second part of Theorem 1, as well.

Theorem 2. *1. Under the conditions of the first part of Theorem 1, assume firstly that g is a convex function on J. Then*

$$0 \leq J_n(g,h;\mathbf{p},x) \leq \max_p [pf(a) + (1-p)f(b) - f(pa + (1-p)b)],$$

where $f := g \circ h$.

2. Assuming that $f = g \circ h$ is a concave function, we have

$$0 \leq J_n(g,h;\mathbf{p},x) \leq \max_p [g(ph(a) + (1-p)h(b)) - (pf(a) + (1-p)f(b))].$$

Now, both maximums can be easily determined by the standard technique.

Proof. By the first part of Theorem 1, we found that there exists $p \in [0,1]$ such that

$$J_n(g,h;\mathbf{p},x) \leq g(ph(a) + (1-p)h(b)) - g(h(pa + (1-p)b)).$$

If additionally g is convex on J, then

$$g(ph(a) + (1-p)h(b)) \leq p(g \circ h)(a) + (1-p)(g \circ h)(b).$$

Hence,

$$J_n(g,h;\mathbf{p},x) \leq p(g \circ h)(a) + (1-p)(g \circ h)(b) - (g \circ h)(pa + (1-p)b)$$

$$= pf(a) + (1-p)f(b) - f(pa + (1-p)b)] \leq \max_p [pf(a) + (1-p)f(b) - f(pa + (1-p)b)].$$

Consequently, if $g \circ h$ is a concave function on J, we have

$$g(h(pa + (1-p)b) = (g \circ h)(pa + (1-p)b) \geq p(g \circ h)(a) + (1-p)(g \circ h)(b),$$

and

$$J_n(g,h;\mathbf{p},x) \leq \max_p [g(ph(a) + (1-p)h(b)) - (pf(a) + (1-p)f(b))].$$

□

3. Applications

The results above are the source of a number of interesting inequalities. For instance, taking $g(x) = \log x$ in Theorem 1, we are enabled to determine converses of the quotient

$$\frac{\sum p_i h(x_i)}{h(\sum p_i x_i)}.$$

Or, taking $g(x) = h^{-1}(x)$, we can estimate the difference

$$\mathcal{A}_h(\mathbf{p},x) - \mathcal{A}(\mathbf{p},x),$$

where
$$\mathcal{A}_h(\mathbf{p}, x) := h^{-1}(\sum p_i h(x_i)),$$
is the quasi-arithmetic mean and
$$\mathcal{A}_x(\mathbf{p}, x) = \mathcal{A}(\mathbf{p}, x) = \sum p_i x_i,$$
is the generalized arithmetic mean.

We shall specialize this argument for the class of generalized power means $\mathcal{B}_s(\mathbf{p}, x)$ of order $s \in \mathbb{R}$, where
$$\mathcal{B}_s(\mathbf{p}, x) := (\sum p_i x_i^s)^{1/s}.$$

Some important particular cases are
$$\mathcal{B}_{-1}(\mathbf{p}, x) = (\sum_1^n p_i/x_i)^{-1} := \mathcal{H}(\mathbf{p}, x);$$

$$\mathcal{B}_0(\mathbf{p}, x) = \lim_{s \to 0} \mathcal{B}_s(\mathbf{p}, x) = \prod_1^n x_i^{p_i} := \mathcal{G}(\mathbf{p}, x);$$

$$\mathcal{B}_1(\mathbf{p}, x) = \sum_1^n p_i x_i := \mathcal{A}(\mathbf{p}, x),$$

that is, the generalized harmonic, geometric and arithmetic means, respectively.

It is well-known that $\mathcal{B}_s(\mathbf{p}, x)$ is monotone increasing in $s \in \mathbb{R}$ (cf. [4]).

Therefore,
$$\mathcal{H}(\mathbf{p}, x) \leq \mathcal{G}(\mathbf{p}, x) \leq \mathcal{A}(\mathbf{p}, x),$$
represents the famous $\mathcal{A} - \mathcal{G} - \mathcal{H}$ inequality.

As an application of Theorem 1, we shall estimate the difference $\mathcal{B}_s(\mathbf{p}, x) - \mathcal{A}(\mathbf{p}, x)$.

Theorem 3. *Let* $x \in [a, b]^n \subset I^n$, $0 < a < b$.
Then

$$0 \leq \mathcal{B}_s(\mathbf{p}, x) - \mathcal{A}(\mathbf{p}, x) \leq \frac{s-1}{s}(E_{s,1}(a,b) - E_{s,s-1}^{-1}(1/a, 1/b)), \ s > 1;$$

$$0 \leq \mathcal{A}(\mathbf{p}, x) - \mathcal{B}_s(\mathbf{p}, x) \leq \frac{1-s}{s}(E_{1,s}(a,b) - E_{1-s,-s}(a,b)), \ 0 < s < 1;$$

$$0 \leq \mathcal{A}(\mathbf{p}, x) - \mathcal{B}_s(\mathbf{p}, x) \leq \frac{s-1}{s}(E_{1-s,-s}(a,b) - E_{1,s}(a,b)), \ s < 0.$$

Proof. Let $h(x) = x^s$, $g(x) = x^{1/s}$, $s \in \mathbb{R}/\{0\}$.

If $s > 1$, then h is a convex function and g is monotone increasing on $(0, \infty)$. Hence, by the first part of Theorem 1, we obtain

$$0 \leq \mathcal{B}_s(\mathbf{p}, x) - \mathcal{A}(\mathbf{p}, x) \leq \max_p((pa^s + (1-p)b^s)^{1/s}) - (pa + (1-p)b) := M_s(p_0; a, b).$$

This maximum is easy to calculate and we obtain

$$p_0 a^s + (1 - p_0) b^s = \left(\frac{b^s - a^s}{s(b-a)}\right)^{s/(s-1)} = E_{s,1}^s(a, b).$$

Therefore,
$$p_0 = \frac{b^s - E_{s,1}^s(a, b)}{b^s - a^s}; \ 1 - p_0 = \frac{E_{s,1}^s(a, b) - a^s}{b^s - a^s},$$

and
$$p_0 a + (1 - p_0) b = \frac{ab^s - ba^s}{b^s - a^s} + \frac{b - a}{b^s - a^s} E_{s,1}^s(a, b).$$

Since,
$$E_{s,1}^s(a,b) = \frac{b^s - a^s}{s(b-a)} E_{s,1}(a,b),$$

we obtain
$$M_s(p_0;a,b) = (p_0 a^s + (1-p_0)b^s)^{1/s} - (p_0 a + (1-p_0)b)$$
$$= E_{s,1}(a,b) - \left(\frac{(1/a)^{s-1} - (1/b)^{s-1}}{(1/a)^s - (1/b)^s} + \frac{1}{s} E_{s,1}(a,b)\right)$$
$$= \frac{s-1}{s}(E_{s,1}(a,b) - E_{s,s-1}^{-1}(1/a,1/b)).$$

In cases $0 < s < 1$ and $s < 0$ one should apply the second part of Theorem 1, since then h is concave and g is increasing in the first case and h is convex and g is decreasing in the second case. Proceeding as above, the result follows. □

As a consequence, we obtain some converses of the $\mathcal{A}(\mathbf{p},x) - \mathcal{G}(\mathbf{p},x) - \mathcal{H}(\mathbf{p},x)$ inequality.

Corollary 1. *Let* $\mathbf{x} \in [a,b]^n \subset I^n$, $b > a > 0$.
Then
$$0 \leq \mathcal{A}(\mathbf{p},x) - \mathcal{H}(\mathbf{p},x) \leq 2(A(a,b) - G(a,b)).$$

Proof. Putting $s = -1$, we obtain
$$0 \leq \mathcal{A}(\mathbf{p},x) - \mathcal{B}_{-1}(\mathbf{p},x) = \mathcal{A}(\mathbf{p},x) - \mathcal{H}(\mathbf{p},x)$$
$$\leq 2(E_{2,1}(a,b) - E_{1,-1}(a,b)) = 2(A(a,b) - G(a,b)).$$
□

Corollary 2. *Let* $\mathbf{x} \in [a,b]^n \subset I^n$, $b > a > 0$.
Then
$$0 \leq \mathcal{A}(\mathbf{p},x) - \mathcal{G}(\mathbf{p},x) \leq L(a,b) \log \frac{L(a,b)I(a,b)}{G^2(a,b)}.$$

Proof. Letting $s \to 0$, we have
$$\mathcal{A}(\mathbf{p},x) - \mathcal{G}(\mathbf{p},x) = \lim_{s \to 0}(\mathcal{A}(\mathbf{p},x) - \mathcal{B}_s(\mathbf{p},x))$$
$$\leq \lim_{s \to 0}\left(\frac{1-s}{s}(E_{1,s}(a,b) - E_{1-s,-s}(a,b))\right).$$

After somewhat laborious calculation using Taylor series, the result follows. □

Remark 1. *Estimating the Jensen functional*
$$\mathcal{J}_n(e^x;\mathbf{p},x) = \sum_1^n p_i e^{x_i} - e^{\sum_1^n p_i x_i}$$

for $\mathbf{x} \in [a,b]^n \subset \mathbb{R}^n$, *and then changing variables* $x_i \to \log x_i$; $a \to \log a$, $b \to \log b$, *we obtain the same result.*

Open problem *Find the exact upper global bound for*
$$\mathcal{G}(p,x) - \mathcal{H}(p,x).$$

The next proposition gives global bounds for the quotient of two power means.

Theorem 4. *For $s > t$ and $\mathbf{x} \in [a,b]^n \subset \mathbb{R}_+^n$, we have*

$$1 \leq \frac{B_s(\mathbf{p}, \mathbf{x})}{B_t(\mathbf{p}, \mathbf{x})} \leq \frac{E_{s,s-t}(a,b)}{E_{t,t-s}(a,b)}.$$

Both bounds are the best possible.

Proof. Applying the method from the proof of Theorem 1, we obtain

$$x_i^t = \lambda_i a^t + \mu_i b^t, \; \lambda_i + \mu_i = 1, \; i = 1, 2, ..., n.$$

In the cases $s > t > 0$ or $s > 0, t < 0$, we have that the function $x^{s/t}$ is convex. Hence,

$$x_i^s = (\lambda_i a^t + \mu_i b^t)^{s/t} \leq \lambda_i (a^t)^{s/t} + \mu_i (b^t)^{s/t} = \lambda_i a^s + \mu_i b^s,$$

and

$$\frac{B_s(\mathbf{p}, \mathbf{x})}{B_t(\mathbf{p}, \mathbf{x})} = \frac{(\sum_1^n p_i x_i^s)^{1/s}}{(\sum_1^n p_i x_i^t)^{1/t}} \leq \frac{(a^s \sum_1^n p_i \lambda_i + b^s \sum_1^n p_i \mu_i)^{1/s}}{(a^t \sum_1^n p_i \lambda_i + b^t \sum_1^n p_i \mu_i)^{1/t}} = \frac{(pa^s + qb^s)^{1/s}}{(pa^t + qb^t)^{1/t}},$$

where we put

$$\sum_1^n p_i \lambda_i := p, \; \sum_1^n p_i \mu_i := q; \; p + q = 1.$$

Therefore, it follows that

$$\frac{B_s(\mathbf{p}, \mathbf{x})}{B_t(\mathbf{p}, \mathbf{x})} \leq \max_p \frac{(pa^s + qb^s)^{1/s}}{(pa^t + qb^t)^{1/t}} = \frac{(p_0 a^s + q_0 b^s)^{1/s}}{(p_0 a^t + q_0 b^t)^{1/t}}.$$

By standard means we obtain that this maximum satisfies the equation

$$\frac{s(p_0 a^s + q_0 b^s)}{a^s - b^s} = \frac{t(p_0 a^t + q_0 b^t)}{a^t - b^t},$$

that is,

$$p_0 = \frac{1}{s-t}\left(\frac{sb^s}{b^s - a^s} - \frac{tb^t}{b^t - a^t}\right); \; q_0 = \frac{1}{s-t}\left(\frac{ta^t}{b^t - a^t} - \frac{sa^s}{b^s - a^s}\right).$$

Consequently,

$$p_0 a^t + q_0 b^t = \frac{s}{s-t} \cdot \frac{a^t b^s - a^s b^t}{b^s - a^s} = \frac{s}{s-t} \cdot \frac{(ab)^t (b^{s-t} - a^{s-t})}{b^s - a^s},$$

and

$$p_0 a^s + q_0 b^s = \frac{t}{s-t} \cdot \frac{a^t b^s - a^s b^t}{b^t - a^t} = \frac{t}{t-s} \cdot \frac{(ab)^s (b^{t-s} - a^{t-s})}{b^t - a^t}.$$

Hence,

$$(p_0 a^t + q_0 b^t)^{1/t} = G^2(a,b) / E_{s,s-t}(a,b);$$
$$(p_0 a^s + q_0 b^s)^{1/s} = G^2(a,b) / E_{t,t-s}(a,b),$$

and we finally obtain

$$\max_p \frac{(pa^s + qb^s)^{1/s}}{(pa^t + qb^t)^{1/t}} = \frac{(p_0 a^s + q_0 b^s)^{1/s}}{(p_0 a^t + q_0 b^t)^{1/t}} = \frac{E_{s,s-t}(a,b)}{E_{t,t-s}(a,b)}.$$

In the third case, for $s > t > 0$, we have

$$1 \leq \frac{B_{-t}(\mathbf{p}, x)}{B_{-s}(\mathbf{p}, x)} = \frac{B_s(\mathbf{p}, 1/x)}{B_t(\mathbf{p}, 1/x)} \leq \frac{E_{s,s-t}(1/a, 1/b)}{E_{t,t-s}(1/a, 1/b)}$$

$$= \frac{E_{s,s-t}(a, b)}{E_{t,t-s}(a, b)},$$

since

$$E_{u,v}(1/a, 1/b) = E_{u,v}(a, b)/G^2(a, b).$$

It is obvious that 1 is the best possible lower global bound. To prove that $M_{s,t}(a,b) := E_{s,s-t}(a,b)/E_{t,t-s}(a,b)$ is also the best possible global bound, denote by $N_{s,t}(a,b)$ an arbitrary upper bound. Then the relation

$$\frac{B_s(\mathbf{p}, x)}{B_t(\mathbf{p}, x)} \leq N_{s,t}(a, b),$$

holds for any **p** and **x**.

Putting $x_1 = x_2 = ... = x_{n-1} = a, x_n = b, p_n = q_0$, we obtain

$$M_{s,t}(a,b) = \frac{(p_0 a^s + q_0 b^s)^{1/s}}{(p_0 a^t + q_0 b^t)^{1/t}} = \frac{B_s(\mathbf{p}, x)}{B_t(\mathbf{p}, x)} \leq N_{s,t}(a, b),$$

and the proof is complete. □

Some important consequences of this theorem are given in the following

Corollary 3. *For $s > 1$, we have*

$$A(\mathbf{p}, x) \leq B_s(\mathbf{p}, x) \leq \frac{E_{s,s-1}(a, b)}{E_{1,1-s}(a, b)} A(\mathbf{p}, x).$$

Corollary 4. *For $s > 0$, we have*

$$G(\mathbf{p}, x) \leq B_s(\mathbf{p}, x) \leq \frac{E_{s,s}(a, b) E_{s,0}(a, b)}{G^2(a, b)} G(\mathbf{p}, x).$$

Corollary 5. *For $s > -1$, we have*

$$H(\mathbf{p}, x) \leq B_s(\mathbf{p}, x) \leq \frac{E_{s+1,s}(a, b) E_{s+1,1}(a, b)}{G^2(a, b)} H(\mathbf{p}, x).$$

In the last two corollaries we used the identity

$$E_{-u,-v}(a, b) E_{u,v}(a, b) = G^2(a, b).$$

Finally, putting $s = 1$ in Corollary 4 and $s = 0, s = 1$ in Corollary 5, since $E_{2,1}(a,b) = A(a,b)$, $E_{1,0}(a,b) = L(a,b)$, $E_{1,1}(a,b) = I(a,b)$, we obtain global converses of the $A - G - H$ inequality.

Corollary 6.

$$G(\mathbf{p}, x) \leq A(\mathbf{p}, x) \leq \frac{L(a, b) I(a, b)}{G^2(a, b)} G(\mathbf{p}, x);$$

$$H(\mathbf{p}, x) \leq A(\mathbf{p}, x) \leq \left(\frac{A(a, b)}{G(a, b)}\right)^2 H(\mathbf{p}, x);$$

$$H(\mathbf{p}, x) \leq G(\mathbf{p}, x) \leq \frac{L(a, b) I(a, b)}{G^2(a, b)} H(\mathbf{p}, x).$$

Therefore, a sort of tight symmetry is established for these inequalities.

4. Conclusions

We give a method for two-sided estimations of the generalized Jensen functional $J_n(g, h; \mathbf{p}, \mathbf{x})$, with applications to the general means. In particular, sharp converses of the famous $\mathcal{A} - \mathcal{G} - \mathcal{H}$ inequality are obtained. Further investigations can be undertaken on more general settings, i.e., $J_n(f, g, h; \mathbf{p}, \mathbf{x}) := f(\sum_1^n p_i h(x_i)) - g(h(\sum_1^n p_i x_i))$ or even $F(\sum_1^n p_i h(x_i), h(\sum_1^n p_i x_i))$, with properly chosen functions f, g, h and $F(x, y)$.

Author Contributions: Theoretical part, S.S.; numerical part with examples, B.B.-M. All authors have read and agreed to the published version of the manuscript.

Funding: Bandar Bin-Mohsin is supported by Researchers Supporting Project number (RSP-2021/158), King Saud University, Riyadh, Saudi Arabia.

Institutional Review Board Statement: Not applicable.

Informed Consent Statement: Not applicable.

Data Availability Statement: Not applicable.

Acknowledgments: The authors are grateful to the referees for their valuable comments.

Conflicts of Interest: The authors declare no conflict of interests.

References

1. Hardy, G.H.; Littlewood, J.E.; Polya, G. *Inequalities*; Cambridge University Press: Cambridge, UK, 1978.
2. Mercer, A. A variant of Jensen's inequality. *J. Inequal. Pure Appl. Math.* **2003**, *4*, 73.
3. Dragomir, S.S. Some reverses of the Jensen inequality for functions of self-adjoint operators in Hilbert spaces. *J. Inequal. Appl.* **2010**, *15*, 496821. [CrossRef]
4. Simić, S. On a converse of Jensen's discrete inequality. *J. Inequal. Appl.* **2009**, *2009*, 153080. [CrossRef]
5. Simic, S. Another converse of Jensen's inequality. *Res. Rep. Collect.* **2009**, *12*. [CrossRef]
6. Simić, S. On a converse of Ky Fan inequality. *Krag. J. Math.* **2010**, *33*, 95–99.
7. Stolarsky, K.B. Generalizations of the logarithmic mean. *Math. Mag.* **1975**, *48*, 87–92. [CrossRef]

Article

Some New Simpson's-Formula-Type Inequalities for Twice-Differentiable Convex Functions via Generalized Fractional Operators

Muhammad Aamir Ali [1,*], Hasan Kara [2], Jessada Tariboon [3], Suphawat Asawasamrit [3], Hüseyin Budak [2] and Fatih Hezenci [2]

[1] Jiangsu Key Laboratory for NSLSCS, School of Mathematical Sciences, Nanjing Normal University, Nanjing 210023, China
[2] Department of Mathematics, Faculty of Science and Arts, Düzce University, Düzce 81620, Turkey; hasan96929@ogr.duzce.edu.tr (H.K.); huseyinbudak@duzce.edu.tr (H.B.); fatihhezenci@duzce.edu.tr (F.H.)
[3] Intelligent and Nonlinear Dynamic Innovations Research Center, Department of Mathematics, Faculty of Applied Science, King Mongkut's University of Technology North Bangkok, Bangkok 10800, Thailand; jessada.t@sci.kmutnb.ac.th (J.T.); suphawat.a@sci.kmutnb.ac.th (S.A.)
* Correspondence: mahr.muhammad.aamir@gmail.com

Abstract: From the past to the present, various works have been dedicated to Simpson's inequality for differentiable convex functions. Simpson-type inequalities for twice-differentiable functions have been the subject of some research. In this paper, we establish a new generalized fractional integral identity involving twice-differentiable functions, then we use this result to prove some new Simpson's-formula-type inequalities for twice-differentiable convex functions. Furthermore, we examine a few special cases of newly established inequalities and obtain several new and old Simpson's-formula-type inequalities. These types of analytic inequalities, as well as the methodologies for solving them, have applications in a wide range of fields where symmetry is crucial.

Keywords: Simpson-type inequalities; convex function; fractional integrals

1. Introduction

Simpson's inequality is widely used in many areas of mathematics. For four times continuously differentiable functions, the classical Simpson's inequality is expressed as follows:

Theorem 1. *Suppose that $f : [a,b] \to \mathbb{R}$ is a four times continuously differentiable mapping on (a,b), and suppose also that $\left\| f^{(4)} \right\|_\infty = \sup_{x \in (a,b)} \left| f^{(4)}(x) \right| < \infty$. Then, one has the inequality*

$$\left| \frac{1}{3} \left[\frac{f(a) + f(b)}{2} + 2f\left(\frac{a+b}{2}\right) \right] - \frac{1}{b-a} \int_a^b f(x)dx \right| \leq \frac{1}{2880} \left\| f^{(4)} \right\|_\infty (b-a)^4.$$

Many researchers have studied various Simpson's inequalities. More precisely, some studies have focused on Simpson's type for the convex function, because this focus has been an effective and powerful way to solve many problems in inequality theory and other areas of mathematics. For example, Alomari et al. established some inequalities of Simpson's type for s-convex functions by using differentiable functions [1]. Subsequently, Sarikaya et al. established new variants of Simpson's-type inequalities based on differentiable convex functions in [2,3]. Additionally, some papers have listed Simpson's-type inequalities in various convex classes [4–8]. Moreover, in the papers [9,10], researchers extended the Simpson inequalities for differentiable functions to Riemann–Liouville fractional integrals. Thereupon, several mathematicians studied fractional Simpson inequalities for these kinds of fractional integral operators [11–19]. For more studies related to different integral operator inequalities, one can see [20–31]. In addition, Sarikaya et al. obtained several Simpson-type inequalities for mappings whose second derivatives are convex [32]. In this article, after giving the definition of the generalized fractional integral operators, we construct a new identity for twice-differentiable functions. Using this equality, we prove several Simpson-type inequalities for functions whose second derivatives are convex. Then, with the help of special choices, the main results in this paper are shown to generalize many studies. In addition to all these, new results for k-Riemann–Liouville fractional integrals are also obtained.

First of all, general definitions and theorems that are used throughout the article are presented.

Definition 1. *Let us consider $f \in L_1[a,b]$. The Riemann–Liouville integrals $J_{a+}^\alpha f$ and $J_{b-}^\alpha f$ of order $\alpha > 0$ with $a \geq 0$ are defined by*

$$J_{a+}^\alpha f(x) = \frac{1}{\Gamma(\alpha)} \int_a^x (x-t)^{\alpha-1} f(t) dt, \quad x > a,$$

and

$$J_{b-}^\alpha f(x) = \frac{1}{\Gamma(\alpha)} \int_x^b (t-x)^{\alpha-1} f(t) dt, \quad x < b,$$

respectively. Here, $\Gamma(\alpha)$ is the gamma function and $J_{a+}^0 f(x) = J_{b-}^0 f(x) = f(x)$.

For further information and several properties of Riemann–Liouville fractional integrals, please refer to [33–35].

In [36], Budak et al. prove the following identity for twice-differentiable functions and they also prove corresponding Simpson-type inequalities.

Lemma 1 ([36]). *Let $f : [a,b] \to \mathbb{R}$ be a twice-differentiable mapping (a,b) such that $f'' \in L_1([a,b])$. Then, the following equality holds:*

$$\frac{1}{6}\left[f(a) + 4f\left(\frac{a+b}{2}\right) + f(b)\right] - \frac{2^{\alpha-1}\Gamma(\alpha+1)}{(b-a)^\alpha}\left[J_{\left(\frac{a+b}{2}\right)+}^\alpha f(b) + J_{\left(\frac{a+b}{2}\right)-}^\alpha f(a)\right]$$

$$= \frac{(b-a)^2}{6} \int_0^1 w(t) f''(tb + (1-t)a) dt,$$

where

$$w(t) = \begin{cases} t\left(1 - \frac{3 \cdot 2^\alpha}{\alpha+1} t^\alpha\right), & t \in \left[0, \frac{1}{2}\right], \\ (1-t)\left(1 - \frac{3 \cdot 2^\alpha}{\alpha+1}(1-t)^\alpha\right), & t \in \left(\frac{1}{2}, 1\right]. \end{cases}$$

In [37], Hezenci et al. prove another version of the results given in [36].

However, the generalized fractional integrals were introduced by Sarikaya and Ertuğral as follows:

Definition 2 ([38]). *Let us note that a function $\varphi : [0, \infty) \to [0, \infty)$ satisfies the following condition:*

$$\int_0^1 \frac{\varphi(t)}{t} dt < \infty.$$

We consider the following left-sided and right-sided generalized fractional integral operators

$$_{a+}I_\varphi f(x) = \int_a^x \frac{\varphi(x-t)}{x-t} f(t) dt, \quad x > a, \qquad (1)$$

and
$$_{b-}I_\varphi f(x) = \int_x^b \frac{\varphi(t-x)}{t-x} f(t)dt, \quad x < b, \qquad (2)$$

respectively.

The most important feature of generalized fractional integrals is that they generalize some types of fractional integrals such as Riemann–Liouville fractional integrals, k-Riemann–Liouville fractional integrals, Hadamard fractional integrals, Katugampola fractional integrals, conformable fractional integrals, etc. These significant special cases of the integral operators (1) and (2) are used as follows:

1. For $\varphi(t) = t$, the operators (1) and (2) reduce to the Riemann integral.
2. If we assign $\varphi(t) = \frac{t^\alpha}{\Gamma(\alpha)}$ and $\alpha > 0$, then the operators (1) and (2) reduce to the Riemann–Liouville fractional integrals $J_{a+}^\alpha f(x)$ and $J_{b-}^\alpha f(x)$, respectively. Here, Γ is the gamma function.
3. Let us consider $\varphi(t) = \frac{1}{k\Gamma_k(\alpha)} t^{\frac{\alpha}{k}}$ and $\alpha, k > 0$. Then, the operators (1) and (2) reduce to the k-Riemann–Liouville fractional integrals $J_{a+,k}^\alpha f(x)$ and $J_{b-,k}^\alpha f(x)$, respectively. Here, Γ_k is k-gamma function.

In recent years, several papers have been devoted to obtaining inequalities for generalized fractional integrals; for some of them please refer to [39–45].

Inspired by the ongoing studies, we give the generalized fractional version of the inequalities proved by Budak et al. in [36] for twice-differentiable convex functions. The fundamental benefit of these inequalities is that they can be turned into classical integral inequalities of Simpson's type [32], Riemann–Liouville fractional integral inequalities of Simpson's type [36], and k-Riemann–Liouville fractional integral inequalities of Simpson's type without having to prove each one separately.

2. Simpson's-Type Inequalities for Twice-Differentiable Functions

In this section, we prove some new inequalities of Simpson's type for twice-differentiable convex functions via the generalized fractional integrals. For brevity in the rest of the paper, we define
$$A(t) = \int_0^t T(s)ds,$$

where
$$T(s) = \int_0^s \frac{\varphi((b-a)u)}{u} du.$$

Lemma 2. Let $f : [a,b] \to \mathbb{R}$ be a twice-differentiable mapping (a,b) such that $f'' \in L_1([a,b])$. Then, the following equality for generalized fractional integrals holds:

$$\frac{1}{6}\left[f(a) + 4f\left(\frac{a+b}{2}\right) + f(b)\right] - \frac{1}{2T\left(\frac{1}{2}\right)}\left[{}_{\left(\frac{a+b}{2}\right)+}I_\varphi f(b) + {}_{\left(\frac{a+b}{2}\right)-}I_\varphi f(a)\right]$$

$$= \frac{(b-a)^2}{6} \int_0^1 \omega(t) f''(tb + (1-t)a) dt,$$

where
$$\omega(t) = \begin{cases} t - \frac{3A(t)}{T(1/2)}, & t \in \left[0, \frac{1}{2}\right], \\ 1 - t - \frac{3A(1-t)}{T(1/2)}, & t \in \left(\frac{1}{2}, 1\right]. \end{cases}$$

Proof. Using integration by parts, we obtain

$$I_1 = \int_0^{1/2} \left(t - \frac{3A(t)}{T(1/2)}\right) f''(tb + (1-t)a) dt$$

$$= \left(t - \frac{3A(t)}{T(1/2)}\right) \frac{f'(tb + (1-t)a)}{b-a} \Big|_0^{1/2}$$

$$- \frac{1}{b-a} \int_0^{1/2} \left(1 - \frac{3T(t)}{T(1/2)}\right) f'(tb + (1-t)a) dt$$

$$= \frac{1}{b-a} \left(\frac{1}{2} - \frac{3A(1/2)}{T(1/2)}\right) f'\left(\frac{a+b}{2}\right)$$

$$- \frac{1}{b-a} \left[\left(1 - \frac{3T(t)}{T(1/2)}\right) \frac{f(tb + (1-t)a)}{(b-a)} \Big|_0^{1/2}\right.$$

$$\left. + \frac{1}{b-a} \int_0^{1/2} \frac{3}{T(1/2)} \frac{\varphi((b-a)t)}{t} f(tb + (1-t)) dt\right]$$

$$= \frac{1}{b-a} \left(\frac{1}{2} - \frac{3A(1/2)}{T(1/2)}\right) f'\left(\frac{a+b}{2}\right) + \frac{2}{(b-a)^2} f\left(\frac{a+b}{2}\right)$$

$$+ \frac{f(a)}{(b-a)^2} + \frac{3}{T(1/2)(b-a)^2} \left(\frac{a+b}{2}\right)_{-} I_\varphi f(a).$$

Similarly, we have

$$I_2 = \int_{1/2}^{1} \left(1 - t - \frac{3A(1-t)}{T(1/2)}\right) f''(tb + (1-t)a) dt$$

$$= -\frac{1}{b-a} \left(\frac{1}{2} - \frac{3A(1/2)}{T(1/2)}\right) f'\left(\frac{a+b}{2}\right) + \frac{2}{(b-a)^2} f\left(\frac{a+b}{2}\right)$$

$$+ \frac{f(b)}{(b-a)^2} + \frac{3}{T(1/2)(b-a)^2} \left(\frac{a+b}{2}\right)_{+} I_\varphi f(b).$$

If I_1 and I_2 are added and then multiplied by $\frac{(b-a)^2}{6}$, the desired result is obtained. □

Remark 1. *If we take $\varphi(t) = t$ in Lemma 2, then Lemma 2 reduces to [32] (Lemma 2.1).*

Remark 2. *Let us note that $\varphi(t) = \frac{t^\alpha}{\Gamma(\alpha)}$, $\alpha > 0$ in Lemma 2, then Lemma 2 reduces to Lemma 1.*

Corollary 1. *If we choose $\varphi(t) = \frac{t^{\frac{\alpha}{k}}}{k\Gamma_k(\alpha)}$, $\alpha, k > 0$ in Lemma 2, then the following equality for k-Riemann–Liouville fractional integrals holds:*

$$\frac{1}{6}\left[f(a) + 4f\left(\frac{a+b}{2}\right) + f(b)\right] - \frac{2^{\frac{\alpha-k}{k}}\Gamma(\alpha+k)}{(b-a)^{\frac{\alpha}{k}}} \left[J^\alpha_{\left(\frac{a+b}{2}\right)_+, k} f(b) + J^\alpha_{\left(\frac{a+b}{2}\right)_-, k} f(a)\right]$$

$$= \frac{(b-a)^2}{6} \int_0^1 m(t) f''(tb + (1-t)a) dt,$$

where

$$m(t) = \begin{cases} t\left(1 - \frac{3k \cdot 2^{\frac{\alpha}{k}}}{\alpha+k} t^{\frac{\alpha}{k}}\right), & t \in \left[0, \frac{1}{2}\right], \\ (1-t)\left(1 - \frac{3k \cdot 2^{\frac{\alpha}{k}}}{\alpha+k}(1-t)^{\frac{\alpha}{k}}\right), & t \in \left(\frac{1}{2}, 1\right]. \end{cases}$$

Proof. For $\varphi(\tau) = \frac{\tau^{\frac{\alpha}{k}}}{k\Gamma_k(\alpha)}$, we have

$$\Lambda(s) = \frac{(\kappa_2 - \kappa_1)^{\frac{\alpha}{k}}}{\alpha \Gamma_k(\alpha)} s^{\frac{\alpha}{k}} = \frac{(\kappa_2 - \kappa_1)^{\frac{\alpha}{k}}}{\Gamma_k(\alpha+k)} s^{\frac{\alpha}{k}}, \qquad (3)$$

$$\Lambda(1/2) = \frac{(\kappa_2 - \kappa_1)^{\frac{\alpha}{k}}}{2^{\frac{\alpha}{k}} \Gamma_k(\alpha+k)} \qquad (4)$$

and

$$\Delta(\tau) = \frac{(\kappa_2 - \kappa_1)^{\frac{\alpha}{k}}}{\Gamma_k(\alpha+k)} \int_0^\tau s^{\frac{\alpha}{k}} ds = \frac{k(\kappa_2 - \kappa_1)^{\frac{\alpha}{k}}}{(\alpha+k)\Gamma_k(\alpha+k)} \tau^{\frac{\alpha}{k}+1}. \qquad (5)$$

Then it follows that

$$\varpi(\tau) = m(\tau)$$

which completes the proof. □

Theorem 2. *Assume that the assumptions of Lemma 2 hold. Assume also that the mapping $|f''|$ is convex on $[a,b]$. Then, we have the following Simpson-type inequality for generalized fractional integrals*

$$\left| \frac{1}{6}\left[f(a) + 4f\left(\frac{a+b}{2}\right) + f(b)\right] - \frac{1}{2T\left(\frac{1}{2}\right)} \left[{}_{\left(\frac{a+b}{2}\right)^+} I\varphi f(b) + {}_{\left(\frac{a+b}{2}\right)^-} I\varphi f(a) \right] \right|$$

$$\leq \frac{(b-a)^2}{6} \left(\int_0^{\frac{1}{2}} \left| t - \frac{3A(t)}{T(1/2)} \right| dt \right) [|f''(a)| + |f''(b)|].$$

Proof. By taking the modulus in Lemma 2, we have

$$\left| \frac{1}{6}\left[f(a) + 4f\left(\frac{a+b}{2}\right) + f(b)\right] - \frac{1}{2T\left(\frac{1}{2}\right)} \left[{}_{\left(\frac{a+b}{2}\right)^+} I\varphi f(b) + {}_{\left(\frac{a+b}{2}\right)^-} I\varphi f(a) \right] \right|$$

$$\leq \frac{(b-a)^2}{6} \int_0^1 |\varpi(t)| |f''(tb + (1-t)a)| dt$$

$$= \frac{(b-a)^2}{6} \left[\int_0^{\frac{1}{2}} \left| t - \frac{3A(t)}{T(1/2)} \right| |f''(tb + (1-t)a)| dt \right. \qquad (6)$$

$$\left. + \int_{\frac{1}{2}}^1 \left| 1 - t - \frac{3A(1-t)}{T(1/2)} \right| |f''(tb + (1-t)a)| dt \right].$$

With the help of the convexity of $|f''|$, we obtain

$$\left| \frac{1}{6}\left[f(a) + 4f\left(\frac{a+b}{2}\right) + f(b)\right] - \frac{1}{2T\left(\frac{1}{2}\right)} \left[{}_{\left(\frac{a+b}{2}\right)^+} I\varphi f(b) + {}_{\left(\frac{a+b}{2}\right)^-} I\varphi f(a) \right] \right|$$

$$\leq \frac{(b-a)^2}{6} \left[\int_0^{\frac{1}{2}} \left| t - \frac{3A(t)}{T(1/2)} \right| [t|f''(b)| + (1-t)|f''(a)|] dt \right.$$

$$+ \left. \int_{\frac{1}{2}}^1 \left| 1 - t - \frac{3A(1-t)}{T(1/2)} \right| [t|f''(b)| + (1-t)|f''(a)|] dt \right]$$

$$= \frac{(b-a)^2}{6} \left\{ \left[\int_0^{\frac{1}{2}} t \left| t - \frac{3A(t)}{T(1/2)} \right| dt + \int_{\frac{1}{2}}^1 t \left| 1 - t - \frac{3A(1-t)}{T(1/2)} \right| dt \right] |f''(b)| \right.$$

$$+ \left. \left[\int_0^{\frac{1}{2}} (1-t) \left| t - \frac{3A(t)}{T(1/2)} \right| dt + \int_{\frac{1}{2}}^1 (1-t) \left| 1 - t - \frac{3A(1-t)}{T(1/2)} \right| dt \right] |f''(a)| \right\}$$

$$= \frac{(b-a)^2}{6} \left[\int_0^{\frac{1}{2}} t \left| t - \frac{3A(t)}{T(1/2)} \right| dt + \int_{\frac{1}{2}}^1 t \left| 1 - t - \frac{3A(1-t)}{T(1/2)} \right| dt \right] [|f''(a)| + |f''(b)|]$$

$$= \frac{(b-a)^2}{6} \left(\int_0^{\frac{1}{2}} \left| t - \frac{3A(t)}{T(1/2)} \right| dt \right) [|f''(a)| + |f''(b)|].$$

This completes the proof of Theorem 2. □

Remark 3. *Consider $\varphi(t) = t$ in Theorem 2, then Theorem 2 reduces to [32] (Theorem 2.2).*

Remark 4. *If we assign $\varphi(t) = \frac{t^\alpha}{\Gamma(\alpha)}, \alpha > 0$ in Theorem 2, then we obtain the following Simpson-type inequality for Riemann–Liouville fractional integrals*

$$\left| \frac{1}{6} \left[f(a) + 4f\left(\frac{a+b}{2}\right) + f(b) \right] - \frac{2^{\alpha-1}\Gamma(\alpha+1)}{(b-a)^\alpha} \left[J^\alpha_{\left(\frac{a+b}{2}\right)^+} f(b) + J^\alpha_{\left(\frac{a+b}{2}\right)^-} f(a) \right] \right|$$

$$\leq \frac{(b-a)^2}{6} \Theta(\alpha)[|f''(a)| + |f''(b)|].$$

Here,

$$\Theta(\alpha) = \frac{1}{4(\alpha+2)} \left(\alpha \left(\frac{\alpha+1}{3} \right)^{\frac{2}{\alpha}} + \frac{3}{\alpha+1} \right) - \frac{1}{8}, \quad (7)$$

which is given by Budak et al. in [36].

Corollary 2. *For $\varphi(t) = \frac{t^{\frac{\alpha}{k}}}{k\Gamma_k(\alpha)}, k, \alpha > 0$ in Theorem 2, we have the following Simpson-type inequality for k-Riemann–Liouville fractional integrals*

$$\left| \frac{1}{6} \left[f(a) + 4f\left(\frac{a+b}{2}\right) + f(b) \right] - \frac{2^{\frac{\alpha-k}{k}}\Gamma(\alpha+k)}{(b-a)^{\frac{\alpha}{k}}} \left[J^\alpha_{\left(\frac{a+b}{2}\right)^+, k} f(b) + J^\alpha_{\left(\frac{a+b}{2}\right)^-, k} f(a) \right] \right|$$

$$\leq \frac{(b-a)^2}{6} \Theta(\alpha, k)[|f''(a)| + |f''(b)|],$$

where

$$\Theta(\alpha, k) = \frac{k}{4(\alpha+2k)} \left(\frac{\alpha}{k} \left(\frac{\alpha+k}{3k} \right)^{\frac{2k}{\alpha}} + \frac{3k}{\alpha+k} \right) - \frac{1}{8}. \quad (8)$$

Proof. Let $\varphi(\tau) = \frac{\tau^{\frac{\alpha}{k}}}{k\Gamma_k(\alpha)}$. By the equalities (3)–(5), we have

$$\int_0^{\frac{1}{2}} \left|\tau - \frac{3\Delta(\tau)}{\Lambda(1/2)}\right| d\tau = \int_0^{\frac{1}{2}} \left|\tau - \frac{3k \cdot 2^{\frac{\alpha}{k}}}{\alpha+k}\tau^{\frac{\alpha}{k}}\right| d\tau$$

$$= \frac{k}{4(\alpha+2k)} \left(\frac{\alpha}{k}\left(\frac{\alpha+k}{3k}\right)^{\frac{2k}{\alpha}} + \frac{3k}{\alpha+k}\right) - \frac{1}{8}.$$

This completes the proof. □

Theorem 3. *Suppose that the assumptions of Lemma 2 hold. Suppose also that the mapping $|f''|^q$, $q > 1$, is convex on $[a,b]$. Then, the following Simpson-type inequality for generalized fractional integrals*

$$\left|\frac{1}{6}\left[f(a) + 4f\left(\frac{a+b}{2}\right) + f(b)\right] - \frac{1}{2T\left(\frac{1}{2}\right)}\left[{}_{(\frac{a+b}{2})+}I_\varphi f(b) + {}_{(\frac{a+b}{2})-}I_\varphi f(a)\right]\right|$$

$$\leq \frac{(b-a)^2}{6} \left(\int_0^{\frac{1}{2}} \left|t - \frac{3A(t)}{T(1/2)}\right|^p dt\right)^{\frac{1}{p}}$$

$$\times \left[\left(\frac{|f''(b)|^q + 3|f''(a)|^q}{8}\right)^{\frac{1}{q}} + \left(\frac{3|f''(b)|^q + |f''(a)|^q}{8}\right)^{\frac{1}{q}}\right]$$

is valid. Here, $\frac{1}{p} + \frac{1}{q} = 1$.

Proof. By applying the Hölder inequality in inequality (6), we obtain

$$\left|\frac{1}{6}\left[f(a) + 4f\left(\frac{a+b}{2}\right) + f(b)\right] - \frac{1}{2T\left(\frac{1}{2}\right)}\left[{}_{(\frac{a+b}{2})+}I_\varphi f(b) + {}_{(\frac{a+b}{2})-}I_\varphi f(a)\right]\right|$$

$$\leq \frac{(b-a)^2}{6} \left[\left(\int_0^{\frac{1}{2}} \left|t - \frac{3A(t)}{T(1/2)}\right|^p dt\right)^{\frac{1}{p}} \left(\int_0^{\frac{1}{2}} |f''(tb + (1-t)a)|^q dt\right)^{\frac{1}{q}}\right.$$

$$\left. + \left(\int_{\frac{1}{2}}^1 \left|1 - t - \frac{3A(1-t)}{T(1/2)}\right|^p dt\right)^{\frac{1}{p}} \left(\int_{\frac{1}{2}}^1 |f''(tb + (1-t)a)|^q dt\right)^{\frac{1}{q}}\right].$$

By using the convexity of $|f''|^q$, we obtain

$$\left|\frac{1}{6}\left[f(a) + 4f\left(\frac{a+b}{2}\right) + f(b)\right] - \frac{1}{2T\left(\frac{1}{2}\right)}\left[{}_{(\frac{a+b}{2})+}I_\varphi f(b) + {}_{(\frac{a+b}{2})-}I_\varphi f(a)\right]\right|$$

$$\leq \frac{(b-a)^2}{6} \left(\int_0^{\frac{1}{2}} \left|t - \frac{3A(t)}{T(1/2)}\right|^p dt\right)^{\frac{1}{p}}$$

$$\times \left[\left(\int_0^{\frac{1}{2}} \left[t|f''(b)|^q + (1-t)|f''(a)|^q \right] dt \right)^{\frac{1}{q}} + \left(\int_{\frac{1}{2}}^{1} \left[t|f''(b)|^q + (1-t)|f''(a)|^q \right] dt \right)^{\frac{1}{q}} \right]$$

$$= \frac{(b-a)^2}{6} \left(\int_0^{\frac{1}{2}} \left| t - \frac{3A(t)}{T(1/2)} \right|^p dt \right)^{\frac{1}{p}}$$

$$\times \left[\left(\frac{|f''(b)|^q + 3|f''(a)|^q}{8} \right)^{\frac{1}{q}} + \left(\frac{3|f''(b)|^q + |f''(a)|^q}{8} \right)^{\frac{1}{q}} \right].$$

This finishes the proof of Theorem 3. □

Remark 5. *If we choose $\varphi(t) = t$ in Theorem 3, then we obtain*

$$\left| \frac{1}{6} \left[f(a) + 4f\left(\frac{a+b}{2}\right) + f(b) \right] - \frac{1}{(b-a)} \int_a^b f(x)dx \right|$$

$$\leq \frac{(b-a)^2}{6} \left(\int_0^{\frac{1}{2}} t^p |1 - 3t|^p dt \right)^{\frac{1}{p}}$$

$$\times \left[\left(\frac{|f''(b)|^q + 3|f''(a)|^q}{8} \right)^{\frac{1}{q}} + \left(\frac{3|f''(b)|^q + |f''(a)|^q}{8} \right)^{\frac{1}{q}} \right],$$

which is given by Budak et al. in [36].

Remark 6. *Let us consider $\varphi(t) = \frac{t^\alpha}{\Gamma(\alpha)}, \alpha > 0$ in Theorem 3, then the Simpson-type inequality for Riemann–Liouville fractional integrals*

$$\left| \frac{1}{6} \left[f(a) + 4f\left(\frac{a+b}{2}\right) + f(b) \right] - \frac{2^{\alpha-1}\Gamma(\alpha+1)}{(b-a)^\alpha} \left[J^\alpha_{\left(\frac{a+b}{2}\right)^+} f(b) + J^\alpha_{\left(\frac{a+b}{2}\right)^-} f(a) \right] \right|$$

$$\leq \frac{(b-a)^2}{6} Y(\alpha, p) \left[\left(\frac{|f''(b)|^q + 3|f''(a)|^q}{8} \right)^{\frac{1}{q}} + \left(\frac{3|f''(b)|^q + |f''(a)|^q}{8} \right)^{\frac{1}{q}} \right]$$

is valid. Here, $\frac{1}{p} + \frac{1}{q} = 1$ and

$$Y(\alpha, p) = \left(\int_0^{\frac{1}{2}} t^p \left| 1 - \frac{3 \cdot 2^\alpha}{\alpha+1} t^\alpha \right|^p dt \right)^{\frac{1}{p}}.$$

which is given by Budak et al. in [36].

Corollary 3. *If we choose $\varphi(t) = \frac{t^{\frac{\alpha}{k}}}{k\Gamma_k(\alpha)}, \alpha, k > 0$ in Theorem 3, then we have the following Simpson-type inequality for k-Riemann–Liouville fractional integrals*

$$\left| \frac{1}{6} \left[f(a) + 4f\left(\frac{a+b}{2}\right) + f(b) \right] - \frac{2^{\frac{\alpha-k}{k}}\Gamma(\alpha+k)}{(b-a)^{\frac{\alpha}{k}}} \left[J^\alpha_{\left(\frac{a+b}{2}\right)^+,k} f(b) + J^\alpha_{\left(\frac{a+b}{2}\right)^-,k} f(a) \right] \right|$$

$$\leq \frac{(b-a)^2}{6} Y(\alpha, p, k) \left[\left(\frac{|f''(b)|^q + 3|f''(a)|^q}{8} \right)^{\frac{1}{q}} + \left(\frac{3|f''(b)|^q + |f''(a)|^q}{8} \right)^{\frac{1}{q}} \right].$$

Here, $\frac{1}{p} + \frac{1}{q} = 1$ and

$$Y(\alpha, p, k) = \left(\int_0^{\frac{1}{2}} t^p \left|1 - \frac{3k \cdot 2^{\frac{\alpha}{k}}}{\alpha + k} t^{\frac{\alpha}{k}}\right|^p dt\right)^{\frac{1}{p}}.$$

Proof. For $\varphi(\tau) = \frac{\tau^{\frac{\alpha}{k}}}{k\Gamma_k(\alpha)}$, the proof can be seen easily by the equalities (3)–(5). □

Theorem 4. *Assume that the assumptions of Lemma 2 hold. If the mapping $|f''|^q$, $q \geq 1$ is convex on $[a,b]$, then we have the following Simpson-type inequality for generalized fractional integrals*

$$\left|\frac{1}{6}\left[f(a) + 4f\left(\frac{a+b}{2}\right) + f(b)\right] - \frac{1}{2T\left(\frac{1}{2}\right)}\left[{}_{(\frac{a+b}{2})^+}I_\varphi f(b) + {}_{(\frac{a+b}{2})^-}I_\varphi f(a)\right]\right|$$

$$\leq \frac{(b-a)^2}{6}\left(\int_0^{\frac{1}{2}}\left|t - \frac{3A(t)}{T(1/2)}\right|dt\right)^{1-\frac{1}{q}}$$

$$\times \left\{\left[\left(\int_0^{\frac{1}{2}} t\left|t - \frac{3A(t)}{T(1/2)}\right|dt\right)|f''(b)|^q + \left(\int_0^{\frac{1}{2}}(1-t)\left|t - \frac{3A(t)}{T(1/2)}\right|dt\right)|f''(a)|^q\right]^{\frac{1}{q}}\right.$$

$$\left. + \left[\left(\int_0^{\frac{1}{2}}(1-t)\left|t - \frac{3A(t)}{T(1/2)}\right|dt\right)|f''(b)|^q + \left(\int_0^{\frac{1}{2}} t\left|t - \frac{3A(t)}{T(1/2)}\right|dt\right)|f''(a)|^q\right]^{\frac{1}{q}}\right\}.$$

Proof. By applying the power-mean inequality in (6), we obtain

$$\left|\frac{1}{6}\left[f(a) + 4f\left(\frac{a+b}{2}\right) + f(b)\right] - \frac{1}{2T\left(\frac{1}{2}\right)}\left[{}_{(\frac{a+b}{2})^+}I_\varphi f(b) + {}_{(\frac{a+b}{2})^-}I_\varphi f(a)\right]\right| \quad (9)$$

$$\leq \frac{(b-a)^2}{6}\left[\left(\int_0^{\frac{1}{2}}\left|t - \frac{3A(t)}{T(1/2)}\right|dt\right)^{1-\frac{1}{q}}\right.$$

$$\times \left(\int_0^{\frac{1}{2}}\left|t - \frac{3A(t)}{T(1/2)}\right||f''(tb + (1-t)a)|^q dt\right)^{\frac{1}{q}}$$

$$+ \left(\int_{\frac{1}{2}}^1\left|1 - t - \frac{3A(1-t)}{T(1/2)}\right|dt\right)^{1-\frac{1}{q}}$$

$$\left.\times \left(\int_{\frac{1}{2}}^1\left|1 - t - \frac{3A(1-t)}{T(1/2)}\right||f''(tb + (1-t)a)|^q dt\right)^{\frac{1}{q}}\right].$$

Since $|f''|^q$ is convex, we obtain

$$\int_0^{\frac{1}{2}}\left|t-\frac{3A(t)}{T(1/2)}\right||f''(tb+(1-t)a)|^q dt \tag{10}$$

$$\leq \int_0^{\frac{1}{2}}\left|t-\frac{3A(t)}{T(1/2)}\right|\left[t|f''(b)|^q+(1-t)|f''(a)|^q\right]dt$$

$$= |f''(b)|^q \int_0^{\frac{1}{2}} t\left|t-\frac{3A(t)}{T(1/2)}\right|dt + |f''(a)|^q \int_0^{\frac{1}{2}}(1-t)\left|t-\frac{3A(t)}{T(1/2)}\right|dt$$

and similarly

$$\int_{\frac{1}{2}}^1 \left|1-t-\frac{3A(1-t)}{T(1/2)}\right||f''(tb+(1-t)a)|^q dt \tag{11}$$

$$\leq |f''(b)|^q \int_{\frac{1}{2}}^1 t\left|1-t-\frac{3A(1-t)}{T(1/2)}\right|dt + |f''(a)|^q \int_{\frac{1}{2}}^1 (1-t)\left|1-t-\frac{3A(1-t)}{T(1/2)}\right|dt$$

$$= |f''(b)|^q \int_0^{\frac{1}{2}}(1-t)\left|t-\frac{3A(t)}{T(1/2)}\right|dt + |f''(a)|^q \int_0^{\frac{1}{2}} t\left|t-\frac{3A(t)}{T(1/2)}\right|dt.$$

If we substitute the inequalities (10) and (11) in (9), then we obtain the desired result. □

Remark 7. *Consider $\varphi(t)=t$ in Theorem 4, then Theorem 4 reduces to [32] (Theorem 2.5).*

Remark 8. *If we take $\varphi(t)=\frac{t^\alpha}{\Gamma(\alpha)},\alpha>0$ in Theorem 4, then we obtain the following Simpson-type inequality for Riemann–Liouville fractional integrals*

$$\left|\frac{1}{6}\left[f(a)+4f\left(\frac{a+b}{2}\right)+f(b)\right]-\frac{2^{\alpha-1}\Gamma(\alpha+1)}{(b-a)^\alpha}\left[J^\alpha_{(\frac{a+b}{2})^+}f(b)+J^\alpha_{(\frac{a+b}{2})^-}f(a)\right]\right|$$

$$\leq \frac{(b-a)^2}{6}(\Theta(\alpha))^{1-\frac{1}{q}}\left[\left(\Xi(\alpha)|f''(b)|^q+\Omega(\alpha)|f''(a)|^q\right)^{\frac{1}{q}}+\left(\Omega(\alpha)|f''(b)|^q+\Xi(\alpha)|f''(a)|^q\right)^{\frac{1}{q}}\right].$$

Here, $\Theta(\alpha)$ is defined as in (7) and

$$\Xi(\alpha) = \frac{1}{4(\alpha+3)}\left[\frac{\alpha}{3}\left(\frac{\alpha+1}{3}\right)^{\frac{3}{\alpha}}+\frac{3}{2(\alpha+1)}\right]-\frac{1}{24},$$

$$\Omega(\alpha) = \Theta(\alpha)-\Xi(\alpha)$$

$$= \frac{1}{4(\alpha+2)}\left(\alpha\left(\frac{\alpha+1}{3}\right)^{\frac{2}{\alpha}}+\frac{3}{\alpha+1}\right)$$

$$-\frac{1}{4(\alpha+3)}\left[\frac{\alpha}{3}\left(\frac{\alpha+1}{3}\right)^{\frac{3}{\alpha}}+\frac{3}{2(\alpha+1)}\right]-\frac{1}{12},$$

which is given by Budak et al. in [36].

Corollary 4. Let us consider $\varphi(t) = \frac{t^{\frac{a}{k}}}{k\Gamma_k(\alpha)}$, $\alpha, k > 0$ in Theorem 4, then the following Simpson-type inequality for k-Riemann–Liouville fractional integrals holds:

$$\left| \frac{1}{6}\left[f(a) + 4f\left(\frac{a+b}{2}\right) + f(b) \right] - \frac{2^{\frac{a-k}{k}}\Gamma(\alpha+k)}{(b-a)^{\frac{\alpha}{k}}}\left[J^{\alpha}_{\left(\frac{a+b}{2}\right)^+,k}f(b) + J^{\alpha}_{\left(\frac{a+b}{2}\right)^-,k}f(a) \right] \right|$$

$$\leq \frac{(b-a)^2}{6}(\Theta(\alpha,k))^{1-\frac{1}{q}}\left[\left(\Xi(\alpha,k)|f''(b)|^q + \Omega(\alpha,k)|f''(a)|^q\right)^{\frac{1}{q}} + \left(\Omega(\alpha,k)|f''(b)|^q + \Xi(\alpha,k)|f''(a)|^q\right)^{\frac{1}{q}} \right],$$

where $\Theta(\alpha,k)$ is defined as in (8) and

$$\Xi(\alpha,k) = \frac{k}{4(\alpha+3k)}\left[\frac{\alpha}{3k}\left(\frac{\alpha+k}{3k}\right)^{\frac{3k}{\alpha}} + \frac{3k}{2(\alpha+k)}\right] - \frac{1}{24},$$

$$\Omega(\alpha,k) = \Theta(\alpha,k) - \Xi(\alpha,k)$$

$$= \frac{k}{4(\alpha+2k)}\left(\frac{\alpha}{k}\left(\frac{\alpha+k}{3k}\right)^{\frac{2k}{\alpha}} + \frac{3k}{\alpha+k}\right)$$

$$- \frac{k}{4(\alpha+3k)}\left[\frac{\alpha}{3k}\left(\frac{\alpha+k}{3k}\right)^{\frac{3k}{\alpha}} + \frac{3k}{2(\alpha+k)}\right] - \frac{1}{12}.$$

Proof. Let $\varphi(\tau) = \frac{\tau^{\frac{a}{k}}}{k\Gamma_k(\alpha)}$. By the equalities (3)–(5), we have

$$\int_0^{\frac{1}{2}} \tau\left|\tau - \frac{3\Delta(\tau)}{\Lambda(1/2)}\right| d\tau$$

$$= \int_0^{\frac{1}{2}} \tau\left|\tau - \frac{3k \cdot 2^{\frac{a}{k}}}{\alpha+k}\tau^{\frac{a}{k}}\right| d\tau$$

$$= \frac{k}{4(\alpha+3k)}\left[\frac{\alpha}{3k}\left(\frac{\alpha+k}{3k}\right)^{\frac{3k}{\alpha}} + \frac{3k}{2(\alpha+k)}\right] - \frac{1}{24}$$

and

$$\int_0^{\frac{1}{2}} (1-\tau)\left|\tau - \frac{3\Delta(\tau)}{\Lambda(1/2)}\right| d\tau$$

$$= \int_0^{\frac{1}{2}} (1-\tau)\left|\tau - \frac{3k \cdot 2^{\frac{a}{k}}}{\alpha+k}\tau^{\frac{a}{k}}\right| d\tau$$

$$= \frac{k}{4(\alpha+2k)}\left(\frac{\alpha}{k}\left(\frac{\alpha+k}{3k}\right)^{\frac{2k}{\alpha}} + \frac{3k}{\alpha+k}\right)$$

$$- \frac{k}{4(\alpha+3k)}\left[\frac{\alpha}{3k}\left(\frac{\alpha+k}{3k}\right)^{\frac{3k}{\alpha}} + \frac{3k}{2(\alpha+k)}\right] - \frac{1}{12}.$$

□

3. Conclusions

For twice-differentiable functions, we have developed a generalized fractional version of the Simpson-type inequality in this paper. After that, we explained how our findings generalize a number of inequalities found in previous research. For k-Riemann–Liouville fractional integrals, we additionally provided novel Simpson-type inequalities. The findings of this study can be utilized in symmetry. The results for the case of symmetric convex functions can be obtained in future studies. In future studies, researchers can obtain generalized versions of our results by utilizing other kinds of convex function classes or different types of generalized fractional integral operators.

Author Contributions: All authors contributed equally in the preparation of the present work. Theorems and corollaries: M.A.A., H.K., J.T., S.A., H.B. and F.H.; review of the articles and books cited: M.A.A., H.K., J.T., S.A., H.B. and F.H.; formal analysis: M.A.A., H.K., J.T., S.A., H.B. and F.H.; writing—original draft preparation and writing—review and editing: M.A.A., H.K., J.T., S.A., H.B. and F.H. All authors have read and agreed to the published version of the manuscript.

Funding: This research was funded by King Mongkut's University of Technology, North Bangkok. Contract no. KMUTNB-62-KNOW-29.

Institutional Review Board Statement: Not applicable.

Informed Consent Statement: Not applicable.

Data Availability Statement: Not applicable.

Acknowledgments: We thank the referees for their valuable comments.

Conflicts of Interest: The authors declare no conflict of interest.

References

1. Alomari, M.; Darus, M.; Dragomir, S.S. New inequalities of Simpson's type for s-convex functions with applications. *RGMIA Res. Rep. Coll.* **2009**, *12*, 1–18.
2. Sarikaya, M.Z.; Set, E.; Özdemir, M.E. On new inequalities of Simpson's type for convex functions. *RGMIA Res. Rep. Coll.* **2010**, *13*, 2.
3. Sarikaya, M.Z.; Set, E.; Özdemir, M.E. On new inequalities of Simpson's type for s-convex functions. *Comput. Math. Appl.* **2020**, *60*, 2191–2199. [CrossRef]
4. Du, T.; Li, Y.; Yang, Z. A generalization of Simpson's inequality via differentiable mapping using extended (s,m)-convex functions. *Appl. Math. Comput.* **2017**, *293*, 358–369. [CrossRef]
5. İşcan, İ. Hermite-Hadamard and Simpson-like type inequalities for differentiable harmonically convex functions. *J. Math.* **2014**, *2014*, 346305. [CrossRef]
6. Matloka, M. Some inequalities of Simpson type for h-convex functions via fractional integrals. *Abstr. Appl. Anal.* **2015**, *2015*, 956850. [CrossRef]
7. Ozdemir, M.E.; Akdemir, A.O.; Kavurmacı, H. On the Simpson's inequality for convex functions on the coordinates. *Turk. J. Anal. Number Theory* **2014**, *2*, 165–169. [CrossRef]
8. Park, J. On Simpson-like type integral inequalities for differentiable preinvex functions. *Appl. Math. Sci.* **2013**, *7*, 6009–6021. [CrossRef]
9. Chen, J.; Huang, X. Some new inequalities of Simpson's type for s-convex functions via fractional integrals. *Filomat* **2017**, *31*, 4989–4997. [CrossRef]
10. Iqbal, M.; Qaisar, S.; Hussain, S. On Simpson's type inequalities utilizing fractional integrals. *J. Comput. Anal. Appl.* **2017**, *23*, 1137–1145.
11. Abdeljawad, T.; Rashid, S.; Hammouch, Z.; Chu, İ.Y.M. Some new Simpson-type inequalities for generalized p-convex function on fractal sets with applications. *Adv. Differ. Equ.* **2020**, *2020*, 1–26. [CrossRef]
12. Ertuğral, F.; Sarikaya, M.Z. Simpson type integral inequalities for generalized fractional integral. *Rev. Real Acad. Cienc. Exactas Físicas Nat. Ser. A Matemáticas* **2019**, *113*, 3115–3124. [CrossRef]
13. Hussain, S.; Khalid, J.; Chu, Y.M. Some generalized fractional integral Simpson's type inequalities with applications. *AIMS Math.* **2020**, *5*, 5859–5883. [CrossRef]
14. Kermausuor, S. Simpson's type inequalities via the Katugampola fractional integrals for s-convex functions. *Kragujev. J. Math.* **2021**, *45*, 709–720. [CrossRef]
15. Lei, H.; Hu, G.; Nie, J.; Du, T. Generalized Simpson-type inequalities considering first derivatives through the k-Fractional Integrals. *IAENG Int. J. Appl. Math.* **2021**, *50*, 1–8.
16. Luo, C.; Du, T. Generalized Simpson type inequalities involving Riemann-Liouville fractional integrals and their applications. *Filomat* **2020**, *34*, 751–760. [CrossRef]
17. Rashid, S.; Akdemir, A.O.; Jarad, F.; Noor, M.A.; Noor, K.I. Simpson's type integral inequalities for κ-fractional integrals and their applications. *AIMS Math.* **2019**, *4*, 1087–1100. [CrossRef]

18. Sarıkaya, M.Z.; Budak, H.; Erden, S. On new inequalities of Simpson's type for generalized convex functions. *Korean J. Math.* **2019**, *27*, 279–295.
19. Set, E.; Akdemir, A.O.; Özdemir, M.E. Simpson type integral inequalities for convex functions via Riemann-Liouville integrals. *Filomat* **2017**, *31*, 4415–4420. [CrossRef]
20. Asawasamrit, S.; Ali, M.A.; Ntouyas, S.K.; Tariboon, J. Some Parameterized Quantum Midpoint and Quantum Trapezoid Type Inequalities for Convex Functions with Applications. *Entropy* **2021**, *23*, 996. [CrossRef]
21. Budak, H.; Erden, S.; Ali, M.A. Simpson and Newton type inequalities for convex functions via newly defined quantum integrals. *Math. Methods Appl. Sci.* **2021**, *44*, 378–390. [CrossRef]
22. Dragomir, S.S.; Agarwal, R.P.; Cerone, P. On Simpson's inequality and applications. *J. Inequal. Appl.* **2000**, *5*, 533–579. [CrossRef]
23. Hua, J.; Xi, B.Y.; Qi, F. Some new inequalities of Simpson type for strongly s-convex functions. *Afr. Mat.* **2015**, *26*, 741–752. [CrossRef]
24. Hussain, S.; Qaisar, S. More results on Simpson's type inequality through convexity for twice differentiable continuous mappings. *SpringerPlus* **2016**, *5*, 1–9. [CrossRef]
25. Wu, H.K.J.-D.; Hussain, S.; Latif, M.A. Simpson's Type Inequalities for Co-Ordinated Convex Functions on Quantum Calculus. *Symmetry* **2019**, *11*, 768.
26. Li, Y.; Du, T. Some Simpson type integral inequalities for functions whose third derivatives are (α, m)-GA-convex functions. *J. Egypt. Math. Soc.* **2016**, *24*, 175–180. [CrossRef]
27. Liu, B.Z. An inequality of Simpson type. *Proc. R. Soc. A* **2005**, *461*, 2155–2158. [CrossRef]
28. Liu, W. Some Simpson type inequalities for h-convex and (α, m)-convex functions. *J. Comput. Anal. Appl.* **2014**, *16*, 1005–1012.
29. Simic, S.; Bin-Mohsin, B. Simpson's Rule and Hermite-Hadamard Inequality for Non-Convex Functions. *Mathematics* **2020**, *8*, 1248. [CrossRef]
30. Siricharuanun, P.; Erden, S.; Ali, M.A.; Budak, H.; Chasreechai, S.; Sitthiwirattham, T. Some New Simpson's and Newton's Formulas Type Inequalities for Convex Functions in Quantum Calculus. *Mathematics* **2021**, *9*, 1992. [CrossRef]
31. Vivas-Cortez, M.; Abdeljawad, T.; Mohammed, P.O.; Rangel-Oliveros, Y. Simpson's integral inequalities for twice differentiable convex functions. *Math. Probl. Eng.* **2020**, *2020*, 1936461. [CrossRef]
32. Sarikaya, M.Z.; Set, E.; Özdemir, M.E. On new inequalities of Simpson's type for functions whose second derivatives absolute values are convex. *J. Appl. Math. Inform.* **2013**, *9*, 37–45. [CrossRef]
33. Gorenflo, R.; Mainardi, F. *Fractional Calculus: Integral and Differential Equations of Fractional Order*; Springer: Wien, Austria, 1997; pp. 223–276.
34. Kilbas, A.A.; Srivastava, H.M.; Trujillo, J.J. *Theory and Applications of Fractional Differential Equations*; North-Holland Mathematics Studies, 204; Elsevier Science B.V.: Amsterdam, The Nertherland, 2006.
35. Miller, S.; Ross, B. *An Introduction to the Fractional Calculus and Fractional Differential Equations*; Wiley: New York, NY, USA, 1993.
36. Budak, H.; Kara, H.; Hezenci, F. Fractional Simpson type inequalities for twice differentiable functions. *Turk. J. Math.* **2021**, submitted.
37. Hezenci, F.; Budak, H.; Kara, H. New version of Fractional Simpson type inequalities for twice differentiable functions. *Adv. Differ. Equ.* **2021**, *2021*, 460. [CrossRef]
38. Sarikaya, M.Z.; Ertugral, F. On the generalized Hermite-Hadamard inequalities. *Ann. Univ. Craiova Math. Comput. Sci. Ser.* **2020**, *47*, 193–213.
39. Budak, H.; Yildirim, S.K.; Kara, H.; Yildirim, H. On new generalized inequalities with some parameters for coordinated convex functions via generalized fractional integrals. *Math. Methods Appl. Sci.* **2021**, 13069–13098. [CrossRef]
40. Mohammed, P.O.; Sarikaya, M.Z. On generalized fractional integral inequalities for twice differentiable convex functions. *J. Comput. Appl. Math.* **2020**, *372*, 112740. [CrossRef]
41. Budak, H.; Ertuğral, F.; Pehlivan, E. Hermite-Hadamard type inequalities for twice differantiable functions via generalized fractional integrals. *Filomat* **2019**, *33*, 4967–4979. [CrossRef]
42. Budak, H.; Pehlivan, E.; Kösem, P. On New Extensions of Hermite-Hadamard inequalities for generalized fractional integrals. *Sahand Commun. Math. Anal.* **2021**, *18*, 73–88.
43. Kashuri, A.; Set, E.; Liko, R. Some new fractional trapezium-type inequalities for preinvex functions. *Fractal Fract.* **2019**, *3*, 12. [CrossRef]
44. Zhao, D.; Ali, M.A.; Kashuri, A.; Budak, H.; Sarikaya, M.Z. Hermite–Hadamard-type inequalities for the interval-valued approximately h-convex functions via generalized fractional integrals. *J. Inequal. Appl.* **2020**, *2020*, 222. [CrossRef]
45. You, X.X.; Ali, M.A.; Budak, H.; Agarwal, P.; Chu, Y.M. Extensions of Hermite–Hadamard inequalities for harmonically convex functions via generalized fractional integrals. *J. Inequal. Appl.* **2021**, *2021*, 102. [CrossRef]

Article

Phragmén-Lindelöf Alternative Results for a Class of Thermoelastic Plate

Shiguang Luo [1], Jincheng Shi [2,*] and Baiping Ouyang [2]

[1] Department of Applied Mathematics, Guangdong University of Finance, Yingfu Road, Guangzhou 510521, China; 26-047@gduf.edu.cn
[2] School of Data Scinence, Guangzhou Huashang College, Huashang Road, Guangzhou 511300, China; oytengfei79@gdhsc.edu.cn
* Correspondence: shijc0818@gdhsc.edu.cn

Abstract: The spatial properties of solutions for a class of thermoelastic plate with biharmonic operator were studied. The energy method was used. We constructed an energy expression. A differential inequality which the energy expression was controlled by a second-order differential inequality is deduced. The *Phragmén-Lindelöf* alternative results of the solutions were obtained by solving the inequality. These results show that the Saint-Venant principle is also valid for the hyperbolic–hyperbolic coupling equations. Our results can been seen as a version of symmetry in inequality for studying the *Phragmén-Lindelöf* alternative results.

Keywords: thermoelastic plate; *Phragmén-Lindelöf* alternative; Saint-Venant principle; biharmonic equation

1. Introduction

Saint Venant principle points out that for any equilibrium force system on an elastic body, if its action point is limited to a given ball, the displacement and stress generated by the equilibrium force system at any point where the distance from the load is far greater than the radius of the ball can be ignored. This principle is widely used in engineering mechanics in practice. Many papers in the literature dealt with the study of the Saint-Venant principle. For example, Horgan and Knowles [1] and Horgan [2,3] studied the Saint-Venant principle in different equations and different situations. The traditional characteristic of the Saint-Venant theorem is to derive the energy decay estimates of the solutions. Usually, these decays are exponential with the spatial distance from the finite end to the infinity. In order to have some understandings about the study of the Saint-Venant Principle, one could refer to the papers [4–9]. In recent years, the studies of Saint-Venant principle for hyperbolic or quasihyperbolic equations are abundant. Especially for the studies of the spatial behavior of viscoelasticity equations, we could see papers [10–13]. When the spatial variable tends to infinity, the solution is decreasing. In the research of solution spacal decay estimates, people often need to add the solutions must satisfy some constraints at infinity. Many scholars have begun to study the *Phragmén-Lindelöf* alternative results of solutions. The advantage of this situation is that there is no need to add constraints on the solutions at infinity. The classical *Phragmén-Lindelöf* theorem states that the solutions of the harmonic equation must grow exponentially or decay exponentially with distance from the finite end of the cylinder to infinity. Payne and Schaefer [14] extended the study from harmonic equation to biharmonic equation. They obtained the *Phragmén-Lindelöf* alternative results for biharmonic equation in three different regions. Literatures [15–18] studied the spatial behaviors of biharmonic equations by various methods. In particular, we can see that Liu and Lin [19] studied the spatial properties for time-dependent stokes equation. They transformed the equation to a biharmonic equation and obtained the *Phragmén-Lindelöf* results by using a second-order differential inequality. The abovementioned studies from the literature all consider a single equation. Recently, there some new results about the studies of the hyperbolic equations or biharmonic Equations have been published (see [20–25]). For studies of other equations using energy method, see [26–29].

The domain we consider in this paper is defined as follows:

$$\Omega_0 = \{(x_1, x_2) | x_1 > 0, 0 < x_2 < h\}, \tag{1}$$

with h is a given positive number. We now give the following notation:

$$L_z = \{(x_1, x_2) | x_1 = z \geq 0, 0 \leq x_2 \leq h\}. \tag{2}$$

In reference [30], the authors studied the coupled system of wave-plate type with thermal effect. They obtained the results of the analytic property and the exponential stability of the C_0-semigroup. The equations are as follows:

$$\begin{cases} \rho_1 u_{,tt} - \Delta u - \mu \Delta u_{,t} + \lambda \Delta vs. = 0, \\ \rho_2 v_{,tt} + \gamma \Delta^2 vs. + \lambda \Delta u + m \Delta \theta = 0, \\ \tau \theta_{,t} - k \Delta \theta - m \Delta v_{,t} = 0. \end{cases} \tag{3}$$

The model is used to represent the evolution process of a system which contains an elastic membrane and plate. The plate has an elastic force and a thermal effect (see [31]). Here u is the vertical deflection of the membrane and v is the vertical deflection of the plate. θ is the difference of temperature. The coefficients $\rho_1, \rho_2, \mu, \lambda, m, \tau, \gamma$, and k are nonnegative constants. Δ denotes the Laplace operator, and Δ^2 denotes the biharmonic operator.

In the present paper, we consider the case when $\tau = 0$. In this case, Equation (3) can be rewritten as:

$$\rho_1 u_{,tt} - \Delta u - \mu \Delta u_{,t} + \lambda \Delta vs. = 0, \tag{4}$$

$$\rho_2 v_{,tt} + \gamma \Delta^2 v + \lambda \Delta u - \frac{m^2}{k} \Delta v_{,t} = 0. \tag{5}$$

We give the following initial and boundary value conditions:

$$\begin{cases} v(x_1, 0, t) = u(x_1, 0, t) = u_{,2}(x_1, 0, t) = 0, x_1 > 0, t > 0, \\ v(x_1, h, t) = u(x_1, h, t) = u_{,2}(x_1, h, t) = 0, x_1 > 0, t > 0, \\ v(0, x_2, t) = g_1(x_2, t), 0 \leq x_2 \leq h, t > 0, \\ u(0, x_2, t) = g_2(x_2, t), 0 \leq x_2 \leq h, t > 0, \\ u_{,1}(0, x_2, t) = g_3(x_2, t), 0 \leq x_2 \leq h, t > 0, \\ v(x_1, x_2, 0) = u(x_1, x_2, 0) = u_{,t}(x_1, x_2, 0), 0 \leq x_2 \leq h, x_1 > 0, \end{cases} \tag{6}$$

where $g_i(x_2, t), i = 1, 2, 3$ are the given functions and meet the following compatibility conditions:

$$\begin{cases} g_1(0, t) = g_1(h, t) = g_{1,2}(0, t) = g_{1,2}(h, t) = 0, \\ g_2(0, t) = g_2(h, t) = g_{2,2}(0, t) = g_{2,2}(h, t) = 0, \\ g_3(0, t) = g_3(h, t) = g_{3,2}(0, t) = g_{3,2}(h, t) = 0, \\ g_1(x_2, 0) = g_2(x_2, 0) = g_3(x_2, 0) = 0. \end{cases} \tag{7}$$

We try to establish the *Phragmén-Lindelöf* alternative results for the solutions of the biharmonic Equations (4) and (5) under conditions (6) and (7). We firstly define an energy expression of the solutions, then we derive that the energy expression satisfies a second-order differential inequality, and finally we obtain the *Phragmén-Lindelöf* alternative results of the solutions by solving the second-order inequality. For the inequality is symmetry, we show the application of symmetry in mathematical inequalities in practice. Since the system is a hyperbolic–hyperbolic coupling system, how to define the appropriate energy function will be the greatest innovation in this paper. How to control the energy function will be the difficulty of this paper. No similar studies have been found on the spatial properties for the solutions of the biharmonic equations with hyperbolic–hyperbolic coupling equations using the second-order differential inequality. In this paper, we use the comma to represent partial differentiation. $,k$ denotes the differentiation with respect to the direction x_k, thus $u_{,\alpha}$ denotes $\frac{\partial u}{\partial x_\alpha}$, and $u_{,t}$ denotes $\frac{\partial u}{\partial t}$. The usual summation convection is employed with repeated Greek subscripts α summed from 1 to 2. Hence, $u_{\alpha,\alpha} = \sum_{\alpha=1}^{2} \frac{\partial u_\alpha}{\partial x_\alpha}$. The symbol $dA = dx_1 dx_2$.

2. Energy Expression $\Phi(z,t)$

In order to get the *Phragmén-Lindelöf* alternative results, we must define an energy expression for the solutions. This expression plays an important role in obtaining our results. The energy expression will be constructed by the following Lemmas.

Lemma 1. *Let u and v be classical solutions of problems (4)–(7), we define the a function $\varphi_1(z,t)$ as:*

$$\varphi_1(z,t) = \frac{\mu}{2} \int_0^t \int_{L_z} exp(-\omega\eta) u_{,\eta}^2 dx_2 d\eta + \lambda \int_0^t \int_{L_z} exp(-\omega\eta) uv_{,\eta} dx_2 d\eta. \tag{8}$$

$\varphi_1(z,t)$ can also be expressed as:

$$\begin{aligned}
\varphi_1(z,t) = & \frac{\omega\rho_1}{2} \int_0^t \int_0^z \int_{L_\xi} exp(-\omega\eta)(z-\xi) u_{,\eta}^2 dA d\eta \\
& + \frac{\rho_1}{2} \int_0^z \int_{L_\xi} exp(-\omega t)(z-\xi) u_{,t}^2 dA \\
& + \frac{\omega}{2} \int_0^t \int_0^z \int_{L_\xi} exp(-\omega\eta)(z-\xi) u_{,\alpha} u_{,\alpha} dA d\eta \\
& + \frac{1}{2} \int_0^z \int_{L_\xi} exp(-\omega t)(z-\xi) u_{,\alpha} u_{,\alpha} dA \\
& + \mu \int_0^t \int_0^z \int_{L_\xi} exp(-\omega\eta)(z-\xi) u_{,\alpha\eta} u_{,\alpha\eta} dA d\eta \\
& + \lambda \int_0^t \int_0^z \int_{L_\xi} exp(-\omega\eta)(z-\xi) u_{,\alpha} v_{,\alpha\eta} dA d\eta \\
& - \int_0^t \int_0^z \int_{L_\xi} exp(-\omega\eta) u_{,\eta} u_{,1} dA d\eta \\
& + \lambda\omega \int_0^t \int_0^z \int_{L_\xi} exp(-\omega\eta)(z-\xi) u_{,\alpha} v_{,\alpha} dA d\eta \\
& + \lambda \int_0^z \int_{L_\xi} exp(-\omega t)(z-\xi) u_{,\alpha} v_{,\alpha} dA \\
& + \lambda \int_0^t \int_0^z \int_{L_\xi} exp(-\omega\eta) u_{,1} v_{,\eta} dA d\eta \\
& + \lambda\omega \int_0^t \int_0^z \int_{L_\xi} exp(-\omega\eta) uv_{,1} dA d\eta + \lambda \int_0^z \int_{L_\xi} exp(-\omega t) uv_{,1} dA + k_1(z,t),
\end{aligned} \tag{9}$$

where

$$\begin{aligned}
k_1(z,t) = & z \int_0^t \int_{L_0} exp(-\omega\eta) u_{,\eta} u_{,1} dx_2 d\eta + \frac{\mu}{2} \int_0^t \int_{L_0} exp(-\omega\eta) u_{,\eta}^2 dx_2 d\eta \\
& + z\mu \int_0^t \int_{L_0} exp(-\omega\eta) u_{,\eta} u_{,1\eta} dx_2 d\eta + \lambda \int_0^t \int_{L_0} exp(-\omega\eta) uv_{,\eta} dx_2 d\eta.
\end{aligned} \tag{10}$$

Proof. Multiplying both sides of Equation (4) by $exp(-\omega\eta)(z-\xi)u_{,\eta}$ and integrating, we obtain

$$
\begin{aligned}
0 =& \int_0^t \int_0^z \int_{L_\xi} exp(-\omega\eta)(z-\xi)u_{,\eta}(\rho_1 u_{,\eta\eta} - u_{,\alpha\alpha} - \mu u_{,\alpha\alpha\eta} \\
&+ \lambda v_{,\alpha\alpha}) \mathrm{d}A \mathrm{d}\eta \\
=& \frac{\omega \rho_1}{2} \int_0^t \int_0^z \int_{L_\xi} exp(-\omega\eta)(z-\xi)u_{,\eta}^2 \mathrm{d}A \mathrm{d}\eta \\
&+ \frac{\rho_1}{2} \int_0^z \int_{L_\xi} exp(-\omega t)(z-\xi)u_{,t}^2 \mathrm{d}A \\
&+ \frac{\omega}{2} \int_0^t \int_0^z \int_{L_\xi} exp(-\omega\eta)(z-\xi)u_{,\alpha}u_{,\alpha} \mathrm{d}A \mathrm{d}\eta \\
&+ \frac{1}{2} \int_0^z \int_{L_\xi} exp(-\omega t)(z-\xi)u_{,\alpha}u_{,\alpha} \mathrm{d}A \\
&- \int_0^t \int_0^z \int_{L_\xi} exp(-\omega\eta)u_{,\eta}u_{,1} \mathrm{d}A \mathrm{d}\eta \\
&+ z \int_0^t \int_{L_0} exp(-\omega\eta)u_{,\eta}u_{,1} \mathrm{d}x_2 \mathrm{d}\eta \\
&+ \mu \int_0^t \int_0^z \int_{L_\xi} exp(-\omega\eta)(z-\xi)u_{,\alpha\eta}u_{,\alpha\eta} \mathrm{d}A \mathrm{d}\eta \\
&- \frac{\mu}{2} \int_0^t \int_{L_z} exp(-\omega\eta)u_{,\eta}^2 \mathrm{d}x_2 \mathrm{d}\eta \\
&+ \frac{\mu}{2} \int_0^t \int_{L_0} exp(-\omega\eta)u_{,\eta}^2 \mathrm{d}x_2 \mathrm{d}\eta \\
&+ z\mu \int_0^t \int_{L_0} exp(-\omega\eta)u_{,\eta}u_{,1\eta} \mathrm{d}x_2 \mathrm{d}\eta \\
&+ \lambda \int_0^t \int_0^z \int_{L_\xi} exp(-\omega\eta)(z-\xi)u_{,\alpha}v_{,\alpha\eta} \mathrm{d}A \mathrm{d}\eta \\
&+ \lambda\omega \int_0^t \int_0^z \int_{L_\xi} exp(-\omega\eta)(z-\xi)u_{,\alpha}v_{,\alpha} \mathrm{d}A \mathrm{d}\eta \\
&+ \lambda \int_0^z \int_{L_\xi} exp(-\omega t)(z-\xi)u_{,\alpha}v_{,\alpha} \mathrm{d}A + \lambda \int_0^t \int_0^z \int_{L_\xi} exp(-\omega\eta)u_{,1}v_{,\eta} \mathrm{d}A \mathrm{d}\eta \\
&- \lambda \int_0^t \int_{L_z} exp(-\omega\eta)uv_{,\eta} \mathrm{d}x_2 \mathrm{d}\eta + \lambda \int_0^t \int_{L_0} exp(-\omega\eta)uv_{,\eta} \mathrm{d}x_2 \mathrm{d}\eta \\
&+ \lambda\omega \int_0^t \int_0^z \int_{L_\xi} exp(-\omega\eta)uv_{,1} \mathrm{d}A \mathrm{d}\eta \\
&+ \lambda \int_0^z \int_{L_\xi} exp(-\omega t)uv_{,1} \mathrm{d}A.
\end{aligned} \tag{11}
$$

By combining Equations (8) and (11), we can get (9). The proof of Lemma 1 is finished. □

Lemma 2. *We suggest u and v are the classical solutions of problems (4)–(7), and we define a function $\varphi_2(z,t)$ as:*

$$\varphi_2(z,t) = \int_0^t \int_0^z \int_{L_{\xi}} \exp(-\omega\eta)(z-\xi)(u_{,\alpha\alpha})^2 dA d\eta + \mu\omega \int_0^t \int_0^z \int_{L_{\xi}} \exp(-\omega\eta)(z-\xi)(u_{,\alpha\alpha})^2 dA d\eta$$
$$+ \mu \int_0^z \int_{L_{\xi}} \exp(-\omega\eta)(z-\xi)(u_{,\alpha\alpha})^2 dA - \rho_1 \int_0^t \int_0^z \int_{L_{\xi}} \exp(-\omega\eta)(z-\xi)u_{,\beta\eta}u_{,\beta\eta}dAd\eta$$
$$+ \frac{\rho_1}{2} \int_0^t \int_0^z \int_{L_{\xi}} \exp(-\omega\eta)u_{,\eta}^2 dA d\eta - \omega\rho_1 \int_0^t \int_0^z \int_{L_{\xi}} \exp(-\omega\eta)(z-\xi)u_{,\beta\beta}u_{,\eta}dAd\eta \qquad (12)$$
$$- \rho_1 \int_0^z \int_{L_{\xi}} \exp(-\omega t)(z-\xi)u_{,\beta\beta}u_{,t}dA - \lambda \int_0^t \int_0^z \int_{L_{\xi}} \exp(-\omega\eta)(z-\xi)u_{,\beta\beta}v_{,\alpha\alpha}dAd\eta$$
$$+ k_2(z,t),$$

$\varphi_2(z,t)$ can also be expressed as:

$$\varphi_2(z,t) = -\frac{\rho_1}{2} \int_0^t \int_{L_z} \exp(-\omega\eta)u_{,\eta}^2 dx_2 d\eta, \qquad (13)$$

where

$$k_2(z,t) = \frac{\rho_1 z}{2} \int_0^t \int_{L_0} \exp(-\omega\eta)u_{,\eta}^2 dx_2 d\eta - \rho_1 z \int_0^t \int_{L_0} \exp(-\omega\eta)u_{,\eta}u_{,1\eta}dx_2 d\eta.$$

Proof. Multiplying both sides of Equation (4) by $\exp(-\omega\eta)(z-\xi)u_{,\beta\beta}$ and integrating, we can obtain

$$0 = \int_0^t \int_0^z \int_{L_{\xi}} \exp(-\omega\eta)(z-\xi)u_{,\beta\beta}(\rho_1 u_{,\eta\eta} - u_{,\alpha\alpha} - \mu u_{,\alpha\alpha\eta} + \lambda v_{,\alpha\alpha})dAd\eta$$
$$= \rho_1 \int_0^t \int_0^z \int_{L_{\xi}} \exp(-\omega\eta)(z-\xi)u_{,\beta\eta}u_{,\beta\eta}dAd\eta$$
$$- \rho_1 \int_0^t \int_0^z \int_{L_{\xi}} \exp(-\omega\eta)(z-\xi)u_{,\eta}u_{,1\eta}dAd\eta$$
$$+ \rho_1 z \int_0^t \int_{L_0} \exp(-\omega\eta)u_{,\eta}u_{,1\eta}dx_2 d\eta$$
$$+ \omega\rho_1 \int_0^t \int_0^z \int_{L_{\xi}} \exp(-\omega\eta)(z-\xi)u_{,\beta\beta}u_{,\eta}dAd\eta \qquad (14)$$
$$+ \rho_1 \int_0^z \int_{L_{\xi}} \exp(-\omega t)(z-\xi)u_{,\beta\beta}u_{,t}dA$$
$$- \int_0^t \int_0^z \int_{L_{\xi}} \exp(-\omega\eta)(z-\xi)(u_{,\alpha\alpha})^2 dA d\eta$$
$$- \mu\omega \int_0^t \int_0^z \int_{L_{\xi}} \exp(-\omega\eta)(z-\xi)(u_{,\alpha\alpha})^2 dA d\eta$$
$$- \mu \int_0^z \int_{L_{\xi}} \exp(-\omega t)(z-\xi)(u_{,\alpha\alpha})^2 dA$$
$$+ \lambda \int_0^t \int_0^z \int_{L_{\xi}} \exp(-\omega\eta)(z-\xi)u_{,\beta\beta}v_{,\alpha\alpha}dAd\eta.$$

By combining Equations (12) and (14), we can get (13). The proof of Lemma 2 is finished. □

Lemma 3. We suggest u and v are classical solutions of problems (4)–(7), and we define a function $\varphi_3(z,t)$ as:

$$\varphi_3(z,t) = \frac{\omega \rho_2}{2} \int_0^t \int_0^z \int_{L_\xi} exp(-\omega\eta)(z-\xi)v_{,\eta}^2 dAd\eta$$
$$+ \frac{\rho_2}{2} \int_0^z \int_{L_\xi} exp(-\omega t)(z-\xi)v_{,t}^2 dx_2 d\eta$$
$$+ \frac{m^2}{k} \int_0^t \int_0^z \int_{L_\xi} exp(-\omega\eta)(z-\xi)v_{,\alpha\eta}v_{,\alpha\eta} dAd\eta$$
$$+ \frac{\gamma\omega}{2} \int_0^t \int_0^z \int_{L_\xi} exp(-\omega\eta)(z-\xi)v_{,\alpha\beta}v_{,\alpha\beta} dAd\eta$$
$$+ \frac{\gamma}{2} \int_0^z \int_{L_\xi} exp(-\omega t)v_{,\alpha\beta}v_{,\alpha\beta} dA$$
$$- \lambda \int_0^t \int_0^z \int_{L_\xi} exp(-\omega\eta)(z-\xi)v_{,\alpha\eta}u_{,\alpha} dAd\eta \qquad (15)$$
$$+ \lambda \int_0^t \int_0^z \int_{L_\xi} exp(-\omega\eta)v_{,\eta}u_{,1} dAd\eta$$
$$- 2\gamma \int_0^t \int_0^z \int_{L_\xi} exp(-\omega\eta)v_{,\alpha\eta}v_{,\alpha 1} dAd\eta$$
$$+ \frac{2\gamma\kappa\rho_2\omega}{m^2} \int_0^t \int_0^z \int_{L_\xi} exp(-\omega\eta)v_{,\eta}v_{,1} dAd\eta$$
$$+ \frac{2\gamma\kappa\rho_2}{m^2} \int_0^z \int_{L_\xi} exp(-\omega\eta)v_{,t}v_{,1} dA$$
$$- \frac{2\kappa\lambda\gamma}{m^2} \int_0^t \int_0^z \int_{L_\xi} exp(-\omega\eta)u_{,\alpha}v_{,1\alpha} dAd\eta + k_3(z,t).$$

$\varphi_3(z,t)$ can also be expressed as:

$$\varphi_3(z,t) = \frac{m^2}{2k} \int_0^t \int_{L_z} exp(-\omega\eta)v_{,\eta}^2 dx_2 d\eta$$
$$+ 2\gamma \int_0^t \int_{L_z} exp(-\omega\eta)v_{,1\eta}v_{,1} dx_2 d\eta$$
$$- \frac{2k\lambda\gamma}{m^2} \int_0^t \int_{L_z} exp(-\omega\eta)u_{,1}v_{,11} dx_2 d\eta$$
$$- \frac{k\gamma^2}{m^2} \int_0^t \int_{L_z} exp(-\omega\eta)v_{,\alpha\beta}v_{,\alpha\beta} dx_2 d\eta \qquad (16)$$
$$+ \frac{2k\gamma^2}{m^2} \int_0^t \int_{L_z} exp(-\omega\eta)v_{,1\alpha}v_{,1\alpha} dx_2 d\eta$$
$$- \frac{2k\gamma^2}{m^2} \int_0^t \int_{L_z} exp(-\omega\eta)v_{,1}v_{,1\beta\beta} dx_2 d\eta,$$

with

$$k_3(z,t) = (\frac{m^2}{2k} + \frac{k\rho_2\gamma}{m^2})\int_0^t\int_{L_0}exp(-\omega\eta)v_{,\eta}^2dx_2d\eta$$
$$+\frac{m^2}{k}z\int_0^t\int_{L_0}exp(-\omega\eta)v_{,\eta}v_{,1\eta}dx_2d\eta$$
$$+\gamma z\int_0^t\int_{L_0}exp(-\omega\eta)v_{,\alpha\eta}v_{,\alpha1}dx_2d\eta$$
$$-\gamma z\int_0^t\int_{L_0}exp(-\omega\eta)v_{,\eta}v_{,1\beta\beta}dx_2d\eta$$
$$+2\gamma\int_0^t\int_{L_0}exp(-\omega\eta)v_{,1\eta}v_{,1}dx_2d\eta$$
$$-\frac{2k\lambda\gamma}{m^2}\int_0^t\int_{L_0}exp(-\omega\eta)u_{,1}v_{,11}dx_2d\eta$$
$$-\frac{k\gamma^2}{m^2}\int_0^t\int_{L_0}exp(-\omega\eta)v_{,\alpha\beta}v_{,\alpha\beta}dx_2d\eta$$
$$+\frac{2k\gamma^2}{m^2}\int_0^t\int_{L_0}exp(-\omega\eta)v_{,1\alpha}v_{,1\alpha}dx_2d\eta$$
$$-\frac{2k\gamma^2}{m^2}\int_0^t\int_{L_0}exp(-\omega\eta)v_{,1}v_{,1\beta\beta}dx_2d\eta.$$

Proof. Multiplying both sides of Equation (5) by $exp(-\omega\eta)(z-\xi)v_{,\eta}$ and integrating, we can obtain

$$0 = \int_0^t\int_0^z\int_{L_\xi}exp(-\omega\eta)(z-\xi)v_{,\eta}(\rho_2 v_{,\eta\eta} + \gamma v_{,\alpha\alpha\beta\beta} + \lambda u_{,\alpha\alpha} - \frac{m^2}{k}v_{,\alpha\alpha\eta})dAd\eta$$
$$= \frac{\omega\rho_2}{2}\int_0^t\int_0^z\int_{L_\xi}exp(-\omega\eta)(z-\xi)v_{,\eta}^2dAd\eta$$
$$+\frac{\rho_2}{2}\int_0^z\int_{L_\xi}exp(-\omega t)(z-\xi)v_{,t}^2dA$$
$$-\lambda\int_0^t\int_0^z\int_{L_\xi}exp(-\omega\eta)(z-\xi)v_{,\alpha\eta}u_{,\alpha}dAd\eta$$
$$+\lambda\int_0^t\int_0^z\int_{L_\xi}exp(-\omega\eta)v_{,\eta}u_{,1}dAd\eta$$
$$+\gamma\int_0^t\int_0^z\int_{L_\xi}exp(-\omega\eta)(z-\xi)v_{,\eta}v_{,\alpha\alpha\beta\beta}dAd\eta \qquad (17)$$
$$+\frac{m^2}{k}\int_0^t\int_0^z\int_{L_\xi}exp(-\omega\eta)(z-\xi)v_{,\alpha\eta}v_{,\alpha\eta}dAd\eta$$
$$-\frac{m^2}{2k}\int_0^t\int_{L_z}exp(-\omega\eta)v_{,\eta}^2dx_2d\eta$$
$$+\frac{m^2}{2k}\int_0^t\int_{L_0}exp(-\omega\eta)v_{,\eta}^2dx_2d\eta$$
$$+\frac{m^2}{k}z\int_0^t\int_{L_0}exp(-\omega\eta)v_{,\eta}v_{,1\eta}dx_2d\eta.$$

Next, we begin to deal with the term $\gamma \int_0^t \int_0^z \int_{L_\xi} exp(-\omega\eta)(z-\xi)v_{,\eta}v_{,\alpha\alpha\beta\beta}dAd\eta$.

$$
\begin{aligned}
\gamma & \int_0^t \int_0^z \int_{L_\xi} exp(-\omega\eta)(z-\xi)v_{,\eta}v_{,\alpha\alpha\beta\beta}dAd\eta \\
= & \frac{\gamma\omega}{2} \int_0^t \int_0^z \int_{L_\xi} exp(-\omega\eta)(z-\xi)v_{,\alpha\beta}v_{,\alpha\beta}dAd\eta \\
& + \frac{\gamma}{2} \int_0^z \int_{L_\xi} exp(-\omega\eta)(z-\xi)v_{,\alpha\beta}v_{,\alpha\beta}dA \\
& - 2\gamma \int_0^t \int_0^z \int_{L_\xi} exp(-\omega\eta)v_{,\alpha\eta}v_{,\alpha 1}dAd\eta \\
& + \gamma z \int_0^t \int_{L_0} exp(-\omega\eta)v_{,\alpha\eta}v_{,\alpha 1}dx_2 d\eta \\
& - \gamma z \int_0^t \int_{L_0} exp(-\omega\eta)v_{,\eta}v_{,1\beta\beta}dx_2 d\eta.
\end{aligned}
\tag{18}
$$

Now let us deal with $-2\gamma \int_0^t \int_0^z \int_{L_\xi} exp(-\omega\eta)v_{,\alpha\eta}v_{,\alpha 1}dAd\eta$.

$$
\begin{aligned}
& -2\gamma \int_0^t \int_0^z \int_{L_\xi} exp(-\omega\eta)v_{,\alpha\eta}v_{,\alpha 1}dAd\eta \\
= & 2\gamma \int_0^t \int_0^z \int_{L_\xi} exp(-\omega\eta)v_{,\alpha\alpha\eta}v_{,1}dAd\eta \\
& - 2\gamma \int_0^t \int_{L_z} exp(-\omega\eta)v_{,1\eta}v_{,1}dx_2 d\eta \\
& + 2\gamma \int_0^t \int_{L_0} exp(-\omega\eta)v_{,1\eta}v_{,1}dx_2 d\eta.
\end{aligned}
\tag{19}
$$

Using the Equation (5), we can get

$$
\begin{aligned}
& 2\gamma \int_0^t \int_0^z \int_{L_\xi} exp(-\omega\eta)v_{,\alpha\alpha\eta}v_{,1}dAd\eta \\
= & 2\gamma \int_0^t \int_0^z \int_{L_\xi} exp(-\omega\eta)(\frac{k}{m^2}\rho_2 v_{,\eta\eta} + \frac{k}{m^2}\gamma v_{,\alpha\alpha\beta\beta} + \frac{k}{m^2}\lambda u_{,\alpha\alpha})v_{,1}dAd\eta \\
= & -\frac{k\rho_2 \gamma}{m^2} \int_0^t \int_{L_z} exp(-\omega\eta)v_{,\eta}^2 dx_2 d\eta + \frac{k\rho_2 \gamma}{m^2} \int_0^t \int_{L_0} exp(-\omega\eta)v_{,\eta}^2 dx_2 d\eta \\
& + \frac{2k\gamma \rho_2 \omega}{m^2} \int_0^t \int_0^z \int_{L_\xi} exp(-\omega\eta)v_{,\eta}v_{,1}dAd\eta + \frac{2k\gamma \rho_2}{m^2} \int_0^z \int_{L_\xi} exp(-\omega\eta)v_{,t}v_{,1}dA \\
& + \frac{2k\gamma^2}{m^2} \int_0^t \int_0^z \int_{L_\xi} exp(-\omega\eta)v_{,1}v_{,\alpha\alpha\beta\beta}dAd\eta \\
& - \frac{2k\lambda\gamma}{m^2} \int_0^t \int_0^z \int_{L_\xi} exp(-\omega\eta)u_{,\alpha}v_{,1\alpha}dAd\eta \\
& + \frac{2k\lambda\gamma}{m^2} \int_0^t \int_{L_z} exp(-\omega\eta)u_{,1}v_{,11}dx_2 d\eta \\
& - \frac{2k\lambda\gamma}{m^2} \int_0^t \int_{L_0} exp(-\omega\eta)u_{,1}v_{,11}dx_2 d\eta.
\end{aligned}
\tag{20}
$$

Now, let us deal with the term $\frac{2k\gamma^2}{m^2} \int_0^t \int_0^z \int_{L_\xi} exp(-\omega\eta)v_{,1}v_{,\alpha\alpha\beta\beta}dAd\eta$.

$$\frac{2k\gamma^2}{m^2} \int_0^t \int_0^z \int_{L_\xi} exp(-\omega\eta)v_{,1}v_{,\alpha\alpha\beta\beta} dAd\eta$$

$$= -\frac{2k\gamma^2}{m^2} \int_0^t \int_0^z \int_{L_\xi} exp(-\omega\eta)v_{,1\alpha}v_{,\alpha\beta\beta} dAd\eta + \frac{2k\gamma^2}{m^2} \int_0^t \int_{L_z} exp(-\omega\eta)v_{,1}v_{,1\beta\beta} dx_2 d\eta$$

$$- \frac{2k\gamma^2}{m^2} \int_0^t \int_{L_0} exp(-\omega\eta)v_{,1}v_{,1\beta\beta} dx_2 d\eta \qquad (21)$$

$$= \frac{k\gamma^2}{m^2} \int_0^t \int_{L_z} exp(-\omega\eta)v_{,\alpha\beta}v_{,\alpha\beta} dx_2 d\eta - \frac{k\gamma^2}{m^2} \int_0^t \int_{L_0} exp(-\omega\eta)v_{,\alpha\beta}v_{,\alpha\beta} dx_2 d\eta$$

$$- \frac{2k\gamma^2}{m^2} \int_0^t \int_{L_z} exp(-\omega\eta)v_{,1\alpha}v_{,1\alpha} dx_2 d\eta + \frac{2k\gamma^2}{m^2} \int_0^t \int_{L_0} exp(-\omega\eta)v_{,1\alpha}v_{,1\alpha} dx_2 d\eta$$

$$+ \frac{2k\gamma^2}{m^2} \int_0^t \int_{L_z} exp(-\omega\eta)v_{,1}v_{,1\beta\beta} dx_2 d\eta - \frac{2k\gamma^2}{m^2} \int_0^t \int_{L_0} exp(-\omega\eta)v_{,1}v_{,1\beta\beta} dx_2 d\eta.$$

A combination of (15) and (17)–(21), we obtain

$$\varphi_3(z,t) = \frac{m^2}{2k} \int_0^t \int_{L_z} exp(-\omega\eta)v_{,\eta}^2 dx_2 d\eta + 2\gamma \int_0^t \int_{L_z} exp(-\omega\eta)v_{,1\eta}v_{,1} dx_2 d\eta$$

$$- \frac{2k\lambda\gamma}{m^2} \int_0^t \int_{L_z} exp(-\omega\eta)u_{,1}v_{,11} dx_2 d\eta - \frac{k\gamma^2}{m^2} \int_0^t \int_{L_z} exp(-\omega\eta)v_{,\alpha\beta}v_{,\alpha\beta} dx_2 d\eta$$

$$+ \frac{2k\gamma^2}{m^2} \int_0^t \int_{L_z} exp(-\omega\eta)v_{,1\alpha}v_{,1\alpha} dx_2 d\eta - \frac{2k\gamma^2}{m^2} \int_0^t \int_{L_z} exp(-\omega\eta)v_{,1}v_{,1\beta\beta} dx_2 d\eta.$$

The proof of Lemma 3 is finished. □

Lemma 4. *We suggest u and v are classical solutions of problems (4)–(7), and we define a function $\varphi_4(z,t)$ as :*

$$\varphi_4(z,t) = -\frac{\rho_2}{2} \int_0^t \int_{L_z} exp(-\omega\eta)v_{,\eta}^2 dx_2 d\eta + \gamma \int_0^t \int_{L_z} exp(-\omega\eta)v_{,1\alpha\beta}v_{,\alpha\beta} dx_2 d\eta$$

$$- \frac{\gamma}{2} \int_0^t \int_{L_z} exp(-\omega\eta)v_{,1\alpha}v_{,1\alpha} dx_2 d\eta + \frac{\gamma}{2} \int_0^t \int_{L_z} exp(-\omega\eta)v_{,11}^2 dx_2 d\eta \qquad (22)$$

$$- \frac{\gamma}{2} \int_0^t \int_{L_z} exp(-\omega\eta)v_{,12}^2 dx_2 d\eta.$$

Then, $\varphi_4(z,t)$ can also be expressed as:

$$\varphi_4(z,t) = -\rho_2 \int_0^t \int_0^z \int_{L_\xi} exp(-\omega\eta)(z-\xi)v_{,1\eta}^2 dAd\eta + \frac{m^2}{2k} \int_0^t \int_{L_\xi} exp(-\omega t)(z-\xi)v_{,1\alpha}v_{,1\alpha} dA$$

$$+ \gamma \int_0^t \int_0^z \int_{L_\xi} exp(-\omega\eta)v_{,1\alpha\beta}v_{,1\alpha\beta} dAd\eta - \rho_2\omega \int_0^t \int_0^z \int_{L_\xi} exp(-\omega\eta)(z-\xi)v_{,11}v_{,\eta} dAd\eta \qquad (23)$$

$$- \rho_2 \int_0^z \int_{L_\xi} exp(-\omega t)(z-\xi)v_{,11}v_{,t} dA + \lambda \int_0^t \int_0^z \int_{L_\xi} exp(-\omega\eta)(z-\xi)v_{,11\alpha}u_{,\alpha} dAd\eta$$

$$- \lambda \int_0^t \int_0^z \int_{L_\xi} exp(-\omega\eta)v_{,11}u_{,1} dAd\eta + \int_0^t \int_0^z \int_{L_\xi} exp(-\omega\eta)v_{,12}v_{,2\eta} dAd\eta + k_4(z,t),$$

with

$$k_4(z,t) = -\frac{\rho_2}{2}\int_0^t\int_{L_0}\exp(-\omega\eta)v_{,\eta}^2 dx_2 d\eta$$
$$-\rho_2 z\int_0^z\int_{L_0}\exp(-\omega\eta)v_{,1\eta}v_{,\eta}dx_2 d\eta$$
$$+\frac{m^2}{k}z\int_0^t\int_{L_0}\exp(-\omega\eta)v_{,12}v_{,2\eta}dx_2 d\eta$$
$$+\gamma\int_0^t\int_{L_0}\exp(-\omega\eta)v_{,1\alpha\beta}v_{,\alpha\beta}dx_2 d\eta$$
$$-\frac{\gamma}{2}\int_0^t\int_{L_0}\exp(-\omega\eta)v_{,1\alpha}v_{,1\alpha}dx_2 d\eta$$
$$-\gamma z\int_0^t\int_{L_0}\exp(-\omega\eta)v_{,11\alpha}v_{,\alpha 1}dx_2 d\eta$$
$$+\frac{\gamma}{2}\int_0^t\int_{L_0}\exp(-\omega\eta)v_{,11}^2 dx_2 d\eta$$
$$-\frac{\gamma}{2}\int_0^t\int_{L_0}\exp(-\omega\eta)v_{,12}^2 dx_2 d\eta$$
$$+\gamma z\int_0^t\int_{L_0}\exp(-\omega\eta)v_{,11}v_{,1\beta\beta}dx_2 d\eta$$
$$+\lambda z\int_0^t\int_{L_0}\exp(-\omega\eta)v_{,11}u_{,1}dx_2 d\eta.$$

Proof. Multiplying both sides of Equation (5) by $\exp(-\omega\eta)(z-\xi)v_{,11}$ and integrating, we can obtain

$$0 = \rho_2\int_0^t\int_0^z\int_{L_\xi}\exp(-\omega\eta)(z-\xi)v_{,11}v_{,\eta\eta}dAd\eta$$
$$+\gamma\int_0^t\int_0^z\int_{L_\xi}\exp(-\omega\eta)(z-\xi)v_{,11}v_{,\alpha\alpha\beta\beta}dAd\eta \qquad (24)$$
$$+\lambda\int_0^t\int_0^z\int_{L_\xi}\exp(-\omega\eta)(z-\xi)v_{,11}u_{,\alpha\alpha}dAd\eta$$
$$-\frac{m^2}{k}\int_0^t\int_0^z\int_{L_\xi}\exp(-\omega\eta)(z-\xi)v_{,11}v_{,\alpha\alpha\eta}dAd\eta.$$

Using the divergence theorem, the first term on the right of Equation (22) can be rewritten as

$$\rho_2\int_0^t\int_0^z\int_{L_\xi}\exp(-\omega\eta)(z-\xi)v_{,11}v_{,\eta\eta}dAd\eta$$
$$= \rho_2\int_0^t\int_0^z\int_{L_\xi}\exp(-\omega\eta)(z-\xi)v_{,1\eta}v_{,1\eta}dAd\eta - \frac{\rho_2}{2}\int_0^t\int_{L_z}\exp(-\omega\eta)v_{,\eta}^2 dx_2 d\eta$$
$$+\frac{\rho_2}{2}\int_0^t\int_{L_0}\exp(-\omega\eta)v_{,\eta}^2 dx_2 d\eta + \rho_2 z\int_0^t\int_{L_0}\exp(-\omega\eta)v_{,1\eta}v_{,\eta}dx_2 d\eta \qquad (25)$$
$$+\rho_2\omega\int_0^t\int_0^z\int_{L_\xi}\exp(-\omega\eta)(z-\xi)v_{,11}v_{,\eta}dAd\eta$$
$$+\rho_2\int_0^z\int_{L_\xi}\exp(-\omega t)(z-\xi)v_{,11}v_{,t}dA.$$

Similarly, the second term on the right of Equation (22) can be rewritten as

$$\gamma \int_0^t \int_0^z \int_{L_\xi} exp(-\omega\eta)(z-\xi)v_{,11}v_{,\alpha\alpha\beta\beta} dAd\eta$$

$$= -\gamma \int_0^t \int_0^z \int_{L_\xi} exp(-\omega\eta)v_{,1\alpha\beta}v_{,1\alpha\beta} dAd\eta + \gamma \int_0^t \int_{L_z} exp(-\omega\eta)v_{,1\alpha\beta}v_{,\alpha\beta} dx_2 d\eta$$

$$-\gamma \int_0^t \int_{L_0} exp(-\omega\eta)v_{,1\alpha\beta}v_{,\alpha\beta} dx_2 d\eta - \frac{\gamma}{2}\int_0^t \int_{L_z} exp(-\omega\eta)v_{,1\alpha}v_{,1\alpha} dx_2 d\eta$$

$$+\frac{\gamma}{2}\int_0^t \int_{L_0} exp(-\omega\eta)v_{,1\alpha}v_{,1\alpha} dx_2 d\eta + \gamma z \int_0^t \int_{L_0} exp(-\omega\eta)v_{,11\alpha}v_{,\alpha 1} dx_2 d\eta \qquad (26)$$

$$+\frac{\gamma}{2}\int_0^t \int_{L_z} exp(-\omega\eta)v_{,11}^2 dx_2 d\eta - \frac{\gamma}{2}\int_0^t \int_{L_0} exp(-\omega\eta)v_{,11}^2 dx_2 d\eta$$

$$-\frac{\gamma}{2}\int_0^t \int_{L_z} exp(-\omega\eta)v_{,12}^2 dx_2 d\eta + \frac{\gamma}{2}\int_0^t \int_{L_0} exp(-\omega\eta)v_{,12}^2 dx_2 d\eta$$

$$-\gamma z \int_0^t \int_{L_0} exp(-\omega\eta)v_{,11}v_{,1\beta\beta} dx_2 d\eta.$$

The third term on the right of Equation (22) can be rewritten as

$$\lambda \int_0^t \int_0^z \int_{L_\xi} exp(-\omega\eta)(z-\xi)v_{,11}u_{,\alpha\alpha} dAd\eta$$

$$= -\lambda \int_0^t \int_0^z \int_{L_\xi} exp(-\omega\eta)(z-\xi)v_{,11\alpha}u_{,\alpha} dAd\eta \qquad (27)$$

$$+\lambda \int_0^t \int_0^z \int_{L_\xi} exp(-\omega\eta)v_{,11}u_{,1} dAd\eta$$

$$-\lambda z \int_0^t \int_{L_0} exp(-\omega\eta)v_{,11}u_{,1} dx_2 d\eta.$$

The fourth term on the right of Equation (22) can be rewritten as

$$-\frac{m^2}{k}\int_0^t \int_0^z \int_{L_\xi} exp(-\omega\eta)(z-\xi)v_{,11}v_{,\alpha\eta} dAd\eta$$

$$= -\frac{m^2}{2k}\int_0^z \int_{L_\xi} exp(-\omega t)(z-\xi)v_{,1\alpha}v_{,1\alpha} dA \qquad (28)$$

$$-\frac{m^2}{k}z \int_0^t \int_{L_0} exp(-\omega\eta)(z-\xi)v_{,12}v_{,2\eta} dx_2 d\eta$$

$$-\int_0^t \int_0^z \int_{L_\xi} exp(-\omega\eta)v_{,12}v_{,2\eta} dAd\eta.$$

A combination of (24)–(28) gives (23). The proof of Lemma 4 is finished. □

Lemma 5. *We define new energy expressions $\varphi(z,t)$ and $\Phi(z,t)$ as follows:*

$$\varphi(z,t) = \varphi_1(z,t) + k_1\varphi_2(z,t) + \varphi_3(z,t) + k_2\varphi_4(z,t), \qquad (29)$$

and

$$\Phi(z,t) = \int_0^t \varphi(z,s) ds. \qquad (30)$$

The following second-order partial differential inequality holds

$$|\Phi(z,t)| \le k_3 \frac{\partial^2 \Phi(z,t)}{\partial z^2}, \qquad (31)$$

where k_1 k_2 and k_3 are positive constance to be defined later.

Proof. From (9), we can get

$$\begin{aligned}\frac{\partial^2 \varphi_1(z,t)}{\partial z^2} &= \frac{\omega \rho_1}{2} \int_0^t \int_{L_z} \exp(-\omega \eta) u_{,\eta}^2 dx_2 d\eta \\ &+ \frac{\rho_1}{2} \int_{L_z} \exp(-\omega t) u_{,t}^2 dx_2 \\ &+ \frac{\omega}{2} \int_0^t \int_{L_z} \exp(-\omega \eta) u_{,\alpha} u_{,\alpha} dx_2 d\eta \\ &+ \frac{1}{2} \int_{L_z} \exp(-\omega t) u_{,\alpha} u_{,\alpha} dx_2 \\ &- \lambda \int_0^t \int_{L_z} \exp(-\omega \eta) u_{,1\eta} u_{,1} dx_2 d\eta \\ &- \lambda \int_0^t \int_{L_z} \exp(-\omega \eta) u_{,\eta} u_{,11} dx_2 d\eta \\ &+ \lambda \int_0^t \int_{L_z} \exp(-\omega \eta) u_{,11} v_{,\eta} dx_2 d\eta \\ &+ \lambda \int_0^t \int_{L_z} \exp(-\omega \eta) u_{,1} v_{,1\eta} dx_2 d\eta \\ &+ \lambda \omega \int_0^t \int_{L_z} \exp(-\omega \eta) u_{,1} v_{,1} dx_2 d\eta \\ &+ \lambda \omega \int_0^t \int_{L_z} \exp(-\omega \eta) u v_{,11} dx_2 d\eta \\ &+ \mu \int_0^t \int_{L_z} \exp(-\omega \eta) u_{,\alpha \eta} u_{,\alpha \eta} dx_2 d\eta \\ &+ \lambda \int_0^t \int_{L_z} \exp(-\omega \eta) u_{,\alpha} v_{,\alpha \eta} dx_2 d\eta \\ &+ \lambda \int_{L_z} \exp(-\omega t) u_{,1} v_{,1} dx_2 \\ &+ \lambda \int_{L_z} \exp(-\omega t) u v_{,11} dx_2 \\ &+ \lambda \omega \int_0^t \int_{L_z} \exp(-\omega \eta) u_{,\alpha} v_{,\alpha} dx_2 d\eta \\ &+ \lambda \int_{L_z} \exp(-\omega t) u_{,\alpha} v_{,\alpha} dx_2. \end{aligned} \quad (32)$$

From (12), we can get

$$\begin{aligned}\frac{\partial^2 \varphi_2(z,t)}{\partial z^2} &= \int_0^t \int_{L_z} \exp(-\omega \eta)(u_{,\alpha\alpha})^2 dx_2 d\eta \\ &+ \mu \omega \int_0^t \int_{L_z} \exp(-\omega \eta)(u_{,\alpha\alpha})^2 dx_2 d\eta \\ &+ \mu \int_{L_z} \exp(-\omega \eta)(u_{,\alpha\alpha})^2 dx_2 \\ &- \rho_1 \int_0^t \int_{L_z} \exp(-\omega \eta) u_{,\beta \eta} u_{,\beta \eta} dx_2 d\eta \\ &+ \rho_1 \int_0^t \int_{L_z} \exp(-\omega \eta) u_{,1\eta} u_{,1} dx_2 d\eta. \end{aligned} \quad (33)$$

From (15), we can get

$$\frac{\partial^2 \varphi_3(z,t)}{\partial z^2} = \frac{\omega \rho_2}{2} \int_0^t \int_{L_z} exp(-\omega\eta) v_{,\eta}^2 dx_2 d\eta + \frac{\rho_2}{2} \int_{L_z} exp(-\omega t) v_{,t}^2 dx_2$$
$$+ \frac{m^2}{k} \int_0^t \int_{L_z} exp(-\omega\eta) v_{,\alpha\eta} v_{,\alpha\eta} dx_2 d\eta + \frac{\gamma\omega}{2} \int_0^t \int_{L_z} exp(-\omega\eta) v_{,\alpha\beta} v_{,\alpha\beta} dx_2 d\eta$$
$$+ \frac{\gamma}{2} \int_{L_z} exp(-\omega t) v_{,\alpha\beta} v_{,\alpha\beta} dx_2 - \lambda \int_0^t \int_{L_z} exp(-\omega\eta) v_{,\alpha\eta} u_{,\alpha} dx_2 d\eta$$
$$+ \lambda \int_0^t \int_{L_z} exp(-\omega\eta) v_{,1\eta} u_{,1} dx_2 d\eta + \lambda \int_0^t \int_{L_z} exp(-\omega\eta) v_{,\eta} u_{,11} dx_2 d\eta \quad (34)$$
$$+ \frac{2\gamma\kappa\rho_2\omega}{m^2} \int_0^t \int_{L_z} exp(-\omega\eta) v_{,1\eta} v_{,1} dx_2 d\eta + \frac{2\gamma\kappa\rho_2\omega}{m^2} \int_0^t \int_{L_z} exp(-\omega\eta) v_{,\eta} v_{,11} dx_2 d\eta$$
$$+ \frac{2\gamma\kappa\rho_2}{m^2} \int_{L_z} exp(-\omega t) v_{,1t} v_{,1} dx_2 + \frac{2\gamma\kappa\rho_2}{m^2} \int_{L_z} exp(-\omega t) v_{,t} v_{,11} dx_2$$
$$- \frac{2\kappa\lambda\gamma}{m^2} \int_0^t \int_{L_z} exp(-\omega\eta) u_{,1\alpha} v_{,1\alpha} dx_2 d\eta - \frac{2\kappa\lambda\gamma}{m^2} \int_0^t \int_{L_z} exp(-\omega\eta) u_{,\alpha} v_{,11\alpha} dx_2 d\eta.$$

From (23), we can get

$$\frac{\partial^2 \varphi_4(z,t)}{\partial z^2} = -\rho_2 \int_0^t \int_{L_z} exp(-\omega\eta) v_{,1\eta}^2 dx_2 d\eta + \frac{m^2}{2k} \int_{L_z} exp(-\omega t) v_{,1\alpha} v_{,1\alpha} dx_2$$
$$+ \gamma \int_0^t \int_{L_z} exp(-\omega\eta) v_{,1\alpha\beta} v_{,1\alpha\beta} dx_2 d\eta - \rho_2\omega \int_0^t \int_{L_z} exp(-\omega\eta) v_{,11} v_{,\eta} dx_2 d\eta$$
$$+ \rho_2 \int_{L_z} exp(-\omega\eta) v_{,11} v_{,t} dx_2 + \lambda \int_0^t \int_{L_z} exp(-\omega\eta) v_{,11\alpha} u_{,\alpha} dx_2 d\eta \quad (35)$$
$$- \lambda \int_0^t \int_{L_z} exp(-\omega\eta) v_{,111} u_{,1} dx_2 d\eta - \lambda \int_0^t \int_{L_z} exp(-\omega\eta) v_{,11} u_{,11} dx_2 d\eta$$
$$+ \int_0^t \int_{L_z} exp(-\omega\eta) v_{,112} v_{,2\eta} dx_2 d\eta + \int_0^t \int_{L_z} exp(-\omega\eta) v_{,12} v_{,12\eta} dx_2 d\eta.$$

A combination of (8), (13), (21), (22) and (29) leads to

$$\varphi(z,t) = \frac{\mu}{2} \int_0^t \int_{L_z} exp(-\omega\eta) u_{,\eta}^2 dx_2 d\eta + \lambda \int_0^t \int_{L_z} exp(-\omega\eta) u v_{,\eta} dx_2 d\eta$$
$$- k_1 \frac{\rho_1}{2} \int_0^t \int_{L_z} exp(-\omega\eta) u_{,\eta}^2 dx_2 d\eta - k_2 \frac{\gamma}{2} \int_0^t \int_{L_z} exp(-\omega\eta) v_{,12}^2 dx_2 d\eta$$
$$+ \frac{m^2}{2k} \int_0^t \int_{L_z} exp(-\omega\eta) v_{,\eta}^2 dx_2 d\eta + 2\gamma \int_0^t \int_{L_z} exp(-\omega\eta) v_{,1\eta} v_{,1} dx_2 d\eta$$
$$- \frac{2k\lambda\gamma}{m^2} \int_0^t \int_{L_z} exp(-\omega\eta) u_{,1} v_{,11} dx_2 d\eta - \frac{k\gamma^2}{m^2} \int_0^t \int_{L_z} exp(-\omega\eta) v_{,\alpha\beta} v_{,\alpha\beta} dx_2 d\eta \quad (36)$$
$$+ \frac{2k\gamma^2}{m^2} \int_0^t \int_{L_z} exp(-\omega\eta) v_{,1\alpha} v_{,1\alpha} dx_2 d\eta - \frac{2k\gamma^2}{m^2} \int_0^t \int_{L_z} exp(-\omega\eta) v_{,1} v_{,1\beta\beta} dx_2 d\eta$$
$$- k_2 \frac{\rho_2}{2} \int_0^t \int_{L_z} exp(-\omega\eta) v_{,\eta}^2 dx_2 d\eta + k_2 \gamma \int_0^t \int_{L_z} exp(-\omega\eta) v_{,1\alpha\beta} v_{,\alpha\beta} dx_2 d\eta$$
$$- k_2 \frac{\gamma}{2} \int_0^t \int_{L_z} exp(-\omega\eta) v_{,1\alpha} v_{,1\alpha} dx_2 d\eta + k_2 \frac{\gamma}{2} \int_0^t \int_{L_z} exp(-\omega\eta) v_{,11}^2 dx_2 d\eta.$$

Combining (32)–(36), we have

$$\begin{aligned}\frac{\partial^2 \varphi(z,t)}{\partial z^2} &= \frac{\omega\rho_1}{2}\int_0^t\int_{L_z}\exp(-\omega\eta)u_{,\eta}^2\,dx_2\,d\eta + \frac{\rho_1}{2}\int_{L_z}\exp(-\omega t)u_{,t}^2\,dx_2\\ &+ \frac{\omega}{2}\int_0^t\int_{L_z}\exp(-\omega\eta)u_{,\alpha}u_{,\alpha}\,dx_2\,d\eta + \frac{1}{2}\int_{L_z}\exp(-\omega t)u_{,\alpha}u_{,\alpha}\,dx_2\\ &+ u\int_0^t\int_{L_z}\exp(-\omega\eta)u_{,\alpha\eta}u_{,\alpha\eta}\,dx_2\,d\eta + \lambda\omega\int_0^t\int_{L_z}\exp(-\omega\eta)u_{,\alpha}v_{,\alpha}\,dx_2\,d\eta\\ &+ \lambda\int_{L_z}\exp(-\omega t)u_{,\alpha}v_{,\alpha}\,dx_2 + (\rho_1 k_1 - \lambda)\int_0^t\int_{L_z}\exp(-\omega\eta)u_{,1\eta}u_{,1}\,dx_2\,d\eta\\ &- \lambda\int_0^t\int_{L_z}\exp(-\omega\eta)u_{,\eta}u_{,11}\,dx_2\,d\eta + 2\lambda\int_0^t\int_{L_z}\exp(-\omega\eta)u_{,11}v_{,\eta}\,dx_2\,d\eta\\ &+ 2\lambda\int_0^t\int_{L_z}\exp(-\omega\eta)u_{,1}v_{,1\eta}\,dx_2\,d\eta + \lambda\omega\int_0^t\int_{L_z}\exp(-\omega\eta)u_{,1}v_{,1}\,dx_2\,d\eta\\ &+ \lambda\omega\int_0^t\int_{L_z}\exp(-\omega\eta)uv_{,11}\,dx_2\,d\eta + \lambda\int_{L_z}\exp(-\omega t)u_{,1}v_{,1}\,dx_2\\ &+ \lambda\int_{L_z}\exp(-\omega t)uv_{,11}\,dx_2 + (1+\mu\omega)k_1\int_0^t\int_{L_z}\exp(-\omega\eta)(u_{,\alpha\alpha})^2\,dx_2\,d\eta\\ &+ \mu k_1\int_{L_z}\exp(-\omega t)(u_{,\alpha\alpha})^2\,dx_2 - \rho_1 k_1\int_0^t\int_{L_z}\exp(-\omega\eta)u_{,\beta\eta}u_{,\beta\eta}\,dx_2\,d\eta\\ &+ \frac{\rho_2\omega}{2}\int_0^t\int_{L_z}\exp(-\omega\eta)v_{,\eta}^2\,dx_2\,d\eta + \frac{\rho_1}{2}\int_{L_z}\exp(-\omega t)v_{,t}^2\,dx_2\\ &+ \frac{m^2}{k}\int_0^t\int_{L_z}\exp(-\omega\eta)v_{,\alpha\eta}v_{,\alpha\eta}\,dx_2\,d\eta + \frac{\omega\gamma}{2}\int_0^t\int_{L_z}\exp(-\omega t)v_{,\alpha\beta}v_{,\alpha\beta}\,dx_2\,d\eta\\ &+ \frac{\gamma}{2}\int_{L_z}\exp(-\omega t)v_{,\alpha\beta}v_{,\alpha\beta}\,dx_2 + \frac{2\gamma k\rho_2\omega}{m^2}\int_0^t\int_{L_z}\exp(-\omega\eta)v_{,1\eta}v_{,1}\,dx_2\,d\eta\\ &+ \left(\frac{2\gamma k\rho_2\omega}{m^2} - \rho_2\omega k_2\right)\int_0^t\int_{L_z}\exp(-\omega\eta)v_{,\eta}v_{,11}\,dx_2\,d\eta + \frac{2\gamma k\rho_2}{m^2}\int_{L_z}\exp(-\omega t)v_{,1t}v_{,1}\,dx_2\\ &+ \left(\frac{2\gamma k\rho_2}{m^2} + \rho_2 k_2\right)\int_{L_z}\exp(-\omega t)v_{,t}v_{,11}\,dx_2 - \frac{2k\lambda\gamma}{m^2}\int_0^t\int_{L_z}\exp(-\omega\eta)u_{,1\alpha}v_{,1\alpha}\,dx_2\,d\eta\\ &+ \left(\lambda k_2 - \frac{2k\lambda\gamma}{m^2}\right)\int_0^t\int_{L_z}\exp(-\omega\eta)u_{,\alpha}v_{,11\alpha}\,dx_2\,d\eta - \rho_2 k_2\int_0^t\int_{L_z}\exp(-\omega\eta)v_{,1\eta}^2\,dx_2\,d\eta\\ &+ \frac{m^2}{2k}k_2\int_{L_z}\exp(-\omega t)v_{,1\alpha}v_{,1\alpha}\,dx_2 + \gamma k_2\int_0^t\int_{L_z}\exp(-\omega\eta)v_{,1\alpha\beta}v_{,1\alpha\beta}\,dx_2\,d\eta\\ &- \lambda k_2\int_0^t\int_{L_z}\exp(-\omega\eta)v_{,111}u_{,1}\,dx_2\,d\eta - \lambda k_2\int_0^t\int_{L_z}\exp(-\omega\eta)v_{,11}u_{,11}\,dx_2\,d\eta\\ &+ k_2\int_0^t\int_{L_z}\exp(-\omega\eta)v_{,112}v_{,2\eta}\,dx_2\,d\eta + k_2\int_0^t\int_{L_z}\exp(-\omega\eta)v_{,12}u_{,12\eta}\,dx_2\,d\eta.\end{aligned} \quad (37)$$

Using the results (3.1)–(3.3) in [19], we have

$$\int_0^t\int_{L_z}\exp(-\omega\eta)v_{,\alpha}v_{,\alpha}\,dx_2\,d\eta \le c_1\int_0^t\int_{L_z}\exp(-\omega\eta)v_{,\alpha\beta}v_{,\alpha\beta}\,dx_2\,d\eta, \quad (38)$$

$$\int_{L_z}\exp(-\omega t)v_{,\alpha}v_{,\alpha}\,dx_2 \le c_1\int_{L_z}\exp(-\omega t)v_{,\alpha\beta}v_{,\alpha\beta}\,dx_2, \quad (39)$$

$$\int_0^t\int_{L_z}\exp(-\omega\eta)u^2\,dx_2\,d\eta \le c_2\int_0^t\int_{L_z}\exp(-\omega\eta)u_{,\alpha\alpha}u_{,\alpha\alpha}\,dx_2\,d\eta, \quad (40)$$

$$\int_{L_z}\exp(-\omega t)u^2\,dx_2 \le c_2\int_{L_z}\exp(-\omega t)u_{,\alpha\alpha}u_{,\alpha\alpha}\,dx_2, \quad (41)$$

$$\int_{L_z} \exp(-\omega t) v_{,1} v_{,1} dx_2 \leq c_3 \int_{L_z} \exp(-\omega t) v_{,1\alpha} v_{,1\alpha} dx_2 d\eta, \qquad (42)$$

with c_1, c_2, and c_3 are positive constants.

Using the Schwarz inequality, and combining (37)–(42), we obtain

$$\begin{aligned}
\frac{\partial^2 \varphi(z,t)}{\partial z^2} \geq &\ (\frac{\omega \rho_1}{2} - \frac{\lambda}{2}\varepsilon_4) \int_0^t \int_{L_z} \exp(-\omega \eta) u_{,\eta}^2 dx_2 d\eta + \frac{\rho_1}{2} \int_{L_z} \exp(-\omega t) u_{,t}^2 dx_2 \\
& + [\frac{\omega}{2} - \frac{\lambda \omega}{2}\varepsilon_1 - \frac{\rho_1 k_1 - \lambda}{2\varepsilon_3} - \lambda\varepsilon_6 - \frac{\lambda \omega}{2}\varepsilon_7 - \frac{k\lambda\gamma}{m^2}\varepsilon_{15} - (\lambda k_2 - \frac{2k\lambda\gamma}{m^2})\frac{\varepsilon_{16}}{2} \\
& - \frac{\lambda k_2}{2\varepsilon_{17}}] \int_0^t \int_{L_z} \exp(-\omega \eta) u_{,\alpha} u_{,\alpha} dx_2 d\eta + (\frac{1}{2} - \frac{\lambda}{2}\varepsilon_2 - \frac{\lambda}{2}\varepsilon_9) \int_{L_z} \exp(-\omega t) u_{,\alpha} u_{,\alpha} dx_2 \\
& + [\mu - \frac{\rho_1 k_1 - \lambda}{2}\varepsilon_3 - \rho_1 k_1] \int_0^t \int_{L_z} \exp(-\omega \eta) u_{,\alpha\eta} u_{,\alpha\eta} dx_2 d\eta \\
& + [(1 + \mu\omega)k_1 - \frac{1}{2\varepsilon_4} - \lambda\varepsilon_5 - \frac{\lambda\omega c_2}{2}\varepsilon_8 - \frac{k\lambda\gamma}{m^2}\varepsilon_{14} - \frac{\lambda k_2}{2\varepsilon_{18}}] \int_0^t \int_{L_z} \exp(-\omega \eta)(u_{,\alpha\eta})^2 dx_2 d\eta \\
& + (\mu k_1 - \frac{\lambda c_2}{2}\varepsilon_{10}) \int_{L_z} \exp(-\omega t)(u_{,\alpha\alpha})^2 dx_2 \\
& + [\frac{\rho_2 \omega}{2} - \frac{\lambda}{\varepsilon_5} - \frac{1}{2}(\frac{2\gamma k\rho_2 \omega}{m^2} - \rho_2 \omega k_2)\varepsilon_{12}] \int_0^t \int_{L_z} \exp(-\omega \eta) v_{,\eta}^2 dx_2 d\eta \\
& + [\frac{\rho_2}{2} - \frac{1}{2}(\frac{2\gamma k \rho_2}{m^2} + \rho_2 k_2)\varepsilon_{13}] \int_{L_z} \exp(-\omega t) v_{,t}^2 dx_2 \\
& + [\frac{m^2}{k} - \frac{\lambda}{\varepsilon_6} - \frac{\gamma k\rho_2 \omega}{m^2}\varepsilon_{11} - \frac{k_2}{2\varepsilon_{19}} - \rho_2 k_2] \int_0^t \int_{L_z} \exp(-\omega \eta) v_{,\alpha\eta} v_{,\alpha\eta} dx_2 d\eta \\
& + [\frac{\omega \gamma}{2} - \frac{\lambda \omega c_1}{2\varepsilon_1} - \frac{\lambda \omega c_1}{2\varepsilon_7} - \frac{\lambda \omega}{2\varepsilon_8} - \frac{\gamma k\rho_2 \omega c_1}{m^2 \varepsilon_{11}} - \frac{1}{2}(\frac{2\gamma k\rho_2 \omega}{m^2} - \rho_2 \omega k_2)\frac{1}{\varepsilon_{12}} - \frac{k\lambda\gamma}{m^2}\frac{1}{\varepsilon_{14}} \\
& - \frac{\lambda k_2}{2}\varepsilon_{18}] \int_0^t \int_{L_z} \exp(-\omega \eta) v_{,\alpha\beta} v_{,\alpha\beta} dx_2 d\eta + [\frac{\gamma}{2} - \frac{\lambda c_1}{2\varepsilon_2}] \int_{L_z} \exp(-\omega t) v_{,\alpha\beta} v_{,\alpha\beta} dx_2 \\
& + [\frac{m^2}{2k}k_2 - \frac{\lambda c_3}{2\varepsilon_9} - \frac{\lambda}{2\varepsilon_{10}} - \frac{1}{2\varepsilon_{13}}(\frac{2\gamma k\rho_2}{m^2} + \rho_2 k_2)] \int_{L_z} \exp(-\omega t) v_{,1\alpha} v_{,1\alpha} dx_2 \\
& + [\gamma k_2 - \frac{k\lambda\gamma}{m^2\varepsilon_{15}} - (\lambda k_2 - \frac{2k\lambda\gamma}{m^2})\frac{1}{2\varepsilon_{16}} - \frac{\lambda k_2}{2}\varepsilon_{17} - \frac{k_2}{2}\varepsilon_{19}] \int_0^t \int_{L_z} \exp(-\omega \eta) v_{,1\alpha\beta} v_{,1\alpha\beta} dx_2 d\eta \\
& + \frac{k_2}{2} \int_{L_z} \exp(-\omega t) v_{,12} v_{,12} dx_2 + \frac{2\gamma k\rho_2}{m^2} \int_{L_z} \exp(-\omega t) v_{,1t} v_{,1} dx_2,
\end{aligned} \qquad (43)$$

where $\varepsilon_i, (i = 1, 2, \cdots, 20)$ are arbitrary positive constants.

In (43), if we choose $\varepsilon_1 = \varepsilon_2 = \varepsilon_7 = \varepsilon_9 = \frac{1}{4\lambda}, \varepsilon_3 = 2, \varepsilon_4 = \frac{\omega \rho_1}{2\lambda}, \varepsilon_5 = \frac{\omega \rho_2}{8\lambda}, \varepsilon_6 = \lambda, \varepsilon_8 = 1$, $\varepsilon_{10} = \frac{\mu k_1}{\lambda c_2}, \varepsilon_{11} = \varepsilon_{12} = \gamma, \varepsilon_{13} = \frac{1}{2}(\frac{2\gamma k\rho_2}{m^2} + \rho_2 k_2)^{-1}\rho_1, \varepsilon_{14} = \frac{\gamma}{\omega}, \varepsilon_{15} = \frac{k\lambda\gamma}{m^2}, \varepsilon_{16} = \frac{2\lambda}{\gamma}, \varepsilon_{17} = \frac{\gamma}{2\lambda}$, $\varepsilon_{18} = \omega, \varepsilon_{19} = \frac{\gamma}{2}, k_1 = \frac{1}{2\rho_1}(\frac{\mu}{2} + \lambda), k_2 = \frac{4}{\gamma}; m \geq \max\{\sqrt{\frac{4k}{k_2}[2\lambda^2 c_3 + \frac{\lambda^2 c_2}{2\mu k_1} + \frac{(2\gamma k\rho_2 + \rho_2 k_2)^2}{\rho_1}]}$, $1, 8\gamma^2 k, \sqrt{2k(1 + \gamma^2 k\rho_2 \omega + \frac{4}{\gamma^2} + \frac{4\rho_2}{\gamma})}\}, \omega \geq \max\{2k_1\rho_1 + 16\lambda^2 + 8k^2\lambda^2\gamma^2, 1\}, \mu \geq \sqrt{\frac{8\lambda}{\omega^2} + \rho_1\rho_2 + 4\rho_1\lambda c_1 + 8\rho_1 k\lambda\gamma^2}, \gamma \geq \max\{16\lambda^2 c_1 + 10\lambda + 4k\rho_2 c_1 + 4\rho_2 + 4k\lambda, 1\}$, we can get

$$\begin{aligned}
\frac{\partial^2 \varphi(z,t)}{\partial z^2} &\geq \frac{\omega \rho_1}{4} \int_0^t \int_{L_z} exp(-\omega\eta) u_{,\eta}^2 dx_2 d\eta + \frac{\rho_1}{2} \int_{L_z} exp(-\omega t) u_{,t}^2 dx_2 \\
&+ \frac{\omega}{8} \int_0^t \int_{L_z} exp(-\omega\eta) u_{,\alpha} u_{,\alpha} dx_2 d\eta + \frac{1}{4} \int_{L_z} exp(-\omega t) u_{,\alpha} u_{,\alpha} dx_2 \\
&+ \frac{\mu}{2} \int_0^t \int_{L_z} exp(-\omega\eta) u_{,\alpha\eta} u_{,\alpha\eta} dx_2 d\eta + \frac{\mu\omega k_1}{2} \int_0^t \int_{L_z} exp(-\omega\eta) (u_{,\alpha\alpha})^2 dx_2 d\eta \\
&+ \frac{\mu k_1}{2} \int_{L_z} exp(-\omega t)(u_{,\alpha\alpha})^2 dx_2 + \frac{\rho_2 \omega}{4} \int_0^t \int_{L_z} exp(-\omega\eta) v_{,\eta}^2 dx_2 d\eta \\
&+ \frac{\rho_2}{4} \int_{L_z} exp(-\omega t) v_{,t}^2 dx_2 + \frac{m^2}{2k} \int_0^t \int_{L_z} exp(-\omega\eta) v_{,\alpha\eta} v_{,\alpha\eta} dx_2 d\eta \\
&+ \frac{\omega\gamma}{4} \int_0^t \int_{L_z} exp(-\omega\eta) v_{,\alpha\beta} v_{,\alpha\beta} dx_2 d\eta + \frac{\gamma}{4} \int_{L_z} exp(-\omega t) v_{,\alpha\beta} v_{,\alpha\beta} dx_2 \\
&+ \frac{m^2}{4k} k_2 \int_{L_z} exp(-\omega t) v_{,1\alpha} v_{,1\alpha} dx_2 + \int_0^t \int_{L_z} exp(-\omega\eta) v_{,1\alpha\beta} v_{,1\alpha\beta} dx_2 d\eta \\
&+ \frac{k_2}{2} \int_{L_z} exp(-\omega t) v_{,12} v_{,12} dx_2 + \frac{2\gamma k \rho_2}{m^2} \int_{L_z} exp(-\omega t) v_{,1t} v_{,1} dx_2 \\
&= E(z,t).
\end{aligned} \quad (44)$$

We now define a new function $F(z,t)$ as

$$F(z,t) = \int_0^t E(z,s) ds. \quad (45)$$

We get

$$\begin{aligned}
F(z,t) &= \frac{\omega\rho_1}{4} \int_0^t \int_0^s \int_{L_z} exp(-\omega\eta) u_{,\eta}^2 dx_2 d\eta ds + \frac{\rho_1}{2} \int_0^t \int_{L_z} exp(-\omega s) u_{,s}^2 dx_2 ds \\
&+ \frac{\omega}{8} \int_0^t \int_0^s \int_{L_z} exp(-\omega\eta) u_{,\alpha} u_{,\alpha} dx_2 d\eta ds + \frac{1}{4} \int_0^t \int_{L_z} exp(-\omega s) u_{,\alpha} u_{,\alpha} dx_2 ds \\
&+ \frac{\mu}{2} \int_0^t \int_0^s \int_{L_z} exp(-\omega\eta) u_{,\alpha\eta} u_{,\alpha\eta} dx_2 d\eta ds + \frac{\mu\omega k_1}{2} \int_0^t \int_0^s \int_{L_z} exp(-\omega\eta) (u_{,\alpha\alpha})^2 dx_2 d\eta ds \\
&+ \frac{\mu k_1}{2} \int_0^t \int_{L_z} exp(-\omega s)(u_{,\alpha\alpha})^2 dx_2 ds + \frac{\rho_2 \omega}{4} \int_0^t \int_0^s \int_{L_z} exp(-\omega\eta) v_{,\eta}^2 dx_2 d\eta ds \\
&+ \frac{\rho_2}{4} \int_0^t \int_{L_z} exp(-\omega s) v_{,t}^2 dx_2 ds + \frac{m^2}{2k} \int_0^t \int_0^s \int_{L_z} exp(-\omega\eta) v_{,\alpha\eta} v_{,\alpha\eta} dx_2 d\eta ds \\
&+ \frac{\omega\gamma}{4} \int_0^t \int_0^s \int_{L_z} exp(-\omega\eta) v_{,\alpha\beta} v_{,\alpha\beta} dx_2 d\eta ds + \frac{\gamma}{4} \int_0^t \int_{L_z} exp(-\omega s) v_{,\alpha\beta} v_{,\alpha\beta} dx_2 ds \\
&+ \frac{m^2}{4k} k_2 \int_0^t \int_{L_z} exp(-\omega s) v_{,1\alpha} v_{,1\alpha} dx_2 ds + \int_0^t \int_0^s \int_{L_z} exp(-\omega\eta) v_{,1\alpha\beta} v_{,1\alpha\beta} dx_2 d\eta ds \\
&+ \frac{k_2}{2} \int_0^t \int_{L_z} exp(-\omega s) v_{,12}^2 dx_2 ds + \frac{\omega\gamma k \rho_2}{m^2} \int_0^t \int_{L_z} exp(-\omega s) v_{,1}^2 dx_2 ds \\
&+ \frac{\gamma k \rho_2}{m^2} \int_{L_z} exp(-\omega t) v_{,1}^2 dx_2.
\end{aligned} \quad (46)$$

We can easily get

$$F(z,t) \geq 0. \tag{47}$$

Following the same procedures as (37)–(44), we obtain

$$\frac{\partial^2 \varphi(z,t)}{\partial z^2} \leq \frac{3}{2} E(z,t). \tag{48}$$

Inserting (30) into (48), we have

$$\frac{\partial^2 \Phi(z,t)}{\partial z^2} \leq \frac{3}{2} F(z,t). \tag{49}$$

We can also get

$$\frac{\partial^2 \Phi(z,t)}{\partial z^2} \geq F(z,t). \tag{50}$$

Combining (47) and (50), we obtain

$$\frac{\partial^2 \Phi(z,t)}{\partial z^2} = \frac{\partial^2 \int_0^t \varphi(z,s)ds}{\partial z^2} \geq 0. \tag{51}$$

Combining (36), (44) and (51), using the Schwarz's inequality, we can obtain

$$|\Phi(z,t)| \leq k_3 \frac{\partial^2 \Phi(z,t)}{\partial z^2},$$

where k_3 is a computable positive constant. The proof of Lemma 5 is finished. □

3. Phragmén-Lindelöf Alternative Results

Based on Lemmas 1–5, we can get the following Lemmas:

Lemma 6. *We suggest u and v are classical solutions of problems (4)–(7) in the semi-infinite strip Ω_0 defined by (1), if there exists a $z_0 \geq 0$ such that $\frac{\partial \Phi(z_0,t)}{\partial z} > 0$, then the following inequality holds:*

$$\lim_{z \to \infty} e^{-k_4 z} G(z,t) \geq c_1(t), \tag{52}$$

where $c_1(t) = \frac{2}{3}[\frac{\partial}{\partial z}\Phi(z_1,t) + k_4 \Phi(z_1,t)]e^{-k_4 z_1}$, $G(z,t)$ will be defined in (61).

Proof. Since $\frac{\partial^2 \Phi(z_0,t)}{\partial z^2} \geq 0$ for all $z \geq 0$, we can get $\frac{\partial \Phi(z,t)}{\partial z} > 0$ for all $z \geq z_0$.
We know the fact $\Phi(z,t) \geq \Phi(z_0,t) + \frac{\partial \Phi(z_0,t)}{\partial z}(z - z_0)$ for all $z \geq z_0$.
If we let $z \to +\infty$, we can obtain $\Phi(z,t) > 0$.
So, wo have the following results:
There exists a $z_1 > z_0$ such that $\frac{\partial \Phi(z_1,t)}{\partial z} > 0$ and $\Phi(z_1,t) > 0$.
From (31), we can get

$$\frac{\partial^2 \Phi(z,t)}{\partial z^2} - k_4^2 \Phi(z,t) \geq 0, \tag{53}$$

with $k_4 = \sqrt{\frac{1}{k_3}}$.

Equation (53) can be rewritten as

$$\frac{\partial}{\partial z}\left(e^{-k_4 z}\left[\frac{\partial}{\partial z}\Phi(z,t) + k_4\Phi(z,t)\right]\right) \geq 0, \tag{54}$$

or

$$\frac{\partial}{\partial z}\left(e^{k_4 z}\left[\frac{\partial}{\partial z}\Phi(z,t) - k_4\Phi(z,t)\right]\right) \geq 0. \tag{55}$$

Integrating (54) and (55), we obtain

$$\frac{\partial}{\partial z}\Phi(z,t) + k_4\Phi(z,t) \geq [\frac{\partial}{\partial z}\Phi(z_1,t) + k_4\Phi(z_1,t)]e^{k_4(z-z_1)}, \tag{56}$$

or

$$\frac{\partial}{\partial z}\Phi(z,t) - k_4\Phi(z,t) \geq [\frac{\partial}{\partial z}\Phi(z_1,t) - k_4\Phi(z_1,t)]e^{-k_4(z-z_1)}, \tag{57}$$

for all $z \geq z_1$.

Combining (56) and (57), we have

$$\frac{\partial}{\partial z}\Phi(z,t) \geq \frac{\partial}{\partial z}\Phi(z_1,t)\frac{e^{k_4(z-z_1)} + e^{-k_4(z-z_1)}}{2}$$
$$+ k_4\Phi(z_1,t)\frac{e^{k_4(z-z_1)} - e^{-k_4(z-z_1)}}{2}. \tag{58}$$

Integrating (49) from z_1 to z, we obtain

$$\int_{z_1}^{z}\frac{\partial^2\Phi(z,t)}{\partial z^2}d\zeta \leq \frac{3}{2}\int_{z_1}^{z}F(\zeta,t)d\zeta. \tag{59}$$

Inserting (59) into (58), we have

$$\frac{3}{2}\int_{z_1}^{z}F(\zeta,t)d\zeta \geq \frac{\partial}{\partial z}\Phi(z_1,t)\left[\frac{e^{k_4(z-z_1)} + e^{-k_4(z-z_1)}}{2} - 1\right]$$
$$+ k_4\Phi(z_1,t)\frac{e^{k_4(z-z_1)} - e^{-k_4(z-z_1)}}{2}. \tag{60}$$

If we define

$$G(z,t) = \int_{z_1}^{z}F(\zeta,t)d\zeta, \tag{61}$$

Combining (46) and (61), we have

$$G(z,t) = \frac{\omega \rho_1}{4} \int_0^t \int_0^s \int_{z_1}^z \int_{L_\xi} \exp(-\omega \eta) u_{,\eta}^2 dA d\eta ds$$
$$+ \frac{\rho_1}{2} \int_0^t \int_{z_1}^z \int_{L_\xi} \exp(-\omega s) u_{,s}^2 dA ds$$
$$+ \frac{\omega}{8} \int_0^t \int_0^s \int_{z_1}^z \int_{L_\xi} \exp(-\omega \eta) u_{,\alpha} u_{,\alpha} dA d\eta ds$$
$$+ \frac{1}{4} \int_0^t \int_{z_1}^z \int_{L_\xi} \exp(-\omega s) u_{,\alpha} u_{,\alpha} dA ds$$
$$+ \frac{\mu}{2} \int_0^t \int_0^s \int_{z_1}^z \int_{L_\xi} \exp(-\omega \eta) u_{,\alpha \eta} u_{,\alpha \eta} dA d\eta ds$$
$$+ \frac{\mu \omega k_1}{2} \int_0^t \int_0^s \int_{z_1}^z \int_{L_\xi} \exp(-\omega \eta)(u_{,\alpha \alpha})^2 dA d\eta ds$$
$$+ \frac{\mu k_1}{2} \int_0^t \int_{z_1}^z \int_{L_\xi} \exp(-\omega s)(u_{,\alpha \alpha})^2 dA ds$$
$$+ \frac{\rho_2 \omega}{4} \int_0^t \int_0^s \int_{z_1}^z \int_{L_\xi} \exp(-\omega \eta) v_{,\eta}^2 dA d\eta ds$$
$$+ \frac{\rho_2}{4} \int_0^t \int_{z_1}^z \int_{L_\xi} \exp(-\omega s) v_{,s}^2 dA ds \qquad (62)$$
$$+ \frac{m^2}{2k} \int_0^t \int_0^s \int_{z_1}^z \int_{L_\xi} \exp(-\omega \eta) v_{,\alpha \eta} v_{,\alpha \eta} dA d\eta ds$$
$$+ \frac{\omega \gamma}{4} \int_0^t \int_0^s \int_{z_1}^z \int_{L_\xi} \exp(-\omega \eta) v_{,\alpha \beta} v_{,\alpha \beta} dA d\eta ds$$
$$+ \frac{\gamma}{4} \int_0^t \int_{z_1}^z \int_{L_\xi} \exp(-\omega s) v_{,\alpha \beta} v_{,\alpha \beta} dA ds$$
$$+ \frac{m^2}{4k} k_2 \int_0^t \int_{z_1}^z \int_{L_\xi} \exp(-\omega s) v_{,1\alpha} v_{,1\alpha} dA ds$$
$$+ \int_0^t \int_0^s \int_{z_1}^z \int_{L_\xi} \exp(-\omega \eta) v_{,1\alpha \beta} v_{,1\alpha \beta} dA d\eta ds$$
$$+ \frac{k_2}{2} \int_0^t \int_{z_1}^z \int_{L_\xi} \exp(-\omega s) v_{,12}^2 dA ds$$
$$+ \frac{\omega \gamma k \rho_2}{m^2} \int_0^t \int_{z_1}^z \int_{L_\xi} \exp(-\omega s) v_{,1}^2 dA ds$$
$$+ \frac{\gamma k \rho_2}{m^2} \int_{z_1}^z \int_{L_\xi} \exp(-\omega t) v_{,1}^2 dA.$$

we obtain

$$\lim_{z \to \infty} e^{-k_4 z} G(z,t) \geq c_1(t),$$

with $c_1(t) = \frac{2}{3}[\frac{\partial}{\partial z}\Phi(z_1,t) + k_4 \Phi(z_1,t)]e^{-k_4 z_1}$. □

Lemma 7. *We suggest u and v are classical solutions of problems (4)–(7) in the semi-infinite strip Ω_0 defined by (1). If $\frac{\partial \Phi(z,t)}{\partial z} \leq 0$ for all $z \geq 0$, then the following inequality holds:*

$$H(z,t) \leq c_2(t) e^{-k_4 z}. \qquad (63)$$

where $c_2(t) = -\frac{\partial}{\partial z}\Phi(0,t) + k_4 \Phi(0,t)]$, $H(z,t)$ will be defined in (66).

Proof. If we suggest there exists a $z_0 > 0$, such that $\Phi(z_0, t) < 0$. Since $\frac{\partial \Phi(z,t)}{\partial z} \leq 0$ for all $z \geq 0$, we can get $\Phi(z,t) \leq \Phi(z_0, t) < 0$ for all $z \geq z_0$. From (31), we have $\frac{\partial \Phi(z,t)}{\partial z} - \frac{\partial \Phi(z_0,t)}{\partial z} = \frac{\partial^2 \Phi(\xi,t)}{\partial z}(z - z_0) \geq -\frac{1}{k_3}\Phi(\xi,t)(z - z_0)$, with $z_0 < \xi < z$. let $z \to \infty$, we have $\frac{\partial \Phi(z,t)}{\partial z} > 0$. Which gives a contradiction to $\frac{\partial \Phi(z,t)}{\partial z} \leq 0$ for all $z \geq 0$. So we can conclude $\Phi(z,t) \geq 0$ for all $z \geq 0$.

Integrating (53) from 0 to z, we obtain

$$-\frac{\partial \Phi(z,t)}{\partial z} + k_4 \Phi(z,t) \leq c_2(t) e^{-k_4 z}, \qquad (64)$$

with $c_2(t) = -\frac{\partial}{\partial z}\Phi(0,t) + k_4 \Phi(0,t)]$.
Since $\Phi(z,t) \geq 0$ for for all $z \geq 0$, we have

$$-\frac{\partial \Phi(z,t)}{\partial z} \leq c_2(t) e^{-k_4 z}. \qquad (65)$$

From (64), we can get the results $\Phi(z,t)$ and $-\frac{\partial \Phi(z,t)}{\partial z}$ tend to 0 as $z \to \infty$. We thus have

$$\begin{aligned}
-\frac{\partial \Phi(z,t)}{\partial z} &= \int_z^\infty \frac{\partial^2 \Phi(\xi,t)}{\partial z^2} d\xi \\
&\geq \int_z^\infty F(\xi,t) d\xi \\
&= H(z,t).
\end{aligned} \qquad (66)$$

Combining (46) and (66), we have

$$\begin{aligned}
H(z,t) = &\frac{\omega \rho_1}{4} \int_0^t \int_0^s \int_z^\infty \int_{L_\xi} \exp(-\omega\eta) u_{,\eta}^2 dA d\eta ds \\
&+ \frac{\rho_1}{2} \int_0^t \int_z^\infty \int_{L_\xi} \exp(-\omega s) u_{,s}^2 dA ds \\
&+ \frac{\omega}{8} \int_0^t \int_0^s \int_z^\infty \int_{L_\xi} \exp(-\omega\eta) u_{,\alpha} u_{,\alpha} dA d\eta ds \\
&+ \frac{1}{4} \int_0^t \int_z^\infty \int_{L_\xi} \exp(-\omega s) u_{,\alpha} u_{,\alpha} dx_2 ds \\
&+ \frac{\mu}{2} \int_0^t \int_0^s \int_z^\infty \int_{L_\xi} \exp(-\omega\eta) u_{,\alpha\eta} u_{,\alpha\eta} dA d\eta ds \\
&+ \frac{\mu\omega k_1}{2} \int_0^t \int_0^s \int_z^\infty \int_{L_\xi} \exp(-\omega\eta)(u_{,\alpha\alpha})^2 dA d\eta ds \\
&+ \frac{\mu k_1}{2} \int_0^t \int_z^\infty \int_{L_\xi} \exp(-\omega s)(u_{,\alpha\alpha})^2 dA ds \\
&+ \frac{\rho_2 \omega}{4} \int_0^t \int_0^s \int_z^\infty \int_{L_\xi} \exp(-\omega\eta) v_{,\eta}^2 dA d\eta ds \\
&+ \frac{\rho_2}{4} \int_0^t \int_z^\infty \int_{L_\xi} \exp(-\omega s) v_{,t}^2 dA ds \\
&+ \frac{m^2}{2k} \int_0^t \int_0^s \int_z^\infty \int_{L_\xi} \exp(-\omega\eta) v_{,\alpha\eta} v_{,\alpha\eta} dA d\eta ds \\
&+ \frac{\omega\gamma}{4} \int_0^t \int_0^s \int_z^\infty \int_{L_\xi} \exp(-\omega\eta) v_{,\alpha\beta} v_{,\alpha\beta} dA d\eta ds \\
&+ \frac{\gamma}{4} \int_0^t \int_z^\infty \int_{L_\xi} \exp(-\omega s) v_{,\alpha\beta} v_{,\alpha\beta} dA ds \\
&+ \frac{m^2}{4k} k_2 \int_0^t \int_z^\infty \int_{L_\xi} \exp(-\omega s) v_{,1\alpha} v_{,1\alpha} dA ds \\
&+ \int_0^t \int_0^s \int_z^\infty \int_{L_\xi} \exp(-\omega\eta) v_{,1\alpha\beta} v_{,1\alpha\beta} dA d\eta ds \\
&+ \frac{k_2}{2} \int_0^t \int_z^\infty \int_{L_\xi} \exp(-\omega s) v_{,12}^2 dA ds \\
&+ \frac{\omega\gamma k \rho_2}{m^2} \int_0^t \int_z^\infty \int_{L_\xi} \exp(-\omega s) v_{,1}^2 dA ds \\
&+ \frac{\gamma k \rho_2}{m^2} \int_z^\infty \int_{L_\xi} \exp(-\omega t) v_{,1}^2 dA.
\end{aligned} \qquad (67)$$

Inserting (66) into (65), we obtain

$$H(z,t) \leq c_2(t)e^{-k_4 z}.$$

□

Based on Lemmas 6 and 7, we can get the following theorem.

Theorem 1. *We suggest u and v are classical solutions of problems (4)–(7) in the semi-infinite strip Ω_0 defined by (1), then either inequality*

$$\lim_{z \to \infty} e^{-k_4 z} G(z,t) \geq c_1(t)$$

holds or

$$H(z,t) \leq c_2(t)e^{-k_4 z}$$

holds.

Theorem 1 shows that either the energy expression $G(z,t)$ grows exponentially or the energy expression $H(z,t)$ decays exponentially.

4. Conclusions

In this paper, we studied the spatial properties of solutions for a class of thermoelastic plate with biharmonic operator in a semi-infinite cylinder in R^2. The *Phragmén–Lindelöf* alternative results were obtained based on a second-order inequality. Our method is also valid for the hyperbolic–parabolic coupling equations. We can only deal with the linear equations. For the case of nonlinear equations, it is difficult to study the spatial properties. The results of these future studies will be of great interest to researchers in our field.

Author Contributions: Writing–original draft, S.L., original draft preparation J.S. and review and editing, B.O. All authors have read and agreed to the published version of the manuscript.

Funding: The work was supported national natural Science Foundation of China(Grant # 61907010), natural Science in Higher Education of Guangdong, China (Grant # 2018KZDXM048), the General Project of Science Research of Guangzhou (Grant # 201707010126). Guangdong Province Educational Science "Thirteenth Five-Year Plan" 2020 research project approval (NO. 2020JKDY040).

Data Availability Statement: This paper focuses on theoretical analysis, not involving experiments and data.

Acknowledgments: The authors express their heartfelt thanks to the editors and referees who have provided some important suggestions.

Conflicts of Interest: The authors declare no conflict of interest.

References

1. Horgan, C.O.; Knowles, J.K. Recent development concerning Saint-Venant's principle. *Adv. Appl. Mech.* **1983**, *23*, 179–269.
2. Horgan, C.O. Recent development concerning Saint-Venant's principle: An update. *Appl. Mech. Rev.* **1989**, *42*, 295–303. [CrossRef]
3. Horgan, C.O. Recent development concerning Saint-Venant's principle: An second update. *Appl. Mech. Rev.* **1996**, *49*, 101–111. [CrossRef]
4. D'Apice, C. Convexity considerations and spatial behavior for the harmonic vibrations in thermoelastic plates. *J. Math. Anal. Appl.* **2005**, *312*, 44–60. [CrossRef]
5. D'Apice, C. On a generalized biharmonic equation in plane polars with applications to functionally graded material. *Aust. J. Math. Anal. Appl.* **2006**, *3*, 1–15.
6. Chirita, S.; D'Apice, C. On spatial growth or decay of solutions to a non simple heat conduction problem in a semi-infinite strip. *An. Stiintifice Univ. Alexandru Ioan Cuza Iasi Mat.* **2002**, *48*, 75–100.

7. Chirita, S.; Ciarletta, M.; Fabrizio, M. Some spatial decay estimates in time-dependent Stokes slow flows. *Appl. Anal.* **2001**, *77*, 211–231. [CrossRef]
8. Fabrizio, M.; Chirita, S. Some qualitative results on the dynamic viscoelasticity of the Reissner-Mindlin plate model. *Q. J. Mech. Appl. Math.* **2004**, *57*, 59–78. [CrossRef]
9. Li, Y.F.; Lin, C.H. Spatial Decay for Solutions to 2-D Boussinesq System with Variable Thermal Diffusivity. *Acta Appl. Math.* **2018**, *154*, 111–130. [CrossRef]
10. Borrelli, A.; Patria, M.C. Energy bounds in dynamical problems for a semi-infinite magnetoelastic beam. *J. Appl. Math. Phys. ZAMP* **1996**, *47*, 880–893. [CrossRef]
11. Diaz, J.I.; Quintallina, R. Spatial and continuous dependence estimates in linear viscoelasticity. *J. Math. Anal. Appl.* **2002**, *273*, 1–16. [CrossRef]
12. Quintanilla, R. A spatial decay estimate for the hyperbolic heat equation. *SIAM J. Math. Anal.* **1998**, *27*, 78–91. [CrossRef]
13. Quintanilla, R. Phragmen-Lindelof alternative in nonlinear viscoelasticity. *Nonlinear Anal.* **1998**, *14*, 7–16. [CrossRef]
14. Payne, L.E.; Schaefer, P.W. Some Phragmén-Lindelöf Type Results for the Biharmonic Equation. *J. Appl. Math. Phys. ZAMP* **1994**, *45*, 414–432.
15. Lin, C.H. Spatial Decay Estimates and Energy Bounds forth Stokes Flow Equation. *Stab. Appl. Anal. Contin. Media* **1992**, *2*, 249–264.
16. Knowles, J.K. An Energy Estimate for the Biharmonic Equationand its Application to Saint-Venant's Principle in Plane elasto statics. *Indian J. Pure Appl. Math.* **1983**, *14*, 791–805.
17. Flavin, J.N. On Knowles' version of Saint-Venant's Principle in Two-dimensional Elastostatics. *Arch. Ration. Mech. Anal.* **1973**, *53*, 366–375. [CrossRef]
18. Horgan, C.O. Decay Estimates for the Biharmonic Equation with Applications to Saint-Venant's Principles in Plane Elasticity and Stokes flows. *Q. Appl. Math.* **1989**, *47*, 147–157. [CrossRef]
19. Liu, Y.; Lin, C.H. Phragmén-Lindelöftype alternativeresults for the stokes flow equation. *Math. Inequalities Appl.* **2006**, *9*, 671–694. [CrossRef]
20. Chen, W.; Palmieri, A. Nonexistence of global solutions for the semilinear Moore-Gibson-Thompson equation in the conservative case. *Discret. Contin. Dyn. Syst.* **2020**, *40*, 5513–5540. [CrossRef]
21. Chen, W.; Ikehata, R. The Cauchy problem for the Moore-Gibson-Thompson equation in the dissipative case. *J. Differ. Equ.* **2021**, *292*, 176–219. [CrossRef]
22. Palmieri, A.; Takamura, H. Blow-up for a weakly coupled system of semilinear damped wave equations in the scattering case with power nonlinearities. *Nonlinear Anal.* **2019**, *187*, 467–492. [CrossRef]
23. Palmieri, A.; Reissig, M. Semi-linear wave models with power non-linearity and scale-invariant time-dependent mass and dissipation, II. *Math. Nachr.* **2018**, *291*, 1859–1892. [CrossRef]
24. Liu, Y.; Chen, W. Asymptotic profiles of solutions for regularity-loss-type generalized thermoelastic plate equations and their applications. *Z. Angew. Math. Phys.* **2020**, *71*, 1–14. [CrossRef]
25. Liu, Y.; Li, Y.; Shi, J. Estimates for the linear viscoelastic damped wave equation on the Heisenberg group. *J. Differ. Equ.* **2021**, *285*, 663–685. [CrossRef]
26. Liu, Y.; Chen, Y.; Luo, C.; Lin, C. *Phragmén-Lindelöf* alternative results for the shallow water equations for transient compressible viscous flow. *J. Math. Anal. Appl.* **2013**, *398*, 409–420. [CrossRef]
27. Liu, Y. Continuous dependence for a thermal convection model with temperature-dependent solubility. *Appl. Math. Comput.* **2017**, *308*, 18–30. [CrossRef]
28. Liu, Y.; Xiao, S. Structural stability for the Brinkman fluid interfacing with a Darcy fluid in an unbounded domain. *Nonlinear Anal. Real World Appl.* **2018**, *42*, 308–333. [CrossRef]
29. Liu, Y.; Xiao, S.; Lin, Y. Continuous dependence for the Brinkman–Forchheimer fluid interfacing with a Darcy fluid in a bounded domain. *Math. Comput. Simul.* **2018**, *150*, 66–82. [CrossRef]
30. Santos, M.L.; Munoz Rivera, J.E. Analytic property of a coupled system of wave-plate type with thermal effect. *Differ. Integral Equ.* **2011**, *24*, 965–972.
31. Love, A.E.H. *Mathematical Theory of Elasticity*, 4th ed.; Dover Publications: New York, NY, USA, 1942.

Article

Schur-Convexity for Elementary Symmetric Composite Functions and Their Inverse Problems and Applications

Tao Zhang [1,2], Alatancang Chen [1,2], Huannan Shi [3], B. Saheya [1,2,*] and Boyan Xi [4]

1. College of Mathematics Science, Inner Mongolia Normal University, Hohhot 010022, China; zhangtaomath@imnu.edu.cn (T.Z.); alatanca@imu.edu.cn (A.C.)
2. Center for Applied Mathematical Science, Hohhot 010022, China
3. Department of Electronic Information, Teacher's College, Beijing Union University, Beijing 100011, China; sfthuannan@buu.edu.cn
4. College of Mathematics, Inner Mongolia University for Nationalities, Tongliao 028043, China; baoyintu78@imun.edu.cn
* Correspondence: saheya@imnu.edu.cn

Abstract: This paper investigates the Schur-convexity, Schur-geometric convexity, and Schur-harmonic convexity for the elementary symmetric composite function and its dual form. The inverse problems are also considered. New inequalities on special means are established by using the theory of majorization.

Keywords: symmetric function; Schur-convexity; inequality; special means

1. Introduction

Throughout the article, the n-dimensional Euclidean space is denoted by $\mathbb{R}^n$, and $\mathbb{R}_+^n = \{(x_1,\ldots,x_n) \mid x_i > 0, i = 1,\ldots,n\}$. $\mathbb{R}^1$ is denoted by $\mathbb{R}$ for simplicity.

In 1923, Schur [1] introduced the concept of the Schur-convex function. It can be applied to many aspects, including extended mean values [2–7], isoperimetric inequalities on the polyhedron [8], theory of statistical experiments [9], gamma and digamma functions [10], combinational optimization [11], graphs and matrices [12], reliability [13], information theoretic topics [14], stochastic orderings [15], and other related fields.

Zhang [16] and Chu et al. [17] proposed the notations of Schur-geometric convexity (or "Schur-multiplicative convexity") and Schur-harmonic convexity, respectively. Then the theory of majorization was enriched [18–27].

Let $x = (x_1,\ldots,x_n) \in \mathbb{R}^n$, the k-th elementary symmetric function and its dual form, denoted by $E_k(x)$ and $E_k^*(x)$, respectively, are defined as

$$E_k(x) = \sum_{1 \leq i_1 < \cdots < i_k \leq n} \prod_{j=1}^k x_{i_j}, \quad E_k^*(x) = \prod_{1 \leq i_1 < \cdots < i_k \leq n} \sum_{j=1}^k x_{i_j}, \quad k = 1, 2, \ldots, n.$$

Let $f : I \to \mathbb{R}$ be a function on an interval $I \subseteq \mathbb{R}$. In this paper, the k-th elementary symmetric composite function and its dual form are denoted by

$$E_k(f,x) = E_k(f(x_1),\ldots,f(x_n)), \quad E_k^*(f,x) = E_k^*(f(x_1),\ldots,f(x_n)).$$

Clearly $E_1(f,x) = E_n^*(f,x), E_n(f,x) = E_1^*(f,x)$.

Schur [1] obtained that $E_k(x)$ is Schur-concave, increasing on $\mathbb{R}_+^n$. Shi et al. [21–23] proved that $E_k^*(x)$ is increasing Schur-concave on $\mathbb{R}_+^n$, $E_k(x)$ and $E_k^*(x)$ are increasing Schur-geometrically convex and Schur-harmonically convex on $\mathbb{R}_+^n$. Xia et al. [24], Guan [25], Shi et al. [26], Sun [27], Chu et al. [17] constructed and studied the Schur-convexity, Schur-geometric convexity, and Schur-harmonic convexity of various special cases of $E_k(f,x)$ and $E_k^*(f,x)$; many interesting inequalities were established and proved.

Schur [1], Hardy et al. [28] studied the Schur-convexity of $E_1(f,x)$ (or $E_n^*(f,x)$) and obtained that:

Theorem 1 ([1,28]). *$E_1(f,x)$ (or $E_n^*(f,x)$) is Schur-convex on I^n if f is convex on $I \subseteq \mathbb{R}$.*

If f is continuous, the inverse problem of Theorem 1 also holds [29]. That is:

Theorem 2 ([29]). *If f is continuous on I, then f is convex on I if $E_1(f,x)$ (or $E_n^*(f,x)$) is Schur-convex on I^n.*

In 2010, Rovența [30] investigated the Schur-convexity of $E_2(f,x)$ and $E_{n-1}(f,x)$ and obtained that:

Theorem 3 ([30]). *Let $I \subseteq \mathbb{R}_+$ be an interval. If $f : I \to \mathbb{R}_+$ is differentiable in the interior of I and $\log f$ is convex and continuous on I, then $E_2(f,x)$ and $E_{n-1}(f,x)$ are Schur-convex functions on I.*

However, Rovența did not discuss the case of $3 \leq k \leq n-2$.
In 2011, Wang et al. [31] proved the following two results.

Theorem 4 ([31]). *Let $I \subseteq \mathbb{R}_+$ be symmetric and convex with non-empty interior, and let $f : I \to \mathbb{R}_+$ be differentiable in the interior of I and continuous on I. If $\log f$ is convex, then $E_k(f,x)$ is a Schur-convex function on I^n for any $k = 1, 2, \ldots, n$.*

Theorem 5 ([31]). *Let $I \subseteq \mathbb{R}_+$ be symmetric and convex with non-empty interior, and let $f : I \to \mathbb{R}_+$ be differentiable in the interior of I and continuous on I. If $\log f$ is convex and increasing, then $E_k(f,x)$ is a Schur-geometrically convex and Schur-harmonically convex function on I^n for any $k = 1, 2, \ldots, n$.*

In 2013, Zhang and Shi [32] gave a simple proof of Theorems 4 and 5. In 2014, Shi et al. [33] obtained the following two results.

Theorem 6 ([33]). *Let $I \subseteq \mathbb{R}_+$ be symmetric and convex with non-empty interior, and let $f : I \to \mathbb{R}_+$ be differentiable in the interior of I and continuous on I. If $\log f$ is convex, then $E_k^*(f,x)$ is a Schur-convex function on I^n for any $k = 1, 2, \ldots, n$.*

Theorem 7 ([33]). *Let $I \subseteq \mathbb{R}_+$ be symmetric and convex with non-empty interior, and let $f : I \to \mathbb{R}_+$ be differentiable in the interior of I and continuous on I. If $\log f$ is convex and increasing, then $E_k^*(f,x)$ is a Schur-geometrically convex and Schur-harmonically convex function on I^n for any $k = 1, 2, \ldots, n$.*

Theorem 2 is the inverse problem of Theorem 1. Thus, the first aim of this paper is to study the inverse problems from Theorems 3 to 7. In contrast with these results, our study suggests that the functions that do not have to be monotonous and continuous.

The arithmetic mean of $x, y \in \mathbb{R}$ is defined by

$$A(x,y) = \frac{x+y}{2}.$$

The geometric mean, harmonic mean, identity mean, and logarithmic mean of $x, y > 0$ are respectively defined by

$$G(x,y) = \sqrt{xy}, \quad H(x,y) = \frac{2xy}{x+y},$$

$$I(x,y) = \begin{cases} \frac{1}{e}\left(\frac{x^x}{y^y}\right)^{\frac{1}{x-y}}, & x \neq y, \\ x, & x = y, \end{cases} \quad L(x,y) = \begin{cases} \frac{x-y}{\log x - \log y}, & x \neq y, \\ x, & x = y. \end{cases}$$

It is well known that the following inequalities on special means

$$H(x,y) \leq G(x,y) \leq L(x,y) \leq I(x,y) \leq A(x,y), \quad x,y > 0 \tag{1}$$

have many important applications. Another aim of this paper is to establish new inequalities on special means by use of the Schur-convexity of $E_k(f,x)$, $E_k^*(f,x)$, and the theory of majorization.

2. Definitions and Lemmas

First, we introduce the concepts of Schur-convex function, Schur-geometrically convex function, and Schur-harmonically convex function.

For positive vector $x = (x_1, \ldots, x_n) \in \mathbb{R}_+^n$, we denote by

$$\frac{1}{x} := \left(\frac{1}{x_1}, \ldots, \frac{1}{x_n}\right), \quad \log x := (\log x_1, \ldots, \log x_n), \quad e^x := (e^{x_1}, \ldots, e^{x_n}).$$

A function $\varphi : \Omega \subseteq \mathbb{R}^n \to \mathbb{R}$ is said to be increasing on Ω if $x_i \leq y_i (1 \leq i \leq n)$ implies $\varphi(x) \leq \varphi(y)$ for any $x = (x_1, \ldots, x_n), y = (y_1, \ldots, y_n) \in \Omega$.

Definition 1. *Let $x = (x_1, \ldots, x_n), y = (y_1, \ldots, y_n) \in \mathbb{R}^n$.*

(i) *([34]) x is said to be majorized by y (in symbols $x \prec y$) if*

$$\sum_{i=1}^k x_{[i]} \leq \sum_{i=1}^k y_{[i]} \quad \text{for} \quad 1 \leq k \leq n-1 \quad \text{and} \quad \sum_{i=1}^n x_i = \sum_{i=1}^n y_i,$$

where $x_{[1]} \geq \cdots \geq x_{[n]}$ and $y_{[1]} \geq \cdots \geq y_{[n]}$ are rearrangements of x and y in a descending order.

(ii) *([34]) A function $\varphi : \Omega \subseteq \mathbb{R}^n \to \mathbb{R}$ is said to be Schur-convex (Schur-concave) on Ω if*

$$x \prec y \Rightarrow \varphi(x) \leq (\geq) \varphi(y), \quad \forall x, y \in \Omega.$$

(iii) *([16]) A function $\varphi : \Omega \subseteq \mathbb{R}_+^n \to \mathbb{R}_+$ is said to be Schur-geometrically convex (Schur-geometrically concave) on Ω if*

$$\log x \prec \log y \Rightarrow \varphi(x) \leq (\geq) \varphi(y), \quad \forall x, y \in \Omega.$$

(iv) *([23]) A function $\varphi : \Omega \subseteq \mathbb{R}_+^n \to \mathbb{R}_+$ is said to be Schur-harmonically convex (Schur-harmonically concave) on Ω if*

$$\frac{1}{x} \prec \frac{1}{y} \Rightarrow \varphi(x) \leq (\geq) \varphi(y), \quad \forall x, y \in \Omega.$$

Next, we introduce the concepts of convex function, geometrically convex function, and harmonically convex function.

Definition 2 ([22,23]). *Let $I \subseteq \mathbb{R}$ be an interval, and let $f : I \to \mathbb{R}$ be a function.*

(i) *f is called a convex (concave) function on I if*

$$f(\lambda x + (1-\lambda)y) \leq (\geq) \lambda f(x) + (1-\lambda)f(y), \quad \forall x, y \in I, \ 0 \leq \lambda \leq 1.$$

(ii) $f : I \subseteq \mathbb{R}_+ \to \mathbb{R}_+$ is called a geometrically convex (geometrically concave) function on I if

$$f(x^\lambda y^{1-\lambda}) \leq (\geq)[f(x)]^\lambda [f(y)]^{1-\lambda}, \quad \forall\, x, y \in I,\, 0 \leq \lambda \leq 1.$$

(iii) $f : I \subseteq \mathbb{R}_+ \to \mathbb{R}_+$ is called a harmonically convex (harmonically concave) function on I if

$$f\left(\left(\frac{\lambda}{x} + \frac{1-\lambda}{y}\right)^{-1}\right) \leq (\geq) \left(\frac{\lambda}{f(x)} + \frac{1-\lambda}{f(y)}\right)^{-1}, \quad \forall\, x, y \in I,\, 0 \leq \lambda \leq 1.$$

Lemma 1. *Let $f : [a,b] \subseteq \mathbb{R}_+ \to \mathbb{R}_+$ and $\varphi : \Omega \subseteq \mathbb{R}^n_+ \to \mathbb{R}_+$ be functions.*

(i) ([22]) f is geometrically convex (geometrically concave) on $[a,b]$ if and only if $\log f(e^x)$ is convex (concave) on $[\log a, \log b]$.

(ii) ([23,35]) f is harmonically convex (harmonically concave) on $[a,b]$ if and only if $\frac{1}{f(\frac{1}{x})}$ is concave (convex) on $\left[\frac{1}{b}, \frac{1}{a}\right]$.

(iii) ([22]) φ is Schur-geometrically convex (Schur-geometrically concave) on Ω if and only if $\varphi(e^x)$ is Schur-convex (Schur-concave) on $\{\log x \mid x \in \Omega\}$.

(iv) ([23]) φ is Schur-harmonically convex (Schur-harmonically concave) on Ω if and only if $\varphi\left(\frac{1}{x}\right)$ is Schur-convex (Schur-concave) on $\left\{\frac{1}{x} \mid x \in \Omega\right\}$.

Lemma 2 ([16,36]). *Let $I \subseteq \mathbb{R}$ be an interval, and let $f : I \to \mathbb{R}$ be a continuous function.*

(i) f is convex (concave) on I if and only if

$$f(A(x,y)) \leq (\geq) A(f(x), f(y)), \quad \forall\, x, y \in I.$$

(ii) $f : I \subseteq \mathbb{R}_+ \to \mathbb{R}_+$ is geometrically convex (geometrically concave) on I if and only if

$$f(G(x,y)) \leq (\geq) G(f(x), f(y)), \quad \forall\, x, y \in I.$$

(iii) $f : I \subseteq \mathbb{R}_+ \to \mathbb{R}_+$ is harmonically convex (harmonically concave) on I if and only if

$$f(H(x,y)) \leq (\geq) H(f(x), f(y)), \quad \forall\, x, y \in I.$$

Next, we prove the convexity of some functions involving $I(x, a+x)$ and $L(x, a+x)$.

Lemma 3. *Let $a > 0$. Then*

(i) $I(x, a+x)$ and $L(x, a+x)$ are concave on $\mathbb{R}_+$.

(ii) $I(x, a+x)$, $L(x, a+x)$ and $e^{[1/L(x,a+x)]}$ are geometrically convex on $\mathbb{R}_+$, $e^{[1/I(x,a+x)]}$ is geometrically convex on $[a, +\infty)$.

(iii) $I(x, a+x)$ and $L(x, a+x)$ are harmonically convex on $\mathbb{R}_+$.

Proof. For simplicity, we denote $f(x) = I(x, a+x)$, $g(x) = L(x, a+x)$.

(i) By a simple calculation, we can obtain that

$$f''(x) = f(x)\left[(\log f(x))'' + (\log f(x))'^2\right] = \frac{f(x)}{a^2}\left[\frac{-a^2}{x(a+x)} + \left(\log\left(1 + \frac{a}{x}\right)\right)^2\right],$$

$$g''(x) = \frac{-a^2[(2x+a)(\log(x+a) - \log x) - 2a]}{x^2(x+a)^2[\log(x+a) - \log x]^3}.$$

Let

$$f_1(t) = -t - \frac{1}{t} + (\log t)^2 + 2, \quad t > 1;$$
$$\phi_x(s) = (2x+s)(\log(x+s) - \log x) - 2s, \quad s > 0,\ x > 0,$$

then
$$f''(x) = \frac{f(x)f_1(1+\frac{a}{x})}{a^2}, \quad g''(x) = \frac{-a^2\phi_x(a)}{x^2(x+a)^2[\log(x+a)-\log x]^3},$$

and
$$f_1'(t) = \frac{1}{t}(-t+\frac{1}{t}+2\log t) < 0,$$
$$\phi_x'(s) = -\log\frac{x}{x+s} - \frac{s}{x+s} > 0.$$

Note that $f_1(1) = 0$, $\phi_x(0) = 0$, so $f_1(t) < 0 (t > 1)$ and $\phi_x(s) > 0 (s > 0)$. It follows that $f''(x) < 0$ and $g''(x) < 0$ on $\mathbb{R}_+$. Hence, $f(x)$ and $g(x)$ are concave on $\mathbb{R}_+$.

(ii) Note that
$$(\log f(e^x))'' = \frac{e^x}{-a}\left[\frac{a}{a+e^x} + \log\frac{e^x}{a+e^x}\right] > 0, \quad x \in \mathbb{R},$$
$$(\log g(e^x))'' = \frac{g(e^x)^2 e^x[ae^{-x}-\log(1+ae^{-x})]}{a(a+e^x)^2} > 0, \quad x \in \mathbb{R},$$
$$\left(\frac{1}{g(e^x)}\right)'' = \frac{e^x}{(a+e^x)^2} > 0, \quad x \in \mathbb{R}.$$

It means that $\log f(e^x)$, $\log g(e^x)$ and $\frac{1}{g(e^x)}$ are convex on $\mathbb{R}$. So $f(x)$, $g(x)$ and $e^{1/g(x)}$ are geometrically convex on $\mathbb{R}_+$ by Lemma 1(i).

Next we prove that $e^{1/f(x)}$ is geometrically convex on $[a, +\infty)$. Clearly we have
$$\left(\frac{1}{f(e^x)}\right)'' = \frac{e^{2x}}{a^2 f(e^x)}\left[\frac{a}{e^x}\left(\log\frac{e^x}{a+e^x}+1-\frac{e^x}{a+e^x}\right)+\left(\log\frac{e^x}{a+e^x}\right)^2\right], \quad x \geq \log a.$$

Let
$$p(t) = (1/t-1)(\log t+1-t)+(\log t)^2, \quad \frac{1}{2} \leq t < 1,$$

then $\left(\frac{1}{f(e^x)}\right)'' = \frac{e^{2x}p(\frac{e^x}{a+e^x})}{a^2 f(e^x)}$ and
$$p'(t) = \frac{1}{t}\left[(t-1)+\left(2-\frac{1}{t}\right)\log t\right] < 0.$$

Note that $p(1) = 0$, so $p(t) > 0$ ($\frac{1}{2} \leq t < 1$). It follows that $\left(\frac{1}{f(e^x)}\right)'' > 0$ on $[\log a, +\infty)$ and $e^{1/f(x)}$ is geometrically convex on $[a, +\infty)$ by Lemma 1(i).

(iii) Note that
$$\left[\frac{1}{g(\frac{1}{x})}\right]'' = \frac{-a}{(ax+1)^2} < 0, \quad x > 0.$$

So $\frac{1}{g(\frac{1}{x})}$ is concave and $g(x)$ is harmonically convex on $\mathbb{R}_+$ by Lemma 1(ii).

Next, we prove that $f(x)$ is harmonically convex on $\mathbb{R}_+$. Clearly we have
$$\left[\frac{1}{f(\frac{1}{x})}\right]'' = \frac{1}{a^2 x^4 f(\frac{1}{x})}\left[-2ax\log(ax+1)+\frac{a^2 x^2}{ax+1}+(\log(ax+1))^2\right], \quad x > 0.$$

Let
$$h(t) = -2(t-1)\log t + t + \frac{1}{t} - 2 + (\log t)^2, \quad t > 1,$$

then $\left[\frac{1}{f(\frac{1}{x})}\right]'' = \frac{h(ax+1)}{a^2 x^4 f(\frac{1}{x})}$ and
$$h'(t) = -\left(1-\frac{1}{t}\right)\left(1-\frac{1}{t}+2\log t\right) < 0.$$

Note that $h(1) = 0$, so $h(t) < 0 (t > 1)$ and $\left[\frac{1}{f(\frac{1}{x})}\right]'' < 0 (x > 0)$. Hence $\frac{1}{f(\frac{1}{x})}$ is concave and $f(x)$ is harmonically convex on $\mathbb{R}_+$ by Lemma 1(ii). □

In the following, we introduce some relevant conclusions on the Schur-convexity of the composite function. For further details, please refer to [22,23,29].

Lemma 4 ([29]). *Let $I \subseteq \mathbb{R}$ be an interval, and let $\varphi : \mathbb{R}^n \to \mathbb{R}$, $f : I \to \mathbb{R}$ and $\psi(x) = \varphi(f(x_1), \cdots, f(x_n)) : \mathbb{R}^n \to \mathbb{R}$ be functions.*

(i) *If f is convex and φ is increasing Schur-convex, then ψ is Schur-convex on I^n.*
(ii) *If f is concave and φ is increasing Schur-concave, then ψ is Schur-concave on I^n.*

Lemma 5 ([22,23]). *Let $I \subseteq \mathbb{R}_+$ be an interval, and let $\varphi : \mathbb{R}_+^n \to \mathbb{R}_+$, $f : I \to \mathbb{R}_+$ and $\psi(x) = \varphi(f(x_1), \cdots, f(x_n)) : \mathbb{R}_+^n \to \mathbb{R}_+$ be functions.*

(i) *If f is geometrically convex and φ is increasing Schur-geometrically convex, then ψ is Schur-geometrically convex on I^n.*
(ii) *If f is geometrically concave and φ is increasing Schur-geometrically concave, then ψ is Schur-geometrically concave on I^n.*
(iii) *If φ is increasing and Schur-harmonically convex and f is harmonically convex, then ψ is Schur-harmonically convex on I^n.*

Symmetric functions $E_k(x)$ and $E_k^*(x)$ have the following properties.

Lemma 6 ([1,21–23]). *$E_k(x)$ and $E_k^*(x)$ are increasing Schur-concave, Schur-geometrically convex and Schur-harmonically convex on $\mathbb{R}_+^n$.*

Lemma 7 ([29]). *Let $I \subseteq \mathbb{R}_+$ be an interval, and let $\varphi : I^n \to \mathbb{R}$ be a continuous symmetric function. If φ is differentiable on I^n, then φ is Schur-convex (Schur-concave) on I^n if and only if*

$$(x_1 - x_2)\left(\frac{\partial \varphi(x)}{\partial x_1} - \frac{\partial \varphi(x)}{\partial x_2}\right) \geq 0 (\leq 0).$$

Let $E_0(x_3, \cdots, x_n) = 1$, $\sum_{i=1}^{0} x_i = 0$, it is easy to induce that

$$E_1(x) = \sum_{i=1}^{n} x_i, \qquad E_1^*(x) = \prod_{i=1}^{n} x_i,$$

$$E_k(x) = x_1 E_{k-1}(x_3, \cdots, x_n) + x_2 E_{k-1}(x_3, \cdots, x_n) + x_1 x_2 E_{k-2}(x_3, \cdots, x_n) + E_k(x_3, \cdots, x_n), \quad 2 \leq k \leq n,$$

$$\frac{\partial E_k^*(x)}{\partial x_1} = \sum_{3 \leq i_1 < \cdots < i_{k-1} \leq n} \frac{E_k^*(x)}{x_1 + \sum_{j=1}^{k-1} x_{i_j}} + \sum_{3 \leq i_1 < \cdots < i_{k-2} \leq n} \frac{E_k^*(x)}{x_1 + x_2 + \sum_{j=1}^{k-2} x_{i_j}}, \quad 2 \leq k \leq n,$$

$$\frac{\partial E_k^*(x)}{\partial x_2} = \sum_{3 \leq i_1 < \cdots < i_{k-1} \leq n} \frac{E_k^*(x)}{x_2 + \sum_{j=1}^{k-1} x_{i_j}} + \sum_{3 \leq i_1 < \cdots < i_{k-2} \leq n} \frac{E_k^*(x)}{x_1 + x_2 + \sum_{j=1}^{k-2} x_{i_j}}, \quad 2 \leq k \leq n.$$

Hence, by use of Lemma 7, Lemma 1(iii), (iv) and Lemma 6, we have

Lemma 8. *Let $k = 1, 2, \cdots, n$, then*

(i) *$E_k(e^x)$ and $E_k^*(e^x)$ are increasing and Schur-convex on $\mathbb{R}^n$.*
(ii) *$E_k(\log x)$ and $E_k^*(\log x)$ are increasing and Schur-geometrically concave on $\{e^x | x \in \mathbb{R}_+^n\}$.*
(iii) *$E_k(\frac{1}{x})$ and $E_k^*(\frac{1}{x})$ are decreasing and Schur-harmonically concave on $\mathbb{R}_+^n$.*

3. Main Results

In this section, we prove our main results. Firstly, we investigate the Schur-convexity of $E_k(f,x)$ and $E_k^*(f,x)$ and their inverse problems. Note that Theorems 1 and 2 study the cases of $E_1(f,x)$ and $E_n^*(f,x)$, so we only consider the other cases in the following.

Theorem 8. Let $I \subseteq \mathbb{R}$ be an interval, and let $f : I \to \mathbb{R}_+$ be a function.

(i) If $\log f$ is convex, then $E_k(f,x)(2 \le k \le n)$ and $E_k^*(f,x)(1 \le k \le n-1)$ are Schur-convex on I^n. Conversely, if $E_k(f,x)(2 \le k \le n)$ or $E_k^*(f,x)(1 \le k \le n-1)$ is Schur-convex on I^n and f is continuous, then f is convex.

(ii) If f is concave, then $E_k(f,x)(1 \le k \le n)$ and $E_k^*(f,x)(1 \le k \le n)$ are Schur-concave on I^n. Conversely, if $E_1(f,x)$ or $E_n^*(f,x)$ is Schur-concave on I^n and f is continuous, then f is concave. If $E_k(f,x)(2 \le k \le n)$ or $E_k^*(f,x)(1 \le k \le n-1)$ is Schur-concave on I^n and f is continuous, then $\log f$ is concave.

Proof. We only prove that the results hold for $E_k(f,x)$. A similar argument leads to the proof of the results for $E_k^*(f,x)$.

(i) If $\log f$ is convex, then $E_k(f,x) = E_k(e^{\log f}, x)$ is Schur-convex on I^n by Lemmas 4(i) and 8(i). Conversely, if $2 \le k \le n$ and $E_k(f,x)$ is Schur-convex on I^n, note that $E_k(x)$ is Schur-concave on $\mathbb{R}_+^n$, so for all $(x_1, \cdots, x_n) \in I^n$, we have

$$E_k(f(A(x_1,x_2)), f(A(x_1,x_2)), f(x_3), \cdots, f(x_n))$$
$$\le E_k(f(x_1), f(x_2), f(x_3), \cdots, f(x_n))$$
$$\le E_k(A(f(x_1), f(x_2)), A(f(x_1), f(x_2)), f(x_3), \cdots, f(x_n)).$$

Since $E_k(x)$ is increasing on $\mathbb{R}_+^n$, then

$$f(A(x_1, x_2)) \le A(f(x_1), f(x_2)).$$

Since f is continuous, f is convex by Lemma 2(i).

(ii) If f is concave, then $E_k(f,x)$ is Schur-concave on I^n by Lemmas 4(ii) and 6. Conversely, if $E_1(f,x)$ is Schur-concave on I^n and f is continuous, then $-E_1(f,x) = E_1(-f,x)$ is Schur-convex on I^n, so $-f$ is convex on I by Theorem 2. Hence f is concave.
If $2 \le k \le n$ and $E_k(f,x)$ is Schur-concave on I^n, note that $E_k(e^x)$ is Schur-convex by Lemma 8(i), so for all $(x_1, \cdots, x_n) \in I^n$ and $2 \le k \le n$, we have

$$E_k(f(A(x_1,x_2)), f(A(x_1,x_2)), f(x_3), \cdots, f(x_n))$$
$$\ge E_k(f(x_1), f(x_2), f(x_3), \cdots, f(x_n))$$
$$= E_k\left(e^{\log f(x_1)}, e^{\log f(x_2)}, e^{\log f(x_3)}, \cdots, e^{\log f(x_n)}\right)$$
$$\ge E_k\left(e^{A(\log f(x_1), \log f(x_2))}, e^{A(\log f(x_1), \log f(x_2))}, e^{\log f(x_3)}, \cdots, e^{\log f(x_n)}\right)$$
$$= E_k(G(f(x_1), f(x_2)), G(f(x_1), f(x_2)), f(x_3), \cdots, f(x_n)).$$

Since $E_k(x)$ is increasing on $\mathbb{R}_+^n$, then

$$f(A(x_1, x_2)) \ge G(f(x_1), f(x_2)).$$

Since f is continuous, $\log f$ is concave by Lemma 2(i). □

Secondly, we prove the Schur-geometrically convexity of $E_k(f,x)$ and $E_k^*(f,x)$ and their inverse problems.

Theorem 9. Let $1 \leq k \leq n$ and $I \subseteq \mathbb{R}_+$ be an interval, and let $f : I \to \mathbb{R}_+$ be a function.

(i) If f is geometrically convex, then $E_k(f,x)$ and $E_k^*(f,x)$ are Schur-geometrically convex on I^n. Conversely, if $E_n(f,x)$ or $E_1^*(f,x)$ is Schur-geometrically convex on I^n and f is continuous, then f is geometrically convex. If $E_k(f,x)(1 \leq k \leq n-1)$ or $E_k^*(f,x)(2 \leq k \leq n)$ is Schur-geometrically convex on I^n and f is continuous, then e^f is geometrically convex;

(ii) If f is geometrically concave, then $E_n(f,x)$ and $E_1^*(f,x)$ are Schur-geometrically concave on I^n. If e^f is geometrically concave, then $E_k(f,x)(1 \leq k \leq n-1)$ and $E_k^*(f,x)(2 \leq k \leq n)$ are Schur-geometrically concave on I^n. Conversely, if $E_k(f,x)$ or $E_k^*(f,x)$ is Schur-geometrically concave on I^n and f is continuous, then f is geometrically concave.

Proof. We only prove that the results hold for $E_k(f,x)$. A similar argument leads to the proof of the results for $E_k^*(f,x)$.

(i) If f is geometrically convex, then $E_k(f,x)$ is Schur-geometrically convex on I^n by Lemmas 5(i) and 6. Conversely, if $E_n(f,x)$ is Schur-geometrically convex on I^n, then for all $(x_1, \cdots, x_n) \in I^n$, we have

$$E_n(f(G(x_1,x_2)), f(G(x_1,x_2)), f(x_3), \cdots, f(x_n)) = f^2(G(x_1,x_2)) \prod_{i=3}^{n} f(x_i) \leq \prod_{i=1}^{n} f(x_i).$$

So we have

$$f(G(x_1,x_2)) \leq G(f(x_1), f(x_2)).$$

Since f is continuous, f is geometrically convex by Lemma 2(ii).

If $E_k(f,x)(1 \leq k \leq n-1)$ is Schur-geometrically convex on I^n, note that $E_k(\log x)$ is Schur-geometrically concave by Lemma 8(ii), so for all $(x_1, \cdots, x_n) \in I^n$, we have

$$E_k(f(G(x_1,x_2)), f(G(x_1,x_2)), f(x_3), \cdots, f(x_n))$$
$$\leq E_k(f(x_1), f(x_2), f(x_3), \cdots, f(x_n))$$
$$= E_k\left(\log e^{f(x_1)}, \log e^{f(x_2)}, \log e^{f(x_3)}, \cdots, \log e^{f(x_n)}\right)$$
$$\leq E_k\left(\log G(e^{f(x_1)}, e^{f(x_2)}), \log G(e^{f(x_1)}, e^{f(x_2)}), \log e^{f(x_3)}, \cdots, \log e^{f(x_n)}\right)$$
$$= E_k(A(f(x_1), f(x_2)), A(f(x_1), f(x_2)), f(x_3), \cdots, f(x_n)).$$

Which implies that

$$f(G(x_1,x_2)) \leq A(f(x_1), f(x_2)).$$

Since f is continuous, e^f is geometrically convex by Lemma 2(ii).

(ii) If f is geometrically concave, then $\frac{1}{f}$ is geometrically convexity, it follows that the function

$$\frac{1}{E_n(f,x)} = E_n\left(\frac{1}{f}, x\right)$$

is Schur-geometrically convex on I^n by (i); hence, $E_n(f,x)$ is Schur-geometrically concave on I^n.

If e^f is geometrically concave, then for any $1 \leq k \leq n-1$, $E_k(f,x) = E_k(\log e^f, x)$ is Schur-geometrically concave on I^n by Lemmas 5(ii) and 8(ii).

Conversely, if $E_k(f,x)$ is Schur-geometrically concave on I^n, note that $E_k(x)$ is Schur-geometrically convex on I^n, so for all $(x_1, \cdots, x_n) \in I^n$, we have

$$E_k(f(G(x_1,x_2)), f(G(x_1,x_2)), f(x_3), \cdots, f(x_n))$$
$$\geq E_k(f(x_1), f(x_2), f(x_3), \cdots, f(x_n))$$
$$\geq E_k(G(f(x_1), f(x_2)), G(f(x_1), f(x_2)), f(x_3), \cdots, f(x_n)).$$

Which implies that
$$f(G(x_1, x_2)) \geq G(f(x_1), f(x_2)).$$

Since f is continuous, f is geometrically concave by Lemma 2(ii).

□

Finally, we prove the Schur-harmonically convexity of $E_k(f, x)$ and $E_k^*(f, x)$ and their inverse problems.

Theorem 10. *Let $1 \leq k \leq n$ and $I \subseteq \mathbb{R}_+$ be an interval, and let $f : I \to \mathbb{R}_+$ be a function.*

(i) *If f is harmonically convex, then $E_k(f, x)$ and $E_k^*(f, x)$ are Schur-harmonically convex on I^n. Conversely, if $E_k(f, x)$ or $E_k^*(f, x)$ is Schur-harmonically convex on I^n and f is continuous, then $\frac{1}{f}$ is harmonically concave.*

(ii) *If $\frac{1}{f}$ is harmonically convex, then $E_k(f, x)$ and $E_k^*(f, x)$ are Schur-harmonically concave on I^n. Conversely, if $E_k(f, x)$ or $E_k^*(f, x)$ is Schur-harmonically concave on I^n and f is continuous, then f is harmonically concave.*

Proof. We only prove that the results hold for $E_k(f, x)$. A similar argument leads to the proof of the results for $E_k^*(f, x)$.

(i) If f is harmonically convex, then $E_k(f, x)$ is Schur-harmonically convex on I^n by Lemmas 5(iii) and 6. Conversely, if $E_k(f, x)$ is Schur-harmonically convex on I^n, note that $E_k(\frac{1}{x})$ is Schur-harmonically concave by Lemma 8(iii), so for all $(x_1, \cdots, x_n) \in I^n$, we have

$$E_k(f(H(x_1, x_2)), f(H(x_1, x_2)), f(x_3), \cdots, f(x_n))$$
$$\leq E_k(f(x_1), f(x_2), f(x_3), \cdots, f(x_n))$$
$$= E_k\left(\frac{1}{\frac{1}{f(x_1)}}, \frac{1}{\frac{1}{f(x_2)}}, \frac{1}{\frac{1}{f(x_3)}}, \cdots, \frac{1}{\frac{1}{f(x_n)}}\right)$$
$$\leq E_k\left(\frac{1}{H\left(\frac{1}{f(x_1)}, \frac{1}{f(x_2)}\right)}, \frac{1}{H\left(\frac{1}{f(x_1)}, \frac{1}{f(x_2)}\right)}, \frac{1}{\frac{1}{f(x_3)}}, \cdots, \frac{1}{\frac{1}{f(x_n)}}\right).$$

Which implies that
$$\frac{1}{f(H(x_1, x_2))} \geq H\left(\frac{1}{f(x_1)}, \frac{1}{f(x_2)}\right).$$

Since f is continuous, $\frac{1}{f}$ is harmonically concave by Lemma 2(iii).

(ii) If $\frac{1}{f}$ is harmonically convex, note that $\left[E_k(\frac{1}{x})\right]^{-1}$ is increasing Schur-harmonically convex on $\mathbb{R}_+^n$ by Lemma 8(iii), so the function

$$(E_k(f, x))^{-1} = \left(E_k\left(\frac{1}{\frac{1}{f}}, x\right)\right)^{-1}$$

is Schur-harmonically convex on I^n by Lemma 5(iii). It follows that $E_k(f, x)$ is Schur-harmonically concave on I^n. Conversely, if $E_k(f, x)$ is Schur-harmonically concave on I^n, note that $E_k(x)$ is Schur-harmonically convex on I^n by Lemma 6, so for all $(x_1, \cdots, x_n) \in I^n$, we have

$$E_k(f(H(x_1, x_2)), f(H(x_1, x_2)), f(x_3), \cdots, f(x_n))$$
$$\geq E_k(f(x_1), f(x_2), f(x_3), \cdots, f(x_n))$$
$$\geq E_k(H(f(x_1), f(x_2)), H(f(x_1), f(x_2)), f(x_3), \cdots, f(x_n)).$$

Which implies that

$$f(H(x_1,x_2)) \geq H(f(x_1),f(x_2)).$$

Since f is continuous, f is harmonically concave by Lemma 2(iii). □

4. Applications to Means

Now, we use Theorems 8–10 to establish new inequalities on special means.

Let $x = (x_1, \cdots, x_n) \in \mathbb{R}_{++}^n$, the arithmetic mean, geometric mean, harmonic mean of $x_1, \cdots, x_n$ are respectively defined by

$$A_n(x) = \frac{1}{n}\sum_{i=1}^n x_i, \quad G_n(x) = \left(\prod_{i=1}^n x_i\right)^{1/n}, \quad H_n(x) = n\left(\sum_{i=1}^n x_i^{-1}\right)^{-1}.$$

For simplicity, we denote

$$I(x, a+x) = (I(x_1, a+x_1), \cdots, I(x_n, a+x_n)),$$
$$L(x, a+x) = (L(x_1, a+x_1), \cdots, L(x_n, a+x_n)).$$

If we replace $f(x)$ with $I(x, a+x)$ and $L(x, a+x)$, respectively, in Theorem 8(ii), then by Lemma 3(i) and Theorem 8(ii) we can get:

Theorem 11. *Let $a > 0$, $x = (x_1, \cdots, x_n) \in \mathbb{R}_+$, $n \geq 2$, $1 \leq k \leq n$, then*

$$\sum_{1 \leq i_1 < \cdots < i_k \leq n} \prod_{j=1}^k I(x_{i_j}, a+x_{i_j}) \leq \binom{n}{k} I(A_n(x), a+A_n(x))^k, \tag{2}$$

$$\sum_{1 \leq i_1 < \cdots < i_k \leq n} \prod_{j=1}^k L(x_{i_j}, a+x_{i_j}) \leq \binom{n}{k} L(A_n(x), a+A_n(x))^k, \tag{3}$$

$$\prod_{1 \leq i_1 < \cdots < i_k \leq n} \sum_{j=1}^k I(x_{i_j}, a+x_{i_j}) \leq k^{\binom{n}{k}} I(A_n(x), a+A_n(x))^{\binom{n}{k}}, \tag{4}$$

$$\prod_{1 \leq i_1 < \cdots < i_k \leq n} \sum_{j=1}^k L(x_{i_j}, a+x_{i_j}) \leq k^{\binom{n}{k}} L(A_n(x), a+A_n(x))^{\binom{n}{k}}. \tag{5}$$

In particular, if we let $k = 1$ in (2) and (3), respectively, then we have

$$A_n(I(x,a+x)) \leq I(A_n(x), a+A_n(x)), \tag{6}$$
$$A_n(L(x,a+x)) \leq L(A_n(x), a+A_n(x)). \tag{7}$$

If we replace $f(x)$ with $I(x, a+x)$, $L(x, a+x)$, $e^{[1/I(x,a+x)]}$ and $e^{[1/L(x,a+x)]}$ respectively in Theorem 9(i), then by Lemma 3(ii) and Theorem 9(i) we have:

Theorem 12. *Let $a > 0$, $x = (x_1, \cdots, x_n)$, $n \geq 2$, $1 \leq k \leq n$, then*

$$\sum_{1\leq i_1<\cdots<i_k\leq n}\prod_{j=1}^{k}I(x_{i_j},a+x_{i_j})\geq\binom{n}{k}I(G_n(x),a+G_n(x))^k, \quad x\in\mathbb{R}_+^n, \tag{8}$$

$$\sum_{1\leq i_1<\cdots<i_k\leq n}\prod_{j=1}^{k}e^{[1/I(x_{i_j},a+x_{i_j})]}\geq\binom{n}{k}e^{[k/I(G_n(x),a+G_n(x))]}, \quad x\in[a,+\infty)^n, \tag{9}$$

$$\sum_{1\leq i_1<\cdots<i_k\leq n}\prod_{j=1}^{k}L(x_{i_j},a+x_{i_j})\geq\binom{n}{k}L(G_n(x),a+G_n(x))^k, \quad x\in\mathbb{R}_+^n, \tag{10}$$

$$\sum_{1\leq i_1<\cdots<i_k\leq n}\prod_{j=1}^{k}\left(\frac{a+x_{i_j}}{x_{i_j}}\right)^{\frac{1}{a}}\geq\binom{n}{k}\left(\frac{a+G_n(x)}{G_n(x)}\right)^{\frac{k}{a}}, \quad x\in\mathbb{R}_+^n, \tag{11}$$

$$\prod_{1\leq i_1<\cdots<i_k\leq n}\sum_{j=1}^{k}I(x_{i_j},a+x_{i_j})\geq k^{\binom{n}{k}}I(G_n(x),a+G_n(x))^{\binom{n}{k}}, \quad x\in\mathbb{R}_+^n, \tag{12}$$

$$\prod_{1\leq i_1<\cdots<i_k\leq n}\sum_{j=1}^{k}e^{[1/I(x_{i_j},a+x_{i_j})]}\geq k^{\binom{n}{k}}e^{[\binom{n}{k}/I(G_n(x),a+G_n(x))]}, \quad x\in[a,+\infty)^n, \tag{13}$$

$$\prod_{1\leq i_1<\cdots<i_k\leq n}\sum_{j=1}^{k}L(x_{i_j},a+x_{i_j})\geq k^{\binom{n}{k}}L(G_n(x),a+G_n(x))^{\binom{n}{k}}, \quad x\in\mathbb{R}_+^n, \tag{14}$$

$$\prod_{1\leq i_1<\cdots<i_k\leq n}\sum_{j=1}^{k}\left(\frac{a+x_{i_j}}{x_{i_j}}\right)^{\frac{1}{a}}\geq k^{\binom{n}{k}}\left(\frac{a+G_n(x)}{G_n(x)}\right)^{\binom{n}{k}/a}, \quad x\in\mathbb{R}_+^n. \tag{15}$$

In particular, if we let $k=n$ in (8), (9), (10) and (11), respectively, then we have

$$G_n(I(x,a+x))\geq I(G_n(x),a+G_n(x)), \quad x\in\mathbb{R}_+^n, \tag{16}$$
$$H_n(I(x,a+x))\leq I(G_n(x),a+G_n(x)), \quad x\in[a,+\infty)^n, \tag{17}$$
$$G_n(L(x,a+x))\geq L(G_n(x),a+G_n(x)), \quad x\in\mathbb{R}_+^n, \tag{18}$$
$$H_n(L(x,a+x))\leq L(G_n(x),a+G_n(x)), \quad x\in\mathbb{R}_+^n. \tag{19}$$

If we replace $\frac{1}{f(x)}$ with $I(x,a+x)$ and $L(x,a+x)$, respectively, in Theorem 10(ii), then by Lemma 3(iii) and Theorem 10(ii), we can get:

Theorem 13. Let $a>0$, $x=(x_1,\cdots,x_n)\in\mathbb{R}_+^n$, $n\geq 2$, $1\leq k\leq n$, then

$$\sum_{1\leq i_1<\cdots<i_k\leq n}\prod_{j=1}^{k}\frac{1}{I(x_{i_j},a+x_{i_j})}\leq\binom{n}{k}\frac{1}{I(H_n(x),a+H_n(x))^k}, \tag{20}$$

$$\sum_{1\leq i_1<\cdots<i_k\leq n}\prod_{j=1}^{k}\frac{1}{L(x_{i_j},a+x_{i_j})}\leq\binom{n}{k}\frac{1}{L(H_n(x),a+H_n(x))^k}, \tag{21}$$

$$\prod_{1\leq i_1<\cdots<i_k\leq n}\sum_{j=1}^{k}\frac{1}{I(x_{i_j},a+x_{i_j})}\leq k^{\binom{n}{k}}\frac{1}{I(H_n(x),a+H_n(x))^k}, \tag{22}$$

$$\prod_{1\leq i_1<\cdots<i_k\leq n}\sum_{j=1}^{k}\frac{1}{L(x_{i_j},a+x_{i_j})}\leq k^{\binom{n}{k}}\frac{1}{L(H_n(x),a+H_n(x))^k}. \tag{23}$$

In particular, if we let $k=1$ in (20) and (21), respectively, then we have

$$H_n(I(x,a+x))\geq I(H_n(x),a+H_n(x)), \tag{24}$$
$$H_n(L(x,a+x))\geq L(H_n(x),a+H_n(x)). \tag{25}$$

By the inequalities (6), (7), (16)–(19), (24) and (25), we can obtain the following new inequalities.

Theorem 14. Let $a > 0$, $x = (x_1, \cdots, x_n) \in \mathbb{R}_+^n$, $n \geq 2$, then

$$I(H_n(x), a + H_n(x)) \leq H_n(I(x, a + x)) \leq I(G_n(x), a + G_n(x))$$
$$\leq G_n(I(x, a + x)) \leq A_n(I(x, a + x)) \leq I(A_n(x), a + A_n(x)), \quad x \in [a, +\infty)^n, \quad (26)$$
$$L(H_n(x), a + H_n(x)) \leq H_n(L(x, a + x)) \leq L(G_n(x), a + G_n(x))$$
$$\leq G_n(L(x, a + x)) \leq A_n(L(x, a + x)) \leq L(A_n(x), a + A_n(x)), \quad x \in \mathbb{R}_+^n. \quad (27)$$

5. Discussion

In this paper, the Schur-convexity, Schur-geometric convexity, and Schur-harmonic convexity and the inverse problem for $E_k(f, x)$ and $E_k^*(f, x)$ are established in Theorems 8–10, then some results in the papers [1,17,24–33] are generalized.

The inequalities involving special means (arithmetic mean, geometric mean, harmonic mean, identity mean, and logarithmic mean) are very important. In this paper, by use of Theorems 8–10 and the theory of majorization, new inequalities on special means are established in Theorems 11–14.

Author Contributions: Investigation, T.Z., A.C., H.S. and B.X.; writing—original draft, T.Z. and B.X.; validation, B.S. All authors have contributed equally to the preparation of this paper. All authors have read and agreed to the published version of the manuscript.

Funding: This research was funded by the National Natural Science Foundation (no. 11761029, no. 62161044), the Natural Science Foundation of Inner Mongolia (no. 2021LHMS01008, no. 2019LH01001).

Conflicts of Interest: The authors declare no conflict of interest.

References

1. Schur, I. Über eine klasse von mittebildungen mit anwendungen auf die determinanten theorie. *Sitzungsber. Berl. Math. Ges.* **1923**, *22*, 9–20.
2. Elezović, N.; Pečarić, J. A note on Schur-convex functions. *Rocky Mt. J. Math.* **2000**, *30*, 853–856. [CrossRef]
3. Čuljak, V.; Franjić, I.; Ghulam, R.; Pečarić, J. Schur-convexity of averages of convex functions. *J. Inequal. Appl.* **2011**, *1*, 581918. [CrossRef]
4. Chu, Y.M.; Zhang, X.M. Necessary and sufficient conditions such that extended mean values are Schur-convex or Schur-concave. *J. Math. Kyoto Univ.* **2008**, *48*, 229–238. [CrossRef]
5. Qi, F. A note on Schur-convexity of extended mean values. *Rocky Mt. J. Math.* **2005**, *35*, 1787–1797. [CrossRef]
6. Shi, H.N.; Wu, S.H.; Qi, F. An alternative note on the Schur-convexity of extended mean values. *Math. Inequal. Appl.* **2006**, *9*, 219–224. [CrossRef]
7. Qi, F.; Sándor, J.; Deagomir, S.S. Notes on Schur-convexity of extended mean values. *Taiwan. J. Math.* **2005**, *9*, 411–420. [CrossRef]
8. Zhang, X.M. Schur-convex functions and isoperimetric inequalities. *Proc. Am. Math. Soc.* **1998**, *126*, 461–470. [CrossRef]
9. Stepniak, C. Stochastic ordering and Schur-convex functions in comparison of linear experiments. *Metrika* **1989**, *36*, 291–298. [CrossRef]
10. Merkle, M. Convexity, Schur-convexity and bounds for the gamma function involving the digamma function. *Rocky Mt. J. Math.* **1998**, *28*, 1053–1066. [CrossRef]
11. Hwang, F.K.; Rothblum, U.G. Partition-optimization with Schur convex sum objective functions. *SIAM J. Discret. Math.* **2004**, *18*, 512–524. [CrossRef]
12. Constantine, G.M. Schur convex functions on the spectra of graphs. *Discret. Math.* **1983**, *45*, 181–188. [CrossRef]
13. Hwang, F.K.; Rothblum, U.G.; Shepp, L. Monotone optimal multipartitions using Schur-convexity with respect to partial orders. *SIAM J. Discret. Math.* **1993**, *6*, 533–547. [CrossRef]
14. Forcina, A.; Giovagnoli, A. Homogeneity indices and Schur-convex functions. *Statistica* **1982**, *42*, 529–542.
15. Shaked, M.; Shanthikumar, J.G.; Tong, Y.L. Parametric Schur-convexity and arrangement monotonicity properties of partial sums. *J. Multivar. Anal.* **1995**, *53*, 293–310. [CrossRef]
16. Zhang, X.M. *Geometrically Convex Functions*; An'hui University Press: Hefei, China, 2004.
17. Chu, Y.M.; Lv, Y.P. The Schur-harmonic convexity of the Hamy symmetric function and its applications. *J. Inequal. Appl.* **2009**, *1*, 838529. [CrossRef]
18. Xi, B.Y.; Gao, D.D.; Zhang, T.; Guo, B.N.; Qi, F. Shannon Type Inequalities for Kapur's Entropy. *Mathematics* **2019**, *7*, 22. [CrossRef]

19. Safaei, N.; Barani, A. Schur-harmonic convexity related to co-ordinated harmonically convex functions in plane. *J. Inequal. Appl.* **2019**, *2019*, 297. [CrossRef]
20. Xi, B.Y.; Wu, Y.; Shi, H.N.; Qi, F. Generalizations of Several Inequalities Related to Multivariate Geometric Means. *Mathematics* **2019**, *7*, 552. [CrossRef]
21. Shi, H.N. Schur-concavity and Schur-geometrically convexity of dual form for elementary symmetric function with applications. *RGMIA Res. Rep. Collect.* **2007**, *10*, 15. Available online: http://rgmia.org/papers/v10n2/hnshi.pdf (accessed on 15 November 2021).
22. Shi, H.N.; Zhang, J. Compositions involving Schur-geometrically convex functions. *J. Inequal. Appl.* **2015**, *2015*, 320. [CrossRef]
23. Shi, H.N.; Zhang, J. Compositions involving Schur-Harmonically convex functions. *J. Comput. Anal. Appl.* **2017**, *22*, 907–922.
24. Xia, W.F.; Chu, Y.M. On Schur-convexity of some symmetric functions. *J. Inequal. Appl.* **2010**, *1*, 543250. [CrossRef]
25. Guan, K.Z. Some properties of a class of symmetric functions. *J. Math. Anal. Appl.* **2007**, *336*, 70–80. [CrossRef]
26. Shi, H.N.; Zhang, J. Some new judgement theorems of Schur-geometric and Schur-harmonic convexities for a class of symmetric functions. *J. Inequal. Appl.* **2013**, *1*, 527. [CrossRef]
27. Sun, M.B. The Schur-convexity for two calsses of symmetric functions. *Sci. Sin.* **2014**, *44*, 633. [CrossRef]
28. Hardy, G.H.; Littlewood, J.E.; Pólya, G. Some simple inequalities satisfied by convex functions. *Messenger Math.* **1929**, *58*, 145–152.
29. Marshall, A.W.; Olkin, I.; Arnord, B.C. *Inequalities: Theory of Majorization and ITS Application*, 2nd ed.; Springer: New York, NY, USA, 2011; p. 95
30. Rovenţa, I. A note on Schur-concave functions. *J. Inequal. Appl.* **2012**, *2012*, 159. [CrossRef]
31. Wang, S.H.; Zhang, T.Y.; Hua, Z.Q. Schur convexity and Schur multiplicatively convexity and Schur harmonic convexity for a class of symmetric functions. *J. Inn. Mong. Univ. Natl.* **2011**, *26*, 387–390.
32. Zhang, J.; Shi, H.N. Schur convexity of a class of symmetric functions. *Math. Pract. Theory* **2013**, *43*, 292–296. (In Chinese)
33. Shi, H.N.; Zhang, J. Schur-convexity, Schur-geometric and Schur-harmonic convexities of dual form of a class symmetric functions. *J. Math. Inequal.* **2014**, *8*, 349–358. [CrossRef]
34. Wang, W.; Zhang, X.Q. Properties of functions related to Hadamard type inequality and applications. *J. Math. Inequal.* **2019**, *13*, 121–134. [CrossRef]
35. Chu, Y.M.; Wang, G.D.; Zhang, X.H. The Schur multiplicative and harmonic convexities of the complete symmetric function. *Math. Nachrichten* **2011**, *284*, 653–663. [CrossRef]
36. Bullen, P.S. *Handbook of Means and Their Inequalities*; Springer: Dordrecht, The Netherlands, 2003.

Article

Bounds for the Differences between Arithmetic and Geometric Means and Their Applications to Inequalities

Shigeru Furuichi [1] and Nicușor Minculete [2,*]

1. Department of Information Science, College of Humanities and Sciences, Nihon University, Setagaya-ku, Tokyo 156-8550, Japan; furuichi.shigeru@nihon-u.ac.jp
2. Department of Mathematics and Computer Science, Transilvania University of Brașov, 500091 Brașov, Romania
* Correspondence: minculete.nicusor@unitbv.ro

Abstract: Refining and reversing weighted arithmetic-geometric mean inequalities have been studied in many papers. In this paper, we provide some bounds for the differences between the weighted arithmetic and geometric means, using known inequalities. We improve the results given by Furuichi-Ghaemi-Gharakhanlu and Sababheh-Choi. We also give some bounds on entropies, applying the results in a different approach. We explore certain convex or concave functions, which are symmetric functions on the axis $t = 1/2$.

Keywords: Shannon entropy; Tsallis entropy; Fermi–Dirac entropy; Bose–Einstein entropy; arithmetic mean; geometric mean; Young's inequality

MSC: 26D20; 94A15

1. Introduction

We denote a set of all probability distributions by

$$\Delta_n := \left\{ \mathbf{p} = \{p_1, p_2, \cdots, p_n\} \mid p_j > 0, \ (j=1,2,\cdots,n), \ \sum_{j=1}^n p_j = 1 \right\}.$$

In this manuscript, for mathematical simplicity we remove the case $p_j = 0$ for $j = 1, 2, \cdots, n$. For any $\mathbf{p} \in \Delta_n$, Shannon entropy $H(\mathbf{p})$, Rényi entropy $R_q(\mathbf{p})$ and Tsallis entropy $H_q(\mathbf{p})$ are defined as [1–3]

$$H(\mathbf{p}) := -\sum_{j=1}^n p_j \log p_j, \quad R_q(\mathbf{p}) := \frac{1}{1-q} \log \left(\sum_{j=1}^n p_j^q \right), \quad H_q(\mathbf{p}) := -\sum_{j=1}^n p_j^q \ln_q p_j.$$

where $\ln_q(x) := \dfrac{x^{1-q} - 1}{1-q}$ is q-logarithmic function defined for $x > 0$ and $q > 0$ with $q \neq 1$. It is known that $\lim_{q \to 1} R_q(\mathbf{p}) = \lim_{q \to 1} H_q(\mathbf{p}) = H(\mathbf{p})$. An interesting differential relation of the Rényi entropy [4] is

$$\frac{dR_q(\mathbf{p})}{dq} = -\frac{1}{(1-q)^2} \sum_{j=1}^n v_j \log \frac{v_j}{p_j},$$

which is proportional to Kullback–Leibler divergence, where $v_j = p_j^q / \sum_{j=1}^n p_j^q$.

In [5], the Fermi–Dirac-Tsallis entropy was introduced by

$$I_q^{FD}(\mathbf{p}) := \sum_{j=1}^n p_j \ln_q \frac{1}{p_j} + \sum_{j=1}^n (1 - p_j) \ln_q \frac{1}{1 - p_j}$$

for $\mathbf{p} \in \Delta_n$ and the Bose–Einstein–Tsallis entropy was given in [6] as

$$I_q^{BE}(\mathbf{p}) := \sum_{j=1}^n p_j \ln_q \frac{1}{p_j} - \sum_{j=1}^n (1+p_j) \ln_q \frac{1}{1+p_j}.$$

In the limit of $q \to 1$, we have

$$\lim_{q \to 1} I_q^{FD}(\mathbf{p}) = I_1^{FD}(\mathbf{p}) := -\sum_{j=1}^n p_j \log p_j - \sum_{j=1}^n (1-p_j) \log(1-p_j)$$

and

$$\lim_{q \to 1} I_q^{BE}(\mathbf{p}) = I_1^{BE}(\mathbf{p}) := -\sum_{j=1}^n p_j \log p_j + \sum_{j=1}^n (1+p_j) \log(1+p_j),$$

where $I_1^{FD}(\mathbf{p})$ and $I_1^{BE}(\mathbf{p})$ are the Fermi–Dirac entropy and the Bose–Einstein entropy, respectively. See [6] and references therein for their details.

In [7], we used the expression that describes the difference between the arithmetic mean and the weighted geometric mean:

$$d_p(a,b) := pa + (1-p)b - a^p b^{1-p}, \quad (a,b > 0, \ p \in [0,1]).$$

It is well known that $d_p(a,b) \geq 0$ as Young inequality or the weighted arithmetic-geometric mean inequality.

Next, we consider $d_p(a,b)$ for $p \in \mathbb{R}$. We easily find that the following properties:

$$d_p(a,b) \geq 0 \ (\text{when } p \in [0,1]),$$

$$d_p(a,a) = d_0(a,b) = d_1(a,b) = 0, \ d_p(a,b) = d_{1-p}(b,a) \tag{1}$$

and

$$\begin{aligned} d_p\left(\frac{1}{a}, \frac{1}{b}\right) &= \frac{1}{ab} d_p(b,a), \ d_p(a,1) + d_p(b,1) \\ &= d_p(a+b, 2) + 2\left\{\left(\frac{a+b}{2}\right)^p - \frac{a^p + b^p}{2}\right\}. \end{aligned} \tag{2}$$

In [8] Sababheh and Choi prove that if a and b are positive numbers with $p \notin [0,1]$, then $d_{1-p}(a,b) \leq 0$.

Some important results [9–11] on the studies used to estimate bounds on several entropies have been established, recently, via the use of mathematical inequalities. We provide some results on several entropies, applying new and improved inequalities in this paper.

2. Bounds of $d.(\cdot, \cdot)$ and Inequalities for Entropies

We first rewrite the Tsallis entropy, Rényi entropy, the Fermi–Dirac-Tsallis entropy, and the Bose–Einstein-Tsallis entropy by the use of the notation $d.(\cdot, \cdot)$.

Lemma 1. *For $\mathbf{p} \in \Delta_n$ and $q \geq 0$ with $q > 1$, we have*

(i) $H_q(\mathbf{p}) = n - 1 - \dfrac{1}{1-q} \sum_{j=1}^n d_q(p_j, 1),$

(ii) $R_q(\mathbf{p}) = \dfrac{1}{1-q} \log\left\{n(1-q) + q - \sum_{j=1}^n d_q(p_j, 1)\right\},$

(iii) $I_q^{FD}(\mathbf{p}) = n - \dfrac{1}{1-q} \sum_{j=1}^n \{d_q(p_j, 1) + d_q(1-p_j, 1)\},$

(iv) $I_q^{BE}(\mathbf{p}) = n - \dfrac{1}{1-q}\sum_{j=1}^{n}\{d_q(p_j,1) - d_q(1+p_j,1)\}.$

Proof. The proof can be done by the direct calculations.
(i) Simple calculations

$$1 + H_q(\mathbf{p}) = -\sum_{j=1}^{n}\left(\dfrac{p_j - p_j^q}{1-q} - p_j\right) = -\sum_{j=1}^{n}\dfrac{qp_j - p_j^q}{1-q} = n - \sum_{j=1}^{n}\left(\dfrac{qp_j - p_j^q}{1-q} + 1\right)$$

$$= n - \dfrac{1}{1-q}\sum_{j=1}^{n}d_q(p_j,1)$$

show the statement in (i).
(ii) Since we have the relation:

$$\exp((1-q)R_q(\mathbf{p})) = 1 + (1-q)H_q(\mathbf{p}),$$

we have

$$\exp((1-q)R_q(\mathbf{p})) = n(1-q) + q - \sum_{j=1}^{n}d_q(p_j,1)$$

which implies the statement in (ii).
(iii) We can calculate as

$$\sum_{j=1}^{n}(1-p_j)\ln_q\dfrac{1}{1-p_j} = \sum_{j=1}^{n}\dfrac{(1-p_j)^q - (1-p_j)}{1-q}$$

$$= \sum_{j=1}^{n}\left\{\dfrac{(1-p_j)^q - (1-p_j)}{1-q} + 1 - p_j\right\} - n + 1$$

$$= \sum_{j=1}^{n}\left\{\dfrac{(1-p_j)^q - q(1-p_j)}{1-q} - 1\right\} + 1$$

$$= 1 - \dfrac{1}{1-q}\sum_{j=1}^{n}\{q(1-p_j) + 1 - q - (1-p_j)^q\} = 1 - \dfrac{1}{1-q}\sum_{j=1}^{n}d_q(1-p_j,1).$$

Thus, we have with the result of (i),

$$I_q^{FD}(\mathbf{p}) = \sum_{j=1}^{n}p_j\ln_q\dfrac{1}{p_j} + \sum_{j=1}^{n}(1-p_j)\ln_q\dfrac{1}{1-p_j}$$

$$= n - 1 - \dfrac{1}{1-q}\sum_{j=1}^{n}d_q(p_j,1) + 1 - \dfrac{1}{1-q}\sum_{j=1}^{n}d_q(1-p_j,1)$$

$$= n - \dfrac{1}{1-q}\sum_{j=1}^{n}\{d_q(p_j,1) + d_q(1-p_j,1)\}.$$

(iv) We can calculate as

$$\sum_{j=1}^{n}(1+p_j)\ln_q \frac{1}{1+p_j} = \sum_{j=1}^{n} \frac{(1+p_j)^q - (1+p_j)}{1-q}$$

$$= \sum_{j=1}^{n}\left\{\frac{(1+p_j)^q - (1+p_j)}{1-q} + 1 + p_j\right\} - n - 1$$

$$= \sum_{j=1}^{n}\left\{\frac{(1+p_j)^q - q(1+p_j)}{1-q} - 1\right\} - 1$$

$$= -1 - \frac{1}{1-q}\sum_{j=1}^{n} d_q(1+p_j, 1).$$

Thus, we have

$$I_q^{BE}(\mathbf{p}) = \sum_{j=1}^{n} p_j \ln_q \frac{1}{p_j} - \sum_{j=1}^{n}(1+p_j)\ln_q \frac{1}{1+p_j}$$

$$= n - 1 - \frac{1}{1-q}\sum_{j=1}^{n} d_q(p_j, 1) + 1 + \frac{1}{1-q}\sum_{j=1}^{n} d_q(1+p_j, 1)$$

$$= n - \frac{1}{1-q}\sum_{j=1}^{n}\{d_q(p_j, 1) - d_q(1+p_j, 1)\}.$$

□

We give relations on $d.(\cdot, \cdot)$.

Lemma 2. *Let $a, b > 0$. If $p \in \mathbb{R}$, then the following equalities hold:*

$$d_p(a, b) = p\left(\sqrt{a} - \sqrt{b}\right)^2 + d_{2p}\left(\sqrt{ab}, b\right)$$

and

$$d_p(a, b) = (1-p)\left(\sqrt{a} - \sqrt{b}\right)^2 + d_{2p-1}\left(a, \sqrt{ab}\right).$$

Proof. We note that $a^p b^{1-p} = (ab)^{1-p} a^{2p-1} = \left(\sqrt{ab}\right)^{2-2p} a^{2p-1} = \left(\sqrt{ab}\right)^{2p} b^{1-2p}$.

(i) Then,

$$d_p(a, b) = pa + (1-p)b - \left(\sqrt{ab}\right)^{2p} b^{1-2p}$$

$$= pa + (1-p)b - 2p\sqrt{ab} - (1-2p)b + 2p\sqrt{ab} + (1-2p)b - \left(\sqrt{ab}\right)^{2p} b^{1-2p}$$

$$= p\left(\sqrt{a} - \sqrt{b}\right)^2 + d_{2p}\left(\sqrt{ab}, b\right)$$

(ii) We also have

$$d_p(a, b) = pa + (1-p)b - \left(\sqrt{ab}\right)^{2-2p} a^{2p-1}$$

$$= pa + (1-p)b - 2(1-p)\sqrt{ab} - (2p-1)a$$

$$+ 2(1-p)\sqrt{ab} + (2p-1)a - \left(\sqrt{ab}\right)^{2-2p} a^{2p-1}$$

$$= (1-p)\left(\sqrt{a} - \sqrt{b}\right)^2 + d_{2p-1}\left(a, \sqrt{ab}\right).$$

□

In several papers [7,12–14], we find estimations of the bounds of $d_p(a,b)$. For this purpose, we use the following inequalities from (a) to (d).

(a) Kittaneh and Manasrah gave in [12]:

$$r(p)\left(\sqrt{a} - \sqrt{b}\right)^2 \leq d_p(a,b) \leq R(p)\left(\sqrt{a} - \sqrt{b}\right)^2 \qquad (3)$$

where $a, b > 0$, $0 \leq p \leq 1$ and $r(p) = \min\{p, 1-p\}$, $R(p) = \max\{p, 1-p\}$, whose notations are used throughout this paper without mention.

(b) Cartwright and Field proved the inequality (see, e.g., [14]):

$$\frac{1}{2}p(1-p)\frac{(a-b)^2}{\max\{a,b\}} \leq d_p(a,b) \leq \frac{1}{2}p(1-p)\frac{(a-b)^2}{\min\{a,b\}} \qquad (4)$$

for $a, b > 0$ and $0 \leq p \leq 1$.

(c) Alzer, da Fonseca, and Kovačec obtained the following inequalities (see, e.g., [13]):

$$\frac{1}{2}p(1-p)\min\{a,b\}\log^2\frac{a}{b} \leq d_p(a,b) \leq \frac{1}{2}p(1-p)\max\{a,b\}\log^2\frac{a}{b} \qquad (5)$$

and

$$\min\left\{\frac{p}{q}, \frac{1-p}{1-q}\right\}d_q(a,b) \leq d_p(a,b) \leq \max\left\{\frac{p}{q}, \frac{1-p}{1-q}\right\}d_q(a,b), \qquad (6)$$

for $a, b > 0$ and $0 < p, q < 1$.

Taking into account (1), (2) and taking $b = 1$ and changing p by q in the above inequalities given in (a)–(c), we obtain the following.

(a_1)
$$r(q)\left(\sqrt{a} - 1\right)^2 \leq d_q(a,1) \leq R(q)\left(\sqrt{a} - 1\right)^2 \qquad (7)$$

where $a > 0$ and $0 \leq q \leq 1$.

(b_1)
$$\frac{1}{2}q(1-q)(a-1)^2 \leq d_q(a,1) \leq \frac{1}{2}q(1-q)\frac{(a-1)^2}{a} \qquad (8)$$

for $0 < a \leq 1$ and $0 \leq q \leq 1$.

(c_1)
$$\frac{1}{2}q(1-q)a\log^2 a \leq d_q(a,1) \leq \frac{1}{2}q(1-q)\log^2 a \qquad (9)$$

and

$$\min\left\{\frac{q}{p}, \frac{1-q}{1-p}\right\}d_p(a,1) \leq d_q(a,1) \leq \max\left\{\frac{q}{p}, \frac{1-q}{1-p}\right\}d_p(a,1)$$

for $0 < a \leq 1$ and $0 < p, q < 1$.

If we take $a = p_j < 1$, for all $j \in \{1, ..., n\}$, in the above inequalities (a_1)–(c_1) and passing to the sum from 1 to n, we deduce the following inequalities (a_2)–(c_2) on $d.(\cdot,\cdot)$.

(a_2)
$$r(q)\sum_{j=1}^{n}\left(\sqrt{p_j} - 1\right)^2 \leq \sum_{j=1}^{n}d_q(p_j, 1) \leq R(q)\sum_{j=1}^{n}\left(\sqrt{p_j} - 1\right)^2$$

where $0 \leq q \leq 1$.

(b_2)
$$\frac{1}{2}q(1-q)\sum_{j=1}^{n}(p_j - 1)^2 \leq \sum_{j=1}^{n}d_q(p_j, 1) \leq \frac{1}{2}q(1-q)\sum_{j=1}^{n}\frac{(p_j - 1)^2}{p_j}$$

for $0 \leq q \leq 1$.

169

(c_2)
$$\frac{1}{2}q(1-q)\sum_{j=1}^{n}p_j\log^2 p_j \leq \sum_{j=1}^{n}d_q(p_j,1) \leq \frac{1}{2}q(1-q)\sum_{j=1}^{n}\log^2 p_j$$

and

$$\min\left\{\frac{q}{p},\frac{1-q}{1-p}\right\}\sum_{j=1}^{n}d_p(p_j,1) \leq \sum_{j=1}^{n}d_q(p_j,1) \leq \max\left\{\frac{q}{p},\frac{1-q}{1-p}\right\}\sum_{j=1}^{n}d_p(p_j,1)$$

for $0 < p, q < 1$.

Using the point (i) from Lemma 2 and inequalities (a_2)–(c_2), we deduce a series of inequalities for the Tsallis entropy $H_q(\mathbf{p})$ in the following (A)–(C) as the theorem.

Theorem 1. *Let $0 < p, q < 1$. Then we have the following (A)–(C).*

(A)
$$n-1-\frac{R(q)}{1-q}\sum_{j=1}^{n}\left(\sqrt{p_j}-1\right)^2 \leq H_q(\mathbf{p}) \leq n-1-\frac{r(q)}{1-q}\sum_{j=1}^{n}\left(\sqrt{p_j}-1\right)^2. \tag{10}$$

(B)
$$n-1-\frac{q}{2}\sum_{j=1}^{n}\frac{(p_j-1)^2}{p_j} \leq H_q(\mathbf{p}) \leq n-1-\frac{q}{2}\sum_{j=1}^{n}(p_j-1)^2. \tag{11}$$

(C)
$$n-1-\frac{q}{2}\sum_{j=1}^{n}\log^2 p_j \leq H_q(\mathbf{p}) \leq n-1-\frac{q}{2}\sum_{j=1}^{n}p_j\log^2 p_j \tag{12}$$

and

$$(n-1)\left(1-\frac{1-p}{1-q}\max\left\{\frac{q}{p},\frac{1-q}{1-p}\right\}\right)+\frac{1-p}{1-q}\max\left\{\frac{q}{p},\frac{1-q}{1-p}\right\}H_p(\mathbf{p}) \leq H_q(\mathbf{p})$$
$$\leq (n-1)\left(1-\frac{1-p}{1-q}\min\left\{\frac{q}{p},\frac{1-q}{1-p}\right\}\right)+\frac{1-p}{1-q}\min\left\{\frac{q}{p},\frac{1-q}{1-p}\right\}H_p(\mathbf{p}).$$

If $p \leq q$, then we have $\min\left\{\frac{q}{p},\frac{1-q}{1-p}\right\} = \frac{1-q}{1-p}$ and $\max\left\{\frac{q}{p},\frac{1-q}{1-p}\right\} = \frac{q}{p}$, then we obtain

$$(n-1)\frac{p-q}{p(1-q)}+\frac{q(1-p)}{p(1-q)}H_p(\mathbf{p}) \leq H_q(\mathbf{p}) \leq H_p(\mathbf{p}),$$

which implies that $H_q(\mathbf{p})$ is decreasing related to q.

In the limit of $q \to 1$, we find some bounds for Shannon entropy as a corollary of the above theorem.

Corollary 1. *We have the inequalities for Shannon entropy $H(\mathbf{p})$.*

$$H(\mathbf{p}) \leq n-1-\sum_{j=1}^{n}\left(\sqrt{p_j}-1\right)^2 = 2\sum_{j=1}^{n}\left(\sqrt{p_j}-1\right), \tag{13}$$

$$n-1-\frac{1}{2}\sum_{j=1}^{n}\frac{(p_j-1)^2}{p_j} \leq H(\mathbf{p}) \leq n-1-\frac{1}{2}\sum_{j=1}^{n}(p_j-1)^2, \tag{14}$$

$$n-1-\frac{1}{2}\sum_{j=1}^{n}\log^2 p_j \leq H(\mathbf{p}) \leq n-1-\frac{1}{2}\sum_{j=1}^{n}p_j\log^2 p_j \tag{15}$$

and

$$H(\mathbf{p}) \leq H_p(\mathbf{p}), \quad (0 < p < 1).$$

Using the points (ii) and (iii) from Lemma 2 and inequalities (a_2)–(c_2), we deduce several inequalities for Rényi entropy $R_q(\mathbf{p})$ and for the Fermi–Dirac–Tsallis entropy $I_q^{FD}(\mathbf{p})$ in the following:

Theorem 2. *Let $0 < q < 1$. Then we have*

(A_1)

$$\frac{1}{1-q}\log\{n(1-q) + q - R(q)(n + 1 - 2\sum_{j=1}^{n}\sqrt{p_j})\} \leq R_q(\mathbf{p})$$

$$\leq \frac{1}{1-q}\log\{n(1-q) + q - r(q)(n + 1 - 2\sum_{j=1}^{n}\sqrt{p_j})\},$$

(B_1)

$$\frac{1}{1-q}\log\{n(1-q) + q - \frac{1}{2}q(1-q)(1 - 2n + \sum_{j=1}^{n}\frac{1}{p_j})\} \leq R_q(\mathbf{p})$$

$$\frac{1}{1-q}\log\{n(1-q) + q - \frac{1}{2}q(1-q)(n - 2 + \sum_{j=1}^{n}p_j^2)\},$$

(C_1)

$$\frac{1}{1-q}\log\{n(1-q) + q - \frac{1}{2}q(1-q)\sum_{j=1}^{n}\log^2 p_j\} \leq R_q(\mathbf{p})$$

$$\frac{1}{1-q}\log\{n(1-q) + q - \frac{1}{2}q(1-q)\sum_{j=1}^{n}p_j\log^2 p_j\},$$

(A_2)

$$n - \frac{R(q)}{1-q}\{3n - 2\sum_{j=1}^{n}(\sqrt{p_j} + \sqrt{1-p_j})\} \leq I_q^{FD}(\mathbf{p})$$

$$n - \frac{r(q)}{1-q}\{3n - 2\sum_{j=1}^{n}(\sqrt{p_j} + \sqrt{1-p_j})\},$$

(B_2)

$$n - \frac{q}{2}\left(\sum_{j=1}^{n}\frac{1}{p_j(1-p_j)} - 3n\right) \leq I_q^{FD}(\mathbf{p}) \leq n - \frac{q}{2}\left(n - 2 + 2\sum_{j=1}^{n}p_j^2\right)$$

(C_2)

$$n - \frac{q}{2}\sum_{j=1}^{n}\left(\log^2 p_j + \log^2(1-p_j)\right) \leq I_q^{FD}(\mathbf{p}) \leq$$

$$n - \frac{q}{2}\sum_{j=1}^{n}\left(p_j\log^2 p_j + (1-p_j)\log^2(1-p_j)\right).$$

In the limit of $q \to 1$, we find some bounds for the Fermi–Dirac–Tsallis entropy as a corollary of the above theorem.

Corollary 2. We have the following inequalities for the Fermi–Dirac entropy $I_1^{FD}(\mathbf{p})$:

$$I_1^{FD}(\mathbf{p}) \leq 2\sum_{j=1}^n (\sqrt{p_j} + \sqrt{1-p_j} - 1),$$

$$\frac{1}{2}\left(5n - \sum_{j=1}^n \frac{1}{p_j(1-p_j)}\right) \leq I_1^{FD}(\mathbf{p}) \leq \frac{1}{2}\left(n + 2 - 2\sum_{j=1}^n p_j^2\right)$$

and

$$n - \frac{1}{2}\sum_{j=1}^n \left(\log^2 p_j + \log^2(1-p_j)\right) \leq I_1^{FD}(\mathbf{p}) \leq$$

$$n - \frac{1}{2}\sum_{j=1}^n \left(p_j \log^2 p_j + (1-p_j)\log^2(1-p_j)\right).$$

Theorem 3. Let $0 < q < 1$. Then,

(A_3)

$$(2n+1)r(q) - (n+1)R(q) + 2R(q)\sum_{j=1}^n \sqrt{p_j} - 2r(q)\sum_{j=1}^n \sqrt{1+p_j}$$

$$\leq (1-q)\left(I_q^{BE}(\mathbf{p}) - n\right) \tag{16}$$

$$\leq (2n+1)R(q) - (n+1)r(q) + 2r(q)\sum_{j=1}^n \sqrt{p_j} - 2R(q)\sum_{j=1}^n \sqrt{1+p_j},$$

(B_3)

$$n + \frac{q}{2}\left(n - \sum_{j=1}^n \frac{1}{p_j(p_j+1)}\right) \leq I_q^{BE}(\mathbf{p}) \leq n + \frac{q}{2}(2-n) \tag{17}$$

(C_3)

$$\sum_{j=1}^n \left(\log^2(p_j+1) - \log^2 p_j\right)$$

$$\leq \frac{2}{q}\left(I_q^{BE}(\mathbf{p}) - n\right) \tag{18}$$

$$\leq \sum_{j=1}^n \left((p_j+1)\log^2(p_j+1) - p_j \log^2 p_j\right).$$

Proof. From inequality (7), we find

$$r(q)\left(\sqrt{p_j} - 1\right)^2 \leq d_q(p_j, 1) \leq R(q)\left(\sqrt{p_j} - 1\right)^2 \tag{19}$$

and

$$r(q)\left(\sqrt{p_j+1} - 1\right)^2 \leq d_q(p_j+1, 1) \leq R(q)\left(\sqrt{p_j+1} - 1\right)^2. \tag{20}$$

Using inequalities (19), (20) and the definition of the Bose–Einstein–Tsallis entropy $I_q^{BE}(\mathbf{p})$, given above, we find

$$n + \frac{1}{1-q}\left(r(q)\sum_{j=1}^n \left(\sqrt{p_j+1} - 1\right)^2 - R(q)\sum_{j=1}^n \left(\sqrt{p_j} - 1\right)^2\right) \leq I_q^{BE}(\mathbf{p})$$

172

$$\leq n+\frac{1}{1-q}\left(R(q)\sum_{j=1}^{n}\left(\sqrt{p_j+1}-1\right)^2 - r(q)\sum_{j=1}^{n}\left(\sqrt{p_j}-1\right)^2\right),$$

which implies inequality (16). From inequality (8), we have:

$$\frac{1}{2}q(1-q)\frac{p_j^2}{p_j+1} \leq d_q(p_j+1,1) \leq \frac{1}{2}q(1-q)p_j^2$$

and

$$\frac{1}{2}q(1-q)(p_j-1)^2 \leq d_q(p_j,1) \leq \frac{1}{2}q(1-q)\frac{(p_j-1)^2}{p_j}.$$

Summing from 1 to n, we deduce inequality (17).
We apply inequality (9) in the following way:

$$\frac{1}{2}q(1-q)\log^2(p_j+1) \leq d_q(p_j+1,1) \leq \frac{1}{2}q(1-q)(p_j+1)\log^2(p_j+1)$$

and

$$\frac{1}{2}q(1-q)p_j\log^2 p_j \leq d_q(p_j,1) \leq \frac{1}{2}q(1-q)p_j\log^2 p_j.$$

Summing from 1 to n, we deduce inequality (18). □

Corollary 3. *We have the following inequalities for the Bose–Einstein entropy $I_1^{BE}(\mathbf{p})$:*

$$3n - \sum_{j=1}^{n}\frac{1}{p_j(1+p_j)} \leq 2I_1^{BE}(\mathbf{p}) \leq n+1$$

and

$$\sum_{j=1}^{n}\left(\log^2(p_j+1) - \log^2 p_j\right) \leq 2\left(I_1^{BE}(\mathbf{p}) - n\right) \leq \sum_{j=1}^{n}\left((p_j+1)\log^2(p_j+1) - p_j\log^2 p_j\right).$$

3. New Characterizations of Young's Inequality

The inequality of Young is given by:

$$pa + (1-p)b \geq a^p b^{1-p}, \quad (a,b > 0, \ p \in [0,1]),$$

which means $d_p(a,b) \geq 0$.
In this section, we give further bounds on $d.(\cdot,\cdot)$.

Lemma 3. *Let a and b be positive real numbers, and let $p \in \mathbb{R}$. Then,*

$$d_p(a,b) = p\sum_{k=1}^{n}2^{k-1}\sqrt[2^k]{b^{2^{k-1}-1}}\left(\sqrt[2^k]{a} - \sqrt[2^k]{b}\right)^2 + d_{2^n p}(\sqrt[2^n]{ab^{2^n-1}}, b) \tag{21}$$

and

$$d_p(a,b) = (1-p)\sum_{k=1}^{n}2^{k-1}\sqrt[2^k]{a^{2^{k-1}-1}}\left(\sqrt[2^k]{a} - \sqrt[2^k]{b}\right)^2 + d_{2^n(p-1)+1}(a, \sqrt[2^n]{a^{2^n-1}b}). \tag{22}$$

Proof. Using Lemma 2 for $p \in \mathbb{R}$, then

$$d_p(a,b) = p(\sqrt{a} - \sqrt{b})^2 + d_{2p}(\sqrt{ab}, b).$$

We replace p by $2p$ and a by $\sqrt{ab}$, then we get

$$d_{2p}(\sqrt{ab}, b) = 2p(\sqrt[4]{ab} - \sqrt{b})^2 + d_{4p}(\sqrt[4]{ab^3}, b).$$

If we inductively repeat the above substitutions, for $k \geq 1$, then we have

$$d_{2^{k-1}p}(\sqrt[2^{k-1}]{ab^{2^{k-1}-1}}, b) = 2^{k-1}p(\sqrt[2^k]{ab^{2^{k-1}-1}} - \sqrt{b})^2 + d_{2^k p}(\sqrt[2^k]{ab^{2^k-1}}, b).$$

Therefore, summarizing the above relations for $k \in \{1, ..., n\}$, we obtain the relation of the statement. Applying equality (21) and taking into account that $d_p(a,b) = d_{1-p}(b,a)$, we deduce equality (22). □

Remark 1. *From [8], if $a, b > 0$ and $p \notin [0,1]$, we have $d_{1-p}(a,b) \leq 0$, so, we deduce $d_{2^n p}(\sqrt[2^n]{ab^{2^n-1}}, b) \leq 0$, for $p \notin [0, \frac{1}{2^n}]$ and $d_{2^n(p-1)+1}(a, \sqrt[2^n]{a^{2^n-1}b}) \leq 0$, for $p \notin [1 - \frac{1}{2^n}, 1]$. Using the above equalities, we deduce the inequalities:*

$$d_p(a,b) \leq p \sum_{k=1}^{n} 2^{k-1} \sqrt[2^{k-1}]{b^{2^{k-1}-1}} \left(\sqrt[2^k]{a} - \sqrt[2^k]{b} \right)^2 \qquad (23)$$

when $p \notin \left[0, \frac{1}{2^n}\right]$ and

$$d_p(a,b) \leq (1-p) \sum_{k=1}^{n} 2^{k-1} \sqrt[2^{k-1}]{a^{2^{k-1}-1}} \left(\sqrt[2^k]{a} - \sqrt[2^k]{b} \right)^2. \qquad (24)$$

when $p \notin \left[1 - \frac{1}{2^n}, 1\right]$. These inequalities are given by Furuichi et al. in ([15], Theorem 3). We also find that inequality (23) when $p \leq 0$ and inequality (24) when $p \geq 1$ are given by Sababheh–Choi in ([8], Theorem 2.9) and by Sababheh–Moslehian ([16], Theorem 2.2).

Proposition 1. *Let a and b be positive real numbers. We then have the following bounds on $d.(\cdot,\cdot)$.*

(i) *For $p \in \left[0, \frac{1}{2^n}\right]$, we have*

$$r(2^n p) \left(\sqrt[2^{n+1}]{ab^{2^n-1}} - \sqrt{b} \right)^2 + p \sum_{k=1}^{n} 2^{k-1} \sqrt[2^{k-1}]{b^{2^{k-1}-1}} \left(\sqrt[2^k]{a} - \sqrt[2^k]{b} \right)^2 \leq d_p(a,b)$$

$$\leq R(2^n p) \left(\sqrt[2^{n+1}]{ab^{2^n-1}} - \sqrt{b} \right)^2 + p \sum_{k=1}^{n} 2^{k-1} \sqrt[2^{k-1}]{b^{2^{k-1}-1}} \left(\sqrt[2^k]{a} - \sqrt[2^k]{b} \right)^2.$$

where $r(\cdot)$ and $R(\cdot)$ are defined above,

(ii) *For $p \in \left[0, \frac{1}{2^n}\right]$, we have*

$$2^{n-1} p(1 - 2^n p) \frac{\left(\sqrt[2^n]{ab^{2^n-1}} - b \right)^2}{\max\{\sqrt[2^n]{ab^{2^n-1}}, b\}} + p \sum_{k=1}^{n} 2^{k-1} \sqrt[2^{k-1}]{b^{2^{k-1}-1}} \left(\sqrt[2^k]{a} - \sqrt[2^k]{b} \right)^2 \leq d_p(a,b)$$

$$2^{n-1} p(1 - 2^n p) \frac{\left(\sqrt[2^n]{ab^{2^n-1}} - b \right)^2}{\min\{\sqrt[2^n]{ab^{2^n-1}}, b\}} + p \sum_{k=1}^{n} 2^{k-1} \sqrt[2^{k-1}]{b^{2^{k-1}-1}} \left(\sqrt[2^k]{a} - \sqrt[2^k]{b} \right)^2. \qquad (25)$$

(iii) For $p \in \left[0, \frac{1}{2^n}\right]$, we have

$$\frac{p}{2^{n+1}}(1-2^n p) \min\{\sqrt[2^n]{ab^{2^n-1}}, b\} \log^2 \frac{a}{b}$$

$$\leq d_p(a,b) - p \sum_{k=1}^{n} 2^{k-1}\sqrt{b^{2^k-1}-1}\left(\sqrt[2^k]{a} - \sqrt[2^k]{b}\right)^2$$

$$\leq \frac{p}{2^{n+1}}(1-2^n p) \min\{\sqrt[2^n]{ab^{2^n-1}}, b\} \log^2 \frac{a}{b}.$$

Proof. We use the inequalities from (a) to (c), where we replace p by $2^n p$ and a by $\sqrt[2^n]{ab^{2^n-1}}$. For $a, b > 0$ and $p \in \left[0, \frac{1}{2^n}\right]$, we have the following (a3)–(c3).

(a3)

$$r(2^n p)\left(\sqrt[2^{n+1}]{ab^{2^n-1}} - \sqrt{b}\right)^2 \leq d_{2^n p}(\sqrt[2^n]{ab^{2^n-1}}, b)$$

$$\leq R(2^n p)\left(\sqrt[2^{n+1}]{ab^{2^n-1}} - \sqrt{b}\right)^2, \qquad (26)$$

(b3)

$$2^{n-1} p(1-2^n p) \frac{\left(\sqrt[2^n]{ab^{2^n-1}} - b\right)^2}{\max\{\sqrt[2^n]{ab^{2^n-1}}, b\}} \leq d_{2^n p}(\sqrt[2^n]{ab^{2^n-1}}, b)$$

$$\leq 2^{n-1} p(1-2^n p) \frac{\left(\sqrt[2^n]{ab^{2^n-1}} - b\right)^2}{\min\{\sqrt[2^n]{ab^{2^n-1}}, b\}}. \qquad (27)$$

(c3)

$$\frac{p}{2^{n+1}}(1-2^n p) \min\{\sqrt[2^n]{ab^{2^n-1}}, b\} \log^2 \frac{a}{b} \leq d_{2^n p}(\sqrt[2^n]{ab^{2^n-1}}, b)$$

$$\leq \frac{p}{2^{n+1}}(1-2^n p) \max\{\sqrt[2^n]{ab^{2^n-1}}, b\} \log^2 \frac{a}{b}. \qquad (28)$$

Using equality (21) and inequalities (26)–(28), we deduce the inequalities from the statement. □

4. The Connection between $d.(\cdot, \cdot)$ and Different Types of Convexity

In the following, we use the inequality by Kittaneh–Manasrah as noted in (3). We prepare some lemmas to state our results.

Lemma 4. *If $f : J \to \mathbb{R}$, where J is an interval of $\mathbb{R}$, is a concave function, then*

$$f((1+r)x - ry) \leq (1+r)f(x) - rf(y) \qquad (29)$$

for all $x, y \in J$ and all $r > 0$ with $(1+r)x - ry \in J$. If f is a convex function, then the reversed inequality above holds.

Proof. If f is concave, then we have

$$\frac{1}{1+r}f((1+r)x - ry) + \frac{r}{1+r}f(y) \leq f\left(x - \frac{r}{1+r}y + \frac{r}{1+r}y\right) = f(x).$$

□

The following result is given in ([15], Corollary 1). This is the supplemental to the first inequality of (3).

Lemma 5. *Let a and b be positive real numbers and let $p \notin (0,1)$. Then,*

$$d_p(a,b) \leq r(p)\left(\sqrt{a} - \sqrt{b}\right)^2, \qquad (30)$$

where $r(p) := \min\{p, 1-p\}$.

Proof. We set the function $f(t) := t^p - 2pt^{1/2} - (1-2p)$ for $t > 0$ and $p \notin (0, 1/2)$. From $f'(t) = pt^{-1/2}\left(t^{p-1/2} - 1\right)$, we find that $f'(t) = 0 \Leftrightarrow t = 1$, $f'(t) < 0$ for $0 < t < 1$ and $f'(t) > 0$ for $t > 1$. Thus, we have $f(t) \geq f(1) = 0$. Putting $t := a/b$ and multiplying $b > 0$ to both sides in the inequality $f(t) \geq 0$, we have

$$a^p b^{1-p} \geq 2p\sqrt{ab} + (1-2p)b,$$

which is equivalent to

$$pa + (1-p)b - p\left(\sqrt{a} - \sqrt{b}\right)^2 \leq a^p b^{1-p}, \quad p \notin (0, 1/2) \qquad (31)$$

We similarly have

$$pa + (1-p)b - (1-p)\left(\sqrt{a} - \sqrt{b}\right)^2 \leq a^p b^{1-p}, \quad p \notin (1/2, 1). \qquad (32)$$

From (31) and (32), we have (30). □

Note that the supplemental to the second inequality of (3), never generally holds:

$$R(p)\left(\sqrt{a} - \sqrt{b}\right)^2 \leq d_p(a,b), \quad a, b > 0 \quad p \notin (0,1).$$

To state the following result, we review the log-convexity/log-concavity. For the function $f : I \to (0, \infty)$, where $I \subset \mathbb{R}$, $x, y \in I$ and $\lambda \in [0,1]$, if $f((1-\lambda)x + \lambda y) \leq f^{1-\lambda}(x)f^{\lambda}(y)$, then f is often called log-convex function. If the reversed inequality holds, then f is called log-concave function.

In the following two lemmas, we deal with the symmetric function on $\frac{1}{2}$ (i.e., $f(t) = f(1-t)$, for every $t \in [0,1]$). The results are applied to the concrete symmetric function related to entropy, in the end of this section.

Lemma 6. *Let $f : [0,1] \to (0, \infty)$ be a convex function such that $f(t) = f(1-t)$ for every $t \in [0,1]$. Then*

$$2R(t)f(1/2) + (1 - 2R(t))f(0) \leq f(t) \leq 2r(t)f(1/2) + (1 - 2r(t))f(0), \qquad (33)$$

where $r(t) := \min\{t, 1-t\}$ and $R(t) := \max\{t, 1-t\}$. If in addition, f is log-convex, then

$$2R(t)f(1/2) + (1 - 2R(t))f(0)$$
$$\leq 2R(t)f(1/2) + (1 - 2R(t))f(0) - (1 - 2R(t))\left(\sqrt{f(1/2)} - \sqrt{f(0)}\right)^2$$
$$\leq f(1/2)^{2R(t)} f(0)^{1-2R(t)}$$
$$\leq f(t) \qquad (34)$$
$$\leq f(1/2)^{2r(t)} f(0)^{1-2r(t)}$$
$$\leq 2r(t)f(1/2) + (1 - 2r(t))f(0) - r(2r(t))\left(\sqrt{f(1/2)} - \sqrt{f(0)}\right)^2$$
$$\leq 2r(t)f(1/2) + (1 - 2r(t))f(0).$$

Proof. By convexity of f, we have for $t \in [0, 1/2]$,

$$f(t) = f\left(2t \cdot \frac{1}{2} + (1 - 2t) \cdot 0\right) \leq 2tf\left(\frac{1}{2}\right) + (1 - 2t)f(0).$$

Thus, we have
$$2t(f(1/2) - f(0)) \geq f(t) - f(0).$$

For $t \in [1/2, 1]$, by exchanging t with $1 - t$ in the above inequality, we have

$$2(1-t)(f(1/2) - f(0)) \geq f(t) - f(0).$$

Therefore, we have
$$2r(t)(f(1/2) - f(0)) \geq f(t) - f(0),$$

which implies the second inequality in (33). By Lemma 4 with $r := 2t - 1 > 0$ (i.e., $t \in [1/2, 1]$.), we have

$$f(t) = f\left(2t \cdot \frac{1}{2} + (1 - 2t) \cdot 0\right) = f\left((1+r) \cdot \frac{1}{2} - r \cdot 0\right)$$
$$\geq (1+r)f(1/2) - rf(0) = 2tf(1/2) + (1 - 2t)f(0).$$

Thus, we have for $t \in [1/2, 1]$
$$2t(f(1/2) - f(0)) \leq f(t) - f(0).$$

For $t \in [0, 1/2]$, by exchanging t with $1 - t$ in the above inequality, we have

$$2(1-t)(f(1/2) - f(0)) \leq f(t) - f(0).$$

Therefore, we have
$$2R(t)(f(1/2) - f(0)) \leq f(t) - f(0),$$

which implies the first inequality in (33).

By log-convexity of f, $\log f$ is convex so that we have $f(t) \leq f(1/2)^{2r(t)} f(0)^{1-2r(t)}$ which is the forth inequality of (34). The third inequality is from (33) and the second one is obtained by the Young inequality. The last inequality of (34) is trivial. Since $0 \leq r(t) \leq \frac{1}{2}$, we have $0 \leq 2r(t) \leq 1$. So we can use the first inequality of (3) as

$$f(1/2)^{2r(t)} f(0)^{1-2r(t)}$$
$$\leq 2r(t)f(1/2) + (1-2r(t))f(0) - r(2r(t))\left(\sqrt{f(1/2)} - \sqrt{f(0)}\right)^2,$$

which is the fifth inequality of (34). Finally, we prove the first inequality of (34). Since $\frac{1}{2} \leq R(t) \leq 1$, we have $1 \leq 2R(t) \leq 2$ and $-3 \leq 1 - 2R(t) \leq -1$. Namely, we have $1 - 2R(t) \leq 2R(t)$. By using (30), we have

$$f(1/2)^{2R(t)} f(0)^{1-2R(t)}$$
$$\geq 2R(t)f(1/2) + (1-2R(t))f(0) - (1-2R(t))\left(\sqrt{f(1/2)} - \sqrt{f(0)}\right)^2.$$

□

It is notable that the right inequalities in (33) and (34) are also found in ([17], Lemma 1.1). The following lemma is a counterpart by concavity. However, it does not completely corresponded to the above lemma. (See Remark 2 below).

Lemma 7. *Let $f : [0,1] \to (0,\infty)$ be a concave function with $f(t) = f(1-t)$ for every $t \in [0,1]$. Then*

$$2r(t)f(1/2) + (1-2r(t))f(0) \leq f(t) \leq 2R(t)f(1/2) + (1-2R(t))f(0). \quad (35)$$

If in addition, f is log-concave, then

$$2r(t)f(1/2) + (1-2r(t))f(0) - R(2r(t))\left(\sqrt{f(1/2)} - \sqrt{f(0)}\right)^2$$
$$\leq f(1/2)^{2r(t)} f(0)^{1-2r(t)}$$
$$\leq 2r(t)f(1/2) + (1-2r(t))f(0)$$
$$\leq f(t) \quad (36)$$
$$\leq 2R(t)f(1/2) + (1-2R(t))f(0)$$
$$\leq f(1/2)^{2R(t)} f(0)^{1-2R(t)}$$

Proof. By concavity of f, we have for $t \in [0, 1/2]$,

$$f(t) = f\left(2t \cdot \frac{1}{2} + (1-2t) \cdot 0\right) \geq 2tf(1/2) + (1-2t)f(0),$$

which implies

$$2t(f(0) - f(1/2)) \geq f(0) - f(t).$$

For the case of $t \in [1/2, 1]$, by exchanging t with $1 - t$, then we have from the above inequality
$$2(1-t)(f(0) - f(1/2)) \geq f(0) - f(1-t) = f(0) - f(t).$$

Thus, we have for $t \in [0,1]$ and $r(t) := \min\{t, 1-t\}$,

$$2r(t)(f(0) - f(1/2)) \geq f(0) - f(t),$$

which implies the first inequality of (35). For the proof of the second inequality of (35), we use Lemma 4. Putting $r := 2t - 1 > 0$ in (29), we have

$$f(t) = f\left(2t \cdot \frac{1}{2} + (1-2t) \cdot 0\right) = f\left((1+r) \cdot \frac{1}{2} - r \cdot 0\right) \leq (1+r)f(1/2) - rf(0)$$
$$= 2tf(1/2) + (1-2t)f(0),$$

which means

$$2t(f(0) - f(1/2)) \leq f(0) - f(t), \ t \in [1/2, 1].$$

For the case of $t \in [0, 1/2]$, by exchanging t with $1-t$, we have from the above inequality

$$2(1-t)(f(0) - f(1/2)) \leq f(0) - f(1-t), \ t \in [0, 1/2].$$

By the symmetric property of f in $t = 1/2$, we obtain

$$2R(t)(f(0) - f(1/2)) \leq f(0) - f(t),$$

which gives the right hand side in the inequalities (35).

If f is log-concave, then we have from the first inequality of (35) with concave function $\log f$, $f(1/2)^{2R(t)} f(0)^{1-2R(t)} \geq f(t)$, which show the forth inequality in (36). The third inequality is just from (35). The second and last inequalities in (36) are obtained by the Young inequality.

Since we have $0 \leq r(t) \leq 1/2 \leq R(t) \leq 1$ generally, we have $0 \leq 2r(t) \leq 1$ for $t \in [0, 1]$. Then we apply the second inequality of (3), we have

$$f(1/2)^{2r(t)} f(0)^{1-2r(t)} \geq 2r(t)f(1/2) + (1-2r(t))f(0) - R(2r(t))\left(\sqrt{f(1/2)} - \sqrt{f(0)}\right)^2$$

which shows the first inequality in (36). □

Remark 2. *In general, we have the supplement to the Young inequality:*

$$a^v b^{1-v} \geq va + (1-v)b, \quad v \notin (0,1), \quad a, b > 0.$$

Thus, we have

$$f(1/2)^{2R(t)} f(0)^{1-2R(t)} \geq 2R(t)f(1/2) + (1-2R(t))f(0).$$

Therefore, it seems difficult to bound $f(1/2)^{2R(t)} f(0)^{1-2R(t)}$ in (36) from the above by the use of the two terms $2R(t)f(1/2) + (1-2R(t))f(0)$ and $\left(\sqrt{f(1/2)} - \sqrt{f(0)}\right)^2$ as a simple form.

We have some bounds on $f(1/2)^{2R(t)} f(0)^{1-2R(t)}$ by applying (3)–(6). We here show one result by the use of (3). However, we omit the other cases.

Lemma 8. *Let a and b be positive real numbers and let $p \in [1, 2]$. Then,*

$$pa + (1-p)b + \min\{A_p, B_p\}\left(\sqrt{a} - \sqrt{b}\right)^2$$
$$\leq a^p b^{1-p} \qquad (37)$$
$$\leq pa + (1-p)b + \max\{A_p, B_p\}\left(\sqrt{a} - \sqrt{b}\right)^2,$$

where $A_p := (p-1)\left(1 + 2\sqrt{\frac{a}{b}}\right)$ and $B_p := (2p-3)\frac{a}{b} + (p-1)\left(1 + 2\sqrt{\frac{a}{b}}\right)$.

Proof. Since $p - 1 \in [0, 1]$, we can use (3) as

$$r(p-1)\left(\sqrt{a}-\sqrt{b}\right)^2 \leq d_{p-1}(a,b) \leq R(p-1)\left(\sqrt{a}-\sqrt{b}\right)^2. \tag{38}$$

Here we have the relation:

$$b \cdot d_p(a,b) - a \cdot d_{p-1}(a,b) = (1-p)(a-b)^2, \quad (a,b > 0, \quad p \in \mathbb{R}). \tag{39}$$

Combining (39) with (38), we obtain

$$r(p-1)a\left(\sqrt{a}-\sqrt{b}\right)^2 + (1-p)(a-b)^2 \leq b \cdot d_p(a,b)$$
$$\leq R(p-1)a\left(\sqrt{a}-\sqrt{b}\right)^2 + (1-p)(a-b)^2.$$

Elementary calculations imply

$$pa + (1-p)b + \frac{1}{b}\left\{(p-1)\left(\sqrt{a}+\sqrt{b}\right)^2 - R(p-1)a\right\}\left(\sqrt{a}-\sqrt{b}\right)^2$$
$$\leq a^p b^{1-p}$$
$$\leq pa + (1-p)b + \frac{1}{b}\left\{(p-1)\left(\sqrt{a}+\sqrt{b}\right)^2 - r(p-1)a\right\}\left(\sqrt{a}-\sqrt{b}\right)^2.$$

Considering the cases $\max\{p-1, 2-p\}$ and $\min\{p-1, 2-p\}$, we obtain the inequalities (37). □

As for the bounds on $f(1/2)^{2R(t)} f(0)^{1-2R(t)}$, we have the following result.

Proposition 2. *Let $t \in [0,1]$ and a function $f : [0,1] \to (0,\infty)$. Then we have*

$$2R(t)f(1/2) + (1-2R(t))f(0) + \min\{A_t, B_t\}\left(\sqrt{f(1/2)} - \sqrt{f(0)}\right)^2$$
$$\leq f(1/2)^{2R(t)} f(0)^{1-2R(t)}$$
$$\leq 2R(t)f(1/2) + (1-2R(t))f(0) + \max\{A_t, B_t\}\left(\sqrt{f(1/2)} - \sqrt{f(0)}\right)^2,$$

where

$$A_t := (2R(t) - 1)\left(1 + 2\sqrt{\frac{f(1/2)}{f(0)}}\right),$$
$$B_t := (4R(t) - 3)\frac{f(1/2)}{f(0)} + (2R(t) - 1)\left(1 + 2\sqrt{\frac{f(1/2)}{f(0)}}\right).$$

Proof. Since $1 \leq 2R(t) \leq 2$, we set $p := 2R(t)$, $a := f(1/2)$ and $b := f(0)$ in Lemma 8. □

Example 1. *The so-called binary entropy (e.g., [18], example 2.1.1) defined by*

$$h_{bin}(t) := -t \log t - (1-t) \log(1-t) > 0, \quad (0 < t < 1)$$

with convention $0 \log 0 =: 0$, satisfies the conditions in Lemma 7, since

$$\frac{d^2 h_{bin}(t)}{dt^2} = \frac{-1}{t(1-t)} < 0$$

and

$$\frac{d^2}{dt^2}(\log h_{bin}(t)) = \frac{-h_{bin}(t) - t(1-t)\{\log t - \log(1-t)\}^2}{t(1-t)h_{bin}(t)^2} < 0$$

The standard convention $0\log 0 =: 0$ is in information theory, since we have $\lim_{x\downarrow 0} x\log x = 0$ and $\log x$ is undefined for $x \le 0$. In information theory, we use 2 as the base of the logarithmic function, but we here use e for mathematical simplicity. Its selection is not essential in mathematics. Applying (35) to function $h_{bin}(t)$ with convention $h_{bin}(0) =: 0$, we have $2(\log_e 2)r(t) \le h_{bin}(t) \le 2(\log_e 2)R(t)$, which is equivalent to

$$2\min\{t, 1-t\} \le -t\log_2 t - (1-t)\log_2(1-t) \le 2\max\{t, 1-t\}. \tag{40}$$

The above inequalities are equivalent to

$$1 - |1-2p| \le H_b(p) \le 1 + |1-2p|, \quad (0 \le p \le 1), \tag{41}$$

where $H_b(p) := -p\log_2 p - (1-p)\log_2(1-p)$ is the usual binary entropy, whose base is 2.

If we do not adopt the standard convention $0\log 0 =: 0$ in information theory, then we assume $f(0) := \lim_{t\to 0} f(t) =: \varepsilon$ precisely. Applying the inequalities in (36):

$$f(1/2)^{2r(t)} f(0)^{1-2r(t)} \le f(t) \le f(1/2)^{2R(t)} f(0)^{1-2R(t)},$$

we obtain

$$(\log_e 2)^{2r(t)} \varepsilon^{1-2r(t)} \le f(t) \le (\log_e 2)^{2R(t)} \varepsilon^{1-2R(t)},$$

which implies the following result.

$$\left(\frac{\varepsilon}{\log_e 2}\right)^{1-2r(p)} \le H_b(p) \le \left(\frac{\varepsilon}{\log_e 2}\right)^{1-2R(p)}, \quad (0 \le p \le 1).$$

The Fermi–Dirac entropy is defined above by

$$I_1^{FD}(\mathbf{p}) := -\sum_{j=1}^n p_j \log p_j - \sum_{j=1}^n (1-p_j)\log(1-p_j).$$

From the bounds of the binary entropy given in (40) and (41), we obtain the interesting bounds on the Fermi–Dirac entropy as

$$2\sum_{j=1}^n \min\{p_j, 1-p_j\} \le I_1^{FD}(\mathbf{p}) \le 2\sum_{j=1}^n \max\{p_j, 1-p_j\}$$

or

$$n - \sum_{j=1}^n |1-2p_j| \le I_1^{FD}(\mathbf{p}) \le n + \sum_{j=1}^n |1-2p_j|.$$

5. Concluding Remarks

We close this paper by providing some remarks on the log-convex function.

Lemma 9. *For $a, b, c, d > 0$ and $\lambda \in [0,1]$, we have*

$$a^\lambda b^{1-\lambda} + c^\lambda d^{1-\lambda} \le (a+c)^\lambda (b+d)^{1-\lambda}. \tag{42}$$

Proof. Since function $f(t) = t^\lambda$ is concave for $\lambda \in [0,1]$, we use the Jensen inequality for positive real numbers x and y as

$$\frac{bf(x) + df(y)}{b+d} \le f\left(\frac{bx+dy}{b+d}\right).$$

If we take $x := \frac{a}{b}$ and $y := \frac{c}{d}$, then we obtain

$$\frac{b}{b+d}\left(\frac{a}{b}\right)^\lambda + \frac{d}{b+d}\left(\frac{c}{d}\right)^\lambda \leq \left(\frac{a+c}{b+d}\right)^\lambda$$

which implies (42). □

Theorem 4. *If $f, g : I \to (0, \infty)$ are log-convex functions, then function $\mu f + \nu g$ is log-convex, where $I \subset \mathbb{R}$ and $\mu, \nu > 0$.*

Proof. Since f, g are log-convex functions, we have for $\lambda \in [0, 1]$,

$$(\mu f + \nu g)(\lambda x + (1-\lambda)y) = \mu f(\lambda x + (1-\lambda)y) + \nu g(\lambda x + (1-\lambda)y)$$
$$\leq \mu f^\lambda(x) f^{1-\lambda}(y) + \nu g^\lambda(x) g^{1-\lambda}(y) = (\mu f(x))^\lambda (\mu f(y))^{1-\lambda} + (\nu g(x))^\lambda (\nu g(y))^{1-\lambda}$$
$$\leq (\mu f(x) + \nu g(x))^\lambda (\mu f(y) + \nu g(y))^{1-\lambda},$$

where we used Lemma 9 in the last inequality. Therefore, $\mu f + \nu g$ is log-convex. □

Let $\mathbb{M}_n$ be the set of all $n \times n$ complex matrices, and let $\mathbb{M}_n^+$ be the set of all positive semi-definite matrices in $\mathbb{M}_n$.

Corollary 4. *For $A, B \in \mathbb{M}_n^+$, $X \in \mathbb{M}_n$, $t \in [0, 1]$ and $||| \cdot |||$ is the unitarily invariant norm, the following functions are log-convex:*

$$g_1(t) := |||A^t X B^t||| + |||A^{1-t} X B^{1-t}|||,$$
$$g_2(t) := |||A^t X B^{1-t}||| + |||A^{1-t} X B^t|||,$$
$$g_3(t) := |||A^t||| + |||A^{1-t}|||,$$
$$g_4(t) := \operatorname{tr}\left(A^t X B^{1-t} X^* + A^{1-t} X B^t X^*\right).$$

Proof. In [19], it was shown that functions $f_1(t) := |||A^t X B^t|||$, $f_2(t) := |||A^t X B^{1-t}|||$, $f_3(t) := |||A^t|||$ and $f_4(t) := \operatorname{tr}(A^t X B^{1-t} X^*)$ are log-convex on $[0, 1]$. Thus, we have the corollary from Theorem 4. □

Since the functions g_i are log-convex and $g_i(t) = g_i(1-t)$, we can apply Lemma 6 for the symmetric function g_i on an axis $t = \frac{1}{2}$. Therefore, we obtain the chain of inequalities for the functions g_1 in the following, for example. We can obtain the similar inequalities for the other functions g_2, g_3 and g_4. However, we omit them. For $A, B \in \mathbb{M}_n^+$, $X \in \mathbb{M}_n$ and $t \in [0, 1]$, we have

$$4R(t)|||A^{1/2} X B^{1/2}||| + (1 - 2R(t))(|||X||| + |||AXB|||)$$
$$-(1-2R(t))\left(\sqrt{2|||A^{1/2} X B^{1/2}|||} - \sqrt{|||X||| + |||AXB|||}\right)^2$$
$$\leq \left(2|||A^{1/2} X B^{1/2}|||\right)^{2R(t)} (|||X||| + |||AXB|||)^{1-2R(t)}$$
$$\leq |||A^t X B^t||| + |||A^{1-t} X B^{1-t}|||$$
$$\leq \left(2|||A^{1/2} X B^{1/2}|||\right)^{2r(t)} (|||X||| + |||AXB|||)^{1-2r(t)}$$
$$\leq 4r(t)|||A^{1/2} X B^{1/2}||| + (1 - 2r(t))(|||X||| + |||AXB|||)$$
$$-r(2r(t))\left(\sqrt{2|||A^{1/2} X B^{1/2}|||} - \sqrt{|||X||| + |||AXB|||}\right)^2.$$

Author Contributions: This work was carried out in collaboration among all authors. All authors contributed equally and significantly in writing this manuscript. All authors have read and agreed to the published version of the manuscript.

Funding: The first author was supported in part by JSPS KAKENHI grant number 21K03341.

Institutional Review Board Statement: Not applicable.

Informed Consent Statement: Not applicable.

Data Availability Statement: Not applicable.

Acknowledgments: The authors would like to thank the reviewers for their important suggestions and careful reading of our manuscript. The authors would like to thank M. Kian, who let us know the essential estimation for the symmetric function in Lemma 6.

Conflicts of Interest: The authors declare no conflict of interest.

References

1. Rényi, A. On measures of entropy and information. In *Proceedings of the Fourth Berkeley Symposium on Mathematical Statistics and Probability, Volume 1: Contributions to the Theory of Statistics*; University of California Press: Berkeley, CA, USA, 1961; Volume 1, p. 547.
2. Shannon, C.E. A mathematical theory of communication. *Bell Syst. Tech. J.* **1948**, *27*, 379–656. [CrossRef]
3. Tsallis, C. Possible generalization of Bolzmann-Gibbs statistics. *J. Stat. Phys.* **1988**, *52*, 479–487. [CrossRef]
4. Beck, C.; Schlögl, F. *Thermodynamics of Chaotic Systems: An Introduction*; Cambridge University Press: Cambridge, UK, 1993.
5. Conroy, J.M.; Miller, H.G.; Plastino, A.R. Thermodynamic consistency of the q–deformed Fermi–Dirac distribution in nonextensive thermostatics *Phys. Lett. A* **2010**, *374*, 4581–4584. [CrossRef]
6. Furuichi, S.; Mitroi, F.-C. Mathematical inequalities for some divergences. *Phys. A* **2012**, *391*, 388–400. [CrossRef]
7. Furuichi, S.; Minculete, N. Refined Young inequality and its application to divergences. *Entropy* **2021**, *23*, 514. [CrossRef] [PubMed]
8. Sababheh, M.; Choi, D. A complete refinement of Young's inequality. *J. Math. Anal. Appl.* **2016**, *440*, 379–393. [CrossRef]
9. Butt, S.I.; Mehmood, N.; Pečarić, D.P.; Pečarić, J.P. New bounds for Shannon, relative and Mandelbrot entropies via Abel-Gontscharoff interpolating polynomial. *Math. Inequal. Appl.* **2019**, *22*, 1283–1301. [CrossRef]
10. Tohyama, H.; Kamei, E.; Watanabe, M. The n-th residual relative operator entropy $\mathfrak{R}_{x,y}^{[n]}(A|B)$. *Adv. Oper. Theory* **2021**, *6*, 18. [CrossRef]
11. Isa, H.; Kamei, E.; Tohyama, H.; Watanabe, M. The n-th relative operator entropies and the n-th operator divergences. *Ann. Funct. Anal.* **2020**, *11*, 298–313. [CrossRef]
12. Kittaneh, F.; Manasrah, Y. Improved Young and Heinz inequalities for matrix. *J. Math. Anal. Appl.* **2010**, *361*, 262–269. [CrossRef]
13. Alzer, H.; da Fonseca, C.; Cec, A.K. Young-type inequalities and their matrix analogues. *Linear Multilinear Algebra* **2014**, *63*, 622–635. [CrossRef]
14. Cartwright, D.I.; Field, M.J. A refinement of the arithmetic mean-geometric mean inequality. *Proc. Amer. Math. Soc.* **1978**, *71*, 36–38. [CrossRef]
15. Furuichi, S.; Ghaemi, M.B.; Gharakhanlu, N. Generalized reverse Young and Heinz inequalities. *Bull. Malays. Math. Sci. Soc.* **2019**, *42*, 267–284. [CrossRef]
16. Sababheh, M.; Moslehian, M.S. Advanced refinements of Young and Heinz inequalities. *Number Theory* **2017**, *172*, 178–199. [CrossRef]
17. Alakhrass, M.; Sababheh, M. Matrix mixed mean inequalities. *Results Math.* **2019**, *74*, 2. [CrossRef]
18. Cover, T.M.; Thomas, J.A. *Elements of Information Theory*, 2nd ed.; Wiley–Interscience: Hoboken, NJ, USA, 2006.
19. Sababheh, M. Log and harmonically log–convex functions related to matrix norms. *Oper. Matrices* **2016**, *10*, 453–465. [CrossRef]

Article

On Some New Simpson's Formula Type Inequalities for Convex Functions in Post-Quantum Calculus

Miguel J. Vivas-Cortez [1,*,†], Muhammad Aamir Ali [2,*,†], Shahid Qaisar [3,†], Ifra Bashir Sial [4,†], Sinchai Jansem [5,†] and Abdul Mateen [3,†]

1. Facultad de Ciencias Exactas y Naturales, Pontificia Universidad Católica del Ecuador, Escuela de Ciencias Matemáticas y Físicas, Av. 12 de Octubre 1076, Apartado, Quito 17-01-2184, Ecuador
2. Jiangsu Key Laboratory for NSLSCS, School of Mathematical Sciences, Nanjing Normal University, Nanjing 210023, China
3. Department of Mathematics, COMSATS University Islamabad, Sahiwal 57000, Pakistan; shahidqaisar90@cuisahiwal.edu.pk (S.Q.); aabdulmateen1996@gmail.com (A.M.)
4. School of Control Science and Engineering, Jiangsu University, Zhenjiang 212000, China; ifrabashir92@gmail.com
5. Faculty of Education, Suan Dusit University, Bangkok 10300, Thailand; sinchai_jan@dusit.ac.th
* Correspondence: mjvivas@puce.edu.ec (M.J.V.-C.); mahr.muhammad.aamir@gmail.com (M.A.A.)
† These authors contributed equally to this work.

Abstract: In this work, we prove a new (p,q)-integral identity involving a (p,q)-derivative and (p,q)-integral. The newly established identity is then used to show some new Simpson's formula type inequalities for (p,q)-differentiable convex functions. Finally, the newly discovered results are shown to be refinements of comparable results in the literature. Analytic inequalities of this type, as well as the techniques used to solve them, have applications in a variety of fields where symmetry is important.

Keywords: Simpson's inequalities; post-quantum calculus; convex functions

MSC: 26D10; 26D15; 26A51

1. Introduction

During his lifetime, Thomas Simpson created important approaches for numerical integration and the estimation of definite integrals, which became known as Simpson's rule (1710–1761). J. Kepler, who made a comparable calculation roughly a century before Newton, is the inspiration for Kepler's rule. Estimations based exclusively on a three-step quadratic kernel are commonly referred to as Newton-type results because Simpson's technique incorporates the three-point Newton–Cotes quadrature rule.

(1) Simpson's quadrature formula (Simpson's 1/3 rule)

$$\int_{\pi_1}^{\pi_2} \mathcal{F}(x)dx \approx \frac{\pi_2 - \pi_1}{6}\left[\mathcal{F}(\pi_1) + 4\mathcal{F}\left(\frac{\pi_1 + \pi_2}{2}\right) + \mathcal{F}(\pi_2)\right].$$

(2) Simpson's second formula or Newton–Cotes quadrature formula (Simpson's 3/8 rule)

$$\int_{\pi_1}^{\pi_2} \mathcal{F}(x)dx \approx \frac{\pi_2 - \pi_1}{8}\left[\mathcal{F}(\pi_1) + 3\mathcal{F}\left(\frac{2\pi_1 + \pi_2}{3}\right) + 3\mathcal{F}\left(\frac{\pi_1 + 2\pi_2}{3}\right) + \mathcal{F}(\pi_2)\right].$$

The following estimation, known as Simpson's inequality, is one of many linked with these quadrature rules in the literature:

Theorem 1. *Suppose that $\mathcal{F}:[\pi_1,\pi_2]\to\mathbb{R}$ is a four-times continuously differentiable mapping on (π_1,π_2), and let $\left\|\mathcal{F}^{(4)}\right\|_\infty = \sup_{x\in(\pi_1,\pi_2)}\left|\mathcal{F}^{(4)}(x)\right|<\infty$. Then, one has the inequality*

$$\left|\frac{1}{3}\left[\frac{\mathcal{F}(\pi_1)+\mathcal{F}(\pi_2)}{2}+2\mathcal{F}\left(\frac{\pi_1+\pi_2}{2}\right)\right]-\frac{1}{\pi_2-\pi_1}\int_{\pi_1}^{\pi_2}\mathcal{F}(x)dx\right|\leq \frac{1}{2880}\left\|\mathcal{F}^{(4)}\right\|_\infty(\pi_2-\pi_1)^4.$$

Many researchers have focused on Simpson-type inequality in various categories of mappings in recent years. Because convexity theory is an effective and powerful technique to solve a huge number of problems from various disciplines of pure and applied mathematics, some mathematicians have worked on the results of Simpson's and Newton's type in obtaining a convex map. The novel Simpson's inequalities and their applications in numerical integration quadrature formulations were presented by Dragomir et al. [1]. Furthermore, Alomari et al. [2] discovered a number of inequalities in Simpson's kind of s-convex functions. The variance of Simpson-type inequality as a function of convexity was then observed by Sarikaya et al. in [3]. Refs. [4–6] can be consulted for further research on this subject.

On the other hand, quantum and post-quantum integrals for many types of functions have been used to study many integral inequalities. The authors of [7–21] employed left–right q-derivatives and integrals to prove HH integral inequalities and associated left–right estimates for convex and coordinated convex functions. Noor et al. proposed a generalized version of quantum integral inequalities in their paper [22]. In [23], the authors demonstrated some parameterized quantum integral inequalities for generalized quasi-convex functions. In [24], Khan et al. used the green function to prove quantum HH inequality. For convex and coordinated convex functions, the authors of [25–30] constructed new quantum Simpson's and quantum Newton's type inequalities. Consult [31–33] for quantum Ostrowski's inequality for convex and co-ordinated convex functions. Using the left (p,q)-difference operator and integral, the authors of [34] expanded the results of [9] and demonstrated HH-type inequalities and associated left estimates. In [16], the authors discovered the right estimates of HH-type inequalities, as demonstrated in [34]. Vivas-Cortez et al. [35] recently generalized the results of [11] and used the right (p,q)-difference operator and integral to prove HH-type inequalities and associated left estimates.

We use the (p,q)-integral to establish some new post-quantum Simpson's type inequalities for (p,q)-differentiable convex functions, as inspired by recent research. The newly revealed inequalities are also shown to be extensions of previously discovered inequalities.

The structure of this article is as follows. The principles of q-calculus, as well as other relevant topics in this subject, are briefly discussed in Section 2. The basics of (p,q)-calculus, as well as some recent research in this topic, are covered in Section 3. In Section 4, we prove a new (p,q)-integral identity involving a (p,q)-derivative. Section 5 describes the Simpson's type inequalities for (p,q)-differentiable functions via (p,q)-integrals. It is also taken into account the relationship between the findings given here and similar findings in the literature. Section 6 finishes with some research suggestions for the future.

2. Preliminaries of q-Calculus and Some Inequalities

In this section, we revisit several previously regarded ideas. In addition, we utilize the following notation here and elsewhere (see [36]):

$$[n]_q=\frac{1-q^n}{1-q}=1+q+q^2+\ldots+q^{n-1},\quad q\in(0,1).$$

In [37], Jackson gave the q-Jackson integral from 0 to π_2 for $0<q<1$ as follows:

$$\int_0^{\pi_2}\mathcal{F}(x)\,d_qx=(1-q)\pi_2\sum_{n=0}^{\infty}q^n\mathcal{F}(\pi_2 q^n) \qquad (1)$$

provided that the sum converges absolutely.

Definition 1 ([38]). For a function $\mathcal{F} : [\pi_1, \pi_2] \to \mathbb{R}$, the left q-derivative of $\mathcal{F}$ at $x \in [\pi_1, \pi_2]$ is characterized by the expression

$$_{\pi_1}D_q\mathcal{F}(x) = \frac{\mathcal{F}(x) - \mathcal{F}(qx + (1-q)\pi_1)}{(1-q)(x - \pi_1)}, \quad x \neq \pi_1. \tag{2}$$

If $x = \pi_1$, we define $_{\pi_1}D_q\mathcal{F}(\pi_1) = \lim_{x \to \pi_1} {_{\pi_1}D_q\mathcal{F}(x)}$ if it exists and it is finite.

Definition 2 ([11]). For a function $\mathcal{F} : [\pi_1, \pi_2] \to \mathbb{R}$, the right q-derivative of $\mathcal{F}$ at $x \in [\pi_1, \pi_2]$ is characterized by the expression

$$^{\pi_2}D_q\mathcal{F}(x) = \frac{\mathcal{F}(qx + (1-q)\pi_2) - \mathcal{F}(x)}{(1-q)(\pi_2 - x)}, \quad x \neq \pi_2. \tag{3}$$

If $x = \pi_2$, we define $^{\pi_2}D_q\mathcal{F}(\pi_2) = \lim_{x \to \pi_2} {^{\pi_2}D_q\mathcal{F}(x)}$ if it exists and it is finite.

Definition 3 ([38]). Let $\mathcal{F} : [\pi_1, \pi_2] \to \mathbb{R}$ be a function. Then, the left q-definite integral on $[\pi_1, \pi_2]$ is defined as

$$\int_{\pi_1}^{\pi_2} \mathcal{F}(x) \, _{\pi_1}d_q x = (1-q)(\pi_2 - \pi_1) \sum_{n=0}^{\infty} q^n \mathcal{F}(q^n \pi_2 + (1 - q^n)\pi_1) \tag{4}$$

$$= (\pi_2 - \pi_1) \int_0^1 \mathcal{F}((1-t)\pi_1 + t\pi_2) \, d_q t.$$

Definition 4 ([11]). Let $\mathcal{F} : [\pi_1, \pi_2] \to \mathbb{R}$ be a function. Then, the right q-definite integral on $[\pi_1, \pi_2]$ is defined as

$$\int_{\pi_1}^{\pi_2} \mathcal{F}(x) \, ^{\pi_2}d_q x = (1-q)(\pi_2 - \pi_1) \sum_{n=0}^{\infty} q^n \mathcal{F}(q^n \pi_1 + (1 - q^n)\pi_2) \tag{5}$$

$$= (\pi_2 - \pi_1) \int_0^1 \mathcal{F}(t\pi_1 + (1-t)\pi_2) \, d_q t.$$

Alp et al. [9] proved the following Hermite–Hadamard-type inequalities for convex functions via q-integral.

Theorem 2. For the convex mapping $\mathcal{F} : [\pi_1, \pi_2] \to \mathbb{R}$, the following inequality holds

$$\mathcal{F}\left(\frac{q\pi_1 + \pi_2}{[2]_q}\right) \leq \frac{1}{\pi_2 - \pi_1} \int_{\pi_1}^{\pi_2} \mathcal{F}(x) \, _{\pi_1}d_q x \leq \frac{q\mathcal{F}(\pi_1) + \mathcal{F}(\pi_2)}{[2]_q}.$$

In [11], Bermudo et al. established the following quantum Hermite–Hadamard-type inequalities:

Theorem 3. For the convex mapping $\mathcal{F} : [\pi_1, \pi_2] \to \mathbb{R}$, the following inequality holds

$$\mathcal{F}\left(\frac{\pi_1 + q\pi_2}{[2]_q}\right) \leq \frac{1}{\pi_2 - \pi_1} \int_{\pi_1}^{\pi_2} \mathcal{F}(x) \, ^{\pi_2}d_q x \leq \frac{\mathcal{F}(\pi_1) + q\mathcal{F}(\pi_2)}{[2]_q}.$$

$$\mathcal{F}\left(\frac{\pi_1 + \pi_2}{2}\right) \leq \frac{1}{2(\pi_2 - \pi_1)} \left[\int_{\pi_1}^{\pi_2} \mathcal{F}(x) \,^{\pi_1} d_q x + \int_{\pi_1}^{\pi_2} \mathcal{F}(x) \,^{\pi_2} d_q x \right] \leq \frac{\mathcal{F}(\pi_1) + \mathcal{F}(\pi_2)}{2}.$$

Recently, Siricharuanun et al. [29] proved the following Simpson's formula type inequality for convex functions.

Theorem 4. *Let $\mathcal{F} : [\pi_1, \pi_2] \to \mathbb{R}$ be a $^{\pi_2}D_q\mathcal{F}$-differentiable function on (π_1, π_2) such that $^{\pi_2}D_q\mathcal{F}$ is continuous and integrable on $[\pi_1, \pi_2]$. If $|^{\pi_2}D_q\mathcal{F}|$ is convex on $[\pi_1, \pi_2]$, then we have the following inequality for q^{π_2}-integrals:*

$$\left| \frac{1}{(\pi_2 - \pi_1)} \int_{\pi_1}^{\pi_2} \mathcal{F}(s) \,^{\pi_2} d_q s - \frac{1}{[6]_q} \left[\mathcal{F}(\pi_1) + q^2 [4]_q \mathcal{F}\left(\frac{\pi_1 + q\pi_2}{[2]_q}\right) + q\mathcal{F}(\pi_2) \right] \right| \quad (6)$$
$$\leq q(\pi_2 - \pi_1)\{ |^{\pi_2}D_q\mathcal{F}(\pi_1)|[A_1(q) + A_2(q)] + |^{\pi_2}D_q\mathcal{F}(\pi_2)|[B_1(q) + B_2(q)] \},$$

where $0 < q < 1$ and

$$A_1(q) = \frac{2q^2[2]_q^2 + [6]_q^2\left([6]_q - [3]_q\right)}{[2]_q^3[3]_q[6]_q^3},$$

$$B_1(q) = 2\frac{q[3]_q[6]_q - q^2}{[2]_q[3]_q[6]_q^3} + \frac{1}{[2]_q^3}\left(\frac{q+q^2}{[3]_q} - \frac{q^2 + 2q}{[6]_q}\right),$$

$$A_2(q) = \frac{2q^2[5]_q^3}{[2]_q[3]_q[6]_q^3} + \frac{[6]_q\left(1 + [2]_q^3\right) - [3]_q[5]_q\left(1 + [2]_q^2\right)}{[2]_q^3[3]_q[6]_q},$$

$$B_2(q) = 2\frac{q[5]_q^2[6]_q[3]_q - q^2[5]_q^3}{[2]_q[3]_q[6]_q^3} + \frac{q^2}{[2]_q[3]_q} - \frac{q[5]_q}{[2]_q[6]_q}$$
$$- \frac{1}{[2]_q^3}\left[\frac{[5]_q(2q + q^2)}{[6]_q} - \frac{q+q^2}{[3]_q}\right].$$

3. Post-Quantum Calculus and Some Inequalities

In this section, we review some fundamental notions and notations of (p,q)-calculus. The $[n]_{p,q}$ is said to be (p,q)-integers and expressed as:

$$[n]_{p,q} = \frac{p^n - q^n}{p - q}$$

with $0 < q < p \leq 1$. The $[n]_{p,q}!$ and $\begin{bmatrix} n \\ k \end{bmatrix}!$ are called (p,q)-factorial and (p,q)-binomial, respectively, and expressed as:

$$[n]_{p,q}! = \prod_{k=1}^{n} [k]_{p,q}, \quad n \geq 1, \quad [0]_{p,q}! = 1,$$

$$\begin{bmatrix} n \\ k \end{bmatrix}! = \frac{[n]_{p,q}!}{[n-k]_{p,q}![k]_{p,q}!}.$$

Definition 5 ([39]). *The (p,q)-derivative of mapping $\mathcal{F} : [\pi_1, \pi_2] \to \mathbb{R}$ is given as:*

$$D_{p,q}\mathcal{F}(x) = \frac{\mathcal{F}(px) - \mathcal{F}(qx)}{(p-q)x}, \quad x \neq 0$$

with $0 < q < p \leq 1$.

Definition 6 ([40]). The left p,q-derivative of mapping $\mathcal{F} : [\pi_1, \pi_2] \to \mathbb{R}$ is given as:

$$_{\pi_1}D_{p,q}\mathcal{F}(x) = \frac{\mathcal{F}(px + (1-p)\pi_1) - \mathcal{F}(qx + (1-q)\pi_1)}{(p-q)(x - \pi_1)}, \quad x \neq \pi_1 \tag{7}$$

with $0 < q < p \leq 1$. For $x = \pi_1$, we state that $_{\pi_1}D_{p,q}\mathcal{F}(\pi_1) = \lim_{x \to \pi_1} {}_{\pi_1}D_{p,q}\mathcal{F}(x)$ if it exists and it is finite.

Definition 7 ([35]). The right (p,q)-derivative of mapping $\mathcal{F} : [\pi_1, \pi_2] \to \mathbb{R}$ is given as:

$$^{\pi_2}D_{p,q}\mathcal{F}(x) = \frac{\mathcal{F}(qx + (1-q)\pi_2) - \mathcal{F}(px + (1-p)\pi_2)}{(p-q)(\pi_2 - x)}, \quad x \neq \pi_2. \tag{8}$$

with $0 < q < p \leq 1$. For $x = \pi_2$, we state that $^{\pi_2}D_{p,q}\mathcal{F}(\pi_2) = \lim_{x \to \pi_2} {}^{\pi_2}D_{p,q}\mathcal{F}(x)$ if it exists and it is finite.

Remark 1. It is clear that if we use $p = 1$ in (7) and (8), then the equalities (7) and (8) reduce to (2) and (3), respectively.

Definition 8 ([40]). The left (p,q)-integral of mapping $\mathcal{F} : [\pi_1, \pi_2] \to \mathbb{R}$ on $[\pi_1, \pi_2]$ is stated as:

$$\int_{\pi_1}^{x} \mathcal{F}(\tau) \; {}_{\pi_1}d_{p,q}\tau = (p-q)(x - \pi_1) \sum_{n=0}^{\infty} \frac{q^n}{p^{n+1}} \mathcal{F}\left(\frac{q^n}{p^{n+1}}x + \left(1 - \frac{q^n}{p^{n+1}}\right)\pi_1\right) \tag{9}$$

with $0 < q < p \leq 1$.

Definition 9 ([35]). The right (p,q)-integral of mapping $\mathcal{F} : [\pi_1, \pi_2] \to \mathbb{R}$ on $[\pi_1, \pi_2]$ is stated as:

$$\int_{x}^{\pi_2} \mathcal{F}(\tau) \; {}^{\pi_2}d_{p,q}\tau = (p-q)(\pi_2 - x) \sum_{n=0}^{\infty} \frac{q^n}{p^{n+1}} \mathcal{F}\left(\frac{q^n}{p^{n+1}}x + \left(1 - \frac{q^n}{p^{n+1}}\right)\pi_2\right) \tag{10}$$

with $0 < q < p \leq 1$.

Remark 2. It is evident that if we select $p = 1$ in (9) and (10), then the equalities (9) and (10) change into (4) and (5), respectively.

Remark 3. If we take $\pi_1 = 0$ and $x = \pi_2 = 1$ in (9), then we have

$$\int_{0}^{1} \mathcal{F}(\tau) \; {}_0d_{p,q}\tau = (p-q) \sum_{n=0}^{\infty} \frac{q^n}{p^{n+1}} \mathcal{F}\left(\frac{q^n}{p^{n+1}}\right).$$

Similarly, by taking $x = \pi_1 = 0$ and $\pi_2 = 1$ in (10), then we obtain that

$$\int_{0}^{1} \mathcal{F}(\tau) \; {}^1d_{p,q}\tau = (p-q) \sum_{n=0}^{\infty} \frac{q^n}{p^{n+1}} \mathcal{F}\left(1 - \frac{q^n}{p^{n+1}}\right).$$

Remark 4. If f is a symmetric function—that is, $\mathcal{F}(s) = \mathcal{F}(\pi_2 + \pi_1 - s)$, for $s \in [\pi_1, \pi_2]$—then we have

$$\int_{\pi_1}^{p\pi_2 + (1-p)\pi_1} \mathcal{F}(s) \; {}_{\pi_1}d_{p,q}s = \int_{p\pi_1 + (1-p)\pi_2}^{\pi_2} \mathcal{F}(s) \; {}^{\pi_2}d_{p,q}s.$$

Lemma 1 ([35]). *We have the following equalities*

$$\int_{\pi_1}^{\pi_2} (\pi_2 - x)^{\pi_1} \,{}^{\pi_2}d_{p,q}x = \frac{(\pi_2 - \pi_1)^{\pi_1+1}}{[\pi_1+1]_{p,q}} \tag{11}$$

$$\int_{\pi_1}^{\pi_2} (x - \pi_1)^{\pi_1} \,{}_{\pi_1}d_{p,q}x = \frac{(\pi_2 - \pi_1)^{\pi_1+1}}{[\pi_1+1]_{p,q}}, \tag{12}$$

where $\pi_1 \in \mathbb{R} - \{-1\}$.

Recently, M. Vivas-Cortez et al. [35] proved the following HH-type inequalities for convex functions using the $(p,q)^{\pi_2}$-integral.

Theorem 5 ([35]). *For a convex mapping* $\mathcal{F}: [\pi_1, \pi_2] \to \mathbb{R}$, *which is differentiable on* $[\pi_1, \pi_2]$, *the following inequalities hold for the* $(p,q)^{\pi_2}$-*integral:*

$$\mathcal{F}\left(\frac{p\pi_1 + q\pi_2}{[2]_{p,q}}\right) \le \frac{1}{p(\pi_2 - \pi_1)} \int_{p\pi_1+(1-p)\pi_2}^{\pi_2} \mathcal{F}(x) \,{}^{\pi_2}d_{p,q}x \le \frac{p\mathcal{F}(\pi_1) + q\mathcal{F}(\pi_2)}{[2]_{p,q}}, \tag{13}$$

where $0 < q < p \le 1$.

Theorem 6 ([35]). *For a convex function* $\mathcal{F}: [\pi_1, \pi_2] \to \mathbb{R}$, *the following inequality holds:*

$$\mathcal{F}\left(\frac{\pi_1 + \pi_2}{2}\right) \le \frac{1}{2p(\pi_2 - \pi_1)} \left[\int_{\pi_1}^{p\pi_2+(1-p)\pi_1} \mathcal{F}(x) \,{}_{\pi_1}d_{p,q}x + \int_{p\pi_1+(1-p)\pi_2}^{\pi_2} \mathcal{F}(x) \,{}^{\pi_2}d_{p,q}x \right] \tag{14}$$

$$\le \frac{\mathcal{F}(\pi_1) + \mathcal{F}(\pi_2)}{2},$$

where $0 < q < p \le 1$.

4. An Identity

In this section, we deal with an identity that is required to reach our major estimates. In the following lemma, we first build an identity based on a two-stage kernel.

Lemma 2. *Let* $\mathcal{F}: [\pi_1, \pi_2] \to \mathbb{R}$ *be a differentiable function on* (π_1, π_2). *If* ${}_{\pi_1}D_{p,q}\mathcal{F}$ *is continuous and integrable on* $[\pi_1, \pi_2]$, *then one has the identity*

$$\frac{p}{[6]_{p,q}} \left[p^5 \mathcal{F}(\pi_2) + q\left([5]_{p,q} - 1\right)\mathcal{F}\left(\frac{p\pi_2 + q\pi_1}{p+q}\right) + q\mathcal{F}(\pi_1) \right] \tag{15}$$

$$- \frac{1}{(\pi_2 - \pi_1)} \int_{\pi_1}^{p\pi_2+(1-p)\pi_1} \mathcal{F}(s) \,{}_{\pi_1}d_{p,q}s$$

$$= pq(\pi_2 - \pi_1) \int_0^1 \Lambda(s) \,{}_{\pi_1}D_{p,q}\mathcal{F}(s\pi_2 + (1-s)\pi_1) \, d_{p,q}s \,,$$

where

$$\Lambda(s) = \begin{cases} s - \frac{1}{[6]_{p,q}}, & s \in \left[0, \frac{p}{[2]_{p,q}}\right) \\ s - \frac{[5]_{p,q}}{[6]_{p,q}}, & s \in \left[\frac{p}{[2]_{p,q}}, 1\right]. \end{cases}$$

Proof. Using the fundamental properties of (p,q)-integrals and the definition of function $\Lambda(s)$, we find that

$$\int_0^1 \Lambda(s) \, {}_{\pi_1}D_{p,q}\mathcal{F}(s\pi_2 + (1-s)\pi_1) \, d_{p,q}s \tag{16}$$

$$= \frac{[5]_{p,q} - 1}{[6]_{p,q}} \int_0^{\frac{p}{[2]_{p,q}}} {}_{\pi_1}D_{p,q}\mathcal{F}(s\pi_2 + (1-s)\pi_1) \, d_{p,q}s$$

$$+ \int_0^1 \left(s - \frac{[5]_{p,q}}{[6]_{p,q}} \right) {}_{\pi_1}D_{p,q}\mathcal{F}(s\pi_2 + (1-s)\pi_1) \, d_{p,q}s.$$

According to Definition 6, one must also have

$${}_{\pi_1}D_{p,q}\mathcal{F}(s\pi_2 + (1-s)\pi_1) = \frac{\mathcal{F}(ps\pi_2 + (1-ps)\pi_1) - \mathcal{F}(qs\pi_2 + (1-qs)\pi_1)}{(p-q)(\pi_2 - \pi_1)s}.$$

Now, if we substitute the above equation into (16), we obtain

$$\int_0^1 \Lambda(s) \, {}_{\pi_1}D_{p,q}\mathcal{F}(s\pi_2 + (1-s)\pi_1) \, d_{p,q}s \tag{17}$$

$$= \frac{[5]_{p,q} - 1}{[6]_{p,q}} \int_0^{\frac{p}{[2]_{p,q}}} \frac{\mathcal{F}(ps\pi_2 + (1-ps)\pi_1) - \mathcal{F}(qs\pi_2 + (1-qs)\pi_1)}{(p-q)(\pi_2 - \pi_1)s} d_{p,q}s$$

$$+ \int_0^1 \frac{\mathcal{F}(ps\pi_2 + (1-ps)\pi_1) - \mathcal{F}(qs\pi_2 + (1-qs)\pi_1)}{(p-q)(\pi_2 - \pi_1)} d_q s$$

$$- \frac{[5]_{p,q}}{[6]_{p,q}} \int_0^1 \frac{\mathcal{F}(ps\pi_2 + (1-ps)\pi_1) - \mathcal{F}(qs\pi_2 + (1-qs)\pi_1)}{(1-q)(\pi_2 - \pi_1)s} d_{p,q}s.$$

When the first integral on the right-hand side of (17) is calculated using Definition 8, it is discovered that

$$\int_0^{\frac{p}{[2]_{p,q}}} \frac{\mathcal{F}(ps\pi_2 + (1-ps)\pi_1) - \mathcal{F}(qs\pi_2 + (1-qs)\pi_1)}{(p-q)(\pi_2 - \pi_1)s} d_{p,q}s \tag{18}$$

$$= \frac{1}{(\pi_2 - \pi_1)} \left\{ \sum_{k=0}^{\infty} \mathcal{F}\left(\frac{q^k}{p^{k+1}} \frac{p^2}{[2]_{p,q}} \pi_2 + \left(1 - \frac{q^k}{p^{k+1}} \frac{p^2}{[2]_{p,q}}\right) \pi_1 \right) \right.$$

$$\left. - \sum_{k=0}^{\infty} \mathcal{F}\left(\frac{q^{k+1}}{p^{k+1}} \frac{p}{[2]_{p,q}} \pi_2 + \left(1 - \frac{q^{k+1}}{p^{k+1}} \frac{p}{[2]_{p,q}}\right) \pi_1 \right) \right\}$$

$$= \frac{1}{(\pi_2 - \pi_1)} \left\{ \mathcal{F}\left(\frac{p\pi_2 + q\pi_1}{[2]_{p,q}} \right) - \mathcal{F}(\pi_1) \right\}.$$

If we look at the other integrals on the right-hand side of (17), we obtain

$$\int_0^1 \frac{\mathcal{F}(ps\pi_2 + (1-ps)\pi_1) - \mathcal{F}(qs\pi_2 + (1-qs)\pi_1)}{(p-q)(\pi_2 - \pi_1)} d_{p,q}s \qquad (19)$$

$$= \frac{1}{(\pi_2 - \pi_1)} \left\{ \frac{1}{pq(\pi_2 - \pi_1)} \int_{\pi_1}^{p\pi_2 + (1-p)\pi_1} \mathcal{F}(s) \; \pi_1 d_{p,q}s + \frac{1}{q}\mathcal{F}(\pi_2) \right\}$$

and

$$\int_0^1 \frac{\mathcal{F}(ps\pi_2 + (1-ps)\pi_1) - \mathcal{F}(qs\pi_2 + (1-qs)\pi_1)}{(p-q)(\pi_2 - \pi_1)s} d_{p,q}s \qquad (20)$$

$$= \frac{1}{(\pi_2 - \pi_1)} \{\mathcal{F}(\pi_2) - \mathcal{F}(\pi_1)\}$$

Substituting the expressions (18)–(20) into (17), and later multiplying both sides of the resulting identity by $pq(\pi_2 - \pi_1)$, the equality (15) can be captured. □

5. Main Results

For (p,q)-differentiable convex functions, we prove some new Simpson's formula type inequalities in this section. For the sake of brevity, we start this section with certain notations that will be utilized in our new results.

$$A_1(p,q) = \frac{2[2]_{p,q}^2 \left([3]_{p,q} - [2]_{p,q}\right) + p^2[6]_{p,q}^2 \left(p[6]_{p,q} - [3]_{p,q}\right)}{[2]_{p,q}^3 [3]_{p,q} [6]_{p,q}^3}, \qquad (21)$$

$$B_1(p,q) = 2\frac{[2]_{p,q}[3]_{p,q}[6]_{p,q} - [3]_{p,q}[6]_{p,q} - [3]_{p,q} + [2]_{p,q}}{[2]_{p,q}[3]_{p,q}[6]_{p,q}^3}$$

$$+ \left(\frac{p^2[3]_{p,q}[6]_{p,q} - p[2]_{p,q}^2[3]_{p,q} - p^3[6]_{p,q} + p^2[3]_{p,q}}{[2]_{p,q}^3[3]_{p,q}[6]_{p,q}} \right), \qquad (22)$$

$$A_2(p,q) = 2\frac{[3]_{p,q}[5]_{p,q}^3 - [2]_{p,q}[5]_{p,q}^3}{[2]_{p,q}[3]_{p,q}[6]_{p,q}^3} + \frac{p^3[6]_{p,q} - p^2[3]_{p,q}[5]_{p,q} + [2]_{p,q}^3[6]_{p,q} - [2]_{p,q}^2[3]_{p,q}}{[2]_{p,q}^3[3]_{p,q}[6]_{p,q}}, \qquad (23)$$

$$B_2(p,q) = 2\frac{[5]_{p,q}^2[2]_{p,q}[3]_{p,q}[6]_{p,q} - [5]_{p,q}^2[3]_{p,q}[6]_{p,q} - [5]_{p,q}^3[3]_{p,q} + [5]_{p,q}^3[2]_{p,q}}{[2]_{p,q}[3]_{p,q}[6]_{p,q}^3}$$

$$- \left(\frac{p[5]_{p,q}[2]_{p,q}^2[3]_{p,q} - p^2[3]_{p,q}[6]_{p,q} - p^2[5]_{p,q}[3]_{p,q} + p^3[6]_{p,q}}{[2]_{p,q}^3[3]_{p,q}[6]_{p,q}} \right)$$

$$+ \left(\frac{[3]_{p,q}[6]_{p,q} - [5]_{p,q}[2]_{p,q}[3]_{p,q} - [2]_{p,q}[6]_{p,q} + [5]_{p,q}[3]_{p,q}}{[2]_{p,q}[3]_{p,q}[6]_{p,q}} \right) \qquad (24)$$

Theorem 7. Assume that the conditions of Lemma 2 hold. If $|_{\pi_1}D_{p,q}\mathcal{F}|$ is convex on $[\pi_1, \pi_2]$, then we have following inequality for $(p,q)_{\pi_1}$-integrals:

$$\left| \frac{p}{[6]_{p,q}} \left[p^5 \mathcal{F}(\pi_2) + q\left([5]_{p,q} - 1\right) \mathcal{F}\left(\frac{p\pi_2 + q\pi_1}{p+q}\right) + q\mathcal{F}(\pi_1) \right] \right. \tag{25}$$

$$\left. - \frac{1}{(\pi_2 - \pi_1)} \int_{\pi_1}^{p\pi_2 - (1-p)\pi_1} \mathcal{F}(s) \,_{\pi_1}d_{p,q}s \right|$$

$$\leq pq(\pi_2 - \pi_1)\{|_{\pi_1}D_{p,q}\mathcal{F}(\pi_2)|[A_1(p,q) + A_2(p,q)] + |_{\pi_1}D_{p,q}\mathcal{F}(\pi_1)|[B_1(p,q) + B_2(p,q)]\},$$

where $0 < q < p \leq 1$ and $A_1(p,q)$, $A_2(p,q)$, $B_1(p,q)$, $B_2(p,q)$ are given as in (21)–(24), respectively.

Proof. We observe that when we take the modulus in Lemma 2, because of the modulus' characteristics, we have

$$\left| \frac{1}{[6]_{p,q}} \left[p^5 \mathcal{F}(\pi_2) + q\left([5]_{p,q} - 1\right) \mathcal{F}\left(\frac{p\pi_2 + q\pi_1}{p+q}\right) + q\mathcal{F}(\pi_1) \right] \right. \tag{26}$$

$$\left. - \frac{1}{(\pi_2 - \pi_1)} \int_{\pi_1}^{p\pi_2 - (1-p)\pi_1} \mathcal{F}(s) \,_{\pi_1}d_{p,q}s \right|$$

$$\leq pq(\pi_2 - \pi_1) \int_0^{\frac{p}{[2]_{p,q}}} \left| s - \frac{1}{[6]_{p,q}} \right| |_{\pi_1}D_{p,q}\mathcal{F}(s\pi_2 + (1-s)\pi_1)| \, d_{p,q}s$$

$$+ pq(\pi_2 - \pi_1) \int_{\frac{p}{[2]_{p,q}}}^{1} \left| s - \frac{[5]_{p,q}}{[6]_{p,q}} \right| |_{\pi_1}D_{p,q}\mathcal{F}(s\pi_2 + (1-s)\pi_1)| \, d_{p,q}s$$

Using the convexity of $|_{\pi_1}D_{p,q}\mathcal{F}|$, we may calculate integrals on the right-hand side of (26) as follows:

$$\int_0^{\frac{p}{[2]_{p,q}}} \left| s - \frac{1}{[6]_{p,q}} \right| |_{\pi_1}D_{p,q}\mathcal{F}(s\pi_2 + (1-s)\pi_1)| \, d_{p,q}s$$

$$\leq |_{\pi_1}D_{p,q}\mathcal{F}(\pi_2)| \int_0^{\frac{p}{[2]_{p,q}}} s \left| s - \frac{1}{[6]_{p,q}} \right| d_{p,q}s + |_{\pi_1}D_{p,q}\mathcal{F}(\pi_1)| \int_0^{\frac{p}{[2]_{p,q}}} (1-s) \left| s - \frac{1}{[6]_{p,q}} \right| d_{p,q}s.$$

When we apply the equality (12) idea to the aforementioned post-quantum integrals, we obtain

$$\int_0^{\frac{p}{[2]_{p,q}}} s \left| s - \frac{1}{[6]_{p,q}} \right| d_{p,q}s = \int_0^{\frac{1}{[6]_{p,q}}} s\left(\frac{1}{[6]_{p,q}} - s\right) d_{p,q}s + \int_{\frac{1}{[6]_{p,q}}}^{\frac{p}{[2]_{p,q}}} s\left(s - \frac{1}{[6]_{p,q}}\right) d_{p,q}s$$

$$= 2\int_0^{\frac{1}{[6]_{p,q}}} s\left(\frac{1}{[6]_{p,q}} - s\right) d_{p,q}s + \int_0^{\frac{p}{[2]_{p,q}}} s\left(s - \frac{1}{[6]_{p,q}}\right) d_{p,q}s$$

$$= \frac{2[2]_{p,q}^2\left([3]_{p,q} - [2]_{p,q}\right) + p^2[6]_{p,q}^2\left(p[6]_{p,q} - [3]_{p,q}\right)}{[2]_{p,q}^3[3]_{p,q}[6]_{p,q}^3}$$

193

and

$$\int_0^{\frac{p}{[2]_{p,q}}} (1-s) \left| s - \frac{1}{[6]_{p,q}} \right| d_{p,q}s$$

$$= \int_0^{\frac{1}{[6]_{p,q}}} (1-s) \left(\frac{1}{[6]_{p,q}} - s \right) d_{p,q}s + \int_{\frac{1}{[6]_{p,q}}}^{\frac{p}{[2]_{p,q}}} (1-s) \left(s - \frac{1}{[6]_{p,q}} \right) d_{p,q}s$$

$$= 2\int_0^{\frac{1}{[6]_{p,q}}} (1-s) \left(\frac{1}{[6]_{p,q}} - s \right) d_{p,q}s + \int_0^{\frac{p}{[2]_{p,q}}} (1-s) \left(s - \frac{1}{[6]_{p,q}} \right) d_{p,q}s$$

$$= 2\frac{[2]_{p,q}[3]_{p,q}[6]_{p,q} - [3]_{p,q}[6]_{p,q} - [3]_{p,q} + [2]_{p,q}}{[2]_{p,q}[3]_{p,q}[6]_{p,q}^3}$$

$$+ \left(\frac{p^2[3]_{p,q}[6]_{p,q} - p[2]_{p,q}^2[3]_{p,q} - p^3[6]_{p,q} + p^2[3]_{p,q}}{[2]_{p,q}^3[3]_{p,q}[6]_{p,q}} \right).$$

Thus, we obtain

$$\int_0^{\frac{p}{[2]_{p,q}}} \left| s - \frac{1}{[6]_{p,q}} \right| |\pi_1 D_{p,q} \mathcal{F}(s\pi_2 + (1-s)\pi_1)| d_{p,q}s \quad (27)$$

$$\leq |\pi_1 D_{p,q} \mathcal{F}(\pi_2)| \left(\frac{2[2]_{p,q}^2 \left([3]_{p,q} - [2]_{p,q} \right) + p^2[6]_{p,q}^2 \left(p[6]_{p,q} - [3]_{p,q} \right)}{[2]_q^3 [3]_q [6]_q^3} \right)$$

$$+ |\pi_1 D_{p,q} \mathcal{F}(\pi_1)| \left(2\frac{[2]_{p,q}[3]_{p,q}[6]_{p,q} - [3]_{p,q}[6]_{p,q} - [3]_{p,q} + [2]_{p,q}}{[2]_{p,q}[3]_{p,q}[6]_{p,q}^3} \right.$$

$$+ \left. \left(\frac{p^2[3]_{p,q}[6]_{p,q} - p[2]_{p,q}^2[3]_{p,q} - p^3[6]_{p,q} + p^2[6]_{p,q}}{[2]_{p,q}^3[3]_{p,q}[6]_{p,q}} \right) \right).$$

Similarly, we have

$$\int_{\frac{p}{[2]_{p,q}}}^1 \left| s - \frac{[5]_{p,q}}{[6]_{p,q}} \right| |\pi_1 D_{p,q} \mathcal{F}(s\pi_2 + (1-s)\pi_1)| d_{p,q}s \quad (28)$$

$$\leq |\pi_1 D_{p,q} \mathcal{F}(\pi_2)| \left(2\frac{[3]_{p,q}[5]_{p,q}^3 - [5]_{p,q}^3[2]_{p,q}}{[2]_{p,q}[3]_{p,q}[6]_{p,q}^3} + \frac{\begin{array}{c}p^3[6]_{p,q} - p^2[5]_{p,q}[3]_{p,q} + [2]_{p,q}^3[6]_{p,q} \\ -[5]_{p,q}[2]_{p,q}^2[3]_{p,q}\end{array}}{[2]_{p,q}^3[3]_{p,q}[6]_{p,q}} \right)$$

$$+ |\pi_1 D_{p,q} \mathcal{F}(\pi_1)| \left(\begin{array}{c} 2\frac{[5]_{p,q}^2[2]_{p,q}[3]_{p,q}[6]_{p,q}-[5]_{p,q}^2[3]_{p,q}[6]_{p,q}-[5]_{p,q}^3[3]_{p,q}+[5]_{p,q}^3[2]_{p,q}}{[2]_{p,q}[3]_{p,q}[6]_{p,q}^3} \\ -\left[\frac{p[5]_{p,q}[2]_{p,q}^2[3]_{p,q} - p^2[3]_{p,q}[6]_{p,q} - p^2[5]_{p,q}[3]_{p,q} + p^3[6]_{p,q}}{[2]_{p,q}^3[3]_{p,q}[6]_{p,q}} \right] \\ +\left[\frac{[3]_{p,q}[6]_{p,q} - [5]_{p,q}[2]_{p,q}[3]_{p,q} - [2]_{p,q}[6]_{p,q} + [5]_{p,q}[3]_{p,q}}{[2]_{p,q}[3]_{p,q}[6]_{p,q}} \right] \end{array} \right)$$

We obtain the inequality (25) by placing (27) and (28) in (26). This completes the proof. □

Corollary 1. In Theorem 7, if we set $p = 1$, then we have the following new Simpson's type inequality for q-integrals:

$$\left| \frac{1}{[6]_q} \left[\mathcal{F}(\pi_2) + q\left([5]_q - 1 \right) \mathcal{F}\left(\frac{\pi_2 + q\pi_1}{1+q} \right) + q\mathcal{F}(\pi_1) \right] - \frac{1}{(\pi_2 - \pi_1)} \int_{\pi_1}^{\pi_2} \mathcal{F}(s) \; _{\pi_1}d_q s \right|$$

$$\leq q(\pi_2 - \pi_1) \{ |_{\pi_1}D_q\mathcal{F}(\pi_2)| [A_1(1,q) + A_2(1,q)] + |_{\pi_1}D_q\mathcal{F}(\pi_1)| [B_1(1,q) + B_2(1,q)] \}.$$

Remark 5. In Theorem 7, if we assume $p = 1$ and later take the limit as $q \to 1^-$, then we obtain the following Simpson's type inequality:

$$\left| \frac{1}{6} \left[\mathcal{F}(\pi_1) + 4\mathcal{F}\left(\frac{\pi_1 + \pi_2}{2} \right) + \mathcal{F}(\pi_2) \right] - \frac{1}{\pi_2 - \pi_1} \int_{\pi_1}^{\pi_2} \mathcal{F}(s) ds \right|$$

$$\leq \frac{5(\pi_2 - \pi_1)}{72} [|\mathcal{F}'(\pi_1)| + |\mathcal{F}'(\pi_2)|].$$

This is proven by Alomari et al. in [2].

Now, we can see how the inequalities appear when we utilize maps with convex q^{π_2}-derivative powers in an absolute value.

Theorem 8. Assume that the conditions of Lemma 2 hold. If $|_{\pi_1}D_{p,q}\mathcal{F}|^{p_1}$ is convex on $[\pi_1, \pi_2]$ for some $p_1 > 1$, then we have following inequality for $(p,q)_{\pi_1}$-integrals:

$$\left| \frac{p}{[6]_{p,q}} \left[p^5 \mathcal{F}(\pi_2) + q\left([5]_{p,q} - 1 \right) \mathcal{F}\left(\frac{p\pi_2 + q\pi_1}{p+q} \right) + q\mathcal{F}(\pi_1) \right] \right. \quad (29)$$

$$\left. - \frac{1}{(\pi_2 - \pi_1)} \int_{\pi_1}^{p\pi_2 + (1-p)\pi_1} \mathcal{F}(s) \; _{\pi_1}d_{p,q}s \right|$$

$$\leq pq(\pi_2 - \pi_1) \left[\Theta_1^{\frac{1}{r_1}}(p,q) \right.$$

$$\times \left(\frac{p}{[2]_{p,q}^3} |_{\pi_1}D_{p,q}\mathcal{F}(\pi_2)|^{p_1} + \frac{p[2]_{p,q}^2 - p^2}{[2]_{p,q}^3} |_{\pi_1}D_{p,q}\mathcal{F}(\pi_1)|^{p_1} \right)^{\frac{1}{p_1}}$$

$$+ \Theta_2^{\frac{1}{r_1}}(p,q)$$

$$\left. \times \left(\frac{[2]_{p,q}^2 - p^2}{[2]_{p,q}^3} |_{\pi_1}D_{p,q}\mathcal{F}(\pi_2)|^{p_1} + \frac{[2]_{p,q}^3 - [2]_{p,q}^2 - p[2]_{p,q}^2 + p^2}{[2]_{p,q}^3} |_{\pi_1}D_{p,q}\mathcal{F}(\pi_1)|^{p_1} \right)^{\frac{1}{p_1}} \right],$$

where $0 < q < q \leq 1$, $\frac{1}{p_1} + \frac{1}{r_1} = 1$ and

$$\Theta_1(p,q) = \int_0^{\frac{p}{[2]_{p,q}}} \left| s - \frac{1}{[6]_{p,q}} \right|^{r_1} d_{p,q}s,$$

$$\Theta_2(p,q) = \int_{\frac{p}{[2]_{p,q}}}^{1} \left| s - \frac{[5]_q}{[6]_q} \right|^{r_1} d_{p,q}s.$$

Proof. When the integrals on the right-hand side of (26) are subjected to the well-known Hölder's inequality for post-quantum integrals, it is discovered that

$$\left| \frac{p}{[6]_{p,q}} \left[p^5 \mathcal{F}(\pi_2) - q\left([5]_{p,q} - 1\right) \mathcal{F}\left(\frac{p\pi_2 + q\pi_1}{p+q}\right) + q\mathcal{F}(\pi_1) \right] - \frac{1}{(\pi_2 - \pi_1)} \int_{\pi_1}^{p\pi_2 + (1-p)\pi_1} \mathcal{F}(s) \,_{\pi_1}d_{p,q}s \right|$$

$$\leq pq(\pi_2 - \pi_1) \left[\left(\int_0^{\frac{p}{[2]_{p,q}}} \left| s - \frac{1}{[6]_{p,q}} \right|^{r_1} d_{p,q}s \right)^{\frac{1}{r_1}} \right.$$

$$\times \left(\int_0^{\frac{p}{[2]_{p,q}}} \left| _{\pi_1}D_{p,q}\mathcal{F}(s\pi_2 + (1-s)\pi_1) \right|^{p_1} d_{p,q}s \right)^{\frac{1}{p_1}} \right]$$

$$\left[+pq(\pi_2 - \pi_1) \left(\int_{\frac{p}{[2]_{p,q}}}^1 \left| s - \frac{[5]_{p,q}}{[6]_{p,q}} \right|^{r_1} d_{p,q}s \right)^{\frac{1}{r_1}} \right.$$

$$\left. \times \left(\int_{\frac{p}{[2]_{p,q}}}^1 \left| _{\pi_1}D_{p,q}\mathcal{F}(s\pi_2 + (1-s)\pi_1) \right|^{p_1} d_{p,q}s \right)^{\frac{1}{p_1}} \right].$$

By using the convexity of $\left|_{\pi_1}D_{p,q}\mathcal{F}\right|^{p_1}$, we obtain

$$\left| \frac{p}{[6]_{p,q}} \left[p^5 \mathcal{F}(\pi_2) - q\left([5]_{p,q} - 1\right) \mathcal{F}\left(\frac{p\pi_2 + q\pi_1}{p+q}\right) + q\mathcal{F}(\pi_1) \right] \right. \tag{30}$$

$$\left. - \frac{1}{(\pi_2 - \pi_1)} \int_{\pi_1}^{p\pi_2 + (1-p)\pi_1} \mathcal{F}(s) \,_{\pi_1}d_{p,q}s \right|$$

$$\leq pq(\pi_2 - \pi_1) \left[\left(\int_0^{\frac{p}{[2]_{p,q}}} \left| s - \frac{1}{[6]_{p,q}} \right|^{r_1} d_{p,q}s \right)^{\frac{1}{r_1}} \right.$$

$$\left(\left|_{\pi_1}D_{p,q}\mathcal{F}(\pi_2)\right|^{p_1} \int_0^{\frac{p}{[2]_{p,q}}} s d_{p,q}s + \left|_{\pi_1}D_{p,q}\mathcal{F}(\pi_1)\right|^{p_1} \int_0^{\frac{p}{[2]_{p,q}}} (1-s) d_{p,q}s \right)^{\frac{1}{p_1}} \right]$$

$$\left[+pq(\pi_2 - \pi_1) \left(\int_{\frac{p}{[2]_{p,q}}}^1 \left| s - \frac{[5]_{p,q}}{[6]_{p,q}} \right|^{r_1} d_{p,q}s \right)^{\frac{1}{r_1}} \right.$$

$$\left(\left|_{\pi_1}D_{p,q}\mathcal{F}(\pi_2)\right|^{p_1} \int_{\frac{p}{[2]_{p,q}}}^1 s d_{p,q}s + \left|_{\pi_1}D_{p,q}\mathcal{F}(\pi_1)\right|^{p_1} \int_{\frac{p}{[2]_{p,q}}}^1 (1-s) d_{p,q}s \right)^{\frac{1}{p_1}} \right].$$

Using equality (12), we see that, for the other integrals on the right-hand side of (30),

$$\int_0^{\frac{p}{[2]_{p,q}}} s \, d_{p,q}s = \frac{p^2}{[2]_{p,q}^3}, \tag{31}$$

$$\int_0^{\frac{p}{[2]_{p,q}}} (1-s) d_{p,q}s = \frac{p[2]_{p,q}^2 - p^2}{[2]_{p,q}^3}. \tag{32}$$

Similarly, we obtain

$$\int_{\frac{p}{[2]_{p,q}}}^{1} s \, d_{p,q}s = \frac{[2]_{p,q}^2 - p^2}{\left([2]_{p,q}\right)^3} \qquad (33)$$

$$\int_{\frac{p}{[2]_{p,q}}}^{1} (1-s) \, d_{p,q}s = \frac{[2]_{p,q}^3 - [2]_{p,q}^2 - p[2]_{p,q}^2 + p^2}{\left([2]_{p,q}\right)^3}. \qquad (34)$$

We obtain the desired inequality (29) by inserting (31)–(34) into (30), which completes the proof. □

Corollary 2. *In Theorem 8, if we set $p = 1$, then we obtain the following new Simpson's type inequality for q-integrals:*

$$\left| \frac{1}{[6]_q} \left[\mathcal{F}(\pi_2) + q\left([5]_q - 1\right) \mathcal{F}\left(\frac{\pi_2 + q\pi_1}{1+q}\right) + q\mathcal{F}(\pi_1) \right] - \frac{1}{(\pi_2 - \pi_1)} \int_{\pi_1}^{\pi_2} \mathcal{F}(s) \, _{\pi_1}d_q s \right|$$

$$\leq q(\pi_2 - \pi_1) \left[\Theta_1^{\frac{1}{p_1}}(1,q) \right.$$

$$\times \left(\frac{1}{[2]_q^3} |_{\pi_1}D_q\mathcal{F}(\pi_2)|^{p_1} + \frac{[2]_q^2 - 1}{[2]_q^3} |_{\pi_1}D_q\mathcal{F}(\pi_1)|^{p_1} \right)^{\frac{1}{p_1}}$$

$$+ \Theta_2^{\frac{1}{p_1}}(1,q)$$

$$\times \left(\frac{[2]_q^2 - 1}{[2]_q^3} |_{\pi_1}D_q\mathcal{F}(\pi_2)|^{p_1} + \frac{[2]_q^3 - [2]_q^2 - [2]_q + 1}{[2]_q^3} |_{\pi_1}D_q\mathcal{F}(\pi_1)|^{p_1} \right)^{\frac{1}{p_1}} \right].$$

Theorem 9. *Assume that the conditions of Lemma 2 hold. If $|_{\pi_1}D_{p,q}\mathcal{F}|^{p_1}$ is convex on $[\pi_1, \pi_2]$ for some $p_1 \geq 1$, then we have following inequality for $(p,q)_{\pi_1}$-integrals:*

$$\left| \frac{p}{[6]_{p,q}} \left[p^5 \mathcal{F}(\pi_2) - q\left([5]_{p,q} - 1\right) \mathcal{F}\left(\frac{p\pi_2 + q\pi_1}{p+q}\right) + q\mathcal{F}(\pi_1) \right] \right. \qquad (35)$$

$$- \frac{1}{(\pi_2 - \pi_1)} \int_{\pi_1}^{p\pi_2 + (1-p)\pi_1} \mathcal{F}(s) \, _{\pi_1}d_{p,q}s \right|$$

$$\leq pq(\pi_2 - \pi_1) \left[\left(\frac{2([2]_{p,q} - 1)}{[2]_{p,q}[6]_{p,q}^2} + \frac{p^2[6]_{p,q} - p[2]_{p,q}^2}{[6]_{p,q}[2]_{p,q}^3} \right)^{1-\frac{1}{p_1}} \right.$$

$$\times \left(A_1(p,q) |_{\pi_1}D_{p,q}\mathcal{F}(\pi_2)|^{p_1} + B_1(p,q) |_{\pi_1}D_{p,q}\mathcal{F}(\pi_1)|^{p_1} \right)^{\frac{1}{p_1}}$$

$$+ \left(2\frac{[2]_{p,q}[5]_{p,q}^2 - [5]_{p,q}^2}{[2]_{p,q}[6]_{p,q}^2} + \frac{1}{[2]_{p,q}} - \frac{[5]_{p,q}}{[6]_{p,q}} - \frac{p[5]_{p,q}[2]_{p,q}^2 - p^2[6]_{p,q}}{[6]_{p,q}[2]_{p,q}^3} \right)^{1-\frac{1}{p_1}}$$

$$\times \left(A_2(p,q) |_{\pi_1}D_{p,q}\mathcal{F}(\pi_2)|^{p_1} + B_2(p,q) |_{\pi_1}D_{p,q}\mathcal{F}(\pi_1)|^{p_1} \right)^{\frac{1}{p_1}},$$

where $0 < q < p \leq 1$ and $A_1(p,q)$, $A_2(p,q)$, $B_1(p,q)$, $B_2(p,q)$ are given as in (21)–(24), respectively.

Proof. Using the conclusions obtained in the proof of Theorem 7 after applying the well-known power mean inequality to the integrals on the right-hand side of (26), we discover that, due to the convexity of $\left|\pi_1 D_{p,q}\mathcal{F}\right|^{p_1}$,

$$\left|\frac{p}{[6]_{p,q}}\left[p^5\mathcal{F}(\pi_2) - q\left([5]_{p,q} - 1\right)\mathcal{F}\left(\frac{p\pi_2 + q\pi_1}{p+q}\right) + q\mathcal{F}(\pi_1)\right]\right.$$
$$\left. - \frac{1}{(\pi_2 - \pi_1)}\int_{\pi_1}^{p\pi_2+(1-p)\pi_1}\mathcal{F}(s)\,\pi_1 d_{p,q}s\right| \tag{36}$$

$$\leq pq(\pi_2 - \pi_1)\left[\left(\int_0^{\frac{p}{[2]_{p,q}}}\left|s - \frac{1}{[6]_{p,q}}\right|d_{p,q}s\right)^{1-\frac{1}{p_1}}\right.$$
$$\times\left(\left|\pi_1 D_{p,q}\mathcal{F}(\pi_2)\right|^{p_1}\int_0^{\frac{p}{[2]_{p,q}}}s\left|s - \frac{1}{[6]_q}\right|d_{p,q}s\right.$$
$$\left.+\left|\pi_1 D_{p,q}\mathcal{F}(\pi_1)\right|^{p_1}\int_0^{\frac{p}{[2]_{p,q}}}(1-s)\left|s - \frac{1}{[6]_{p,q}}\right|d_{p,q}s\right)^{\frac{1}{p_1}}\right]$$

$$+ pq(\pi_2 - \pi_1)\left[\left(\int_{\frac{p}{[2]_{p,q}}}^1\left|s - \frac{[5]_{p,q}}{[6]_{p,q}}\right|d_{p,q}s\right)^{1-\frac{1}{p_1}}\right.$$
$$\times\left(\left|\pi_1 D_{p,q}\mathcal{F}(\pi_2)\right|^{p_1}\int_{\frac{p}{[2]_{p,q}}}^1 s\left|s - \frac{[5]_{p,q}}{[6]_{p,q}}\right|d_{p,q}s\right.$$
$$\left.+\left|\pi_1 D_{p,q}\mathcal{F}(\pi_1)\right|^{p_1}\int_{\frac{p}{[2]_{p,q}}}^1(1-s)\left|s - \frac{[5]_{p,q}}{[6]_{p,q}}\right|d_{p,q}s\right)^{\frac{1}{p_1}}\right]$$

$$= pq(\pi_2 - \pi_1)\left[\left(\int_0^{\frac{p}{[2]_{p,q}}}\left|s - \frac{1}{[6]_{p,q}}\right|d_{p,q}s\right)^{1-\frac{1}{p_1}}\right.$$
$$\left.\times\left(A_1(p,q)\left|\pi_1 D_{p,q}\mathcal{F}(\pi_2)\right|^{p_1} + B_1(p,q)\left|\pi_1 D_{p,q}\mathcal{F}(\pi_1)\right|^{p_1}\right)^{\frac{1}{p_1}}\right]$$
$$+ pq\left[(\pi_2 - \pi_1)\left(\int_{\frac{p}{[2]_{p,q}}}^1\left|s - \frac{[5]_{p,q}}{[6]_{p,q}}\right|d_{p,q}s\right)^{1-\frac{1}{p_1}}\right.$$
$$\left.\times\left(A_2(p,q)\left|\pi_1 D_{p,q}\mathcal{F}(\pi_2)\right|^{p_1} + B_2(p,q)\left|\pi_1 D_{p,q}\mathcal{F}(\pi_1)\right|^{p_1}\right)^{\frac{1}{p_1}}\right].$$

We also observe that

$$\int_0^{\frac{p}{[2]_{p,q}}}\left|s - \frac{1}{[6]_{p,q}}\right|d_{p,q}s = 2\int_0^{\frac{1}{[6]_{p,q}}}\left(\frac{1}{[6]_{p,q}} - s\right)d_{p,q}s + \int_0^{\frac{p}{[2]_{p,q}}}\left(s - \frac{1}{[6]_{p,q}}\right)d_{p,q}s \tag{37}$$
$$= 2\frac{\left([2]_{p,q} - 1\right)}{[2]_{p,q}[6]_{p,q}^2} + \frac{p^2[6]_{p,q} - p[2]_{p,q}^2}{[6]_{p,q}[2]_{p,q}^3},$$

and by using similar operations, we have

$$\int_{\frac{p}{[2]_{p,q}}}^1\left|s - \frac{[5]_{p,q}}{[6]_{p,q}}\right|d_{p,q}s = 2\frac{[2]_{p,q}[5]_{p,q}^2 - [5]_{p,q}}{[2]_{p,q}[6]_{p,q}^2} + \frac{1}{[2]_{p,q}} - \frac{[5]_{p,q}}{[6]_{p,q}} - \frac{p[5]_{p,q}[2]_{p,q}^2 - p^2[6]_{p,q}}{[6]_{p,q}[2]_{p,q}^3}. \tag{38}$$

We obtain the needed inequality (35) by swapping (37) and (38) in (36). As a result, the proof is complete. □

Corollary 3. *In Theorem 9, if we set $p = 1$, then we obtain the following new Simpson's type inequality for the q-integral:*

$$\left| \frac{1}{[6]_q} \left[\mathcal{F}(\pi_2) - q\left([5]_q - 1\right) \mathcal{F}\left(\frac{\pi_2 + q\pi_1}{1+q}\right) + q\mathcal{F}(\pi_1) \right] - \frac{1}{(\pi_2 - \pi_1)} \int_{\pi_1}^{\pi_2} \mathcal{F}(s) \ _{\pi_1}d_q s \right|$$

$$\leq q(\pi_2 - \pi_1) \left[\left(\frac{2\left([2]_q - 1\right)}{[2]_q [6]_q^2} + \frac{[6]_q - [2]_q^2}{[6]_q [2]_q^3} \right)^{1 - \frac{1}{p_1}} \right.$$

$$\times \left(A_1(1,q) \left| \ _{\pi_1}D_q \mathcal{F}(\pi_2) \right|^{p_1} + B_1(1,q) \left| \ _{\pi_1}D_q \mathcal{F}(\pi_1) \right|^{p_1} \right)^{\frac{1}{p_1}}$$

$$+ \left(2\frac{[2]_q [5]_q^2 - [5]_q^2}{[2]_q [6]_q^2} + \frac{1}{[2]_q} - \frac{[5]_q}{[6]_q} - \frac{[5]_q [2]_q^2 - [6]_q}{[6]_q [2]_q^3} \right)^{1 - \frac{1}{p_1}}$$

$$\left. \times \left(A_2(1,q) \left| \ _{\pi_1}D_q \mathcal{F}(\pi_2) \right|^{p_1} + B_2(1,q) \left| \ _{\pi_1}D_q \mathcal{F}(\pi_1) \right|^{p_1} \right)^{\frac{1}{p_1}} \right].$$

Remark 6. *In Theorem 9, if we set $p = 1$ and later take the limit as $q \to 1^-$, then we have the following Simpson's type inequality:*

$$\left| \frac{1}{6} \left[\mathcal{F}(\pi_1) + 4\mathcal{F}\left(\frac{\pi_1 + \pi_2}{2}\right) + \mathcal{F}(\pi_2) \right] - \frac{1}{\pi_2 - \pi_1} \int_{\pi_1}^{\pi_2} \mathcal{F}(s) ds \right|$$

$$\leq \frac{1}{(1296)^{\frac{1}{p_1}}} \left(\frac{5}{72} \right)^{1 - \frac{1}{p_1}} (\pi_2 - \pi_1)$$

$$\times \left[61|\mathcal{F}'(\pi_1)|^{p_1} + 29|\mathcal{F}'(\pi_2)|^{p_1} \right]^{\frac{1}{p_1}} + \left[29|\mathcal{F}'(\pi_1)|^{p_1} + 61|\mathcal{F}'(\pi_2)|^{p_1} \right]^{\frac{1}{p_1}}.$$

This is given by Alomari et al. in [2].

6. Conclusions

In this investigation, we have proven different variants of Simpson's formula type inequalities for (p,q)-differentiable convex functions via post-quantum calculus. We conclude that the findings of this research are universal in nature and contribute to inequality theory, as well as applications in quantum boundary value problems, quantum mechanics, and special relativity theory for determining solution uniqueness. The findings of this study can be utilized in symmetry. Results for the case of symmetric functions can be obtained by applying the concept in Remark 4, which will be studied in future work. Future researchers will be able to obtain similar inequalities for different types of convexity and co-ordinated convexity in their future work, which is a new and important problem.

Author Contributions: All authors contributed equally in the preparation of the present work. Theorems and corollaries: M.J.V.-C., M.A.A., S.Q., I.B.S., S.J. and A.M.; review of the articles and books cited: M.J.V.-C., M.A.A., S.Q., I.B.S., S.J. and A.M.; formal analysis: M.J.V.-C., M.A.A., S.Q., I.B.S., S.J. and A.M.; writing—original draft preparation and writing—review and editing: M.J.V.-C., M.A.A., S.Q., I.B.S., S.J. and A.M. All authors have read and agreed to the published version of the manuscript.

Funding: This research was funded by the Science, Research and Innovation Promotion Fund under the Basic Research Plan–Suan Dusit University. Contract no.65-FF-010.

Institutional Review Board Statement: Not applicable.

Informed Consent Statement: Not applicable.

Data Availability Statement: Not applicable.

Acknowledgments: Miguel Vivas-Cortez wishes to thank to Dirección de Investigación from Pontificia Universidad Católica del Ecuador. In addition, all the authors wish to thank those appointed to review this article and the editorial team of *Symmetry*.

Conflicts of Interest: The authors declare no conflict of interest.

References

1. Dragomir, S.S.; Agarwal, R.P.; Cerone, P. On Simpson's inequality and applications. *J. Inequal. Appl.* **2000**, *5*, 533–579. [CrossRef]
2. Alomari, M.; Darus, M.; Dragomir, S.S. New inequalities of Simpson's type for s-convex functions with applications. *RGMIA Res Rep Coll.* **2009**, 2.
3. Sarikaya, M.Z.; Set, E.; Özdemir, M.E. On new inequalities of Simpson's type for convex functions. *RGMIA Res. Rep. Coll.* **2010**, *13*, 2.
4. Erden, S.; Iftikhar, S.; Delavar, M.R.; Kumam, P.; Thounthong, P.; Kumam, W. On generalizations of some inequalities for convex functions via quantum integrals. *RACSAM* **2020**, *114*, 1–15. [CrossRef]
5. Iftikhar, S.; Erden, S.; Kumam, P.; Awan, M.U. Local fractional Newton's inequalities involving generalized harmonic convex functions. *Adv. Differ. Equ.* **2020**, *2020*, 1–14.
6. Özdemir, M.E.; Akdemir, A.O.; Kavurmaci, H.; Avci, M. On the Simpson's inequality for co-ordinated convex functions. *arXiv* **2010**, arXiv:1101.0075.
7. Ali, M.A.; Budak, H.; Abbas, M.; Chu, Y.-M. Quantum Hermite–Hadamard-type inequalities for functions with convex absolute values of second q^{π_2}-derivatives. *Adv. Differ. Equ.* **2021**, *2021*, 1–12. [CrossRef]
8. Ali, M.A.; Alp, N.; Budak, H.; Chu, Y.; Zhang, Z. On some new quantum midpoint type inequalities for twice quantum differentiable convex functions. *Open Math.* **2021**, *19*, 427–439. [CrossRef]
9. Alp, N.; Sarikaya, M.Z.; Kunt, M. q-Hermite Hadamard inequalities and quantum estimates for midpoint type inequalities via convex and quasi-convex functions. *J. King Saud Univ. -Sci.* **2018**, *30*, 193–203. [CrossRef]
10. Alp, N.; Sarikaya, M.Z. Hermite Hadamard's type inequalities for co-ordinated convex functions on quantum integral. *Appl. Math. E-Notes* **2020**, *20*, 341–356.
11. Bermudo, S.; Kórus, P.; Valdés, J.N. On q-Hermite-Hadamard inequalities for general convex functions. *Acta Math. Hung.* **2020**, *162*, 364–374. [CrossRef]
12. Budak, H. Some trapezoid and midpoint type inequalities for newly defined quantum integrals. *Proyecciones* **2021**, *40*, 199–215. [CrossRef]
13. Budak, H.; Ali, M.A.; Tarhanaci, M. Some new quantum Hermite-Hadamard-like inequalities for coordinated convex functions. *J. Optim. Theory Appl.* **2020**, *186*, 899–910. [CrossRef]
14. Jhanthanam, S.; Tariboon, J.; Ntouyas, S.K.; Nonlapon, K. On q-Hermite-Hadamard inequalities for differentiable convex functions. *Mathematics* **2019**, *7*, 632. [CrossRef]
15. Kalsoom, H.; Rashid, S.; Idrees, M.; Safdar, F.; Akram, S.; Baleanu, D.; Chu, Y.-M. Post quantum inequalities of Hermite-Hadamard type associated with co-ordinated higher-order generalized strongly pre-invex and quasi-pre-invex mappings. *Symmetry* **2020**, *12*, 443. [CrossRef]
16. Latif, M.A.; Dragomir, S.S.; Momoniat, E. Some q-analogues of Hermite-Hadamard inequality of functions of two variables on finite rectangles in the plane. *J. King Saud-Univ. -Sci.* **2017**, *29*, 263–273. [CrossRef]
17. Liu, W.; Hefeng, Z. Some quantum estimates of Hermite-Hadamard inequalities for convex functions. *J. Appl. Anal. Comput.* **2016**, *7*, 501–522.
18. Noor, M.A.; Noor, K.I.; Awan, M.U. Some quantum estimates for Hermite-Hadamard inequalities. *Appl. Math. Comput.* **2015**, *251*, 675–679. [CrossRef]
19. Sial, I.B.; Ali, M.A.; Murtaza, G.; Ntouyas, S.K.; Soontharanon, J.; Thanin, S. On Some New Inequalities of Hermite–Hadamard Midpoint and Trapezoid Type for Preinvex Functions in (p,q)-Calculus. *Symmetry* **2021**, *13*, 1864. [CrossRef]
20. Sitho, S.; Ali, M.A.; Budak, H.; Ntouyas, S.K. Tariboon, J.; Trapezoid and Midpoint Type Inequalities for Preinvex Functions via Quantum Calculus. *Mathematics* **2021**, *9*, 1996. [CrossRef]
21. Wannalookkhee, F.; Nonlaopon, K.; Tariboon, J.; Ntouyas, S.K. On Hermite-Hadamard type inequalities for coordinated convex functions via (p,q)-calculus. *Mathematics* **2021**, *9*, 698. [CrossRef]
22. Noor, M.A.; Noor, K.I.; Awan, M.U. Some quantum integral inequalities via preinvex functions. *Appl. Math. Comput.* **2015**, *269*, 242–251. [CrossRef]
23. Nwaeze, E.R.; Tameru, A.M. New parameterized quantum integral inequalities via η-quasiconvexity. *Adv. Differ. Equ.* **2019**, *2019*, 1–12. [CrossRef]
24. Khan, M.A.; Noor, M.; Nwaeze, E.R.; Chu, Y.-M. Quantum Hermite–Hadamard inequality by means of a Green function. *Adv. Differ. Equ.* **2020**, *2020*, 1–20.

25. Ali, M.A.; Budak, H.; Zhang, Z.; Yildrim, H. Some new Simpson's type inequalities for co-ordinated convex functions in quantum calculus. *Math. Meth. Appl. Sci.* **2021**, *44*, 4515–4540. [CrossRef]
26. Ali, M.A.; Abbas, M.; Budak, H.; Agarwal, P.; Murtaza, G.; Chu, Y. New quantum boundaries for quantum Simpson's and quantum Newton's type inequalities for preinvex functions. *Adv. Differ. Equ.* **2021**, *2021*, 1–21. [CrossRef]
27. Budak, H.; Erden, S.; Ali, M.A. Simpson and Newton type inequalities for convex functions via newly defined quantum integrals. *Math. Meth. Appl. Sci.* **2020**, *44*, 378–390. [CrossRef]
28. Budak, H.; Ali, M.A.; Tunç, T. Quantum Ostrowski-type integral inequalities for functions of two variables. *Math. Meth. Appl. Sci.* **2021**, *44*, 5857–5872. [CrossRef]
29. Siricharuanun, P.; Erden, S.; Ali, M.A.; Budak, H.; Chasreechai, S.; Thanin, S. Some New Simpson's and Newton's Formulas Type Inequalities for Convex Functions in Quantum Calculus. *Mathematics* **2021**, *9*, 1992. [CrossRef]
30. Vivas-Cortez, M.; Ali, M.A.; Kashuri, A.; Sial, I.B.; Zhang, Z. Some New Newton's Type Integral Inequalities for Co-Ordinated Convex Functions in Quantum Calculus. *Symmetry* **2020**, *12*, 1476. [CrossRef]
31. Ali, M.A.; Chu, Y.-M.; Budak, H.; Akkurt, A.; Yildrim, H. Quantum variant of Montgomery identity and Ostrowski-type inequalities for the mappings of two variables. *Adv. Differ. Equ.* **2021**, *2021*, 1–26. [CrossRef]
32. Ali, M.A.; Budak, H.; Akkurt, A.; Chu, Y.-M. Quantum Ostrowski type inequalities for twice quantum differentiable functions in quantum calculus. *Open Math.* **2021**, *19*, 440–449. [CrossRef]
33. Budak, H.; Ali, M.A.; Alp, N.; Chu, Y.-M. Quantum Ostrowski type integral inequalities. *J. Math. Inequal.* **2021**, in press.
34. Kunt, M.; İşcan, İ.; Alp, N.; Sarikaya, M.Z. (p,q)−Hermite-Hadamard inequalities and (p,q)−estimates for midpoint inequalities via convex quasi-convex functions. *Rev. R. Acad. Cienc. Exactas F s. Nat. Ser. A Mat. RACSAM* **2018**, *112*, 969–992. [CrossRef]
35. Vivas-Cortez, M.; Ali, M.A.; Budak, H.; Kalsoom, H.; Agarwal, P. Some New Hermite–Hadamard and Related Inequalities for Convex Functions via (p,q)-Integral. *Entropy* **2021**, *23*, 828. [CrossRef]
36. Kac, V.; Cheung, P. *Quantum Calculus*; Springer: New York, NY, USA, 2002.
37. Jackson, F.H. On a q-definite integrals. *Quarterly J. Pure Appl. Math.* **1910**, *41*, 193–203.
38. Tariboon, J.; Ntouyas, S.K. Quantum calculus on finite intervals and applications to impulsive difference equations. *Adv. Differ. Equ.* **2013**, *2013*, 1–19. [CrossRef]
39. Sadjang, P.N. On the fundamental theorem of (p,q)-calculus and some (p,q)-Taylor formulas. *Results Math.* **2018**, *73*, 1–21.
40. Tunç, M.; Göv, E. Some integral inequalities via (p,q)-calculus on finite intervals. *RGMIA Res. Rep. Coll.* **2016**, *19*, 1–12. [CrossRef]

Article

Spatial Decay Bounds for the Brinkman Fluid Equations in Double-Diffusive Convection

Xuejiao Chen [†], Yuanfei Li *,[†] and Dandan Li

School of Data Science, Guangzhou Huashang College, Guangzhou 511300, China; cxjsky@gdhsc.edu.cn (X.C.); li20201101@126.com (D.L.)
* Correspondence: 201610104816@mail.scut.edu.cn
† These authors contributed equally to this work.

Abstract: In this paper, we consider the Brinkman equations pipe flow, which includes the salinity and the temperature. Assuming that the fluid satisfies nonlinear boundary conditions at the finite end of the cylinder, using the symmetry of differential inequalities and the energy analysis methods, we establish the exponential decay estimates for homogeneous Brinkman equations. That is to prove that the solutions of the equation decay exponentially with the distance from the finite end of the cylinder. To make the estimate of decay explicit, the bound for the total energy is also derived.

Keywords: spatial decay estimates; Brinkman equations; Saint-Venant principle

1. Introduction

The Brinkman equations are one of the most important models in fluid mechanics. This model are mainly used to describe flow in a porous medium. For more details, one can refer to Nield and Bejan [1] and Straughan [2]. In the present paper, we define the Brinkman flow depending on the salinity and the temperature in a semi-infinite cylindrical pipe and derive the spatial decay properties. When the homogeneous initial-boundary conditions are applied on the lateral surface of the cylinder, We prove that the solutions of Brinkman equations decays exponentially with spatial variable.

In fact, the Brinkman equations have been studied by many papers in the literature. For example, Straughan [2] considered the mathematical properties of Brinkman equations as well as Darcy and Forchheimer equations, and stated how these equations describe the flow of porous media. Ames and Payne [3] studied the structural stability for the solutions to the viscoelasticity in an ill-posed problem. Franchi and Straughan [4] proved the structural stability for the solutions to the Brinkman equations in porous media in a bounded region. More relevant results one can see [5–10]. Paper [11] studied the double diffusive convection in porous medium and obtained the structural stability for the solutions. The continuous dependence for a thermal convection model with temperature-dependent solubility can be found in [12]. For more recent work about continuous dependence, one may refer to [13–19].

In this paper, let R be a semi-infinite cylinder and ∂R represents the boundary of R. D denotes the cross section of the cylinder with the smooth boundary ∂D (see Figure 1).

In this paper, we also use the following notations

$$R_z = \left\{(x_1, x_2, x_3) \big| (x_1, x_2) \in D, \quad x_3 > z \geq 0\right\},$$

$$D_z = \left\{(x_1, x_2, x_3) \big| (x_1, x_2) \in D, \quad x_3 = z \geq 0\right\},$$

where z is a point along the x_3 axis. Clearly, $R_0 = R$ and $D_0 = D$. Letting u_i, T, C and p denote the fluid velocity, temperature, salt concentration and pressure, respectively.

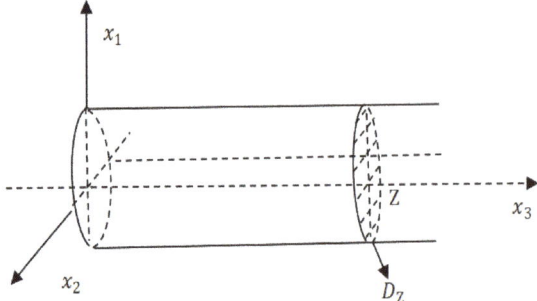

Figure 1. Cylindrical pipe.

The Brinkman equations we study can be written as [20]

$$\frac{\partial u_i}{\partial t} = \nu \Delta u_i - k_1 u_i - p_{,i} + g_i T + h_i C, \quad \text{in } R \times \{t \geq 0\}, \tag{1}$$

$$\frac{\partial T}{\partial t} + u_i \frac{\partial T}{\partial x_i} = k_2 \Delta T, \quad \text{in } R \times \{t \geq 0\}, \tag{2}$$

$$\frac{\partial C}{\partial t} + u_i \frac{\partial C}{\partial x_i} = k_3 \Delta C + \sigma \Delta T, \quad \text{in } R \times \{t \geq 0\}, \tag{3}$$

$$u_{i,i} = 0, \quad \text{in } R \times \{t \geq 0\}, \tag{4}$$

where $\nu, \sigma > 0$ denote the Brinkman coefficient, and the Soret coefficient, respectively. $k_1, k_2, k_3 > 0$. Without losing generality, we take them equal to 1. Δ is the Laplacian operator. $g_i(x)$ and $h_i(x)$ are gravity field, which are given functions. We suppose that (1)–(4) have the following initial-boundary conditions

$$u_i = 0, \quad T = C = 0, \qquad \text{on } \partial D \times \{t \geq 0\}, \tag{5}$$

$$u_i = 0, \quad T = C = 0, \qquad \text{on } R \times \{t = 0\}. \tag{6}$$

$$u_i = f_i(x_1, x_2, t), \ T = F(x_1, x_2, t), \ C = G(x_1, x_2, t), \quad \text{on } D_0 \times \{t \geq 0\}, \tag{7}$$

$$u_i, u_{i,j}, u_{i,t}, T, T_{,i}, C, C_{,i}, p = o(x_3^{-1}) \text{ uniformly in } x_1, x_2, t, \quad \text{as } x_3 \to \infty. \tag{8}$$

In (1)–(8) and in the following, the usual summation convention is employed with repeated Latin subscripts summed from 1 to 3 and repeat Greek subscript summed from 1 to 2. The comma is used to indicate partial differentiation, i.e., $u_{i,j} u_{i,j} = \sum_{i,j=1}^{3} \left(\frac{\partial u_i}{\partial x_j} \right)^2$, $\varphi_{\alpha,\beta} \varphi_{\alpha,\beta} = \sum_{\alpha,\beta=1}^{2} \left(\frac{\partial \varphi_\alpha}{\partial x_\beta} \right)^2$.

The purpose of this paper is to consider the spatial decay properties of the Equations (1)–(8) in a semi-infinite cylindrical pipe by using the symmetry of differential inequalities, that is, to prove that the solutions of the equations decay exponentially with the distance from the finite end of the cylindrical pipe.

In Section 2, some auxiliary inequalities are presented. We establish some useful lemmas in Section 3. The spatial exponential decay estimate for the solution is established in Section 4. Finally, in Section 5 we derive the bounds for the total energies.

2. Auxiliary Results

In this paper, we will use some inequalities in the following sections. Thus, we firstly list them as follows.

Lemma 1. Let D be a plane domain D with the smooth boundary ∂D. If $w = 0$ on ∂D, then

$$\int_D w_{,\alpha} w_{,\alpha} dA \geq \lambda_1 \int_{R_z} w^2 dx, \tag{9}$$

where λ_1 is the smallest eigenvalue of the problem

$$\Delta \phi + \lambda \phi = 0 \quad \text{in } D,$$

$$\phi = 0 \quad \text{on } \partial D.$$

Many papers have studied this inequality, e.g., one may see [21,22].

A representation theorem will be also used in next sections. We write this theorem as

Lemma 2. Let D be a plane Lipschitz bound region and w be a differential function in D which satisfies $\int_D w dA = 0$, then there exists a vector function $\varphi_\alpha(x_1, x_2)$ such that

$$\varphi_{\alpha,\alpha} = w \quad \text{in } D,$$

$$\varphi_\alpha = 0 \quad \text{on } \partial D,$$

and a positive constant Λ depending only on the geometry of D such that

$$\int_D \varphi_{\alpha,\beta} \varphi_{\alpha,\beta} dA \leq \Lambda \int_D \varphi_{\alpha,\alpha}^2 dA. \tag{10}$$

The Lemma 2 was proofed by Babuška and Aziz [23] and Horgan and Wheeler [24] have used the Lemma 1 to viscous flow problems. The explicit upper bound of Λ can be found in Horgan and Payne [25]. In this paper, this Lemma 2 is used to eliminate the pressure function difference terms p, since we can prove that u_3 satisfy the hypothesis of this Lemma 2 later.

If $w \in C_0^1(D)$ and $w \in C_0^1(R)$, the following Sobolev inequalities hold

$$\int_D w^4 dA \leq \frac{1}{2} \left[\int_D w^2 dA \right] \left[\int_D w_{,\alpha} w_{,\alpha} dA \right], \tag{11}$$

$$\int_{R_z} w^6 dx \leq \Omega \left[\int_{R_z} w_{,i} w_{,i} dx \right]^3. \tag{12}$$

For (11), we assume that $w \to 0$ as $x_3 \to \infty$. Payne [26] has given the derivation of (12). For a special case of the results one can see [27,28]. They have obtained the optimal value of Ω

$$\Omega = \frac{1}{27} \left(\frac{3}{4} \right)^4.$$

In the following, we also use the following lemma.

Lemma 3. If $w \in C^1(R_z)$, $w_i \big|_{\partial D} = 0$ and $w_i \to 0$ as $x_3 \to \infty$, then

$$\int_{D_z} \left(w_i w_i \right)^2 dA \leq 4\sqrt{\Omega} \left[\int_{R_z} w_{i,j} w_{i,j} dx \right]^2. \tag{13}$$

We will also use the following lemmas which were derived in [29].

Lemma 4. Let that the function φ is the solution of the problem

$$\Delta \varphi = 0 \quad \text{in } R_z,$$
$$\frac{\partial \varphi}{\partial n} = 0 \quad \text{on } \partial D_z, \tag{14}$$
$$\frac{\partial \varphi}{\partial n} = g \quad \text{in } D_z,$$

where $\int_{D_z} g dA = 0$. Then

$$\int_{D_z} \varphi_{,\alpha} \varphi_{,\alpha} dA = \int_{D_z} g^2 dA, \tag{15}$$

$$\int_{R_z} \varphi_{,i} \varphi_{,i} dA = \frac{1}{\sqrt{\mu}} \int_{D_z} g^2 dA, \tag{16}$$

3. Some Useful Lemmas

In this section, we derive some useful lemmas which will be used in next section. First, we define a weighted energy expression

$$\begin{aligned}
E(z,t) &= k \int_0^t \int_{R_z} (\xi - z) u_{i,\eta} u_{i,\eta} dx d\eta + \nu \int_0^t \int_{R_z} (\xi - z) u_{i,j} u_{i,j} dx d\eta \\
&+ \rho_1 \int_0^t \int_{R_z} (\xi - z) T_{,j} T_{,j} dx d\eta + \rho_2 \int_0^t \int_{R_z} (\xi - z) C_{,j} C_{,j} dx d\eta \\
&= E_1(z,t) + E_2(z,t) + E_3(z,t) + E_4(z,t),
\end{aligned} \tag{17}$$

where k, ρ_1, ρ_2 are positive parameters and $\xi > z > 0$.

By using the divergence theorem and Equations (1) and (4), we obtain

$$\begin{aligned}
E_1(z,t) &= k \int_0^t \int_{R_z} (\xi - z) u_{i,\eta} \Big[\nu \Delta u_i - u_i - p_{,i} + g_i T + h_i C \Big] dx d\eta \\
&= k\nu \int_0^t \int_{R_z} u_{i,\eta} u_{i,3} dx d\eta + k \int_0^t \int_{R_z} u_{3,\eta} p dx d\eta \\
&\quad + k \int_0^t \int_{R_z} (\xi - z) u_{i,\eta} g_i T dx d\eta + k \int_0^t \int_{R_z} (\xi - z) u_{i,\eta} h_i C dx d\eta \\
&\quad - k\nu \int_{R_z} (\xi - z) u_{i,j} u_{i,j} dx \Big|_{\eta=t} - k \int_{R_z} (\xi - z) u_i u_i dx \Big|_{\eta=t} \\
&\doteq \sum_{i=1}^4 A_i \\
&\quad - \frac{1}{2} k\nu \int_{R_z} (\xi - z) u_{i,j} u_{i,j} dx \Big|_{\eta=t} - \frac{1}{2} k \int_{R_z} (\xi - z) u_i u_i dx \Big|_{\eta=t}.
\end{aligned} \tag{18}$$

Using the Schwarz inequality, the arithmetic geometric mean inequality and (9), we can obtain

$$\begin{aligned}
A_1 &\leq k\nu \left[\int_0^t \int_{R_z} u_{i,\eta} u_{i,\eta} dx d\eta \int_0^t \int_{R_z} u_{i,3} u_{i,3} dx d\eta \right]^{\frac{1}{2}} \\
&\leq \frac{\sqrt{k\nu}}{2} \left[k \int_0^t \int_{R_z} u_{i,\eta} u_{i,\eta} dx d\eta + \nu \int_0^t \int_{R_z} u_{i,3} u_{i,3} dx d\eta \right],
\end{aligned} \tag{19}$$

$$\begin{aligned}
A_3 &\leq \frac{k}{\sqrt{\lambda_1}} \left[\int_0^t \int_{R_z} (\xi - z) u_{i,\eta} u_{i,\eta} dx d\eta \int_0^t \int_{R_z} (\xi - z) T_{,\alpha} T_{,\alpha} dx d\eta \right]^{\frac{1}{2}} \\
&\leq \frac{\varepsilon_1}{2} k \int_0^t \int_{R_z} (\xi - z) u_{i,\eta} u_{i,\eta} dx d\eta + \frac{k \delta_1^2}{2 \lambda_1 \varepsilon_1} \int_0^t \int_{R_z} (\xi - z) T_{,\alpha} T_{,\alpha} dx d\eta,
\end{aligned} \tag{20}$$

and

$$A_4 \leq \frac{\varepsilon_2}{2}k\int_0^t\int_{R_z}(\xi-z)u_{i,\eta}u_{i,\eta}dxd\eta + \frac{k\delta_2^2}{2\lambda_1\varepsilon_2}\int_0^t\int_{R_z}(\xi-z)C_{,\alpha}C_{,\alpha}dxd\eta, \tag{21}$$

where $\varepsilon_1, \varepsilon_2 > 0$ will be determined later and

$$\delta_1^2 = \max_D(g_ig_i), \quad \delta_2^2 = \max_D(h_ih_i), \tag{22}$$

We note that for any $z^* > 0$, using (4) and (5),

$$\int_{D_z} u_{3,\eta}dA = \int_{D_{z^*}} u_{3,\eta}dA - \int_z^{z^*}\int_{D_\xi} u_{3,3\eta}dAd\xi$$

$$= \int_{D_{z^*}} u_{3,\eta}dA + \int_z^{z^*}\int_{D_\xi} u_{\alpha,\alpha\eta}dAd\xi$$

$$= \int_{D_{z^*}} u_{3,\eta}dA.$$

Since

$$\int_{D_0} f_{3,\eta}dA = 0, \quad t \geq 0, \tag{23}$$

then,

$$\int_{D_z} u_{3,\eta}dA = 0.$$

Under this assumption, using Lemma 2, there exist vector functions (φ_1, φ_2) such that

$$\varphi_{\alpha,\alpha} = u_{3,\eta} \quad \text{in } D, \quad \varphi_\alpha = 0 \quad \text{on } \partial D. \tag{24}$$

Hence we have

$$A_2 = k\int_0^t\int_{R_z}\varphi_{\alpha,\alpha}pdxd\eta = -k\int_0^t\int_{R_z}\varphi_\alpha p_{,\alpha}dxd\eta$$

$$= k\int_0^t\int_{R_z}\varphi_\alpha\left[u_{\alpha,\eta} - \nu\Delta u_\alpha + u_\alpha - g_\alpha T - h_\alpha C\right]dxd\eta$$

$$= k\int_0^t\int_{R_z}\varphi_\alpha u_{\alpha,\eta}dxd\eta + k\nu\int_0^t\int_{R_z}\varphi_{\alpha,\beta}u_{\alpha,\beta}dxd\eta \tag{25}$$

$$+ k\nu\int_0^t\int_{D_z}\varphi_\alpha u_{\alpha,3}dxd\eta + k\int_0^t\int_{R_z}\varphi_\alpha u_\alpha dxd\eta$$

$$- k\int_0^t\int_{R_z}\varphi_\alpha g_\alpha Tdxd\eta - k\int_0^t\int_{R_z}\varphi_\alpha h_\alpha Cdxd\eta$$

$$= A_{21} + A_{22} + A_{23} + A_{24} + A_{25} + A_{26}.$$

Using the Schwarz, Poincaré and the AG mean inequalities, (9) and (10), we can obtain

$$A_{21} \leq \left(\int_0^t \int_{R_z} \varphi_\alpha \varphi_\alpha dxd\eta\right)^{\frac{1}{2}} \left(\int_0^t \int_{R_z} u_{\alpha,\eta} u_{\alpha,\eta} dxd\eta\right)^{\frac{1}{2}}$$

$$\leq \frac{1}{\sqrt{\lambda_1}} \left(\int_0^t \int_{R_z} \varphi_{\alpha,\beta} \varphi_{\alpha,\beta} dxd\eta\right)^{\frac{1}{2}} \left(\int_0^t \int_{R_z} u_{\alpha,\eta} u_{\alpha,\eta} dxd\eta\right)^{\frac{1}{2}}$$

$$\leq \frac{\Lambda^{\frac{1}{2}}}{\sqrt{\lambda_1}} \left(\int_0^t \int_{R_z} u_3^2 d\eta\right)^{\frac{1}{2}} \left(\int_0^t \int_{R_z} u_{\alpha,\eta} u_{\alpha,\eta} dxd\eta\right)^{\frac{1}{2}}$$

$$\leq \frac{k\Lambda^{\frac{1}{2}}}{2\sqrt{\lambda_1}} \int_0^t \int_{R_z} u_{i,\eta} u_{i,\eta} dxd\eta, \tag{26}$$

$$A_{22} \leq k\nu \left(\int_0^t \int_{R_z} \varphi_{\alpha,\beta} \varphi_{\alpha,\beta} dxd\eta\right)^{\frac{1}{2}} \left(\int_0^t \int_{R_z} u_{\alpha,\beta} u_{\alpha,\beta} dxd\eta\right)^{\frac{1}{2}}$$

$$\leq k\nu \Lambda^{\frac{1}{2}} \left(\int_0^t \int_{R_z} u_{3,\eta}^2 dxd\eta\right)^{\frac{1}{2}} \left(\int_0^t \int_{R_z} u_{\alpha,\beta} u_{\alpha,\beta} dxd\eta\right)^{\frac{1}{2}}$$

$$\leq \frac{k\nu\Lambda^{\frac{1}{2}}}{2} \int_0^t \int_{R_z} u_{3,\eta}^2 dxd\eta + \frac{k\nu\Lambda^{\frac{1}{2}}}{2} \int_0^t \int_{R_z} u_{\alpha,\beta} u_{\alpha,\beta} dxd\eta, \tag{27}$$

$$A_{23} \leq k\nu \left(\int_0^t \int_{D_z} \varphi_\alpha \varphi_\alpha dxd\eta\right)^{\frac{1}{2}} \left(\int_0^t \int_{D_z} u_{\alpha,3} u_{\alpha,3} dxd\eta\right)^{\frac{1}{2}}$$

$$\leq \frac{k\nu\Lambda^{\frac{1}{2}}}{\sqrt{\lambda_1}} \left(\int_0^t \int_{D_z} u_{3,\eta}^2 dxd\eta\right)^{\frac{1}{2}} \left(\int_0^t \int_{D_z} u_{\alpha,3} u_{\alpha,3} dxd\eta\right)^{\frac{1}{2}}$$

$$\leq \frac{k\nu\Lambda^{\frac{1}{2}}}{2\sqrt{\lambda_1}} \int_0^t \int_{D_z} u_{3,\eta}^2 dxd\eta + \frac{k\nu\Lambda^{\frac{1}{2}}}{2\sqrt{\lambda_1}} \int_0^t \int_{D_z} u_{\alpha,3} u_{\alpha,3} dxd\eta, \tag{28}$$

$$A_{24} \leq k \left(\int_0^t \int_{R_z} \varphi_\alpha \varphi_\alpha dxd\eta\right)^{\frac{1}{2}} \left(\int_0^t \int_{R_z} u_\alpha u_\alpha dxd\eta\right)^{\frac{1}{2}}$$

$$\leq \frac{k\Lambda^{\frac{1}{2}}}{\lambda_1} \left(\int_0^t \int_{R_z} u_{3,\eta}^2 dxd\eta\right)^{\frac{1}{2}} \left(\int_0^t \int_{R_z} u_{\alpha,\beta} u_{\alpha,\beta} dxd\eta\right)^{\frac{1}{2}}$$

$$\leq \frac{k\Lambda^{\frac{1}{2}}}{2\lambda_1} \int_0^t \int_{R_z} u_{3,\eta}^2 dxd\eta + \frac{k\Lambda^{\frac{1}{2}}}{2\lambda_1} \int_0^t \int_{R_z} u_{\alpha,\beta} u_{\alpha,\beta} dxd\eta, \tag{29}$$

$$A_{25} \leq k \left(\int_0^t \int_{R_z} \varphi_\alpha \varphi_\alpha dxd\eta\right)^{\frac{1}{2}} \left(\int_0^t \int_{R_z} g_\alpha g_\alpha T^2 dxd\eta\right)^{\frac{1}{2}}$$

$$\leq \frac{k\delta_1 \Lambda^{\frac{1}{2}}}{\lambda_1} \left(\int_0^t \int_{R_z} u_{3,\eta}^2 dxd\eta\right)^{\frac{1}{2}} \left(\int_0^t \int_{R_z} T_{,i} T_{,i} dxd\eta\right)^{\frac{1}{2}}$$

$$\leq \frac{k\delta_1 \Lambda^{\frac{1}{2}}}{2\lambda_1} \int_0^t \int_{R_z} u_{3,\eta}^2 dxd\eta + \frac{k\delta_1 \Lambda^{\frac{1}{2}}}{2\lambda_1} \int_0^t \int_{R_z} T_{,i} T_{,i} dxd\eta, \tag{30}$$

$$A_{26} \leq \frac{k\delta_2 \Lambda^{\frac{1}{2}}}{2\lambda_1} \int_0^t \int_{R_z} u_{3,\eta}^2 dxd\eta + \frac{k\delta_2 \Lambda^{\frac{1}{2}}}{2\lambda_1} \int_0^t \int_{R_z} C_{,i} C_{,i} dxd\eta. \tag{31}$$

Inserting (26)–(31) into (25), then (19)–(21) and (25) into (18), and choosing $\varepsilon_1 = \varepsilon_2 = \frac{1}{2}$, we obtain the following lemma.

Lemma 5. Let u, T, C, p be solutions of Equations (1)–(8) with $g, h \in L_\infty(R \times \{t > 0\})$ and $\int_D f_3 dA = 0$. Then

$$E_1(z,t) + kv \int_{R_z} (\xi - z) u_{i,j} u_{i,j} dx \bigg|_{\eta=t} + k \int_{R_z} (\xi - z) u_i u_i dx \bigg|_{\eta=t}$$

$$\leq a_1 k \int_0^t \int_{R_z} u_{i,\eta} u_{i,\eta} dx d\eta + a_2 v \int_0^t \int_{R_z} u_{i,j} u_{i,j} dx d\eta$$

$$+ \frac{k\delta_1 \Lambda^{\frac{1}{2}}}{\lambda_1} \int_0^t \int_{R_z} T_{,i} T_{,i} dx d\eta + \frac{k\delta_2 \Lambda^{\frac{1}{2}}}{\lambda_1} \int_0^t \int_{R_z} C_{,i} C_{,i} dx d\eta$$

$$+ \frac{kv \Lambda^{\frac{1}{2}}}{2\sqrt{\lambda_1}} \int_0^t \int_{D_z} u_{3,\eta}^2 dx d\eta + \frac{kv \Lambda^{\frac{1}{2}}}{2\sqrt{\lambda_1}} \int_0^t \int_{D_z} u_{\alpha,3} u_{\alpha,3} dx d\eta$$

$$+ \frac{2k\delta_1^2}{\lambda_1} \int_0^t \int_{R_z} (\xi - z) T_{,\alpha} T_{,\alpha} dx d\eta + \frac{2k\delta_2^2}{\lambda_1} \int_0^t \int_{R_z} (\xi - z) C_{,\alpha} C_{,\alpha} dx d\eta,$$

where

$$a_1 = \sqrt{kv} + \frac{\Lambda^{\frac{1}{2}}}{\sqrt{\lambda_1}} + v \Lambda^{\frac{1}{2}} + \frac{\Lambda^{\frac{1}{2}}}{\lambda_1} + \frac{2\delta_1 \Lambda^{\frac{1}{2}}}{\lambda_1} + \frac{2\delta_2 \Lambda^{\frac{1}{2}}}{\lambda_1},$$

$$a_2 = \frac{\sqrt{kv}}{2} + \frac{k\Lambda^{\frac{1}{2}}}{2} + \frac{k\Lambda^{\frac{1}{2}}}{2v\sqrt{\lambda_1}}.$$

Similar to Lemma 5, for $E_2(z,t)$ we can obtain the following lemma.

Lemma 6. Let u, T, C, p be solutions of Equations (1)–(8) with $g, h \in L_\infty(R \times \{t > 0\})$ and $\int_D f_3 dA = 0$. Then

$$E_2(z,t) + \frac{1}{2} \int_0^t \int_{R_z} (\xi - z) u_i u_i dx d\eta + \frac{1}{2} \int_{R_z} (\xi - z) u_i u_i dx \bigg|_{\eta=t}$$

$$\leq a_3 \int_0^t \int_{R_z} u_{i,j} u_{i,j} dx d\eta + \frac{v}{2} \int_0^t \int_{R_z} u_i u_i dx d\eta$$

$$+ \frac{\Lambda^{\frac{1}{2}}}{2\lambda_1} \int_0^t \int_{R_z} u_{i,\eta} u_{i,\eta} dx d\eta + \frac{\delta_1 \Lambda^{\frac{1}{2}}}{2\lambda_1} \int_0^t \int_{R_z} T_{,\alpha} T_{,\alpha} dx d\eta$$

$$+ \frac{\delta_2 \Lambda^{\frac{1}{2}}}{2\lambda_1} \int_0^t \int_{R_z} C_{,\alpha} C_{,\alpha} dx d\eta$$

$$+ \frac{\delta_1^2}{2\lambda_1 \varepsilon_3} \int_0^t \int_{R_z} (\xi - z) T_{,\alpha} T_{,\alpha} dx d\eta + \frac{\delta_2^2}{2\lambda_1 \varepsilon_2} \int_0^t \int_{R_z} (\xi - z) C_{,\alpha} C_{,\alpha} dx d\eta,$$

where

$$a_3 = \frac{v}{2} + \frac{\Lambda^{\frac{1}{2}}}{2\lambda_1} + \frac{v\Lambda^{\frac{1}{2}}}{2\sqrt{\lambda_1}} + \frac{v\Lambda^{\frac{1}{2}}}{2\lambda_1} + \frac{k\Lambda^{\frac{1}{2}}}{2\lambda_1} + \frac{\delta_1 \Lambda^{\frac{1}{2}}}{2\lambda_1} + \frac{\delta_2 \Lambda^{\frac{1}{2}}}{2\lambda_1}.$$

Proof. By the divergence theorem and Equations (1)–(8), we have

$$
\begin{aligned}
E_2(z,t) &= -\int_0^t \int_{R_z} (\xi-z) u_i u_i dx d\eta - \frac{1}{2} \int_{R_z} (\xi-z) u_i u_i dx \Big|_{\eta=t} \\
&\quad - \nu \int_0^t \int_{R_z} u_i u_{i,3} dx d\eta + \int_0^t \int_{R_z} (\xi-z) u_i g_i T dx d\eta \\
&\quad + \int_0^t \int_{R_z} (\xi-z) u_i h_i C dx d\eta + \int_0^t \int_{R_z} u_3 p dx d\eta \\
&\doteq -\int_0^t \int_{R_z} (\xi-z) u_i u_i dx d\eta - \frac{1}{2} \int_{R_z} (\xi-z) u_i u_i dx \Big|_{\eta=t} \\
&\quad + \sum_{i=1}^4 B_i.
\end{aligned}
\tag{32}
$$

Using the Schwarz inequality, the Poincaré inequality and the AG mean inequality, we can obtain

$$
\begin{aligned}
B_1 &\leq \nu \left[\int_0^t \int_{R_z} u_{i,3} u_{i,3} dx d\eta \int_0^t \int_{R_z} u_i u_i dx d\eta \right]^{\frac{1}{2}} \\
&\leq \frac{\nu}{2} \left[\int_0^t \int_{R_z} u_{i,3} u_{i,3} dx d\eta + \int_0^t \int_{R_z} u_i u_i dx d\eta \right].
\end{aligned}
\tag{33}
$$

Similar to (20) and (21), we have for B_2 and B_3

$$
B_2 \leq \frac{\varepsilon_3}{2} \int_0^t \int_{R_z} (\xi-z) u_i u_i dx d\eta + \frac{\delta_1^2}{2\lambda_1 \varepsilon_3} \int_0^t \int_{R_z} (\xi-z) T_{,\alpha} T_{,\alpha} dx d\eta,
\tag{34}
$$

and

$$
B_3 \leq \frac{\varepsilon_4}{2} \int_0^t \int_{R_z} (\xi-z) u_i u_i dx d\eta + \frac{\delta_2^2}{2\lambda_1 \varepsilon_2} \int_0^t \int_{R_z} (\xi-z) C_{,\alpha} C_{,\alpha} dx d\eta,
\tag{35}
$$

where $\varepsilon_3, \varepsilon_4$ are positive constants.

To bound B_4 in (32), we also require that

$$
\int_D f_3 dA = 0.
$$

Then using to the Lemma 2 in Section 2, there exist vector functions $(\hat{\varphi}_1, \hat{\varphi}_2)$ such that

$$
\hat{\varphi}_{\alpha,\alpha} = u_3, \quad \text{in } D, \quad \hat{\varphi}_\alpha = 0, \quad \text{on } \partial D.
\tag{36}
$$

Therefore, we have

$$
\begin{aligned}
B_4 &= \int_0^t \int_{R_z} \hat{\varphi}_{\alpha,\alpha} p dx d\eta \\
&= -\int_0^t \int_{R_z} \hat{\varphi}_\alpha p_{,\alpha} dx d\eta \\
&= \int_0^t \int_{R_z} \hat{\varphi}_\alpha \left[u_{\alpha,\eta} - \nu \Delta u_\alpha + u_\alpha - g_\alpha T - h_\alpha C \right] dx d\eta \\
&= \int_0^t \int_{R_z} \hat{\varphi}_\alpha u_{\alpha,\eta} dx d\eta + \nu \int_0^t \int_{R_z} \hat{\varphi}_{\alpha,\beta} u_{\alpha,\beta} dx d\eta + \nu \int_0^t \int_{D_z} \hat{\varphi}_\alpha u_{\alpha,3} dA d\eta \\
&\quad + \int_0^t \int_{R_z} \hat{\varphi}_\alpha u_\alpha dx d\eta - \int_0^t \int_{R_z} g_\alpha T \hat{\varphi}_\alpha dx d\eta - \int_0^t \int_{R_z} h_\alpha C \hat{\varphi}_\alpha dx d\eta \\
&\doteq \sum_{i=1}^6 B_{4i}.
\end{aligned}
\tag{37}
$$

As the derivation of (26)–(32), we conclude that

$$B_{41} \leq \left(\int_0^t \int_{R_z} \widehat{\varphi}_\alpha \widehat{\varphi}_\alpha dxd\eta\right)^{\frac{1}{2}} \left(\int_0^t \int_{R_z} u_{\alpha,\eta} u_{\alpha,\eta} dxd\eta\right)^{\frac{1}{2}}$$

$$\leq \frac{1}{\sqrt{\lambda_1}} \left(\int_0^t \int_{R_z} \widehat{\varphi}_{\alpha,\beta} \widehat{\varphi}_{\alpha,\beta} dxd\eta\right)^{\frac{1}{2}} \left(\int_0^t \int_{R_z} u_{\alpha,\eta} u_{\alpha,\eta} dxd\eta\right)^{\frac{1}{2}}$$

$$\leq \frac{\Lambda^{\frac{1}{2}}}{\sqrt{\lambda_1}} \left(\int_0^t \int_{R_z} u_3^2 xd\eta\right)^{\frac{1}{2}} \left(\int_0^t \int_{R_z} u_{\alpha,\eta} u_{\alpha,\eta} dxd\eta\right)^{\frac{1}{2}}$$

$$\leq \frac{\Lambda^{\frac{1}{2}}}{2\lambda_1} \left[\int_0^t \int_{R_z} u_{3,\alpha} u_{3,\alpha} xd\eta + \int_0^t \int_{R_z} u_{i,\eta} u_{i,\eta} dxd\eta\right], \tag{38}$$

$$B_{42} \leq \nu \left(\int_0^t \int_{R_z} \widehat{\varphi}_{\alpha,\beta} \widehat{\varphi}_{\alpha,\beta} dxd\eta\right)^{\frac{1}{2}} \left(\int_0^t \int_{R_z} u_{\alpha,\beta} u_{\alpha,\beta} dxd\eta\right)^{\frac{1}{2}}$$

$$\leq \nu \Lambda^{\frac{1}{2}} \left(\int_0^t \int_{R_z} u_3^2 dxd\eta\right)^{\frac{1}{2}} \left(\int_0^t \int_{R_z} u_{\alpha,\beta} u_{\alpha,\beta} dxd\eta\right)^{\frac{1}{2}}$$

$$\leq \frac{\nu \Lambda^{\frac{1}{2}}}{2\sqrt{\lambda_1}} \int_0^t \int_{R_z} u_{i,j} u_{i,j} dxd\eta, \tag{39}$$

$$B_{43} \leq \nu \left(\int_0^t \int_{D_z} \widehat{\varphi}_\alpha \widehat{\varphi}_\alpha dxd\eta\right)^{\frac{1}{2}} \left(\int_0^t \int_{D_z} u_{\alpha,3} u_{\alpha,3} dxd\eta\right)^{\frac{1}{2}}$$

$$\leq \frac{\nu \Lambda^{\frac{1}{2}}}{\sqrt{\lambda_1}} \left(\int_0^t \int_{D_z} u_3^2 dxd\eta\right)^{\frac{1}{2}} \left(\int_0^t \int_{D_z} u_{\alpha,3} u_{\alpha,3} dxd\eta\right)^{\frac{1}{2}}$$

$$\leq \frac{\nu \Lambda^{\frac{1}{2}}}{2\lambda_1} \int_0^t \int_{D_z} u_{i,j} u_{i,j} dxd\eta, \tag{40}$$

$$B_{44} \leq \left(\int_0^t \int_{R_z} \widehat{\varphi}_\alpha \widehat{\varphi}_\alpha dxd\eta\right)^{\frac{1}{2}} \left(\int_0^t \int_{R_z} u_\alpha u_\alpha dxd\eta\right)^{\frac{1}{2}}$$

$$\leq \frac{\Lambda^{\frac{1}{2}}}{\lambda_1} \int_0^t \int_{R_z} u_i u_i dxd\eta$$

$$\leq \frac{k\Lambda^{\frac{1}{2}}}{2\lambda_1} \int_0^t \int_{R_z} u_{i,\alpha} u_{i,\alpha} dxd\eta, \tag{41}$$

$$B_{45} \leq \left(\int_0^t \int_{R_z} \widehat{\varphi}_\alpha \widehat{\varphi}_\alpha dxd\eta\right)^{\frac{1}{2}} \left(\int_0^t \int_{R_z} g_\alpha g_\alpha T^2 dxd\eta\right)^{\frac{1}{2}}$$

$$\leq \frac{\delta_1 \Lambda^{\frac{1}{2}}}{\lambda_1} \left(\int_0^t \int_{R_z} u_{3,\alpha} u_{3,\alpha} dxd\eta\right)^{\frac{1}{2}} \left(\int_0^t \int_{R_z} T_{,\alpha} T_{,\alpha} dxd\eta\right)^{\frac{1}{2}}$$

$$\leq \frac{\delta_1 \Lambda^{\frac{1}{2}}}{2\lambda_1} \left[\int_0^t \int_{R_z} u_{3,\alpha} u_{3,\alpha} dxd\eta + \int_0^t \int_{R_z} T_{,\alpha} T_{,\alpha} dxd\eta\right], \tag{42}$$

$$B_{46} \leq \frac{\delta_2 \Lambda^{\frac{1}{2}}}{2\lambda_1} \left[\int_0^t \int_{R_z} u_{3,\alpha} u_{3,\alpha} dxd\eta + \int_0^t \int_{R_z} C_{,\alpha} C_{,\alpha} dxd\eta\right]. \tag{43}$$

Inserting (38)–(43) into (37), we obtain

$$B_4 \leq \left[\frac{\Lambda^{\frac{1}{2}}}{2\lambda_1} + \frac{\nu \Lambda^{\frac{1}{2}}}{2\sqrt{\lambda_1}} + \frac{\nu \Lambda^{\frac{1}{2}}}{2\lambda_1} + \frac{k\Lambda^{\frac{1}{2}}}{2\lambda_1} + \frac{\delta_1 \Lambda^{\frac{1}{2}}}{2\lambda_1} + \frac{\delta_2 \Lambda^{\frac{1}{2}}}{2\lambda_1}\right] \int_0^t \int_{R_z} u_{i,j} u_{i,j} dxd\eta$$

$$+ \frac{\Lambda^{\frac{1}{2}}}{2\lambda_1} \int_0^t \int_{R_z} u_{i,\eta} u_{i,\eta} dxd\eta + \frac{\delta_1 \Lambda^{\frac{1}{2}}}{2\lambda_1} \int_0^t \int_{R_z} T_{,\alpha} T_{,\alpha} dxd\eta \tag{44}$$

$$+ \frac{\delta_2 \Lambda^{\frac{1}{2}}}{2\lambda_1} \int_0^t \int_{R_z} C_{,\alpha} C_{,\alpha} dxd\eta.$$

Inserting (33), (34), (35) and (44) into (32) and choosing $\varepsilon_3 = \varepsilon_4 = \frac{1}{2}$, we can obtain Lemma 5.

Next we may bound $E_3(z,t)$. First we let T_M denotes that the maximum of T by using the maximum principle in R, i.e.,

$$T_M = \max_{D \times \{t>0\}} F(x_1, x_2, t). \tag{45}$$

Integrating by parts, using (3), (5), (6), (7) together with (9) and the AG mean inequality, we have

$$\begin{aligned} E_3(z,t) &= -\rho_1 \int_0^t \int_{R_z} TT_{,3} dx d\eta - \rho_1 \int_0^t \int_{R_z} T(T_{,\eta} + u_i T_{,i}) dx d\eta \\ &= -\frac{\rho_1}{2} \int_{R_z} (\xi - z) T^2 dx \Big|_{\eta=t} + \frac{\rho_1}{2} \int_0^t \int_{D_z} T^2 dA d\eta + \frac{\rho_1}{2} \int_0^t \int_{R_z} u_3 T^2 dx d\eta \\ &\leq -\frac{\rho_1}{2} \int_{R_z} (\xi - z) T^2 dx \Big|_{\eta=t} + \frac{\rho_1}{2\lambda_1} \int_0^t \int_{D_z} T_{,\alpha} T_{,\alpha} dA d\eta \\ &\quad + \frac{\rho_1 T_M}{2} \left(\int_0^t \int_{R_z} u_3^2 dx d\eta \right)^{\frac{1}{2}} \left(\int_0^t \int_{R_z} T^2 dx d\eta \right)^{\frac{1}{2}} \\ &\leq -\frac{\rho_1}{2} \int_{R_z} (\xi - z) T^2 dx \Big|_{\eta=t} + \frac{\rho_1}{2\lambda_1} \int_0^t \int_{D_z} T_{,\alpha} T_{,\alpha} dA d\eta \\ &\quad + \frac{\rho_1 T_M}{4\lambda_1} \left(\int_0^t \int_{R_z} u_{3,\alpha} u_{3,\alpha} dx d\eta + \int_0^t \int_{R_z} T_{,i} T_{,i} dx d\eta \right). \end{aligned} \tag{46}$$

Using Equations (3)–(7) and integrating by parts, we obtain

$$\begin{aligned} E_4(z,t) &= -\rho_2 \int_0^t \int_{R_z} CC_{,3} dx d\eta - \rho_2 \int_0^t \int_{R_z} (\xi - z) C \left[C_{,\eta} + u_i C_{,i} - \sigma \Delta T \right] dx d\eta \\ &\leq \frac{\rho_2}{2} \int_0^t \int_{D_z} C^2 dA d\eta - \frac{\rho_2}{2} \int_{R_z} (\xi - z) C^2 dx \Big|_{\eta=t} + \frac{\rho_2}{2} \int_0^t \int_{R_z} u_3 C^2 dx d\eta \\ &\quad - \sigma \rho_2 \int_0^t \int_{R_z} CT_{,3} dx d\eta - \sigma \rho_2 \int_0^t \int_{R_z} (\xi - z) C_{,i} T_{,i} dx d\eta. \end{aligned} \tag{47}$$

By the Schwarz and the AG mean inequalities, it follows that from (47)

$$\begin{aligned} E_4(z,t) + \frac{\rho_2}{2} \int_{R_z} (\xi - z) C^2 dx \Big|_{\eta=t} \\ \leq \frac{\rho_2}{2\lambda_1} \int_0^t \int_{D_z} C^2 dA d\eta + \frac{\sigma \rho_2}{2\sqrt{\lambda_1}} \int_0^t \int_{R_z} C_{,i} C_{,i} dx d\eta \\ + \frac{\sigma \rho_2}{2\sqrt{\lambda_1}} \int_0^t \int_{R_z} T_{,3} T_{,3} dx d\eta + \frac{\sigma \rho_2 \varepsilon_5}{2} \int_0^t \int_{R_z} (\xi - z) C_{,i} C_{,i} dx d\eta \\ + \frac{\sigma \rho_2}{2\varepsilon_5} \int_0^t \int_{R_z} (\xi - z) T_{,i} T_{,i} dx d\eta + \frac{\rho_2}{2} \int_0^t \int_{R_z} u_3 C^2 dx d\eta, \end{aligned} \tag{48}$$

for an arbitrary constant $\varepsilon_5 > 0$.

In order to bound the last term on the right of (48), using the Equations (9), (11) and (13), the Schwarz inequality and the AG mean inequality to obtain

$$\frac{\rho_2}{2}\int_0^t \int_{R_z} u_3 C^2 dx d\eta \leq \frac{\rho_2}{2}\int_0^t \Big(\int_{R_z}(u_3 C)^2 dx\Big)^{\frac{1}{2}}\Big(\int_{R_z} C^2 dx\Big)^{\frac{1}{2}} d\eta$$

$$\leq \frac{\rho_2}{2}\max_t\Big\{\Big(\int_{R_z} C^2 dx\Big)^{\frac{1}{2}}\Big\}\int_0^t \int_z^\infty \Big(\int_{D_\xi} u_3^4 dA\Big)^{\frac{1}{4}}\Big(\int_{D_\xi} C^4 dA\Big)^{\frac{1}{4}} d\xi d\eta$$

$$\leq \frac{\rho_2 \Omega^{\frac{1}{8}}}{2^{\frac{3}{4}}\lambda_1^{\frac{1}{4}}}\max_t\Big\{\Big(\int_{R_z} C^2 dx\Big)^{\frac{1}{2}}\Big\}\Big(\int_0^t \int_{R_z} u_{i,j} u_{i,j} dxd\eta\Big)^{\frac{1}{2}}\Big(\int_0^t \int_{R_z} C_{,i} C_{,i} dxd\eta\Big)^{\frac{1}{2}} \quad (49)$$

$$\leq \frac{\rho_2 \Omega^{\frac{1}{8}}}{2^{\frac{7}{4}}\lambda_1^{\frac{1}{4}}}\max_t\Big\{\Big(\int_{R_z} C^2 dx\Big)^{\frac{1}{2}}\Big\}\Big(\int_0^t \int_{R_z} u_{i,j} u_{i,j} dxd\eta + \int_0^t \int_{R_z} C_{,i} C_{,i} dxd\eta\Big),$$

where the bound for $\max_t\Big\{\Big(\int_{R_z} C^2 dx\Big)^{\frac{1}{2}}\Big\}$ will be derived later.

Inserting (49) back into (48), we have

$$E_4(z,t) + \frac{\rho_2}{2}\int_{R_z}(\xi - z)C^2 dx\Big|_{\eta = t}$$

$$\leq \frac{\rho_2}{2\lambda_1}\int_0^t \int_{D_z} C_{,\alpha} C_{,\alpha} dA d\eta + \frac{\sigma\rho_2}{2\sqrt{\lambda_1}}\int_0^t \int_{R_z} C_{,i} C_{,i} dxd\eta + \frac{\sigma\rho_2}{2\sqrt{\lambda_1}}\int_0^t \int_{R_z} T_{,3} T_{,3} dxd\eta$$

$$+ \frac{\sigma\rho_2\varepsilon_6}{2}\int_0^t \int_{R_z}(\xi - z)C_{,i} C_{,i} dxd\eta + \frac{\sigma\rho_2}{2\varepsilon_6}\int_0^t \int_{R_z}(\xi - z)T_{,i} T_{,i} dxd\eta \quad (50)$$

$$+ \frac{\rho_2 \Omega^{\frac{1}{8}}}{2^{\frac{7}{4}}\lambda_1^{\frac{1}{4}}}\max_t\Big\{\Big(\int_{R_z} C^2 dx\Big)^{\frac{1}{2}}\Big\}\Big(\int_0^t \int_{R_z} u_{i,j} u_{i,j} dxd\eta + \int_0^t \int_{R_z} C_{,i} C_{,i} dxd\eta\Big).$$

Combining (46) and (50), we obtain the following Lemma.

Lemma 7. Let u, T, C, p be solutions of Equations (1)–(8) with $g, h \in L_\infty(R \times \{t > 0\})$ and $\int_D f_3 dA = 0$. Then

$$E_3(z,t) + E_4(z,t)\frac{1}{2}\int_{R_z}(\xi - z)\big[\rho_1 T^2 + \rho_2 C^2\big] dx\Big|_{\eta = t}$$

$$\leq \frac{\rho_1}{2\lambda_1}\int_0^t \int_{D_z} T_{,\alpha} T_{,\alpha} dA d\eta + \frac{\rho_2}{2\lambda_1}\int_0^t \int_{D_z} C_{,\alpha} C_{,\alpha} dA d\eta$$

$$+ \Big[\frac{\sigma\rho_2}{2\sqrt{\lambda_1}} + \frac{\rho_2 \Omega^{\frac{1}{8}}}{2^{\frac{7}{4}}\lambda_1^{\frac{1}{4}}}\max_t\Big\{\Big(\int_{R_z} C^2 dx\Big)^{\frac{1}{2}}\Big\}\Big]\int_0^t \int_{R_z} C_{,i} C_{,i} dxd\eta$$

$$+ \Big[\frac{\sigma\rho_2}{2\sqrt{\lambda_1}} + \frac{\rho_1 T_M}{4\lambda_1}\Big]\int_0^t \int_{R_z} T_{,i} T_{,i} dxd\eta$$

$$+ \frac{\sigma\rho_2\varepsilon_6}{2}\int_0^t \int_{R_z}(\xi - z)C_{,i} C_{,i} dxd\eta + \frac{\sigma\rho_2}{2\varepsilon_6}\int_0^t \int_{R_z}(\xi - z)T_{,i} T_{,i} dxd\eta$$

$$+ \Big[\frac{\rho_1 T_M}{4\lambda_1} + \frac{\rho_2 \Omega^{\frac{1}{8}}}{2^{\frac{7}{4}}\lambda_1^{\frac{1}{4}}}\max_t\Big\{\Big(\int_{R_z} C^2 dx\Big)^{\frac{1}{2}}\Big\}\Big]\int_0^t \int_{R_z} u_{i,j} u_{i,j} dxd\eta,$$

where ε_6 is a positive constant. Next, we use Lemmas 5–7 to prove our main result. □

4. Main Result

First, we introduce a new function

$$\psi(z,t) = k \int_0^t \int_{R_z} (\xi - z) u_{i,\eta} u_{i,\eta} dx d\eta + \nu \int_0^t \int_{R_z} (\xi - z) u_{i,j} u_{i,j} dx d\eta$$
$$+ \rho_1 \int_0^t \int_{R_z} (\xi - z) T_{,i} T_{,i} dx d\eta + \rho_2 \int_0^t \int_{R_z} (\xi - z) C_{,i} C_{,i} dx d\eta$$
$$+ k\nu \int_{R_z} (\xi - z) u_{i,j} u_{i,j} dx \Big|_{\eta=t} + \left(k + \frac{1}{2}\right) \int_{R_z} (\xi - z) u_i u_i dx \Big|_{\eta=t} \qquad (51)$$
$$+ \frac{1}{2} \int_0^t \int_{R_z} (\xi - z) u_i u_i dx d\eta + \frac{1}{2} \int_{R_z} (\xi - z) \left[\rho_1 T^2 + \rho_2 C^2\right] dx \Big|_{\eta=t}.$$

Using Lemmas 4–6 and in view of (51), we have

$$\psi(z,t) \leq a_4 \int_0^t \int_{R_z} u_{i,\eta} u_{i,\eta} dx d\eta + a_5 \int_0^t \int_{R_z} u_{i,j} u_{i,j} dx d\eta$$
$$+ a_6 \int_0^t \int_{R_z} T_{,i} T_{,i} dx d\eta + \frac{\nu}{2} \int_0^t \int_{R_z} u_i u_i dx d\eta + a_7 \int_0^t \int_{R_z} C_{,i} C_{,i} dx d\eta$$
$$+ \frac{k\nu \Lambda^{\frac{1}{2}}}{2\sqrt{\lambda_1}} \int_0^t \int_{D_z} u_{3,\eta}^2 dA d\eta + \frac{k\nu \Lambda^{\frac{1}{2}}}{2\sqrt{\lambda_1}} \int_0^t \int_{D_z} u_{\alpha,3} u_{\alpha,3} dA d\eta$$
$$+ \frac{\rho_1}{2\lambda_1} \int_0^t \int_{D_z} T_{,\alpha} T_{,\alpha} dA d\eta + \frac{\rho_2}{2\lambda_1} \int_0^t \int_{D_z} C_{,\alpha} C_{,\alpha} dA d\eta \qquad (52)$$
$$+ \frac{2k\delta_1^2}{\lambda_1} \int_0^t \int_{R_z} (\xi - z) T_{,\alpha} T_{,\alpha} dx d\eta + \frac{2k\delta_2^2}{\lambda_1} \int_0^t \int_{R_z} (\xi - z) C_{,\alpha} C_{,\alpha} dx d\eta$$
$$+ \frac{\delta_1^2}{2\lambda_1 \varepsilon_3} \int_0^t \int_{R_z} (\xi - z) T_{,\alpha} T_{,\alpha} dx d\eta + \frac{\delta_2^2}{2\lambda_1 \varepsilon_2} \int_0^t \int_{R_z} (\xi - z) C_{,\alpha} C_{,\alpha} dx d\eta$$
$$+ \frac{\sigma \rho_2 \varepsilon_6}{2} \int_0^t \int_{R_z} (\xi - z) C_{,i} C_{,i} dx d\eta + \frac{\sigma \rho_2}{2\varepsilon_6} \int_0^t \int_{R_z} (\xi - z) T_{,i} T_{,i} dx d\eta,$$

where

$$a_4 = a_1 k + \frac{\Lambda^{\frac{1}{2}}}{2\lambda_1}, a_5 = a_2 \nu + a_3 + \frac{\rho_1 T_M}{4\lambda_1} + \frac{\rho_2 \Omega^{\frac{1}{8}}}{2^{\frac{7}{4}} \lambda_1^{\frac{1}{4}}} \max_t \left\{\left(\int_{R_z} C^2 dx\right)^{\frac{1}{2}}\right\},$$

$$a_6 = \frac{k\delta_1 \Lambda^{\frac{1}{2}}}{\lambda_1} + \frac{\delta_1 \Lambda^{\frac{1}{2}}}{2\lambda_1}, a_7 = \frac{k\delta_2 \Lambda^{\frac{1}{2}}}{\lambda_1} + \frac{\delta_2 \Lambda^{\frac{1}{2}}}{2\lambda_1} + \frac{\sigma \rho_2}{2\sqrt{\lambda_1}} + \frac{\rho_2 \Omega^{\frac{1}{8}}}{2^{\frac{7}{4}} \lambda_1^{\frac{1}{4}}} \max_t \left\{\left(\int_{R_z} C^2 dx\right)^{\frac{1}{2}}\right\}.$$

Choosing $\varepsilon_6 = \frac{1}{2\sigma}, \rho_2 = \frac{8k\delta_2^2}{\lambda_1} + \frac{2\delta_2^2}{\lambda_1 \varepsilon_2}, \rho_1 = \frac{4k\delta_1^2}{\lambda_1} + \frac{\delta_1^2}{\lambda_1 \varepsilon_3} + \frac{\sigma \rho_2}{\varepsilon_6}$ and define

$$\Psi(z,t) = k \int_0^t \int_{R_z} (\xi - z) u_{i,\eta} u_{i,\eta} dx d\eta + \nu \int_0^t \int_{R_z} (\xi - z) u_{i,j} u_{i,j} dx d\eta$$
$$+ \frac{1}{2}\rho_1 \int_0^t \int_{R_z} (\xi - z) T_{,i} T_{,i} dx d\eta + \frac{1}{2}\rho_2 \int_0^t \int_{R_z} (\xi - z) C_{,i} C_{,i} dx d\eta$$
$$+ k\nu \int_{R_z} (\xi - z) u_{i,j} u_{i,j} dx \Big|_{\eta=t} + \left(k + \frac{1}{2}\right) \int_{R_z} (\xi - z) u_i u_i dx \Big|_{\eta=t} \qquad (53)$$
$$+ \frac{1}{2} \int_0^t \int_{R_z} (\xi - z) u_i u_i dx d\eta + \frac{1}{2} \int_{R_z} (\xi - z) \left[\rho_1 T^2 + \rho_2 C^2\right] dx \Big|_{\eta=t},$$

we can have from (52)

$$\Psi(z,t) \leq a_4 \int_0^t \int_{R_z} u_{i,\eta} u_{i,\eta} dx d\eta + a_5 \int_0^t \int_{R_z} u_{i,j} u_{i,j} dx d\eta$$
$$+ a_6 \int_0^t \int_{R_z} T_{,i} T_{,i} dx d\eta + \frac{\nu}{2} \int_0^t \int_{R_z} u_i u_i dx d\eta + a_7 \int_0^t \int_{R_z} C_{,i} C_{,i} dx d\eta$$
$$+ \frac{k\nu \Lambda^{\frac{1}{2}}}{2\sqrt{\lambda_1}} \int_0^t \int_{D_z} u_{3,\eta}^2 dA d\eta + \frac{k\nu \Lambda^{\frac{1}{2}}}{2\sqrt{\lambda_1}} \int_0^t \int_{D_z} u_{\alpha,3} u_{\alpha,3} dA d\eta$$
$$+ \frac{\rho_1}{2\lambda_1} \int_0^t \int_{D_z} T_{,\alpha} T_{,\alpha} dA d\eta + \frac{\rho_2}{2\lambda_1} \int_0^t \int_{D_z} C_{,\alpha} C_{,\alpha} dA d\eta. \quad (54)$$

From (53), we have

$$-\frac{\partial \Psi(z,t)}{\partial z} = k \int_0^t \int_{R_z} u_{i,\eta} u_{i,\eta} dx d\eta + \nu \int_0^t \int_{R_z} u_{i,j} u_{i,j} dx d\eta$$
$$+ \frac{1}{2}\rho_1 \int_0^t \int_{R_z} T_{,i} T_{,i} dx d\eta + \frac{1}{2}\rho_2 \int_0^t \int_{R_z} C_{,i} C_{,i} dx d\eta$$
$$+ k\nu \int_{R_z} u_{i,j} u_{i,j} dx \Big|_{\eta=t} + (k+\frac{1}{2}) \int_{R_z} u_i u_i dx \Big|_{\eta=t}$$
$$+ \frac{1}{2} \int_0^t \int_{R_z} u_i u_i dx d\eta + \frac{1}{2} \int_{R_z} \left[\rho_1 T^2 + \rho_2 C^2\right] dx \Big|_{\eta=t} \quad (55)$$

and

$$\frac{\partial^2 \Psi(z,t)}{\partial z^2} = k \int_0^t \int_{D_z} u_{i,\eta} u_{i,\eta} dA d\eta + \nu \int_0^t \int_{D_z} u_{i,j} u_{i,j} dA d\eta$$
$$+ \frac{1}{2}\rho_1 \int_0^t \int_{D_z} T_{,i} T_{,i} dA d\eta + \frac{1}{2}\rho_2 \int_0^t \int_{D_z} C_{,i} C_{,i} dA d\eta$$
$$+ k\nu \int_{D_z} u_{i,j} u_{i,j} dA \Big|_{\eta=t} + (k+\frac{1}{2}) \int_{D_z} u_i u_i dA \Big|_{\eta=t}$$
$$+ \frac{1}{2} \int_0^t \int_{D_z} u_i u_i dA d\eta + \frac{1}{2} \int_{D_z} \left[\rho_1 T^2 + \rho_2 C^2\right] dA \Big|_{\eta=t}. \quad (56)$$

Combining (54), (55) and (56), we have
Thus

$$\Psi(z,t) \leq K_1 \left[-\frac{\partial \Psi(z,t)}{\partial z}\right] + K_2 \frac{\partial^2 \Psi(z,t)}{\partial z^2}, \quad (57)$$

where

$$K_1 = \max\{\frac{a_4}{k}, \frac{a_5}{\nu}, \nu, \frac{a_6}{\rho_1}, \frac{a_7}{\rho_2}\},$$

$$K_2 = \max\{\frac{\nu \Lambda^{\frac{1}{2}}}{2\sqrt{\lambda_1}}, \frac{k\Lambda^{\frac{1}{2}}}{2\sqrt{\lambda_1}}, \frac{1}{2\lambda_1}\}.$$

Inequality (57) can be rewritten as

$$\frac{\partial}{\partial z}\left\{e^{-\ell_1 z}\left(\frac{\partial \Psi}{\partial z} + \ell_2 \Psi\right)\right\} \geq 0, \quad (58)$$

where

$$\ell_1 = \frac{K_1}{2K_2} + \frac{1}{2}\sqrt{\frac{K_1^2}{K_2^2} + \frac{4}{K_2}}, \quad \ell_2 = -\frac{K_1}{2K_2} + \frac{1}{2}\sqrt{\frac{K_1^2}{K_2^2} + \frac{4}{K_2}}.$$

Integrating (58) from z to ∞ leads to

$$\frac{\partial \Psi}{\partial z} + \ell_2 \Psi \leq 0,$$

and hence

$$\Psi(z,t) \leq \Psi(0,t)e^{-\ell_2 z}. \tag{59}$$

Combining (53) and (59), we can obtain the following theorem.

Theorem 1. *Let u, T, C, p be solutions of Equations (1)–(8) with $g, h \in L_\infty(R \times \{t > 0\})$ and $\int_D f_3 dA = 0$. Then*

$$k \int_0^t \int_{R_z} (\xi - z) u_{i,\eta} u_{i,\eta} dx d\eta + \nu \int_0^t \int_{R_z} (\xi - z) u_{i,j} u_{i,j} dx d\eta$$
$$+ \frac{1}{2} \rho_1 \int_0^t \int_{R_z} (\xi - z) T_{,i} T_{,i} dx d\eta + \frac{1}{2} \rho_2 \int_0^t \int_{R_z} (\xi - z) C_{,i} C_{,i} dx d\eta$$
$$+ k\nu \int_{R_z} (\xi - z) u_{i,j} u_{i,j} dx \Big|_{\eta=t} + (k + \frac{1}{2}) \int_{R_z} (\xi - z) u_i u_i dx \Big|_{\eta=t} \tag{60}$$
$$+ \frac{1}{2} \int_0^t \int_{R_z} (\xi - z) u_i u_i dx d\eta + \frac{1}{2} \int_{R_z} (\xi - z) [\rho_1 T^2 + \rho_2 C^2] dx \Big|_{\eta=t}$$
$$\leq \Psi(0,t)e^{-\ell_2 z}.$$

Remark 1. *The result of Theorem 1 belongs to the study of Saint-Venant principle, which shows that the fluid decays exponentially with spatial variables on the cylinder.*

Remark 2. *Theorem 1 shows that the solutions of Equations (1)–(8) decays exponentially as $z \to \infty$. To make the decay bound explicit, we have to derive the bounds for $\Psi(0,t)$ and $\max_t \int_R C^2 dx$ in next section.*

5. Bounds of $\Psi(0,t)$ and $\max_t \int_R C^2 dx$

From the previous section, we can see that a_3 involves the quantities $\max_t \int_R C^2 dx$. To make our main result explicit, we have to derive bounds of $\Psi(0,t)$ and $\max_t \int_R C^2 dx$ in term of the physical parameters σ, ν, g_i, h_i, the boundary data and so on. To do this, we begin with

$$\int_0^t \int_R T_{,i} T_{,i} dx d\eta = -\int_0^t \int_D FT_{,3} dA d\eta - \int_0^t \int_R T\Delta T dx d\eta. \tag{61}$$

Now we assume that S is a sufficiently smooth function satisfying the same initial and boundary conditions as T. Thus,

$$\int_0^t \int_R T_{,i} T_{,i} dx d\eta = -\int_0^t \int_D ST_{,3} dA d\eta - \int_0^t \int_R T\Delta T dx d\eta$$
$$= \int_0^t \int_R S_{,i} T_{,i} dx d\eta - \int_0^t \int_R (T-S)\Delta T dx d\eta$$
$$= \int_0^t \int_R S_{,i} T_{,i} dx d\eta - \int_0^t \int_R (T-S)(T_{,\eta} + u_i T_{,i}) dx d\eta \tag{62}$$
$$= \int_0^t \int_R S_{,i} T_{,i} dx d\eta - \int_R T^2 dx \Big|_{\eta=t} + \int_R TS dx \Big|_{\eta=t}$$
$$- \int_0^t \int_R S_{,\eta} T dx d\eta - \int_0^t \int_R S_{,i} T u_i dx d\eta - \frac{1}{2} \int_0^t \int_D fF^2 dA d\eta.$$

Using the Schwarz and the arithmetic-geometric mean inequalities, we can obtain

$$\int_R T^2 dx\Big|_{\eta=t} + \int_0^t \int_R T_{,i}T_{,i}dxd\eta \leq \frac{1}{2}\int_R S^2 dx\Big|_{\eta=t} - \frac{1}{2}\int_0^t \int_D fF^2 dAd\eta$$
$$+ \left(\frac{\epsilon_1}{2}\int_0^t \int_R T_{,i}T_{,i}dxd\eta + \frac{1}{2\epsilon_1}\int_0^t \int_R S_{,i}S_{,i}dxd\eta\right)$$
$$+ \left(\frac{\epsilon_2}{2\lambda_1}\int_0^t \int_R T_{,i}T_{,i}dxd\eta + \frac{1}{2\epsilon_2\lambda_1}\int_0^t \int_R S_{,\eta}S_{,\eta}dxd\eta\right)$$
$$+ \left(\frac{\epsilon_3 T_M}{2}\int_0^t \int_R u_i u_i dxd\eta + \frac{T_M}{2\epsilon_3}\int_0^t \int_R S_{,i}S_{,i}dxd\eta\right), \quad (63)$$

where $\epsilon_1, \epsilon_2, \epsilon_3$ are positive constants. Choosing

$$\epsilon_1 = \frac{1}{2}, \quad \epsilon_2 = \frac{\lambda_1}{2}, \quad (64)$$

we can obtain

$$\int_R T^2 dx\Big|_{\eta=t} + \int_0^t \int_R T_{,i}T_{,i}dxd\eta \leq \frac{\epsilon_3 T_M}{2}\int_0^t \int_R u_i u_i dxd\eta + \text{data}. \quad (65)$$

Obviously, the data terms in (65) involve $\frac{1}{2}\int_R S^2 dx\Big|_{\eta=t}$, $\int_0^t \int_R S_{,i}S_{,i}dxd\eta$, $\int_0^t \int_R S_{,\eta}S_{,\eta}dxd\eta$ and $-\frac{1}{2}\int_0^t \int_D fF^2 dAd\eta$. Similarly, we can bound $\int_0^t \int_R C_{,i}C_{,i}dxd\eta$ as well as $\max_t \int_R C^2 dx$. Firstly, we introduce a function H:

$$\begin{aligned}
\frac{\partial H}{\partial t} + u_i H_{,i} &= \Delta H, & &\text{in } R \times \{t > 0\}, \\
H &= 0, & &\text{in } R \times \{t = 0\}, \\
H &= 0, & &\text{on } \partial D \times \{x_3 > 0\} \times \{t \geq 0\}, \\
H &= G(x_1, x_2, t), & &\text{on } D \times \{t > 0\},
\end{aligned} \quad (66)$$

Then we have

$$\begin{aligned}
(C - H)_{,t} + u_i(C - H)_{,i} &= \Delta(C - H) + \sigma \Delta T, & &\text{in } R \times \{t > 0\}, \\
C - H &= 0 & &\text{in } R \times \{t = 0\}, \\
C - H &= 0 & &\text{on } \partial D \times \{x_3 > 0\} \times \{t \geq 0\}, \\
C - H &= 0 & &\text{on } D \times \{t > 0\}.
\end{aligned} \quad (67)$$

By the triangle inequality, we obtain that

$$\left(\int_0^t \int_R C_{,i}C_{,i}dxd\eta\right)^{\frac{1}{2}} \leq \left[\int_0^t \int_R (C - H)_{,i}(C - H)_{,i}dxd\eta\right]^{\frac{1}{2}} + \left[\int_0^t \int_R H_{,i}H_{,i}dxd\eta\right]^{\frac{1}{2}}, \quad (68)$$

and

$$\left[\max_t \int_R C^2 dx\right]^{\frac{1}{2}} \leq \left[\max_t \int_R (C - H)^2 dx\right]^{\frac{1}{2}} + \left[\max_t \int_R H^2 dx\right]^{\frac{1}{2}}. \quad (69)$$

Then,

$$\frac{1}{2}\int_R (C - H)^2 dx\Big|_{\eta=t} + \int_0^t \int_R (C - H)_{,i}(C - H)_{,i}dxd\eta = -\sigma \int_0^t \int_R (C - H)_{,i}T_{,i}dxd\eta, \quad (70)$$

which follows that

$$\frac{1}{2}\int_R (C-H)^2 dx\Big|_{\eta=t} + \int_0^t \int_R (C-H)_{,i}(C-H)_{,i} dx d\eta$$
$$\leq \sigma^2 \int_0^t \int_R T_{,i}T_{,i} dx d\eta \qquad (71)$$
$$\leq \frac{\epsilon_3 T_M \sigma^2}{2} \int_0^t \int_R u_i u_i dx d\eta + data.$$

Just as in the computation for T, we have the following inequality

$$\frac{1}{2}\int_R H^2 dx\Big|_{\eta=t} + \int_0^t \int_R H_{,i}H_{,i} dx d\eta \leq \epsilon_4 \int_0^t \int_R u_i u_i dx d\eta + data. \qquad (72)$$

Thus,

$$\frac{1}{2}\int_R C^2 dx\Big|_{\eta=t} + \int_0^t \int_R C_{,i}C_{,i} dx d\eta \leq \epsilon_5 \int_0^t \int_R u_i u_i dx d\eta + data, \qquad (73)$$

where $\epsilon_5 > 0$ depends on ϵ_3, ϵ_4 and σ. Next we have to derive a bound for $\int_0^t \int_R u_i u_i dx d\eta$ in term of data. To do this, we define a function

$$\varpi_i = f_i e^{-\varsigma_1 z}, \qquad (74)$$

for some positive constant ϖ_i. Then,

$$\left[\int_0^t \int_R u_{i,j} u_{i,j} dx d\eta\right]^{\frac{1}{2}} \leq \left[\int_0^t \int_R (u_i - \varpi_i)_{,j}(u_i - \varpi_i)_{,j} dx d\eta\right]^{\frac{1}{2}}$$
$$+ \left[\int_0^t \int_R \varpi_{i,j}\varpi_{i,j} dx d\eta\right]^{\frac{1}{2}}.$$

Obviously, we find that the last term of (75) is a data term. Now

$$\nu \int_0^t \int_R (u_i - \varpi_i)_{,j}(u_i - \varpi_i)_{,j} dx d\eta$$
$$= -\int_0^t \int_R (u_i - \varpi_i)_{,j}\left[(u_i - \varpi_i) + p_{,i} - g_i T - h_i C + \varpi_i - \nu\Delta\varpi_i\right] dx d\eta \qquad (75)$$

or

$$\frac{\nu}{2}\int_0^t \int_R (u_i - \varpi_i)_{,j}(u_i - \varpi_i)_{,j} dx d\eta$$
$$\leq -\int_0^t \int_R p\varpi_{i,i} dx d\eta + \frac{\delta_1^2}{2}\int_0^t \int_R T^2 dx d\eta + \frac{\delta_2^2}{2}\int_0^t \int_R C^2 dx d\eta + data. \qquad (76)$$

Noting that

$$\varpi_{i,i} = (f_{\alpha,\alpha} - \varsigma_1 f_3)e^{-\varsigma_1 z} = 0, \qquad (77)$$

in R for $\varsigma_1 = \frac{f_{\alpha,\alpha}}{f_3}$, we can rewrite (76) as

$$\frac{\nu}{2}\int_0^t \int_R (u_i - \varpi_i)_{,j}(u_i - \varpi_i)_{,j} dx d\eta$$
$$\leq \frac{\delta_1^2}{2\lambda_1}\int_0^t \int_R T_{,i}T_{,i} dx d\eta + \frac{\delta_2^2}{2\lambda_1}\int_0^t \int_R C_{,i}C_{,i} dx d\eta + data. \qquad (78)$$

218

Inserting (78) back into (75), we may have a bound of the form

$$\int_0^t \int_R u_{i,j}u_{i,j}dxd\eta \leq C_1 \int_0^t \int_R T_{,i}T_{,i}dxd\eta + C_2 \int_0^t \int_R C_{,i}C_{,i}dxd\eta + data, \quad (79)$$

for computable C_1 and C_2. Combining (65) and (73) and by inequality (17), we have

$$\int_0^t \int_R u_{i,j}u_{i,j}dxd\eta \leq \frac{C_1 T_M}{2\lambda_1}\epsilon_3 \int_0^t \int_R u_{i,j}u_{i,j}dxd\eta + \frac{C_2}{\lambda_1}\epsilon_5 \int_0^t \int_R u_{i,j}u_{i,j}dxd\eta + data. \quad (80)$$

It is clear to see that

$$\int_0^t \int_R u_{i,j}u_{i,j}dxd\eta \leq data, \quad (81)$$

for $\epsilon_3 = \frac{\lambda_1}{2C_1 T_M}, \epsilon_5 = \frac{\lambda_1}{4C_2}$. From (65) and (73), we can obtain

$$\max_t \int_R T^2 dx \leq data, \quad \max_t \int_R C^2 dx \leq data, \quad (82)$$

and

$$\int_0^t \int_R T_{,i}T_{,i}dxd\eta \leq data, \quad \int_0^t \int_R C_{,i}C_{,i}dxd\eta \leq data. \quad (83)$$

Next we seek bound for the total energy $\Psi(0,t)$. From (54) we can obtain for $\Psi(0,t)$

$$\Psi(0,t) \leq a_4 \int_0^t \int_R u_{i,\eta}u_{i,\eta}dxd\eta + \frac{\nu}{2}\int_0^t \int_R u_i u_i dxd\eta$$
$$+ b_1 \int_0^t \int_D u_{\alpha,3}u_{\alpha,3}dAd\eta + data. \quad (84)$$

We are left to derive bounds for $\int_0^t \int_{R_z} u_{i,\eta}u_{i,\eta}dxd\eta$ and $\int_0^t \int_D u_{\alpha,3}u_{\alpha,3}dAd\eta$. Multiplying (1) with $u_{i,\eta}$ and integrating in the region $R \times [0,t]$, we have

$$\int_0^t \int_R u_{i,\eta}u_{i,\eta}dxd\eta = \int_0^t \int_R u_{i,\eta}\left[\nu\Delta u_i - u_i - p_{,i} + g_i T + h_i C\right]dxd\eta, \quad (85)$$

which follows that

$$\int_0^t \int_R u_{i,\eta}u_{i,\eta}dxd\eta \leq -2\nu \int_0^t \int_D u_{\alpha,3}u_{\alpha,\eta}dAd\eta + 2\int_0^t \int_D u_{3,\eta}pdAd\eta$$
$$+ \frac{\delta_1^2}{2\lambda_1}\int_0^t \int_R T_{,i}T_{,i}dxd\eta + \frac{\delta_1^2}{2\lambda_1}\int_0^t \int_R C_{,i}C_{,i}dxd\eta + data \quad (86)$$
$$\leq -2\nu \int_0^t \int_D u_{\alpha,3}f_{\alpha,\eta}dAd\eta + 2\int_0^t \int_D f_{3,\eta}pdAd\eta + data,$$

where we have used the fact $u_{3,3} = -u_{\alpha,\alpha} = -f_{\alpha,\alpha}$ on D_0 and (83), and ϵ_6 is a positive constants. For the first term of (86), using the Schwarz and the AG mean inequalities we have

$$-2\nu \int_0^t \int_{D_0} f_{\alpha,\eta}u_{\alpha,3}dxd\eta \leq 2\nu\left(\int_0^t \int_{D_0} u_{\alpha,3}u_{\alpha,3}dAd\eta\right)^{\frac{1}{2}}\left(\int_0^t \int_{D_0} f_{\alpha,\eta}f_{\alpha,\eta}dAd\eta\right)^{\frac{1}{2}}$$
$$\leq \int_0^t \int_{D_0} u_{\alpha,3}u_{\alpha,3}dAd\eta + data. \quad (87)$$

To bound the second term on the right of (86), we define $\bar{p}$ to be the mean value of p over D_0, i.e.,

$$\bar{p} = \frac{1}{|D_0|} \int_{D_0} p \, dA, \tag{88}$$

where $|D_0|$ is the measure of D_0. Since

$$\int_{D_0} f_{3,\eta} \bar{p} \, dA = \bar{p} \int_{D_0} f_{3,\eta} \, dA = 0, \tag{89}$$

we obtain

$$\int_{D_0} f_{3,\eta} p \, dA = \int_{D_0} f_{3,\eta} (p - \bar{p}) \, dA. \tag{90}$$

It follows by using Schwarz inequality that

$$\int_0^t \int_{D_0} f_{3,\eta} p \, dx d\eta = \int_0^t \int_{D_0} f_{3,\eta} (p - \bar{p}) \, dA d\eta \leq data + \epsilon_6 \int_0^t \int_{D_0} (p - \bar{p})^2 \, dA d\eta, \tag{91}$$

where ϵ_6 is a positive constant to be determined later.

To deal with the integral $\int_0^t \int_{D_0} (p - \bar{p})^2 \, dA d\eta$, we let an auxiliary function χ satisfying:

$$\Delta \chi = 0, \quad \frac{\partial \chi}{\partial n} = 0 \quad \text{on } \partial D_0, \quad \frac{\partial \chi}{\partial n} = p - \bar{p}, \quad \text{in } D_0. \tag{92}$$

From the definition of $\bar{p}$ in (88), it is clear that $\int_{D_0} (p - \bar{p}) dA = 0$. Thus, the necessary condition for the existence of a solution is satisfied and we compute

$$\int_0^t \int_{D_0} (p - \bar{p})^2 \, dA d\eta = \int_0^t \int_{\partial R} (p - \bar{p}) \frac{\partial \chi}{\partial n} dx d\eta = \int_0^t \int_R (p - \bar{p})_{,i} \chi_{,i} dx d\eta$$

$$= \int_0^t \int_R \chi_{,i} \left[-u_{i,\eta} + v u_{i,jj} - u_i + g_i T + h_i C \right] dx d\eta. \tag{93}$$

Since

$$v \int_0^t \int_R \chi_{,i} u_{i,jj} dx d\eta = -v \int_0^t \int_D \chi_{,i} u_{i,3} dx d\eta - v \int_0^t \int_R \chi_{,ij} u_{i,j} dx d\eta$$

$$= v \int_0^t \int_D \chi_{,3} f_{\alpha,\alpha} dx d\eta - v \int_0^t \int_D \chi_{,\alpha} u_{\alpha,3} dx d\eta$$

$$+ v \int_0^t \int_D \chi_{,j} u_{3,j} dx d\eta + v \int_0^t \int_R \chi_{,j} u_{i,ij} dx d\eta \tag{94}$$

$$= -v \int_0^t \int_D \chi_{,\alpha} u_{\alpha,3} dx d\eta + v \int_0^t \int_D \chi_{,\alpha} f_{3,\alpha} dx d\eta.$$

From (93), we can obtain

$$\int_0^t \int_{D_0} (p - \bar{p})^2 dA d\eta = \int_0^t \int_R \chi_{,i} \left[-u_{i,\eta} + \nu u_{i,jj} - u_i + g_i T + h_i C \right] dxd\eta$$

$$\leq \left(\int_0^t \int_R \chi_{,i} \chi_{,i} dxd\eta \right)^{\frac{1}{2}} \left(\int_0^t \int_R u_{i,\eta} u_{i,\eta} dxd\eta \right)^{\frac{1}{2}}$$

$$+ \nu \left(\int_0^t \int_D \chi_{,\alpha} \chi_{,\alpha} dA d\eta \right)^{\frac{1}{2}} \left(\int_0^t \int_D u_{3,\alpha} u_{3,\alpha} dA d\eta \right)^{\frac{1}{2}}$$

$$+ \nu \left(\int_0^t \int_D \chi_{,\alpha} \chi_{,\alpha} dA d\eta \right)^{\frac{1}{2}} \left(\int_0^t \int_D f_{3,\alpha} f_{3,\alpha} dA d\eta \right)^{\frac{1}{2}} \quad (95)$$

$$+ \frac{1}{\sqrt{\lambda_1}} \left(\int_0^t \int_R \chi_{,i} \chi_{,i} dxd\eta \right)^{\frac{1}{2}} \left(\int_0^t \int_R u_{i,j} u_{i,j} dxd\eta \right)^{\frac{1}{2}}$$

$$+ \frac{\delta_1}{\sqrt{\lambda_1}} \left(\int_0^t \int_R \chi_{,i} \chi_{,i} dxd\eta \right)^{\frac{1}{2}} \left(\int_0^t \int_R T_{,j} T_{,j} dxd\eta \right)^{\frac{1}{2}}$$

$$+ \frac{\delta_2}{\sqrt{\lambda_1}} \left(\int_0^t \int_R \chi_{,i} \chi_{,i} dxd\eta \right)^{\frac{1}{2}} \left(\int_0^t \int_R C_{,j} C_{,j} dxd\eta \right)^{\frac{1}{2}}.$$

Making use of (15), (16), (81) and (83) with $g = p - \bar{p}$, we have

$$\left[\int_0^t \int_{D_0} (p - \bar{p})^2 dA d\eta \right]^{\frac{1}{2}}$$

$$\leq \frac{1}{\sqrt{\mu}} \left(\int_0^t \int_R u_{i,\eta} u_{i,\eta} dxd\eta \right)^{\frac{1}{2}} + \nu \left(\int_0^t \int_{D_0} u_{\alpha,3} u_{\alpha,3} dxd\eta \right)^{\frac{1}{2}}$$

$$+ \nu \left(\int_0^t \int_{D_0} f_{3,\alpha} f_{3,\alpha} dxd\eta \right)^{\frac{1}{2}} + \frac{1}{\sqrt{\mu \lambda_1}} \left(\int_0^t \int_R u_{i,j} u_{i,j} dxd\eta \right)^{\frac{1}{2}} \quad (96)$$

$$+ \frac{\delta_1}{\sqrt{\mu \lambda_1}} \left(\int_0^t \int_R T_{,j} T_{,j} dxd\eta \right)^{\frac{1}{2}} + \frac{\delta_2}{\sqrt{\mu \lambda_1}} \left(\int_0^t \int_R C_{,j} C_{,j} dxd\eta \right)^{\frac{1}{2}},$$

which follows that

$$\int_0^t \int_{D_0} (p - \bar{p})^2 dA d\eta \leq data + c_3 \int_0^t \int_{D_0} u_{\alpha,3} u_{\alpha,3} dxd\eta + c_4 \int_0^t \int_R u_{i,\eta} u_{i,\eta} dxd\eta. \quad (97)$$

Obviously, from (97) we must establish a bound for the term $\int_0^t \int_{D_0} u_{\alpha,3} u_{\alpha,3} dxd\eta$. To do this, we begin with the identity

$$\int_0^t \int_R u_{i,3} \left[\nu u_{i,jj} - u_i - p_{,i} - u_{i,\eta} + g_i T + h_i C \right] dxd\eta = 0. \quad (98)$$

Integrating (98) by parts, we can have

$$-\nu \int_0^t \int_{D_0} u_{i,3} u_{i,3} dxd\eta + \nu \int_0^t \int_R u_{i,j3} u_{i,j} dxd\eta + \int_0^t \int_R u_{i,3} u_i dxd\eta$$

$$+ \int_0^t \int_R u_{i,3} p_{,i} dxd\eta + \int_0^t \int_R u_{i,3} u_{i,\eta} dxd\eta + \int_0^t \int_R u_{i,3} g_i T dxd\eta \quad (99)$$

$$+ \int_0^t \int_R u_{i,3} h_i C dxd\eta = 0,$$

which follows that

$$\int_0^t \int_{D_0} u_{\alpha,3} u_{\alpha,3} dxd\eta \leq data + \int_0^t \int_{D_0} u_{\alpha,3} p dA d\eta + \epsilon_7 \int_0^t \int_R u_{i,\eta} u_{i,\eta} dxd\eta. \quad (100)$$

where ϵ_7 is a positive constant.

As the derivation of (91), for the term $\int_0^t \int_{D_0} u_{\alpha,3} p \, dA d\eta$ we can obtain

$$\int_0^t \int_{D_0} u_{\alpha,3} p \, dA d\eta \leq data + \epsilon_8 \int_0^t \int_{D_0} (p-\bar{p})^2 dA d\eta, \quad (101)$$

where ϵ_8 is a positive constant.

Combining (97), (100) and (101), we have

$$(1-\epsilon_8 c_3) \int_0^t \int_{D_0} (p-\bar{p})^2 dx d\eta \leq data + c_3 \epsilon_7 \int_0^t \int_R u_{i,\eta} u_{i,\eta} dx d\eta. \quad (102)$$

Combing (86), (87), (91) and (100), we obtain

$$(1-\epsilon_7) \int_0^t \int_R u_{i,\eta} u_{i,\eta} dx d\eta \leq data + (\epsilon_6 + \epsilon_7) \int_0^t \int_{D_0} (p-\bar{p})^2 dx d\eta. \quad (103)$$

Choosing ϵ_7 and ϵ_8 small enough such that $1 - \epsilon_8 c_3 > 0$ and $1 - \epsilon_7 > 0$, from (102) and (103) we can obtain

$$\int_0^t \int_R u_{i,\eta} u_{i,\eta} dx d\eta \leq data, \quad (104)$$

and

$$\int_0^t \int_{D_0} (p-\bar{p})^2 dA d\eta \leq data. \quad (105)$$

Inserting (101) back into (100), we obtain

$$\int_0^t \int_{D_0} u_{\alpha,3} u_{\alpha,3} dx d\eta \leq data + \epsilon_8 \int_0^t \int_{D_0} (p-\bar{p})^2 dA d\eta + \epsilon_7 \int_0^t \int_R u_{i,\eta} u_{i,\eta} dx d\eta. \quad (106)$$

In light of (104) and (105), we have

$$\int_0^t \int_{D_0} u_{\alpha,3} u_{\alpha,3} dx d\eta \leq data. \quad (107)$$

Recalling (84) and using (104) and (107), we obtain

$$\Psi(0,t) \leq data, \quad (108)$$

which is to say that we have bounded the total energy.

6. Conclusions

In this paper, we consider the spatial decay bounds for the Brinkman equations in double-diffusive convection in a semi-infinite pipe. Using the results of this paper, we can continue to study the continuous dependence of the solution on the parameters in the system of equations. In addition, Using the results of this paper, we can continue to study the continuous dependence of the solution on the parameters in the system of equations. This research can refer to the method of [30,31]. In addition, if Equation (1) is replaced by a nonlinear problem (e.g., Forchheimer equations), it will be a more interesting topic.

Author Contributions: Conceptualization, and validation, Y.L.; formal analysis and investigation, X.C. and D.L. All authors have read and agreed to the published version of the manuscript.

Funding: This research was funded by Key projects of universities in Guangdong Province (NATURAL SCIENCE) (2019KZDXM042) and the Research team project of Guangzhou Huashang College(2021HSKT01).

Institutional Review Board Statement: Not applicable.

Informed Consent Statement: Not applicable.

Data Availability Statement: Not applicable.

Acknowledgments: The authors would like to deeply thank all the reviewers for their insightful and constructive comments.

Conflicts of Interest: The authors declare no conflict of interest.

References

1. Nield, D.A.; Bejan, A. *Convection in Porous Media*; Springer: New York, NY, USA, 1992.
2. Straughan, B. *Mathematical Aspects of Penetrative Convection*; Pitman Research Notes in Mathematics Series; CRC Press: Boca Raton, FL, USA, 1993; p. 288.
3. Ames, K.A.; Payne, L.E. Continuous dependence results for an ill-posed problem in nonlinear viscoelasticity. *Z. Angew. Math. Phys.* **1997**, *48*, 20–29. [CrossRef]
4. Franchi, F.; Straughan, B. Structural stability for the Brinkman equations of porous media. *Math. Meth. Appl. Sci.* **1996**, *19*, 1335–1347. [CrossRef]
5. Payne, L.E.; Straughan, B. Stability in the initial-time geometry problem for the Brinkman and Darcy equations of flow in porous media. *J. Math. Pures Appl.* **1996**, *75*, 225–271.
6. Ames, K.A.; Payne, L.E. On stabilizing against modeling errors in a penetrative convection problem for a porous medium. *Math. Models Meth. Appl. Sci.* **1994**, *4*, 733–740. [CrossRef]
7. Franchi, F. Stabilization estimates for penetrative motions in porous media. *Math. Meth. Appl. Aci.* **1994**, *17*, 11–20. [CrossRef]
8. Morro, A.; Straughan, B. Continuous dependence on the source parameters for convective motion in porous media. *Nonlinear Anal. Theory Methods Appl.* **1992**, *18*, 307–315. [CrossRef]
9. Qin, Y.; Kaloni, P.N. Steady convection in a porous convection based upon the Brinkman model. *IMA J. Appl. Math.* **1992**, *35*, 85–95. [CrossRef]
10. Richardson, L.L.; Straughan, B. Convection with temperature dependent viscosity in a porous medium: Nonlinear stability and the Brinkman effect. *Atti Acad. Naz. Lincei. (Ser. IX)* **1993**, *4*, 223–230.
11. Hameed, A.A.; Harfash, A.J. Continuous dependence of double diffusive convection in a porous medium with temperature-dependent density. *Basrah J. Sci.* **2019**, *37*, 1–15.
12. Liu, Y.; Xiao, S.Z.; Lin, Y.W. Continuous dependence for the Brinkman-Forchheimer fluid interfacing with a Darcy fluid in a bounded domain. *Math. Comput. Simul.* **2018**, *150*, 66–82. [CrossRef]
13. Liu, Y. Continuous dependence for a thermal convection model with temperature-dependent solubility. *Appl. Math. Comput.* **2017**, *308*, 18–30.
14. Chen, W.H. Dissipative structure and diffusion phenomena for doubly dissipative elastic waves in two space dimensions. *J. Math. Anal. Appl.* **2020**, *486*, 123922. [CrossRef]
15. Scott, N.L. Continuous dependence on boundary reaction terms in a porous mediu od Darcy type. *J. Math. Anal. Appl.* **2013**, *399*, 667–675. [CrossRef]
16. Scott, N.L.; Straughan, B. Continuous dependence on the reaction terms in porous convection with surface reactions. *Quart. Appl. Math.* **2013**, *71*, 501–508. [CrossRef]
17. Li, Y.F.; Xiao, S.Z.; Zeng, P. The applications of some basic mathematical inequalities on the convergence of the primitive equations of moist atmosphere. *J. Math. Inequalit.* **2021**, *15*, 293–304. [CrossRef]
18. Li, Y.F.; Chen, X.J.; Shi, J.C. Structural stability in resonant penetrative convection in a Brinkman-Forchheimer fluid interfacing with a Darcy fluid. *Appl. Math. Opt.* **2021**, *84*, 979–999. [CrossRef]
19. Li, Y.; Zeng, P. Continuous Dependence on the Heat Source of 2D Large-Scale Primitive Equations in Oceanic Dynamics. *Symmetry* **2021**, *13*, 1961. [CrossRef]
20. Liu, Y.; Du, Y.; Lin, C.H. Convergence and continuous dependence results for the Brinkman equations. *Appl. Math. Comput.* **2010**, *215*, 4443–4455. [CrossRef]
21. Payne, L.E. Isopermetric inequalities and their applications. *SIAM Rev.* **1967**, *9*, 453–488. [CrossRef]
22. Pólya, G.; Szegö, G. *Isopermetric Inequalities in Mathematical Physics*; Annals of Mathematics Studies; Princeton University Press: Princeton, NJ, USA, 1951; Volume 27.
23. Babuska, I.; Aziz, A.K. Survey lectures on the mathematical foundations of the finite element method. In *The Mathematical Foundation of the Finite Element Method with Application to Partial Differential Equation*; Academic Press: New York, NY, USA, 1972; pp. 3–359.
24. Horgan, C.O.; Wheeler, L.T. Spatial decay estimates for the Navier–Stokes equations with application to the problem of entry flow. *SIAM J. Appl. Math.* **1978**, *35*, 97–116. [CrossRef]
25. Horgan, C.O.; Payne, L.E. Inequalities of Korn, Friedrichs and Babuška-Aziz. *Arch. Rational Mech. Anal.* **1983**, *82*, 165–179. [CrossRef]
26. Payne, L.E. Uniqueness criteria for steady state solutions of the Navier-Stokes equation. In Proceedings of the Simposio Internazionale Sulle Applicazioni Dell'analisi alla Fisica Matematica, Roma, Italy, 28 September–4 October 1964; pp. 130–153.

27. Levine, H.A. An estimate for the best constant in a sobolev inequality involving three integral norms. *Ann. Mat. Pura Appl.* **1980**, *4*, 181–197. [CrossRef]
28. Talenti, G. Best constant in Sobolev inequality. *Ann. Mat. Pura Appl.* **1976**, 110, 353–372. [CrossRef]
29. Ames, K.A.; Payne, L.E.; Schaefer, P.W. Spatial decay estimates in time-dependent stokes flow. *SIAM J. Math. Anal.* **1993**, *24*, 1395–1413. [CrossRef]
30. Song, J.C. Phragmén-Lindelöf and continuous dependence type results in a Stokes flow. *Appl. Math. Mech.* **2010**, *31*, 875–882. [CrossRef]
31. Li, Y.F.; Lin, C.H. Continuous dependence for the nonhomogeneous Brinkman-Forchheimer equations in a semi-infinite pipe. *Appl. Math. Comput.* **2014**, *244*, 201–208. [CrossRef]

Article

On Generalization of Different Integral Inequalities for Harmonically Convex Functions

Jiraporn Reunsumrit [1], Miguel J. Vivas-Cortez [2,*], Muhammad Aamir Ali [3] and Thanin Sitthiwirattham [4]

[1] Department of Mathematics, Faculty of Applied Science, King Mongkut's University of Technology North Bangkok, Bangkok 10800, Thailand; jiraporn.r@sci.kmutnb.ac.th
[2] Escuela de Ciencias Matemáticas y Físicas, Facultad de Ciencias Exactas y Naturales, Pontificia Universidad Católica del Ecuador, Av. 12 de Octubre 1076, Apartado, Quito 17-01-2184, Ecuador
[3] Jiangsu Key Laboratory for NSLSCS, School of Mathematical Sciences, Nanjing Normal University, Nanjing 210023, China; mahr.muhammad.aamir@gmail.com
[4] Mathematics Department, Faculty of Science and Technology, Suan Dusit University, Bangkok 10300, Thailand; thanin_sit@dusit.ac.th
* Correspondence: mjvivas@puce.edu.ec

Abstract: In this study, we first prove a parameterized integral identity involving differentiable functions. Then, for differentiable harmonically convex functions, we use this result to establish some new inequalities of a midpoint type, trapezoidal type, and Simpson type. Analytic inequalities of this type, as well as the approaches for solving them, have applications in a variety of domains where symmetry is important. Finally, several particular cases of recently discovered results are discussed, as well as applications to the special means of real numbers.

Keywords: midpoint and trapezoidal inequality; Simpson's inequality; harmonically convex functions

MSC: 26D10; 26D15; 26A51

1. Introduction

The Hermite–Hadamard inequality, which was independently found by C. Hermite and J. Hadamard (see, also [1], and [2] (p. 137)), is particularly important in the convex functions theory:

$$\mathcal{F}\left(\frac{\kappa_1 + \kappa_2}{2}\right) \leq \frac{1}{\kappa_2 - \kappa_1} \int_{\kappa_1}^{\kappa_2} \mathcal{F}(x)dx \leq \frac{\mathcal{F}(\kappa_1) + \mathcal{F}(\kappa_2)}{2} \quad (1)$$

where $\mathcal{F} : I \subset \mathbb{R} \to \mathbb{R}$ is a convex function over I, and $\kappa_1, \kappa_2 \in I$, with $\kappa_1 < \kappa_2$. In the case of concave mappings, the above inequality is satisfied in reverse order.

Several researches have concentrated on obtaining trapezoid and midpoint-type inequalities that offer bounds for the right-hand side and left-hand side of the inequality (1), respectively, throughout the previous two decades. In [3,4], for example, authors first obtained trapezoid and midpoint-type inequalities for convex functions. In [5], Sarikaya et al. obtained the inequalities (1) for the Riemann–Liouville fractional integrals and the authors also proved some corresponding trapezoid-type inequalities for fractional integrals. Iqbal et al. presented some fractional midpoint-type inequalities for convex functions in [6]. On the other hand, İşcan defined the harmonically convex functions and obtained Hermite–Hadamard-type inequalities for these kinds of functions in [7]. The author also established some trapezoid-type inequalities for harmonically convex functions in [7]. Furthermore, using the Riemann–Liouville fractional integrals, the authors proved Hermite–Hadamard-type inequalities for harmonically convex functions in [8]. They also proved some fractional trapezoid-type inequalities for mapping whose derivatives in absolute value are harmonically convex. In [9], Şanlı proved several fractional midpoint-type inequalities utilizing differentiable convex functions. In [10], Butt et al. presented a new generalization of Hermite–Hadamard inequalities for harmonically convex functions using the notions of the Jensen–Mercer inequality and, in [11], Butt et al. gave a new definition of general harmonically convex functions and proved Hermite–Hadamard-type inequalities. In [12], the authors used fractional operators and proved some new inequalities for general harmonic convex functions. In [13], the authors established Hermite–Hadamard-type inequalities for harmonically convex functions on n-co-ordinates. Some generalizations of Hermite–Hadamard-type inequalities for harmonically convex functions on fractal sets are also given in [14]. Moreover, Liu and Xu extended this class of functions and defined a general harmonic convexity for interval-valued functions in [15]. In the literature, there are several papers on inequalities for harmonically convex functions. For some recent developments in integral inequalities and harmonical convexity, one can consult [16–26].

Inspired by these ongoing studies, we prove several Simpson's type generalized integral inequalities for differentiable convex functions. The key benefit of these inequalities is that they can be turned into midpoint and trapezoidal-type inequalities for differentiable convex functions without having to prove each one independently. These newly established inequalities are the generalizations of inequalities proved in [7,9].

The following is the structure of this paper: In Section 2, we present the definition of the harmonically convex functions and some related results. In Section 3, we prove several new results for harmonically convex functions depending on parameters. We also prove some new integral inequalities to highlight the relationship between the results reported here and related results in the literature. By specially choosing one of the parameters, we give some new results in Section 4. Some applications of newly established inequalities to special means of real numbers are given in Section 5. In Section 6, we give some recommendations for future studies.

2. Preliminaries

In [7], İşcan gave the concept of harmonically convex functions and proved associated Hermite–Hadamard inequalities as follows:

Definition 1 ([7]). *If the mapping $\mathcal{F} : I \subset \mathbb{R}\backslash\{0\} \to \mathbb{R}$ satisfies the inequality*

$$\mathcal{F}\left(\frac{1}{\frac{\tau}{\kappa_2} + \frac{1-\tau}{\kappa_1}}\right) \leq \tau \mathcal{F}(\kappa_2) + (1-\tau)\mathcal{F}(\kappa_1), \tag{2}$$

for all $x, y \in I$ and $\tau \in [0,1]$; then, $\mathcal{F}$ is called the harmonically convex function. In the case of harmonically concave mappings, the above inequality is satisfied in reverse order.

Theorem 1 ([7]). *For any harmonically convex mapping $\mathcal{F} : I \subset \mathbb{R}\backslash\{0\} \to \mathbb{R}$ and $\kappa_1, \kappa_2 \in I$, with $\kappa_1 < \kappa_2$, the following inequality holds:*

$$\mathcal{F}\left(\frac{2\kappa_1\kappa_2}{\kappa_1 + \kappa_2}\right) \leq \frac{\kappa_1\kappa_2}{\kappa_2 - \kappa_1}\int_{\kappa_1}^{\kappa_2}\frac{\mathcal{F}(x)}{x^2}dx \leq \frac{\mathcal{F}(\kappa_1) + \mathcal{F}(\kappa_2)}{2}. \tag{3}$$

In [7], İşcan established the following Lemma to prove trapezoidal-type inequalities for harmonically convex functions.

Lemma 1. *Consider a mapping $\mathcal{F}: I \subset \mathbb{R}\setminus\{0\} \to \mathbb{R}$, which is differentiable mapping on $I°$ (interior of I) and $\kappa_1, \kappa_2 \in I°$ with $\kappa_1 < \kappa_2$. If $\mathcal{F}'$ is integrable over $[\kappa_1, \kappa_2]$, then we would have the following equality:*

$$\frac{\mathcal{F}(\kappa_1) + \mathcal{F}(\kappa_2)}{2} - \frac{\kappa_1 \kappa_2}{\kappa_2 - \kappa_1} \int_{\kappa_1}^{\kappa_2} \frac{\mathcal{F}(x)}{x^2} dx \qquad (4)$$

$$= \frac{\kappa_1 \kappa_2 (\kappa_2 - \kappa_1)}{2} \int_0^1 \frac{1 - 2\tau}{(\tau\kappa_2 + (1-\tau)\kappa_1)^2} \mathcal{F}'\left(\frac{\kappa_1 \kappa_2}{\tau\kappa_2 + (1-\tau)\kappa_1}\right) d\tau.$$

Theorem 2. *Consider a mapping $\mathcal{F}: I \subset (0, \infty) \to \mathbb{R}$, which is differentiable mapping on $I°$ and $\kappa_1, \kappa_2 \in I°$ with $\kappa_1 < \kappa_2$, and $\mathcal{F}'$ is integrable over $[\kappa_1, \kappa_2]$. If $|\mathcal{F}'|$ is harmonically convex on $[\kappa_1, \kappa_2]$, then the following inequality satisfies:*

$$\left| \frac{\mathcal{F}(\kappa_1) + \mathcal{F}(\kappa_2)}{2} - \frac{\kappa_1 \kappa_2}{\kappa_2 - \kappa_1} \int_{\kappa_1}^{\kappa_2} \frac{\mathcal{F}(x)}{x^2} dx \right| \qquad (5)$$

$$\leq \frac{\kappa_1 \kappa_2 (\kappa_2 - \kappa_1)}{2} \theta_1^{1-\frac{1}{q}} \left(\theta_2 |\mathcal{F}'(\kappa_1)|^q + \theta_3 |\mathcal{F}'(\kappa_2)|^q \right)^{\frac{1}{q}},$$

where

$$\theta_1 = \frac{1}{\kappa_1 \kappa_2} - \frac{2}{(\kappa_2 - \kappa_1)^2} \ln\left(\frac{(\kappa_1 + \kappa_2)^2}{4\kappa_1 \kappa_2}\right),$$

$$\theta_2 = \frac{1}{\kappa_2(\kappa_1 - \kappa_2)} + \frac{3\kappa_1 + \kappa_2}{(\kappa_2 - \kappa_1)^3} \ln\left(\frac{(\kappa_1 + \kappa_2)^2}{4\kappa_1 \kappa_2}\right),$$

$$\theta_3 = \theta_1 - \theta_2.$$

Recently, Şanli [9] proved the following Lemma to find the left estimates of the inequality (3).

Lemma 2. *Consider a mapping $\mathcal{F}: I \subset \mathbb{R}\setminus\{0\} \to \mathbb{R}$, which is differentiable mapping on $I°$ and $\kappa_1, \kappa_2 \in I°$ with $\kappa_1 < \kappa_2$. If $\mathcal{F}'$ is integrable over $[\kappa_1, \kappa_2]$, then we would have the following equality:*

$$\mathcal{F}\left(\frac{2\kappa_1 \kappa_2}{\kappa_1 + \kappa_2}\right) - \frac{\kappa_1 \kappa_2}{\kappa_2 - \kappa_1} \int_{\kappa_1}^{\kappa_2} \frac{\mathcal{F}(x)}{x^2} dx \qquad (6)$$

$$= \kappa_1 \kappa_2 (\kappa_2 - \kappa_1) \left[\int_0^{\frac{1}{2}} \frac{\tau}{(\tau\kappa_2 + (1-\tau)\kappa_1)^2} \mathcal{F}'\left(\frac{\kappa_1 \kappa_2}{\tau\kappa_2 + (1-\tau)\kappa_1}\right) d\tau \right.$$

$$\left. + \int_{\frac{1}{2}}^1 \frac{\tau - 1}{(\tau\kappa_2 + (1-\tau)\kappa_1)^2} \mathcal{F}'\left(\frac{\kappa_1 \kappa_2}{\tau\kappa_2 + (1-\tau)\kappa_1}\right) d\tau \right].$$

3. New Parameterized Inequalities for Harmonically Convex Function

Lemma 3. *Consider a mapping $\mathcal{F}: I \subset \mathbb{R}\setminus\{0\} \to \mathbb{R}$, which is differentiable mapping on $I°$ and $\kappa_1, \kappa_2 \in I°$ with $\kappa_1 < \kappa_2$. If $\mathcal{F}'$ is integrable over $[\kappa_1, \kappa_2]$, then for $\lambda \in \mathbb{R}$ we would have the following equality:*

$$\lambda[\mathcal{F}(\kappa_1) + \mathcal{F}(\kappa_2)] - (2\lambda - 1)\mathcal{F}\left(\frac{2\kappa_1 \kappa_2}{\kappa_1 + \kappa_2}\right) - \frac{\kappa_1 \kappa_2}{\kappa_2 - \kappa_1} \int_{\kappa_1}^{\kappa_2} \frac{\mathcal{F}(x)}{x^2} dx \qquad (7)$$

$$= \kappa_1 \kappa_2 (\kappa_2 - \kappa_1) \int_0^1 \frac{m(\tau)}{(\tau\kappa_2 + (1-\tau)\kappa_1)^2} \mathcal{F}'\left(\frac{\kappa_1 \kappa_2}{\tau\kappa_2 + (1-\tau)\kappa_1}\right) d\tau,$$

where

$$m(\tau) = \begin{cases} \lambda - \tau, & \text{if } \tau \in \left[0, \frac{1}{2}\right) \\ 1 - \lambda - \tau, & \text{if } \tau \in \left[\frac{1}{2}, 1\right]. \end{cases}$$

Proof. From the fundamental concepts of integration, we had:

$$\kappa_1\kappa_2(\kappa_2 - \kappa_1)\int_0^1 \frac{m(\tau)}{(\tau\kappa_2 + (1-\tau)\kappa_1)^2}\mathcal{F}'\left(\frac{\kappa_1\kappa_2}{\tau\kappa_2 + (1-\tau)\kappa_1}\right)d\tau$$

$$= \kappa_1\kappa_2(\kappa_2 - \kappa_1)\left[\int_0^{\frac{1}{2}} \frac{\lambda - \tau}{(\tau\kappa_2 + (1-\tau)\kappa_1)^2}\mathcal{F}'\left(\frac{\kappa_1\kappa_2}{\tau\kappa_2 + (1-\tau)\kappa_1}\right)d\tau \right.$$

$$\left. + \int_{\frac{1}{2}}^1 \frac{1 - \lambda - \tau}{(\tau\kappa_2 + (1-\tau)\kappa_1)^2}\mathcal{F}'\left(\frac{\kappa_1\kappa_2}{\tau\kappa_2 + (1-\tau)\kappa_1}\right)d\tau\right]$$

$$= \left[(\tau - \lambda)\mathcal{F}\left(\frac{\kappa_1\kappa_2}{\tau\kappa_2 + (1-\tau)\kappa_1}\right)\Big|_0^{\frac{1}{2}} - \int_0^{\frac{1}{2}}\mathcal{F}\left(\frac{\kappa_1\kappa_2}{\tau\kappa_2 + (1-\tau)\kappa_1}\right)d\tau\right]$$

$$+ \left[(\tau + \lambda - 1)\mathcal{F}\left(\frac{\kappa_1\kappa_2}{\tau\kappa_2 + (1-\tau)\kappa_1}\right)\Big|_{\frac{1}{2}}^1 - \int_{\frac{1}{2}}^1\mathcal{F}\left(\frac{\kappa_1\kappa_2}{\tau\kappa_2 + (1-\tau)\kappa_1}\right)d\tau\right]$$

$$= \lambda[\mathcal{F}(\kappa_1) + \mathcal{F}(\kappa_2)] - (2\lambda - 1)\mathcal{F}\left(\frac{2\kappa_1\kappa_2}{\kappa_1 + \kappa_2}\right) - \frac{\kappa_1\kappa_2}{\kappa_2 - \kappa_1}\int_{\kappa_1}^{\kappa_2}\frac{\mathcal{F}(x)}{x^2}dx$$

and the proof was completed. □

Remark 1. *In Lemma 3, if we set* $\lambda = \frac{1}{2}$, *then we recaptured the identity* (4).

Remark 2. *In Lemma 3, if we assume* $\lambda = 0$, *then we recaptured the identity* (6).

Theorem 3. *Consider a mapping* $\mathcal{F} : I \subset (0, \infty) \to \mathbb{R}$, *which is differentiable mapping on* $I°$ *and* $\kappa_1, \kappa_2 \in I°$ *with* $\kappa_1 < \kappa_2$, *and* $\mathcal{F}'$ *is integrable over* $[\kappa_1, \kappa_2]$. *If* $|\mathcal{F}'|$ *is harmonically convex on* $[\kappa_1, \kappa_2]$, *then the following inequality satisfies:*

$$\left|\lambda[\mathcal{F}(\kappa_1) + \mathcal{F}(\kappa_2)] - (2\lambda - 1)\mathcal{F}\left(\frac{2\kappa_1\kappa_2}{\kappa_1 + \kappa_2}\right) - \frac{\kappa_1\kappa_2}{\kappa_2 - \kappa_1}\int_{\kappa_1}^{\kappa_2}\frac{\mathcal{F}(x)}{x^2}dx\right|$$
$$\leq \kappa_1\kappa_2(\kappa_2 - \kappa_1)$$
$$\times \begin{cases} \{[\Delta_1(\kappa_1,\kappa_2;\lambda) + \Delta_3(\kappa_1,\kappa_2;\lambda) + \Delta_5(\kappa_1,\kappa_2;\lambda) + \Delta_7(\kappa_1,\kappa_2;\lambda)]|\mathcal{F}'(\kappa_1)| \\ +[\Delta_2(\kappa_1,\kappa_2;\lambda) + \Delta_4(\kappa_1,\kappa_2;\lambda) + \Delta_6(\kappa_1,\kappa_2;\lambda) + \Delta_8(\kappa_1,\kappa_2;\lambda)]|\mathcal{F}'(\kappa_2)|\}, & \text{if } 0 \leq \lambda < \frac{1}{2} \\ \{[\Delta_9(\kappa_1,\kappa_2;\lambda) + \Delta_{11}(\kappa_1,\kappa_2;\lambda)]|\mathcal{F}'(\kappa_1)| \\ +[\Delta_{10}(\kappa_1,\kappa_2;\lambda) + \Delta_{12}(\kappa_1,\kappa_2;\lambda)]|\mathcal{F}'(\kappa_2)|\}, & \text{if } \frac{1}{2} \leq \lambda \leq 1 \end{cases},$$

where

$$\Delta_1(\kappa_1,\kappa_2;\lambda) = \frac{\lambda}{(\kappa_2-\kappa_1)^2}\ln(\kappa_1.(\lambda\kappa_2+(1-\lambda)\kappa_1))$$
$$-\frac{2\lambda}{(\kappa_2-\kappa_1)^2}+\frac{2\kappa_1}{(\kappa_2-\kappa_1)^3}\ln\left(\frac{\lambda\kappa_2+(1-\lambda)\kappa_1}{\kappa_1}\right),$$

$$\Delta_2(\kappa_1,\kappa_2;\lambda) = \frac{\lambda}{\kappa_1(\kappa_2-\kappa_1)}+\frac{1}{(\kappa_2-\kappa_1)^2}\ln\left(\frac{\kappa_1}{\lambda\kappa_2+(1-\lambda)\kappa_1}\right)-\Delta_1(\kappa_1,\kappa_2;\lambda),$$

$$\Delta_3(\kappa_1,\kappa_2;\lambda) = \frac{2\lambda-1}{2(\kappa_2^2-\kappa_1^2)}+\frac{\lambda}{(\kappa_2-\kappa_1)^2}\ln\left(\frac{(\kappa_1+\kappa_2)(\lambda\kappa_2+(1-\lambda)\kappa_1)}{2}\right)$$
$$+\frac{1-2\lambda}{(\kappa_2-\kappa_1)^2}+\frac{2\kappa_1}{(\kappa_2-\kappa_1)^3}\ln\left(\frac{2(\lambda\kappa_2+(1-\lambda\kappa_1))}{\kappa_1+\kappa_2}\right),$$

$$\Delta_4(\kappa_1,\kappa_2;\lambda) = \frac{2\lambda-1}{\kappa_2^2-\kappa_1^2}+\frac{1}{(\kappa_2-\kappa_1)^2}\ln\left(\frac{\kappa_1+\kappa_2}{2(\lambda\kappa_2+(1-\lambda\kappa_1))}\right)-\Delta_3(\kappa_1,\kappa_2;\lambda),$$

$$\Delta_5(\kappa_1,\kappa_2;\lambda) = \frac{2\lambda-1}{2(\kappa_2^2-\kappa_1^2)}+\frac{\kappa_1+\kappa_2}{(\kappa_2-\kappa_1)^3}\ln\left(\frac{\kappa_1+\kappa_2}{2}\right)$$
$$+\frac{1-2\lambda}{(\kappa_2-\kappa_1)^2}(1+\ln(\lambda\kappa_1+(1-\lambda)\kappa_2))$$
$$-\frac{2}{(\kappa_2-\kappa_1)^3}(\lambda\kappa_1+(1-\lambda)\kappa_2)\ln(\lambda\kappa_1+(1-\lambda)\kappa_2),$$

$$\Delta_6(\kappa_1,\kappa_2;\lambda) = \frac{2\lambda-1}{\kappa_2^2-\kappa_1^2}+\frac{1}{(\kappa_2-\kappa_1)^2}\ln\left(\frac{2(\lambda\kappa_1+(1-\lambda)\kappa_2)}{\kappa_1+\kappa_2}\right)-\Delta_5(\kappa_1,\kappa_2;\lambda),$$

$$\Delta_7(\kappa_1,\kappa_2;\lambda) = \frac{1-2\lambda}{(\kappa_2-\kappa_1)^2}\ln(\lambda\kappa_1+(1-\lambda)\kappa_2)$$
$$-\frac{2}{(\kappa_2-\kappa_1)^3}(\lambda\kappa_1+(1-\lambda)\kappa_2)\ln(\lambda\kappa_1+(1-\lambda)\kappa_2)$$
$$+\frac{\lambda}{\kappa_2(\kappa_2-\kappa_1)}-\frac{2\lambda}{(\kappa_2-\kappa_1)^2}+\frac{\kappa_1+\kappa_2}{\kappa_2-\kappa_1}\ln(\kappa_2),$$

$$\Delta_8(\kappa_1,\kappa_2;\lambda) = \frac{1}{(\kappa_2-\kappa_1)^2}\ln\left(\frac{\lambda\kappa_1+(1-\lambda)\kappa_2}{\kappa_2}\right)+\frac{\lambda}{\kappa_2(\kappa_2-\kappa_1)}-\Delta_7(\kappa_1,\kappa_2;\lambda),$$

$$\Delta_9(\kappa_1,\kappa_2;\lambda) = \frac{1-2\lambda}{2(\kappa_2^2-\kappa_1^2)}+\frac{\kappa_1+\kappa_2}{(\kappa_2-\kappa_1)^3}\ln\left(\frac{\kappa_1+\kappa_2}{2}\right)$$
$$-\frac{1}{(\kappa_2-\kappa_1)^2}-\frac{\lambda}{(\kappa_2-\kappa_1)^2}\ln(\kappa_1)-\frac{2}{(\kappa_2-\kappa_1)^3}\kappa_1\ln(\kappa_1),$$

$$\Delta_{10}(\kappa_1,\kappa_2;\lambda) = \frac{1-2\lambda}{\kappa_2^2-\kappa_1^2}+\frac{\kappa_1+\kappa_2}{2(\kappa_2-\kappa_1)^2}\ln\left(\frac{\kappa_1+\kappa_2}{2}\right)$$
$$-\frac{\kappa_2-\kappa_1}{2}+\frac{\lambda}{\kappa_1(\kappa_2-\kappa_1)}-\frac{1}{(\kappa_2-\kappa_1)^2}\kappa_1\ln(\kappa_1)-\Delta_9(\kappa_1,\kappa_2;\lambda),$$

$$\Delta_{11}(\kappa_1,\kappa_2;\lambda) = \frac{\lambda}{\kappa_2(\kappa_1-\kappa_2)}+\ln\left(\frac{(1+\lambda)(\kappa_2-\kappa_1)+2\kappa_2}{(\kappa_2-\kappa_1)^3}\right)$$
$$-\frac{1}{(\kappa_2-\kappa_1)^2}+\frac{2\lambda-1}{2(\kappa_2^2-\kappa_1^2)}+\ln\left(\frac{\lambda(\kappa_2-\kappa_1)+\kappa_1+\kappa_2}{(\kappa_2-\kappa_1)^3}\right),$$

$$\Delta_{12}(\kappa_1,\kappa_2;\lambda) = \frac{\lambda}{\kappa_2(\kappa_1-\kappa_2)}+\frac{1}{(\kappa_2-\kappa_1)^2}\kappa_2\ln(\kappa_2)$$
$$-\frac{1}{2(\kappa_2-\kappa_1)}+\frac{2\lambda-1}{\kappa_2^2-\kappa_1^2}-\frac{\kappa_1+\kappa_2}{2(\kappa_2-\kappa_1)^2}\ln\left(\frac{\kappa_1+\kappa_2}{2}\right).$$

Proof. Taking modulus in (7), we had:

$$\left| \lambda[\mathcal{F}(\kappa_1) + \mathcal{F}(\kappa_2)] - (2\lambda - 1)\mathcal{F}\left(\frac{2\kappa_1\kappa_2}{\kappa_1 + \kappa_2}\right) - \frac{\kappa_1\kappa_2}{\kappa_2 - \kappa_1}\int_{\kappa_1}^{\kappa_2} \frac{\mathcal{F}(x)}{x^2}dx \right|$$

$$\leq \kappa_1\kappa_2(\kappa_2 - \kappa_1)\left[\int_0^{\frac{1}{2}} \frac{|\lambda - \tau|}{(\tau\kappa_2 + (1-\tau)\kappa_1)^2}\left|\mathcal{F}'\left(\frac{\kappa_1\kappa_2}{\tau\kappa_2 + (1-\tau)\kappa_1}\right)\right|d\tau \right.$$

$$\left. + \int_{\frac{1}{2}}^1 \frac{|1 - \lambda - \tau|}{(\tau\kappa_2 + (1-\tau)\kappa_1)^2}\left|\mathcal{F}'\left(\frac{\kappa_1\kappa_2}{\tau\kappa_2 + (1-\tau)\kappa_1}\right)\right|d\tau\right]$$

$$= \kappa_1\kappa_2(\kappa_2 - \kappa_1)[S_1 + S_2].$$

From the convexity of $|\mathcal{F}'|$ and for $0 \leq \lambda \leq \frac{1}{2}$, we have:

$$S_1 \leq \int_0^{\frac{1}{2}} \frac{|\lambda - \tau|}{(\tau\kappa_2 + (1-\tau)\kappa_1)^2}[\tau|\mathcal{F}'(\kappa_1)| + (1-\tau)|\mathcal{F}'(\kappa_1)|]d\tau$$

$$= \int_0^{\lambda} \frac{(\lambda - \tau)}{(\tau\kappa_2 + (1-\tau)\kappa_1)^2}[\tau|\mathcal{F}'(\kappa_1)| + (1-\tau)|\mathcal{F}'(\kappa_1)|]d\tau$$

$$+ \int_{\lambda}^{\frac{1}{2}} \frac{(\tau - \lambda)}{(\tau\kappa_2 + (1-\tau)\kappa_1)^2}[\tau|\mathcal{F}'(\kappa_1)| + (1-\tau)|\mathcal{F}'(\kappa_1)|]d\tau$$

$$= \left[\int_0^{\lambda} \frac{\tau(\lambda - \tau)}{(\tau\kappa_2 + (1-\tau)\kappa_1)^2}d\tau + \int_{\lambda}^{\frac{1}{2}} \frac{\tau(\tau - \lambda)}{(\tau\kappa_2 + (1-\tau)\kappa_1)^2}d\tau\right]|\mathcal{F}'(\kappa_1)|$$

$$+ \left[\int_0^{\lambda} \frac{(1-\tau)(\lambda - \tau)}{(\tau\kappa_2 + (1-\tau)\kappa_1)^2}d\tau + \int_{\lambda}^{\frac{1}{2}} \frac{(1-\tau)(\tau - \lambda)}{(\tau\kappa_2 + (1-\tau)\kappa_1)^2}d\tau\right]|\mathcal{F}'(\kappa_2)|$$

$$= [\Delta_1(\kappa_1, \kappa_2; \lambda) + \Delta_3(\kappa_1, \kappa_2; \lambda)]|\mathcal{F}'(\kappa_1)| + [\Delta_2(\kappa_1, \kappa_2; \lambda) + \Delta_4(\kappa_1, \kappa_2; \lambda)]|\mathcal{F}'(\kappa_2)|.$$

Similarly, we have:

$$S_2 \leq \int_{\frac{1}{2}}^1 \frac{|1 - \lambda - \tau|}{(\tau\kappa_2 + (1-\tau)\kappa_1)^2}[\tau|\mathcal{F}'(\kappa_1)| + (1-\tau)|\mathcal{F}'(\kappa_1)|]d\tau$$

$$= \int_{\frac{1}{2}}^{1-\lambda} \frac{(1 - \lambda - \tau)}{(\tau\kappa_2 + (1-\tau)\kappa_1)^2}[\tau|\mathcal{F}'(\kappa_1)| + (1-\tau)|\mathcal{F}'(\kappa_1)|]d\tau$$

$$+ \int_{1-\lambda}^1 \frac{(\tau + \lambda - 1)}{(\tau\kappa_2 + (1-\tau)\kappa_1)^2}[\tau|\mathcal{F}'(\kappa_1)| + (1-\tau)|\mathcal{F}'(\kappa_1)|]d\tau$$

$$= \left[\int_{\frac{1}{2}}^{1-\lambda} \frac{\tau(1 - \lambda - \tau)}{(\tau\kappa_2 + (1-\tau)\kappa_1)^2}d\tau + \int_{1-\lambda}^1 \frac{\tau(\tau + \lambda - 1)}{(\tau\kappa_2 + (1-\tau)\kappa_1)^2}d\tau\right]|\mathcal{F}'(\kappa_1)|$$

$$+ \left[\int_{\frac{1}{2}}^{1-\lambda} \frac{(1-\tau)(1 - \lambda - \tau)}{(\tau\kappa_2 + (1-\tau)\kappa_1)^2}d\tau + \int_{1-\lambda}^1 \frac{(1-\tau)(\tau + \lambda - 1)}{(\tau\kappa_2 + (1-\tau)\kappa_1)^2}d\tau\right]|\mathcal{F}'(\kappa_2)|$$

$$= [\Delta_5(\kappa_1, \kappa_2; \lambda) + \Delta_7(\kappa_1, \kappa_2; \lambda)]|\mathcal{F}'(\kappa_1)| + [\Delta_6(\kappa_1, \kappa_2; \lambda) + \Delta_8(\kappa_1, \kappa_2; \lambda)]|\mathcal{F}'(\kappa_2)|.$$

Now, from the convexity of $|\mathcal{F}'|$ and for $\frac{1}{2} \leq \lambda \leq 1$, we have:

$$S_1 \leq \int_0^{\frac{1}{2}} \frac{|\lambda - \tau|}{(\tau\kappa_2 + (1-\tau)\kappa_1)^2}[\tau|\mathcal{F}'(\kappa_1)| + (1-\tau)|\mathcal{F}'(\kappa_1)|]d\tau$$

$$= \int_0^{\frac{1}{2}} \frac{(\lambda - \tau)}{(\tau\kappa_2 + (1-\tau)\kappa_1)^2}[\tau|\mathcal{F}'(\kappa_1)| + (1-\tau)|\mathcal{F}'(\kappa_1)|]d\tau$$

$$= |\mathcal{F}'(\kappa_1)|\int_0^{\frac{1}{2}} \frac{\tau(\lambda - \tau)}{(\tau\kappa_2 + (1-\tau)\kappa_1)^2}d\tau + |\mathcal{F}'(\kappa_2)|\int_0^{\frac{1}{2}} \frac{(1-\tau)(\lambda - \tau)}{(\tau\kappa_2 + (1-\tau)\kappa_1)^2}d\tau$$

$$= \Delta_9(\kappa_1, \kappa_2; \lambda)|\mathcal{F}'(\kappa_1)| + \Delta_{10}(\kappa_1, \kappa_2; \lambda)|\mathcal{F}'(\kappa_2)|$$

and

$$S_2 \leq \int_{\frac{1}{2}}^{1} \frac{|1-\lambda-\tau|}{(\tau\kappa_2+(1-\tau)\kappa_1)^2}[\tau|\mathcal{F}'(\kappa_1)|+(1-\tau)|\mathcal{F}'(\kappa_1)|]d\tau$$

$$= \int_{\frac{1}{2}}^{1} \frac{(\tau+\lambda-1)}{(\tau\kappa_2+(1-\tau)\kappa_1)^2}[\tau|\mathcal{F}'(\kappa_1)|+(1-\tau)|\mathcal{F}'(\kappa_1)|]d\tau$$

$$= |\mathcal{F}'(\kappa_1)|\int_{\frac{1}{2}}^{1}\frac{\tau(\tau+\lambda-1)}{(\tau\kappa_2+(1-\tau)\kappa_1)^2}d\tau + |\mathcal{F}'(\kappa_2)|\int_{\frac{1}{2}}^{1}\frac{(1-\tau)(\tau+\lambda-1)}{(\tau\kappa_2+(1-\tau)\kappa_1)^2}d\tau$$

$$= \Delta_{11}(\kappa_1,\kappa_2;\lambda)|\mathcal{F}'(\kappa_1)|+\Delta_{12}(\kappa_1,\kappa_2;\lambda)|\mathcal{F}'(\kappa_2)|.$$

Thus, the proof is completed. □

Remark 3. *In Theorem 3, if we set $\lambda = \frac{1}{2}$, then we recaptured the inequality (5) for $q = 1$.*

Remark 4. *In Theorem 3, if we set $\lambda = 0$, then Theorem 3 reduced to [9] (Theorem 3.1 for $q = 1$).*

Corollary 1. *In Theorem 3, if we set $\lambda = \frac{1}{6}$, then we had the following inequality of Simpson's type:*

$$\left|\frac{1}{6}\left[\mathcal{F}(\kappa_1)+4\mathcal{F}\left(\frac{2\kappa_1\kappa_2}{\kappa_1+\kappa_2}\right)+\mathcal{F}(\kappa_2)\right]-\frac{\kappa_1\kappa_2}{\kappa_2-\kappa_1}\int_{\kappa_1}^{\kappa_2}\frac{\mathcal{F}(x)}{x^2}dx\right|$$

$$\leq \kappa_1\kappa_2(\kappa_2-\kappa_1)$$

$$\times\left\{\left[\Delta_1\left(\kappa_1,\kappa_2;\frac{1}{6}\right)+\Delta_3\left(\kappa_1,\kappa_2;\frac{1}{6}\right)+\Delta_5\left(\kappa_1,\kappa_2;\frac{1}{6}\right)+\Delta_7\left(\kappa_1,\kappa_2;\frac{1}{6}\right)\right]|\mathcal{F}'(\kappa_1)|\right.$$

$$\left.+\left[\Delta_2\left(\kappa_1,\kappa_2;\frac{1}{6}\right)+\Delta_4\left(\kappa_1,\kappa_2;\frac{1}{6}\right)+\Delta_6\left(\kappa_1,\kappa_2;\frac{1}{6}\right)+\Delta_8\left(\kappa_1,\kappa_2;\frac{1}{6}\right)\right]|\mathcal{F}'(\kappa_2)|\right\}.$$

Theorem 4. *Consider a mapping $\mathcal{F}: I \subset (0,\infty) \to \mathbb{R}$, which is differentiable mapping on I° and $\kappa_1, \kappa_2 \in I^\circ$ with $\kappa_1 < \kappa_2$, and $\mathcal{F}'$ is integrable over $[\kappa_1,\kappa_2]$. If $|\mathcal{F}'|^q$, $q \geq 1$ is harmonically convex on $[\kappa_1,\kappa_2]$, then the following inequality satisfies:*

$$\left|\lambda(\mathcal{F}(\kappa_1)+\mathcal{F}(\kappa_2))-(2\lambda-1)\mathcal{F}\left(\frac{2\kappa_1\kappa_2}{\kappa_1+\kappa_2}\right)-\frac{\kappa_1\kappa_2}{\kappa_2-\kappa_1}\int_{\kappa_1}^{\kappa_2}\frac{\mathcal{F}(x)}{x^2}dx\right|$$

$$= \kappa_1\kappa_2(\kappa_2-\kappa_1)$$

$$\times \begin{cases} \begin{aligned}&\left[(\Delta_1(\kappa_1,\kappa_2;\lambda)+\Delta_2(\kappa_1,\kappa_2;\lambda))^{1-\frac{1}{q}}\right.\\&\times\left([\Delta_1(\kappa_1,\kappa_2;\lambda)+\Delta_3(\kappa_1,\kappa_2;\lambda)]|\mathcal{F}'(\kappa_1)|^q\right.\\&\left.+[\Delta_2(\kappa_1,\kappa_2;\lambda)+\Delta_4(\kappa_1,\kappa_2;\lambda)]|\mathcal{F}'(\kappa_2)|^q\right)^{\frac{1}{q}}\\&+(\Delta_5(\kappa_1,\kappa_2;\lambda)+\Delta_6(\kappa_1,\kappa_2;\lambda))^{1-\frac{1}{q}}\\&\left([\Delta_5(\kappa_1,\kappa_2;\lambda)+\Delta_7(\kappa_1,\kappa_2;\lambda)]|\mathcal{F}'(\kappa_1)|^q\right.\\&\left.\left.+[\Delta_6(\kappa_1,\kappa_2;\lambda)+\Delta_8(\kappa_1,\kappa_2;\lambda)]|\mathcal{F}'(\kappa_2)|^q\right)^{\frac{1}{q}}\right]\end{aligned} & \text{if } 0 \leq \lambda \leq \frac{1}{2} \\[2ex] \begin{aligned}&\left[(\Delta_9(\kappa_1,\kappa_2;\lambda)+\Delta_{10}(\kappa_1,\kappa_2;\lambda))^{1-\frac{1}{q}}\right.\\&\times\left(\Delta_9(\kappa_1,\kappa_2;\lambda)|\mathcal{F}'(\kappa_1)|^q+\Delta_{10}(\kappa_1,\kappa_2;\lambda)|\mathcal{F}'(\kappa_2)|^q\right)^{\frac{1}{q}}\\&+(\Delta_{11}(\kappa_1,\kappa_2;\lambda)+\Delta_{12}(\kappa_1,\kappa_2;\lambda))^{1-\frac{1}{q}}\\&\left.\left(\Delta_{11}(\kappa_1,\kappa_2;\lambda)|\mathcal{F}'(\kappa_1)|^q+\Delta_{12}(\kappa_1,\kappa_2;\lambda)|\mathcal{F}'(\kappa_2)|^q\right)^{\frac{1}{q}}\right]\end{aligned} & \text{if } \frac{1}{2} \leq \lambda \leq 1 \end{cases}$$

where $\Delta_1(\kappa_1,\kappa_2;\lambda) - \Delta_{12}(\kappa_1,\kappa_2;\lambda)$ are defined as in Theorem 3.

Proof. Taking modulus in (7) and applying the power mean inequality, we had:

$$\left|\lambda[\mathcal{F}(\kappa_1)+\mathcal{F}(\kappa_2)]-(2\lambda-1)\mathcal{F}\left(\frac{2\kappa_1\kappa_2}{\kappa_1+\kappa_2}\right)-\frac{\kappa_1\kappa_2}{\kappa_2-\kappa_1}\int_{\kappa_1}^{\kappa_2}\frac{\mathcal{F}(x)}{x^2}dx\right|$$

$$\leq \kappa_1\kappa_2(\kappa_2-\kappa_1)\left[\int_0^{\frac{1}{2}}\frac{|\lambda-\tau|}{(\tau\kappa_2+(1-\tau)\kappa_1)^2}\left|\mathcal{F}'\left(\frac{\kappa_1\kappa_2}{\tau\kappa_2+(1-\tau)\kappa_1}\right)\right|d\tau\right.$$

$$\left.+\int_{\frac{1}{2}}^{1}\frac{|1-\lambda-\tau|}{(\tau\kappa_2+(1-\tau)\kappa_1)^2}\left|\mathcal{F}'\left(\frac{\kappa_1\kappa_2}{\tau\kappa_2+(1-\tau)\kappa_1}\right)\right|d\tau\right].$$

$$\leq \kappa_1\kappa_2(\kappa_2-\kappa_1)\left[\left(\int_0^{\frac{1}{2}}\frac{|\lambda-\tau|}{(\tau\kappa_2+(1-\tau)\kappa_1)^2}d\tau\right)^{1-\frac{1}{q}}\right.$$

$$\left(\int_0^{\frac{1}{2}}\frac{|\lambda-\tau|}{(\tau\kappa_2+(1-\tau)\kappa_1)^2}\left|\mathcal{F}'\left(\frac{\kappa_1\kappa_2}{\tau\kappa_2+(1-\tau)\kappa_1}\right)\right|^q d\tau\right)^{\frac{1}{q}}$$

$$+\left(\int_{\frac{1}{2}}^{1}\frac{|1-\lambda-\tau|}{(\tau\kappa_2+(1-\tau)\kappa_1)^2}d\tau\right)^{1-\frac{1}{q}}$$

$$\left.\left(\int_{\frac{1}{2}}^{1}\frac{|1-\lambda-\tau|}{(\tau\kappa_2+(1-\tau)\kappa_1)^2}\left|\mathcal{F}'\left(\frac{\kappa_1\kappa_2}{\tau\kappa_2+(1-\tau)\kappa_1}\right)\right|^q d\tau\right)^{\frac{1}{q}}\right].$$

From the convexity of $|\mathcal{F}'|^q$ and $0 \leq \lambda < \frac{1}{2}$, we have:

$$\left|\lambda[\mathcal{F}(\kappa_1)+\mathcal{F}(\kappa_2)]-(2\lambda-1)\mathcal{F}\left(\frac{2\kappa_1\kappa_2}{\kappa_1+\kappa_2}\right)-\frac{\kappa_1\kappa_2}{\kappa_2-\kappa_1}\int_{\kappa_1}^{\kappa_2}\frac{\mathcal{F}(x)}{x^2}dx\right|$$

$$\leq \kappa_1\kappa_2(\kappa_2-\kappa_1)\Big[(\Delta_1(\kappa_1,\kappa_2;\lambda)+\Delta_2(\kappa_1,\kappa_2;\lambda))^{1-\frac{1}{q}}$$

$$\times\Big([\Delta_1(\kappa_1,\kappa_2;\lambda)+\Delta_3(\kappa_1,\kappa_2;\lambda)]|\mathcal{F}'(\kappa_1)|^q+[\Delta_2(\kappa_1,\kappa_2;\lambda)+\Delta_4(\kappa_1,\kappa_2;\lambda)]|\mathcal{F}'(\kappa_2)|^q\Big)^{\frac{1}{q}}$$

$$+(\Delta_5(\kappa_1,\kappa_2;\lambda)+\Delta_6(\kappa_1,\kappa_2;\lambda))^{1-\frac{1}{q}}$$

$$\times\Big([\Delta_5(\kappa_1,\kappa_2;\lambda)+\Delta_7(\kappa_1,\kappa_2;\lambda)]|\mathcal{F}'(\kappa_1)|^q+[\Delta_6(\kappa_1,\kappa_2;\lambda)+\Delta_8(\kappa_1,\kappa_2;\lambda)]|\mathcal{F}'(\kappa_2)|^q\Big)^{\frac{1}{q}}\Big].$$

Now, from the convexity of $|\mathcal{F}'|^q$ and $\frac{1}{2} < \lambda \leq 1$, we have:

$$\left|\lambda[\mathcal{F}(\kappa_1)+\mathcal{F}(\kappa_2)]-(2\lambda-1)\mathcal{F}\left(\frac{2\kappa_1\kappa_2}{\kappa_1+\kappa_2}\right)-\frac{\kappa_1\kappa_2}{\kappa_2-\kappa_1}\int_{\kappa_1}^{\kappa_2}\frac{\mathcal{F}(x)}{x^2}dx\right|$$

$$\leq \kappa_1\kappa_2(\kappa_2-\kappa_1)\Big[(\Delta_9(\kappa_1,\kappa_2;\lambda)+\Delta_{10}(\kappa_1,\kappa_2;\lambda))^{1-\frac{1}{q}}$$

$$\times\Big(\Delta_9(\kappa_1,\kappa_2;\lambda)|\mathcal{F}'(\kappa_1)|^q+\Delta_{10}(\kappa_1,\kappa_2;\lambda)|\mathcal{F}'(\kappa_2)|^q\Big)^{\frac{1}{q}}$$

$$+(\Delta_{11}(\kappa_1,\kappa_2;\lambda)+\Delta_{12}(\kappa_1,\kappa_2;\lambda))^{1-\frac{1}{q}}$$

$$\times\Big(\Delta_{11}(\kappa_1,\kappa_2;\lambda)|\mathcal{F}'(\kappa_1)|^q+\Delta_{12}(\kappa_1,\kappa_2;\lambda)|\mathcal{F}'(\kappa_2)|^q\Big)^{\frac{1}{q}}\Big]$$

and the proof was completed. □

Remark 5. *In Theorem 4, if we set $\lambda = \frac{1}{2}$, then we recaptured the inequality (5).*

Remark 6. *In Theorem 4, if we set $\lambda = 0$, then Theorem 4 reduced to [9] (Theorem 3.1).*

Corollary 2. *In Theorem 4, if we set $\lambda = \frac{1}{6}$, then we obtain the following Simpson's type inequality:*

$$\left| \frac{1}{6}\left[\mathcal{F}(\kappa_1) + 4\mathcal{F}\left(\frac{2\kappa_1\kappa_2}{\kappa_1+\kappa_2}\right) + \mathcal{F}(\kappa_2)\right] - \frac{\kappa_1\kappa_2}{\kappa_2-\kappa_1}\int_{\kappa_1}^{\kappa_2}\frac{\mathcal{F}(x)}{x^2}dx \right|$$

$$\leq \kappa_1\kappa_2(\kappa_2-\kappa_1)\left[\left(\Delta_1\left(\kappa_1,\kappa_2;\frac{1}{6}\right) + \Delta_2\left(\kappa_1,\kappa_2;\frac{1}{6}\right)\right)^{1-\frac{1}{q}}\right.$$

$$\times \left(\left[\Delta_1\left(\kappa_1,\kappa_2;\frac{1}{6}\right) + \Delta_3\left(\kappa_1,\kappa_2;\frac{1}{6}\right)\right]|\mathcal{F}'(\kappa_1)|^q\right.$$

$$+\left.\left[\Delta_2\left(\kappa_1,\kappa_2;\frac{1}{6}\right) + \Delta_4\left(\kappa_1,\kappa_2;\frac{1}{6}\right)\right]|\mathcal{F}'(\kappa_2)|^q\right)^{\frac{1}{q}}$$

$$+\left(\Delta_5\left(\kappa_1,\kappa_2;\frac{1}{6}\right) + \Delta_6\left(\kappa_1,\kappa_2;\frac{1}{6}\right)\right)^{1-\frac{1}{q}}$$

$$\times \left(\left[\Delta_5\left(\kappa_1,\kappa_2;\frac{1}{6}\right) + \Delta_7\left(\kappa_1,\kappa_2;\frac{1}{6}\right)\right]|\mathcal{F}'(\kappa_1)|^q\right.$$

$$\times + \left.\left[\Delta_6\left(\kappa_1,\kappa_2;\frac{1}{6}\right) + \Delta_8\left(\kappa_1,\kappa_2;\frac{1}{6}\right)\right]|\mathcal{F}'(\kappa_2)|^q\right)^{\frac{1}{q}}\right].$$

4. Some Special Cases of Main Results

In this section, we gave some new inequalities as special cases of the newly established results.

Corollary 3. *Under the assumptions of Theorem 3 with $\lambda = 1$, the following inequality held:*

$$\left| \mathcal{F}(\kappa_1) + \mathcal{F}(\kappa_2) - \mathcal{F}\left(\frac{2\kappa_1\kappa_2}{\kappa_1+\kappa_2}\right) - \frac{\kappa_1\kappa_2}{\kappa_2-\kappa_1}\int_{\kappa_1}^{\kappa_2}\frac{\mathcal{F}(x)}{x^2}dx \right|$$
$$\leq \kappa_1\kappa_2(\kappa_2-\kappa_1)$$
$$\times \{[\Delta_9(\kappa_1,\kappa_2;1) + \Delta_{11}(\kappa_1,\kappa_2;1)]|\mathcal{F}'(\kappa_1)| + [\Delta_{10}(\kappa_1,\kappa_2;1) + \Delta_{12}(\kappa_1,\kappa_2;1)]|\mathcal{F}'(\kappa_2)|\}.$$

Corollary 4. *Under the assumptions of Theorem 3 with $\lambda = \frac{1}{3}$, the following inequality held:*

$$\left| \frac{1}{3}\left[\mathcal{F}(\kappa_1) + \mathcal{F}\left(\frac{2\kappa_1\kappa_2}{\kappa_1+\kappa_2}\right) + \mathcal{F}(\kappa_2)\right] - \frac{\kappa_1\kappa_2}{\kappa_2-\kappa_1}\int_{\kappa_1}^{\kappa_2}\frac{\mathcal{F}(x)}{x^2}dx \right|$$
$$\leq \kappa_1\kappa_2(\kappa_2-\kappa_1)$$
$$\times \left\{\left[\Delta_1\left(\kappa_1,\kappa_2;\frac{1}{3}\right) + \Delta_3\left(\kappa_1,\kappa_2;\frac{1}{3}\right) + \Delta_5\left(\kappa_1,\kappa_2;\frac{1}{3}\right) + \Delta_7\left(\kappa_1,\kappa_2;\frac{1}{3}\right)\right]|\mathcal{F}'(\kappa_1)|\right.$$
$$+\left.\left[\Delta_2\left(\kappa_1,\kappa_2;\frac{1}{3}\right) + \Delta_4\left(\kappa_1,\kappa_2;\frac{1}{3}\right) + \Delta_6\left(\kappa_1,\kappa_2;\frac{1}{3}\right) + \Delta_8\left(\kappa_1,\kappa_2;\frac{1}{3}\right)\right]|\mathcal{F}'(\kappa_2)|\right\}.$$

Corollary 5. *Under the assumptions of Theorem 3 with $\lambda = \frac{1}{4}$, the following inequality held:*

$$\left| \frac{1}{2}\left[\frac{\mathcal{F}(\kappa_1) + \mathcal{F}(\kappa_1)}{2} + \mathcal{F}\left(\frac{2\kappa_1\kappa_2}{\kappa_1+\kappa_2}\right)\right] - \frac{\kappa_1\kappa_2}{\kappa_2-\kappa_1}\int_{\kappa_1}^{\kappa_2}\frac{\mathcal{F}(x)}{x^2}dx \right|$$
$$\leq \kappa_1\kappa_2(\kappa_2-\kappa_1)$$
$$\times \left\{\left[\Delta_1\left(\kappa_1,\kappa_2;\frac{1}{4}\right) + \Delta_3\left(\kappa_1,\kappa_2;\frac{1}{4}\right) + \Delta_5\left(\kappa_1,\kappa_2;\frac{1}{4}\right) + \Delta_7\left(\kappa_1,\kappa_2;\frac{1}{4}\right)\right]|\mathcal{F}'(\kappa_1)|\right.$$
$$+\left.\left[\Delta_2\left(\kappa_1,\kappa_2;\frac{1}{4}\right) + \Delta_4\left(\kappa_1,\kappa_2;\frac{1}{4}\right) + \Delta_6\left(\kappa_1,\kappa_2;\frac{1}{4}\right) + \Delta_8\left(\kappa_1,\kappa_2;\frac{1}{4}\right)\right]|\mathcal{F}'(\kappa_2)|\right\}.$$

Corollary 6. *Under the assumptions of Theorem 4 with $\lambda = 1$, the following inequality held:*

$$\left| 2\frac{\mathcal{F}(\kappa_1) + \mathcal{F}(\kappa_2)}{2} - \mathcal{F}\left(\frac{2\kappa_1\kappa_2}{\kappa_1 + \kappa_2}\right) - \frac{\kappa_1\kappa_2}{\kappa_2 - \kappa_1}\int_{\kappa_1}^{\kappa_2}\frac{\mathcal{F}(x)}{x^2}dx \right|$$

$$\leq \kappa_1\kappa_2(\kappa_2 - \kappa_1)$$

$$\times \left\{ (\Delta_9(\kappa_1,\kappa_2;1) + \Delta_{10}(\kappa_1,\kappa_2;1))^{1-\frac{1}{q}} \left(\Delta_9(\kappa_1,\kappa_2;1)|\mathcal{F}'(\kappa_1)|^q + \Delta_{10}(\kappa_1,\kappa_2;1)|\mathcal{F}'(\kappa_2)|^q \right)^{\frac{1}{q}} \right.$$

$$\left. + (\Delta_{11}(\kappa_1,\kappa_2;1) + \Delta_{12}(\kappa_1,\kappa_2;1))^{1-\frac{1}{q}} \left(\Delta_{11}(\kappa_1,\kappa_2;1)|\mathcal{F}'(\kappa_1)|^q + \Delta_{12}(\kappa_1,\kappa_2;1)|\mathcal{F}'(\kappa_2)|^q \right)^{\frac{1}{q}} \right\}.$$

Corollary 7. *Under the assumptions of Theorem 4 with $\lambda = \frac{1}{3}$, the following inequality held:*

$$\left| \frac{1}{3}\left[\mathcal{F}(\kappa_1) + \mathcal{F}\left(\frac{2\kappa_1\kappa_2}{\kappa_1 + \kappa_2}\right) + \mathcal{F}(\kappa_2)\right] - \frac{\kappa_1\kappa_2}{\kappa_2 - \kappa_1}\int_{\kappa_1}^{\kappa_2}\frac{\mathcal{F}(x)}{x^2}dx \right|$$

$$\leq \kappa_1\kappa_2(\kappa_2 - \kappa_1)\left[\left(\Delta_1\left(\kappa_1,\kappa_2;\frac{1}{3}\right) + \Delta_2\left(\kappa_1,\kappa_2;\frac{1}{3}\right)\right)^{1-\frac{1}{q}}\right.$$

$$\times \left(\left[\Delta_1\left(\kappa_1,\kappa_2;\frac{1}{3}\right) + \Delta_3\left(\kappa_1,\kappa_2;\frac{1}{3}\right)\right]|\mathcal{F}'(\kappa_1)|^q + \left[\Delta_2\left(\kappa_1,\kappa_2;\frac{1}{3}\right) + \Delta_4\left(\kappa_1,\kappa_2;\frac{1}{3}\right)\right]|\mathcal{F}'(\kappa_2)|^q \right)^{\frac{1}{q}}$$

$$+ \left(\Delta_5\left(\kappa_1,\kappa_2;\frac{1}{3}\right) + \Delta_6\left(\kappa_1,\kappa_2;\frac{1}{3}\right)\right)^{1-\frac{1}{q}}$$

$$\left. \times \left(\left[\Delta_5\left(\kappa_1,\kappa_2;\frac{1}{3}\right) + \Delta_7\left(\kappa_1,\kappa_2;\frac{1}{3}\right)\right]|\mathcal{F}'(\kappa_1)|^q + \left[\Delta_6\left(\kappa_1,\kappa_2;\frac{1}{3}\right) + \Delta_8\left(\kappa_1,\kappa_2;\frac{1}{3}\right)\right]|\mathcal{F}'(\kappa_2)|^q \right)^{\frac{1}{q}}\right].$$

Corollary 8. *Under the assumptions of Theorem 4 with $\lambda = \frac{1}{4}$, the following inequality held:*

$$\left| \frac{1}{2}\left[\frac{\mathcal{F}(\kappa_1) + \mathcal{F}(\kappa_1)}{2} + \mathcal{F}\left(\frac{2\kappa_1\kappa_2}{\kappa_1 + \kappa_2}\right)\right] - \frac{\kappa_1\kappa_2}{\kappa_2 - \kappa_1}\int_{\kappa_1}^{\kappa_2}\frac{\mathcal{F}(x)}{x^2}dx \right|$$

$$\leq \kappa_1\kappa_2(\kappa_2 - \kappa_1)\left[\left(\Delta_1\left(\kappa_1,\kappa_2;\frac{1}{4}\right) + \Delta_2\left(\kappa_1,\kappa_2;\frac{1}{4}\right)\right)^{1-\frac{1}{q}}\right.$$

$$\times \left(\left[\Delta_1\left(\kappa_1,\kappa_2;\frac{1}{4}\right) + \Delta_3\left(\kappa_1,\kappa_2;\frac{1}{4}\right)\right]|\mathcal{F}'(\kappa_1)|^q + \left[\Delta_2\left(\kappa_1,\kappa_2;\frac{1}{4}\right) + \Delta_4\left(\kappa_1,\kappa_2;\frac{1}{4}\right)\right]|\mathcal{F}'(\kappa_2)|^q \right)^{\frac{1}{q}}$$

$$+ \left(\Delta_5\left(\kappa_1,\kappa_2;\frac{1}{4}\right) + \Delta_6\left(\kappa_1,\kappa_2;\frac{1}{4}\right)\right)^{1-\frac{1}{q}}$$

$$\left. \times \left(\left[\Delta_5\left(\kappa_1,\kappa_2;\frac{1}{4}\right) + \Delta_7\left(\kappa_1,\kappa_2;\frac{1}{4}\right)\right]|\mathcal{F}'(\kappa_1)|^q + \left[\Delta_6\left(\kappa_1,\kappa_2;\frac{1}{4}\right) + \Delta_8\left(\kappa_1,\kappa_2;\frac{1}{4}\right)\right]|\mathcal{F}'(\kappa_2)|^q \right)^{\frac{1}{q}}\right].$$

5. Application to Special Means

For arbitrary positive numbers κ_1, κ_2 ($\kappa_1 \neq \kappa_2$), we considered the means as follows:

1. The arithmetic mean;
$$\mathcal{A} = \mathcal{A}(\kappa_1, \kappa_2) = \frac{\kappa_1 + \kappa_2}{2}.$$

2. The geometric mean;
$$\mathcal{G} = \mathcal{G}(\kappa_1, \kappa_2) = \sqrt{\kappa_1\kappa_2}.$$

3. The harmonic mean;
$$\mathcal{H} = \mathcal{H}(\kappa_1, \kappa_2) = \frac{2\kappa_1\kappa_2}{\kappa_1 + \kappa_2}.$$

4. The logarithmic mean;
$$\mathcal{L} = \mathcal{L}(\kappa_1, \kappa_2) = \frac{\kappa_2 - \kappa_1}{\ln \kappa_2 - \ln \kappa_1}.$$

5. The generalize logarithmic mean;
$$\mathcal{L}_p = \mathcal{L}_p(\kappa_1, \kappa_2) = \left[\frac{\kappa_2^{p+1} - \kappa_1^{p+1}}{(\kappa_2 - \kappa_1)(p+1)}\right]^{\frac{1}{p}}, \ p \in \mathbb{R}\setminus\{-1, 0\}.$$

6. The identric mean.
$$\mathcal{I} = \mathcal{I}(\kappa_1, \kappa_2) = \begin{cases} \frac{1}{e}\left(\frac{\kappa_2^{\kappa_2}}{\kappa_1^{\kappa_1}}\right)^{\frac{1}{\kappa_2-\kappa_1}}, & \text{if } \kappa_1 \neq \kappa_2, \\ \kappa_1, & \text{if } \kappa_1 = \kappa_2, \end{cases} \kappa_1, \kappa_2 > 0.$$

These means are often employed in numerical approximations and other fields. However, the following straightforward relationship has been stated in the literature.

$$\mathcal{H} \leq \mathcal{G} \leq \mathcal{L} \leq \mathcal{I} \leq \mathcal{A}.$$

Proposition 1. *For $\kappa_1, \kappa_2 \in (0, \infty)$ with $\kappa_1 < \kappa_2$, the following inequality was true:*

$$\left|2\lambda \mathcal{A}(\kappa_1, \kappa_2) - (2\lambda - 1)\mathcal{H}(\kappa_1, \kappa_2) - \frac{\mathcal{G}^2(\kappa_1, \kappa_2)}{\mathcal{L}(\kappa_1, \kappa_2)}\right|$$
$$\leq \kappa_1\kappa_2(\kappa_2 - \kappa_1)$$
$$\times \begin{cases} \{[\Delta_1(\kappa_1,\kappa_2;\lambda) + \Delta_3(\kappa_1,\kappa_2;\lambda) + \Delta_5(\kappa_1,\kappa_2;\lambda) + \Delta_7(\kappa_1,\kappa_2;\lambda)] \\ +[\Delta_2(\kappa_1,\kappa_2;\lambda) + \Delta_4(\kappa_1,\kappa_2;\lambda) + \Delta_6(\kappa_1,\kappa_2;\lambda) + \Delta_8(\kappa_1,\kappa_2;\lambda)]\kappa_2^{p+1}\}, & \text{if } 0 \leq \lambda < \frac{1}{2} \\ \{[\Delta_9(\kappa_1,\kappa_2;\lambda) + \Delta_{11}(\kappa_1,\kappa_2;\lambda)] + [\Delta_{10}(\kappa_1,\kappa_2;\lambda) + \Delta_{12}(\kappa_1,\kappa_2;\lambda)]\}, & \text{if } \frac{1}{2} \leq \lambda \leq 1 \end{cases}$$

Proof. The inequality in Theorem 3 for mapping $\mathcal{F}: (0, \infty) \to \mathbb{R}$, $\mathcal{F}(x) = x$ leads to this conclusion. □

Proposition 2. *For $\kappa_1, \kappa_2 \in (0, \infty)$ with $\kappa_1 < \kappa_2$, the following inequality was true:*

$$\left|2\lambda \mathcal{A}\left(\kappa_1^{p+2}, \kappa_2^{p+2}\right) - (2\lambda - 1)\mathcal{H}^{p+2}(\kappa_1, \kappa_2) - \mathcal{G}^2(\kappa_1, \kappa_2)\mathcal{L}_p^p(\kappa_1, \kappa_2)\right|$$
$$\leq \kappa_1\kappa_2(\kappa_2 - \kappa_1)(p+2)$$
$$\times \begin{cases} \{[\Delta_1(\kappa_1,\kappa_2;\lambda) + \Delta_3(\kappa_1,\kappa_2;\lambda) + \Delta_5(\kappa_1,\kappa_2;\lambda) + \Delta_7(\kappa_1,\kappa_2;\lambda)]\kappa_1^{p+1} \\ +[\Delta_2(\kappa_1,\kappa_2;\lambda) + \Delta_4(\kappa_1,\kappa_2;\lambda) + \Delta_6(\kappa_1,\kappa_2;\lambda) + \Delta_8(\kappa_1,\kappa_2;\lambda)]\kappa_2^{p+1}\}, & \text{if } 0 \leq \lambda < \frac{1}{2} \\ \{[\Delta_9(\kappa_1,\kappa_2;\lambda) + \Delta_{11}(\kappa_1,\kappa_2;\lambda)]\kappa_1^{p+1} \\ +[\Delta_{10}(\kappa_1,\kappa_2;\lambda) + \Delta_{12}(\kappa_1,\kappa_2;\lambda)]\kappa_2^{p+1}\}, & \text{if } \frac{1}{2} \leq \lambda \leq 1. \end{cases}$$

Proof. The inequality in Theorem 3 for mapping $\mathcal{F}: (0, \infty) \to \mathbb{R}$, $\mathcal{F}(x) = x^{p+2}$, $p \in (-1, \infty)\{0\}$ leads to this conclusion. □

Proposition 3. For $\kappa_1, \kappa_2 \in (0, \infty)$ with $\kappa_1 < \kappa_2$, the following inequality was true:

$$\left| 2\lambda \mathcal{A}\left(\kappa_1^2 \ln \kappa_1, \kappa_2^2 \ln \kappa_2\right) - (2\lambda - 1)\mathcal{H}^2(\kappa_1, \kappa_2) \ln(\mathcal{H}(\kappa_1, \kappa_2)) - \mathcal{G}^2(\kappa_1, \kappa_2) \ln(\mathcal{I}(\kappa_1, \kappa_2)) \right|$$
$$\leq \kappa_1 \kappa_2 (\kappa_2 - \kappa_1)$$
$$\times \begin{cases} \{[\Delta_1(\kappa_1,\kappa_2;\lambda) + \Delta_3(\kappa_1,\kappa_2;\lambda) \\ +\Delta_5(\kappa_1,\kappa_2;\lambda) + \Delta_7(\kappa_1,\kappa_2;\lambda)]\kappa_1(\kappa_1 + 2\ln\kappa_1) \\ +[\Delta_2(\kappa_1,\kappa_2;\lambda) + \Delta_4(\kappa_1,\kappa_2;\lambda) \\ +\Delta_6(\kappa_1,\kappa_2;\lambda) + \Delta_8(\kappa_1,\kappa_2;\lambda)]\kappa_2(\kappa_2 + 2\ln\kappa_2)\}, & \text{if } 0 \leq \lambda < \frac{1}{2} \\[1em] \{[\Delta_9(\kappa_1,\kappa_2;\lambda) + \Delta_{11}(\kappa_1,\kappa_2;\lambda)]\kappa_1(\kappa_1 + 2\ln\kappa_1) \\ +[\Delta_{10}(\kappa_1,\kappa_2;\lambda) + \Delta_{12}(\kappa_1,\kappa_2;\lambda)]\kappa_2(\kappa_2 + 2\ln\kappa_2)\}, & \text{if } \frac{1}{2} \leq \lambda \leq 1. \end{cases}$$

Proof. The inequality in Theorem 3 for mapping $\mathcal{F}: (0, \infty) \to \mathbb{R}$, $\mathcal{F}(x) = x^2 \ln x$ leads to this conclusion. □

6. Conclusions

In this research, we proved some new inequalities of a midpoint type, trapezoidal type, and Simpson type for differentiable harmonically convex functions. We also showed that the results proved in this research were the refinements of some existing results in [7,9]. The findings of this study can be utilized in symmetry. The results for the case of symmetric harmonically convex functions can be obtained in future studies. It is an interesting and new problem that upcoming researchers can develop similar inequalities for in their future work, with regards to differentiable coordinated harmonically convex functions.

Author Contributions: Funding acquisition, J.R., M.J.V.-C. and T.S.; Investigation, J.R., M.J.V.-C., M.A.A. and T.S.; Methodology, J.R., M.J.V.-C., M.A.A. and T.S.; Supervision, M.J.V.-C., M.A.A. and T.S.; Writing—original draft, J.R., M.J.V.-C., M.A.A. and T.S.; Writing—review & editing, J.R., M.J.V.-C., M.A.A. and T.S. All authors have read and agreed to the published version of the manuscript.

Funding: This research was funded by the King Mongkut's University of Technology, North Bangkok. Contract no.KMUTNB-62-KNOW-26.

Institutional Review Board Statement: Not applicable.

Informed Consent Statement: Not applicable.

Data Availability Statement: Not applicable.

Acknowledgments: We want to give thanks to the Dirección de investigación from Pontificia Universidad Católica del Ecuador for technical support to our research project entitled: "Algunas desigualdades integrales para funciones convexas generalizadas y aplicaciones". All the authors want to thank those appointed to review this article and the editorial team of *Symmetry*.

Conflicts of Interest: The authors declare no conflict of interest.

References

1. Dragomir, S.S.; Pearce, C.E.M. *Selected Topics on Hermite-Hadamard Inequalities and Applications*; RGMIA Monographs; Victoria University, Melbourne, Australia, 2000.
2. Pečarić, J.E.; Proschan, F.; Tong, Y.L. *Convex Functions, Partial Orderings and Statistical Applications*; Academic Press: Boston, MA, USA, 1992.
3. Dragomir, S.S.; Agarwal, R.P. Two inequalities for differentiable mappings and applications to special means of real numbers and to trapezoidal formula. *Appl. Math. Lett.* **1998**, *11*, 91–95. [CrossRef]
4. Kirmaci, U.S. Inequalities for differentiable mappings and applications to special means of real numbers to midpoint formula. *Appl. Math. Comput.* **2004**, *147*, 137–146. [CrossRef]
5. Sarikaya, M.Z.; Set, E.; Yaldiz, H.; Basak, N. Hermite–Hadamard's inequalities for fractional integrals and related fractional inequalities. *Math. Comput. Model.* **2013**, *57*, 2403–2407. [CrossRef]
6. Iqbal, M.; Qaisar, S.; Muddassar, M. A short note on integral inequality of type Hermite-Hadamard through convexity. *J. Comput. Analaysis Appl.* **2016**, *21*, 946–953.
7. İşcan, İ. Hermite-Hadamard type inequaities for harmonically functions. *Hacet. J. Math. Stat.* **2014**, *43*, 935–942.

8. İşcan, İ.; Wu, S. Hermite-Hadamard type inequalities for harmonically convex functions via fractional integrals. *Appl. Math. Comput.* **2014**, *238*, 237–244. [CrossRef]
9. Şanli, Z. Some midpoint type inequalities for Riemann–Liouville fractional integrals. *Appl. Appl. Math.* **2019**, *2019*, 58–73.
10. Butt, S.I.; Yousaf, S.; Asghar, A.; Khan, K.A.; Moradi, H.R. New Fractional Hermite-Hadamard-Mercer Inequalities for Harmonically Convex Function. *J. Funct. Spaces* **2021**, *2021*, 5868326. [CrossRef]
11. Butt, S.I.; Tariq, M.; Aslam, A.; Ahmad, H.; Nofal, T.A. Hermite-Hadamard Type Inequalities via Generalized Harmonic Exponential Convexity and Applications. *J. Funct. Spaces* **2021**, *2021*, 5533491. [CrossRef]
12. Nwaeze, E.R.; Khan, M.A.; Ahmadian, A.; Ahmed, M.N.; Mahmood, A.K. Fractional inequalities of the Hermite-Hadamard type for m-polynomial convex and harmonically convex functions. *AIMS Math.* **2021**, *6*, 1889–1904. [CrossRef]
13. Viloria, J.M.; Vivas-Cortez, M.J. Hermite-Hadamard type inequalities for harmonically convex functions on n-coordinates. *Appl. Math. Inf. Sci. Lett.* **2018**, *6*, 1–6. [CrossRef]
14. Sun, W. Generalized harmonically convex functions on fractal sets and related Hermite-Hadamard type inequalities. *J. Nonlinear Sci. Appl.* **2017**, *10*, 5869–5880. [CrossRef]
15. Liu, R.; Xu, R. Hermite-Hadamard type inequalities for harmonical (h_1, h_2)-convex interval-valued functions. *AIMS Math.* **2021**, *4*, 89–103. [CrossRef]
16. Awan, M.U.; Akhtar, N.; Iftikhar, S.; Noor, M.A.; Chu, Y.M. New Hermite-Hadamard type inequalities for n-polynomial harmonically convex functions. *J. Inequal. Appl.* **2020**, *2020*, 1–12. [CrossRef]
17. Baloch, I.A.; Chu, Y.M. Petrović-type inequalities for harmonic h-convex functions. *J. Funct. Space* **2020**, *2020*, 1–7. [CrossRef]
18. Baloch, I.A.; Mughal, A.A.; Chu, Y.-M.; Haq, A.U.; Sen, M.D.L. A variant of Jensen-type inequality and related results for harmonic convex functions. *AIMS Math.* **2020**, *5*, 6404–6418. [CrossRef]
19. Chen, F. Extensions of the Hermite–Hadamard inequality for harmonically convex functions via fractional integrals. *Appl. Math. Comput.* **2015**, *268*, 121–128. [CrossRef]
20. Dragomir, S.S. Inequalities of Jensen type for HA-convex functions. *An. Univ. Oradea Fasc. Mat.* **2020**, *27*, 103–124.
21. Kunt, M.; İşcan, İ.; Yazici, N. Hermite-Hadamard type inequalities for product of harmonically convex functions via Riemann–Liouville fractional integrals. *J. Math. Anal.* **2016**, *7*, 74–82.
22. Set, E.; İşcan, İ.; Zehir, F. On some new inequalities of Hermite-Hadamard type involving harmonically convex functions via fractional integrals. *Konuralp J. Math.* **2015**, *3*, 42–55.
23. Sitthiwirattham, T.; Budak, H.; Kara, H.; Ali, M.A.; Reunsumrit, J. On Some New Fractional Ostrowski- and Trapezoid-Type Inequalities for Functions of Bounded Variations with Two Variables. *Symmetry* **2021**, *13*, 1724. [CrossRef]
24. You, X.X.; Ali, M.A.; Budak, H.; Agarwal, P.; Chu, Y.M. Extensions of Hermite–Hadamard inequalities for harmonically convex functions via generalized fractional integrals. *J. Inequal. Appl.* **2021**, *2021*, 1–22. [CrossRef]
25. You, X.X.; Ali, M.A.; Budak, H.; Reunsumrit, J.; Sitthiwirattham, T. Hermite-Hadamard-Mercer-Type Inequalities for Harmonically Convex Mappings. *Mathematics* **2021**, *9*, 2556. [CrossRef]
26. Zhao, D.; Ali, M.A.; Kashuri, A.; Budak, H. Generalized fractional integral inequalities of Hermite-Hadamard type for harmonically convex functions. *Adv. Differ. Equ.* **2020**, *2020*, 1–37. [CrossRef]

Article

New Generalized Class of Convex Functions and Some Related Integral Inequalities

Artion Kashuri [1], Ravi P. Agarwal [2], Pshtiwan Othman Mohammed [3], Kamsing Nonlaopon [4,*], Khadijah M. Abualnaja [5] and Yasser S. Hamed [5]

[1] Department of Mathematics, Faculty of Technical Science, University "Ismail Qemali", 9400 Vlora, Albania; artion.kashuri@univlora.edu.al
[2] Department of Mathematics, Texas A & M University-Kingsville, Kingsville, TX 78363, USA; Ravi.Agarwal@tamuk.edu
[3] Department of Mathematics, College of Education, University of Sulaimani, Sulaimani 46001, Kurdistan Region, Iraq; pshtiwan.muhammad@univsul.edu.iq
[4] Department of Mathematics, Faculty of Science, Khon Kaen University, Khon Kaen 40002, Thailand
[5] Department of Mathematics and Statistics, College of Science, Taif University, P. O. Box 11099, Taif 21944, Saudi Arabia; Kh.abualnaja@tu.edu.sa (K.M.A.); yasersalah@tu.edu.sa (Y.S.H.)
* Correspondence: nkamsi@kku.ac.th; Tel.: +66-86642-1582

Abstract: There is a strong correlation between convexity and symmetry concepts. In this study, we investigated the new generic class of functions called the (n, m)–generalized convex and studied its basic algebraic properties. The Hermite–Hadamard inequality for the (n, m)–generalized convex function, for the products of two functions and of this type, were proven. Moreover, this class of functions was applied to several known identities; midpoint-type inequalities of Ostrowski and Simpson were derived. Our results are extensions of many previous contributions related to integral inequalities via different convexities.

Keywords: Hermite–Hadamard inequality; Ostrowski inequality; Simpson inequality; (n, m)–generalized convexity

MSC: 26A33; 26A51; 26D07; 26D10; 26D15; 26D20

1. Introduction and Preliminaries

The twenty-first century began with the introduction and establishment of new tools used to solve linear and nonlinear differential and difference equations. In terms of the convexity theory, one important development involves defining a new class of convex functions, which is then tested on the well-known inequalities. "As it is known, inequalities aim to develop different mathematical methods. Nowadays, we need to seek accurate inequalities for proving the existence and uniqueness of the mathematical methods. In recent years, especially over the past two decades, several authors have been engaged in the study of inequalities, including various function classes (symmetric or asymmetric)", see [1]. Moreover, the modern convexity theory has motivated researchers to propose a new generalized class of convex functions and to investigate their special models, which could effectively be used in different fields, in particular, agriculture, medicine, reliability engineering, demography, actuarial study, survival analysis, and others. Kasamsetty et al. in [2] defined a new class of convex functions used to delay modeling and established an application to the transistor sizing problem. Awan et al. in [3] obtained new classes of convex functions and inequalities. Hudzik and Maligranda in [4] investigated the class of s-convex functions. Eftekhari in [5] derived new results using (s, m)–convexity in the second sense. Kadakal and İşcan in [6] established related inequalities via the exponential type convexity. Agarwal and Choi in [7] used fractional operators and found their image formulas. Rekhviashvili et al. in [8] described damped vibrations via a fractional oscillator model.

In much of the literature, we can see various Hermite–Hadamard (HH) inequality types, in which one of the known classes of convex functions is utilized (e.g., [9–11]). Moreover, some generalizations of the HH integral inequalities, such as HH–Fejér, AB HH, midpoint HH, mid-end-point HH, conformable HH, and HH–Mercer integral inequalities are found (e.g., [12–14]). In addition, different integral inequalities using those convexities are investigated. Ujević in [15] obtained sharp inequalities for Simpson and Ostrowski types. Liu et al. in [16], using the MT–convexity class derived Ostrowski fractional inequalities. Kaijser et al. in [17] established Hardy-type inequalities via convexity. Rashid et al. in [18], using generalized k–fractional integrals, found Grüss inequalities. For more recent published papers on HH, see [19,20].

Let us review some fundamental and preliminary results on convexity and inequality.

Definition 1. *Function* $\Theta : \tau \subseteq \mathrm{R} \to \mathrm{R}$ *is called convex, if*

$$\Theta(\varrho\chi_1 + (1-\varrho)\chi_2) \leq \varrho\Theta(\chi_1) + (1-\varrho)\Theta(\chi_2), \tag{1}$$

holds for all $\chi_1, \chi_2 \in \tau$ *(τ is an interval with real numbers and* R *is the set of real numbers) and* $\varrho \in [0,1]$. *Moreover,* Θ *is concave if* $(-\Theta)$ *is convex.*

Definition 2 ([4])**.** *Let* $s \in (0,1]$ *be a real number. A function* $\Theta : \tau \subseteq \mathrm{R} \to \mathrm{R}$ *is called s-convex (in the second sense), if*

$$\Theta(\varrho\chi_1 + (1-\varrho)\chi_2) \leq \varrho^s\Theta(\chi_1) + (1-\varrho)^s\Theta(\chi_2), \tag{2}$$

holds for all $\chi_1, \chi_2 \in \tau$, *and* $\varrho \in [0,1]$.

Definition 3 ([21])**.** *Let* $\tau, \mathcal{J}$ *be intervals in* R, $(0,1) \subseteq \mathcal{J}$ *and let* $h : \mathcal{J} \to \mathrm{R}$ *be a nonnegative function, and* $h \neq 0$. *A nonnegative function* $\Theta : \tau \to \mathrm{R}$ *is called h-convex, if*

$$\Theta(\varrho\chi_1 + (1-\varrho)\chi_2) \leq h(\varrho)\Theta(\chi_1) + h(1-\varrho)\Theta(\chi_2), \tag{3}$$

holds for all $\chi_1, \chi_2 \in \tau$, $\varrho \in (0,1)$.

Toply et al. [22] introduced the following class of convex functions:

Definition 4. *Let* $n \in \mathbb{N}$. *A function* $\Theta : \tau \to \mathrm{R}$ *is called n–polynomial convex, if*

$$\Theta(\varrho\chi_1 + (1-\varrho)\chi_2) \leq \frac{1}{n}\sum_{\ell_1=1}^{n}\left[1-(1-\varrho)^{\ell_1}\right]\Theta(\chi_1) + \frac{1}{n}\sum_{\ell_1=1}^{n}\left[1-\varrho^{\ell_1}\right]\Theta(\chi_2), \tag{4}$$

holds for every $\chi_1, \chi_2 \in \tau$, *and* $\varrho \in [0,1]$.

Recently, Rashid et al. [23] defined the following class of convex functions:

Definition 5 ([23])**.** *Assume that* $s \in [0,1]$ *and* $n \in \mathbb{N}$. *A function* $\Theta : \tau \to \mathrm{R}$ *is said to be n–polynomial s–type convex, if*

$$\Theta(\varrho\chi_1 + (1-\varrho)\chi_2) \leq \frac{1}{n}\sum_{\ell_1=1}^{n}\left[1-(s(1-\varrho))^{\ell_1}\right]\Theta(\chi_1) + \frac{1}{n}\sum_{\ell_1=1}^{n}\left[1-(s\varrho)^{\ell_1}\right]\Theta(\chi_2), \tag{5}$$

holds for every $\chi_1, \chi_2 \in \tau$, *and* $\varrho \in [0,1]$.

The following double inequality, namely the HH inequality, is remarkable, and it played an important role in the analysis.

Theorem 1 (HH inequality [24]). *Let $\Theta : \tau \subseteq \mathbb{R} \to \mathbb{R}$ be a convex function on τ for $\chi_1, \chi_2 \in \tau$ and $\chi_1 < \chi_2$, then*

$$\Theta\left(\frac{\chi_1 + \chi_2}{2}\right) \leq \frac{1}{\chi_2 - \chi_1} \int_{\chi_1}^{\chi_2} \Theta(\varrho) d\varrho \leq \frac{\Theta(\chi_1) + \Theta(\chi_2)}{2}. \tag{6}$$

The following well-known inequality is called the Ostrowski inequality:

Theorem 2 (Ostrowski inequality [16]). *Let $\Theta : \tau \subseteq \mathbb{R} \to \mathbb{R}$ a differentiable function in the interval τ and let $\chi_1, \chi_2 \in \tau$ with $\chi_1 < \chi_2$. If $|\Theta'(x)| \leq M$ for all $x \in [\chi_1, \chi_2]$, then*

$$\left|\Theta(x) - \frac{1}{\chi_2 - \chi_1} \int_{\chi_1}^{\chi_2} \Theta(\varrho) d\varrho\right| \leq M(\chi_2 - \chi_1)\left[\frac{1}{4} + \frac{\left(x - \frac{\chi_1 + \chi_2}{2}\right)^2}{(\chi_2 - \chi_1)^2}\right]. \tag{7}$$

Another type of inequality is obtained by Dragomir et al. [25], which is as follows:

Theorem 3 (Simpson inequality [25]). *Assume that $\Theta : [\chi_1, \chi_2] \to \mathbb{R}$ is a four-time continuous and differentiable function on (χ_1, χ_2) such that $\|\Theta^{(4)}\|_\infty := \sup_{x \in (\chi_1, \chi_2)} |\Theta^{(4)}(x)| < \infty$ with $\chi_1 < \chi_2$, then*

$$\left|\frac{1}{6}\left[\Theta(\chi_1) + 4\Theta\left(\frac{\chi_1 + \chi_2}{2}\right) + \Theta(\chi_2)\right] - \frac{1}{\chi_2 - \chi_1}\int_{\chi_1}^{\chi_2} \Theta(x) dx\right| \leq \frac{1}{2880}(\chi_2 - \chi_1)^4 \|\Theta^{(4)}\|_\infty. \tag{8}$$

For brevity, we denote by $\mathcal{D} = \{h_1, h_2, \ldots, h_n, g_1, g_2, \ldots, g_m\}$ the convex set in the sequel. Motivated by the above results, we introduce the following generic class of convex functions:

Definition 6. *Suppose that $1 \leq n \leq m$, where $n, m \in \mathbb{N}$, and assume that $h_{\ell_1}, g_{\ell_2} : [0,1] \to [0, +\infty)$ are continuous functions for all $\ell_1 = 1, 2, \ldots, n$ and $\ell_2 = 1, 2, \ldots, m$. A function $\Theta : \tau \to \mathbb{R}$, which is nonnegative, is said to be (n, m)–generalized convex with respect to $\mathcal{D}$, if*

$$\Theta(\varrho \chi_1 + (1-\varrho)\chi_2) \leq \left(\frac{1}{n}\sum_{\ell_1=1}^{n} h_{\ell_1}(\varrho)\right)\Theta(\chi_1) + \left(\frac{1}{m}\sum_{\ell_2=1}^{m} g_{\ell_2}(\varrho)\right)\Theta(\chi_2), \tag{9}$$

holds for every $\chi_1, \chi_2 \in \tau$ and $\varrho \in [0,1]$.

Remark 1. *From Definition 6, we can observe that:*

1. *If $n = m = 1$, $h_{\ell_1}(\varrho) = 1 - (1-\varrho)^{\ell_1}$ and $g_{\ell_2}(\varrho) = 1 - \varrho^{\ell_2}$, then we have Definition 1.*
2. *If $n = m = 1$, $h_{\ell_1}(\varrho) = \varrho^s$ and $g_{\ell_2}(\varrho) = (1-\varrho)^s$, then we obtain Definition 2.*
3. *If $n = m = 1$, $h_{\ell_1}(\varrho) = h(\varrho)$ and $g_{\ell_2}(\varrho) = h(1-\varrho)$, then we obtain Definition 3.*
4. *If $n = m$, $h_{\ell_1}(\varrho) = 1 - (1-\varrho)^{\ell_1}$ and $g_{\ell_2}(\varrho) = 1 - \varrho^{\ell_2}$, then we obtain Definition 4.*
5. *If $n = m$, $h_{\ell_1}(\varrho) = 1 - (s(1-\varrho))^{\ell_1}$ and $g_{\ell_2}(\varrho) = 1 - (s\varrho)^{\ell_2}$, then we obtain Definition 5.*

Interested readers can derive many other known and unknown classes for suitable choices of the above functions h_{ℓ_1} and g_{ℓ_2}.

This article is divided into five sections: in Section 2, algebraic properties of the (n, m)–generalized convex function are presented. In Section 3, a new version of the HH inequality is presented; by using this definition, we will also derive the products of two functions of this type. In Section 4, we obtain general results by using the well-known identities of midpoint-type inequalities of Ostrowski and Simpson for our new defined convex functions; we obtain special cases from these. Section 5 concludes the article.

2. Algebraic Properties of the New Convex Function

This section deals with algebraic properties of our new definition.

Theorem 4. *Suppose that $1 \leq n \leq m$, where $n, m \in \mathbb{N}$, and assume that $h_{\ell_1}, g_{\ell_2} : [0,1] \to [0, +\infty)$ are continuous functions for all $\ell_1 = 1, 2, \ldots, n$ and $\ell_2 = 1, 2, \ldots, m$, and $\Theta, \Theta_1, \Theta_2 : \tau \to \mathbb{R}$. If $\Theta, \Theta_1,$ and Θ_2 are three nonnegative (n, m)-generalized convex functions with respect to $\mathcal{D}$, then*

1. $\Theta_1 + \Theta_2$ *is the (n, m)-generalized convex with respect to $\mathcal{D}$;*
2. $c\Theta$ *is the (n, m)-generalized convex with respect to $\mathcal{D}$ for any nonnegative real number c.*

Proof. The proof is evident, so we omit it. □

Theorem 5. *Suppose that $1 \leq n \leq m$, where $n, m \in \mathbb{N}$, and assume that $h_{\ell_1}, g_{\ell_2} : [0,1] \to [0, +\infty)$ are continuous functions for all $\ell_1 = 1, 2, \ldots, n$ and $\ell_2 = 1, 2, \ldots, m$. Let $\Theta_1 : \tau \to \mathbb{R}$ be a convex function and $\Theta_2 : \mathbb{R} \to \mathbb{R}$ is a non-decreasing and nonnegative (n, m)-generalized convex function with respect to $\mathcal{D}$. Then the function $\Theta_2 \circ \Theta_1 : \tau \to \mathbb{R}$ is an (n, m)-generalized convex with respect to $\mathcal{D}$.*

Proof. For all $\chi_1, \chi_2 \in \tau$ and $\varrho \in [0, 1]$, we have

$$(\Theta_2 \circ \Theta_1)(\varrho\chi_1 + (1-\varrho)\chi_2) = \Theta_2(\Theta_1(\varrho\chi_1 + (1-\varrho)\chi_2))$$
$$\leq \Theta_2(\varrho\Theta_1(\chi_1) + (1-\varrho)\Theta_1(\chi_2))$$
$$\leq \left(\frac{1}{n}\sum_{\ell_1=1}^{n} h_{\ell_1}(\varrho)\right)\Theta_2(\Theta_1(\chi_1)) + \left(\frac{1}{m}\sum_{\ell_2=1}^{m} g_{\ell_2}(\varrho)\right)\Theta_2(\Theta_1(\chi_2))$$
$$= \left(\frac{1}{n}\sum_{\ell_1=1}^{n} h_{\ell_1}(\varrho)\right)(\Theta_2 \circ \Theta_1)(\chi_1) + \left(\frac{1}{m}\sum_{\ell_2=1}^{m} g_{\ell_2}(\varrho)\right)(\Theta_2 \circ \Theta_1)(\chi_2),$$

which ends our proof. □

Theorem 6. *Suppose that $1 \leq n \leq m$, where $n, m \in \mathbb{N}$, and assume that $h_{\ell_1}, g_{\ell_2} : [0,1] \to [0, +\infty)$ are continuous functions for all $\ell_1 = 1, 2, \ldots, n$ and $\ell_2 = 1, 2, \ldots, m$. Let $\Theta_k : [\chi_1, \chi_2] \to \mathbb{R}$ be a family of nonnegative (n, m)-generalized convex functions with respect to $\mathcal{D}$ and $\Theta(\chi) = \sup_k \Theta_k(\chi)$. Then Θ is an (n, m)-generalized convex function with respect to $\mathcal{D}$ and $\mathcal{U} = \{\chi \in [\chi_1, \chi_2] : \Theta(\chi) < +\infty\}$ is an interval.*

Proof. Let $\chi_1, \chi_2 \in \mathcal{U}$ and $\varrho \in [0, 1]$, then

$$\Theta(\varrho\chi_1 + (1-\varrho)\chi_2) = \sup_k \Theta_k(\varrho\chi_1 + (1-\varrho)\chi_2)$$
$$\leq \left(\frac{1}{n}\sum_{\ell_1=1}^{n} h_{\ell_1}(\varrho)\right)\sup_k \Theta_k(\chi_1) + \left(\frac{1}{m}\sum_{\ell_2=1}^{m} g_{\ell_2}(\varrho)\right)\sup_k \Theta_k(\chi_2)$$
$$= \left(\frac{1}{n}\sum_{\ell_1=1}^{n} h_{\ell_1}(\varrho)\right)\Theta(\chi_1) + \left(\frac{1}{m}\sum_{\ell_2=1}^{m} g_{\ell_2}(\varrho)\right)\Theta(\chi_2) < +\infty,$$

which ends our proof. □

Theorem 7. *Suppose that $1 \leq n \leq m$, where $n, m \in \mathbb{N}$, and assume that $h_{\ell_1}, g_{\ell_2} : [0,1] \to [0, +\infty)$ are continuous functions for all $\ell_1 = 1, 2, \ldots, n$ and $\ell_2 = 1, 2, \ldots, m$. If $\Theta : [\chi_1, \chi_2] \to \mathbb{R}$ is a nonnegative (n, m)-generalized convex function with respect to $\mathcal{D}$, then Θ is bounded on $[\chi_1, \chi_2]$.*

Proof. Let $K = \max\{\Theta(\chi_1), \Theta(\chi_2)\}$ and $x \in [\chi_1, \chi_2]$. Then, there exists $\varrho \in [0,1]$, such that $x = \varrho\chi_1 + (1-\varrho)\chi_2$. Moreover, since h_{ℓ_1}, g_{ℓ_2} are continuous functions on $[0,1]$ for all $\ell_1 = 1, 2, \ldots, n$ and $\ell_2 = 1, 2, \ldots, m$, then we denote, respectively, $L_1 = \max\{h_1, h_2, \ldots, h_n\}$ and $L_2 = \max\{g_1, g_2, \ldots, g_m\}$. Hence,

$$\Theta(x) = \Theta(\varrho\chi_1 + (1-\varrho)\chi_2) \leq \left(\frac{1}{n}\sum_{\ell_1=1}^{n} h_{\ell_1}(\varrho)\right)\Theta(\chi_1) + \left(\frac{1}{m}\sum_{\ell_2=1}^{m} g_{\ell_2}(\varrho)\right)\Theta(\chi_2)$$

$$\leq K\left[\frac{1}{n}\sum_{\ell_1=1}^{n} h_{\ell_1}(\varrho) + \frac{1}{m}\sum_{\ell_2=1}^{m} g_{\ell_2}(\varrho)\right]$$

$$\leq K\left[\frac{1}{n}\sum_{\ell_1=1}^{n} L_1 + \frac{1}{m}\sum_{\ell_2=1}^{m} L_2\right]$$

$$= K(L_1 + L_2) = M.$$

Moreover, for all $x \in [\chi_1, \chi_2]$, there exists $\xi \in \left[0, \frac{\chi_2-\chi_1}{2}\right]$, such that $x = \frac{\chi_1+\chi_2}{2} + \xi$ or $x = \frac{\chi_1+\chi_2}{2} - \xi$. Let us suppose that $x = \frac{\chi_1+\chi_2}{2} + \xi$ without loss of generality. So, we have

$$\Theta\left(\frac{\chi_1+\chi_2}{2}\right) = \Theta\left(\frac{1}{2}\left[\frac{\chi_1+\chi_2}{2}+\xi\right] + \frac{1}{2}\left[\frac{\chi_1+\chi_2}{2}-\xi\right]\right)$$

$$\leq \left(\frac{1}{n}\sum_{\ell_1=1}^{n} h_{\ell_1}\left(\frac{1}{2}\right)\right)\Theta(x) + \left(\frac{1}{m}\sum_{\ell_2=1}^{m} g_{\ell_2}\left(\frac{1}{2}\right)\right)\Theta\left(\frac{\chi_1+\chi_2}{2}-\xi\right)$$

$$\leq L_1\Theta(x) + L_2\Theta\left(\frac{\chi_1+\chi_2}{2}-\xi\right).$$

By making use of M as the upper bound, we can deduce

$$\Theta(x) \geq \frac{1}{L_1}\Theta\left(\frac{\chi_1+\chi_2}{2}\right) - M = m,$$

which ends our proof. □

3. The HH Inequality for the New Convex Function

In this section, we will establish some integral inequalities of the HH-type pertaining to the (n,m)–generalized convex functions.

Theorem 8. *Assume that $1 \leq n \leq m$, where $n, m \in \mathbb{N}$, and assume that $h_{\ell_1}, g_{\ell_2} : [0,1] \to [0, +\infty)$ are continuous functions for all $\ell_1 = 1, 2, \ldots, n$ and $\ell_2 = 1, 2, \ldots, m$. If $\Theta : [\chi_1, \chi_2] \to \mathbb{R}$ is a nonnegative (n,m)–generalized convex function with respect to $\mathcal{D}$, then we have*

$$\frac{1}{\frac{1}{n}\sum_{\ell_1=1}^{n} h_{\ell_1}\left(\frac{1}{2}\right) + \frac{1}{m}\sum_{\ell_2=1}^{m} g_{\ell_2}\left(\frac{1}{2}\right)}\Theta\left(\frac{\chi_1+\chi_2}{2}\right) \leq \frac{1}{\chi_2-\chi_1}\int_{\chi_1}^{\chi_2}\Theta(x)dx$$

$$\leq \left(\frac{\Theta(\chi_1)+\Theta(\chi_2)}{2}\right)\left[\frac{1}{n}\sum_{\ell_1=1}^{n} H_{\ell_1} + \frac{1}{m}\sum_{\ell_2=1}^{m} G_{\ell_2}\right], \quad (10)$$

where

$$H_{\ell_1} := \int_0^1 h_{\ell_1}(\varrho)d\varrho, \quad \forall \ell_1 = 1, 2, \ldots, n \quad \text{and} \quad G_{\ell_2} := \int_0^1 g_{\ell_2}(\varrho)d\varrho, \quad \forall \ell_2 = 1, 2, \ldots, m.$$

Proof. Let $w_1, w_2 \in [\chi_1, \chi_2]$. Applying the (n,m)-generalized convexity with respect to $\mathcal{D}$ of Θ on $[\chi_1, \chi_2]$, we have

$$\Theta\left(\frac{w_1+w_2}{2}\right) \leq \frac{1}{n}\sum_{\ell_1=1}^{n} h_{\ell_1}\left(\frac{1}{2}\right)\Theta(w_1) + \frac{1}{m}\sum_{\ell_2=1}^{m} g_{\ell_2}\left(\frac{1}{2}\right)\Theta(w_2). \tag{11}$$

Let us denote, respectively, $w_1 = \varrho\chi_2 + (1-\varrho)\chi_1$ and $w_2 = \varrho\chi_1 + (1-\varrho)\chi_2$. From inequality (11), we obtain

$$\Theta\left(\frac{\chi_1+\chi_2}{2}\right) \leq \frac{1}{n}\sum_{\ell_1=1}^{n} h_{\ell_1}\left(\frac{1}{2}\right)\Theta(\varrho\chi_2 + (1-\varrho)\chi_1) + \frac{1}{m}\sum_{\ell_2=1}^{m} g_{\ell_2}\left(\frac{1}{2}\right)\Theta(\varrho\chi_1 + (1-\varrho)\chi_2). \tag{12}$$

Integrating on both sides (12), with respect to ϱ from 0 to 1, we obtain

$$\Theta\left(\frac{\chi_1+\chi_2}{2}\right) \leq \left(\frac{1}{n}\sum_{\ell_1=1}^{n} h_{\ell_1}\left(\frac{1}{2}\right)\right) \int_0^1 \Theta(\varrho\chi_2 + (1-\varrho)\chi_1) d\varrho$$

$$+ \left(\frac{1}{m}\sum_{\ell_2=1}^{m} g_{\ell_2}\left(\frac{1}{2}\right)\right) \int_0^1 \Theta(\varrho\chi_1 + (1-\varrho)\chi_2) d\varrho$$

$$= \left(\frac{1}{n}\sum_{\ell_1=1}^{n} h_{\ell_1}\left(\frac{1}{2}\right) + \frac{1}{m}\sum_{\ell_2=1}^{m} g_{\ell_2}\left(\frac{1}{2}\right)\right) \frac{1}{\chi_2 - \chi_1} \int_{\chi_1}^{\chi_2} \Theta(x) dx,$$

which gives the proof of the left hand side of (10). For the right hand side of (10), we use the definition of (n,m)-generalized convexity with respect to $\mathcal{D}$ of Θ, where $\varrho \in [0,1]$. Hence,

$$\Theta(\varrho\chi_1 + (1-\varrho)\chi_2) \leq \left(\frac{1}{n}\sum_{\ell_1=1}^{n} h_{\ell_1}(\varrho)\right)\Theta(\chi_1) + \left(\frac{1}{m}\sum_{\ell_2=1}^{m} g_{\ell_2}(\varrho)\right)\Theta(\chi_2),$$

and

$$\Theta(\varrho\chi_2 + (1-\varrho)\chi_1) \leq \left(\frac{1}{n}\sum_{\ell_1=1}^{n} h_{\ell_1}(\varrho)\right)\Theta(\chi_2) + \left(\frac{1}{m}\sum_{\ell_2=1}^{m} g_{\ell_2}(\varrho)\right)\Theta(\chi_1).$$

Adding both of them, we have

$$\Theta(\varrho\chi_1 + (1-\varrho)\chi_2) + \Theta(\varrho\chi_2 + (1-\varrho)\chi_1) \leq \left(\frac{1}{n}\sum_{\ell_1=1}^{n} h_{\ell_1}(\varrho)\right)\Theta(\chi_1) + \left(\frac{1}{m}\sum_{\ell_2=1}^{m} g_{\ell_2}(\varrho)\right)\Theta(\chi_2)$$

$$+ \left(\frac{1}{n}\sum_{\ell_1=1}^{n} h_{\ell_1}(\varrho)\right)\Theta(\chi_2) + \left(\frac{1}{m}\sum_{\ell_2=1}^{m} g_{\ell_2}(\varrho)\right)\Theta(\chi_1). \tag{13}$$

Integrating on both sides (13) with respect to ϱ from 0 to 1, we obtain

$$\int_0^1 \Theta(\varrho\chi_1 + (1-\varrho)\chi_2) d\varrho + \int_0^1 \Theta(\varrho\chi_2 + (1-\varrho)\chi_1) d\varrho$$

$$\leq \int_0^1 \left[\left(\frac{1}{n}\sum_{\ell_1=1}^{n} h_{\ell_1}(\varrho)\right)\Theta(\chi_1) + \left(\frac{1}{m}\sum_{\ell_2=1}^{m} g_{\ell_2}(\varrho)\right)\Theta(\chi_2)\right] d\varrho$$

$$+ \int_0^1 \left[\left(\frac{1}{n}\sum_{\ell_1=1}^{n} h_{\ell_1}(\varrho)\right)\Theta(\chi_2) + \left(\frac{1}{m}\sum_{\ell_2=1}^{m} g_{\ell_2}(\varrho)\right)\Theta(\chi_1)\right] d\varrho,$$

which leads to

$$\frac{1}{\chi_2 - \chi_1}\int_{\chi_1}^{\chi_2} \Theta(x) dx \leq \left(\frac{\Theta(\chi_1) + \Theta(\chi_2)}{2}\right)\left[\frac{1}{n}\sum_{\ell_1=1}^{n} H_{\ell_1} + \frac{1}{m}\sum_{\ell_2=1}^{m} G_{\ell_2}\right],$$

which ends our proof. □

Remark 2. *We have particular cases from Theorem 8:*
- *If $h_{\ell_1}(\varrho) = \varrho$ and $g_{\ell_2}(\varrho) = \varrho$ for all $\ell_1 = 1, 2, \ldots, n$ and $\ell_2 = 1, 2, \ldots, m$, we have Theorem 1.*
- *If $n = m$, $h_{\ell_1}(\varrho) = 1 - (s(1-\varrho))^{\ell_1}$ and $g_{\ell_2}(\varrho) = 1 - (s\varrho)^{\ell_2}$ for $s \in [0,1]$, $\ell_1 = 1, 2, \ldots, n$ and $\ell_2 = 1, 2, \ldots, m$, we obtain ([23], Theorem 2.1).*
- *If $n = m$, $h_{\ell_1}(\varrho) = 1 - (1-\varrho)^{\ell_1}$ and $g_{\ell_2}(\varrho) = 1 - \varrho^{\ell_2}$ for all $\ell_1 = 1, 2, \ldots, n$ and $\ell_2 = 1, 2, \ldots, m$, we obtain ([22], Theorem 4).*

Theorem 9. *Let $1 \leq n_1 \leq m_1$ and $1 \leq n_2 \leq m_2$ where $n_1, n_2, m_1, m_2 \in \mathbb{N}$. Assume that $h_{\ell_1}^{(1)}, g_{\ell_2}^{(1)}, h_k^{(2)}, g_l^{(2)} : [0,1] \to [0, +\infty)$ are continuous functions for all $\ell_1 = 1, \ldots, n_1$, $\ell_2 = 1, \ldots, m_1$, $k = 1, \ldots, n_2$ and $l = 1, \ldots, m_2$. If $\Theta, \psi : [\chi_1, \chi_2] \to \mathbb{R}$ are nonnegative (n_1, m_1) and (n_2, m_2)–generalized convex functions with respect to*
$$\mathcal{D}^{(1)} = \left\{h_1^{(1)}, h_2^{(1)}, \ldots, h_{n_1}^{(1)}, g_1^{(1)}, g_2^{(1)}, \ldots, g_{m_1}^{(1)}\right\}, \text{ and}$$
$$\mathcal{D}^{(2)} = \left\{h_1^{(2)}, h_2^{(2)}, \ldots, h_{n_2}^{(2)}, g_1^{(2)}, g_2^{(2)}, \ldots, g_{m_2}^{(2)}\right\}, \text{ respectively, then we have}$$

$$\frac{1}{\chi_2 - \chi_1} \int_{\chi_1}^{\chi_2} \Theta(x)\psi(x)dx$$
$$\leq \left(\frac{1}{n_1 n_2} \sum_{\ell_1=1}^{n_1} \sum_{k=1}^{n_2} A_{\ell_1,k}\right) \Theta(\chi_1)\psi(\chi_1) + \left(\frac{1}{n_1 m_2} \sum_{\ell_1=1}^{n_1} \sum_{l=1}^{m_2} B_{\ell_1,l}\right) \Theta(\chi_1)\psi(\chi_2)$$
$$+ \left(\frac{1}{n_2 m_1} \sum_{k=1}^{n_2} \sum_{\ell_2=1}^{m_1} C_{k,\ell_2}\right) \Theta(\chi_2)\psi(\chi_1) + \left(\frac{1}{m_1 m_2} \sum_{\ell_2=1}^{m_1} \sum_{l=1}^{m_2} D_{\ell_2,l}\right) \Theta(\chi_2)\psi(\chi_2), \quad (14)$$

where
$$A_{\ell_1,k} := \int_0^1 h_{\ell_1}^{(1)}(\varrho) h_k^{(2)}(\varrho) d\varrho, \quad \forall \ell_1 = 1, 2, \ldots, n_1, \ \forall k = 1, 2, \ldots, n_2,$$
$$B_{\ell_1,l} := \int_0^1 h_{\ell_1}^{(1)}(\varrho) g_l^{(2)}(\varrho) d\varrho, \quad \forall \ell_1 = 1, 2, \ldots, n_1, \ \forall l = 1, 2, \ldots, m_2,$$
$$C_{k,\ell_2} := \int_0^1 h_k^{(2)}(\varrho) g_{\ell_2}^{(1)}(\varrho) d\varrho, \quad \forall k = 1, 2, \ldots, n_2, \ \forall \ell_2 = 1, 2, \ldots, m_1,$$

and
$$D_{\ell_2,l} := \int_0^1 g_{\ell_2}^{(1)}(\varrho) g_l^{(2)}(\varrho) d\varrho, \quad \forall \ell_2 = 1, 2, \ldots, m_1, \ \forall l = 1, 2, \ldots, m_2.$$

Proof. Applying (n_1, m_1) and (n_2, m_2)–generalized convexity with respect to $\mathcal{D}^{(1)}$ and $\mathcal{D}^{(2)}$ of Θ, ψ on $[\chi_1, \chi_2]$, respectively, we have

$$\Theta(\varrho \chi_1 + (1-\varrho)\chi_2) \leq \left(\frac{1}{n_1} \sum_{\ell_1=1}^{n_1} h_{\ell_1}^{(1)}(\varrho)\right) \Theta(\chi_1) + \left(\frac{1}{m_1} \sum_{\ell_2=1}^{m_1} g_{\ell_2}^{(1)}(\varrho)\right) \Theta(\chi_2) \quad (15)$$

and

$$\psi(\varrho \chi_1 + (1-\varrho)\chi_2) \leq \left(\frac{1}{n_2} \sum_{k=1}^{n_2} h_k^{(2)}(\varrho)\right) \psi(\chi_1) + \left(\frac{1}{m_2} \sum_{l=1}^{m_2} g_l^{(2)}(\varrho)\right) \psi(\chi_2). \quad (16)$$

Multiplying inequalities (15) and (16) on both sides, we obtain

$$\Theta(\varrho\chi_1 + (1-\varrho)\chi_2)\psi(\varrho\chi_1 + (1-\varrho)\chi_2)$$
$$\leq \left(\frac{1}{n_1}\sum_{\ell_1=1}^{n_1}h_{\ell_1}^{(1)}(\varrho)\right)\left(\frac{1}{n_2}\sum_{k=1}^{n_2}h_k^{(2)}(\varrho)\right)\Theta(\chi_1)\psi(\chi_1)$$
$$+ \left(\frac{1}{n_1}\sum_{\ell_1=1}^{n_1}h_{\ell_1}^{(1)}(\varrho)\right)\left(\frac{1}{m_2}\sum_{l=1}^{m_2}g_l^{(2)}(\varrho)\right)\Theta(\chi_1)\psi(\chi_2)$$
$$+ \left(\frac{1}{n_2}\sum_{k=1}^{n_2}h_k^{(2)}(\varrho)\right)\left(\frac{1}{m_1}\sum_{\ell_2=1}^{m_1}g_{\ell_2}^{(1)}(\varrho)\right)\Theta(\chi_2)\psi(\chi_1)$$
$$+ \left(\frac{1}{m_1}\sum_{\ell_2=1}^{m_1}g_{\ell_2}^{(1)}(\varrho)\right)\left(\frac{1}{m_2}\sum_{l=1}^{m_2}g_l^{(2)}(\varrho)\right)\Theta(\chi_2)\psi(\chi_2). \quad (17)$$

Integrating inequality (17) with respect to ϱ from 0 to 1 on both sides, we obtain

$$\int_0^1 \Theta(\varrho\chi_1 + (1-\varrho)\chi_2)\psi(\varrho\chi_1 + (1-\varrho)\chi_2)d\varrho = \frac{1}{\chi_2 - \chi_1}\int_{\chi_1}^{\chi_2}\Theta(x)\psi(x)dx$$
$$\leq \left(\frac{1}{n_1 n_2}\sum_{\ell_1=1}^{n_1}\sum_{k=1}^{n_2}\int_0^1 h_{\ell_1}^{(1)}(\varrho)h_k^{(2)}(\varrho)d\varrho\right)\Theta(\chi_1)\psi(\chi_1)$$
$$+ \left(\frac{1}{n_1 m_2}\sum_{\ell_1=1}^{n_1}\sum_{l=1}^{m_2}\int_0^1 h_{\ell_1}^{(1)}(\varrho)g_l^{(2)}(\varrho)d\varrho\right)\Theta(\chi_1)\psi(\chi_2)$$
$$+ \left(\frac{1}{n_2 m_1}\sum_{k=1}^{n_2}\sum_{\ell_2=1}^{m_1}\int_0^1 h_k^{(2)}(\varrho)g_{\ell_2}^{(1)}(\varrho)d\varrho\right)\Theta(\chi_2)\psi(\chi_1)$$
$$+ \left(\frac{1}{m_1 m_2}\sum_{\ell_2=1}^{m_1}\sum_{l=1}^{m_2}\int_0^1 g_{\ell_2}^{(1)}(\varrho)g_l^{(2)}(\varrho)d\varrho\right)\Theta(\chi_2)\psi(\chi_2).$$

$$= \left(\frac{1}{n_1 n_2}\sum_{\ell_1=1}^{n_1}\sum_{k=1}^{n_2}A_{\ell_1,k}\right)\Theta(\chi_1)\psi(\chi_1) + \left(\frac{1}{n_1 m_2}\sum_{\ell_1=1}^{n_1}\sum_{l=1}^{m_2}B_{\ell_1,l}\right)\Theta(\chi_1)\psi(\chi_2)$$
$$+ \left(\frac{1}{n_2 m_1}\sum_{k=1}^{n_2}\sum_{\ell_2=1}^{m_1}C_{k,\ell_2}\right)\Theta(\chi_2)\psi(\chi_1) + \left(\frac{1}{m_1 m_2}\sum_{\ell_2=1}^{m_1}\sum_{l=1}^{m_2}D_{\ell_2,l}\right)\Theta(\chi_2)\psi(\chi_2),$$

which ends our proof. □

4. Further Results

We denote by $\mathcal{L}[\chi_1, \chi_2]$ the set of all integrable functions on $[\chi_1, \chi_2]$. Let us recall the following lemmas in order to establish our following results.

Lemma 1 (Midpoint identity [26]). *Let $\Theta : \tau \subseteq \mathbb{R} \to \mathbb{R}$ be a differentiable function on τ and $\chi_1, \chi_2 \in \tau$ with $\chi_1 < \chi_2$. If $\Theta' \in \mathcal{L}[\chi_1, \chi_2]$, then*

$$\mathcal{T}(\Theta; \chi_1, \chi_2) := \frac{1}{\chi_2 - \chi_1}\int_{\chi_1}^{\chi_2}\Theta(\varrho)d\varrho - \Theta\left(\frac{\chi_1 + \chi_2}{2}\right)$$
$$= \frac{(\chi_2 - \chi_1)}{4}\left\{\int_0^1 \varrho\Theta'\left(\frac{\varrho}{2}\chi_1 + \frac{2-\varrho}{2}\chi_2\right)d\varrho - \int_0^1 \varrho\Theta'\left(\frac{\varrho}{2}\chi_2 + \frac{2-\varrho}{2}\chi_1\right)d\varrho\right\}. \quad (18)$$

Lemma 2 (Ostrowski identity [27]). *Let $\Theta : \tau \subseteq \mathbb{R} \to \mathbb{R}$ be a differentiable function on τ and $\chi_1, \chi_2 \in \tau$ with $\chi_1 < \chi_2$. If $\Theta' \in \mathcal{L}[\chi_1, \chi_2]$, then*

$$\mathcal{T}_1(\Theta; x, \chi_1, \chi_2) := \Theta(x) - \frac{1}{\chi_2 - \chi_1} \int_{\chi_1}^{\chi_2} \Theta(\varrho) d\varrho$$

$$= \frac{(x - \chi_1)^2}{\chi_2 - \chi_1} \int_0^1 \varrho \Theta'(\varrho x + (1 - \varrho)\chi_1) d\varrho - \frac{(\chi_2 - x)^2}{\chi_2 - \chi_1} \int_0^1 \varrho \Theta'(\varrho x + (1 - \varrho)\chi_2) d\varrho. \quad (19)$$

Lemma 3 (Simpson identity [28])**.** *Let $\Theta : \tau \subseteq \mathbb{R} \to \mathbb{R}$ be a differentiable function on τ and $\chi_1, \chi_2 \in \tau$ with $\chi_1 < \chi_2$. If $\Theta' \in \mathcal{L}[\chi_1, \chi_2]$, then*

$$\mathcal{T}_2(\Theta; \chi_1, \chi_2) := \frac{1}{6}\left[\Theta(\chi_1) + 4\Theta\left(\frac{\chi_1 + \chi_2}{2}\right) + \Theta(\chi_2)\right] - \frac{1}{\chi_2 - \chi_1} \int_{\chi_1}^{\chi_2} \Theta(\varrho) d\varrho$$

$$= (\chi_2 - \chi_1)\left\{\int_0^{\frac{1}{2}}\left(\varrho - \frac{1}{6}\right)\Theta'(\varrho\chi_2 + (1 - \varrho)\chi_1) d\varrho + \int_{\frac{1}{2}}^1\left(\varrho - \frac{5}{6}\right)\Theta'(\varrho\chi_2 + (1 - \varrho)\chi_1) d\varrho\right\}. \quad (20)$$

Theorem 10. *Suppose that $1 \leq n \leq m$, where $n, m \in \mathbb{N}$, and assume that $h_{\ell_1}, g_{\ell_2} : [0, 1] \to [0, +\infty)$ are continuous functions for all $\ell_1 = 1, 2, \ldots, n$ and $\ell_2 = 1, 2, \ldots, m$, and $\Theta : [\chi_1, \chi_2] \to \mathbb{R}$ be a differentiable function on (χ_1, χ_2) such that $\Theta' \in \mathcal{L}[\chi_1, \chi_2]$. If $|\Theta'|$ is an (n, m)-generalized convex function with respect to $\mathcal{D}$ on $[\chi_1, \chi_2]$, then we have*

$$|\mathcal{T}(\Theta; \chi_1, \chi_2)| \leq \frac{(\chi_2 - \chi_1)}{4}(|\Theta'(\chi_1)| + |\Theta'(\chi_2)|)\left[\frac{1}{n}\sum_{\ell_1=1}^n U_{\ell_1} + \frac{1}{m}\sum_{\ell_2=1}^m V_{\ell_2}\right], \quad (21)$$

where

$$U_{\ell_1} := \int_0^1 \varrho h_{\ell_1}\left(\frac{\varrho}{2}\right) d\varrho, \quad \forall \ell_1 = 1, 2, \ldots, n \quad \text{and} \quad V_{\ell_2} := \int_0^1 \varrho g_{\ell_2}\left(\frac{\varrho}{2}\right) d\varrho, \quad \forall \ell_2 = 1, 2, \ldots, m.$$

Proof. By using Lemma 1 and the (n, m)-generalized convexity of $|\Theta'|$ with respect to $\mathcal{D}$, we have

$$|\mathcal{T}(\Theta; \chi_1, \chi_2)| \leq \frac{(\chi_2 - \chi_1)}{4}\left\{\int_0^1 \varrho\left|\Theta'\left(\frac{\varrho}{2}\chi_1 + \frac{(2-\varrho)}{2}\chi_2\right)\right| d\varrho + \int_0^1 \varrho\left|\Theta'\left(\frac{\varrho}{2}\chi_2 + \frac{(2-\varrho)}{2}\chi_1\right)\right| d\varrho\right\}$$

$$\leq \frac{(\chi_2 - \chi_1)}{4}\left\{\int_0^1 \varrho\left[\left(\frac{1}{n}\sum_{\ell_1=1}^n h_{\ell_1}\left(\frac{\varrho}{2}\right)\right)|\Theta'(\chi_1)| + \left(\frac{1}{m}\sum_{\ell_2=1}^m g_{\ell_2}\left(\frac{\varrho}{2}\right)\right)|\Theta'(\chi_2)|\right] d\varrho\right.$$

$$\left. + \int_0^1 \varrho\left[\left(\frac{1}{n}\sum_{\ell_1=1}^n h_{\ell_1}\left(\frac{\varrho}{2}\right)\right)|\Theta'(\chi_2)| + \left(\frac{1}{m}\sum_{\ell_2=1}^m g_{\ell_2}\left(\frac{\varrho}{2}\right)\right)|\Theta'(\chi_1)|\right] d\varrho\right\}$$

$$= \frac{(\chi_2 - \chi_1)}{4}(|\Theta'(\chi_1)| + |\Theta'(\chi_2)|)\left[\frac{1}{n}\sum_{\ell_1=1}^n U_{\ell_1} + \frac{1}{m}\sum_{\ell_2=1}^m V_{\ell_2}\right],$$

which ends our proof. □

Corollary 1. *We have particular cases from Theorem 10:*

- *If $h_{\ell_1}(\varrho) = \varrho$ and $g_{\ell_2}(\varrho) = 1 - \varrho$ for all $\ell_1 = 1, 2, \ldots, n$, and $\ell_2 = 1, 2, \ldots, m$, we obtain*

$$|\mathcal{T}(\Theta; \chi_1, \chi_2)| \leq \frac{(\chi_2 - \chi_1)}{8}[|\Theta'(\chi_1)| + |\Theta'(\chi_2)|].$$

- If $h_{\ell_1}(\varrho) = \varrho^{\ell_1}$ and $g_{\ell_2}(\varrho) = (1-\varrho)^{\ell_2}$ for all $\ell_1 = 1,2,\ldots,n$, and $\ell_2 = 1,2,\ldots,m$, we obtain

$$|T(\Theta;\chi_1,\chi_2)| \leq \frac{(\chi_2-\chi_1)}{4}\left[|\Theta'(\chi_1)| + |\Theta'(\chi_2)|\right]$$

$$\times \left[\frac{1}{n}\sum_{\ell_1=1}^{n}\frac{1}{2^{\ell_1}(\ell_1+2)} + \frac{1}{m}\sum_{\ell_2=1}^{m}\frac{1}{2^{\ell_2}}\left(\frac{2}{\ell_2+1}\left(2^{\ell_2+1}-1\right) - \frac{1}{\ell_2+2}\left(2^{\ell_2+2}-1\right)\right)\right].$$

- If $h_{\ell_1}(\varrho) = \varrho^s$ and $g_{\ell_2}(\varrho) = (1-\varrho)^s$ for all $\ell_1 = 1,\ldots,n$, $\ell_2 = 1,\ldots,m$, and $s \in (0,1]$, we obtain

$$|T(\Theta;\chi_1,\chi_2)| \leq \frac{(\chi_2-\chi_1)}{4}\left[|\Theta'(\chi_1)| + |\Theta'(\chi_2)|\right]$$

$$\times \left[\frac{1}{2^s(s+2)} + \frac{1}{2^s}\left(\frac{2}{s+1}\left(2^{s+1}-1\right) - \frac{1}{s+2}\left(2^{s+2}-1\right)\right)\right].$$

Theorem 11. *Suppose that $1 \leq n \leq m$, where $n,m \in \mathbb{N}$, and assume that $h_{\ell_1}, g_{\ell_2} : [0,1] \to [0,+\infty)$ are continuous functions for all $\ell_1 = 1,2,\ldots,n$ and $\ell_2 = 1,2,\ldots,m$, and $\Theta : [\chi_1,\chi_2] \to \mathbb{R}$ be a differentiable function on (χ_1,χ_2), such that $\Theta' \in \mathcal{L}[\chi_1,\chi_2]$. If $|\Theta'|^q$ is an (n,m)-generalized convex function with respect to $\mathcal{D}$ on $[\chi_1,\chi_2]$, then for $q > 1$ and $\frac{1}{p} + \frac{1}{q} = 1$, we have*

$$|T(\Theta;\chi_1,\chi_2)| \leq \frac{(\chi_2-\chi_1)}{4}\left(\frac{1}{p+1}\right)^{\frac{1}{p}}\left\{\left[\left(\frac{1}{n}\sum_{\ell_1=1}^{n}M_{\ell_1}\right)|\Theta'(\chi_1)|^q + \left(\frac{1}{m}\sum_{\ell_2=1}^{m}N_{\ell_2}\right)|\Theta'(\chi_2)|^q\right]^{\frac{1}{q}}\right.$$

$$\left. + \left[\left(\frac{1}{n}\sum_{\ell_1=1}^{n}M_{\ell_1}\right)|\Theta'(\chi_2)|^q + \left(\frac{1}{m}\sum_{\ell_2=1}^{m}N_{\ell_2}\right)|\Theta'(\chi_1)|^q\right]^{\frac{1}{q}}\right\}, \quad (22)$$

where

$$M_{\ell_1} := \int_0^1 h_{\ell_1}\left(\frac{\varrho}{2}\right)d\varrho, \quad \forall \ell_1 = 1,2,\ldots,n \quad \text{and} \quad N_{\ell_2} := \int_0^1 g_{\ell_2}\left(\frac{\varrho}{2}\right)d\varrho, \quad \forall \ell_2 = 1,2,\ldots,m.$$

Proof. By using Lemma 1, Hölder's inequality and the (n,m)-generalized convexity of $|\Theta'|^q$ with respect to $\mathcal{D}$, we have

$$|T(\Theta;\chi_1,\chi_2)| \leq \frac{(\chi_2-\chi_1)}{4}\left\{\int_0^1 \varrho\left|\Theta'\left(\frac{\varrho}{2}\chi_1 + \frac{(2-\varrho)}{2}\chi_2\right)\right|d\varrho + \int_0^1 \varrho\left|\Theta'\left(\frac{\varrho}{2}\chi_2 + \frac{(2-\varrho)}{2}\chi_1\right)\right|d\varrho\right\}$$

$$\leq \frac{(\chi_2-\chi_1)}{4}\left(\int_0^1 \varrho^p d\varrho\right)^{\frac{1}{p}}$$

$$\times \left\{\left(\int_0^1\left|\Theta'\left(\frac{\varrho}{2}\chi_1 + \frac{(2-\varrho)}{2}\chi_2\right)\right|^q d\varrho\right)^{\frac{1}{q}} + \left(\int_0^1\left|\Theta'\left(\frac{\varrho}{2}\chi_2 + \frac{(2-\varrho)}{2}\chi_1\right)\right|^q d\varrho\right)^{\frac{1}{q}}\right\}$$

$$\leq \frac{(\chi_2-\chi_1)}{4}\left(\frac{1}{p+1}\right)^{\frac{1}{p}}$$

$$\times \left\{\left[\int_0^1\left(\left(\frac{1}{n}\sum_{\ell_1=1}^{n}h_{\ell_1}\left(\frac{\varrho}{2}\right)\right)|\Theta'(\chi_1)|^q + \left(\frac{1}{m}\sum_{\ell_2=1}^{m}g_{\ell_2}\left(\frac{\varrho}{2}\right)\right)|\Theta'(\chi_2)|^q\right)d\varrho\right]^{\frac{1}{q}}\right.$$

$$\left. + \left[\int_0^1\left(\left(\frac{1}{n}\sum_{\ell_1=1}^{n}h_{\ell_1}\left(\frac{\varrho}{2}\right)\right)|\Theta'(\chi_2)|^q + \left(\frac{1}{m}\sum_{\ell_2=1}^{m}g_{\ell_2}\left(\frac{\varrho}{2}\right)\right)|\Theta'(\chi_1)|^q\right)d\varrho\right]^{\frac{1}{q}}\right\}$$

$$= \frac{(\chi_2 - \chi_1)}{4} \left(\frac{1}{p+1}\right)^{\frac{1}{p}} \left\{ \left[\left(\frac{1}{n}\sum_{\ell_1=1}^{n} M_{\ell_1}\right) |\Theta'(\chi_1)|^q + \left(\frac{1}{m}\sum_{\ell_2=1}^{m} N_{\ell_2}\right) |\Theta'(\chi_2)|^q \right]^{\frac{1}{q}} \right.$$

$$\left. + \left[\left(\frac{1}{n}\sum_{\ell_1=1}^{n} M_{\ell_1}\right) |\Theta'(\chi_2)|^q + \left(\frac{1}{m}\sum_{\ell_2=1}^{m} N_{\ell_2}\right) |\Theta'(\chi_1)|^q \right]^{\frac{1}{q}} \right\},$$

which ends our proof. □

Corollary 2. *We have particular cases from Theorem 11:*

- *If $h_{\ell_1}(\varrho) = \varrho$ and $g_{\ell_2}(\varrho) = 1 - \varrho$ for all $\ell_1 = 1, 2, \ldots, n$, and $\ell_2 = 1, 2, \ldots, m$, we have*

$$|T(\Theta; \chi_1, \chi_2)| \le \frac{(\chi_2 - \chi_1)}{4\sqrt[q]{4}} \left(\frac{1}{p+1}\right)^{\frac{1}{p}} \left\{ \left[|\Theta'(\chi_1)|^q + 3|\Theta'(\chi_2)|^q\right]^{\frac{1}{q}} + \left[3|\Theta'(\chi_1)|^q + |\Theta'(\chi_2)|^q\right]^{\frac{1}{q}} \right\}.$$

- *If $h_{\ell_1}(\varrho) = \varrho^{\ell_1}$ and $g_{\ell_2}(\varrho) = (1-\varrho)^{\ell_2}$ for all $\ell_1 = 1, 2, \ldots, n$, and $\ell_2 = 1, 2, \ldots, m$, we obtain*

$$|T(\Theta; \chi_1, \chi_2)| \le \frac{(\chi_2 - \chi_1)}{4} \left(\frac{1}{p+1}\right)^{\frac{1}{p}}$$

$$\times \left\{ \left[\left(\frac{1}{n}\sum_{\ell_1=1}^{n} \frac{1}{2^{\ell_1}(\ell_1+1)}\right) |\Theta'(\chi_1)|^q + \left(\frac{1}{m}\sum_{\ell_2=1}^{m} \frac{2^{\ell_2+1}-1}{2^{\ell_2}(\ell_2+1)}\right) |\Theta'(\chi_2)|^q \right]^{\frac{1}{q}} \right.$$

$$\left. + \left[\left(\frac{1}{n}\sum_{\ell_1=1}^{n} \frac{1}{2^{\ell_1}(\ell_1+1)}\right) |\Theta'(\chi_2)|^q + \left(\frac{1}{m}\sum_{\ell_2=1}^{m} \frac{2^{\ell_2+1}-1}{2^{\ell_2}(\ell_2+1)}\right) |\Theta'(\chi_1)|^q \right]^{\frac{1}{q}} \right\}.$$

- *If $h_{\ell_1}(\varrho) = \varrho^s$ and $g_{\ell_2}(\varrho) = (1-\varrho)^s$ for all $\ell_1 = 1, \ldots, n$, $\ell_2 = 1, \ldots, m$, and $s \in (0, 1]$, we obtain*

$$|T(\Theta; \chi_1, \chi_2)| \le \frac{(\chi_2 - \chi_1)}{4\sqrt[q]{2^s(s+1)}} \left(\frac{1}{p+1}\right)^{\frac{1}{p}}$$

$$\times \left\{ \left[|\Theta'(\chi_1)|^q + (2^{s+1}-1)|\Theta'(\chi_2)|^q\right]^{\frac{1}{q}} + \left[(2^{s+1}-1)|\Theta'(\chi_1)|^q + |\Theta'(\chi_2)|^q\right]^{\frac{1}{q}} \right\}.$$

Theorem 12. *Suppose that $1 \le n \le m$, where $n, m \in \mathbb{N}$, and assume that $h_{\ell_1}, g_{\ell_2} : [0, 1] \to [0, +\infty)$ are continuous functions for all $\ell_1 = 1, 2, \ldots, n$ and $\ell_2 = 1, 2, \ldots, m$, and $\Theta : [\chi_1, \chi_2] \to \mathbb{R}$ be a differentiable function on (χ_1, χ_2), such that $\Theta' \in L[\chi_1, \chi_2]$. If $|\Theta'|^q$ is an (n, m)-generalized convex function with respect to $\mathcal{D}$ on $[\chi_1, \chi_2]$, then for $q > 1$, we have*

$$|T(\Theta; \chi_1, \chi_2)| \le \frac{(\chi_2 - \chi_1)}{4} \left(\frac{1}{2}\right)^{1-\frac{1}{q}} \left\{ \left[\left(\frac{1}{n}\sum_{\ell_1=1}^{n} U_{\ell_1}\right) |\Theta'(\chi_1)|^q + \left(\frac{1}{m}\sum_{\ell_2=1}^{m} V_{\ell_2}\right) |\Theta'(\chi_2)|^q \right]^{\frac{1}{q}} \right.$$

$$\left. + \left[\left(\frac{1}{n}\sum_{\ell_1=1}^{n} U_{\ell_1}\right) |\Theta'(\chi_2)|^q + \left(\frac{1}{m}\sum_{\ell_2=1}^{m} V_{\ell_2}\right) |\Theta'(\chi_1)|^q \right]^{\frac{1}{q}} \right\}, \quad (23)$$

where U_{ℓ_1} and V_{ℓ_2} are defined as in Theorem 10.

Proof. By using Lemma 1, the well-known power mean inequality and the (n, m)-generalized convexity of $|\Theta'|^q$ with respect to $\mathcal{D}$, we have

$$|T(\Theta; \chi_1, \chi_2)| \le \frac{(\chi_2 - \chi_1)}{4} \left\{ \int_0^1 \varrho \left|\Theta'\left(\frac{\varrho}{2}\chi_1 + \frac{(2-\varrho)}{2}\chi_2\right)\right| d\varrho + \int_0^1 \varrho \left|\Theta'\left(\frac{\varrho}{2}\chi_2 + \frac{(2-\varrho)}{2}\chi_1\right)\right| d\varrho \right\}$$

$$\leq \frac{(\chi_2-\chi_1)}{4}\left(\int_0^1 \varrho\, d\varrho\right)^{1-\frac{1}{q}}$$

$$\times\left\{\left(\int_0^1 \varrho\left|\Theta'\left(\frac{\varrho}{2}\chi_1+\frac{(2-\varrho)}{2}\chi_2\right)\right|^q d\varrho\right)^{\frac{1}{q}}+\left(\int_0^1 \varrho\left|\Theta'\left(\frac{\varrho}{2}\chi_2+\frac{(2-\varrho)}{2}\chi_1\right)\right|^q d\varrho\right)^{\frac{1}{q}}\right\}$$

$$\leq \frac{(\chi_2-\chi_1)}{4}\left(\frac{1}{2}\right)^{1-\frac{1}{q}}$$

$$\times\left\{\left[\int_0^1 \varrho\left(\left(\frac{1}{n}\sum_{\ell_1=1}^n h_{\ell_1}\left(\frac{\varrho}{2}\right)\right)|\Theta'(\chi_1)|^q+\left(\frac{1}{m}\sum_{\ell_2=1}^m g_{\ell_2}\left(\frac{\varrho}{2}\right)\right)|\Theta'(\chi_2)|^q\right) d\varrho\right]^{\frac{1}{q}}\right.$$

$$\left.+\left[\int_0^1 \varrho\left(\left(\frac{1}{n}\sum_{\ell_1=1}^n h_{\ell_1}\left(\frac{\varrho}{2}\right)\right)|\Theta'(\chi_2)|^q+\left(\frac{1}{m}\sum_{\ell_2=1}^m g_{\ell_2}\left(\frac{\varrho}{2}\right)\right)|\Theta'(\chi_1)|^q\right) d\varrho\right]^{\frac{1}{q}}\right\}$$

$$=\frac{(\chi_2-\chi_1)}{4}\left(\frac{1}{2}\right)^{1-\frac{1}{q}}\left\{\left[\left(\frac{1}{n}\sum_{\ell_1=1}^n U_{\ell_1}\right)|\Theta'(\chi_1)|^q+\left(\frac{1}{m}\sum_{\ell_2=1}^m V_{\ell_2}\right)|\Theta'(\chi_2)|^q\right]^{\frac{1}{q}}\right.$$

$$\left.+\left[\left(\frac{1}{n}\sum_{\ell_1=1}^n U_{\ell_1}\right)|\Theta'(\chi_2)|^q+\left(\frac{1}{m}\sum_{\ell_2=1}^m V_{\ell_2}\right)|\Theta'(\chi_1)|^q\right]^{\frac{1}{q}}\right\},$$

which ends our proof. □

Corollary 3. *We have particular cases from Theorem 12:*

- If $h_{\ell_1}(\varrho)=\varrho$ and $g_{\ell_2}(\varrho)=1-\varrho$ for all $\ell_1=1,2,\ldots,n$, and $\ell_2=1,2,\ldots,m$, we obtain

$$|\mathcal{T}(\Theta;\chi_1,\chi_2)|\leq \frac{(\chi_2-\chi_1)}{8\sqrt[q]{3}}\left\{\left[|\Theta'(\chi_1)|^q+2|\Theta'(\chi_2)|^q\right]^{\frac{1}{q}}+\left[2|\Theta'(\chi_1)|^q+|\Theta'(\chi_2)|^q\right]^{\frac{1}{q}}\right\}.$$

- If $h_{\ell_1}(\varrho)=\varrho^{\ell_1}$ and $g_{\ell_2}(\varrho)=(1-\varrho)^{\ell_2}$ for all $\ell_1=1,2,\ldots,n$, and $\ell_2=1,2,\ldots,m$, we obtain

$$|\mathcal{T}(\Theta;\chi_1,\chi_2)|\leq \frac{(\chi_2-\chi_1)}{4}\left(\frac{1}{2}\right)^{1-\frac{1}{q}}$$

$$\times\left\{\left[\left(\frac{1}{n}\sum_{\ell_1=1}^n \frac{1}{2^{\ell_1}(\ell_1+2)}\right)|\Theta'(\chi_1)|^q\right.\right.$$

$$\left.\left.+\left(\frac{1}{m}\sum_{\ell_2=1}^m \frac{1}{2^{\ell_2}}\left(\frac{2}{\ell_2+1}\left(2^{\ell_2+1}-1\right)-\frac{1}{\ell_2+2}\left(2^{\ell_2+2}-1\right)\right)\right)|\Theta'(\chi_2)|^q\right]^{\frac{1}{q}}\right.$$

$$+\left[\left(\frac{1}{n}\sum_{\ell_1=1}^n \frac{1}{2^{\ell_1}(\ell_1+2)}\right)|\Theta'(\chi_2)|^q\right.$$

$$\left.\left.+\left(\frac{1}{m}\sum_{\ell_2=1}^m \frac{1}{2^{\ell_2}}\left(\frac{2}{\ell_2+1}\left(2^{\ell_2+1}-1\right)-\frac{1}{\ell_2+2}\left(2^{\ell_2+2}-1\right)\right)\right)|\Theta'(\chi_1)|^q\right]^{\frac{1}{q}}\right\}.$$

- If $h_{\ell_1}(\varrho)=\varrho^s$ and $g_{\ell_2}(\varrho)=(1-\varrho)^s$ for all $\ell_1=1,\ldots,n$, $\ell_2=1,\ldots,m$, and $s\in(0,1]$, we obtain

$$|\mathcal{T}(\Theta;\chi_1,\chi_2)| \leq \frac{(\chi_2-\chi_1)}{4}\left(\frac{1}{2}\right)^{1-\frac{1}{q}}$$

$$\times \left\{\left[\frac{1}{2^s(s+2)}|\Theta'(\chi_1)|^q + \frac{1}{2^s}\left(\frac{2}{s+1}\left(2^{s+1}-1\right) - \frac{1}{s+2}\left(2^{s+2}-1\right)\right)|\Theta'(\chi_2)|^q\right]^{\frac{1}{q}}\right.$$

$$\left. + \left[\frac{1}{2^s(s+2)}|\Theta'(\chi_2)|^q + \frac{1}{2^s}\left(\frac{2}{s+1}\left(2^{s+1}-1\right) - \frac{1}{s+2}\left(2^{s+2}-1\right)\right)|\Theta'(\chi_1)|^q\right]^{\frac{1}{q}}\right\}.$$

Theorem 13. *Suppose that $1 \leq n \leq m$, where $n, m \in \mathbb{N}$, and assume that $h_{\ell_1}, g_{\ell_2} : [0,1] \to [0,+\infty)$ are continuous functions for all $\ell_1 = 1, 2, \ldots, n$ and $\ell_2 = 1, 2, \ldots, m$, and $\Theta : [\chi_1, \chi_2] \to \mathbb{R}$ be a differentiable function on (χ_1, χ_2), such that $\Theta' \in \mathcal{L}[\chi_1, \chi_2]$. If $|\Theta'|$ is an (n,m)-generalized convex function with respect to $\mathcal{D}$ on $[\chi_1, \chi_2]$, then we have*

$$|\mathcal{T}_1(\Theta;x,\chi_1,\chi_2)| \leq \frac{(x-\chi_1)^2}{\chi_2-\chi_1}\left[\left(\frac{1}{n}\sum_{\ell_1=1}^{n}E_{\ell_1}\right)|\Theta'(x)| + \left(\frac{1}{m}\sum_{\ell_2=1}^{m}F_{\ell_2}\right)|\Theta'(\chi_1)|\right]$$

$$+ \frac{(\chi_2-x)^2}{\chi_2-\chi_1}\left[\left(\frac{1}{n}\sum_{\ell_1=1}^{n}E_{\ell_1}\right)|\Theta'(x)| + \left(\frac{1}{m}\sum_{\ell_2=1}^{m}F_{\ell_2}\right)|\Theta'(\chi_2)|\right], \quad (24)$$

where

$$E_{\ell_1} := \int_0^1 \varrho h_{\ell_1}(\varrho) d\varrho, \quad \forall \ell_1 = 1, 2, \ldots, n \quad \text{and} \quad F_{\ell_2} := \int_0^1 \varrho g_{\ell_2}(\varrho) d\varrho, \quad \forall \ell_2 = 1, 2, \ldots, m.$$

Proof. By using Lemma 2 and the (n,m)-generalized convexity of $|\Theta'|$ with respect to $\mathcal{D}$, we have

$$|\mathcal{T}_1(\Theta;x,\chi_1,\chi_2)| \leq \frac{(x-\chi_1)^2}{\chi_2-\chi_1}\int_0^1 \varrho|\Theta'(\varrho x + (1-\varrho)\chi_1)|d\varrho$$

$$+ \frac{(\chi_2-x)^2}{\chi_2-\chi_1}\int_0^1 \varrho|\Theta'(\varrho x + (1-\varrho)\chi_2)|d\varrho$$

$$\leq \frac{(x-\chi_1)^2}{\chi_2-\chi_1}\int_0^1 \varrho\left[\left(\frac{1}{n}\sum_{\ell_1=1}^{n}h_{\ell_1}(\varrho)\right)|\Theta'(x)| + \left(\frac{1}{m}\sum_{\ell_2=1}^{m}g_{\ell_2}(\varrho)\right)|\Theta'(\chi_1)|\right]d\varrho$$

$$+ \frac{(\chi_2-x)^2}{\chi_2-\chi_1}\int_0^1 \varrho\left[\left(\frac{1}{n}\sum_{\ell_1=1}^{n}h_{\ell_1}(\varrho)\right)|\Theta'(x)| + \left(\frac{1}{m}\sum_{\ell_2=1}^{m}g_{\ell_2}(\varrho)\right)|\Theta'(\chi_2)|\right]d\varrho$$

$$= \frac{(x-\chi_1)^2}{\chi_2-\chi_1}\left[\left(\frac{1}{n}\sum_{\ell_1=1}^{n}E_{\ell_1}\right)|\Theta'(x)| + \left(\frac{1}{m}\sum_{\ell_2=1}^{m}F_{\ell_2}\right)|\Theta'(\chi_1)|\right]$$

$$+ \frac{(\chi_2-x)^2}{\chi_2-\chi_1}\left[\left(\frac{1}{n}\sum_{\ell_1=1}^{n}E_{\ell_1}\right)|\Theta'(x)| + \left(\frac{1}{m}\sum_{\ell_2=1}^{m}F_{\ell_2}\right)|\Theta'(\chi_2)|\right],$$

which ends our proof. □

Corollary 4. *We have particular cases from Theorem 13:*

- *If $h_{\ell_1}(\varrho) = \varrho$ and $g_{\ell_2}(\varrho) = 1 - \varrho$ for all $\ell_1 = 1, 2, \ldots, n$, and $\ell_2 = 1, 2, \ldots, m$, we obtain*

$$|\mathcal{T}_1(\Theta;x,\chi_1,\chi_2)| \leq \frac{(x-\chi_1)^2}{6(\chi_2-\chi_1)}[2|\Theta'(x)| + |\Theta'(\chi_1)|] + \frac{(\chi_2-x)^2}{6(\chi_2-\chi_1)}[2|\Theta'(x)| + |\Theta'(\chi_2)|].$$

- *If $h_{\ell_1}(\varrho) = \varrho^{\ell_1}$ and $g_{\ell_2}(\varrho) = (1-\varrho)^{\ell_2}$ for all $\ell_1 = 1, 2, \ldots, n$, and $\ell_2 = 1, 2, \ldots, m$, we obtain*

$$'|\mathcal{T}_1(\Theta;x,\chi_1,\chi_2)| \leq \frac{(x-\chi_1)^2}{\chi_2-\chi_1}\left[\left(\frac{1}{n}\sum_{\ell_1=1}^n \frac{1}{\ell_1+2}\right)|\Theta'(x)| + \left(\frac{1}{m}\sum_{\ell_2=1}^m \frac{1}{(\ell_2+1)(\ell_2+2)}\right)|\Theta'(\chi_1)|\right]$$
$$+ \frac{(\chi_2-x)^2}{\chi_2-\chi_1}\left[\left(\frac{1}{n}\sum_{\ell_1=1}^n \frac{1}{\ell_1+2}\right)|\Theta'(x)| + \left(\frac{1}{m}\sum_{\ell_2=1}^m \frac{1}{(\ell_2+1)(\ell_2+2)}\right)|\Theta'(\chi_2)|\right].$$

- If $h_{\ell_1}(\varrho) = \varrho^s$ and $g_{\ell_2}(\varrho) = (1-\varrho)^s$ for all $\ell_1 = 1,\ldots,n$, $\ell_2 = 1,\ldots,m$, and $s \in (0,1]$, we obtain

$$|\mathcal{T}_1(\Theta;x,\chi_1,\chi_2)| \leq \frac{1}{(s+1)(s+2)}$$
$$\times \left\{\frac{(x-\chi_1)^2}{\chi_2-\chi_1}\left[(s+1)|\Theta'(x)| + |\Theta'(\chi_1)|\right] + \frac{(\chi_2-x)^2}{\chi_2-\chi_1}\left[(s+1)|\Theta'(x)| + |\Theta'(\chi_2)|\right]\right\}.$$

Theorem 14. Suppose that $1 \leq n \leq m$, where $n,m \in \mathbb{N}$, and assume that $h_{\ell_1}, g_{\ell_2} : [0,1] \to [0,+\infty)$ are continuous functions for all $\ell_1 = 1,2,\ldots,n$ and $\ell_2 = 1,2,\ldots,m$, and $\Theta : [\chi_1,\chi_2] \to \mathbb{R}$ be a differentiable function on (χ_1,χ_2) such that $\Theta' \in \mathcal{L}[\chi_1,\chi_2]$. If $|\Theta'|^q$ is (n,m)–generalized convex function with respect to $\mathcal{D}$ on $[\chi_1,\chi_2]$, then for $q > 1$ and $\frac{1}{p} + \frac{1}{q} = 1$, we obtain

$$|\mathcal{T}_1(\Theta;x,\chi_1,\chi_2)| \leq \left(\frac{1}{p+1}\right)^{\frac{1}{p}}$$
$$\times \left\{\frac{(x-\chi_1)^2}{\chi_2-\chi_1}\left[\left(\frac{1}{n}\sum_{\ell_1=1}^n H_{\ell_1}\right)|\Theta'(x)|^q + \left(\frac{1}{m}\sum_{\ell_2=1}^m G_{\ell_2}\right)|\Theta'(\chi_1)|^q\right]^{\frac{1}{q}}\right.$$
$$\left.+ \frac{(\chi_2-x)^2}{\chi_2-\chi_1}\left[\left(\frac{1}{n}\sum_{\ell_1=1}^n H_{\ell_1}\right)|\Theta'(x)|^q + \left(\frac{1}{m}\sum_{\ell_2=1}^m G_{\ell_2}\right)|\Theta'(\chi_2)|^q\right]^{\frac{1}{q}}\right\}, \quad (25)$$

where H_{ℓ_1} and G_{ℓ_2} are defined as in Theorem 8.

Proof. By using Lemma 2, Hölder's inequality and the (n,m)–generalized convexity of $|\Theta'|^q$ with respect to $\mathcal{D}$, we obtain

$$|\mathcal{T}_1(\Theta;x,\chi_1,\chi_2)| \leq \frac{(x-\chi_1)^2}{\chi_2-\chi_1}\int_0^1 \varrho|\Theta'(\varrho x + (1-\varrho)\chi_1)|d\varrho$$
$$+ \frac{(\chi_2-x)^2}{\chi_2-\chi_1}\int_0^1 \varrho|\Theta'(\varrho x + (1-\varrho)\chi_2)|d\varrho$$
$$\leq \frac{(x-\chi_1)^2}{\chi_2-\chi_1}\left(\int_0^1 \varrho^p d\varrho\right)^{\frac{1}{p}}\left(\int_0^1 |\Theta'(\varrho x + (1-\varrho)\chi_1)|^q d\varrho\right)^{\frac{1}{q}}$$
$$+ \frac{(\chi_2-x)^2}{\chi_2-\chi_1}\left(\int_0^1 \varrho^p d\varrho\right)^{\frac{1}{p}}\left(\int_0^1 |\Theta'(\varrho x + (1-\varrho)\chi_2)|^q d\varrho\right)^{\frac{1}{q}}$$
$$\leq \left(\frac{1}{p+1}\right)^{\frac{1}{p}}\left\{\frac{(x-\chi_1)^2}{\chi_2-\chi_1}\left[\int_0^1 \left(\left(\frac{1}{n}\sum_{\ell_1=1}^n h_{\ell_1}(\varrho)\right)|\Theta'(x)|^q + \left(\frac{1}{m}\sum_{\ell_2=1}^m g_{\ell_2}(\varrho)\right)|\Theta'(\chi_1)|^q\right)d\varrho\right]^{\frac{1}{q}}\right.$$
$$\left.+ \frac{(\chi_2-x)^2}{\chi_2-\chi_1}\left[\int_0^1 \left(\left(\frac{1}{n}\sum_{\ell_1=1}^n h_{\ell_1}(\varrho)\right)|\Theta'(x)|^q + \left(\frac{1}{m}\sum_{\ell_2=1}^m g_{\ell_2}(\varrho)\right)|\Theta'(\chi_2)|^q\right)d\varrho\right]^{\frac{1}{q}}\right\}$$

$$= \left(\frac{1}{p+1}\right)^{\frac{1}{p}} \Bigg\{ \frac{(x-\chi_1)^2}{\chi_2-\chi_1} \left[\left(\frac{1}{n}\sum_{\ell_1=1}^{n} H_{\ell_1}\right) |\Theta'(x)|^q + \left(\frac{1}{m}\sum_{\ell_2=1}^{m} G_{\ell_2}\right) |\Theta'(\chi_1)|^q \right]^{\frac{1}{q}}$$

$$+ \frac{(\chi_2-x)^2}{\chi_2-\chi_1} \left[\left(\frac{1}{n}\sum_{\ell_1=1}^{n} H_{\ell_1}\right) |\Theta'(x)|^q + \left(\frac{1}{m}\sum_{\ell_2=1}^{m} G_{\ell_2}\right) |\Theta'(\chi_2)|^q \right]^{\frac{1}{q}} \Bigg\},$$

which ends our proof. □

Corollary 5. *We have particular cases from Theorem 14:*

- *If $h_{\ell_1}(\varrho) = \varrho$ and $g_{\ell_2}(\varrho) = 1 - \varrho$ for all $\ell_1 = 1, 2, \ldots, n$, and $\ell_2 = 1, 2, \ldots, m$, we obtain*

$$|T_1(\Theta; x, \chi_1, \chi_2)| \leq \left(\frac{1}{2}\right)^{\frac{1}{q}} \left(\frac{1}{p+1}\right)^{\frac{1}{p}}$$

$$\times \Bigg\{ \frac{(x-\chi_1)^2}{\chi_2-\chi_1} [|\Theta'(x)|^q + |\Theta'(\chi_1)|^q]^{\frac{1}{q}} + \frac{(\chi_2-x)^2}{\chi_2-\chi_1} [|\Theta'(x)|^q + |\Theta'(\chi_2)|^q]^{\frac{1}{q}} \Bigg\}.$$

- *If $h_{\ell_1}(\varrho) = \varrho^{\ell_1}$ and $g_{\ell_2}(\varrho) = (1-\varrho)^{\ell_2}$ for all $\ell_1 = 1, 2, \ldots, n$, and $\ell_2 = 1, 2, \ldots, m$, we obtain*

$$|T_1(\Theta; x, \chi_1, \chi_2)| \leq \left(\frac{1}{p+1}\right)^{\frac{1}{p}}$$

$$\times \Bigg\{ \frac{(x-\chi_1)^2}{\chi_2-\chi_1} \left[\left(\frac{1}{n}\sum_{\ell_1=1}^{n} \frac{1}{\ell_1+1}\right) |\Theta'(x)|^q + \left(\frac{1}{m}\sum_{\ell_2=1}^{m} \frac{1}{\ell_2+1}\right) |\Theta'(\chi_1)|^q \right]^{\frac{1}{q}}$$

$$+ \frac{(\chi_2-x)^2}{\chi_2-\chi_1} \left[\left(\frac{1}{n}\sum_{\ell_1=1}^{n} \frac{1}{\ell_1+1}\right) |\Theta'(x)|^q + \left(\frac{1}{m}\sum_{\ell_2=1}^{m} \frac{1}{\ell_2+1}\right) |\Theta'(\chi_2)|^q \right]^{\frac{1}{q}} \Bigg\}.$$

- *If $h_{\ell_1}(\varrho) = \varrho^s$ and $g_{\ell_2}(\varrho) = (1-\varrho)^s$ for all $\ell_1 = 1, \ldots, n$, $\ell_2 = 1, \ldots, m$, and $s \in (0,1]$, we obtain*

$$|T_1(\Theta; x, \chi_1, \chi_2)| \leq \left(\frac{1}{s+1}\right)^{\frac{1}{q}} \left(\frac{1}{p+1}\right)^{\frac{1}{p}}$$

$$\times \Bigg\{ \frac{(x-\chi_1)^2}{\chi_2-\chi_1} [|\Theta'(x)|^q + |\Theta'(\chi_1)|^q]^{\frac{1}{q}} + \frac{(\chi_2-x)^2}{\chi_2-\chi_1} [|\Theta'(x)|^q + |\Theta'(\chi_2)|^q]^{\frac{1}{q}} \Bigg\}.$$

Theorem 15. *Suppose that $1 \leq n \leq m$, where $n, m \in \mathbb{N}$, and assume that $h_{\ell_1}, g_{\ell_2} : [0,1] \to [0, +\infty)$ are continuous functions for all $\ell_1 = 1, 2, \ldots, n$ and $\ell_2 = 1, 2, \ldots, m$, and $\Theta : [\chi_1, \chi_2] \to \mathbb{R}$ be a differentiable function on (χ_1, χ_2), such that $\Theta' \in \mathcal{L}[\chi_1, \chi_2]$. If $|\Theta'|^q$ is the (n, m)-generalized convex function with respect to $\mathcal{D}$ on $[\chi_1, \chi_2]$, then for $q > 1$, we have*

$$|T_1(\Theta; x, \chi_1, \chi_2)| \leq \left(\frac{1}{2}\right)^{1-\frac{1}{q}} \Bigg\{ \frac{(x-\chi_1)^2}{\chi_2-\chi_1} \left[\left(\frac{1}{n}\sum_{\ell_1=1}^{n} E_{\ell_1}\right) |\Theta'(x)|^q + \left(\frac{1}{m}\sum_{\ell_2=1}^{m} F_{\ell_2}\right) |\Theta'(\chi_1)|^q \right]^{\frac{1}{q}}$$

$$+ \frac{(\chi_2-x)^2}{\chi_2-\chi_1} \left[\left(\frac{1}{n}\sum_{\ell_1=1}^{n} E_{\ell_1}\right) |\Theta'(x)|^q + \left(\frac{1}{m}\sum_{\ell_2=1}^{m} F_{\ell_2}\right) |\Theta'(\chi_2)|^q \right]^{\frac{1}{q}} \Bigg\}, \quad (26)$$

where E_{ℓ_1} and F_{ℓ_2} are defined as in Theorem 13.

Proof. By using Lemma 2, the well-known power mean inequality and the (n, m)-generalized convexity of $|\Theta'|^q$ with respect to $\mathcal{D}$, we have

$$|\mathcal{T}_1(\Theta; x, \chi_1, \chi_2)| \leq \frac{(x - \chi_1)^2}{\chi_2 - \chi_1} \int_0^1 \varrho |\Theta'(\varrho x + (1 - \varrho)\chi_1)| d\varrho$$

$$+ \frac{(\chi_2 - x)^2}{\chi_2 - \chi_1} \int_0^1 \varrho |\Theta'(\varrho x + (1 - \varrho)\chi_2)| d\varrho$$

$$\leq \frac{(x - \chi_1)^2}{\chi_2 - \chi_1} \left(\int_0^1 \varrho d\varrho \right)^{1-\frac{1}{q}} \left(\int_0^1 \varrho |\Theta'(\varrho x + (1 - \varrho)\chi_1)|^q d\varrho \right)^{\frac{1}{q}}$$

$$+ \frac{(\chi_2 - x)^2}{\chi_2 - \chi_1} \left(\int_0^1 \varrho d\varrho \right)^{1-\frac{1}{q}} \left(\int_0^1 \varrho |\Theta'(\varrho x + (1 - \varrho)\chi_2)|^q d\varrho \right)^{\frac{1}{q}}$$

$$\leq \left(\frac{1}{2}\right)^{1-\frac{1}{q}} \left\{ \frac{(x-\chi_1)^2}{\chi_2 - \chi_1} \left[\int_0^1 \varrho \left(\left(\frac{1}{n}\sum_{\ell_1=1}^n h_{\ell_1}(\varrho)\right) |\Theta'(x)|^q + \left(\frac{1}{m}\sum_{\ell_2=1}^m g_{\ell_2}(\varrho)\right) |\Theta'(\chi_1)|^q \right) d\varrho \right]^{\frac{1}{q}} \right.$$

$$+ \frac{(\chi_2 - x)^2}{\chi_2 - \chi_1} \left[\int_0^1 \varrho \left(\left(\frac{1}{n}\sum_{\ell_1=1}^n h_{\ell_1}(\varrho)\right) |\Theta'(x)|^q + \left(\frac{1}{m}\sum_{\ell_2=1}^m g_{\ell_2}(\varrho)\right) |\Theta'(\chi_2)|^q \right) d\varrho \right]^{\frac{1}{q}} \right\}$$

$$= \left(\frac{1}{2}\right)^{1-\frac{1}{q}} \left\{ \frac{(x-\chi_1)^2}{\chi_2 - \chi_1} \left[\left(\frac{1}{n}\sum_{\ell_1=1}^n E_{\ell_1}\right) |\Theta'(x)|^q + \left(\frac{1}{m}\sum_{\ell_2=1}^m F_{\ell_2}\right) |\Theta'(\chi_1)|^q \right]^{\frac{1}{q}} \right.$$

$$\left. + \frac{(\chi_2 - x)^2}{\chi_2 - \chi_1} \left[\left(\frac{1}{n}\sum_{\ell_1=1}^n E_{\ell_1}\right) |\Theta'(x)|^q + \left(\frac{1}{m}\sum_{\ell_2=1}^m F_{\ell_2}\right) |\Theta'(\chi_2)|^q \right]^{\frac{1}{q}} \right\},$$

which ends our proof. □

Corollary 6. We have particular cases from Theorem 15:

- If $h_{\ell_1}(\varrho) = \varrho$ and $g_{\ell_2}(\varrho) = 1 - \varrho$ for all $\ell_1 = 1, 2, \ldots, n$, and $\ell_2 = 1, 2, \ldots, m$, we obtain

$$|\mathcal{T}_1(\Theta; x, \chi_1, \chi_2)| \leq \frac{1}{2\sqrt[q]{3}}$$

$$\times \left\{ \frac{(x - \chi_1)^2}{\chi_2 - \chi_1} \left[2|\Theta'(x)|^q + |\Theta'(\chi_1)|^q \right]^{\frac{1}{q}} + \frac{(\chi_2 - x)^2}{\chi_2 - \chi_1} \left[2|\Theta'(x)|^q + |\Theta'(\chi_2)|^q \right]^{\frac{1}{q}} \right\}.$$

- If $h_{\ell_1}(\varrho) = \varrho^{\ell_1}$ and $g_{\ell_2}(\varrho) = (1 - \varrho)^{\ell_2}$ for all $\ell_1 = 1, 2, \ldots, n$, and $\ell_2 = 1, 2, \ldots, m$, we obtain

$$|\mathcal{T}_1(\Theta; x, \chi_1, \chi_2)| \leq \left(\frac{1}{2}\right)^{1-\frac{1}{q}}$$

$$\times \left\{ \frac{(x-\chi_1)^2}{\chi_2 - \chi_1} \left[\left(\frac{1}{n}\sum_{\ell_1=1}^n \frac{1}{\ell_1 + 2}\right) |\Theta'(x)|^q + \left(\frac{1}{m}\sum_{\ell_2=1}^m \frac{1}{(\ell_2 + 1)(\ell_2 + 2)}\right) |\Theta'(\chi_1)|^q \right]^{\frac{1}{q}} \right.$$

$$\left. + \frac{(\chi_2 - x)^2}{\chi_2 - \chi_1} \left[\left(\frac{1}{n}\sum_{\ell_1=1}^n \frac{1}{\ell_1 + 2}\right) |\Theta'(x)|^q + \left(\frac{1}{m}\sum_{\ell_2=1}^m \frac{1}{(\ell_2 + 1)(\ell_2 + 2)}\right) |\Theta'(\chi_2)|^q \right]^{\frac{1}{q}} \right\}.$$

- If $h_{\ell_1}(\varrho) = \varrho^s$ and $g_{\ell_2}(\varrho) = (1 - \varrho)^s$ for all $\ell_1 = 1, \ldots, n$, $\ell_2 = 1, \ldots, m$, and $s \in (0, 1]$, we obtain

$$|\mathcal{T}_1(\Theta; x, \chi_1, \chi_2)| \leq \left(\frac{1}{2}\right)^{1-\frac{1}{q}} \left(\frac{1}{(s+1)(s+2)}\right)^{\frac{1}{q}}$$
$$\times \left\{ \frac{(x-\chi_1)^2}{\chi_2 - \chi_1} [(s+1)|\Theta'(x)|^q + |\Theta'(\chi_1)|^q]^{\frac{1}{q}} + \frac{(\chi_2 - x)^2}{\chi_2 - \chi_1} [(s+1)|\Theta'(x)|^q + |\Theta'(\chi_2)|^q]^{\frac{1}{q}} \right\}.$$

Theorem 16. *Suppose that $1 \leq n \leq m$, where $n, m \in \mathbb{N}$, and assume that $h_{\ell_1}, g_{\ell_2} : [0,1] \to [0, +\infty)$ are continuous functions for all $\ell_1 = 1, 2, \ldots, n$ and $\ell_2 = 1, 2, \ldots, m$, and $\Theta : [\chi_1, \chi_2] \to \mathbb{R}$ be a differentiable function on (χ_1, χ_2), such that $\Theta' \in \mathcal{L}[\chi_1, \chi_2]$. If $|\Theta'|$ is the (n, m)-generalized convex function with respect to $\mathcal{D}$ on $[\chi_1, \chi_2]$, then we have*

$$|\mathcal{T}_2(\Theta; \chi_1, \chi_2)| \leq (\chi_2 - \chi_1)$$
$$\times \left\{ \frac{1}{n} \sum_{\ell_1=1}^{n} \left[\left(A_{\ell_1}^{(1)} + A_{\ell_1}^{(3)}\right) - \left(A_{\ell_1}^{(2)} + A_{\ell_1}^{(4)}\right) + \left(B_{\ell_1}^{(2)} + B_{\ell_1}^{(4)}\right) - \left(B_{\ell_1}^{(1)} + B_{\ell_1}^{(3)}\right) \right] |\Theta'(\chi_1)| \right.$$
$$\left. + \frac{1}{m} \sum_{\ell_2=1}^{m} \left[\left(C_{\ell_2}^{(1)} + C_{\ell_2}^{(3)}\right) - \left(C_{\ell_2}^{(2)} + C_{\ell_2}^{(4)}\right) + \left(D_{\ell_2}^{(2)} + D_{\ell_2}^{(4)}\right) - \left(D_{\ell_2}^{(1)} + D_{\ell_2}^{(3)}\right) \right] |\Theta'(\chi_2)| \right\}, \quad (27)$$

where

$$A_{\ell_1}^{(1)} := \int_0^{\frac{1}{6}} h_{\ell_1}(\varrho) d\varrho, \quad A_{\ell_1}^{(2)} := \int_{\frac{1}{6}}^{\frac{1}{2}} h_{\ell_1}(\varrho) d\varrho,$$

$$A_{\ell_1}^{(3)} := \int_{\frac{1}{2}}^{\frac{5}{6}} h_{\ell_1}(\varrho) d\varrho, \quad A_{\ell_1}^{(4)} := \int_{\frac{5}{6}}^{1} h_{\ell_1}(\varrho) d\varrho,$$

$$B_{\ell_1}^{(1)} := \int_0^{\frac{1}{6}} \varrho h_{\ell_1}(\varrho) d\varrho, \quad B_{\ell_1}^{(2)} := \int_{\frac{1}{6}}^{\frac{1}{2}} \varrho h_{\ell_1}(\varrho) d\varrho,$$

$$B_{\ell_1}^{(3)} := \int_{\frac{1}{2}}^{\frac{5}{6}} \varrho h_{\ell_1}(\varrho) d\varrho, \quad B_{\ell_1}^{(4)} := \int_{\frac{5}{6}}^{1} \varrho h_{\ell_1}(\varrho) d\varrho,$$

and

$$C_{\ell_2}^{(1)} := \int_0^{\frac{1}{6}} g_{\ell_2}(\varrho) d\varrho, \quad C_{\ell_2}^{(2)} := \int_{\frac{1}{6}}^{\frac{1}{2}} g_{\ell_2}(\varrho) d\varrho,$$

$$C_{\ell_2}^{(3)} := \int_{\frac{1}{2}}^{\frac{5}{6}} g_{\ell_2}(\varrho) d\varrho, \quad C_{\ell_2}^{(4)} := \int_{\frac{5}{6}}^{1} g_{\ell_2}(\varrho) d\varrho,$$

$$D_{\ell_2}^{(1)} := \int_0^{\frac{1}{6}} \varrho g_{\ell_2}(\varrho) d\varrho, \quad D_{\ell_2}^{(2)} := \int_{\frac{1}{6}}^{\frac{1}{2}} \varrho g_{\ell_2}(\varrho) d\varrho,$$

$$D_{\ell_2}^{(3)} := \int_{\frac{1}{2}}^{\frac{5}{6}} \varrho g_{\ell_2}(\varrho) d\varrho, \quad D_{\ell_2}^{(4)} := \int_{\frac{5}{6}}^{1} \varrho g_{\ell_2}(\varrho) d\varrho,$$

for all $\ell_1 = 1, 2, \ldots, n$ and $\ell_2 = 1, 2, \ldots, m$.

Proof. By using Lemma 3 and the (n, m)-generalized convexity of $|\Theta'|$ with respect to $\mathcal{D}$, we have

$$|\mathcal{T}_2(\Theta; \chi_1, \chi_2)| \leq (\chi_2 - \chi_1) \left\{ \int_0^{\frac{1}{2}} \left| \varrho - \frac{1}{6} \right| |\Theta'(\varrho \chi_2 + (1-\varrho)\chi_1)| d\varrho \right.$$
$$\left. + \int_{\frac{1}{2}}^{1} \left| \varrho - \frac{5}{6} \right| |\Theta'(\varrho \chi_2 + (1-\varrho)\chi_1)| d\varrho \right\}$$

$$\leq (\chi_2 - \chi_1)\left\{\int_0^{\frac{1}{2}}\left|\varrho - \frac{1}{6}\right|\left[\left(\frac{1}{n}\sum_{\ell_1=1}^n h_{\ell_1}(\varrho)\right)|\Theta'(\chi_2)| + \left(\frac{1}{m}\sum_{\ell_2=1}^m g_{\ell_2}(\varrho)\right)|\Theta'(\chi_1)|\right]d\varrho\right.$$

$$\left.+\int_{\frac{1}{2}}^1\left|\varrho - \frac{5}{6}\right|\left[\left(\frac{1}{n}\sum_{\ell_1=1}^n h_{\ell_1}(\varrho)\right)|\Theta'(\chi_2)| + \left(\frac{1}{m}\sum_{\ell_2=1}^m g_{\ell_2}(\varrho)\right)|\Theta'(\chi_1)|\right]d\varrho\right\}$$

$$= (\chi_2 - \chi_1)\left\{\frac{1}{n}\sum_{\ell_1=1}^n\left[\left(A_{\ell_1}^{(1)} + A_{\ell_1}^{(3)}\right) - \left(A_{\ell_1}^{(2)} + A_{\ell_1}^{(4)}\right) + \left(B_{\ell_1}^{(2)} + B_{\ell_1}^{(4)}\right) - \left(B_{\ell_1}^{(1)} + B_{\ell_1}^{(3)}\right)\right]|\Theta'(\chi_1)|\right.$$

$$\left.+\frac{1}{m}\sum_{\ell_2=1}^m\left[\left(C_{\ell_2}^{(1)} + C_{\ell_2}^{(3)}\right) - \left(C_{\ell_2}^{(2)} + C_{\ell_2}^{(4)}\right) + \left(D_{\ell_2}^{(2)} + D_{\ell_2}^{(4)}\right) - \left(D_{\ell_2}^{(1)} + D_{\ell_2}^{(3)}\right)\right]|\Theta'(\chi_2)|\right\},$$

which ends our proof. □

Corollary 7. *If we take $h_{\ell_1}(\varrho) = \varrho^{\ell_1}$, $\forall \ell_1 = 1,\ldots,n$ and $g_{\ell_2}(\varrho) = (1-\varrho)^{\ell_2}$, $\forall \ell_2 = 1,\ldots,m$ in Theorem 16, we obtain*

$$|T_2(\Theta;\chi_1,\chi_2)| \leq (\chi_2 - \chi_1)$$

$$\times\left\{\frac{1}{n}\sum_{\ell_1=1}^n\left[\left(U_{\ell_1}^{(1)} + U_{\ell_1}^{(3)}\right) - \left(U_{\ell_1}^{(2)} + U_{\ell_1}^{(4)}\right) + \left(V_{\ell_1}^{(2)} + V_{\ell_1}^{(4)}\right) - \left(V_{\ell_1}^{(1)} + V_{\ell_1}^{(3)}\right)\right]|\Theta'(\chi_1)|\right.$$

$$\left.+\frac{1}{m}\sum_{\ell_2=1}^m\left[\left(P_{\ell_2}^{(1)} + P_{\ell_2}^{(3)}\right) - \left(P_{\ell_2}^{(2)} + P_{\ell_2}^{(4)}\right) + \left(Q_{\ell_2}^{(2)} + Q_{\ell_2}^{(4)}\right) - \left(Q_{\ell_2}^{(1)} + Q_{\ell_2}^{(3)}\right)\right]|\Theta'(\chi_2)|\right\},$$

where

$$U_{\ell_1}^{(1)} := \frac{1}{6^{\ell_1+1}(\ell_1+1)}, \quad U_{\ell_1}^{(2)} := \frac{1}{\ell_1+1}\left(\frac{1}{2^{\ell_1+1}} - \frac{1}{6^{\ell_1+1}}\right),$$

$$U_{\ell_1}^{(3)} := \frac{1}{\ell_1+1}\left(\left(\frac{5}{6}\right)^{\ell_1+1} - \frac{1}{2^{\ell_1+1}}\right), \quad U_{\ell_1}^{(4)} := \frac{1}{\ell_1+1}\left(1 - \left(\frac{5}{6}\right)^{\ell_1+1}\right),$$

$$V_{\ell_1}^{(1)} := \frac{1}{6^{\ell_1+2}(\ell_1+2)}, \quad V_{\ell_1}^{(2)} := \frac{1}{\ell_1+2}\left(\frac{1}{2^{\ell_1+2}} - \frac{1}{6^{\ell_1+2}}\right),$$

$$V_{\ell_1}^{(3)} := \frac{1}{\ell_1+2}\left(\left(\frac{5}{6}\right)^{\ell_1+2} - \frac{1}{2^{\ell_1+2}}\right), \quad V_{\ell_1}^{(4)} := \frac{1}{\ell_1+2}\left(1 - \left(\frac{5}{6}\right)^{\ell_1+2}\right),$$

$$P_{\ell_2}^{(1)} := \frac{1}{\ell_2+1}\left(1 - \left(\frac{5}{6}\right)^{\ell_2+1}\right), \quad P_{\ell_2}^{(2)} := \frac{1}{\ell_2+1}\left(\left(\frac{5}{6}\right)^{\ell_2+1} - \frac{1}{2^{\ell_2+1}}\right),$$

$$P_{\ell_2}^{(3)} := \frac{1}{\ell_2+1}\left(\frac{1}{2^{\ell_2+1}} - \frac{1}{6^{\ell_2+1}}\right), \quad P_{\ell_2}^{(4)} := \frac{1}{6^{\ell_2+1}(\ell_2+1)},$$

and

$$Q_{\ell_2}^{(1)} := \frac{1}{(\ell_2+1)(\ell_2+2)} - \left(\frac{1}{\ell_2+1}\left(\frac{5}{6}\right)^{\ell_2+1} - \frac{1}{\ell_2+2}\left(\frac{5}{6}\right)^{\ell_2+2}\right),$$

$$Q_{\ell_2}^{(2)} := \left(\frac{1}{\ell_2+1}\left(\frac{5}{6}\right)^{\ell_2+1} - \frac{1}{\ell_2+2}\left(\frac{5}{6}\right)^{\ell_2+2}\right) - \left(\frac{1}{\ell_2+1}\left(\frac{1}{2}\right)^{\ell_2+1} - \frac{1}{\ell_2+2}\left(\frac{1}{2}\right)^{\ell_2+2}\right),$$

$$Q_{\ell_2}^{(3)} := \left(\frac{1}{\ell_2+1}\left(\frac{1}{2}\right)^{\ell_2+1} - \frac{1}{\ell_2+2}\left(\frac{1}{2}\right)^{\ell_2+2}\right) - \left(\frac{1}{\ell_2+1}\left(\frac{1}{6}\right)^{\ell_2+1} - \frac{1}{\ell_2+2}\left(\frac{1}{6}\right)^{\ell_2+2}\right),$$

$$Q_{\ell_2}^{(4)} := \frac{1}{\ell_2+1}\left(\frac{1}{6}\right)^{\ell_2+1} - \frac{1}{\ell_2+2}\left(\frac{1}{6}\right)^{\ell_2+2}.$$

Theorem 17. Suppose that $1 \leq n \leq m$, where $n, m \in \mathbb{N}$, and assume that $h_{\ell_1}, g_{\ell_2} : [0,1] \to [0, +\infty)$ are continuous functions for all $\ell_1 = 1, 2, \ldots, n$ and $\ell_2 = 1, 2, \ldots, m$, and $\Theta : [\chi_1, \chi_2] \to \mathbb{R}$ be a differentiable function on (χ_1, χ_2) such that $\Theta' \in \mathcal{L}[\chi_1, \chi_2]$. If $|\Theta'|^q$ is the (n, m)-generalized convex function with respect to $\mathcal{D}$ on $[\chi_1, \chi_2]$, then for $q > 1$ and $\frac{1}{p} + \frac{1}{q} = 1$, we have

$$|T_2(\Theta; \chi_1, \chi_2)| \leq (\chi_2 - \chi_1) \left[\frac{2}{p+1} \left(\frac{2^{p+1}+1}{6^{p+1}} \right) \right]^{\frac{1}{p}}$$

$$\times \left[\left(\frac{1}{n} \sum_{\ell_1=1}^{n} H_{\ell_1} \right) |\Theta'(\chi_2)|^q + \left(\frac{1}{m} \sum_{\ell_2=1}^{m} G_{\ell_2} \right) |\Theta'(\chi_1)|^q \right]^{\frac{1}{q}}, \quad (28)$$

where H_{ℓ_1} and G_{ℓ_2} are as defined in Theorem 8.

Proof. By using Lemma 3, Hölder's inequality and the (n, m)-generalized convexity of $|\Theta'|^q$ with respect to $\mathcal{D}$, we have

$$|T_2(\Theta; \chi_1, \chi_2)| \leq (\chi_2 - \chi_1) \left\{ \int_0^{\frac{1}{2}} \left| \varrho - \frac{1}{6} \right| |\Theta'(\varrho \chi_2 + (1-\varrho) \chi_1)| d\varrho \right.$$

$$\left. + \int_{\frac{1}{2}}^{1} \left| \varrho - \frac{5}{6} \right| |\Theta'(\varrho \chi_2 + (1-\varrho) \chi_1)| d\varrho \right\}$$

$$\leq (\chi_2 - \chi_1) \left[\left(\int_0^{\frac{1}{2}} \left| \varrho - \frac{1}{6} \right|^p d\varrho \right)^{\frac{1}{p}} + \left(\int_{\frac{1}{2}}^{1} \left| \varrho - \frac{5}{6} \right|^p d\varrho \right)^{\frac{1}{p}} \right] \left(\int_0^1 |\Theta'(\varrho \chi_2 + (1-\varrho) \chi_1)|^q d\varrho \right)^{\frac{1}{q}}$$

$$\leq (\chi_2 - \chi_1) \left[\left(\int_0^{\frac{1}{2}} \left| \varrho - \frac{1}{6} \right|^p d\varrho \right)^{\frac{1}{p}} + \left(\int_{\frac{1}{2}}^{1} \left| \varrho - \frac{5}{6} \right|^p d\varrho \right)^{\frac{1}{p}} \right]$$

$$\times \left[\int_0^1 \left(\left(\frac{1}{n} \sum_{\ell_1=1}^{n} h_{\ell_1}(\varrho) \right) |\Theta'(\chi_2)|^q + \left(\frac{1}{m} \sum_{\ell_2=1}^{m} g_{\ell_2}(\varrho) \right) |\Theta'(\chi_1)|^q \right) d\varrho \right]^{\frac{1}{q}}$$

$$= (\chi_2 - \chi_1) \left[\frac{2}{p+1} \left(\frac{2^{p+1}+1}{6^{p+1}} \right) \right]^{\frac{1}{p}} \left[\left(\frac{1}{n} \sum_{\ell_1=1}^{n} H_{\ell_1} \right) |\Theta'(\chi_2)|^q + \left(\frac{1}{m} \sum_{\ell_2=1}^{m} G_{\ell_2} \right) |\Theta'(\chi_1)|^q \right]^{\frac{1}{q}},$$

which ends our proof. □

Corollary 8. We have particular cases from Theorem 17:

- If $h_{\ell_1}(\varrho) = \varrho$ and $g_{\ell_2}(\varrho) = 1 - \varrho$ for all $\ell_1 = 1, 2, \ldots, n$, and $\ell_2 = 1, 2, \ldots, m$, we obtain

$$|T_2(\Theta; \chi_1, \chi_2)| \leq (\chi_2 - \chi_1) \left[\frac{2}{p+1} \left(\frac{2^{p+1}+1}{6^{p+1}} \right) \right]^{\frac{1}{p}} \left[\frac{|\Theta'(\chi_1)|^q + |\Theta'(\chi_2)|^q}{2} \right]^{\frac{1}{q}}.$$

- If $h_{\ell_1}(\varrho) = \varrho^{\ell_1}$ and $g_{\ell_2}(\varrho) = (1-\varrho)^{\ell_2}$ for all $\ell_1 = 1, 2, \ldots, n$, and $\ell_2 = 1, 2, \ldots, m$, we obtain

$$|T_2(\Theta; \chi_1, \chi_2)| \leq (\chi_2 - \chi_1) \left[\frac{2}{p+1} \left(\frac{2^{p+1}+1}{6^{p+1}} \right) \right]^{\frac{1}{p}}$$

$$\times \left[\left(\frac{1}{n} \sum_{\ell_1=1}^{n} \frac{1}{\ell_1+1} \right) |\Theta'(\chi_2)|^q + \left(\frac{1}{m} \sum_{\ell_2=1}^{m} \frac{1}{\ell_2+1} \right) |\Theta'(\chi_1)|^q \right]^{\frac{1}{q}}.$$

- If $h_{\ell_1}(\varrho) = \varrho^s$ and $g_{\ell_2}(\varrho) = (1-\varrho)^s$ for all $\ell_1 = 1,\ldots,n$, $\ell_2 = 1,\ldots,m$, and $s \in (0,1]$, we obtain

$$|\mathcal{T}_2(\Theta;\chi_1,\chi_2)| \leq (\chi_2 - \chi_1)\left[\frac{2}{p+1}\left(\frac{2^{p+1}+1}{6^{p+1}}\right)\right]^{\frac{1}{p}}\left[\frac{|\Theta'(\chi_1)|^q + |\Theta'(\chi_2)|^q}{s+1}\right]^{\frac{1}{q}}.$$

Theorem 18. *Suppose that $1 \leq n \leq m$, where $n,m \in \mathbb{N}$, and assume that $h_{\ell_1}, g_{\ell_2} : [0,1] \to [0,+\infty)$ are continuous functions for all $\ell_1 = 1,2,\ldots,n$ and $\ell_2 = 1,2,\ldots,m$, and $\Theta : [\chi_1,\chi_2] \to \mathbb{R}$ be a differentiable function on (χ_1,χ_2), such that $\Theta' \in \mathcal{L}[\chi_1,\chi_2]$. If $|\Theta'|^q$ is the (n,m)-generalized convex function with respect to $\mathcal{D}$ on $[\chi_1,\chi_2]$, then for $q > 1$, we have*

$$|\mathcal{T}_2(\Theta;\chi_1,\chi_2)| \leq (\chi_2 - \chi_1)\left(\frac{5}{36}\right)^{1-\frac{1}{q}} \tag{29}$$

$$\times \left\{\left[\left(\frac{1}{n}\sum_{\ell_1=1}^{n}\left(\frac{A_{\ell_1}^{(1)}}{6} - B_{\ell_1}^{(1)}\right)\right)|\Theta'(\chi_2)|^q + \left(\frac{1}{m}\sum_{\ell_2=1}^{m}\left(\frac{C_{\ell_2}^{(1)}}{6} - D_{\ell_2}^{(1)}\right)\right)|\Theta'(\chi_1)|^q\right]^{\frac{1}{q}}\right.$$

$$+ \left[\left(\frac{1}{n}\sum_{\ell_1=1}^{n}\left(B_{\ell_1}^{(2)} - \frac{A_{\ell_1}^{(2)}}{6}\right)\right)|\Theta'(\chi_2)|^q + \left(\frac{1}{m}\sum_{\ell_2=1}^{m}\left(D_{\ell_2}^{(2)} - \frac{C_{\ell_2}^{(2)}}{6}\right)\right)|\Theta'(\chi_1)|^q\right]^{\frac{1}{q}}$$

$$+ \left[\left(\frac{1}{n}\sum_{\ell_1=1}^{n}\left(\frac{5A_{\ell_1}^{(3)}}{6} - B_{\ell_1}^{(3)}\right)\right)|\Theta'(\chi_2)|^q + \left(\frac{1}{m}\sum_{\ell_2=1}^{m}\left(\frac{5C_{\ell_2}^{(3)}}{6} - D_{\ell_2}^{(3)}\right)\right)|\Theta'(\chi_1)|^q\right]^{\frac{1}{q}}$$

$$\left. + \left[\left(\frac{1}{n}\sum_{\ell_1=1}^{n}\left(B_{\ell_1}^{(4)} - \frac{5A_{\ell_1}^{(4)}}{6}\right)\right)|\Theta'(\chi_2)|^q + \left(\frac{1}{m}\sum_{\ell_2=1}^{m}\left(D_{\ell_2}^{(4)} - \frac{5C_{\ell_2}^{(4)}}{6}\right)\right)|\Theta'(\chi_1)|^q\right]^{\frac{1}{q}}\right\},$$

where $A_{\ell_1}^{(k)}$, $B_{\ell_1}^{(k)}$, $C_{\ell_2}^{(k)}$, and $D_{\ell_2}^{(k)}$ for all $k = 1,2,3,4$ are defined as in Theorem 16.

Proof. By using Lemma 3, the well-known power mean inequality and (n,m)-generalized convexity $|\Theta'|^q$ with respect to $\mathcal{D}$, we have

$$|\mathcal{T}_2(\Theta;\chi_1,\chi_2)| \leq (\chi_2 - \chi_1)\left\{\int_0^{\frac{1}{2}}\left|\varrho - \frac{1}{6}\right||\Theta'(\varrho\chi_2 + (1-\varrho)\chi_1)|d\varrho\right.$$

$$\left. + \int_{\frac{1}{2}}^{1}\left|\varrho - \frac{5}{6}\right||\Theta'(\varrho\chi_2 + (1-\varrho)\chi_1)|d\varrho\right\}$$

$$\leq (\chi_2 - \chi_1)\left[\left(\int_0^{\frac{1}{2}}\left|\varrho - \frac{1}{6}\right|d\varrho\right)^{1-\frac{1}{q}} + \left(\int_{\frac{1}{2}}^{1}\left|\varrho - \frac{5}{6}\right|d\varrho\right)^{1-\frac{1}{q}}\right]$$

$$\times \left\{\left(\int_0^{\frac{1}{2}}\left|\varrho - \frac{1}{6}\right||\Theta'(\varrho\chi_2 + (1-\varrho)\chi_1)|^q d\varrho\right)^{\frac{1}{q}} + \left(\int_{\frac{1}{2}}^{1}\left|\varrho - \frac{5}{6}\right||\Theta'(\varrho\chi_2 + (1-\varrho)\chi_1)|^q d\varrho\right)^{\frac{1}{q}}\right\}$$

$$\leq (\chi_2 - \chi_1)\left[\left(\int_0^{\frac{1}{2}}\left|\varrho - \frac{1}{6}\right|d\varrho\right)^{1-\frac{1}{q}} + \left(\int_{\frac{1}{2}}^{1}\left|\varrho - \frac{5}{6}\right|d\varrho\right)^{1-\frac{1}{q}}\right]$$

$$\times \left\{\left[\int_0^{\frac{1}{2}}\left|\varrho - \frac{1}{6}\right|\left(\left(\frac{1}{n}\sum_{\ell_1=1}^{n}h_{\ell_1}(\varrho)\right)|\Theta'(\chi_2)|^q + \left(\frac{1}{m}\sum_{\ell_2=1}^{m}g_{\ell_2}(\varrho)\right)|\Theta'(\chi_1)|^q\right)d\varrho\right]^{\frac{1}{q}}\right.$$

$$+\left[\int_{\frac{1}{2}}^{1}\left|\varrho-\frac{5}{6}\right|\left(\left(\frac{1}{n}\sum_{\ell_1=1}^{n}h_{\ell_1}(\varrho)\right)|\Theta'(\chi_2)|^q + \left(\frac{1}{m}\sum_{\ell_2=1}^{m}g_{\ell_2}(\varrho)\right)|\Theta'(\chi_1)|^q\right)d\varrho\right]^{\frac{1}{q}}\Bigg\}$$

$$= (\chi_2 - \chi_1)\left(\frac{5}{36}\right)^{1-\frac{1}{q}}$$

$$\times\left\{\left[\left(\frac{1}{n}\sum_{\ell_1=1}^{n}\left(\frac{A_{\ell_1}^{(1)}}{6} - B_{\ell_1}^{(1)}\right)\right)|\Theta'(\chi_2)|^q + \left(\frac{1}{m}\sum_{\ell_2=1}^{m}\left(\frac{C_{\ell_2}^{(1)}}{6} - D_{\ell_2}^{(1)}\right)\right)|\Theta'(\chi_1)|^q\right]^{\frac{1}{q}}\right.$$

$$+\left[\left(\frac{1}{n}\sum_{\ell_1=1}^{n}\left(B_{\ell_1}^{(2)} - \frac{A_{\ell_1}^{(2)}}{6}\right)\right)|\Theta'(\chi_2)|^q + \left(\frac{1}{m}\sum_{\ell_2=1}^{m}\left(D_{\ell_2}^{(2)} - \frac{C_{\ell_2}^{(2)}}{6}\right)\right)|\Theta'(\chi_1)|^q\right]^{\frac{1}{q}}$$

$$+\left[\left(\frac{1}{n}\sum_{\ell_1=1}^{n}\left(\frac{5A_{\ell_1}^{(3)}}{6} - B_{\ell_1}^{(3)}\right)\right)|\Theta'(\chi_2)|^q + \left(\frac{1}{m}\sum_{\ell_2=1}^{m}\left(\frac{5C_{\ell_2}^{(3)}}{6} - D_{\ell_2}^{(3)}\right)\right)|\Theta'(\chi_1)|^q\right]^{\frac{1}{q}}$$

$$+\left[\left(\frac{1}{n}\sum_{\ell_1=1}^{n}\left(B_{\ell_1}^{(4)} - \frac{5A_{\ell_1}^{(4)}}{6}\right)\right)|\Theta'(\chi_2)|^q + \left(\frac{1}{m}\sum_{\ell_2=1}^{m}\left(D_{\ell_2}^{(4)} - \frac{5C_{\ell_2}^{(4)}}{6}\right)\right)|\Theta'(\chi_1)|^q\right]^{\frac{1}{q}}\right\},$$

which ends our proof. □

Corollary 9. *If we take $h_{\ell_1}(\varrho) = \varrho^{\ell_1}$ and $g_{\ell_2}(\varrho) = (1-\varrho)^{\ell_2}$ in Theorem 18 for all $\ell_1 = 1, 2, \ldots, n$ and $\ell_2 = 1, 2, \ldots, m$, we obtain*

$$|\mathcal{T}_2(\Theta; \chi_1, \chi_2)| \leq (\chi_2 - \chi_1)\left(\frac{5}{36}\right)^{1-\frac{1}{q}}$$

$$\times\left\{\left[\left(\frac{1}{n}\sum_{\ell_1=1}^{n}\left(\frac{U_{\ell_1}^{(1)}}{6} - V_{\ell_1}^{(1)}\right)\right)|\Theta'(\chi_2)|^q + \left(\frac{1}{m}\sum_{\ell_2=1}^{m}\left(\frac{P_{\ell_2}^{(1)}}{6} - Q_{\ell_2}^{(1)}\right)\right)|\Theta'(\chi_1)|^q\right]^{\frac{1}{q}}\right.$$

$$+\left[\left(\frac{1}{n}\sum_{\ell_1=1}^{n}\left(V_{\ell_1}^{(2)} - \frac{U_{\ell_1}^{(2)}}{6}\right)\right)|\Theta'(\chi_2)|^q + \left(\frac{1}{m}\sum_{\ell_2=1}^{m}\left(Q_{\ell_2}^{(2)} - \frac{P_{\ell_2}^{(2)}}{6}\right)\right)|\Theta'(\chi_1)|^q\right]^{\frac{1}{q}}$$

$$+\left[\left(\frac{1}{n}\sum_{\ell_1=1}^{n}\left(\frac{5U_{\ell_1}^{(3)}}{6} - V_{\ell_1}^{(3)}\right)\right)|\Theta'(\chi_2)|^q + \left(\frac{1}{m}\sum_{\ell_2=1}^{m}\left(\frac{5P_{\ell_2}^{(3)}}{6} - Q_{\ell_2}^{(3)}\right)\right)|\Theta'(\chi_1)|^q\right]^{\frac{1}{q}}$$

$$+\left[\left(\frac{1}{n}\sum_{\ell_1=1}^{n}\left(V_{\ell_1}^{(4)} - \frac{5U_{\ell_1}^{(4)}}{6}\right)\right)|\Theta'(\chi_2)|^q + \left(\frac{1}{m}\sum_{\ell_2=1}^{m}\left(Q_{\ell_2}^{(4)} - \frac{5P_{\ell_2}^{(4)}}{6}\right)\right)|\Theta'(\chi_1)|^q\right]^{\frac{1}{q}}\right\},$$

where $U_{\ell_1}^{(k)}$, $V_{\ell_1}^{(k)}$, $P_{\ell_2}^{(k)}$ and $Q_{\ell_2}^{(k)}$ for all $k = 1, 2, 3, 4$ are as defined in Corollary 7.

5. Conclusions

In this article, we studied algebraic properties of a new generic class of functions called the (n, m)–generalized convex function; based on this, we proposed HH inequalities. Moreover, we obtained new midpoint-type inequalities of Ostrowski and Simpson based on our new definition, using well-known integral identities. Finally, we observed that the new, defined convex function is a powerful type of function used to investigate various inequalities in the real analysis field.

Author Contributions: Conceptualization, A.K. and P.O.M.; methodology, A.K., R.P.A. and P.O.M.; software, K.N.; K.M.A. and Y.S.H.; validation, A.K., P.O.M. and Y.S.H.; formal analysis, R.P.A., P.O.M., K.N. and K.M.A.; investigation, A.K., P.O.M. and Y.S.H.; resources, P.O.M., K.N. and K.M.A.; data curation, K.N. and Y.S.H.; writing—original draft preparation, A.K., P.O.M. and R.P.A.; writing—review and editing, A.K., P.O.M., K.M.A. and Y.S.H.; visualisation, A.K., R.P.A. and P.O.M.; supervision, R.P.A., P.O.M., K.N. and Y.S.H.; project administration, P.O.M. and K.N.; funding acquisition, K.N. All authors have read and agreed to the published version of the manuscript.

Funding: Not applicable.

Institutional Review Board Statement: Not applicable.

Informed Consent Statement: Not applicable.

Data Availability Statement: Not applicable.

Acknowledgments: This Research was supported by Taif University Researchers Supporting Project Number (TURSP2020/217), Taif University, Taif, Saudi Arabia, and the National Science, Research, and Innovation Fund (NSRF), Thailand.

Conflicts of Interest: The authors declare no conflict of interest.

References

1. Kashuri, A.; Meftah, B.; Mohammed, P.O.; Lupaş, A.A.; Abdalla, B.; Hamed, Y.S.; Abdeljawad, T. Fractional weighted Ostrowski-type inequalities and their applications. *Symmetry* **2021**, *13*, 968. [CrossRef]
2. Kasamsetty, K.; Ketkar, M.; Sapatnekar, S.S. A new class of convex functions for delay modeling and its application to the transistor sizing problem [CMOS gates]. *IEEE Trans.-Comput.-Aided Des. Integr. Circuits Syst.* **2020**, *19*, 779–788. [CrossRef]
3. Awan, M.U.; Noor, M.A.; Noor, K.I.; Khan, A.G. Some new classes of convex functions and inequalities. *Miskolc Math. Notes* **2018**, *19*, 77–94. [CrossRef]
4. Hudzik, H.; Maligranda, L. Some remarks on s–convex functions. *Aequationes Math.* **1994**, *48*, 100–111. [CrossRef]
5. Eftekhari, N. Some remarks on (s,m)–convexity in the second sense. *J. Math. Inequal.* **2014**, *8*, 489–495. [CrossRef]
6. Kadakal, M.; İşcan, İ. Exponential type convexity and some related inequalities. *J. Inequal. Appl.* **2020**, *1*, 82. [CrossRef]
7. Agarwal, P.; Choi, J. Fractional calculus operators and their image formulas. *J. Korean Math. Soc.* **2016**, *53*, 1183–1210. [CrossRef]
8. Rekhviashvili, S.; Pskhu, A.; Agarwal, P.; Jain, S. Application of the fractional oscillator model to describe damped vibrations. *Turk. J. Phys.* **2019**, *43*, 236–242. [CrossRef]
9. Dragomir, S.S.; Fitzpatrick, S. The Hadamard's inequality for s–convex functions in the second sense. *Demonstr. Math.* **1999**, *32*, 687–696.
10. Han, J.; Mohammed, P.O.; Zeng, H. Generalized fractional integral inequalities of Hermite–Hadamard-type for a convex function. *Open Math.* **2020**, *18*, 794–806. [CrossRef]
11. Rashid, S.; Noor, M.A.; Noor, K.I.; Akdemir, A.O. Some new generalizations for exponentially s–convex functions and inequalities via fractional operators. *Int. J. Sci. Innov. Tech.* **2014**, *1*, 1–12. [CrossRef]
12. İşcan, İ. Hermite–Hadamard–Fejér type inequalities for convex functions via fractional integrals. *Stud. Univ. Babeş-Bolyai Math.* **2015**, *60*, 355–366.
13. Abdeljawad, T.; Mohammed, P.O.; Kashuri, A. New modified conformable fractional integral inequalities of Hermite–Hadamard type with applications. *J. Funct. Spaces* **2020**, *2020*, 4352357. [CrossRef]
14. Fernandez, A.; Mohammed, P.O. Hermite–Hadamard inequalities in fractional calculus defined using Mittag–Leffler kernels. *Math. Meth. Appl. Sci.* **2020**, *44*, 8414–8431. [CrossRef]
15. Ujević, N. Sharp inequalities of Simpson type and Ostrowski type. *Comput. Math. Appl.* **2004**, *48*, 145–151. [CrossRef]
16. Liu, W.; Wen, W.; Park, J. Ostrowski type fractional integral inequalities for MT–convex functions. *Miskolc Math. Notes* **2015**, *16*, 249–256. [CrossRef]
17. Kaijser, S.; Nikolova, L.; Persson, L.E.; Wedestig, A. Hardy type inequalities via convexity. *Math. Inequal. Appl.* **2005**, *8*, 403–417. [CrossRef]
18. Rashid, S.; Jarad, F.; Noor, M.A.; Noor, K.I.; Baleanu, D.; Liu, J.B. On Grüss inequalities within generalized k–fractional integrals. *Adv. Differ. Equ.* **2020**, *2020*, 203. [CrossRef]
19. Mohammed, P.O.; Sarikaya, M.Z.; Baleanu, D. On the generalized Hermite–Hadamard Inequalities via the tempered fractional integrals. *Symmetry* **2020**, *12*, 595. [CrossRef]
20. Kalsoom, H.; Rashid, S.; Idrees, M.; Safdar, F.; Akram, S.; Baleanu, D.; Chu, Y.M. Post quantum integral inequalities of Hermite–Hadamard-type associated with co-ordinated higher-order generalized strongly pre-invex and quasi-pre-invex mappings. *Symmetry* **2020**, *12*, 443. [CrossRef]
21. Bombardelli, M.; Varošanec, S. Properties of h–convex functions related to the Hermite–Hadamard–Fejér inequalities. *Comput. Math. Appl.* **2009**, *58*, 1869–1877. [CrossRef]

22. Toply, T.; Kadakal, M.; İşcan, İ. On n–polynomial convexity and some related inequalities. *AIMS Math.* **2020**, *5*, 1304–1318. [CrossRef]
23. Rashid, S.; İşcan, İ.; Baleanu, D.; Chu, Y.M. Generation of new fractional inequalities via n–polynomials s–type convexity with applications. *Adv. Differ. Equ.* **2020**, *2020*, 264. [CrossRef]
24. Hadamard, J. Étude sur les propriétés des fonctions entières en particulier d'une fonction considérée par Riemann. *J. Math. Pures Appl.* **1893**, *58*, 171–215.
25. Dragomir, S.S.; Agarwal, R.P.; Cerone, P. On Simpson's inequality and applications. *J. Inequal. Appl.* **2000**, *5*, 533–579. [CrossRef]
26. Sarikaya, M.Z.; Yildirim, H. On Hermite–Hadamard type inequalities for Riemann–Liouville fractional integrals. *Miskolc Math. Notes* **2017**, *17*, 1049–1059. [CrossRef]
27. Alomari, M.; Darus, M.; Dragomir, S.S.; Cerone, P. Ostrowski type inequalities for functions whose derivatives are s–convex in the second sense. *Appl. Math. Lett.* **2010**, *23*, 1071–1076. [CrossRef]
28. Qaisar, S.; He, C.; Hussain, S. A generalizations of Simpson's type inequality for differentiable functions using (α, m)–convex functions and applications. *J. Inequal. Appl.* **2013**, *2013*, 158. [CrossRef]

MDPI
St. Alban-Anlage 66
4052 Basel
Switzerland
Tel. +41 61 683 77 34
Fax +41 61 302 89 18
www.mdpi.com

Symmetry Editorial Office
E-mail: symmetry@mdpi.com
www.mdpi.com/journal/symmetry

www.ingramcontent.com/pod-product-compliance
Lightning Source LLC
LaVergne TN
LVHW070511100526
838202LV00014B/1830